www.wadsworth.com

www.wadsworth.com is the World Wide Web site for Wadsworth and is your direct source to dozens of online resources.

At *www.wadsworth.com* you can find out about supplements, demonstration software, and student resources. You can also send email to many of our authors and preview new publications and exciting new technologies.

www.wadsworth.com
Changing the way the world learns®

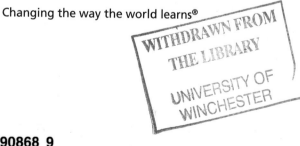

Culture and Psychology

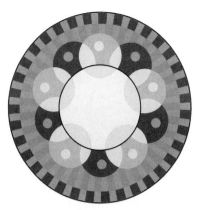

THIRD EDITION

David Matsumoto
San Francisco State University

Linda Juang
San Francisco State University

THOMSON ™

WADSWORTH

Australia ▪ Canada ▪ Mexico ▪ Singapore ▪ Spain
United Kingdom ▪ United States

THOMSON

WADSWORTH

Psychology Editor: *Michele Sordi*
Assistant Editor: *Dan Moneypenny*
Editorial Assistant: *Chelsea Junget*
Technology Project Manager: *Darin Derstine*
Marketing Manager: *Chris Caldeira*
Marketing Assistant: *Laurel Anderson*
Advertising Project Manager: *Brian Chaffee*
Project Manager, Editorial Production: *Emily Smith*
Print/Media Buyer: *Karen Hunt*
Permissions Editor: *Sarah Harkrader*

Production Service and Compositor: *Scratchgravel Publishing Services*
Photo Researcher: *Laura Molmud*
Copy Editor: *Margaret C. Tropp*
Cover Designer: *Lisa Henry*
Cover Image: © *Jose Ortega/Images.com, Inc.*
Text Printer: *Maple-Vail Book Manufacuring Group/ Binghamton*
Cover Printer: *The Lehigh Press, Inc.*

For more information about our products, contact us at:

**Thomson Learning Academic Resource Center
1-800-423-0563**

For permission to use material from this text, contact us by:

Phone: 1-800-730-2214
Fax: 1-800-730-2215
Web: http://www.thomsonrights.com

Library of Congress Control Number: 2003106359

ISBN 0-534-53591-7

**Wadsworth/Thomson Learning
10 Davis Drive
Belmont, CA 94002-3098
USA**

Asia
Thomson Learning
5 Shenton Way #01-01
UIC Building
Singapore 068808

Australia/New Zealand
Thomson Learning
102 Dodds Street
Southbank, Victoria 3006
Australia

Canada
Nelson
1120 Birchmount Road
Toronto, Ontario M1K 5G4
Canada

Europe/Middle East/Africa
Thomson Learning
High Holborn House
50/51 Bedford Row
London WC1R 4LR
United Kingdom

Latin America
Thomson Learning
Seneca, 53
Colonia Polanco
11560 Mexico D.F.
Mexico

Spain/Portugal
Paraninfo
Calle/Magallanes, 25
28015 Madrid, Spain

To the memories of my mom and dad, for their wonderful teachings and the great family they gave to me.

David Matsumoto

To my mom and dad for instilling in me the importance of family, to Margaret for being the older sister I could look up to, and to Bodo, for his kindness.

Linda Juang

About the Authors

David Matsumoto is Professor of Psychology and Director of the Culture and Emotion Research Laboratory at San Francisco State University. He has studied culture, emotion, social interaction, and communication for 20 years, and has written more than 250 works in these areas. His books include well-known titles such as *Culture and Psychology: People Around the World* (2nd edition, translated into Dutch and Japanese), *The Handbook of Culture and Psychology* (Oxford University Press, translated into Russian), and *The New Japan* (Intercultural Press). He is the recipient of many awards and honors, including being named a G. Stanley Hall lecturer by the American Psychological Association. He also holds a sixth-degree black belt in judo, a Class A Coaching Certificate from USA Judo, and a Class A International Referee License from the International Judo Federation. He is the recipient of the 1999 U.S. Olympic Committee's Developmental Coach of the Year Award in Judo, the 2001 U.S. Judo Federation's Senior and Junior Female Coach of the Year Award, and an acclamation from the City and County of Honolulu in 1977. In addition to his works in psychology, he is the author of *The History and Philosophy of Kodokan Judo* (Hon no Tomosha) and *Judo: A Sport and a Way of Life* (International Judo Federation).

Linda Juang is an Assistant Professor of Psychology at San Francisco State University. She earned her B.A. in Child Development from the University of Minnesota and her M.A. and Ph.D. in Developmental Psychology from Michigan State University, and she was also a postdoctoral fellow at the University of Jena in Germany for three years. Her research focuses on adolescent development in various family and cultural contexts. She has published and presented studies concerning issues of ethnic identity, autonomy, acculturation, and competence of adolescents in the United States and Germany.

Brief Contents

Preface   xv

1 An Introduction to the Study of Culture and Psychology   1

2 Cross-Cultural Research Methods   29

3 Ethnocentrism, Prejudice, and Stereotypes   61

4 Culture and Basic Psychological Processes   93

5 Enculturation   133

6 Culture and Developmental Processes   157

7 Culture and Gender   179

8 Culture and Health   201

9 Culture and Emotion   225

10 Culture, Language, and Communication   261

11 Culture, Self, and Personality   299

12 Culture and Abnormal Psychology   339

13 Culture and the Treatment of Abnormal Behavior   365

14 Culture and Social Behavior   385

15 Culture and Organizations   429

16 Conclusion   469

References   486

Name Index   531

Subject Index   540

Contents

Preface   **xv**

 **1 An Introduction to the Study
of Culture and Psychology**   **1**

The Goals of Psychology   2
Cross-Cultural Research and Psychology   3
Defining Culture   5
Culture and Diversity   16
Pancultural Principles versus Culture-Specific Differences:
    Etics and Emics   20
How Does Culture Influence Human Behaviors
    and Mental Processes?   21
The Contribution of the Study of Culture   22
The Goal of This Book   25
Glossary   27
InfoTrac College Edition   27

2 Cross-Cultural Research Methods   **29**

Why It Is Important to Understand Cross-Cultural
    Research Methods   29
Types of Cross-Cultural Research   30
Special Issues Concerning Cross-Cultural Comparisons   32

Transforming Culture into a Measurable Construct 46
Guidelines for Reviewing Cross-Cultural Research 54
Conclusion 58
Glossary 59
InfoTrac College Edition 60

3 Ethnocentrism, Prejudice, and Stereotypes 61

Ethnocentrism and Intergroup Attitudes 62
Stereotypes 69
Prejudice, Discrimination, and "Isms" 80
Going Beyond Prejudice and Discrimination 85
Conclusion 89
Glossary 91
InfoTrac College Edition 91

4 Culture and Basic Psychological Processes 93

Culture and the Biological Bases of Behavior 93
Culture and Perception 97
Culture and Cognition 104
Culture and Consciousness 114
Culture and Intelligence 119
Conclusion 129
Glossary 131
InfoTrac College Edition 131

5 Enculturation 133

Enculturation and Socialization 133
Culture, Child Rearing, Parenting, and Families 135
Culture and Peers 143
Culture and Day Care 144
Culture and Education 145
Religion 152
Summary 153
Conclusion 154
Glossary 156
InfoTrac College Edition 156

6 Culture and Developmental Processes 157

Culture and Temperament   157
Culture and Attachment   161
Temperament and Attachment: A Summary   166
Cognitive Development   167
Moral Reasoning   172
Other Developmental Processes   176
Conclusion   177
Glossary   177
InfoTrac College Edition   178

7 Culture and Gender 179

The Relationship of Gender and Culture
    to Mainstream Psychology   180
Some Definitions   181
Cross-Cultural Research on Gender   182
How Does Culture Influence Gender?   193
Ethnicity and Gender in the United States   195
Conclusion   197
Glossary   198
InfoTrac College Edition   199

8 Culture and Health 201

Cultural Differences in the Definition of Health   202
Culture and Conceptions of the Body   204
Sociocultural Influences on Physical Health
    and Medical Disease Processes   205
Cultural Influences on Attitudes and Beliefs
    Related to Health and Disease   216
A Model of Cultural Influences on Physical Health   219
Cultural Differences in Dealing with Illness   220
Conclusion   223
Glossary   224
InfoTrac College Edition   224

9 Culture and Emotion 225

The Importance of Emotion in Our Lives 225
Culture and Emotion Expression 226
Culture and Emotion Perception 236·
Culture and the Experience of Emotion 241
Culture and the Antecedents of Emotion 247
Culture and Emotion Appraisal 250
Culture and the Concept and Language of Emotion 254
Conclusion 258
Glossary 260
InfoTrac College Edition 260

10 Culture, Language, and Communication 261

The Structure of Language 262
Language Differences across Cultures 263
Culture, Language, and Cognition: The Sapir–Whorf Hypothesis 268
Bilingualism and Culture 273
The Components of Communication 278
The Role of Culture in the Communication Process 283
Intracultural versus Intercultural Communication 288
Improving Intercultural Communication 292
Conclusion 296
Glossary 297
InfoTrac College Edition 298

11 Culture, Self, and Personality 299

Culture and Concepts of Self 300
An Example of Different Cultural Conceptualizations of Self:
    Independent and Interdependent Selves 302
Beyond Independent and Interdependent Self-Construals:
    Interrelated and Isolated Self-Concepts 316
Culture and Personality 320
Cross-Cultural Research on Personality 322
Culture and the Five Factor Model of Personality 329
The Measurement of Personality across Cultures 332
Culture and Indigenous Personalities 333

Conclusion   336
Glossary   337
InfoTrac College Edition   338

12 Culture and Abnormal Psychology   339

Defining Abnormality: Some Core Issues   340
Cross-Cultural Research on Abnormal Behaviors   342
Culture and the Assessment of Abnormal Behavior   352
Mental Health of Ethnic Minorities and Migrants   358
Conclusion   362
Glossary   362
InfoTrac College Edition   363

13 Culture and the Treatment of Abnormal Behavior   365

Culture and Psychotherapy   365
Treatment of Abnormal Behavior across Diverse Cultures
    in the United States   368
Treatment of Abnormal Behavior in Other Cultures   378
An Alternative Approach to Treatment   380
Culture and Clinical Training   381
Conclusion   382
Glossary   383
InfoTrac College Edition   383

14 Culture and Social Behavior   385

Culture and Ingroup/Outgroup Relationships   385
Culture, Person Perception, and Attractiveness   392
Culture and Attributions   404
Culture and Aggression   417
Culture and Conformity, Compliance, Obedience, and Cooperation   420
Conclusion   425
Glossary   426
InfoTrac College Edition   427

15 **Culture and Organizations** **429**

Organizational Culture and Organizational Climate   430
Culture and Organizational Structure   432
Cultural Differences in Work-Related Values   433
Recent Research on Organizational Culture   441
Culture and the Meaning of Work   450
Culture, Motivation, and Productivity   451
Culture, Leadership, and Management Styles   453
Culture and Decision-Making Processes   456
Intercultural Issues Regarding Business and Work   459
Conclusion   466
Glossary   467
InfoTrac College Edition   467

 16 **Conclusion** **469**

Implications for Mainstream Psychology   470
Implications for Our Everyday Lives   475
Conclusion   483

References   **486**

Name Index   **531**

Subject Index   **540**

Preface

Cultural diversity continues to be one of the most important issues in psychology, with more cross-cultural and intercultural studies being conducted on all facets and domains of psychology today than ever before. The boom of culture studies that started a few years ago seems not to have reached its peak yet, as the highest-level mainstream journals in psychology continue to publish an increasing number of culture-related studies. And this trend promises to continue for the near future.

With the proliferation of these studies and the increased awareness of the role of culture in shaping mental processes and human behavior (and vice versa), knowledge and theory in psychology are continually evolving. Models of morality, cognition, development, abnormal behavior, and social psychology are all being revised and shaped by cross-cultural research. Slowly but surely, psychological truth is beginning to reflect the cultural diversity of the people out there in the world that psychology is trying to describe. This point in the history of psychology is indeed an interesting and important time in the evolution of psychological knowledge.

Moreover, cultural studies continue to contribute to the development of critical thinking not only for the field but also for students and researchers. Asking questions about the validity of psychological processes across cultures is healthy for producers and consumers of research and challenges previous knowledge and the philosophy underlying psychological science. Learning about culture in this fashion gives the discipline of psychology another tool with which to help tomorrow's citizens improve their critical thinking skills, preparing them for their lives and the betterment of society.

We live in tumultuous times, and the world all around us seems to be in need of increased awareness, understanding, tolerance, and respect for cultural diversity. At the same time, psychology would benefit from the search for and discovery of pancultural similarities—human universals if you will—to aid in improving the human condition. It is with the hope for a better world—a world of peace and understanding among peoples, nations, and cultures—that this book was revised. We sincerely hope that it helps all of us achieve these ultimate goals of education.

Major Improvements to the Third Edition

1. *Expansion of material related to development.* In this edition, we have considerably expanded the material related to psychological development. This material, covered in a single chapter in the previous edition, now encompasses two separate chapters—one concerning socialization and enculturation, the other covering cultural influences on psychological processes. We opted for this change to better reflect the close relationship between studies of culture and development and to highlight the cultural issues raised with regard to development.

2. *Expansion of material related to abnormal behavior, assessment, and psychotherapy.* Likewise, in this edition, we have expanded coverage of the material related to abnormal behavior, assessment, and psychotherapy. This material, covered in a single chapter in the previous edition, has also been expanded to two chapters.

3. *Restructuring of the initial chapters that provide a framework for understanding culture and psychology.* The previous edition included a separate introductory chapter, a chapter on culture, and a chapter on research methods (Chapters 1, 2, and 5, respectively). In this edition, we have incorporated material from the culture chapter into Chapters 1 and 5, and we have moved the research methods material to Chapter 2. This presentation sharpens the focus and content on culture and the role of cross-cultural psychology in psychology, as well as highlighting the importance of research methods.

4. *Consolidation of material on language, nonverbal behavior, and intercultural communication.* The previous edition covered these materials in three separate chapters. The current edition consolidates the most important aspects of those three chapters into a single chapter focusing on the impact of verbal and nonverbal language on intercultural communication.

5. *Consolidation of material on self and personality.* The previous edition contained a chapter each on personality and self. This edition consolidates that material into a single chapter.

6. *Increased attention to studies comparing ethnic groups within the United States.* The bulk of the cross-cultural studies reviewed in the previous edition were cross-national; in this edition, we have substantially increased our coverage of studies examining cross-ethnic group differences here in the United States. Expanded coverage of these types of studies will be evident throughout the book in all major topic areas.

7. *A reduction in length but an increase in the references cited.* We have shortened the book slightly to better fit the confines of a single course in a quarter or a semester. We have done so, however, with no sacrifice to the amount of research coverage or content. In fact, the previous edition contained about 1,200 references; this edition contains almost 1,500. Achieving an increase in references cited along with a decrease in page length means that the presentation is sharper and more concise than in the past.

Chapter-by-Chapter Improvements

In addition to the major changes described above, each individual chapter has been updated and improved.

Chapter 3: Ethnocentrism, Prejudice, and Stereotypes
- Updated with recent studies, such as the relationship between selective attention and stereotypes and Bodenhausen's work on positive and negative emotions in stereotypical thinking (Bodenhausen, Kramer, & Suesser, 1994).
- Elaborated on racial, gender, and class stereotypes seen on television.
- Elaborated on how social context (such as the context of war) can change stereotypes.
- Added information about Gurin's (1997) study of affirmative action at the University of Michigan.
- Added information on Aronson's (2002) work on "jigsaw classrooms" to reduce prejudice in schoolchildren.

Chapter 4: Culture and Basic Psychological Processes
- Elaborated on the interaction between genes and environment in understanding intelligence. For instance, described Scarr's genotype–environment theory suggesting three kinds of gene–environment interactions: passive, evocative, and active. Also described a recent study by Caspi and colleagues (2002) that very clearly illustrates the interaction between genes (predisposition to violent behavior) and environment (abusive versus nurturing parenting).
- Added current literature on dreaming that challenges Freud's notions of dreaming.
- Added recent cross-cultural studies on pain—for instance, on acceptable expressions of pain in Indian and American college students, and pain response in Chinese versus Canadian babies.
- Added Claude Steele's (1998) work on "stereotype threat" as another possible explanation for racial differences in performance on IQ tests.

Chapter 5: Enculturation
- Added a description of Bronfenbrenner's ecological systems theory early in the chapter to highlight bidirectional influences between children and their environments .

- Added a section on the reciprocal nature of parent–child relationships.
- Included a section on how parenting styles are linked to child and adolescent development.
- Included a section on parenting styles in ethnic minority families. Discussed the work of Chao (1994, 1996), who developed an indigenous parenting style measure for Chinese parents.
- Elaborated on how developmental goals of parents lead to variation in parenting behaviors across cultures, and how parental beliefs also lead to different parenting behaviors.
- Added a section on siblings as another important socializing agent.
- Added a section on peers, describing Mead's ideas on postfigurative, cofigurative, and refigurative cultures to understand importance of peers.
- Described how cultures differ in the availability and amount of time children spend with their peers, and described Davis and Davis's (1989) study of friendships in a Moroccan town.
- Added information on day care cross-culturally, describing how its quality and availability differ across cultures and how cultural attitudes toward children's development may account for some of those differences. Described some findings regarding how day care may be beneficial to the development of children, especially those from disadvantaged families.
- Added a section on the role of religion in enculturation.

Chapter 6: Culture and Developmental Processes
- Added a section on cross-cultural studies using Brazelton's Neonatal Behavior Assessment Scale. This scale, which assesses aspects of temperament, has been used in many different parts of the world, including in Peru and Nepal, and among Hmong immigrants in the United States. The studies suggest the existence of temperamental differences cross-culturally, even a few days after birth.
- Added a paragraph on how temperament can give us a clue to what kinds of personality and behaviors are valued in a culture as an adult.
- Added a section on the goodness of fit between an infant's temperament and his or her cultural context. For instance, having a difficult temperament is usually thought to predict poorer development in infants; however, in some extreme cultural contexts, such as during a drought in Kenya, having a difficult temperament leads to a greater chance of survival.
- Added more basic information on attachment.
- Described Ainsworth's (1967) well-known study of mothers and infants in Uganda, which led to the tripartite classification system of attachment.
- Added more studies that address the question, Is "secure" attachment really the ideal across cultures? In this ongoing debate, there is some evidence of the universality of the idea of secure attachment as optimal; however, other leading researchers of attachment disagree. Crittendon (2000) suggests that viewing attachment through the lens of being "adaptive" and "maladaptive" may be more useful than the evaluative terms "secure" and "insecure."

- Added a section on the relationship between attachment styles and child competence, such as social and cognitive competence.
- Added a section on the cross-cultural validity of assessing attachment.
- Discussed the importance of examining attachment to multiple caretakers in addition to focusing on the mother–infant relationship. Attachment to multiple caretakers is the norm in many cultures.
- Added more detail to Piaget's theory of cognitive development.
- Added more information on different concepts of morality, such the morality of community and the morality of divinity described by Miller (2001).

Chapter 7: Culture and Gender
- Added how recent events around the world (Taliban rule in Afghanistan, World Conference on Women in Beijing, global concern over female circumcision) have brought international attention to gender issues.
- Added a section on how media contribute to the development of gender role stereotypes.
- Added work by Gibbons and colleagues (1989, 1990, 1991) on gender role ideologies in adolescents from Spain, Guatemala, Sri Lanka, and the Netherlands.
- Discussed how, because of globalization, gender role ideologies are changing in countries such as Sri Lanka (de Silva, Stiles, & Gibbons, 1992). However, we also added evidence that gender role ideologies are maintained, as found in a study of Palestinian women (Huntington, Fronk, & Chadwick, 2001).
- Discussed how gender role socialization begins very early in life.
- Mentioned Sandra Bem (1981) and her argument that gender is one of the fundamental ways we organize and understand our world.

Chapter 8: Culture and Health
- Added the World Health Organization's definition of health.
- Updated with current studies.
- Elaborated on other cultures' concepts of health, such as the Chinese principles of *yin* and *yang*.
- Discussed how concepts of health can differ within pluralistic cultures such as the United States or Canada (Huff, 1999; Mulatu & Berry, 2001). For instance, many Native Americans view health holistically, considering good health to be living in harmony with oneself and one's environment, in sharp contrast to the Western biomedical model in which health is typically thought of as confined to the individual.
- Elaborated on how culture and religious beliefs may be related to suicide. For instance, suicide is strictly forbidden in the Muslin and Jewish religions and was considered a mortal sin in the early history of Christianity.
- Reported recent cross-cultural studies of suicide (Kelleher et al., 1998), as well as within-culture studies (Shiang, 1998, on different ethnic groups in San Francisco).
- Discussed how perspectives on health may vary depending on level of acculturation.

Chapter 9: Culture and Emotion
- Condensed by eliminating details of some studies.
- Added a table describing the latent content of emotion antecedents, which we argue is universal.

Chapter 10: Culture, Language, and Communication
- Combined and condensed former Language, Nonverbal Communication, and Intercultural Communication chapters.
- Condensed section on the Sapir–Whorf hypothesis.

Chapter 11: Culture, Self, and Personality
- Cut down details of studies.
- Added the idea of the universality of self-enhancement.
- Updated with studies from current literature, including Kitayama, Markus, & Kurokawa's (2000) "good feelings" study; Oyserman, Coon, & Kemmelmeier's (2002) meta-analysis of I-C; and Matsumoto's (1999) critique of Markus and Kitayama's self-construal paper.
- Added recent cross-cultural studies of self-esteem in children and studies using the FFM.
- Added more indigenous concepts of personality summarized by Church (2000).

Chapter 12: Culture and Abnormal Psychology
- Added more detail to the World Health Organization (WHO) studies.
- Incorporated the section on personality tests to assess abnormal behavior from the Personality chapter in the previous edition.
- Added a case study (P. M., a Korean woman who experienced spirit sickness).
- Added another perspective on what is considered "abnormal" (Rhi, 2000).
- Described in more detail what specific changes were made to the DSM-IV to make it more culturally sensitive.
- Updated with current literature.
- Added information about indigenously created classification manuals of mental disorders, such as those in China and North Africa.
- Elaborated on increasing cases of anorexia reported in other cultures.
- Added Paniagua's (1998, 2000) four assessment guidelines for practitioners to distinguish psychopathology from culture-related conditions.
- Reported how the Child Behavior Checklist (Achenbach, 2001) has been used to assess emotional and behavioral problems of children in various parts of the world.
- Described research demonstrating that the cultural backgrounds of the therapist and the client may contribute to the perception and assessment of mental health.
- Added a section on the mental health of ethnic minority groups, as well as of immigrants and refugees, in the United States.

Chapter 13: Culture and the Treatment of Abnormal Behavior
- Expanded the section on treatment in diverse cultures within the United States.
- Added more detail on utilization of treatment services by African Americans, Native Americans, Asian Americans, and Latino Americans.
- Added a section on barriers to seeking treatment, such as stigma and clinician bias, among different ethnic minority populations.
- Added case studies.
- Added a section on indigenous healing (Sue & Sue, 1999).
- Added a section on community-based treatment.

Chapter 14: Culture and Social Behavior
- Updated with current studies (such as those on the concepts of passionate love and aggression).
- Described an alternative explanation for interpersonal attraction from a social construction perspective (Beall & Sternberg, 1995).
- Elaborated on passionate love across cultures and arranged marriages.
- Described studies that analyzed newspaper articles in the United States and Hong Kong to study attributions about "real-life" (as opposed to laboratory) behaviors.

Chapter 15: Culture and Organizations
- Condensed the chapter by eliminating details of some studies.
- Added recent reviews on industrial and organizational psychology (Aycan, 2000) and culture and negotiation (Gelfand & Dyer, 2000).

Summary of the Improvements

This edition of *Culture and Psychology* continues to reflect the breadth, scope, depth, and understanding of the influence of culture on human behavior, and the intimate relationship between culture and psychology. It still carries a singular message to its intended audience, which remains students in undergraduate and graduate cross-cultural psychology courses. Its purpose is to recast knowledge and truth in psychology by incorporating culture and context as important frameworks, as it reflects the current evolution in thinking about human behavior in psychology. Ultimately, all psychologists share an implicit goal of increased human understanding, and we hope this book gives us one more tool in that struggle for improved understanding and a better, more peaceful, global community. We sincerely hope that you will share our enthusiasm and challenge your minds and hearts to the messages contained within.

Acknowledgments

We are both fortunate to have enjoyed the collaboration of many scholars over the years who have helped forge our thinking about culture and psychology. For this third edition, David Matsumoto would like to thank Paul Ekman, Susumu Yamaguchi, Hiroshi Yamada, Kyoko Yashiro, Masayuki Takeuchi,

Hidenaka Wakayama, Ryuji Okada, Shoko Araki, Bob Grissom, and Dale Dinnel for their collaboration in cross-cultural research that has aided in his thinking about culture and psychology. Linda Juang would like to thank Jacqueline Lerner, Richard Lerner, Rainer Silbereisen, Huong Nguyen, Angela Ittel, and David Matsumoto for lively discussions and research collaborations on understanding human development in a cultural context.

We continue to be indebted to our laboratory staffs for their hard work and dedication in our research programs on culture. David Matsumoto thanks the current and former students, lab assistants, and visiting scholars who have been a part of the Culture and Emotion Research Laboratory in the Psychology Department of San Francisco State University. In particular, he owes a debt of gratitude to Jungwook Choi, Rachael Noble, Heather Gray, Lani Singer, Satoko Hirayama, and Seung Hee Yoo for their help in teaching cross-cultural psychology at San Francisco State University, for contributing countless hours of hard work and dedication to this course, and for helping him refine his ideas about culture and psychology. Linda Juang thanks David Rogers and Tiffeny Jimenez for their help in gathering literature for this third edition. She would also like to thank current and former students from her Culture and Adolescence Lab, especially Miyuki Takagi, Violet Cheung, Gwen Agustin, Cheryl Gordon, Raul Beccerra, Jen Ibardolaza, and Cathryn Fabian, who make her feel so lucky to work with such a culturally diverse and smart group of students.

As in the past, we are grateful for the warm friendships we are fortunate to experience with the people at Wadsworth/Thomson Learning. We thank our previous editor Marianne Taflinger and welcome our new editor Michele Sordi to this work, along with her assistant Chelsea Junget and our representative Tracy Rashbrook. We appreciate the time, patience, concern, and guidance they have all given us in the completion of this project. We also extend our thanks to the reviewers who provided us with advice and guidance concerning strengths and weaknesses of the previous edition: David Chavez, California State University, San Bernadino; Ganie DeHart, SUNY, Geneseo; Sue Nash, University of Houston; Ann Powers, Sul Ross State University; Carla Reyes, University of Utah; and Michael Sloane, University of Alabama at Birmingham.

Our ability to bring together such a large and comprehensive review that improves on our previous work is no small tribute to the love and support we both receive from our families. David Matsumoto gives his deepest appreciation and respect to his wife Mimi for being the best wife, mother, and partner in the whole wide world. Linda Juang thanks her parents, jie jie, and Bodo for keeping her life balanced.

Finally, we thank you—the students and teachers who have used *Culture and Psychology* in your coursework, research, or studies. The many inquiries, challenges, questions, and notes of appreciation we have received over the years have always served to motivate both of us to continue our research programs, to improve this book, and to study that complex, fuzzy, yet fascinating thing we know of as culture. You have our profound thanks and appreciation.

David Matsumoto
Linda Juang

Introducing the Coauthor

The changes from the previous editions of this book have been made possible to a great extent by the addition of a coauthor, Linda Juang. As you can read in her biography on page vi, Linda is a developmental psychologist with interests in culture and ethnicity not only across nations but especially within the United States. Her research interests and expertise were a perfect match with mine, complementing the gaps in my knowledge in these important areas, which are essential areas of inquiry for many students of culture here in the United States. In fact, the expansion of the material on development and the incorporation of the many studies examining ethnic groups are both due in large part to her expertise and contributions. Her assistance in these and all other areas were essential to the improvements made in this edition of *Culture and Psychology*, and I appreciate the time and effort she put in to helping make this text a better one. Linda—you're a gem!

David Matsumoto

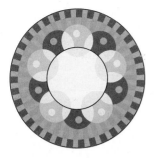

An Introduction to the Study of Culture and Psychology

Cultural diversity is one of the most important topics in the world today. Here in the United States, we live, work, and play with an increasing number of people from all cultures, countries, and walks of life. New immigrants alone make up 10% of the total U.S. population, and that does not include all of the cultural diversity that has existed in this country for decades. In many other countries as well—in Europe, Africa, Asia, and Oceania—people of different countries and cultures come together more today than ever before. While this increasingly diversifying world has created a wonderful environment for personal challenge and growth, it also brings with it an increased potential for misunderstandings that can lead to confusion and anger. "Diversity" is a buzzword for "difference," and conflicts and misunderstandings often arise because of these differences.

Cultural diversity is one of our biggest challenges. Corporate America is attempting to address that challenge through workshops, seminars, and education in diversity throughout the workforce. The educational system has addressed diversity by hiring and retaining faculty of color and infusing material related to different cultures throughout the curriculum. Government has attempted to deal with diversity through policies such as equal employment opportunity and affirmative action.

At the same time, the challenges that face us in the name of cultural diversity and intercultural relations also represent our biggest opportunities. If we can meet those challenges and turn them to our favor, we can actualize a potential in diversity and intercultural relations that will result in far more than the sum of the individual components that comprise that diverse universe. This sum will result in tremendous personal growth for many individuals, as well as positive social evolution.

It is in this belief that this book was written—to meet the challenge of diversity and turn that challenge into opportunity. Doing so is not easy. It requires each of us to take an honest look at our own cultural background and heritage, their merits and limitations. Fear, rigidity, and sometimes stubborn pride come with any type of honest assessment. Yet without that assessment, we cannot meet the challenge of diversity and improve intercultural relations.

In academia, that assessment brings with it fundamental questions about what is taught in our colleges and universities today. To ask how cultural diversity colors the nature of the truths and principles of human behavior delivered in the halls of science is to question the pillars of much of our knowledge about the world and about human behavior. From time to time, we need to shake those pillars to see just how sturdy they are. This is especially true in the social sciences and particularly in psychology—the science specifically concerned with the mental processes and behavioral characteristics of people.

The Goals of Psychology

No field is better equipped to meet the challenge of cultural diversity than psychology. And in fact, psychology has met, and continues to meet, the challenge of culture through a subfield known as cross-cultural psychology. To get a better handle on what cross-cultural psychology is all about, it is important first to have a good grasp of the goals of psychology.

Psychology essentially has two main goals. The first is to build a body of knowledge about people. Psychologists seek to understand behavior when it happens, explain why it happens, and even predict it before it happens. Two aspects of psychology are important in achieving this goal: the conduct of psychological research and the creation of theoretical models of behavior. Research and theory go hand in hand in psychology.

The second goal of psychology involves taking that body of knowledge and applying it to intervene in people's lives, hopefully to make those lives better. Psychologists perform various important roles in pursuit of this goal: as therapists for individuals, families, and groups; as counselors in schools, universities, churches, and other community organizations; as trainers in businesses and work organizations; and as consultants for police, lawyers, courts, sport organizations, athletes, and teams. Psychologists work on the front lines, dealing directly with people to affect their lives in a positive fashion.

The two goals of psychology—creating a body of knowledge and applying that knowledge—are not mutually exclusive. They share a close relationship, as well they should. Psychologists who are on the front lines do not work in a vacuum; they take what psychology as a field has collectively learned about human behavior and use that knowledge as a basis for their applications and interventions. This learning initially comes in the form of academic training of counselors, therapists, and consultants as they achieve academic degrees from universities. But it continues well after formal education has ended, through continuing education programs and individual scholarship—reviewing the literature, attending conferences, joining and participating in professional organizations. Applied psychologists engage in a lifelong learning process that helps them intervene in people's lives more effectively. Likewise, research psychologists are cognizant of the practical and applied implications of their work. In fact, most researchers and theoreticians are well aware that the value of psychological theory and research is often judged by its practical usefulness in society (see, for example, Gergen, Gulerce, Lock, & Misra, 1996). Theories are often tested for their validity not only in the halls of science but also on the streets, and they often have to be revised because of what happens in those streets.

Theory/research and application/intervention are thus the two goals of psychology as we see them. Although some psychologists may choose to focus on one or the other, it is important to remember that psychology as a collective whole seeks to achieve both. Cross-cultural psychology has a special meaning to mainstream psychology because of these goals.

Cross-Cultural Research and Psychology

Most research on human behavior conducted in the United States involves American university students as study participants. The reasons are largely pragmatic. University faculty need to do research, for themselves as much as for the field, and the easiest population to access is often university student volunteers. Another reason has been a lack of concern about issues of diversity and its impact on theory and research, and quite frankly, some of the political ramifications of doing such research. As a result, the majority of the information and research you read about in textbooks and research articles in mainstream psychology is based on studies involving American college or university student participants or samples.

There is nothing wrong with such research, and the findings obtained from such samples are definitely true for those samples. These findings may be replicated across multiple samples using different methodologies. In short, many findings may weather tests for scientific rigor that would normally render them acceptable as a truth or principle about human behavior. However, a basic question still remains: Is what we know as truth or principle about human behavior true for all people, regardless of gender, race, ethnicity, culture, class, or lifestyle? This question has particular import when you consider the nature of the samples generally included in psychological research.

Cross-cultural research* asks these questions by examining and testing them in people of differing cultural backgrounds. In cross-cultural research, these questions are addressed quite simply—by including participants of more than one cultural background and then comparing data obtained across the

---

***Boldface** terms are defined in the glossary at the end of the chapter.

cultural groups. This research approach is primarily concerned with examining how our knowledge about people and their behaviors from one culture may or may not hold for people from another culture.

Cross-cultural research can be understood in relation to mainstream academic psychology as a matter of scientific philosophy. This term refers to the logic underlying the methods used to conduct research and generate knowledge in psychology. Knowledge depends on research to confirm or disconfirm hypotheses; research involves a methodology designed to collect data that can falsify or support hypotheses. Methods involve many specific parameters, one of which includes decisions about the number and nature of the participants in the study. Cross-cultural research involves the inclusion of people of different cultural backgrounds—a specific type of change in one of the parameters of methodology.

What is the difference between cross-cultural research and other types of research that change a parameter of a study? If we consider cross-cultural research from the standpoint of scientific philosophy, other studies that change other parameters of research—such as the specific tests or measures that are used, or the procedures by which data are collected—also raise important questions about the generalizability of findings. Changes can also occur in characteristics of the participants other than their cultural background, such as their socioeconomic class, age, gender, or place of residence. All these types of changes are important in relation to the philosophy underlying psychology's science. But the meaning of a study and its findings differs if it compares different cultures than if it compares different ways of measuring a variable, for example. This difference is related to what may be considered the **cross-cultural approach.**

The cross-cultural approach that cross-cultural research brings to mainstream psychology goes far beyond simple methodological changes in the studies conducted to test hypotheses related to truth and knowledge. It is a way of understanding truth and principles about human behaviors within a global, cross-cultural perspective. Cross-cultural research not only tests similarities and differences in behaviors; it also tests possible limitations of our traditional knowledge by studying people of different cultures. In its narrowest sense, cross-cultural research simply involves including participants from different cultural backgrounds and testing possible differences between these different groups of participants. In its broadest sense, however, the cross-cultural approach is concerned with understanding truth and psychological principles as either universal (true for all people of all cultures) or **culture-specific** (true for some people of some cultures).

Some truths are true for all. Psychologists call these universals. Some truths and principles, however, are not absolutes; they are culturally relative and culturally bound. There is much about the world and about human behavior that is true for one culture but not for others. It may very well be the case, therefore, that even though a finding is replicated in studies involving subjects from a given culture and society, it is not true for another culture or society, and vice versa. The results of psychological research are bound by our methods, and the very standards of care we use when we evaluate the scientific rigor and quality of research are also bound by the cultural frameworks within which our science occurs (Pe-Pua, 1989).

In the United States, as in many countries, psychology is segmented into specific topic areas—for example, clinical, social, developmental, personality, and the like. Cross-cultural psychology and cross-cultural approaches are not topic-specific. Cross-cultural researchers are interested in a broad range of phenomena related to human behavior—from perception to language, child rearing to psychopathology. Cross-cultural psychologists and cross-cultural research can be found in any specific area or subdiscipline within psychology. What distinguishes a cross-cultural approach from a traditional or mainstream approach, therefore, is not the phenomenon of interest but the testing of limitations to knowledge by examining whether that knowledge is applicable to people of different cultural backgrounds. The approach, not the topic, is what is important in cross-cultural psychology.

In the past few years, cross-cultural research in psychology has gained newfound popularity. Much of this popularity is due to the current focus on cultural diversity and intergroup relations and the increasing diversity of the U.S. population. Increasing problems and tensions in intercultural relations and a growing recognition of the limitations of the psychological literature have also enhanced awareness of the need for a cross-cultural approach. Interest in cross-cultural research is certain to increase, especially with events such as the terrorist attacks in the United States on September 11, 2001.

In a much larger sense, an increased interest in cross-cultural psychology is a normal and healthy development, questioning the nature of the truths and principles amassed to date and searching for ways to provide an even more accurate picture of human behavior across people of different cultural backgrounds. As psychology has matured and such questions have been raised, many scientists and writers have come to recognize that much (but not all) of the research and the literature once thought to be universal for all people is indeed culture-bound. The increasing importance and recognition of cross-cultural approaches in the social sciences, and in psychology in particular, are reactions to this realization. Cross-cultural research and scholarship have had a profound impact on our understanding of truths and principles about human behavior.

Defining Culture

It is fashionable today in mainstream psychology to talk about culture. Unfortunately, many psychologists and laypersons alike use the words *culture, race, nationality,* and *ethnicity* interchangeably, as if they were all the same terms denoting the same concepts. Do these terms all refer to the same concept? Although there is clearly some overlap among them, there are also important differences among them. Recognition of these differences is important for a clearer understanding of cross-cultural research and its impact on psychological knowledge.

We will examine first how the term *culture* is used in everyday language and assess the breadth of life it refers to. After examining some previous definitions of culture, we will then discuss a definition of culture for this book. We will contrast this definition of culture with race, ethnicity, and nationality, and suggest that culture is what makes these terms important, especially in relation to understanding psychological similarities and differences among these social constructs. We will also suggest that the constructs of gender, sexual orientation, and disability can be understood in terms of culture as it is defined here. Later in the chapter, we will discuss how culture influences human behavior, and the contribution of culture to the field of psychology and to our own lives as well.

The Use of the Term *Culture* in Everyday Language

Common usages of the word *culture*. We use the word *culture* in many different ways in everyday language and discourse. Sometimes we use the word *culture* to mean race, nationality, or ethnicity. For example, we often refer to people of African American ancestry as coming from African American culture, or Chinese people as coming from Chinese culture. But we also use the word *culture* to reflect trends in music and art, food and clothing, rituals, traditions, and heritage. In short, we use the word *culture* to refer to many different things about people—physical and biological characteristics, behaviors, music, dance, and other activities. Kroeber and Kluckholn (1952) and later Berry, Poortinga, Segall, and Dasen (1992) have described six general categories in which culture is discussed:

- *Descriptive* uses highlight the different types of activities or behaviors associated with a culture.
- *Historical* definitions refer to the heritage and tradition associated with a group of people.
- *Normative* uses describe the rules and norms that are associated with a culture.
- *Psychological* descriptions emphasize learning, problem solving, and other behavioral approaches associated with culture.
- *Structural* definitions emphasize the societal or organizational elements of a culture.
- *Genetic* descriptions refer to the origins of a culture.

We use the concept and term *culture* to describe and explain a broad range of activities, behaviors, events, and structures in our lives. In the United States, we speak of cultural diversity, cultural pluralities, and multiculturalism in many areas of life, including school and the workplace.

It is also important to recognize, however, that the word *culture* may have different meanings or emphases in other cultures. If you refer to culture in Japan, for instance, a Japanese person may think first of flower arranging or a tea ceremony rather than the aspects of culture we normally associate with the word. Likewise, while learning about culture in this book, it is important to remember that this view of culture is only one view and other cultures may have other views. We should not forget that our studies of culture and the ways in which we understand cultural influences on behavior conceptually (this book included) all stem from a particular view of culture—one that is rooted in American thinking and science.

Because we use *culture* to refer to so many different things about life, it is no wonder that it generates so much confusion and ambiguity. We can get a better understanding of the complex nature of culture if we look at all the aspects of life referred to by the word *culture*.

Aspects of life touched on by culture.

The word *culture* is used in many different ways because it touches on so many aspects of life. In an early work, Murdock, Ford, and Hudson (1971) described 79 different aspects of life that culture had something to do with. Barry (1980) rearranged this list into eight broad categories, which were also reported by Berry et al. (1992):

- General characteristics
- Food and clothing
- Housing and technology
- Economy and transportation
- Individual and family activities
- Community and government
- Welfare, religion, and science
- Sex and the life cycle

Culture is a complex concept embedded in many aspects of life and living. Some aspects involve material things, such as food and clothing. Some refer to societal and structural entities, such as government organization and community structure. Others refer to individual behaviors, to reproduction, or to organized activities, such as religion and science.

Culture, in its truest and broadest sense, cannot simply be swallowed in a single gulp (Malpass, 1993)—not in this book, not in a university course, not in any training program. Although we will attempt to bring you closer to a better understanding of what culture is and how it influences our lives, we must begin by recognizing and admitting the breadth, scope, and enormity of culture. Culture cannot possibly be contained within the pages of a book or the confines of a university semester or quarter. Culture, in all its richness and complexity, is huge.

Culture as an abstraction.

Culture itself cannot be seen, felt, heard, or tasted. What is concrete and observable to us is not culture per se but differences in human behavior—actions, thoughts, rituals, traditions, and the like. We see the manifestations of culture, but we never see culture itself.

For example, in American culture we learn to shake hands when we greet others, and handshaking has become ritualistic and automatic for many of us. People of other cultures have different ways of greeting others. People of some cultures, for instance, greet each other with a slight bow of the head. Some cultures encourage this bow with hands together in front as in prayer. Some cultures encourage a bow from the waist with the face lowered out of sight. Some cultures engage only in an eyebrow flash. We can witness these actions and many other behavioral manifestations of culture, and we infer that a cultural difference underlies these various behaviors—that the behaviors are different because the culture is different.

Culture is used as an explanatory concept to describe the reason we see differences in behaviors such as greetings. In this sense, culture is an abstract, explanatory concept. We invoke the concept of culture to describe similarities among individuals within a group and differences between groups. We use the concept of culture as an explanatory construct to help us understand and categorize those within-group similarities and between-group differences. It is a theoretical or conceptual entity that helps us understand why we do the things we do and explains the differences in the behaviors of different groups of people. As an abstract concept, culture is a label.

The cyclical and dynamic nature of culture. But like many labels, culture has a life of its own. Just as similarities within groups and differences between groups give rise to culture as an abstract concept, that abstract concept feeds back on those behaviors, reinforcing our understanding of those similarities and differences. Culture helps to reinforce, promulgate, and strengthen the behavioral similarities and differences that produced it in the first place, producing a cycle of reciprocity between actual behaviors and our theoretical understanding of them as culture (see Figure 1.1).

This reciprocal relationship helps to explain why we are taught to do many things simply because "that is the way they have always been done and it is how they should be done." Learning to eat a certain way, with a certain etiquette, with certain foods, with certain utensils or with one's fingers, in a certain order, simply because "that's the way things are done" is just one of many examples of how the abstract concept of culture drives behaviors. Engaging in those behaviors further reinforces these aspects of culture. It is in this fashion that culture and the actual behaviors culture describes share a close, intimate relationship. And changing behaviors will be associated with a change in culture.

Differences in behaviors between younger and older generations surely signal differences in the underlying culture of these two groups and contribute to what we call the "generation gap." There is always some degree of discrepancy between behaviors mandated by culture and the abstract concept of culture. There is never a one-to-one correspondence across people in the behaviors mandated by an underlying culture and the actual behaviors that occur. Instead, there will always be some degree of discrepancy, however small, between behaviors and culture, despite their close and intimate relationship. Thus, there is always a dynamic tension in this relationship. In this sense, even as an abstract concept or principle, culture is never a static entity. It is always dynamic and changing, existing within a tensive relationship with the actual behaviors it is supposed to explain and predict. The degree of tension between culture as

Figure 1.1 Cycle of reciprocity: Observing, labeling, feedback, and reinforcing. When something is *labeled* culture, it *becomes* culture; then the culture reinforces the label.

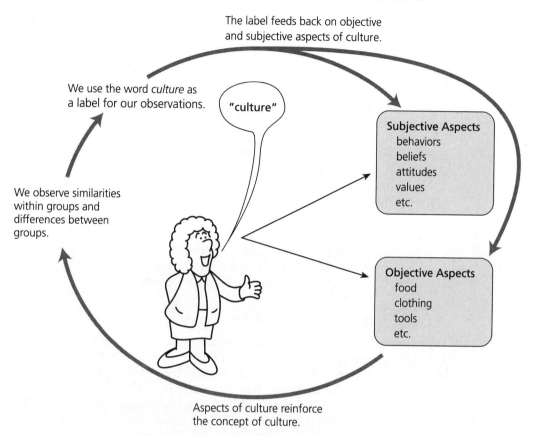

The label feeds back on objective and subjective aspects of culture.

We use the word *culture* as a label for our observations.

"culture"

We observe similarities within groups and differences between groups.

Subjective Aspects
behaviors
beliefs
attitudes
values
etc.

Objective Aspects
food
clothing
tools
etc.

Aspects of culture reinforce the concept of culture.

an underlying construct and the behaviors that it mandates may be an important aspect of culture itself. Some cultures may be characterized by a high degree of tension, whereas others may be characterized by relatively less tension. This difference in the degree of tension is most likely related to Pelto's (1968) distinction of tight versus loose societies.

Previous Definitions of Culture

Over the past 100 years or so, many scholars have made explicit their and the field's definitions of culture. There are probably as many definitions of culture as there are theorists and students of culture. Although these definitions share many similarities, they sometimes exhibit important differences as well. Well over 100 years ago, for example, Tylor (1865) defined culture as all capabilities and habits learned as members of a society. Linton (1936) referred to culture as social heredity. Kroeber and Kluckhohn (1952) defined culture as patterns of and for behavior acquired and transmitted by symbols, constituting the distinct achievements of human groups, including their embodiments in artifacts (p. 181). Rohner (1984) defined culture as the totality of equivalent and complementary learned meanings maintained by a human population, or by identifiable segments of a population, and transmitted from one generation to the next (pp. 119–120). Triandis (1972) contrasted objective aspects of culture, such as tools, with subjective aspects, such as words, shared beliefs, attitudes, norms, roles, and values. This distinction is also related to Kroeber and Kluckhohn's (1952) concept of explicit and implicit culture. Jahoda (1984) argued that *culture* is a descriptive term that captures not only rules and meanings but also behaviors. Some theorists have defined culture in terms of personality (Pelto & Pelto, 1975; Schwartz, 1978) and others as shared symbol systems transcending individuals (Geertz, 1973). Berry et al. (1992) define culture simply as the shared way of life of a group of people (p. 1).

More than a decade ago, Soudijn, Hutschemaekers, and Van de Vijver (1990) analyzed 128 definitions of culture in order to identify common dimensions among them. Their analysis revealed five semantic dimensions within which the definitions could be placed. These researchers argued, however, that instead of integrating all five dimensions into a single, cohesive definition of culture, students of culture should be free to emphasize specific dimensions to highlight particular concerns they may have about human behavior.

A Definition of Culture for This Book

Given the enormity of culture, the approach we have taken in researching the literature, conducting our own research programs involving cross-cultural issues, and writing this book is to adopt a definition of culture that is most germane and relevant for understanding the influence of culture on individuals at different levels of analysis. Even with these parameters, culture is a rather difficult concept to define formally. We define **culture** as a dynamic system of rules, explicit and implicit, established by groups in order to ensure their survival, involving attitudes, values, beliefs, norms, and behaviors, shared by a group but harbored differently by each specific unit within the group, communicated across generations, relatively stable but with the potential to change across time. Let's examine some of the key components of this definition.

Dynamic. Culture describes average, mainstream tendencies. It cannot describe all behaviors of all people in any culture. There will always be some degree of discrepancy, however small, between behaviors and culture. This discrepancy creates a dynamic tension as mentioned earlier. In this sense, culture is not static. It is always dynamic and changing, existing within a tensive relationship with the actual behaviors it is supposed to explain and predict. This degree of tension may be an important aspect of culture itself. Some cultures may be characterized by a high degree of tension, whereas others may be characterized by relatively less.

System of rules. Culture does not refer to any single behavior, rule, attitude, or value. It refers to the entire system of these constructs. In this sense, culture is like a syndrome (Triandis, 1994), involving a constellation of separate but interrelated psychological components. We prefer the metaphor of a system rather than a syndrome, however. Syndrome implies a core element with manifestations emanating from it, not unlike a disease pathogen with symptomatology, whereas system focuses on the functional, working relationship among the various components.

Groups and units. Culture exists on multiple levels—across individuals within groups, and across groups within a larger group (such as a business corporation). This definition of culture is applicable at multiple levels of analysis. When applied to a group of individuals, the units are specific individuals within the group. This is probably the most common usage. But other levels of analyses are also possible. For example, a large corporation often comprises multiple departments or sections. The company as a whole will have a system of rules—both official company policy (explicit) and the unofficial way things are done (implicit)—that constitutes that company's organizational culture. In this context, the group may be the company as a whole and the units the various sections or departments within it.

To ensure their survival. The system of rules that comprise culture exists essentially to ensure survival of the group. These rules also allow for units within the group to coexist with one another, providing a framework for social order instead of the potential chaos of a free-for-all. In many senses, culture is humans' way of capturing, controlling, and avoiding chaos. The rules also allow for groups and units to balance the needs of the group's survival with the desires, wishes, and needs of the unit, taking into account the larger social context and the resources at hand. This concept is related to Poortinga's (1990) definition involving constraints on behavior.

Attitudes, values, beliefs, norms, and behaviors. This definition of culture focuses on ideas, attitudes, values, beliefs—the contents of the mind of each and every individual who lives in that culture. Not only do these aspects of culture exist in people's minds, but they also exist as a social consciousness above and beyond individuals. The behaviors that are shared are indeed observable and are often seen in rituals or common, automatic behavior patterns that arise because of shared cultural values and behavioral norms. These elements collectively constitute the subjective aspects of culture (Triandis, 1972), as opposed to the objective, tangible aspects. Without seeking to diminish the importance of the objective elements of culture, we deem the subjective elements more important for our understanding of cultural influences on behavior.

Harbored differently by each specific unit. Individuals harbor their culture's values, beliefs, behaviors, and the like, to differing degrees. That is, there are individual differences in adherence or conformity to culture. The recognition of individual differences in culture forms one of the bases for understanding the limitations of stereotypes, and is also related to Pelto's (1968) classification of tight versus loose societies.

Communicated across generations, relatively stable. Fads that come and go, even though they have a life of their own and are shared by many people at any one time, are not necessarily considered culture in the sense used here. Instead, culture is that system of rules that is durable, relatively stable over time, and hence especially important in helping units within the group. Core aspects of the system of rules are transmitted across generations.

But with the potential to change across time. Despite the relative stability of culture, it is never static. Culture is a dynamic entity, always in a tensive relationship with the behaviors, attitudes, values, beliefs, and norms it is supposed to describe. Units change over time, and because culture exists in a reciprocal relationship with its components, the tension allows for the possibility that culture itself may change over time. Change is inevitable when the system described by culture no longer accurately describes the mainstream average tendency of the group. We have been witness to drastic cultural changes over the past 30 years in the American culture, as well as in other cultures (such as in Japan; see Matsumoto, 2002).

This definition of culture is similar to many previous definitions, especially with regard to the sharing of psychological attributes and characteristics and the communication of cultural elements across generations. It differs from previous definitions primarily in its broader concept of units within groups—not only groups of individuals but also groups of groups. Thus, it enables us to understand culture in social structures and societies with multiple levels, such as individuals within a family, families within communities, communities in regions, and regions in countries; or individuals within a section, sections within departments, departments within organizations, and organizations within an international community. Culture can be described at all of these levels of analysis, referring to individuals, groups, and social structures.

This definition of culture is "fuzzy," in that it provides no hard-and-fast rules to determine what a culture is or who belongs to that culture. Culture is a sociopsychological construct, a sharing across people of psychological phenomena such as values, attitudes, beliefs, and behaviors. What defines members of the same culture is whether they share these psychological phenomena. What distinguishes members of one culture from another is the absence of these shared phenomena.

Factors That Influence Culture

Cultures help to ensure the survival of groups and individuals by balancing the needs of the individuals and groups with the resources available to meet those needs. This is generally true whether we are talking about primitive cultures with few resources and limited technology or the modern, urban societies that exist in many countries of the world today. Given the necessity to survive, cultures help to select behaviors, attitudes, values, and opinions that may optimize the tapping of resources to meet survival needs. Thus, as suggested by Poortinga (1990), out of all the myriad behaviors possible in the human repertoire, cultures help to focus people's behaviors and attention on a few limited alternatives in order to maximize their effectiveness, given their resources and their environment.

Several factors affect this balancing act, and all of them influence culture in some way. For example, the environment in which the culture exists will influence the nature of that culture. A land void of natural resources may encourage teamwork and community spirit among its members and interrelationships with other groups that have abundant resources in order to survive. These needs and relationships will foster certain psychological characteristics and attributes that complement teamwork, community spirit, and interdependence. In a land with abundant resources, however, a society would have less need for such values and attitudes, and they would be less important in its culture.

Population density also affects culture. Societies with higher population densities may require greater social order in order to function effectively. These societies may encourage hierarchy and groupism, with related psychological attributes, more than societies with relatively less population density.

Affluence is associated with culture. It has been shown to be related not only to a cultural dimension known as individualism (Hofstede, 1980, 1983) but also to national characteristics in emotionality (Wallbott & Scherer, 1988). As societies become more affluent, they are more able to obtain resources with less reliance on others, fostering these types of psychological characteristics.

Technology affects culture. Communication technology (such as cellular phones and electronic mail), for instance, brings with it its own brand of communication culture, in which rules regarding interactions and interpersonal engagement change rather rapidly. The widespread use of computers has brought with it the ability to work independently, loosening the reliance on others to get work accomplished and the need to interact with coworkers. These types of changes have the potential to bring about changes in psychological functioning and behavior, which, in turn, lead to changes in culture.

Climate is yet another factor that affects culture. Groups that live near the equator, in hot, humid, tropical areas, will exhibit a lifestyle that is very different from that of groups living in temperate or arctic zones, with seasonal changes and weather extremes. Differences in climate will affect the clothes people wear, the types of foods they eat, storage and container systems for food supplies, health (infectious and parasitic diseases tend to be more frequent in hotter climates), and many other facets of living. People in hotter climates tend to organize their daily activities more around shelter, shade, and temperature changes that occur during the day. People who live nearer the poles may organize their lives around available sunlight. All of these factors are likely to influence people's attitudes, beliefs, and behaviors, and hence their culture.

An Individual as Well as a Social Construct

We often speak of the culture of a group as if it were a single, unitary concept equally applicable to all members of the group. When we speak of Middle Eastern culture, for instance, we tend to assume that all people with roots in the

Middle East are relatively homogeneous with regard to some psychological trait, characteristic, or behavior. This assumption is also prevalent in cross-cultural research. When a study compares people from the United States, Brazil, and Puerto Rico, the implicit assumption is that individuals within the groups are relatively homogeneous. At some level, culture is relevant for all members of the group that comprise that culture. But the definition of culture adopted in this book suggests something more than a single, unitary concept that is inflexible across individuals. The definition of culture used here suggests that culture is as much an individual, psychological construct as it is a social construct. To some extent, culture exists in each and every one of us individually as much as it exists as a global, social construct. Individual differences in culture can be observed among people in the degree to which they adopt and engage in the attitudes, values, beliefs, and behaviors that, by consensus, constitute their culture. If you act in accordance with those shared values or behaviors, then that culture resides in you; if you do not share those values or behaviors, then you do not share that culture.

While the norms of any culture should be relevant to all the people within that culture, it is also true that those norms will be relevant to different degrees for different people. It is this interesting blend of culture in anthropology and sociology as a macroconcept and in psychology as an individual construct that makes understanding culture difficult but fascinating.

Culture versus Personality

That there can be individual differences within a culture raises questions about the difference between culture and personality. If culture exists as a psychological phenomenon and if different people harbor it to different degrees, then aren't we really talking about personality and not culture? The fact that we have defined culture as a sociopsychological phenomenon does indeed blur the distinction between culture and personality. Many personality traits are sociopsychological in nature. Treating culture as an abstract phenomenon, not based on physical characteristics or national citizenship, contributes to this ambiguity, as does the notion that culture can be different for different people.

Many attributes shared across members of a cultural group are psychological in nature and are common referents in discussions of personality as well. But there are important distinctions between this definition of culture and what is traditionally considered personality. First, culture is a conglomeration of attributes that are shared with other members of a cultural group. Although there may be individual differences in the degree to which members of a cultural group harbor those attributes, most members of the group do share the attribute. This is not necessarily true for personality traits, which by definition refer to individual differences in traits across people and not to differences in the degree to which an attribute is shared.

A second important aspect of culture is stability, which is defined by cross-generational education and transmission of cultural values and behaviors. Parents, extended families, and peers serve as human socialization and enculturation agents across generations, ensuring that rituals, customs, beliefs, and norms are communicated to younger generations in much the same way as they were learned before. Schools, businesses, government agencies, laws, and the like serve as institutional agents in enculturation and fill the same role toward similar outcomes as do human agents. Consequently there is a great deal of consistency in culture over time (despite the ever-present tension between culture and behavior). Such continuity is not necessarily true for personality traits. Personality is usually discussed in terms of traits or attributes of individual people within their own lifetimes.

A final distinction between culture and personality revolves around the idea of culture as a macroconcept, a social phenomenon. Not only does culture exist in each and every individual, but it also exists as a social phenomenon, a label depicting the programmed patterns of life we have learned and become accustomed to. As a social label, culture has a life of its own, reinforcing the behaviors it influences. These behaviors then feed back onto the social label of culture, so that the label is reinforced as well. Culture thus has a cyclical nature between its properties as a social label and the individual behaviors of its members. Concepts of personality do not share commonality with social labeling, nor with the cyclical nature of a social label (although it can be said that a personality label can cycle with individual behaviors).

Culture versus Popular Culture

From time to time, it is fashionable to refer to fads that come and go as "culture." This is also referred to as "popular culture" by the mass media and in everyday conversation. Popular culture generally refers to trends in music, art, and other expressions that become popular among a group of people.

Certainly popular culture and culture as we have defined it share some similarities—perhaps most important, the sharing of an expression and its value by a group of people. But there are also important differences. For one, popular culture does not necessarily involve sharing a wide range of psychological attributes across various psychological domains. Culture as defined in this chapter involves a system of rules that cuts across attitudes, values, opinions, beliefs, norms, and behaviors. Popular culture may involve sharing in the value of a certain type of expression, but does not necessarily involve a way of life.

A second important difference concerns cultural transmission across generations. Popular culture refers to values or expressions that come and go as fads or trends within a few years. Culture is relatively stable over time and even across generations (despite its dynamic quality and potential for change).

Thus, although culture and popular culture have some similarities, there are important differences as well. The cross-cultural literature in psychology and the culture described in this book is the culture defined in this chapter, not popular culture (although the psychology of popular culture is a topic well deserving of consideration).

Culture and Diversity

Given our functional definition of culture—one that is based on the functioning of psychological processes, rather than on social categories or constructs—we believe that many categories and descriptions of people can be considered as cultural groups. These categories include some that are typically associated with culture, such as race, ethnicity, and nationality, but they also include others not usually associated with culture, such as gender, sexual orientation, and disability. Not only are people who belong to these groups similar in terms of the defining characteristic, such as their nationality or sex, they also share something else—a culture—and their underlying culture is one of the most important features of these individuals. Their culture makes them unique and diverse, especially in relation to their psychology.

Culture and Race

Race is not culture, although many people use the terms interchangeably. Two people of the same race may be very similar or very different in their cultural dispositions and in their actual behaviors, thoughts, and feelings. People of the same racial heritage may share the same socialization processes and thus be enculturated in similar ways. But it is also true that there need not be a one-to-one correspondence between race and culture. Just because you are born with certain physical or biological characteristics defined as "race" does not necessarily mean you adopt the culture that is stereotypic of that race. Culture is learned behavior; race is not.

In fact, although we use the term *race* as if we all know what we are talking about, there is actually considerable controversy surrounding it. Many contemporary scholars suggest that there are three major races—Caucasoid, Mongoloid, and Negroid—but past studies of the origins of race have proposed as many as 37 different races (Yee, Fairchild, Weizmann, & Wyatt, 1993). Although laypersons typically use skin color, hair, and other physical characteristics to define race, most physical anthropologists use population gene frequencies. Regardless of which biological or physical characteristics one uses to define race, the very concept of race is much less clear-cut than previously believed (Lewontin, Rose, & Kamin, 1984). Some authors have suggested that the distinctions among races are arbitrary and dubious at best (Zuckerman, 1990).

Even studies of genetic systems, including blood groups, serum proteins, and enzymes, have shown considerably more within-group than between-group variation, suggesting that racially defined groups are actually more similar than different. There is also controversy about the origins of race. Prevalent theories posit a common ancestor originating in Africa 200,000 years ago, whose descendants then migrated to other parts of the world. Evidence for these theories comes from physical anthropology and archaeology. Other theories and apparently conflicting sets of evidence, however, suggest that humans may have existed in multiple regions of the world as far back as 2,000,000 years ago and that intermixing among regions occurred (Wolpoff & Caspari, 1997).

Many psychologists today agree that race is more of a social construction than a biological essential. Hirschfield (1996) suggests that people have a natural propensity to create categories, especially those dealing with human characteristics. Because easily identifiable physical characteristics are often used in this category-formation process, "race" becomes central to these folk theories and thus gains cognitive and social meaning and importance.

Race as a social construction raises a number of other problems. Category boundaries among the socially constructed races are ambiguous and vary with social context (Davis, 1991; Eberhardt & Randall, 1997; Omi & Winant, 1994). And people of different societies and cultures differ in their definitions of race. In some cultures, race is a continuum along a dimensional scale, not a categorical or nominal entity (Davis, 1991). Many Brazilians believe that race is not heritable and varies according to economic or geographic mobility (Degler, 1971, reported in Eberhardt & Randall, 1997). In some countries, socioeconomic mobility is associated with changes in perceptions of physical properties such as skin color and hair texture (Eberhardt & Randall, 1997).

The study of psychological differences between races is of little scientific or practical use without a clear understanding of the underlying causes of the similarities and differences observed (Betancourt & Lopez, 1993; Zuckerman, 1990). These causes will necessarily involve culture, as defined in this book, because culture as a functional psychological phenomenon determines what is psychologically meaningful and important for different races. Culture is what gives race its meaning, and it is culture that psychologists should be concerned with.

Culture and Ethnicity

Ethnicity is another term used interchangeably with *race* and *culture*. It is most widely used to describe different groups of peoples in the United States and appears to include concepts of both race and culture. Examples of categories typically referred to as ethnic groups include African Americans, Asians and Pacific Islanders, Latinos, and Native Americans. Thus, ethnicity is generally used in reference to groups characterized by a common nationality, geographic origin, culture, or language (Betancourt & Lopez, 1993). The concept of ethnicity is derived from the Greek word *ethnos,* meaning people of a nation or tribe.

Psychologists usually use ethnicity as a category to describe differences among people—reporting, for example, ethnic differences in learning styles, emotion, or parenting. When ethnicity is used only as a category, however, the outcome can be more destructive than constructive. Although information about ethnic differences on a broad range of psychological phenomena can be useful, such information by itself does not explain the nature of the relationship between ethnicity and psychology. Exactly what variables related to ethnicity account for psychological differences among individuals and groups of individuals? The use of ethnicity (or race, for that matter) as a categorical descriptor does little to address this important concern. Put simply, just knowing the ethnicity (or race, or nationality) of a person does little to explain psychological outcomes in cognition, emotion, motivation, or health (Phinney, 1996).

Given the limitations of ethnicity as a category descriptor, it is incumbent on psychologists to go beyond the mere use of ethnic labels to explain individual and group differences in psychology. Phinney (1996) has outlined three key aspects of ethnicity that deserve further attention: cultural norms and values; the strength, salience, and meaning of ethnic identity; and attitudes associated with minority status. We agree with the emphasis on culture as an underlying determinant of psychological functioning. Culture makes ethnic group differences meaningful, and psychologists should focus on it, as well as the other two aspects outlined by Phinney (1996), in understanding and describing ethnicity.

Culture and Nationality

Nationality refers to a person's country of origin and is yet another grouping variable that is often used interchangeably with culture. It is not uncommon, for example, for people to speak of French culture, German culture, Chinese culture, and even American culture. That is, in our language, we often equate nationality with culture.

Nowhere is this clearer than in cross-cultural research. In many cross-cultural studies, researchers obtain data from samples in different countries. When they find differences between the samples, they interpret the differences as a function of culture, not country. That is, researchers often assume that culture underlies country.

It may not be a bad assumption to make. Certainly different countries and nationalities are associated with different cultures as we understand them. And this method of understanding culture and doing research has had its place in the history of cross-cultural psychology.

But such practices are not without their share of problems. Nationality per se is not culture. Just because a person is from France does not necessarily mean that he or she will act in accordance with what we would consider the dominant French culture or with our stereotypes of French people. Just as culture does not necessarily conform to race or racial stereotypes, culture does not necessarily conform to nationality or citizenship. One's passport does not necessarily determine one's cultural values.

Equating nationality with culture is also problematic in that it ignores the possibility of multiple and equally important cultures coexisting within a nation. To assume that everyone from the United States harbors the values, attitudes, and opinions of the "dominant" American culture would be to ignore the multiple cultures that exist within this country. Such multiculturalism probably exists in many countries.

Again, as with race and ethnicity, what is important about nationality in relation to psychology is not citizenship per se, but the underlying cultural attitudes and values that affect individual and group psychology. It is incumbent on psychologists to go beyond describing national differences and calling them culture to examine what aspects of functional psychological culture contribute to national differences in various areas of psychological functioning.

Culture and Gender

Psychologists draw important distinctions between the terms *sex* and *gender*. *Sex* refers to the biological and physiological differences between men and women, the most obvious being the anatomical differences in their reproductive systems. Accordingly, the term *sex roles* is used to describe the behaviors and patterns of activities men and women may engage in that are directly related to their biological differences and the process of reproduction (such as breastfeeding). In contrast, *gender* refers to the behaviors or patterns of activities that a society or culture deems appropriate for men and women. These behavior patterns may or may not be related to sex and sex roles, although they oftentimes are. *Gender role* refers to the degree to which a person adopts the gender-specific and appropriate behaviors ascribed by his or her culture.

Describing and understanding psychological gender differences requires us to go beyond the biological, anatomical, or physiological differences between men and women. Gender differences arise because of differences in the psychological cultures transmitted to men and women. Gender differences are thus cultural differences, and men and women can be said to belong to different cultures. Of course, they may also belong to a larger culture (such as a national culture), and their gender cultures may coexist within the larger culture. This is yet another example of how culture can be understood on multiple levels of analysis, as the definition of culture presented earlier in the chapter suggests.

Culture and Disability

Persons with disabilities differ from those without in that they share some type of physical impairment in their senses, limbs, or other parts of their bodies. Although the lay public has generally viewed the main distinction of persons with disabilities as the physical impairments they have, a growing body of work in psychology has found important sociopsychological characteristics of disability as well (for example, E. C. Clymer, 1995; Hughes & Paterson, 1997; Marks, 1997). Persons with disabilities share the same feelings, ways of thinking, and motivations as everyone else. Beyond that, however, they also share some unique ways of thinking and feeling that may be specific to the fact of their impairment. To the extent that they share certain unique psychological attitudes, opinions, beliefs, behaviors, norms, and values, they share a unique culture.

In recent years, a number of authors have begun to describe the culture of disability (for example, Rose, 1995; Slee & Cook, 1994). These works highlight the unique psychological and sociocultural characteristics of this group of people, refocusing our attention on a broader picture of the person in understanding the psychological characteristics of persons with disabilities. Seen in this light, psychological studies involving participants with disabilities can be viewed as yet another example of cross-cultural studies, as they involve comparisons not only of the presence or absence of impairment, but of more important conditions of culture.

Culture and Sexual Orientation

People form different sexual relationships with others, and the persons with whom they form such relationships constitute a major aspect of their sexual orientation. We often view these relationships as the sole or major defining characteristic of a person's sexual orientation. Yet one of the most important aspects of any sexual orientation—whether straight or gay, mono or bi—is the particular psychological outlook and characteristics that are shared by and unique to each orientation.

These distinctive psychological characteristics may indeed be cultural. Understanding shared psychological attributes among people sharing the same sexual orientation as cultural (for example, gay culture) has become not only fashionable in recent years but well accepted in psychology (Abramson & Pinkerton, 1995; Suggs & Miracle, 1993).

The common thread in this section is that people are often grouped on the basis of shared characteristics that are oftentimes visible or otherwise easily identifiable (race, ethnicity, nationality, sex, disability, or sexual orientation). While there may or may not be objective bases underlying these classifications or groupings, we cannot forget that they are important social constructs and categories. We use these groupings as mental categories, as Hirschfield (1996) has suggested with race. Problems occur, however, when we consider these mental categories as endpoints in and of themselves, instead of as gatekeepers to important sociopsychological—that is, cultural—differences (and similarities) among the categories. Thus, it is crucial to recognize that one of the most important features of each of these social categories is its underlying culture—that unique set of shared attributes that influences its members' psychologies.

Is culture the only important underlying feature of these social groupings? Of course not. There may be a host of other factors, personal and social, psychological and biological, innate and environmental, that affects the psychologies and behaviors of these, and all, individuals. Culture is not the only factor, although it is probably a very important one, in understanding individuals. The interaction between culture and social categories—such as race, nationality, disability, or sexual orientation—is a challenge for future research to uncover. For now, it is important to recognize that culture is one of the most important factors that gives each of these social categories its unique psychological meaning, and it is culture that many psychologists should be concerned with.

Pancultural Principles versus Culture-Specific Differences: Etics and Emics

One way of conceptualizing principles in cross-cultural studies is by using the concepts of etics and emics. **Etics** refer to those aspects of life that appear to be consistent across different cultures; that is, etics refer to universal or pancultural truths or principles. **Emics** refer to those aspects of life that appear to differ across cultures; emics, therefore, refer to truths or principles that are culture-specific. These terms originated in the study of language (Pike, 1954), with phonetics referring to aspects of language and verbal behaviors that are common across cultures, and phonemes referring to aspects of language that are specific to a particular culture and language. Berry (1969) was one of the first to use these linguistic concepts to describe universal versus culturally relative aspects of behavior.

The concepts of etics and emics are powerful because of their implications for what we may know as truth. If we know something about human behavior that we regard as a truth and it is an etic, then it is true for all regardless of culture. However, if that something we know about human behavior is an emic, then what we regard as truth is not necessarily what someone from another culture regards as truth. In this sense, truth may be relative, not absolute. This definition of truth should force us all to reconsider what we believe to be true.

How Does Culture Influence Human Behaviors and Mental Processes?

How can we understand the influence of culture on human behaviors and mental processes? Clearly, with the distinctions we have drawn here, cultures are learned phenomena. Newborns have no culture (although they may very well have biological and temperamental dispositions to learning certain cultural tendencies; see Chapters 5 and 6). As children grow older, they learn specific behaviors and patterns of activities appropriate and inappropriate for their culture, and they either adopt or reject those cultural values and mores.

Berry and his colleagues (1992) have suggested that the model presented in Figure 1.2 describes how cultural practices can affect psychology. In this model, three factors—the ecological environment, the sociopolitical context, and biology—all affect cultural practices. These cultural practices, in turn, influence psychological characteristics and traits. As Berry and colleagues point out, culture is not the only factor influencing psychology; biology and the sociopolitical context influence individual psychologies as well. We would suggest that a host of other factors also influence psychology, including familial and community characteristics, cultural identity, affluence, and the like.

An important point to remember is that the factors involved in understanding culture and psychology, as outlined in Figure 1.2, are not static or unidimensional. The entire system is dynamic and interrelated; it feeds back on and reinforces itself. As mentioned earlier in this chapter, there is a continual tension between individual behaviors within any culture and the cultural labels that are used to describe them. Cultural changes occur when the cultural labels no longer describe a majority of the individuals within that culture; thus, psychological characteristics influence culture as well. As a result, the system is not linear with influences going in a single direction; it acquires a life of its own. And the glue we know as culture reinforces this system.

Figure 1.2 A framework for understanding the contributions of culture, biology, ecology, and sociopolitical context to behavior.

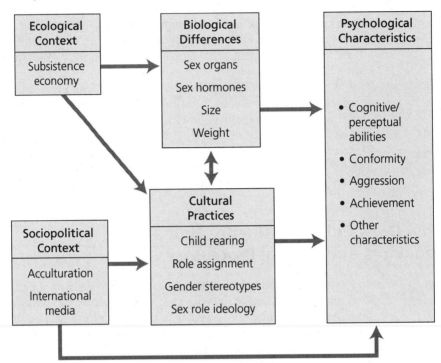

Source: Cross-Cultural Psychology: Research and Applications, by J. W. Berry, Y. H. Pootinga, M. H. Segall, and P. R. Dasen, p. 58. Copyright © 1992 Cambridge University Press. Reprinted with permission of Cambridge University Press.

The Contribution of the Study of Culture

Cross-cultural psychology has contributed much wonderful and important new information to psychological knowledge. Studies comparing people of different cultures date back almost 100 years. The International Association of Cross-Cultural Psychology was founded in 1972. Its flagship journal, the *Journal of Cross-Cultural Psychology,* has been in existence since 1970 and has published many original research articles documenting similarities and differences between cultures. As the field embraces larger, broader-based definitions of culture, psychological studies on cultural diversity are more numerous today than ever before, spanning all the topics of psychology and appearing in mainstream as well as specialty academic journals. The impact of this growth in cross-cultural research on mainstream psychology has been enormous, and is related to both goals described earlier: the creation of knowledge, and the application of that knowledge.

On Psychological Truths:
The Cultural Revolution in Psychology

Despite the wealth of knowledge that has already been gathered in mainstream psychology, it is vitally important to incorporate a cross-cultural approach into our knowledge and learning base. We need to examine whether the information we have learned (or will learn in the future) is applicable to all people of all cultures or only to some people of some cultures. Scientific philosophy suggests that we have a duty and an obligation to ask these questions about the scientific process and about the nature of the truths we have learned, or will learn, about human behavior.

Why is it important to ask and answer these questions? The knowledge that is created in psychology should be accurate and descriptive of all people, not only people of a certain culture (or race, ethnicity, nationality, gender, or sexual orientation). For too many years, students and faculty alike in psychology have been handed information garnered from research that they have questioned as being truly applicable to themselves. Certainly psychology instructors can learn and understand a theory and the research that supports it and then teach it; likewise, students can learn and memorize these theories and facts. But the mere fact that people can teach and learn something does not mean that it accurately reflects all people, and students and faculty members alike have lamented about this issue for years.

The field of psychology has an obligation—to its teachers, students, practitioners, and especially all the people whose lives are touched by its knowledge—to produce accurate knowledge that reflects and applies to them. Cross-cultural research plays an important role in helping psychologists produce that accurate knowledge for all because it tests whether or not what is true for some is also true for others. If it is true for others, then we know that whatever findings were generated from the studies, and whatever theories or models of human behavior were supported by those findings, accurately describe many people. If findings from these studies suggest, however, that truth is relative—true for some but not necessarily true in the same way for others—then they suggest that we need to change our theories, adapt our models and our knowledge, so that they can incorporate those differences among people.

This is not an easy challenge for the field to embrace. In almost any contemporary resource in psychology, cultural diversity in findings and cultural differences in research are widespread and commonplace in all areas of psychology. These differences are forcing psychologists to take a good, hard look at their theories and in many cases to call for revisions, sometimes major, in the way we have conceptualized many aspects of behavior. As a result, many psychologists see an evolution in psychology with culture incorporated as a necessary and important ingredient in mainstream psychology.

In contemporary psychology, cultural similarities and differences in behavior—in thoughts, feelings, attitudes, opinions, motivations, and so on—are part of mainstream theories, not merely interesting side theories by those solely interested in culture. In some cases, incorporating culture as a standard part of any conceptual model may require only minor adjustments to the original theory; in most cases, however, the incorporation of culture requires fundamental and sometimes profound changes in the essence of those theories.

This is only part of the picture. Much of current psychology as a science is a product of traditionally American and European ways of thinking about the mind. The entire scientific process and its products—the theories and models that summarize our understanding of human behavior—are themselves bound and limited by the cultural contexts in which they were derived and existed. These theories and the procedures used to test them may or may not have relevance to people in other cultures. Some authors have even argued that the move toward a cultural psychology should really be a move toward a multicultural psychology—one that incorporates the unique psychologies of the multitude of cultures around the world that may not be assimilable into a single psychology (Gergen et al., 1996). Whether or not that position is accepted, current mainstream psychology clearly needs to move in this direction, finding ways to educate and be educated by other psychological approaches in other cultures. This move involves basic changes in the way psychologists understand many aspects of human behavior. We are in the midst of this evolution in knowledge right now, making it a very exciting time for psychology.

In Our Own Lives and Interactions with Others

The field of psychology also has an obligation to ensure that its knowledge is accurate and applicable for all people of all backgrounds because of the second goal of psychology—to have a positive impact on people's lives. Research and theories in psychology are not simply shelved in libraries; rather, this knowledge forms the basis on which many psychologists intervene in people's lives as counselors, therapists, consultants, and in many other roles. Psychological theories are only as good as their applicability to people in their real lives (Amir & Sharon, 1988; Gergen et al., 1996). And because we touch people's lives, we have to get it right.

As we come more and more in contact with people from different cultural backgrounds, it becomes increasingly important to learn about universals and culture-specifics in our truths—that is, in the beliefs we hold about people and the way they are. More important, we need to use those universals and specifics to help us formulate guiding principles that can be used as resources in our relations with others. To be ignorant of such resources would render us inflexible in our ability to deal with those around us in a dynamic, ever diversifying world.

Yet the content that is produced in cross-cultural psychology is only half the picture. Indeed, one of the main contributions of cross-cultural approaches to applied psychology is the process it fosters in asking questions. Cross-cultural psychology has questions inherently built into its core: Is what we know true for all people regardless of their cultural backgrounds? If not, under what conditions do differences occur, and why? What is it about culture that produces such differences? What factors other than culture, such as socioeconomic class, heredity, or environment, may contribute to these differences? The process of asking these and other important questions about human behavior lies at the core of cross-cultural psychology. The generation of these questions, the harboring of skepticism, and the inquisitive, voyaging nature of the cross-cultural approach together define its process. And this process is even more important than the content. It is impossible to learn everything that has been discovered about enough topics in psychology spanning all the cultures of the world to be effective in intercultural situations in our everyday lives. It makes more sense, therefore, to learn about the process of asking those questions that define a cross-cultural approach because it is the process that we can take with us to all areas of our lives.

This process is as much one of critical thinking as it is anything else. Cross-cultural approaches to psychology, in fact, can be understood as an extension of critical thinking. Improving one's thinking skills in this fashion will aid in everyday life, especially in an increasingly multicultural world.

The Goal of This Book

When we think of cultural diversity and intercultural relations in the United States, some of the most pressing concerns have to do with interethnic and interracial relations in our own states, cities, and communities. Although U.S. society has never been homogeneous, the diversity in the American population and culture is greater today than ever before. This diversity is due to many factors, including immigration trends, technological advances, and increasing global economic and social interdependence. This increasing diversity is not without its share of tension and struggle. Very few universities in today's world are totally free from intergroup conflict regarding issues of race, ethnicity, or culture. Congruent with such concerns, most students want to learn about cultural diversity as it relates to them within this perspective—that is, with a focus on ethnic and racial minorities and intergroup relations within the United States. As you will discover in the remaining chapters of this book, a considerable number of studies conducted in the United States pertain to ethnic differences in a variety of behaviors.

This book has a broader perspective, however, focusing not only on those questions but also on work from other countries and cultures, providing students with a perspective on the United States and American culture in relation to the rest of the world. Much of the information learned in this process can be applied to better our understanding of ethnic and racial groups within the United States. Gaining a broader perspective on our own intracountry differences in relation to the rest of the world will refocus relationships among different groups here in this country. Oftentimes the problems we think are huge because they are right in our faces seem smaller when we understand that they are part of a larger picture of cultural diversity that occurs throughout the world.

Even as we gain a multicultural perspective, we need to realize that we in the United States have a special role with regard to how we deal with cultural diversity and intercultural conflict. The United States is a microcosm of the world, with people of many different cultures coexisting. The problems, issues, and pitfalls that face the entire world face us, and many of the problems we face are or will be faced by others in the future. How we address this challenge bodes well or ill not only for our own future but for the larger global community within which we exist.

As we dive into cross-cultural research and psychology, we must realize that it is neither a panacea nor a utopia of human knowledge. Studying culture does not automatically make cultural conflicts disappear. Instead, studying culture and psychology should give us a better basis on which to understand, respect and appreciate, and empathize with cultural differences when they occur. Liking these differences, or accepting them, is an entirely different question.

Cross-cultural research has its own limitations. Research examining ethnic and cultural differences among groups within the United States is typically not considered cross-cultural and has generally remained separate from the cross-cultural literature. The politics of looking at such differences within the United States has made relevant literature more difficult to assimilate. In cross-cultural research, it is much easier to find or conduct studies that compare Americans as a whole with Japanese or Germans than studies of African Americans versus European Americans or Hispanics versus Asians. The former studies often suffer because they assume that Americans are homogeneous in comparison to other cultural groups in other countries. The participants in such studies are usually middle-class Americans of European ancestry.

But these problems should not deter us from our quest for the truth about human behavior. Just as we need to take what we can from previous, culture-bound research, we must do the same with the cross-cultural literature. We must recognize the limitations and the parameters under which the information was derived and somehow build a foundation from little bits and pieces of information that will come together into a larger, coherent structure.

After all is said and done, what do we intend that you gain from this book? In challenging the traditional, we do not mean to disregard its importance or the importance of the work that produced that knowledge. Instead, we seek to raise questions about the traditional, mainstream knowledge of human behavior. We want to know whether what we know of organizations, development, personality, emotion, communication, and many other aspects of human behavior is applicable to people of all cultural backgrounds. We want to challenge the traditional by seeking out answers to these questions in the cross-cultural literature. And if the research suggests that people are different from what is typically believed, we want to find better ways to understand those differences than are available today. We want to impart the flavor of the evolution in science and knowledge that is now occurring.

We offer this book to you as a way to understand, appreciate, respect, and feel cultural diversity and its influence on human behavior. In this book, there should be no right and wrong, no good and bad. In learning about others—in meeting the challenge of cultural diversity—our biggest challenge is within ourselves.

Glossary

cross-cultural approach A viewpoint for understanding truth and principles about human behaviors across cultures.

cross-cultural research Any type of research on human behavior that compares specific behaviors across two or more cultures. This approach is primarily concerned with testing the possible limitations of knowledge gleaned from one culture by studying people of different cultures.

culture The set of attitudes, values, beliefs, and behaviors shared by a group of people, but different for each individual, communicated from one generation to the next.

culture-specific A research finding considered to be true for some people of some cultures but not for others.

emics Aspects of life that appear to differ across cultures; truths or principles that are culture-specific.

etics Aspects of life that appear to be consistent across different cultures; universal or pancultural truths or principles.

InfoTrac College Edition

Use InfoTrac College Edition® to search for additional readings on topics of interest to you. For more information on topics in this chapter, use the following as a search term:

cross-cultural psychology

Cross-Cultural Research Methods

Why It Is Important to Understand Cross-Cultural Research Methods

Learning basic concepts underlying cross-cultural research is important because the ability to read and understand cross-cultural research is an integral part of understanding the relationship between culture and psychology. It is a skill that is crucial to understanding and evaluating the work that will be presented in the remainder of the book. It is a skill that many of you will need to conduct literature reviews and evaluate that literature. And it is a skill that many of you will need in your continued work in the field, conducting your own studies and evaluating those of others.

Not only is it important to be able to read and understand cross-cultural research; you also need to be able to evaluate it on its own merits. As active consumers of research in your everyday and academic lives, you need to review research with a critical but fair and open mind, accepting information or conclusions not because your teacher told you or because you read about it in an abstract or discussion section of a paper. Instead, you need to be able to access the literature directly, read everything about a study from the theoretical framework and hypotheses through the methods of data collection and analysis to the interpretation of the findings, and make up your own mind as to whether you believe the findings are valid and reliable. You need to have established criteria for making those judgments, and you need to know which questions to raise when reviewing that research.

This chapter presents the information necessary to allow you to do so. First, we will review different types of cross-cultural research. Next, we will discuss in detail the specific issues involved in cross-cultural research, from theory and method to data to interpretation. Then, we will discuss how to transform the abstract concept of culture into a measurable construct. Finally, we will provide you with a chart that you can use to systematically review research on your own.

Types of Cross-Cultural Research

We introduce five types of cross-cultural research: cross-cultural comparison studies, unpackaging studies, ecological-level studies, cross-validation studies, and ethnographies. Each of them is important in its own right, and all have been used to make important contributions to our understanding of culture and psychology.

Cross-Cultural Comparison Studies

By far the most prevalent type of hypothesis-testing study is the **cross-cultural comparison study**—one that compares two or more cultures on some psychological variable of interest. These studies examine whether the cultures in the study differ from each other on the variable, often with the hypothesis that one culture will have significantly higher scores on the variable than the other. These studies are important to the psychological literature because they test the limitations to knowledge generated in mainstream psychological research and help to advance our theoretical and conceptual thinking in all areas of psychology.

Unpackaging Studies

Another type of hypothesis-testing cross-cultural study is one that examines *why* cultural differences occur. These **unpackaging studies** not only look for differences among cultures on their target variables but also include measurements of other variables that researchers believe will account for those differences. Poortinga, Van de Vijver, Joe, and van de Koppel (1987) have likened these types of studies to the peeling of an onion—layer after layer until nothing is left. These researchers view culture in the following way:

> In our approach culture is a summary label, a catchword for all kinds of behavior differences between cultural groups, but within itself, of virtually no explanatory value. Ascribing intergroup differences in behavior, e.g., in test performance, to culture does not shed much light on the nature of these differences. It is one of the main tasks of cross-cultural psychology to peel off cross-cultural differences, i.e., to explain these differences in terms of specific antecedent variables, until in the end they have disappeared and with them the variable culture. In our approach culture is taken as a concept without a core. From a method-

ological point of view, culture can be considered as an immense set of often loosely interrelated independent variables. (p. 22; see also Segall, 1984; Strodtbeck, 1964)

In unpackaging studies, culture as an unspecified variable is replaced by more specific variables in order to truly explain cultural differences. These variables, called *context variables,* should be measured to examine the degree to which they can statistically account for cultural differences. Inferences about the nature of cultural differences can then incorporate the degree of contribution by the context variables. If the context variable included in any study does not account for all of the differences between cultures, then other context variables should be incorporated in subsequent research to account for more of the differences among cultures, until all the differences have been accounted for.

Ecological-Level Studies

Although most hypothesis-testing cross-cultural research uses individual participants as the unit of analysis, **ecological-level studies** use countries or cultures as the unit of analysis. Data may be obtained from individuals in different cultures, but they are often summarized or averaged for each culture, and those averages are used as data points for each culture. Examples of such ecological-level studies include Hofstede's (1980, 1983) studies of cultural values across 50+ cultures; Triandis, Bontempo, Villareal, Asai, and Lucca's (1988) study of the relationship between individualism–collectivism and incidence of heart attacks in eight cultures; Matsumoto and Fletcher's (1996) study of the relationship between four cultural dimensions and incidence rates for six disease states; and Matsumoto's (1989) study of the relationship between cultural dimensions and judgments of emotion in 15 cultures.

There are important differences in the interpretations justified on the basis of ecological- versus individual-level research. A relationship between a cultural variable and a target variable (for example, individualism and the incidence of cardiovascular disease) on the ecological level does not necessarily mean that such a relationship exists on the individual level. The relationship may or may not exist on the individual level within the cultures studied, and if it does, it may or may not be in the same direction (also see Leung, 1989.)

Cross-Cultural Validation Studies

Cross-cultural validation studies examine whether a measure of a psychological construct that was originally generated in a single culture is applicable, meaningful, and thus equivalent in another culture. These studies do not test a specific hypothesis about cultural differences; rather, they test the equivalence of psychological measures and tests for use in other cross-cultural comparative research. Although these types of studies are not as common as hypothesis-testing cross-cultural research, they serve an important purpose in investigating the cross-cultural applicability of many of the methodological techniques used in research.

Ethnographies

Ethnographies are conducted mainly by anthropologists, but also by some cross-cultural psychologists. They involve considerable observation and field-work, with the researchers visiting and oftentimes living together with the people they are interested in studying. Being immersed in a culture for an extended period of time, these researchers learn firsthand the customs, rituals, traditions, beliefs, and ways of life of the culture to which they are exposed. Comparisons to other cultures are done on the basis of their own knowledge, experience, and education about their own and other cultures. This approach is not unlike the case study of individual lives, with cultures serving as the larger unit of analysis. As such, it shares many of the advantages of that approach, including the richness and complexity of the data obtained, as well as the disadvantages in terms of generalizability. These ethnographic studies make an important contribution to the field, complementing existing hypothesis-testing research on specific psychological variables.

These five typologies describe the general range of approaches to cross-cultural research. Like all research, however, studies are as varied as the individuals who design and conduct them. The descriptions provided here, therefore, are not intended as exhaustive categories of the breadth of cross-cultural approaches; rather they are guidelines for the types of cross-cultural studies typically conducted and seen in the literature.

Special Issues Concerning Cross-Cultural Comparisons

In this section, we discuss issues concerning the conduct of cross-cultural comparisons because this is the most prevalent type of study, the one that underlies much of the information in this book, and the basis of unpacking research. Many of the issues in cross-cultural comparisons are really extensions of issues pertaining to all types of research; the issues of equivalence in concept and method and of validity and reliability in measurement are the same for all types of studies. Some issues, however, pertain solely to the conduct of research in different cultures and countries—among them, the issue of language comparability and translation, and the possibility of cultural response sets in the data. This section will give you a flavor of just what these issues are, to better equip you for reading, understanding, and evaluating cross-cultural research on your own.

Equivalence

One concept that is of crucial importance in the conduct and evaluation of cross-cultural research is that of equivalence. **Equivalence** in cross-cultural research can be defined as a state or condition of similarity in conceptual meaning and empirical method between cultures that allows comparisons to be meaningful. In its strictest sense, if any aspect of a cross-cultural study is not entirely equivalent in meaning or method across the cultures being compared, then the comparison loses its meaning. Lack of equivalence in a cross-cultural study creates the proverbial situation of comparing apples and oranges. Only if the theoretical framework and hypotheses have equivalent meaning in the cultures being compared, and if the methods of data collection, management, and analysis have equivalent meaning, will the results from that comparison be meaningful. Apples in one culture can be compared only to apples in another. Lack of equivalence is also known as *bias*.

Theoretical Issues

Researchers decide what hypotheses to test based on some theoretical model. But especially in cross-cultural work, it is important to realize that theories are bound and influenced by the cultural framework of the theorist. How we think about people, interpersonal relationships, basic human nature, fate, luck, supernatural forces, and the like are all influenced by our culture. Thus, when psychologists create theories about human behavior, the cultural framework of the people who create them binds those theories themselves.

As every hypothesis-testing study examines hypotheses that are generated from culture-bound theories, a major concern of cross-cultural research is the equivalence in meaning of the overall theoretical framework being tested, and the meaning and importance of the specific hypotheses being addressed. If these are not equivalent across the cultures participating in the study, then the data obtained from them are not comparable, because they mean different things. If, however, the theoretical framework and hypotheses are equivalent across the participating cultures, the study may be meaningful and relevant.

For example, people trained to do research in the United States or Europe may be bound by a sense of "logical determinism" and "rationality" that is characteristic of such formal and systematic educational systems. In addition, because we are so used to drawing two-dimensional theories of behavior on paper, that medium affects the way we think about people and psychology. Other people of the world who have not been exposed to such an educational system or who are not used to reducing their thoughts about the world onto a two-dimensional space may not think in the same way. If this is the case, then a real question arises as to whether a theory created within a Western cultural framework is meaningful in the same way to people who do not share that culture. If the theory is not meaningful in the same way, then it is not equivalent.

Researchers who formulate research questions and specific hypotheses have their own cultural upbringing and backgrounds, and hence their own biases. Whether good or bad, right or wrong, conscious or unconscious, these biases influence the types of questions we think are important and, subsequently, those questions we believe should be studied in cross-cultural research.

Will a hypothesis that we believe is important to test be important or meaningful in the same way to someone from a different cultural background? For example, suppose researchers want to examine cultural differences in how quickly people can solve maze-type puzzles presented to them on a computer. It might be interesting and relevant to conduct this type of study in the United

States, Hong Kong, and France and compare the results for these participants. But this study might not be as relevant for people from other cultures. People in some cultures may actually be afraid of using a computer.

Or suppose researchers decided to study cultural differences in problem-solving ability in the United States and among tribespeople in Africa. One method might be to present subjects in both cultures with a device that had to be manipulated in some way to obtain a reward, such as money. The Americans might be able to approach this task and be successful at it. The tribespeople, however, might believe the task to be entirely meaningless, might view the contraption with fear, and might not care one bit about money. In contrast, if the problem-solving task involved tracking different animals by using scents and footprints, the tribespeople might respond very positively to the task. Imagine American subjects performing such a task!

Methodological Issues

Among the many methodological issues affecting cross-cultural research are those involving definitions of culture, sampling, noncultural demographic equivalence, definitions of variables, language barriers, and research procedures.

Definitions of culture. When cross-cultural researchers do a study, they may decide to gather data from different countries. Researchers therefore often make the assumption that country equals culture. However, most cross-cultural scholars define culture as the shared conglomeration of attitudes, values, behaviors, and beliefs communicated from one generation to the next via language. This definition of culture is subjective not objective, and sociopsychological not biological.

Despite this definition of culture, cross-cultural researchers have lacked an adequate way of measuring this "sharing" of psychological characteristics in their research. Instead, they have relied on aspects of people that are easier to measure—typically, race (for example, black versus white), ethnicity (for example, Latino versus Asian American), or nationality (for example, American, Japanese, German, Brazilian). Although there is certainly overlap between culture and these other social constructs, reliance on these constructs can be problematic.

As noted in Chapter 1, a number of writers have pointed out the inadequacy of using race as a grouping variable in comparative research. Zuckerman (1990), for example, observed that there is more variability within racial groups than between them on such items as skin color, hair type and color, eye color, stature, head shape and size, facial features, and blood type. Further, these features are not correlated with one another, and none can unequivocally distinguish among racial groups. He then went on to analyze cross-racial differences in temperament, crime, and personality and suggested that there are considerably more differences within groups than between them on these variables as well. Rather than working to help bridge gaps among people, Zuckerman (1990) concluded, psychological research using self-classification by participants into a racial grouping can actually undermine such attempts, allowing the findings from such research to foster racism instead. By reducing culture to race, these procedures promote stereotypic beliefs and opinions about people.

Most, if not all, of the studies conducted to date and presented in this book have measured culture by either race, ethnicity, or nationality. Still, we should not categorically dismiss these studies or their findings; they provide us with valuable information about possible cultural differences because cultural differences do underlie countries. These studies alert us to the limitations of what we know and regard as truth based on research from mainstream academia. Thus, it is still important for us to consider them, but we must consider them with a degree of caution because of the discrepancy between our definition of culture and the definition of culture used in the research.

Besides the issue of how to measure culture, researchers must decide which cultures to include in a study. More often than not, cross-cultural researchers have studied cultures as a matter of convenience rather than on the basis of compelling theoretical, empirical, or practical questions. Technology has now advanced to the point where conducting a study almost anywhere has become possible for most people who want to do so. As the ease of such choices increases, it becomes even more incumbent on cross-cultural researchers to exercise those choices wisely based on compelling reasons rather than convenience. Thus, the choice of cultures to include in a study and to compare becomes another dimension on which to evaluate cross-cultural research.

Sampling adequacy.   More often than not, researchers assume that a group of people who participate in a cross-cultural study (the **sample**) are "good" representatives of that particular culture. For instance, in the simplest cross-cultural research design, researchers obtain a sample of people in one culture, obtain data from them, and compare those data to data collected in another culture or to known values. Let's say a researcher obtained a sample of 50 Americans as part of a cross-cultural study. Are the 50 Americans adequate representatives of American culture? If they were recruited from Beverly Hills in California, would that be the same as recruiting 50 participants from the Bronx in New York? Or 50 people from Wichita, Kansas? If the 50 participants were all of European descent, would they be an "adequate" sample? If not, what percentage of people of different racial and ethnic backgrounds would the researcher need to include? If the sample required 25 % to be of African descent, does it matter which African Americans are included? What criteria can be used to decide whether the sample of 50 people are representative of American culture? What is "American" culture anyway?

These questions are endless, not easy to answer, and pertain to any sample of participants in any culture. Cross-cultural researchers need to pay particular attention to issues of **sampling** in the conduct of their research. The unrealistic and unacceptable assumption of homogeneity among group members can only serve to perpetuate stereotypic impressions and interpretations based on the findings. That is, when differences are found, researchers assume that the differences are "cultural" because they assume that the samples are representatives of culture. In reality, the differences a researcher finds in a study of the United States, Japan, Brazil, and Mexico may be the same as the differences that would be found in a study of Minneapolis, Los Angeles, Miami, and Newark.

Addressing this issue is extremely difficult. In its strictest sense, proper addressing of this issue would require the following steps: (1) The researcher would have to be able to theoretically define exactly what the cultures are that are being tested. (2) The researcher would have to be able to access a pool of individuals from the larger population that embodied those characteristics. (3) The researcher would have to randomly sample from that larger population. (4) The researcher would have to measure those social, cultural, and psychological characteristics in the participants and empirically demonstrate that the culture manipulations occurred as intended.

This is a tall order that is not, and perhaps cannot, be filled by current researchers because of the limitations on our ability to theorize about and subsequently measure culture on the individual level, and because of our inability to randomly access all members of any given cultural population. Given that we cannot currently achieve this ideal, the real issue facing researchers concerns the degree to which they understand how far from this ideal they are and the extent to which they use this information to temper their interpretations. In a practical sense, a sound cross-cultural comparison would entail the collection of data from multiple sites within the same cultural group, either in the same study or across studies, to demonstrate the replicability of a finding across different samples within the same culture.

Noncultural demographic equivalence. A different question involving sampling is whether the samples are equivalent in all possible ways except culture so that a comparison among them is a comparison of culture and not something else. For the research to be methodologically sound, researchers need to make sure the samples they compare are somehow equivalent on noncultural demographic variables. If they are not equivalent on demographic variables, then those variables on which they are not equivalent would confound the comparison in the study.

For example, imagine comparing data from a sample of 50 Americans from Los Angeles with 50 individuals from Bombay, India. Clearly, the Americans and the Indians come from entirely different backgrounds—different socioeconomic classes, different educational levels, different social experiences, different forms of technology, different religious backgrounds, and so on. How can you know that any differences, if found, are due to culture rather than other factors?

There are basically two ways of dealing with this problem, which also affects monocultural studies. The first and best way to deal with this issue is to identify the major participant characteristics that need to be controlled and to select individuals for participation by holding those variables constant in the selection. In doing so, the experimenter can either hold those variables constant within and between groups (for example, including only females of a certain age in the entire study in all cultures) or just between groups (including the same ratio of males and females in all cultures). Sex and age are relatively easy to hold constant, and certainly should be. They are not, however, the only variables that should be held constant by far.

The conceptual problem that arises in cross-cultural research is that some noncultural demographic characteristics are inextricably intertwined with culture such that researchers cannot hold them constant across samples in a comparison. Religion is an example. There are differences in the meaning and practice of religions across cultures that make them oftentimes inextricably bound to culture. Holding religion constant across cultures does not address the issue because being Catholic in the United States does not mean the same thing as being Catholic in Japan or Malaysia. Randomly sampling without regard to religion will result in samples that differ not only on culture but also on religion (to the extent that one can separate the two's influences). Thus, presumed cultural differences often reflect religious differences across samples as well. The same is often true also for socioeconomic status (SES) as there are vast differences in SES across cultural samples from around the world.

The second way of dealing with this problem is to statistically assess and eliminate the possible effects of noncultural demographic variables. That is, researchers can find some solace in the fact that if their samples differ on religion, SES, or other demographic variables, they can engage in specific analyses to examine their contribution to the group differences based on the distributions of these data across the samples. Of course, such analyses depend on the researchers' having measured these variables reliably in the first place—a step that many researchers fail to accomplish—and that the variables are distributed in all cultures tested. Examining within-culture correlations between scalar demographic variables and the target dependent variables will assess the degree to which the demographics are related to the dependents; if they are related, covariance or regression analyses may be used to eliminate their effects in testing between-culture differences (assuming other assumptions of covariance and regression are met).

Still, if the cultures are confounded by noncultural demographics, after-the-fact analyses can only "take care" of noncultural demographic confounds to a certain degree. As with all methodologies, no amount of sophisticated analyses can "fix" real methodological problems. The larger issue, therefore, is not whether the cultural groups also differ on noncultural demographic characteristics, but whether the researchers who conducted the study are aware of these differences. When differences are found on their target variables, researchers who are not aware of the noncultural demographic factors usually assume that the observed differences reflect cultural differences—which may not be the case. Researchers who are aware of demographic differences, however, will present data concerning their sample characteristics, engage in some formal statistical tests to examine the contribution of these characteristics to their variables of interest, and temper their interpretations according to what they find. As consumers of cross-cultural research, we need to be aware of such alternative interpretations of the data even when the researchers are not.

The conceptual and empirical definitions of variables. Of all the issues involving cross-cultural equivalence, those concerning the **validity** and **reliability** of the conceptual meaning and methodological operationalization of variables are arguably the most crucial to any cross-cultural study. Different cultures may conceptually define a construct differently and/or measure it differently. Just because something has the same name in two or more cultures does not mean that it has the same meaning (Wittgenstein, 1953/1968, cited in Poortinga, 1989) or that it can be measured in the same way. If a concept means different things to people of different cultures, or if it is measured in different ways in different cultures, then comparisons can be meaningless. Cross-cultural researchers need to be keenly aware of the issue of equivalence with regard to their conceptual definitions and empirical **operationalization** of the variables (the way researchers conceptually define a variable and measure it) in their study.

Debate concerning cross-cultural studies of intelligence highlights these issues. Many researchers in the United States in the past have considered intelligence to consist mainly of verbal and analytical types of critical thinking skills. Tests (such as the WAIS) assessing these skills have been widely used in this research. This definition may have been fine for the United States, but a different culture may have a different conception of what constitutes intelligence. For example, let's say a culture considers nobility of character and sincerity as markers of intelligence. If we test a sample of people from this culture on the WAIS and compare these data to American data, are we really studying cross-cultural differences in intelligence? Another culture may consider the ability to have smooth, conflict-free interpersonal relationships a marker for intelligence. Yet another culture may consider creativity and artistic abilities to be indices of intelligence. Would comparisons of WAIS data from all of these cultures constitute cross-cultural comparisons of intelligence? Of course, researchers may be interested in the specific traits being measured; the problem occurs when we interpret them as defining a concept of "intelligence" that is assumed to be true for everyone.

Even if a researcher can establish equivalence in the conceptual definition of a variable, the empirical operationalization of it is another question. Let's say, for example, that two cultures do indeed define intelligence in terms of verbal and analytic abilities, such as those measured by the WAIS. Now let's look at the exact ways in which the WAIS measures this definition of intelligence. If the test includes a question about American presidents, can we use the test in this study? Would it be fair to give subjects in France this test to measure their intelligence? With regard to ability tests (such as intelligence and aptitude testing), some writers go as far as to suggest that such tests are inherently nonequivalent across cultures. Greenfield (1997), for example, argues that constructs such as intelligence and cognitive ability are inherently symbolic products of a culture. As such, the constructs and tests of it presuppose a certain cultural framework in order to be valid. Because these frameworks are not universally shared, cross-cultural comparisons of ability and intelligence are meaningless. A totally opposite viewpoint, however, is that concepts of intelligence, aptitudes, and abilities are shared across cultures and thus comparable for research purposes.

Similar questions may arise concerning the equivalence in construct and operation of values. Peng, Nisbett, and Wong (1997), for example, have argued that common methods for assessing values, such as giving participants a list of values and asking them to rate them or rank them in order of importance, may not be valid across cultures. They suggest that such methods may be invalid because of cultural differences in the meanings of specific value items and because some value judgments may be based on inherent social comparisons with others rather than on direct inferences about a private, personal value system. In order to investigate this possibility, these researchers examined four different value survey methods: the traditional ranking, rating, and attitude scaling procedures and a behavioral scenario rating method. The only method that yielded reasonable validity estimates was the behavioral scenario rating method, the most unorthodox of all the measures tested.

Questions concerning equivalence in construct and measurement of variables not only involve those measures that yield single scores, but extend also to methods involving multiple item measurement and multiple scale score computation. If a researcher uses a scale with 50 items that score to five different scales, questions arise as to whether each of the 50 items represents the construct equivalently in all cultures tested and whether the five scales are equivalently represented in all cultures. As factor analysis is often used to derive scale scores from a larger pool of items on a measure, similar factor analytic results in all cultures being studied would be one way to assess the degree of equivalence across cultures, at least in the scale structure of the measure.

A simple way to illustrate these issues regarding equivalence of conceptual definitions and empirical methods is to use the analogy of a cross-cultural study on temperature. Let's say we are interested in conducting such a study between two cultures, A and B. The first question is whether both cultures have a concept of temperature, and whether it refers to the same thing in both cultures. If the answer is no, then it may be pointless to continue with a comparative study of temperature (although other study possibilities do exist). If the answer is yes, then the next question is how to measure it. If culture A measures temperature on the Celsius (C) scale, while culture B measures temperature on the Fahrenheit (F) scale, then clearly those methods of measuring temperature are not directly comparable. It is incumbent on the researchers to find a way to measure temperature that is equivalent in both cultures, and then to compare those scores.

Poortinga (1989) has suggested that when a measure has high content validity in all cultures being tested (it has been shown to mean the same thing in all cultures), and when the construct being measured is in a psychological domain that is similar or identical across cultures (such as color schemes or pitch scale for tones), valid comparisons are generally possible. When unobservable psychological traits and attributes are being measured, comparison may still be possible as long as equivalence in the conceptual meaning of the psychological domain and its measurement has been established for all participating cultures. All other research situations, according to Poortinga (1989), preclude valid comparison across cultures.

Language and translation issues. Cross-cultural research typically involves conducting studies in multiple languages, and researchers need to establish the linguistic equivalence of the research protocols. There are generally two procedures used to establish linguistic equivalence. One is known as back translation (Brislin, 1970); the other uses a committee approach.

Back translation involves taking the research protocol in one language, translating it to the other language(s), and having someone else translate it back to the original. If the back-translated version is the same as the original, they are generally considered equivalent. If it is not, the procedure is repeated until the back-translated version is the same as the original. The concept underlying this procedure is that the end product must be a semantic equivalent to the original English. The original language is **decentered** through this process (Brislin, 1970, 1993), with any culture-specific concepts of the original language eliminated or translated equivalently into the target language. That is, culture-specific meanings and connotations are gradually eliminated from the research protocols so that what remains is something that is the closest semantic equivalents in both languages. Because they are linguistic equivalents, successfully back-translated protocols are comparable in cross-cultural hypothesis-testing research.

The second approach to establishing language equivalence is the committee approach, in which several bilingual informants collectively translate a research protocol into a target language. They debate the various forms, words, and phrases that can be used in the target language, comparing them with their understanding of the language of the original protocol. The product of this process reflects a translation that is the shared consensus of a linguistically equivalent protocol across languages and cultures.

Researchers may combine the two approaches. Here, a protocol may be initially translated and back-translated. Then, the translation and back-translation can be used as an initial platform from which a translation committee works on the protocol, modifying the translation in ways they deem most appropriate, using the back-translation as a guideline.

Even if the words being used in the two languages are the same, there is no guarantee that those words have exactly the same meanings, with the same nuances, in the two cultures. A successful translation gives the researcher protocols that are the closest linguistic equivalents in two or more different languages. However, they still may not be exactly the same. In translating the English word *anger,* for example, we might indeed find an equivalent word in Russian or Swahili. But would it have the same connotations, strength, and interpretation in those languages as it does in English? It is very difficult to find exact translation equivalents of most words.

Such subtle differences are inherent and inevitable when doing cross-cultural research. Cross-cultural researchers need to be aware of issues of language equivalence so as not to confuse language differences with the cultural differences they want to test. "Perfect" equivalence between any two languages is unattainable, and this fact should be considered when evaluating cross-cultural research. The astute researcher and research consumer should be able to incorporate such subtle influences in their interpretations of the data.

The research environment, setting, and procedures.   The issue of equivalence also applies to the environment, setting, and procedures used to collect data in different cultures. In many universities across the United States, students enrolled in introductory psychology classes are strongly encouraged to participate as research subjects in partial fulfillment of class requirements. U.S. students generally expect to participate in research as part of their academic experience, and many American students are "research-wise."

Customs differ in other countries. In some countries, professors simply collect data from their students or require them to participate at a research laboratory. In some countries, students may consider it a privilege rather than a chore or course requirement to participate in an international study. Thus, expectations about and experience with research participation may differ.

All the decisions researchers make in any other type of study are made in cross-cultural studies as well. But those decisions can mean different things in different countries. Laboratory or field, day or night, questionnaire or observation—all these decisions may have different meanings in different cultures. Cross-cultural researchers need to confront these differences in their work and establish procedures, environment, and setting that are equivalent across the cultures being compared. By the same token, consumers need to be aware of these possible differences when evaluating cross-cultural research.

Data Analysis Issues

Although the major issues regarding equivalence in cross-cultural research are methodological, issues regarding data and data analysis are not devoid of such influence. In fact, one of the most important issues that researchers and consumers alike need to be aware of is the possibility of cultural response sets.

Cultural response sets.   A **cultural response set** is the tendency for members of a culture to use certain parts of a scale when responding. For example, suppose participants in the United States and Korea are asked to judge the intensity of a certain stimulus, using a 7-point scale. When examining the data, the researcher may find that Americans generally scored around 6 or 7, whereas Koreans generally scored around 4 or 5. The researcher may interpret these findings to mean that the Americans perceived more intensity in the stimulus than did the Koreans. But what if Koreans actually rate everything lower than Americans, not just this stimulus? What if they actually perceive a considerable degree of intensity in the stimulus but have a cultural tendency to use the lower part of the scale? If cultural response sets exist, any differences found among cultures may reflect these response tendencies rather than actual differences on the items the researcher intended to measure.

Cultural response sets may act in different ways. Members of collectivistic cultures may hesitate to use the extreme endpoints of a scale, consistent with a cultural reluctance to "stick out." Members of other cultural groups may be more inclined to use the endpoints. Bachman and O'Malley (1984), for example, found evidence of extreme response styles among African Americans, and Marin, Gamba, and Marin (1992) found similar evidence for Latinos.

To the extent that these cultural differences result in different uses of response alternatives on questionnaires or interviews, they contribute to nonequivalence in the data, making valid comparisons difficult. Fortunately, statistical manipulations allow researchers to assess whether cultural response sets may be operating in a data set, and to deal with them if found. Researchers need to be aware of cultural response sets and the statistical techniques available to deal with them (see Matsumoto, 1994, for an introduction), and consumers of that research need to be similarly aware.

Effect size analysis. In testing cultural differences on target variables of interest, researchers often use inferential statistics such as chi-square or analysis of variance (ANOVA). These statistics compare the differences observed between the groups to the differences one would normally expect on the basis of chance alone and then compute the probability that the results would have been obtained solely by chance. If the probability of obtaining the findings they did is very low (less than 5%), then researchers infer that the findings did not occur because of chance—that is, that the findings reflect actual differences between the cultural groups from which their samples were drawn. This "proof by negation of the opposite" is at the heart of the logic underlying hypothesis testing and statistical inference.

Just because differences between group means are statistically significant, however, does not by itself give an indication of the degree of practical difference between the groups. Group means may be statistically different even though there is considerable overlap among the scores of individuals comprising the two groups.

One mistake that researchers and consumers of research alike make when interpreting group differences is that they assume that most people of those groups differ in ways corresponding to the mean values. Thus, if a statistically significant difference is found between Americans and Japanese, for instance, on emotional expressivity such that Americans had statistically significantly higher scores than the Japanese, people often conclude that all Americans are more expressive than all Japanese. This, of course, is a mistake in interpretation that is fueled by the field's fascination and single-minded concern with statistical significance.

Statistical procedures are available that help to determine the degree to which differences in mean values reflect meaningful differences among individuals. The general class of statistics that do this is called effect size statistics; when used in a cross-cultural setting, Matsumoto and his colleagues call them *cultural effect size statistics* (Matsumoto, Grissom, & Dinnel, 2001). Matsumoto et al. present four such statistics that they deem most relevant for cross-cultural analyses, with reanalyses from two previously published studies as examples. Whether cross-cultural researchers use these or other statistics, it is incumbent on them to include some kind of effect size analysis when comparing cultures so that informed readers can determine the degree to which the differences reported reflect meaningful differences among people. With these statistics, researchers and consumers can have an idea of the degree to which the between-group cultural differences actually reflect differences among the individuals tested, helping to break the hold of stereotypic interpretations based on group difference findings.

Interpretation Issues

Several issues are especially pertinent to interpreting findings obtained in cross-cultural research—among them, cause–effect versus correlational interpretations, the role of researcher bias and value judgments, and dealing with nonequivalent data.

Cause–effect versus correlational interpretations.

In hypothesis-testing cross-cultural studies, cultural groups are often treated as independent variables in research design and data analysis, making these studies a form of quasi-experiment. Data from such studies are basically correlational, and inferences drawn from them can only be correlational inferences. For example, if a researcher compared data from the United States and Japan on social judgments and found that Americans had significantly higher scores on a person perception task, any interpretations of these data would be limited to the association between cultural membership (American or Japanese) and the scores. Cause–effect inferences (for example, being American causes one to have higher person perception scores) are unwarranted. For such causal statements to be justified, the researcher would have had to (1) create the conditions of the experiment (the cultural groups) and (2) randomly assign people to each of the conditions. These experimental conditions cannot apply in any study in which one of the main variables is cultural group. It makes no more sense to assume a causal relationship between cultural membership and a variable of interest than it does to assume such a relationship on the basis of sex, hair color, or height.

A related type of mistaken interpretation is to suggest specific reasons why cultural differences occurred even though the specific reasons were never measured in the study. For instance, a researcher might take the significant American–Japanese differences found in the previous example and suggest that these differences occurred because of differences between individualism and collectivism in the two cultures. Unless the researchers actually measured individualism and collectivism in their study, found that the two cultures differed on this dimension, and showed that it accounted for the cultural group differences on social judgments, the interpretation that this construct (IC) is responsible for the group differences is unwarranted. Such interpretations about why a cultural group difference has occurred often appear in cross-cultural research articles, but they should be taken only as suggesting a possible context variable for further investigation. Problems arise when researchers and consumers assume that there is a relationship between the cultures and the context variable, and that the context variable actually accounts for the cultural differences. In accordance with Poortinga et al.'s (1987) suggestions, we believe that these types of context variables need to be measured directly in cross-cultural research for such interpretations to be warranted.

Researcher bias and value judgments.   Just as culture can bias formulation of the research questions in a cross-cultural study, it can also bias the ways researchers interpret their findings. Most researchers inevitably interpret the data they obtain through their own cultural filters, and these biases can affect their interpretations to varying degrees. For example, if the mean response for Americans on a rating scale is 6.0 and the mean for Hong Kong Chinese is 4.0, one interpretation is that the Americans simply scored higher on the scale. Another interpretation may be that the Chinese are suppressing their responses. This type of interpretation is common, especially in research with Asian samples. But how do we know the Chinese are suppressing their responses? What if it is the Americans who are exaggerating their responses? What if the Chinese mean response of 4.0 is actually the more "correct" one, and the American mean is the one that is off? What if we surveyed the rest of the world and found that the overall mean was 3.0, suggesting that both the Chinese and the Americans inflated their ratings? In other words, the interpretation that the Chinese are suppressing their responses is based on an implicit assumption that the American data are "correct." One of us has made this sort of ethnocentric interpretation of research findings in a study involving American and Japanese judgments of the intensity of facial expressions of emotion, without really giving much consideration to other possibilities (Matsumoto & Ekman, 1989). In later research (Matsumoto, Kasri, & Kooken, 1999), we were able to show that in fact the Americans exaggerated their intensity ratings of faces, relative to inferences about subjective experience of the posers; the Japanese did not suppress.

Anytime researchers make a **value judgment** or interpretation of a finding, it is always possible that this interpretation is bound by a cultural bias. Interpretations of good or bad, right or wrong, suppressing or exaggerating, important or not important, are all value interpretations that may be made in a cross-cultural study. These interpretations may reflect the value orientations of the researchers as much as they do the cultures of the samples included in the study. As researchers, we may make those interpretations without giving them a second thought—and without the slightest hint of malicious intent—only because we are so accustomed to seeing the world in a certain way. As consumers of research, we may agree with such interpretations when they agree with the ways we have learned to understand and view the world, and we often do so unconsciously and automatically.

Dealing with nonequivalent data.   Despite the best attempts to establish equivalence in theory, hypothesis, method, and data management, cross-cultural research is often inextricably, inherently, and inevitably nonequivalent. It is impossible to create any cross-cultural study that means exactly the same thing to all participating cultures, both conceptually and empirically. What cross-cultural researchers often end up with are best approximations of the closest equivalents in terms of theory and method in a study. Thus, researchers are often faced with the question of how to deal with nonequivalent data. Poortinga (1989) outlines four different ways in which the problem of nonequivalence of cross-cultural data can be handled:

1. *Preclude comparison.* The most conservative thing a researcher could do is not make the comparison in the first place, concluding that it would be meaningless.
2. *Reduce the nonequivalence in the data.* Many researchers take steps to iden- tify equivalent and nonequivalent parts of their methods, and then refocus their comparisons solely on the equivalent parts. For example, if a re- searcher used a 20-item scale to measure anxiety in two cultures and found evidence for nonequivalence on the scale, he or she might then examine each of the 20 items for equivalence and rescore the test using only those items that are shown to be equivalent. Comparisons would then be based on the rescored items.
3. *Interpret the nonequivalence.* A third strategy is for the researcher to inter- pret the nonequivalence as an important piece of information concerning cultural differences.
4. *Ignore the nonequivalence.* Unfortunately, what many cross-cultural re- searchers end up doing is simply ignoring the problem, clinging to beliefs concerning scale invariance across cultures despite a lack of evidence to support those beliefs.

How researchers handle the interpretation of their data given nonequiva- lence depends on their experience and biases and on the nature of the data and the findings. Because of the lack of equivalence in much cross-cultural re- search, researchers are often faced with many gray areas in interpreting their findings. Culture itself is a complex phenomenon, neither black nor white but replete with gray. It is the objective and experienced researcher who can deal with these gray areas, creating sound, valid, and reliable interpretations that are justified by the data. And it is the astute consumer of that research who can sit back and judge those interpretations relative to the data in their own minds and not be unduly swayed by the arguments of the researchers.

We have reviewed some of the fundamental issues that one must be aware of as a researcher and/or a consumer of cross-cultural research. We now turn to the important question of how to transform the abstract construct of culture into something that is measurable.

Transforming Culture into a Measurable Construct

One of the challenges that has faced cross-cultural psychology throughout its history has been how to conceptualize culture in theories of human behavior and how to measure it in research. Most cross-cultural studies operationalize culture as country. But if you examine them closely, most are not actually cross-country studies but cross-city studies (for example, San Francisco versus Tokyo versus Frankfurt versus Istanbul). Also, many samples are really samples of convenience, meaning that the researcher has a friend at a university in one of these cities who will collect data for the project. Because many studies are conducted this way, researchers often have to resort to stereotype, impression, or anecdote to interpret observed differences. Thus, despite the fact that thinking about cultures has progressed steadily over the years, the way in which researchers generally study culture has not. In short, there has been a discrepancy between how theorists talk about culture and its effects on human behavior and how researchers actually study it in their research.

Fortunately, the gap between theory and method with regard to culture is closing fast, thanks to recent developments not only in the measurement of culture but in conceptualizations of it that make it amenable to measurement. These developments have major positive impacts, not only empirically in cross-cultural research but also theoretically on cross-cultural theories and models of behavior.

Reducing Culture from an Abstract, Fuzzy Construct to Specific, Finite Elements

As described earlier, culture in all its complexity is an enormous construct that describes many aspects of a people's way of life. One of the ways previous writers have begun to get a handle on culture is to separate aspects of culture into two components: objective and subjective elements (Triandis, 1972; also see explicit and implicit culture in Kroeber & Kluckhohn, 1952). Objective elements of culture are the physical manifestations of culture—things that we can actually see and touch, such as clothing, artifacts, utensils, foods, and architecture. Subjective elements of culture are all those aspects that we cannot see and touch but we know exist, such as social norms, customs, attitudes, and values. It is the subjective elements of culture that most psychologists are interested in and that are most consonant with the definition of culture proposed in this book.

Cross-cultural psychologists have characterized the subjective elements of culture in two ways: by domain and by dimension. *Domain* refers to specific sociopsychological characteristics that are considered to be meaningful outcomes, products, or constituents of culture, including attitudes, values, beliefs, opinions, norms, customs, and rituals. These are all separate and different psychological processes, and are considered psychological domains. *Dimensions* refer to general tendencies that affect behavior and reflect meaningful aspects of cultural variability. Figure 2.1 summarizes this reduction of culture from a large, abstract, fuzzy concept to subjective domains and dimensions.

Figure 2.1 "Reducing" culture to domains and dimensions

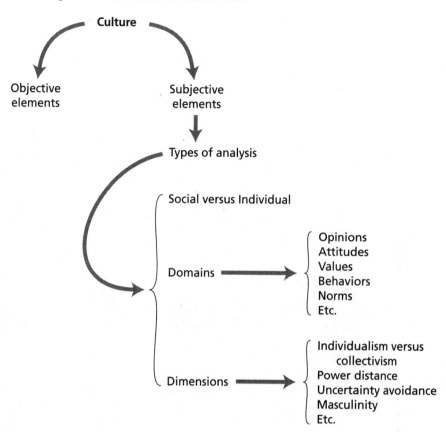

Subjective domains and dimensions of culture exist both socially—that is, across individuals within groups—and individually within each member of a cultural group. To the extent that subjective domains and dimensions of culture can be identified on the individual level, they can be measured in psychological research. Research on the various domains of psychology—attitudes, values, beliefs, and the like—has been standard fare for psychologists for many years. The real challenge for cross-cultural psychology has been to identify meaningful dimensions of cross-cultural variability on which the domains may vary and to develop psychometrically valid and reliable ways of assessing these dimensions within these domains.

To the extent that such assessment procedures can be developed, cross-cultural researchers can specify exactly what it is about culture that they think influences behavior, and why. They will be able to measure those dimensions and domains in their research and assess directly the contribution of those domains and dimensions to the behaviors of interest. Should such measures of culture exist, then we can break free from the lock that stereotypes and anecdotes, derived from a reliance on country and race definitions, has on cross-cultural research. The trick is to find meaningful dimensions of cultural variability with which to assess the psychological domains in individuals.

The Search for Meaningful Dimensions of Cultural Variability

Many scholars have searched for meaningful dimensions of culture and have provided a number of alternatives. Probably the best-known dimension of cultural variability is individualism–collectivism (IC). Anthropologists, sociologists, and psychologists alike have used this dimension to explain differences between cultures (Hofstede, 1980; Kluckholn & Strodtbeck, 1961; Mead, 1961; Triandis, 1972). IC refers to the degree to which a culture encourages, fosters, and facilitates the needs, wishes, desires, and values of an autonomous and unique self over those of a group. Members of individualistic cultures see themselves as separate and autonomous individuals, whereas members of collectivistic cultures see themselves as fundamentally connected with others (Markus & Kitayama, 1991a). In individualistic cultures, personal needs and goals take precedence over the needs of others; in a collectivistic culture, individual needs are sacrificed to satisfy the group.

Numerous other dimensions of cultural variability have been proposed. Mulder (1976, 1977) and later Hofstede (1980, 1984) used the dimension of power distance (PD)—the degree of inequality in power between a less powerful individual (I) and a more powerful other (O). Matsumoto (1991) suggested a slightly modified version of PD called status differentiation (SD)—the degree to which cultures maintain status differences among their members. Hofstede (1980, 1984) also proposed uncertainty avoidance (UA)—the degree to which cultures develop institutions and rituals to deal with the anxiety created by uncertainty and ambiguity—and masculinity (MA)—the degree to which cultures foster traditional gender differences among their members. Pelto (1968) suggested classifying cultures along a dimension of tightness—that is, their degree of internal homogeneity. Hall (1966) suggested that cultures can be differentiated along a dimension of contextualization: High-context cultures foster differential behaviors according to the specific context within which the behavior occurs; low-context cultures minimize differences in behavior from one context to another.

Most of the cross-cultural research and theorizing on the psychological dimensions of culture has focused on individualism–collectivism. Research over the years has focused on its definition, attributes, geographic distribution around the world, consequences for interpersonal and intergroup relations, and applications (see Triandis, 1995, for a comprehensive review of this construct). Thus, IC is the prime example of an attempt to identify a meaningful dimension of cultural variability and to develop ways of measuring its influence in various psychological domains. At the same time, it is important to recognize that this focus on IC may represent a bias among American researchers, working and thinking in an American system, studying a concept so important to American culture—individualism—and its counterpart, collectivism.

Theoretical work on individualism–collectivism.   A considerable body of literature demonstrates the theoretical relevance and empirical utility of IC. Cultural dimensions such as IC are advantageous to theory and research because they can be used to predict and interpret cultural differences without relying on stereotypes, personal anecdotes, or impressions. Also, there is congruence in the conceptual understanding of IC among cross-cultural researchers around the world (Hui & Triandis, 1986). Although it had been discussed in the past, IC received renewed attention through the work of Hofstede (1980, 1984), who collected and analyzed data from a questionnaire assessing IC tendencies among employees in an international corporation with sites in more than 50 countries. Each country was rank-ordered by the degree to which people endorsed IC values. The United States, Australia, and Great Britain were the most individualistic; Venezuela, Colombia, and Pakistan were the most collectivistic (see Table 2.1).

Table 2.1 IC Scores across Countries in Hofstede's Study

Country	Actual IDV	Country	Actual IDV
U.S.A.	91	Argentina	46
Australia	90	Iran	41
Great Britain	89	Brazil	38
Canada	80	Turkey	37
Netherlands	80	Greece	35
New Zealand	79	Philippines	32
Italy	76	Mexico	30
Belgium	75	Portugal	27
Denmark	74	Hong Kong	25
Sweden	71	Chile	23
France	71	Singapore	20
Ireland	70	Thailand	20
Norway	69	Taiwan	17
Switzerland	68	Peru	16
Germany (F.R.)	67	Pakistan	14
South Africa	65	Colombia	13
Finland	63	Venezuela	12
Austria	55	Mean of 39 countries (HERMES)	51
Israel	54		
Spain	51		
India	48	Yugoslavia (same industry)	27
Japan	46		

Work goal scores were computed for a stratified sample of seven occupations at two points in time. Actual values and values predicted on the basis of multiple regression on wealth, latitude, and organization size.

Source: Geert Hofstede, *Culture's Consequences: Comparing Values, Behaviors, Institutions, and Organizations across Nations,* 2nd ed., 2001. Used by permission of the author.

Triandis et al. (1988) suggest that cultural differences on IC are related to differences in self–ingroup versus self–outgroup relationships. (See Brewer & Kramer, 1985; Messick & Mackie, 1989; and Tajfel, 1982, for reviews of the ingroups–outgroups classification.) Individualistic cultures tend to have more ingroups. Because numerous ingroups are available to individuals, members are not strongly attached to any single ingroup. Members of these cultures tend to drop out of groups that are too demanding, and their relationships within their groups are marked by a high level of independence or detachment. Collectivistic cultures depend much more on the effective functioning of groups, so a member's commitment to an ingroup is greater. Collectivists keep stable relationships with their ingroups no matter what the cost and exhibit a high level of interdependence with members of their groups. We will discuss this topic more fully in Chapter 14, Culture and Social Behavior.

Triandis, Leung, Villareal, and Clack (1985) suggest that IC orientations for individuals are both setting-specific and group-specific. They argue that collectivism must be viewed as a syndrome relating to interpersonal concern rather than as a unitary disposition. The results from a subsequent study on IC values in the United States, Japan, and Puerto Rico support this position (Triandis et al., 1988).

Empirical work on individualism–collectivism. Many studies demonstrate the utility of IC in explaining cultural differences in behavior. For example, IC has been used to predict cultural differences in the expression, perception, and antecedents of emotion (Gudykunst & Ting-Toomey, 1988; Matsumoto, 1989, 1991; Wallbott & Scherer, 1988). IC has been used to examine cultural differences in self-monitoring and communication outcomes in ingroup and outgroup relationships in four cultures (Gudykunst et al., 1992), as well as the differential effects of speech rate on perceptions of speaker credibility (Lee & Boster, 1992).

Georgas (1989, 1991) used the IC dimension to explain changes in family values in Greece. He found that the current transition of Greece from an agriculture- and trade-based society with an extended family system to an industrialized, service-oriented society "is accompanied by the rejection of collectivistic values and the gradual adoption of individualist values" (p. 90).

Hamilton, Blumenfeld, Akoh, and Miura (1991) compared teaching styles in American and Japanese elementary classrooms. American teachers directed their instruction toward individuals during both full class instruction and private study time. Japanese teachers, however, consistently addressed the group as a collective. Even when children were working individually, the Japanese teachers checked to make sure all of the children were working on the same task.

Leung (1988) used IC to compare the United States and Hong Kong on conflict avoidance. People rating high on collectivism were more likely to pursue a dispute with a stranger, and Leung concluded that the cultural differences found were consistent with previous conceptualizations of IC.

Recently, Oyserman, Coon, and Kemmelmeier (2002) conducted a meta-analysis of 83 studies examining group differences on IC and the possible contribution of IC to various psychological processes. They found that European Americans were more individualistic and less collectivistic than others in general. But they were not more individualistic than African Americans or Latinos, nor were they less collectivistic than Japanese or Koreans, contrary to common stereotypes. In addition, their review indicated that IC had moderate effects on self-concept and relationality, and large effects on attributions and cognitive styles across the studies examined.

These works highlight the importance of individualism–collectivism in conceptualizing, predicting, and explaining cultural similarities and differences. A number of researchers have even gone beyond identifying the IC concept in understanding cultural differences—they have developed ways of measuring it.

Measuring IC. One of the best-known attempts to measure IC comes from Hofstede's (1980, 1984) previously mentioned study of IBM employees in 50 countries. His survey consisted of 126 questions clustered around four major themes: satisfaction, perception, personal goals and beliefs, and demographics. Hofstede's measurement method, however, was not designed to generate scores for individuals; rather, the unit of analysis was country. His study, therefore, was an ecological rather than individual analysis of culture. In comparative research, it is important to have a measure of IC on the level of the individual because we deal with a relatively small number of people in a cultural sample. By examining the influence of culture at the individual level, we can characterize a psychological culture underlying the samples in our research and examine its influence on other aspects of human behavior.

Triandis (1995) reviewed 20 studies that designed and tested different scales to measure IC on the individual level. (Some of these works are outlined briefly here; interested readers are directed to Triandis, 1995, Appendix, or Oyserman et al., 2002, for a comprehensive review and discussion of method.) By far the most concerted effort has been that of Triandis and his colleagues. These attempts have resulted in the use of a number of different scales across a number of studies. Hui (1984, 1988), for example, developed the INDCOL scale to measure an individual's IC tendencies in relation to six collectivities (spouse, parents and children, kin, neighbors, friends, and coworkers and classmates). Respondents indicate their agreement with statements describing key IC concepts—such as sharing, decision making, and cooperation—in relation to each target collective. Scores are then summed across items within each collective and then across collectives to generate a General Collectivism Index (GCI). Later Triandis et al. (1985) used items from the INDCOL and further broadened them by adding scenarios and other ratings. Triandis et al. (1986) used items from Hui (1984), Triandis et al. (1985), and items suggested by colleagues in other cultures to measure IC. Triandis et al. (1988) used items from the INDCOL and U.S.-originated emic items to measure IC.

Triandis, McCusker, and Hui (1990) used a multimethod approach to measuring IC that represented an evolution not only in method but also in thinking. These researchers viewed IC as a cultural syndrome that includes values, beliefs, attitudes, and behaviors (see also Triandis, 1996); they treated the various psychological domains of subjective culture as an entire collective rather than as separate aspects of culture. Their multimethod approach included ratings of the social content of the self, perceptions of homogeneity of ingroups and outgroups, attitude and value ratings, and perceptions of social behavior as a function of social distance. Participants were classified as either individualist or collectivist on the basis of their scores on each method. On the individual level, Triandis refers to individualism and collectivism as idiocentrism and allocentrism, respectively (Triandis et al., 1986).

Most recently, Triandis and his colleagues (Singelis, Triandis, Bhawuk, & Gelfand, 1995) have developed measures that include items assessing a revised concept of individualism and collectivism they call horizontal and vertical individualism and collectivism, representing yet further advances in the conceptual understanding of IC. In horizontal collectivism, individuals see themselves as members of ingroups in which all members are equal. In vertical collectivism, individuals see themselves as members of ingroups that are characterized by hierarchical or status relationships. In horizontal individualism, individuals are autonomous and equal. In vertical individualism, individuals are autonomous but unequal.

The work of other writers (reviewed in Triandis, 1995) covers a broad range of psychological constructs in their assessment of IC, including attitudinal, value, and norm ratings, self-perceptions, and independent and interdependent self-construals. These works offer researchers a number of alternatives for IC assessment, but Triandis' multimethod system and his latest efforts in assessing horizontal and vertical IC are by far the most advanced and sophisticated assessment tools available. These measures assess IC tendencies in different psychological domains, combining IC tendencies across a wide range of phenomena into a single measurement technique.

It is also important, however, to be able to measure IC tendencies across different contexts as well different psychological domains. No single score can capture context-specific tendencies, either in terms of their conceptual implications or empirical applications, because IC-related processes should vary in different social contexts (Triandis et al., 1988). People act differently depending on whom they are interacting with and the situation in which the interaction is occurring. A person may have collectivistic tendencies at home and with close friends and individualistic tendencies with strangers or at work, or vice versa. If a culture fosters collectivistic tendencies within self–ingroup relationships, that means that certain behaviors are encouraged with ingroups while simultaneously discouraged with outgroups, and vice versa. This difference, in fact, is fundamental to an understanding of collectivism. This view of IC suggests the value of generating context-specific scores on IC rather than producing single scores collapsed across contexts. This view of IC also suggests that IC tendencies on the individual level should be understood as profiles of IC tendencies across contexts rather than as single scores that globally summarize IC tendencies.

Matsumoto and his colleagues (Matsumoto, Weissman, Preston, Brown, & Kupperbusch, 1997) have developed a measure of IC for use on the individual level that assesses context-specific IC tendencies in interpersonal situations. Their measure, called the IC Interpersonal Assessment Inventory (ICIAI), includes a list of 19 items compiled from previous work on IC by Triandis and colleagues (1990), Hui (1984, 1988), and Schwartz and Bilsky (1987). (See the box "Sample Items from the Individualism–Collectivism Interpersonal Assessment Inventory.") The items are described in general value terms (for example, obedience to authority, social responsibility, sacrifice, loyalty) rather than by specific statements tied to single actions. Universal values, such as love and security, are not included, based on Schwartz's (1990) assertion that those "maturity" values serve both individualists and collectivists. The 25 items are presented in relation to four social groups of interactants: (1) family, (2) close

---

Sample Items from the Individualism–Collectivism Interpersonal Assessment Inventory (ICIAI)

Below is a list of general descriptions of behavior. We want to know how important you believe each is as a *value* in relation to four social groups. Consider each of the descriptions as a general, hypothetical value. Also, consider the value separately in each of the four social groups. Please tell us how important each is in terms of being a *guiding principle* for you, regardless of whether you actually find yourself in these situations. Please make an attempt to answer each item.

Please use the following rating scale when giving your answers. Write the appropriate number in the space provided for each of the four social groups.

NOT IMPORTANT AT ALL						VERY IMPORTANT
0	1	2	3	4	5	6

	Family	Friends	Colleagues	Strangers
To comply with direct requests from	_____	_____	_____	_____
To maintain self-control toward	_____	_____	_____	_____
To share credit for accomplishments of	_____	_____	_____	_____
To share blame for failures of	_____	_____	_____	_____
To sacrifice your goals for	_____	_____	_____	_____
To sacrifice your possessions for	_____	_____	_____	_____
To compromise your wishes in order to act together with	_____	_____	_____	_____
To maintain harmonious relationships among	_____	_____	_____	_____

Source: Matsumoto, Weissman, Preston, Brown, & Kupperbusch, 1997.

friends, (3) colleagues, and (4) strangers. These four groups were selected based on their collective differences and the supposition that they maximized context-specific differences in a manageable number of contexts. All the items are rated twice, once in terms of general values as guiding principles for each person's behaviors and a second time in terms of the frequency of actual behaviors. This measure has been used to demonstrate IC differences across different countries as well as across different ethnic groups within the United States (Matsumoto, Weissman, et al., 1997).

The ICIAI and Triandis and colleagues' multimethod assessment techniques described earlier represent major advances for cross-cultural research and our understanding of the influence of cultural dimensions of variability on human behavior. Being able to measure IC, or any other cultural dimension, on the individual level is advantageous for a variety of reasons. First, it allows us to characterize the IC nature of different groups and to examine the relative importance of I or C in those groups. Triandis and his colleagues have administered their measures of IC to samples in different cultures and countries around the world, and on the basis of these data have been able not only to characterize the cultures as relatively I or C but also to estimate the proportion of the population in each of these cultures with primarily I or C tendencies at the individual level. Second, measurement of IC allows for an important methodological check in our research. Using such measures, researchers no longer have to assume that the groups in their studies are I or C; they can demonstrate it empirically. Third, given individual differences in IC within samples, IC scores can be used as covariates in statistical analyses that test group differences with the effects of IC statistically controlled.

Guidelines for Reviewing Cross-Cultural Research

Students, teachers, and researchers alike are all consumers of research. We all need to be able to pick up a research article published in a scientific journal and read, understand, and evaluate it. We need these skills in order to know the literature, understand the state of knowledge in an area, write papers, plan research, and teach.

In this section, we provide a systematic way of evaluating cross-cultural research on your own. We created the summary sheet shown in Table 2.2 to highlight most of the important issues discussed in this chapter, listing in summary form all of the questions you need to ask about individual research articles that you read and review for your own course requirements, research projects, or interests. These guidelines apply specifically to hypothesis-testing cross-cultural research. Photocopy this summary sheet, and use it when conducting your literature reviews and evaluating articles. Remember, your goal is to judge for yourself the merits of individual studies in terms of their potential contribution to truth and knowledge in psychology.

Table 2.2 Summary Sheet for Evaluating Cross-Cultural Research

Author(s): _____

Title: _____

Journal: _____

Pub. Info.: _____

Theory and Hypotheses
1. Does the theory "make sense" for all the cultures being tested in the study? Why or why not?
2. Are the hypotheses meaningfully equivalent for all participants?

Methods
3. Is the design appropriate for the question being addressed?
4. Are the subjects adequate representatives of their culture?
5. Is culture operationalized according to sociopsychological constructs? If not, how is it operationalized?
6. Are the subjects equivalent for comparison purposes—no other characteristics or demographic confounds?
7. Are the concepts being measured equivalent in all cultures in the study?
8. Do the scales, subscales, and items being used have the same reliability and validity characteristics in all cultures in the study?
9. Are the scales/constructs contextualized meaningfully for all subjects?
10. Do subjects come to the laboratory or complete testing procedures with equivalent expectations?
11. Is procedural equivalence established across nuisance parameters of the study?
12. Did the researchers establish linguistic equivalence in their methods and research protocols by using back-translation procedures?

Data and Analyses
13. Do subjects provide data on a level of measurement that is meaningful to them while at the same time equivalent across cultures?
14. Are there cultural response sets operating in the data set?
15. Do the researchers take adequate steps to check for cultural response sets, and control them if necessary?
16. If cultural differences are found, do the researchers provide an index of the size of those differences (effect size statistics)?

(continued on next page)

Table 2.2 Summary Sheet for Evaluating Cross-Cultural Research *(continued)*

Interpretations and Conclusions

17. Are the interpretations of the findings bound by the cultural filters and biases of the researcher, or of the theories?

18. Do the researchers make value judgments based on the findings?

19. Are the interpretations sufficiently tempered by awareness of the unconscious cultural processes that may have affected the research or theory?

20. Do the researchers make unwarranted cause–effect interpretations of the relationship between culture and their target variables?

21. Are the interpretations of cultural mediators justified in relation to how culture was operationalized in the study?

22. Are there sufficient methodological concerns to preclude any meaningful conclusions based on the data presented?

Other Questions about the Study

23. How do the findings contribute to our knowledge with regard to cultural influences on the target variables of interest?

24. How would changes in any aspect of the methodology affect the outcomes of the study (for example, cultural or demographic backgrounds of the participants, methods of measuring key variables)?

25. Can the findings be used by some to foster stereotypes of members of the cultures represented in the study?

26. Can the findings be used by some to foster prejudice or discrimination against members of the cultures represented in the study?

Theory and Hypotheses

Theories, and the hypotheses generated from theories, are bounded by the cultural framework within which they originated. The issue raised in Questions 1 and 2 is whether the theory and hypotheses being tested are equivalent for all cultures participating in the study. In order to make this evaluation, you need to sit back and try to understand conceptually the theoretical framework being presented in the Introduction section of the article—its logic, premises, and assumptions—and then evaluate the cultural framework within which these premises and assumptions do and do not hold true.

Methods

Question 3 asks whether the design chosen by the researchers provides an appropriate way to test their hypotheses. Each of the concepts described in the hypothesis should be manipulated in some fashion in the study so that (1) the hypothesis can be falsified, and (2) if not falsified, rival hypotheses can be eliminated.

Questions 4, 5, and 6 bear on the issues of sampling adequacy and equivalence in noncultural demographic variables.

Questions 7 and 8 address the conceptual and empirical definitions of variables. Issues of cross-cultural validity may be addressed in other research, which should be cited.

Question 9 also relates to the conceptual and empirical definition of variables. In many cultures, questions about abstract psychological constructs are not very meaningful (see, for example, the discussion regarding self-construals in Chapter 11). In these cultures, questions about psychological traits and characteristics make sense only if a specific context is provided (when you are at home, with friends in a public place, at work). If the cultures participating in the study are of this nature, then psychological data will be meaningful only if their measures are sufficiently contextualized.

Questions 10 and 11 bear on the issue of equivalence across cultures in the setting, environment, and procedures of the study.

Question 12 asks whether or not the researchers took care to establish linguistic equivalence in their protocols.

Data and Analyses

Question 13 asks whether the scale of measurement provided to the participants is equivalent in all cultures being tested. Even though the concepts being tested are equivalent in all cultures, different scales may have different meanings for different cultures. Participants from one culture, for example, may not hesitate to give scalar ratings about their attitudes using a 7-point scale (1 through 7). Participants in another culture, however, may be unfamiliar with such scales and unaccustomed to grading their responses in this way, preferring to respond in an open-ended fashion. If such differences exist, the data may be nonequivalent.

Questions 14 and 15 bear on the issue of cultural response sets.

Question 16 addresses the issue of calculating and presenting effect sizes when documenting group differences.

Interpretations and Conclusions

Questions 17, 18, and 19 address the possibility that researcher bias and value judgments may affect interpretations of the data.

Questions 20 and 21 focus on the nature of the interpretations—that is, cause–effect versus correlational.

Question 22 is an overall, summary question about the study as a whole. There is no such thing as a perfect, flawless study; every study is compromised in some fashion, to some degree. The real question facing researchers and consumers of research is whether the limitations are sufficient to preclude drawing any meaningful conclusions about any part of the data, or whether some kind of conclusion is still warranted despite the flaws or limitations. This evaluation is totally subjective, based on your review and evaluation of all the points discussed here and the weight you give to each in relation to the possible contribution of the study and its findings to the literature.

Other Questions about the Study

In addition to questions that can be raised directly about the validity and reliability of the findings reported in a study, we have listed some questions that need to be raised with regard to what it all might mean. Researchers need to consider these important questions from the outset. Consumers need to ask difficult questions about the impact and ramifications of each study not only in terms of the existing literature and current state of knowledge, but also in terms of potential applications of that knowledge, good and bad, by all types of consumers.

 **Conclusion**

Research is the primary way in which scholars and scientists generate knowledge about the world. Cross-cultural research brings with it its own special set of issues. Many of these are extensions of general experimental research issues in the cross-cultural arena. Other issues, however, are specific to cross-cultural research. To be a critical reader and evaluator of cross-cultural research, you need to be alert to these issues.

All in all, the issues discussed in this chapter are so daunting that you may well wonder whether any cross-cultural study can tell us anything. All studies have at least some imperfections, and every study has its limitations. But that does not necessarily mean we cannot learn something from those studies. The real question is whether the flaws of a study so outweigh its procedures as to severely compromise the trust you place in its data. If a study is so compromised that you don't trust the data, you shouldn't believe it, whether it is cross-cultural or not, even if you agree with its nebulous conclusions. But if a study's problems are less serious, you should be able to glean information from it about cultural differences. If you can do this over a number of studies in an area, they might cumulatively or collectively say something about that area, even though any single study might not.

Despite all the inherent difficulties, cross-cultural research offers a number of exciting and interesting opportunities not available with traditional research approaches. Through cross-cultural research, we can test the limits and boundaries of our knowledge in psychology and about human behavior. We can push the envelope of knowledge and understanding about people in ways that are impossible with traditional research approaches. The cross-cultural enterprise itself offers a process by which scientists and laypersons from disparate and divergent cultures can come together and work toward common goals, thereby improving human relations across what otherwise may seem a considerable chasm. The findings from cross-cultural research offer scientists, scholars, and the public ways to further our understanding of human diversity that can serve as the basis for renewed personal and professional interrelationships and can help to focus public and social policy. Methodologically, cross-cultural studies offer researchers a way to deal with empirical problems related to the conduct of research, such as confounding variables present in traditional research approaches.

This process of evaluating the merits of each study in terms of the trust you would place in the data and then accumulating bits and pieces of information across the studies you trust is integral to learning about a field. In this chapter, we have tried to provide a solid basis for developing and practicing these skills. The material presented in this chapter is just the tip of the iceberg. Many excellent resources, other than those cited throughout this chapter, explain cross-cultural research issues to a greater level of specification for specialists in the field, including issues of methodology (for example, Van de Vijver & Leung, 1997a, 1997b), interpretation (Leung, 1989), and data analysis (Leung & Bond, 1989; Matsumoto, 1994). It is this cumulative process that we went through in selecting studies and findings from the various fields of cross-cultural psychology to present to you in the remainder of this book. But don't take our word for it; you need to evaluate that research for yourself. It is a skill that takes practice in order to do well, but like many skills, it can be learned. As you read and evaluate the studies presented in this book and elsewhere, we hope you will find that while cross-cultural research has its own problems and limitations, it has advantages and potentialities that far outweigh the difficulties.

 Glossary

back translation A technique of translating research protocols that involves taking the protocol as it was developed in one language, translating it into the target language, and having someone else translate it back to the original. If the back-translated version is the same as the original, they are generally considered equivalent. If it is not, the procedure is repeated until the back-translated version is the same as the original.

cross-cultural comparison study A study that compares two or more cultures on some psychological variable of interest, often with the hypothesis that one culture will have significantly higher scores on the variable than the other(s).

cross-cultural validation study A study that examines whether a measure of a psychological construct that was originally generated in a single culture is applicable, meaningful, and thus equivalent in another culture.

cultural response set Cultural influences on the use of response scales; the cultural tendency to use certain parts of a scale, irrespective of question content.

decenter The concept underlying the procedure of back translation that involves eliminating any culture-specific concepts of the original language or translating them equivalently into the target language.

ecological-level studies A study in which countries or cultures, not individuals, are the unit of analysis.

equivalence A state or condition of similarity in conceptual meaning and empirical method between cultures that allows comparisons to be meaningful.

ethnography A type of study of a culture that involves in-depth immersion in the culture, often requiring the researcher to spend a considerable amount of time learning the ways and customs of that culture.

operationalization   The ways researchers conceptually define a variable and measure it.

reliability   The degree to which a finding, measurement, or statistic is consistent.

sample   The final group of units that is included in a study.

sampling   The procedures researchers use in determining their sample.

unpackaging studies   Studies that unpackage the contents of the global, unspecific concept of

culture into specific, measurable psychological constructs, and examine their contribution to cultural differences.

validity   The degree to which a finding, measurement, or statistic is accurate, or represents what it is supposed to.

value judgment   An interpretation of data that involves attribution of a value, such as good or bad, right or wrong, based on one's own cultural framework.

InfoTrac College Edition

Use InfoTrac College Edition to search for additional readings on topics of interest to you. For more information on topics in this chapter, use the following as search terms:

collectivism
ethnography
individualism
operationalization

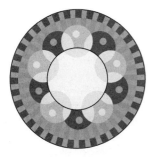

Ethnocentrism, Prejudice, and Stereotypes

In dealing with cultural differences in thoughts, opinions, attitudes, and behaviors, as you will in the rest of this book, it is easy to have cognitive or emotional reactions to the material, to make generalizations and negative stereotypes of others, and even to prejudge those differences and the people who engage in those behaviors before you truly understand their basis. These processes and reactions are commonplace in the world today, and the terms *ethnocentrism, stereotypes, prejudice,* and *discrimination* are often used to describe them. Unfortunately, the terms are often used without being clearly understood, in ways that actually foster the problems they are supposed to clarify.

Some of today's most pressing social issues concern these processes—both domestically within the United States because of our increasingly diverse and multicultural society, and internationally as borders between countries and cultures become increasingly permeable as a result of advances in transportation, technology, and business. You cannot pick up a newspaper or magazine or turn on the television news without seeing a story about problems related to ethnocentrism or racial or national stereotypes. These problems range from doing business internationally to violence and wars based on racial or ethnic differences. These issues promise to become even more salient in the future as technology brings the diverse cultures of the world ever closer together.

Our biases in this chapter are twofold. First, meaningful discussion about these topics is impossible without first defining them thoroughly. Many differences of opinion arise, in fact, not out of disagreement over the meaning or importance of these terms in our everyday lives but over differences in definitions. For this reason, it is important to place those definitions on the table, at least as "working definitions," to be used in discussions as we encounter the cultural differences presented in the rest of the book.

Second, defining these terms leads to a better understanding of how they are created, how they are maintained, and how they might be changed. Certainly, changes are possible without conscious awareness and deliberate cognitive understanding. But the goal of this book is to analyze processes related to cultural similarities and differences, and to understand the contribution of psychology to those processes. This understanding can also provide a basis for change.

A great deal has been written about these topics in the social science literature, particularly in disciplines such as sociology and ethnic relations. In this chapter, we borrow from the existing literature in psychology to develop a psychological explanation of the processes associated with ethnocentrism, stereotypes, prejudice, and discrimination. The first part of the chapter deals with ethnocentrism, building upon our earlier definition of culture and suggesting that ethnocentrism is a normal consequence of learning the ways of society and culture in everyday life. In this view, we are all ethnocentric; the important question is whether we recognize it or not.

The second part of the chapter deals with stereotypes—positive as well as negative, and stereotypes about one's own group as well as other groups. As with ethnocentrism, we believe that stereotypes are inevitable consequences of everyday psychological functioning, building upon other psychological processes that we all use in our daily lives. Again, the issue is not whether or not we harbor stereotypes, but whether or not we recognize them and their limitations.

The third part of the chapter deals with prejudice, discrimination, and a host of "isms" (such as racism), using the previous material on ethnocentrism and stereotypes to understand them. Ethnocentrism and stereotypes are inevitable psychological processes; prejudice and discrimination are not (although not all writers agree, as we shall see). We will discuss the nature of these processes and how they develop.

Finally, the chapter ends with a discussion of how we can go beyond prejudice and discrimination in dealing with cultural differences. Not only is this discussion important as a basis for engaging effectively with the rest of the material in this book; it is also important in our everyday lives. Although these topics have been addressed elsewhere, it is most often from a social or cultural perspective. One of the overall goals of this chapter is to examine the contribution not only of social but also of psychological factors in the creation and maintenance of all these processes, as well as the interaction between culture and psychology.

Ethnocentrism and Intergroup Attitudes

Different Definitions of Ethnocentrism

One of the fundamental concepts concerning intergroup relations is ethnocentrism. This term is often used in a negative way, defined as the inability to view others in a manner outside of your own cultural background. A related definition of ethnocentrism suggests a tendency to judge people of other groups, societies, or lifestyles according to the standards of one's own ingroup or culture, often viewing outgroups as inferior (for example, see Healey, 1998; Noel, 1968). Because many people talk about ethnocentrism in such negative terms, much discussion centers around the need to "rid" ourselves of ethnocentrism.

But can we really rid ourselves of ethnocentrism? A different analysis of this problem suggests not; in fact, ethnocentrism may be a normal psychological function and an inevitable part of our lives. Indeed, although this word is often used in a way that carries negative connotations, it need not have these connotations. We define **ethnocentrism** as the tendency to view the world through one's own cultural filters. With this definition, and knowledge about how we acquire those filters, it follows that just about everyone in the world is ethnocentric. That is, everyone learns a certain way of behaving, and in doing so learns a certain way of perceiving and interpreting the behaviors of others. This way of perceiving and making interpretations about others is a normal consequence of growing up in society. In this sense, ethnocentrism per se is neither bad nor good; it merely reflects the state of affairs—that we all have our cultural filters on when we perceive others.

Ethnocentrism as a Normal Consequence of Socialization and Enculturation

As we grow up, we learn many rules about how to behave. These rules form the basis of culture. Culture consists of the many rules concerning the regulation and control of our behavior via socially appropriate channels. For example, we learn that "Big boys don't cry" and "You don't scratch yourself in public." As these rules shape our behavior, we learn that many rules come with sanctions for transgressing them. If a boy cries in public, for example, he may be ridiculed by his friends or family; he may be called a sissy or some other name.

When we are very little, these rules must be constantly reinforced in us. Our parents, friends, teachers, and other agents of socialization continually remind us of the rules. Many of these rules are also transmitted and reinforced by organizations and institutions. All of these lessons contribute to the process of enculturation discussed in Chapter 5. As we get older, we need to be reminded less and less about these rules. We begin to act upon them with less and less conscious effort.

During adolescence, we begin to question authority and the rules that authority dictates to us. We begin to seek out new ways and rules of behavior. We search for "ourselves." After adolescence, however, many people seem to come back to their roots, to the ways and rules with which they were brought up. Often this happens after college or university life, when a person needs to step out into the workforce and relearn the rules of society. By this time, we have learned how to act according to those rules. Generally, no one around us needs to remind us of the rules as our parents, teachers, and friends did when we were little. Indeed, not only have we internalized the rules of behavior by the time we are adults, but we have learned them so well that we can act according to those rules automatically without thinking very much about them. Many of these rules make up what we know as our culture—the conglomeration of learned rules about how to behave. To the extent that we share these rules about behavior with others, we share a certain culture with them.

But rules of behavior are not the only things we learn as we grow. We also learn how to perceive others, how to interpret the behaviors of others, and how to make judgments of those behaviors. Because we share a set of rules with a certain group of people, we develop a set of expectations about the kinds of behaviors people should exhibit. That is, we implicitly learn that the rules with which we were raised and that are true for us must also be true for others who share the same cultural heritage. This tacit knowledge need not be spoken each time we, as adults, operate on that knowledge. It is similar to communication between two computers that have the same basic operating system and "speak" the same language.

Not only do we have certain expectations about people's behaviors, but we also have learned patterns of judgments about those behaviors. We have emotional reactions associated with those expectations and judgments that range from acceptance and pleasure to outrage, hostility, and frustration. When we interact with someone of our own cultural background, we interact using the same "ground rules." Whatever discussions or negotiations we have will be held above and beyond those ground rules because we both implicitly and tacitly share them. Thus, there is an underlying current of acceptance about those ground rules as we interact (even though we may or may not like the specific content of the interaction).

When we observe or interact with people who engage in transgressions against what we view as "normal" or "socially appropriate," we have negative reactions. We become upset or frustrated or annoyed because we have learned that those types of behaviors are not appropriate, and negative emotions have become associated with that learning. Of course, these types of reactions will be more common when interacting with people of different cultural backgrounds because they operate with different ground rules. But these reactions often occur when interacting with people of our own cultural heritage as well.

Our emotional reactions often lead us to make judgments about others. When the behaviors we observe are what we would normally expect in a given situation, we make an implicit judgment that the person is a member of our culture or that the person is engaging in socially appropriate behavior. We may consider the individual to have been socialized "well" into our culture; they are "good." But when the behavior we observe is what we do not expect, we begin to question that person. Often we interpret the behavior to mean that the person is "bad" or "stupid" or "had a bad upbringing." At the very least, there is uncertainty and ambiguity.

We often make these judgments of good and bad, right and wrong, without a second thought. Indeed, why should we give those judgments second thought? The judgments are often rooted in our upbringing since childhood and are the only types of judgments we have learned to make. As such, they are colored by our emotions, which serve as guidelines in helping us form opinions about ourselves and others.

Thus, as we become enculturated, not only do we learn how to act, but we also learn how to perceive and interpret how other people act. Our learning is associated with strong emotions of acceptance or rejection, with moral judgments of good or bad, right or wrong, and with judgments of personality. These rules of perceiving and interpreting form the basis of our own "filters" that we use in seeing the world. As we become more and more enculturated, we add more layers to those filters. These filters have lenses that allow us to perceive the world in a certain way, from a certain angle, or through a certain color. By the time we are adults, we share the same filters, with the same prescription and color filtering, as other people in our cultural group. It is as if we had all purchased a camera filter with the same properties. We have these filters on all the time, so that by the time we are adults, we hardly notice they are there. They become part of our self, inseparable and invisible. They are a normal part of our psychological composition because of the way we were socialized and enculturated. Culture exists in each and every individual as a set of psychological rules, attitudes, values, and beliefs, and strong associations exist between those rules and our emotions and judgments of morality and personality.

Recognizing One's Own Ethnocentrism

Given that we are all ethnocentric to some degree, an important issue is whether or not we are aware of that ethnocentrism. Some people are well aware that they relate to others and to diversity through the cultural filters of their own particular lifestyle and culture. They understand that the way they perceive and interpret others and the world around them is only one way of doing so, that other interpretations exist, and that their interpretations may not be accurate in relation to the actual intent of the actors producing the differences they perceive. Other people are not aware that they relate to diversity with their cultural filters on; they believe that their way of perceiving and interpreting the world is the only way of perceiving and interpreting. Such people do not recognize the existence of other possible interpretations, nor the possibility that they themselves may be wrong. The question, therefore, is not whether ethnocentrism exists, but whether or not people recognize that they are ethnocentric.

It is important to consider ways to develop flexibility when interacting with others, while at the same time accepting our own ethnocentrism. The work of several researchers (for example, Bochner, 1982; Boucher, Landis, & Clark, 1987; Brislin, 1993) suggest a number of ways to attain this flexibility. First, it is important to know how our own culture filters reality, distorting, rotating, and coloring images so we see things a certain way. Second, it is important to recognize that people of different cultural backgrounds have different filters that produce their own distortions, rotations, and coloring of reality, and that their version of reality will seem as real and valid to them as ours is to us. Third, although knowledge of our own and other people's cultures and their influences on the filtering process is a necessary condition to gaining flexibility, it is not sufficient. We have to learn to deal somehow with the emotions, judgments of morality, and judgments of personality that are associated with our ethnocentrism and cultural filters. We are not suggesting that our potential negative reactions are not valid; what we are suggesting is that we must give ourselves a chance to go beyond those reactions and try to learn about other people's viewpoints. In doing so, we may have to force ourselves to take a crash course on cultural filters from different cultures and superimpose them over our own filters so we can come closer to seeing the world from another person's vantage point. Above all, this process means learning to put our emotional reactions and moral judgments on hold, however briefly, even though we have learned them so well that they are generally automatic.

All of this requires a substantial degree of learning and effort. These new filters are superimposed over and above our existing cultural filters, not substituted for them. Our own cultural filters become a permanent and fixed part of ourselves (although it is true that because they are learned, we are constantly modifying them as we go along). We do not get rid of our own filters when learning to be flexible; we learn ways to add onto them to help us see things from different perspectives. We don't necessarily lose ourselves in this process—a realistic fear of many people—rather, we gain new skills and knowledge.

We think of this entire process of perspective seeking as **flexible ethnocentrism.** It is important to realize that flexible ethnocentrism does not mean you must accept or like the other viewpoint. Some may argue, for example, that the criminal mentality constitutes a culture in itself. You can engage in flexible ethnocentrism to attempt to understand the criminal culture and viewpoint; accepting or liking it, however, is another matter entirely.

The alternative to this process of gaining flexibility is **inflexible ethnocentrism.** This term refers to the traditional notion of ethnocentrism as an inability to go beyond one's own cultural filters in interpreting the behavior of others. Inflexible ethnocentrism may arise from ignorance of the processes necessary to gain a different cultural viewpoint or from a refusal to engage in such a process. It is important to differentiate between ethnocentrism as a general process applicable to people of all cultures, and the flexible or inflexible use of that ethnocentrism in positive or negative ways.

If you ask people which type of ethnocentrism they have, most will probably say they are flexible. But people's subjective judgments of themselves and their own abilities are tempered by culture as well. The best indicator of the type of ethnocentrism a person has is his or her actual interpretations of the behaviors of others. A person who interprets the behavior of someone from a different cultural background solely from his or her own perspective, attaching value statements such as "They are terrible" or "That's why people hate them," is reacting inflexibly. Those who interpret behavior from a flexible ethnocentric viewpoint are likely to use qualifying statements such as "That's the way they have learned to do things" or "We can't judge that right or wrong from our perspective."

As you were reading this section, you had your own cultural filters on. Most people have one of two types of reactions to this section. One type acknowledges these types of ethnocentrism (the "mm-hmm" and "ah-hah" reaction). The other type questions what was described in this section (the "Is that really true?" reaction). Which type of reaction did you have? Which type of ethnocentrism do you think you operate with?

The Contribution of Psychological Factors to Ethnocentrism and Intergroup Attitudes

More than three decades ago, Campbell and Levine (1965; cited in Seelye & Brewer, 1970) suggested that a number of psychological factors contribute to ethnocentrism. (In terms of the previous discussion, we believe all the studies cited in this section defined ethnocentrism as the inflexible type.) On the individual level, they cited variables such as ingroup loyalty, ethnocentric hostility, authoritarianism, rigidity, self-esteem, and extent or frequency of contact with outgroup members. They tested the relationship between these variables and acculturation in a study of Americans who were living in Guatemala. Data were collected in open-ended interviews that covered many aspects of daily life, as well as attitudes, opinions, beliefs, and behaviors. They then related all of the variables collectively to acculturation to Guatemalan life. They concluded that "actual contact with the Guatemalan culture, especially to the extent that it increases the individual's sense of security within the new culture and reduces his commitment to the original ingroup, has more impact on adaptation to the culture than attitudinal variables" (p. 154). Their findings suggest the important role of emotion, self, and values in the formation of ethnocentrism discussed earlier in this chapter, as well as their role in developing flexibility in one's ethnocentrism.

Other studies, however, suggest that exposure to differences can lead to negative attitudes and emotions. Vrij and Winkel (1994), for example, showed Dutch police officers slides of either black (Surinamer) or white (Dutch) actors, supposedly being interrogated about a crime, and asked for their impressions. In addition to skin color and appearance, the researchers manipulated accent, fluency, and speech style to correspond to either the Surinamer or Dutch individual. The results indicated that speech style and fluency of the Surinamers were both related to more negative impressions of nervousness, unpleasantness, and suspiciousness. Thus, differences evoked more negative attitudes than did similarities.

Likewise, Bochner and Osako (1977) presented Hawaiian Japanese, Japanese, and Australian participants with a slide depicting either a Japanese or a Caucasian couple. The participants were asked to describe how the couples were similar. The responses were then scored for the presence or absence of ethnic or racial references involving skin color, race, outgroups, or physiognomy. The Australians described the Japanese but not the Caucasians in ethnic terms, whereas the Japanese described the Caucasians but not the Japanese in ethnic terms. The Hawaiian Japanese used ethnic terms equally in describing both couples. These findings suggest that people use stereotypic ethnic terms and ethnic role salience when describing others perceived as outgroup members—that is, those who are different from themselves. These results also confirm the analysis of ethnocentrism presented earlier.

That ethnocentrism and intergroup attitudes are highly dependent on sociocultural factors was also supported in a study of anti-Semitism in Quebec, Canada (Sniderman, Northrup, Fletcher, Russell, & Tetlock, 1993). The researchers conducted a telephone survey of 2,084 respondents, 60% of whom also completed and mailed back a questionnaire. English- and French-speaking respondents were asked five questions in their native language about their attitudes toward Jews. Their responses were then correlated with responses from corresponding samples in Quebec on relevant personality, political, and sociocultural variables. The French-speaking Canadians were more likely to agree with negative characterizations of Jews, and less likely to agree with positive characterizations, than were English-speaking Canadians. These differences were correlated with the French-speaking participants' support for conformity as a value, and not correlated with personality or political variables. These findings were interpreted to suggest that Quebecers are more likely to distrust and dislike people who are different, and fear that too much freedom to differ can threaten an orderly society.

In yet another study, Greek Canadians were questioned about their attitudes toward culture and language maintenance; economic and cultural security, measured by their own family's economic situation, perceived economic standing of own group, anticipated own group survival, and perceived social status of own group; social distance to seven other Canadian ethnic groups; trait attribution; and ethnocentrism (Lambert, Mermigis, & Taylor, 1986). The Greek Canadians clearly viewed their own group most positively—as hardworking, intelligent, law-abiding, and the like. They also preferred social contacts within their own group over those with people of other groups. Interestingly, the security variables relating to economic and social status and group survival were positively correlated with positive evaluations of other groups, and with closeness on social distance measures. Again, these findings highlight the importance of emotions, self, and values in the maintenance of ethnocentrism and the development of flexible ethnocentrism.

These studies are indicative of the psychological factors that contribute to ethnocentrism, and to the recognition (or lack thereof) of one's own ethnocentric attitudes. Because ethnocentrism is so often discussed in negative terms and not as an inevitable consequence of enculturation and socialization as defined earlier, many readers may have difficulty accepting the premise that ethnocentrism is a normal part of everyday psychological functioning. Yet some degree of ethnocentrism is essential to social order and cohesion. Without such implicit positive evaluations of one's own cultural ways, there would be no reason to observe norms of behavior and laws of society or to work together with others in daily life. Thus, ethnocentrism plays an important role and function, helping to hold society and culture together. A larger question concerns how we can become more flexible in our use of our ethnocentrism, a topic to which we will return at the end of this chapter. First, however, we turn our attention to a closely related psychological construct, stereotypes.

Stereotypes

Definition and Types of Stereotypes

Stereotypes are generalized images that we have about groups of people, particularly about their underlying psychological characteristics or personality traits (Lee, Jussin, & McCauley, 1995). Common, everyday parlance suggests that stereotypes are "bad." But as with ethnocentrism, the situation is not that simple.

First, stereotypes can be either positive or negative. For example, a common positive stereotype is that Asians are hardworking, the "model minority." Another positive stereotype is that Germans are industrious and scientifically minded.

Second, stereotypes can be generally true or completely false. Stereotypes based on some degree of "factual" observation are called sociotypes (Triandis, 1994). But stereotypes can also be totally baseless. Because stereotypes can be perpetuated without direct observation of the behaviors of others, some stereotypes have no factual connection to the target group. Even when we convince ourselves that a stereotype is based on direct observations, we have to question the validity of those observations and the interpretations based on them because of the cultural and psychological biases inherent in those processes.

Finally, people hold stereotypes about their own groups as well as about other groups. Stereotypes about one's own group are called **autostereotypes;** stereotypes about other groups are called **heterostereotypes.** In fact, there is often a considerable degree of overlap between a group's autostereotypes and the heterostereotypes that others hold about that group. Iwao and Triandis (1993), for example, asked Japanese and American undergraduates to respond to three scenarios describing conflicts among individuals and to rate stereotypes of Americans and Japanese. When respondents from the two different cultures were similar in their interpretations of an episode, the relationship between auto- and heterostereotypes was high; when they were dissimilar in their interpretations, the relationship was low. The Japanese viewed themselves as passively accepting inconsistencies between their public and private selves, acting according to group norms, whereas Americans tried to reduce the discrepancy between their private and public selves. Similarities between autostereotypes held by people about their own group and heterostereotypes about that group held by others have also been reported by Nichols and McAndrew (1984) and Walkey and Chung (1996).

Not only do we have auto- as well as heterostereotypes, but autostereotypes are just as variable as heterostereotypes. In one study (Nichols & McAndrew, 1984), for example, four groups of students—Americans in the United States, Americans living in Spain, Spaniards, and Malays—rated their stereotypes of Spanish, Malaysian, and American college students using seven pairs of bipolar adjectives. The results indicated unanimous or near unanimous agreement across the four groups on some stereotypes, and large disagreements on others. More important, the variability in autostereotypes was comparable to the variability in stereotypes of others, both within and across groups.

Thus, stereotypes can be either positive or negative, generally true or totally false, and held about one's own group as well as about other groups. Understanding not only a definition of stereotypes but the different ways in which they can manifest themselves is important to understanding their role in intergroup relations and improving those relationships.

The Content of Stereotypes

A number of studies spanning many years have examined the content of stereotypes. In one of the oldest and most often cited studies, Katz and Braly (1933) gave undergraduates at Princeton University a list of adjectives and asked the students to select the traits they considered representative of ten different racial/ethnic groups. The 12 traits most frequently assigned to each group by the students are shown in Table 3.1.

This study was followed up on the same university campus in 1951 (Gilbert, 1951) and again in 1967 (Karlins, Coffman, & Walters, 1969). The researchers found a number of surprising changes over the years, both in stereotypes and in students' willingness to ascribe stereotypic traits to the various groups. Other researchers have conducted similar studies of American university students, using similar methodologies (for example, Clark & Person, 1982; Wood & Chesser, 1994). The most recent study replicating and extending the original Princeton study reports that most of the stereotypes of the various ethnic and national groups have changed into more favorable stereotypes. The greatest change in stereotype content was for African Americans (Madon et al., 2001).

These studies and others like them (for example, Nichols & McAndrew, 1984; Smith, Griffith, Griffith, & Steger, 1980) used perhaps the most common approach to measuring stereotypes—providing participants with a list of adjectives describing psychological traits or characteristics and asking them to select those they considered representative of the target groups specified. Recent studies, however, have used more sophisticated methods and data analysis techniques to examine the possible psychological factors or dimensions that underlie such ratings. For example, Forgas and O'Driscoll (1984) asked participants from two cultures, Australia and Papua New Guinea, to give similarity ratings between pairs of 20 different countries. These similarity ratings were then subjected to a multidimensional scaling procedure that reduced the ratings to a limited number of underlying dimensions. The researchers found that three dimensions summarized the ratings for both cultural groups: European/non-European, communism/capitalism, and development (underdeveloped/developed). Although there were some differences between the two groups in the relative importance of each of these dimensions, both groups were similar in that the same dimensions described their ratings of the 20 countries.

Walkey and Chung (1996) recruited Chinese and European adolescents living in New Zealand and asked them to rate both Chinese and Europeans on 21 pairs of adjectives. Before conducting any data analyses, the researchers subjected the ratings to a procedure known as factor analysis, which identifies the psychological factors underlying the ratings and reduces the ratings to a smaller

Table 3.1 The Twelve Traits Most Frequently Assigned to Various Racial and National Groups by 100 Princeton Students

Traits	Frequency	Traits	Frequency	Traits	Frequency
Germans		Very religious	29	Aggressive	20
Scientifically minded	78	Industrious	21	Straightforward	19
Industrious	65	Extremely nationalistic	21	Practical	19
Stolid	44	Superstitious	18	Sportsmanlike	19
Intelligent	32	Quarrelsome	14		
Methodical	31	Imaginative	13	**Chinese**	
Extremely nationalistic	24	Aggressive	13	Superstitious	34
Progressive	16	Stubborn	13	Sly	29
Efficient	16			Conservative	29
Jovial	15	**English**		Tradition-loving	26
Musical	13	Sportsmanlike	53	Loyal to family ties	22
Persistent	11	Intelligent	46	Industrious	18
Practical	11	Conventional	34	Meditative	18
		Tradition-loving	31	Reserved	17
Italians		Conservative	30	Very religious	15
Artistic	53	Reserved	29	Ignorant	15
Impulsive	44	Sophisticated	27	Deceitful	14
Passionate	37	Courteous	21	Quiet	13
Quick-tempered	35	Honest	20		
Musical	32	Industrious	18	**Japanese**	
Imaginative	30	Extremely nationalistic	18	Intelligent	45
Very religious	21	Humorless	17	Industrious	43
Talkative	21			Progressive	24
Revengeful	17	**Jews**		Shrewd	22
Physically dirty	13	Shrewd	79	Sly	20
Lazy	12	Mercenary	49	Quiet	19
Unreliable	11	Industrious	48	Imitative	17
		Grasping	34	Alert	16
Negroes		Intelligent	29	Suave	16
Superstitious	84	Ambitious	21	Neat	16
Lazy	75	Sly	20	Treacherous	13
Happy-go-lucky	38	Loyal to family ties	15	Aggressive	13
Ignorant	38	Persistent	13		
Musical	26	Talkative	13	**Turks**	
Ostentatious	26	Aggressive	12	Cruel	47
Very religious	24	Very religious	12	Very religious	26
Stupid	22			Treacherous	21
Physically dirty	17	**Americans**		Sensual	20
Naïve	14	Industrious	48	Ignorant	15
Slovenly	13	Intelligent	47	Physically dirty	15
Unreliable	12	Materialistic	33	Deceitful	13
		Ambitious	33	Sly	12
Irish		Progressive	27	Quarrelsome	12
Pugnacious	45	Pleasure-loving	26	Revengeful	12
Quick-tempered	39	Alert	23	Conservative	12
Witty	38	Efficient	21	Superstitious	11
Honest	32				

Source: Katz & Braly, 1933.

number of factors. Two factors emerged from the data: work ethic, and social versus individual control. Both groups rated the Chinese as high on work ethic and moderate on individual versus social control. Both groups also rated the Europeans less positively on work ethic and more individually rather than socially controlled.

These last two studies exemplify more recent approaches to identifying and examining the content of stereotypes that people hold about themselves and others. Williams and Best (1994) used a similar approach in their research on gender stereotypes across countries and cultures (reported in Chapter 7), reducing 300 adjectives to a much more manageable and interpretable three scales. These approaches enable us to gain better insight into the psychological structure of stereotypes and allow for improved research on this issue for years to come. Forgas and O'Driscoll (1984), for example, extended their findings by correlating the three underlying dimensions with demographic variables to see how the structure of stereotypes is associated with factors such as age, gender, and socioeconomic status. These approaches provide a much better understanding of stereotypes than previously offered in the literature.

The Development of Stereotypes: A Psychological Analysis

Stereotypes are products of normal, everyday psychological processes that lead, naturally and inevitably, to the formation and maintenance of stereotypes. To understand how stereotypes are developed and maintained, therefore, it is important to have a basic understanding of the psychological processes on which they are built. These processes include selective attention, appraisal, concept formation and categorization, attributions, emotion, and memory—all of which should be familiar to you from your introductory psychology classes. They are also discussed elsewhere throughout this book (for example, perception and memory in Chapter 4, emotion and appraisal in Chapter 9, categorization of colors in Chapter 10). Here we limit the discussion to a basic presentation of these principles as they relate specifically to stereotypes.

Selective attention.   The amount of stimulation we receive through our senses is too much for us to process and make sense of in our everyday lives. There is no way in which we can attend to all the signals and stimuli we receive from the world. Because our sensation and perceptual systems have limited capacities, we must learn ways to limit the amount of information we actually receive and process. Thus, we pick and choose which stimuli to attend to (for example, the words on this page, the voice of someone talking to you) and the sensory modalities or channels through which we will attend to them (for example, sight or hearing). This process is called **selective attention.** Generally studied by psychologists interested in perception, selective attention refers to the process by which we filter out many of the stimuli that bombard our senses, thus receiving a more meaningful, finite amount of information that we can then process.

Inherent in this selection process is a certain degree of bias. The cocktail party phenomenon illustrates this selection process: People can often hear their own names across the room at a party even though myriad other sounds are occurring at the same time. Some research has examined the role of attention in the development and maintenance of stereotypic beliefs. For instance, one study reports that people who believe an individual's characteristics are relatively fixed traits tend to pay more attention to stereotypic-consistent information than do people who believe an individual's characteristics are malleable, which may work to reinforce stereotypic thinking in the former group and hinder revising their stereotypes (Plaks, Stroessner, Dweck, & Sherman, 2001).

Appraisal. When we witness events or situations or engage with others, we are constantly appraising those stimuli (compare Lazarus, 1991). **Appraisal** refers to the process by which we evaluate the relevance of stimuli in terms of their meaning to our lives. On the basis of the appraisal process, we have emotional reactions, then make decisions concerning appropriate behavioral responses, which Lazarus (1991) refers to as coping. The process of appraisal is relevant to stereotypes because it provides a psychological mechanism by which we actively operate on incoming stimuli and process them in terms of their meaning to us.

Concept formation and categorization. In our everyday lives, we encounter a multitude of stimuli—objects in the environment, people we meet, things we hear or say—and it is literally impossible for us to keep track of them all. That is, as our minds create mental representations of all of the people, places, events, situations, and activities with which we engage, it is impossible to represent all of these stimuli as single, independent units of information. Thus, we develop concepts by which we can mentally represent these events, situations, places, and people so that our minds can deal with them. A **concept** is a mental category we use to classify events, objects, situations, behaviors, or even people with respect to what we perceive as common properties. (Cultures differ on exactly what these common properties may be; this matter is discussed more fully in Chapter 4.) We use these common properties to aid us in classification or **categorization,** which refers to the process by which psychological concepts are grouped together.

We form concepts so that we can evaluate information, make decisions, and act accordingly. It is far easier and more efficient to create concepts or categories of information and to evaluate and act on those categories than it is to process each individual item. In psychology, the study of concept formation involves examining how people classify or categorize events, objects, situations, and people into concepts.

Concept formation and categorization provide us with a way to organize the diversity of the world around us into a finite number of categories. Those categories, in turn, are based on particular properties of the objects that we perceive or deem to be similar in some psychologically meaningful way. For example, we may classify all objects of a certain color together, all types of facial expressions representing a particular emotion together, and so on. Once such concepts have formed, we can access the individual stimulus through the category and gather information about that stimulus based on that category.

Social identity theory (Tajfel & Turner, 1986) is also helpful in understanding stereotyping and prejudice. According to this theory, we categorize people into social groups and place ourselves within a category. We are motivated to positively evaluate our own social group (ingroup) in comparison to other groups (outgroups) in order to maintain a positive social identity. Thus, according to this perspective, stereotyping and prejudice may grow out of the desire to attain or maintain a positive social identity.

There are a variety of theories about how concept formation occurs. However, what is most germane to our discussion here is recognition of the existence of concepts and categorizations and their general utility in organizing the world around us.

Attribution.   One common characteristic of people is a felt need to explain, in our own minds, the causes of events and behaviors. **Attribution** refers to this process by which we infer the causes of our own and other people's behavior. For instance, in a study of junior high school students, girls were less likely than boys to attribute their academic success to high ability, but were more likely than boys to attribute failure to low ability (Stipek & Gralinski, 1991). These attributions could reinforce the stereotypes these adolescents have about appropriate gender roles and expectations. (This process will be mentioned in Chapter 11 and will be discussed in more detail in Chapter 14.).

Attributions serve important functions in our lives. They allow us to organize information in psychologically meaningful ways. This psychic organization is necessary at the very least because of the sheer number of events that occur around us. Some research has shown that attributions are related to control and that people who desire control are more likely than others to make attributions (Burger & Hemans, 1988). Attributions also help people to accommodate new information about their world and help resolve discrepancies between new and old ways of understanding the intentions and behaviors of others (Snyder & Higgins, 1988).

Emotion.   Emotions are an integral and important part of our normal, everyday lives. Emotions are important motivators of our behaviors, telling us to run when we are afraid and fight when we are angry (Tomkins, 1962, 1963). Emotions are important readout devices (Buck, 1984), telling us how we are interpreting the events and situations around us at a moment's notice. Emotions are also important interpersonal markers, informing us about the status of our relationships with others.

A recent study by Islam and Jahjah (2001) reports that emotions such as anxiety and distrust were better predictors of attitudes toward three minority groups (Aboriginals, Asians, and Arabs) in Australia than were cognitive aspects of attitudes, such as knowledge structures and facts about the different minority groups. They argue that this finding has important implications for interventions aimed at reducing racism and prejudice.

In the past decade, Forgas and his colleagues have reported an interesting and important line of research on the role of emotion in person perception, intergroup discrimination, and stereotype judgments. This research suggests the existence of mood-congruent bias in such judgments of others. In one study, for example, Forgas and Moylan (1991) induced happy, sad, or neutral moods in participants who then formed impressions about Asians or Caucasians interacting with same-race or other-race partners. Participants who were happy had more positive judgments of the target persons; participants who were sad had more negative judgments. In addition, the degree of influence of mood on judgment was larger when the participants were judging mixed-race dyads. On the basis of these and similar findings (for example, Forgas & Bower, 1987; Forgas & Fiedler, 1996), Forgas has suggested that the role of emotion or mood in these types of judgments may be greatest when participants engage in substantive processing, which requires them to select, learn, and interpret novel stimuli and to relate this information to preexisting knowledge (for a review of this affect infusion model, see Forgas, 1992, 1994).

Work by Bodenhausen, Kramer, and Suesser (1994) suggests that both positive and negative emotions play an important role in how stereotypically one judges situations. Other researchers have mainly focused on how negative emotions are associated with the inclination to view the world through stereotypic lenses (Greenberg et al., 1990; Sherif & Sherif, 1953), but Bodenhausen has focused on how positive emotions such as happiness may also relate to stereotypical thinking. He has shown that positive affect (and not just negative) can elicit stereotypical responses.

Nonetheless, Forgas (1994) suggests that stereotype judgments of others are probably the least affected by emotion or mood because these judgments involve a direct access strategy—the direct retrieval of preexisting information. Although this notion has not been tested directly, Forgas (1994) cites some evidence to support this claim (for example, Salovey & Birnbaum, 1989; Schwarz, Strack, Kommer, & Wagner, 1987; Srull, 1983). These studies, however, did not test two issues about emotion that we believe are important to the stereotypic judgment process. One concerns the holding off of negative emotions that arise from the mismatch between expectations due to one's cultural filters and the reality of differences. The second concerns the positive emotions associated with the stereotyping process that reinforce one's stereotypes and, in turn, the sense of self. Thus, it would appear that emotion plays a much more important role in the stereotyping process than is elucidated by current research.

Memory.   Memory refers to our ability to remember past events, actions, people, objects, situations, learned skills, and so forth. It also refers to how we store such information. Psychologists generally differentiate among three subtypes of memory and memory-related processes: sensory memory, the initial coding of memory-related stimuli; short-term memory, the "working" memory that serves as an intermediary between sensory and long-term memory (Baddeley & Hitch, 1974); and long-term memory, the storage and retrieval of information over long, sometimes indefinite, periods of time.

Semantic memory is a special type of long-term memory for rules, ideas, and general concepts about the world, including other people; it is usually based on generalizations or images about events, experiences, and learned knowledge. Semantic memory can also be based on verbal knowledge communicated from one person to the next without any basis in actual experience or interaction with the target of the memory. It refers to knowledge that is gathered over a long period of time and continually modified or reinforced as the individual engages with related facts, events, or experiences (Bahrick & Hall, 1991). These properties of semantic memory make it especially relevant to our understanding of stereotypes.

Exactly what we choose to remember reflects our social beliefs, attitudes, and expectations, including stereotypes. For example, in a study of 103 school-age children, those with the most stereotyped views of gender-appropriate behavior recalled seeing more pictures of traditional (for example, female secretary) as opposed to nontraditional (male secretary) activities (Signorella & Liben, 1984) than did their less stereotyped peers. In addition, the children sometimes even reconstructed the pictures—for example, recalling that a secretary was female when in fact the person was male.

Putting it all together. All of the psychological processes discussed here interact to make stereotypes an inevitable aspect of our psychological life. Actually, as general categories of mental concepts, stereotypes are invaluable aids, helping us keep information about the world organized in our mental representations. We have such categorical representations about many objects in the world, and there is no way we could keep track of the world without them. Categorical representations of people happen to be called stereotypes.

As a special type of category—that is, having to do with people—stereotypes are important in helping us interact effectively with, or act as a hindrance to, others in our world. The problem is that it is relatively easy for negative stereotypes to develop, because our own cultural upbringing, cultural filters, and ethnocentrism create a set of expectations in us about the behaviors and traits of others. When we observe people from a different cultural background, we are often exposed to behaviors, activities, or situations that do not match our initial expectations based on our own cultural backgrounds. These observations can lead to negative attributions about the causes of those events or the underlying intentions or psychological characteristics of the actors being observed. Because such events are unexpected, they often require what Forgas (1994) would call substantive processing, which is the type of processing most affected by induced emotion. If the emotion induced at the time is negative, which is a natural reaction to our witnessing something outside of our expectations, then that negative emotion will be more likely to contribute to negatively valenced attributions about the other person. Such negatively valenced attributions can form the core of a mental concept that may then be placed in a category of such people. This negative attribution will also have a reinforcing effect on the value and expectation system that began the process. The result is a negative stereotype.

Once developed, stereotypes are easily reinforced. Our expectations change according to our stereotypes. We may selectively attend to events that appear to support our stereotypes, ignoring, albeit unconsciously, events and situations that challenge those stereotypes (Johnston, Hewstone, Pendry, & Frankish, 1994). For instance, one study found that when people were presented with stereotypical and nonstereotypical information about a certain group (in this case, football players), they tended to remember and communicate to other people the stereotypical information rather than the nonstereotypical (Lyons & Kashima, 2001). Our negative attributions may be reenacted, thus reinforcing the negative stereotypes held as categorical representations of that group of people.

Even when we attend to events that are contrary to our stereotypic beliefs, we often come up with unique attributional processes to convince ourselves that our stereotype is correct. We may suggest that the observed event was a fluke or that the person observed was not a good representative of the group to which the stereotype applies. Such dismissals can occur quickly, with little conscious thought or effort, and are resistant to infusion of emotion at the time.

To suggest that our attention, attributional, and emotional processes may be biased is nothing new. Indeed, we have made this point throughout the first few chapters of this book and will return to it in later chapters as well. These and other psychological processes make up an integrated psychological system that we know of as our sense of self or self-concept. The core concept underlying the entire discussion in this section is that these psychological processes are all biased so as to reinforce that self-concept. Our emotions, attributions, and attention processes are all constructed so as to help us reinforce the cultural knowledge we have learned from many years of enculturation and socialization. Even the content of our stereotypes probably serves to reinforce our sense of self; as we confirm those stereotypes, we are reinforcing that self-concept.

Thus, stereotypes are an integral and important part of a complete package of psychological processes that constitute our sense of self and self-concept. They are intimately tied to our emotions, values, and core self and, as such, are difficult to change once we acquire them. Yet other factors, too, contribute to the formation and maintenance of stereotypes.

Other Contributing Factors

Stereotypes may develop from several different sources. One, as we have seen, is ethnocentrism. When we observe the behavior of others, we perceive that behavior and make interpretations (attributions) about underlying causes based on rules we have learned from our own cultural upbringing. Those interpretations serve as mental categories or concepts that help us organize and assimilate information about people. As we grow up, we may selectively attend to particular behaviors and even ignore the existence of evidence or behaviors to the contrary, reinforcing the mental categories we have created. These categories are stored as verbal labels in long-term memory and play a major role in the way we interact with the world. All of these processes may be influenced by personal preference, cultural factors, and the like, and all are open to errors in the processing of information. Because of the cyclical nature of the interaction between basic psychological processes and our culturally based ethnocentrism, these processes form a feedback loop, reinforcing errors and creating and maintaining mental categories of people we come to know as stereotypes.

Stereotypes can also be created and perpetuated in individuals merely by communication of verbal labels from generation to generation, with no actual interaction with the people who are the target of the stereotype (Brislin, 1993). Research suggests that stereotypes that are most communicable (most easily talked about) are most likely to persist over time. An understanding of the communicability of stereotypes is helpful in predicting the maintenance and modification in the contents of stereotypes of real groups in the real world (Schaller, Conway, & Tanchuk, 2002).

Stereotypes can be created and reinforced by television, movies, magazines, and other media. For example, gender and class stereotypes are reinforced in popular American television shows (Croteau & Hoynes, 2000). Men are more likely than women to be portrayed as having high-status, traditionally male jobs (such as doctors or lawyers) and are less likely to be shown in the home. Fathers in working-class families are usually portrayed as incompetent yet lovable buffoons (for example, Al Bundy, Homer Simpson), while middle-class fathers are depicted as competent at their jobs and as parents (as in *The Cosby Show* and *The Brady Bunch*) (Butsch, 1992). These portrayals may reinforce stereotypes we have of individuals from different class backgrounds. In another example, Taylor and Stern's (1997) analysis of 1,300 prime time television advertisements shows that Asians are overrepresented in business settings and underrepresented in home settings and family or social relationships, which, they argue, feeds into the stereotype of the successful model minority.

Stereotypes may be formed through limited exposure to members of the target group or to exposure based on a "biased" sample. Thus, stereotypes can be formed and reinforced in a person on the basis of very limited exposure, or no exposure at all, to the target group. The complex interplay of these external factors with our own cultural and psychological processes make stereotypes a difficult problem to deal with.

Sometimes a stereotype is a product of our own observation of something we have interpreted as negative. Because of our need to classify information about people and to verify such classifications based on selective attention and memory processes, we often associate our interpretations with inferred traits of the target person; generalize those traits to observable, identifiable characteristics of that person (for example, skin color); and then make a generalized statement that can be used to describe all people sharing that identifiable characteristic. Thus, we come up with statements such as "Blacks, or Japanese, or Arabs, or Whites are ———." To be sure, many stereotypes are associated with groups whose defining characteristics are not visible—such as lawyers or homosexuals—and these stereotypes are equally limiting, intense, and resistant to change.

Whether positive or negative, stereotypes are generally limiting and potentially discriminatory. This is so because stereotypes as mental categories of people tend to take on a life of their own. Rather than using stereotypes as "best guess" generalizations about a group of people, which we then adjust based on interactions with specific individuals, we often use stereotypes as a rigid set of assumptions about all people of that group, regardless of individual differences or evidence to the contrary. Data (that is, actual observed behavior) that might seem to challenge the stereotype will be "massaged" to the point where they can be used to support the stereotype. Data that cannot be reinterpreted to support the stereotype will simply be discarded as random chance occurrences.

Stereotypes used in this way become more and more entrenched because all our experiences serve to reinforce the stereotype regardless of how true or false it is. Stereotypes exist even in the most pluralistic of people. What is important is how we go beyond them, using them only as basic guides to interacting with people of other cultural backgrounds. As guides, stereotypes are not written in stone but give us ideas, impressions, or images of people that can be used for an initial encounter, after which they can be discarded or reinforced depending on the exact nature of the interaction and behavior observed.

There is a fine line between using a generalization as a guide and using a stereotype to vindicate your personal view of the world. Vindicating your view of the world by using stereotypes rigidly and inflexibly allows you only a limited view of the world, its people and events. Vindicating your view of the world by using stereotypes inflexibly also provides a framework within which prejudice and discrimination are likely to occur.

Current theories underscore the importance of distinguishing between stereotype activation and application (Bargh, 1996; Devine, 1989; Gilbert & Hixon, 1991). Well-learned stereotypes are activated automatically (Blair, 2001), but whether people apply the stereotype or not depends on factors such as whether they are motivated to be nonprejudiced (Monteith, Sherman, & Devine, 1998) or are encouraged to be aware of egalitarian norms and standards (Macrae, Bodenhausen, & Milne, 1998).

Stereotypes can also change depending on major events, such as war. A study by Bal-Tal and Labin (2001) of Israeli adolescents and their stereotypes of Palestinians, Jordanians, and Arabs was conducted longitudinally on three separate occasions. The researchers administered surveys at a relatively peaceful time, directly after an attack by an extreme Palestinian group, and a few months later. They found that stereotypic judgments concerning Palestinians became more negative directly after the attack, but after a few months they returned to the initial baseline level. The researchers argue for more real-life investigations of stereotypes and how they can change over time. They emphasize that stereotypes are not fixed and can change in response to new events and situations. Their results support the view of Oakes, Haslam, and Turner (1994) that stereotypes are "fluid, variable, and context-dependent" (p. 211). Thus, in addition to a recognition of the cognitive and emotional factors that contribute to stereotypical thinking, situational factors are also important.

Prejudice, Discrimination, and "Isms"

Prejudice

Although ethnocentrism and stereotypes are normal and inevitable consequences of daily psychological functioning and enculturation into society, they often form the basis of limited and detrimental patterns of thinking about, and dealing with, others in the world. These processes are called prejudice, discrimination, and a host of terms ending with the suffix *-ism*.

Prejudice refers to the tendency to prejudge others on the basis of their group membership. That is, prejudiced people think about others solely in terms of their stereotypes. The term *prejudice* is often used to describe the tendency to think of others in a negative way based on a negative stereotype. But just as stereotypes can be both positive and negative, so too can people be prejudiced in both positive and negative ways.

Although ethnocentrism and stereotypes are normal and inevitable consequences of psychological functioning, prejudice is not. Prejudice results solely from an individual's inability to realize the limitations in his or her ethnocentric and stereotypic thinking. Those individuals who realize that they have stereotypes, that their stereotypes may or may not be accurate, and that stereotypes never describe all the members of any group, are less likely to be prejudiced. Conversely, less prejudiced individuals are less likely to apply stereotypes in their judgments of others. For example, Devine (1989) found that although people high and low in prejudice articulated similar cultural stereotypes of African Americans, those lower in prejudice personally endorsed these stereotypes to a lesser degree. Those who do not recognize the limitations in their ethnocentric and stereotypic thinking and who do not even recognize that their ethnocentrism and stereotypes exist will be more likely to exhibit prejudicial thinking about themselves as well as others.

Prejudice can have two components: a cognitive (thinking) component, and an affective (feeling) component. Stereotypes form the basis of the cognitive component of prejudice—the stereotypic beliefs, opinions, and attitudes one harbors toward others. The affective component comprises one's personal feelings toward other groups of people. These feelings may include anger, contempt, resentment, or disdain, or even compassion, sympathy, and closeness. Although the cognitive and affective components are often related, they need not be, and may actually exist independently of each other within the same person. That is, a person may have feelings about a particular group of people without being able to specify a stereotype about them; and a person may have stereotypic beliefs about others that are detached from their feelings.

Discrimination

Most social scientists make a distinction between prejudice and discrimination. Whereas prejudice involves stereotypic cognitions and/or feelings about groups of people, **discrimination** typically refers to the unfair treatment of others based on their group membership. The difference between prejudice and discrimination is the difference between thinking/feeling (prejudice) and doing (discrimination).

Like stereotypes and prejudice, discrimination can include preferential or positive treatment as well as deferred or negative treatment. If one harbors positive stereotypes about a group of people and is prejudiced in their favor, for example, one may engage in behaviors that actively promote or enhance individual members of that group solely on the basis of their group membership. Discrimination is often negative, resulting in unfair, less favorable treatment of others. The important issue in defining discrimination revolves around the concept of fairness and treatment based on group membership.

Although prejudice and discrimination are often linked, they need not be. Merton (1968) highlighted the ways in which prejudice and discrimination may be related to each other in any single person. Those who are unprejudiced may or may not discriminate, and those who discriminate may or may not be prejudiced. Prejudice and discrimination are processes that occur on the individual level. When similar processes occur on the group or organizational level, they are known as various "isms" and institutional discrimination.

"Isms" and Institutional Discrimination

Racism, classism, and sexism are just a few of the many examples of the prejudicial thoughts and feelings that can be harbored by large groups of people about other groups based on their biological, sociological, or psychological characteristics. The particular characteristic used is generally attached to the *-ism* suffix. Thus, racism is group-based prejudicial thought based on race, classism is prejudice based on social class, and sexism is prejudice based on sex.

Although prejudice can be either positive or negative in content, isms are usually negative and derogatory, used to justify inferior status on the part of the people being characterized. The term *prejudice* describes preferential thoughts and feelings held by an individual; isms are prejudices that are held by one group of people about another. As such, they generally constitute systems of ideas, beliefs, and opinions held by a large group of people and are often woven into the social and cultural fabric of that group. Thus, they constitute an ideology that can be communicated from one generation to the next, much as other elements of culture are communicated (see Healey, 1998).

Institutional discrimination is discrimination that occurs on the level of a large group, society, organization, or institution. It is unequal or unfair patterns of behavior or preferential treatment of people by a large group or organization solely on the basis of group membership. These patterns of treatment may or may not be conscious and deliberate. Allegations concerning such institutional discrimination are all around us in the daily news, involving the educational system, places of business and work, the legal and criminal justice systems, and professional sports.

One of the most immediate and controversial issues regarding possible institutional discrimination concerns affirmative action policies in admissions to colleges and universities. Several years ago, officers of the University of California voted to repeal affirmative action admissions procedures. Proponents of the repeal point to data suggesting that, despite many years of affirmative action policies for underrepresented populations, there has been no real change in the numbers of people from these groups being educated because many drop out or fail. They also point to the cost of remedial education needed to compensate for poor academic preparation, detracting from the university's ability to provide quality education to those students who were admitted based on non–affirmative action criteria.

On the other side, opponents of the repeal point to their own data suggesting that affirmative action policies were working to educate far greater numbers of individuals from underrepresented groups. They suggest that other problems, such as the need for remediation, merely highlight the other racist and discriminatory programs and policies of the university system and society as a whole. Patricia Gurin (1997) from the University of Michigan analyzed longitudinal data from several survey studies involving more than 10,000 students from almost 200 colleges and universities nationwide. These studies examined the relationship between the diversity of the school campus and student learning outcomes. Based on the results of these studies, she concluded that students who experienced more racial and ethnic diversity in the classroom, as measured by proportion of minorities in the classroom and extent and quality of interaction with students of different racial and ethnic backgrounds, "showed the greatest engagement in active thinking processes, growth in intellectual engagement and motivation, and growth in intellectual and academic skills." She argued that diversity created through affirmative action policies enhances education.

This debate promises to continue for years to come, in California and throughout the United States. At the time of this writing, the U.S. Supreme Court is hearing arguments on affirmative action policies at the University of Michigan undergraduate and law schools. The outcome of this case will be one of the most significant decisions on equal opportunity in education in the United States. As Americans engage in these debates, it is important to study both sides of the issue, leaving our individual prejudices aside, and to weigh the pros and cons of any proposed policy changes with an open mind. In doing so, we need to keep in mind all of the possible ramifications of such policies, not only in terms of their overt consequences for education but also in terms of their social and psychological consequences.

A recent study by Maio and Esses (1998) throws an interesting light on this subject. These authors examined the degree to which knowledge about affirmative action policies may produce negative perceptions about people who benefit from such policies. They presented participants with a fictitious editorial describing an unfamiliar group in a positive manner. In one condition, the editorial indicated that the group benefited from affirmative action policies; in another condition, there was no mention of such benefit. When affirmative action was mentioned, participants expressed less favorable perceptions of and attitudes toward the group. The participants even expressed less favorable attitudes toward immigration by the group, and toward immigration in general. These findings highlight the need for us, as psychologists and concerned citizens of the world, to gather as much data as possible about the social and psychological consequences of programs and policies related to allegations of isms or institutional discrimination and to become fully educated and informed about the issues.

Origins of and Factors Contributing to Prejudice

Social scientists have been concerned for many years about the factors that contribute to the origin and maintenance of prejudice and discrimination. By far the most common theories involve issues of intergroup conflict and power. In general, these theories (for reviews, see Duckitt, 1992; Healey, 1998) suggest that the competition that naturally occurs among groups in any society—whether for power, prestige, status, or wealth—produces prejudicial and discriminatory thoughts, feelings, and actions among both those in power (the "haves") and those without (the "have-nots"). Such prejudice and discrimination on both sides, but especially on the part of the haves, can serve as a justification to exploit the have-nots. As such prejudice and discrimination require an identifying variable or characteristic to which they can become attached, race, ethnicity, or social class is often used as that marker (see also Mirande, 1985; Moore, 1988).

Another argument that has gained attention in recent history is that prejudice and discrimination are inevitable outcomes of social biology and evolution (see, for example, van den Berghe, 1981). This argument suggests that sentiments about ethnicity and race are logical extensions of kinship sentiment—that is, the favoring of kin over nonkin. Kinship sentiments are biologically and evolutionarily functional, increasing the likelihood of one's own genes' being transmitted to future generations. Because racial and ethnic groups can be viewed as extensions of kin, these sentiments may predispose people to behave more favorably to such kin. If kinship sentiments do apply to ethnicity and race, this argument continues, prejudice and discrimination may indeed be fundamental and inevitable.

Other factors have also been suggested as contributing to the origin and maintenance of prejudice and discrimination. Some theories focus on social and cultural factors, suggesting that society promotes ideological prejudice and institutional discrimination in order to impose inferior status on some groups. This inferior status, in turn, reinforces the ideological prejudice and institutional discrimination, which themselves further reinforce the inferior status.

Children growing up in such societies, whether as members of the "inferior" or the "superior" group, become enculturated in these ways of thinking, feeling, and acting, which become a part of their own operating culture, thus ensuring the reenactment of this cycle of exploitation. Jane Elliot, a schoolteacher in the 1960s, is well known for her Blue-Eyed/Brown-Eyed classroom exercises, in which she demonstrated how quickly children can learn to become discriminatory simply based on the messages they are told about a particular group. In this exercise, she divided the children into brown-eyed and blue-eyed groups and told one group they were superior, more talented, and better than the other. She found that in a short amount of time the children actually took on the stereotypes of these groups and, furthermore, began to act in discriminatory ways toward one another. Her exercise demonstrated how harmful stereotyping and prejudice can be and, perhaps more important, that if they can be learned, they can also be unlearned.

A study by Hampel and Krupp (1977) highlights the importance of cultural factors over other social and political factors in maintaining prejudicial stereotypes. This study assessed prejudicial attitudes in three samples of participants: Britons in England; Caucasian, English-speaking South Africans; and Caucasian, Afrikaans-speaking South Africans. Attitudes were assessed about racial minorities in England (for the British sample) and about the Bantu in South Africa. The results indicated that English-speaking South Africans were more similar in their attitudes to Britons in England than to the Afrikaans-speaking South Africans, even though the latter group shared the same social and political environment. Two earlier studies involving South African high school students (Orpen, 1971a, 1971b) also confirmed the strong relationship between adherence to cultural norms among English-speaking South Africans and prejudicial attitudes, above and beyond the existence of personality variables thought to contribute to prejudice.

Other theories have focused on aspects of personality that contribute to the formation and maintenance of prejudice and discrimination. Of particular note is the work on the relationship between authoritarian personality and prejudice (Adorno et al., 1950, cited in Healey, 1998). This work suggests that prejudicial thoughts and feelings and discriminatory behaviors are an integral part of authoritarian personalities, and that people with such personalities in fact require prejudicial thoughts and feelings to function effectively in their lives and in society.

More recent research, however, suggests a more precise relationship between authoritarianism and prejudice. Verkuyten and Hagendoorn (1998), for example, conducted two studies that examined the interaction of self-categorization, authoritarian personality, ingroup stereotypes, and prejudicial attitudes. Participants were instructed to focus on themselves either as unique individuals (personal identity condition) or as members of a larger group (national identity condition). They also completed an authoritarian personality questionnaire, provided data about their stereotypes regarding their own group, and rated three different outgroups in terms of prejudicial attitudes. The results indicated that authoritarian personality predicted prejudicial attitudes only when the participants focused on their personal identities. When participants focused on their national identities, their ingroup stereotypes predicted their prejudicial attitudes, but individual differences on the authoritarian measure did not. These findings suggest that personality variables may be salient only when the reference for prejudicial thought is oneself as an individual, and not as a member of a larger group.

Recent research is also beginning to explore the bases of institutional racism and discrimination. Jeanquart-Barone and Sekaran (1996), for example, tested employees of a national, predominantly minority, organization. Participants provided data on perceived racism in their organization, supportiveness of the climate at work, perceived supervisory discrimination, general supervisory support, procedural justice, and indoctrination—the degree to which the employees' values meshed with those of the organization. The results indicated that the last five variables were all significant predictors of institutional racism.

In particular, supportive climate was negatively correlated with racism; that is, higher levels of a supportive climate were associated with decreased perceptions of institutional racism. Perceived supervisory discrimination, in contrast, was positively correlated with institutional racism.

Which of these factors is responsible for prejudice and discrimination, both on the individual and group levels? The answer, of course, is all of them—intergroup power conflicts, sociobiology, sociocultural history, personality, and others. There is no single cause of prejudice and discrimination—which is why they plague so many societies of the world today and why it is often so difficult to work through these issues. Still it is important to try, especially as we continue in the rest of this book to uncover differences around the world in psychology and behavior.

Going Beyond Prejudice and Discrimination

Recognizing One's Own Ethnocentrism and Stereotypic Thinking

Although ethnocentrism and stereotypes may be inevitable, there is a fine but important distinction between them and prejudice and discrimination. Whether people "cross the line" between prejudicial and nonprejudicial thought depends, first, on whether they recognize their own ethnocentrism and stereotypic thoughts. Individuals who are unaware of the inevitably ethnocentric basis of their own worldviews will not likely be able to recognize that other worldviews are possible. Likewise, individuals who are unaware of the stereotypic biases in their thoughts, attitudes, and opinions will not be able to recognize that those attitudes cannot accurately describe all the individuals with whom they come in contact. Without recognizing one's own ethnocentrism and stereotypic thinking, one cannot develop empathy for another person's viewpoint and worldview. And empathy, as we will see at the end of this book, is the key to true intercultural sensitivity.

Only those individuals who realize that ethnocentrism and stereotypic thoughts are normal and inevitable psychological processes have the ability to recognize the limitations inherent in those processes. Recognizing one's own ethnocentrism makes it possible to recognize the existence of a separate, and potentially different, ethnocentrism in others. Likewise, recognizing the stereotypic attitudes in one's own thinking enables one to recognize the limits and fallibility of stereotypes. Thus, a major first step in moving beyond prejudice and discrimination is to increase awareness of ethnocentrism and stereotypes, their inevitability and their inherent limitations.

Working to Reduce Prejudice

Because prejudicial attitudes are based on fixed and rigid stereotypes, methods to reduce prejudicial thought would necessarily include intervention on the level of those stereotypes. If the first step is to recognize the existence of stereotypes, the next step is to recognize their inherent limitations:

1. Stereotypes are based on interpretations we produce based on our own cultural filters and background, or on communication from external sources.
2. Stereotypes are often associated with identifiable characteristics.
3. Stereotypes are generalizations about a group of people.

By examining each of these three points, we can find ways to use stereotypes more flexibly. Our interpretations may be wrong, based on wrong facts or no facts. Our stereotypes are based on interpretations we have made about the underlying meaning, psychological characteristic, or personality trait of a person. These interpretations are based on the cultural rules we have learned that are applicable to ourselves, and they are made about behavior observed through our own cultural filters. In some cases, stereotypes may not be based on facts at all, having simply been told to us by others or reinforced by the media.

Other people may engage in behavior we interpret to be rude or offensive as viewed through our own cultural filters. In fact, that behavior may not have been intended as rude or offensive from the other person's viewpoint. Furthermore, the behavior we observed may not even be the behavior that actually occurred because our cultural filters may have distorted our perceptions of it or because we selectively attended to parts of an action sequence but not the whole. Thus, it may be that our perceptions of the event and/or our interpretations of its underlying causes are incorrect. When interacting with people of a culture that is obviously different from our own, the potential for being mistaken is much greater than when interacting with someone of the same culture.

On the other hand, your interpretations may be correct despite the fact that you and the other person come from different cultural backgrounds. It may be the case that the person was trying to be rude and offensive. You may actually be correct in your perceptions and interpretations—or you may not be. The point is that we don't really know. All we know is that we perceive events and behaviors and make interpretations about those events and behaviors based on our own cultural filters and rules. We may not know whether we are exactly correct in our perceptions and interpretations (although there are times when we are more sure of our interpretations than others). We usually believe that we are absolutely, entirely correct, because we interpret the world through our own cultural filters. But the very fact that we may be incorrect should make us more flexible in our assumptions about others and their behaviors. When we are mistaken in our judgments, the costs can be high, whether in business, love, or everyday relationships.

The characteristics we identify are often selected without reason. In creating stereotypes, we generally associate our images and impressions with identifiable characteristics of a group of people. Often these characteristics are racial or ethnic; thus, we hear that African Americans, Asians, or Hispanics are a certain way. But race and ethnicity are not the only types of visible characteristics for which we have stereotypes. Stereotypes also exist about other observable, physical characteristics. Thus, we hear stereotypes about blondes or redheads. Sometimes stereotypes are formed on the basis of other characteristics that identify a group of people, such as lawyers, homosexuals, or politicians.

Why do we define our stereotypes according to characteristics that identify groups? The answer lies in basic psychological processes related to concept formation and categorization. Such categories make it easier for us to summarize the wealth of information about the world around us. Indeed, it is impossible to keep track of all the possible information about people we come in contact with. One of the easiest ways to group or categorize is by observable, physical characteristics. Thus, it is easy to make generalizations or stereotypes on the basis of race because racial differences are generally visible and easy to verify. Because they are easy to verify, such stereotypes can also be reinforced rather easily. Besides race, it is also easy to make stereotypes based on sex or class or occupation. Thus, we have stereotypes about men and women, rich and poor, lawyers, doctors, and many other groups.

This aspect of stereotypes highlights how they are limited. The important elements of stereotypes are not the characteristics we can see but the aspects of the person we cannot observe. It is this invisible aspect of people that produces differences and diversity in the first place; this invisible aspect is culture. Indeed, it is culture as a sociopsychological phenomenon and not race, sex, class, or occupation that produces differences in behavior. Learned patterns of behaviors, rituals, values, attitudes, and opinions produce behavior differences. Neither race, sex, class, nor occupation per se can produce such differences; culture can and does. Other authors writing on ethnic and race relations, including Sowell (1983), Steele (1990), Steinberg (1989), and Taylor (1992), have expressed the same idea in different ways. It is the central message of Martin Luther King's "I Have a Dream" speech.

Generalizations about a group may not describe any single individual within the group. Stereotypes are generalizations about a group of individuals that share some identifiable characteristic. Aside from whether those generalizations are true, we must also realize that within any group there are considerable individual differences. For example, saying that African Americans, Asians, Hispanics, or Arabs are _____, even if the generalization has some validity, doesn't mean that each and every African American, Asian, Hispanic, or Arab person you meet is _____. As with any other aspect of culture, there are bound to be individual differences in the degree to which any description of a culture or group of people applies to specific individuals within the group. Some people will indeed be rude and offensive; others will be polite and deferent. Some will be untrustworthy and devious; others will be totally trustworthy and forthright.

A stereotype, or any statement about a group of people, is at best merely a summary of a tendency of the group as a whole. (At worst, it reflects a generalization about a group of people that has no basis in fact and serves as an excuse for discrimination.) As with any summary, there are bound to be people that summary fits and those it doesn't fit. While group tendencies may differ substantially, individuals within those groups may or may not differ at all depending on their individual placement within their respective groups.

We need to challenge the bases of group stereotypes and the generalizations underlying them. We need to recognize individual differences within groups and the fact that no stereotype can adequately describe all people within a certain group. Stereotypes are not likely to disappear. It is human nature to develop guidelines and to use categories and groups to store the wealth of information about people that we gain in our lives. We cannot ignore stereotypes, but we can realize their potential abuses and use them more wisely. Stereotypes should be used as guidelines for interaction, not as rigid and inflexible descriptors of people. We need to validate or invalidate stereotypes, not use them to vindicate ourselves. Only by understanding the bases for stereotypes can we begin the process of using them better.

Working to Reduce Discrimination

One of the most important aspects of the stereotypic thought process that contributes to discrimination is the emotions involved. As noted earlier, negative emotions are often infused in the stereotypic thought process because negative emotions are likely consequences of mismatches between reality and one's expectations based on culture. As the research by Forgas and his colleagues suggests, these negative emotions may color the attributions people make about such mismatches and the other people involved, and these negative attributions may be precisely those that are committed to long-term memory. As stereotypic attitudes crystallize, this process becomes less affected by emotion infusion (direct access judgments), while positive emotions that occur because of a match between perceived reality and held stereotypes reinforce this system.

As negative emotions about outgroups and self-serving emotions reinforce stereotypic attitudes (prejudice), they serve as the primary motivators for behavior and action, and thus form the basis for discrimination. Again, the major difference between prejudice and discrimination is that discrimination involves external actions or behaviors against outgroup others, whereas prejudice involves internal thoughts or feelings. Once negative and self-serving emotions are activated, it may very well be human nature for people to regress in their level of critical and open thinking, to revert back to a more primitive cognitive style. Witness young children who get hurt or angry; once overcome by their emotions, their thinking reverts back to a more primitive level—a phenomenon known as regression. Adults are no different. Once we feel hurt or angry, it is only natural to revert to a more primitive way of thinking and to respond behaviorally by lashing out and treating others unfairly—in short, by discriminating against others.

It thus follows that one of the most important ways of working to reduce discrimination (in addition to recognizing our own ethnocentrism and stereotypes and thinking critically about the limitations of those stereotypes) is learning to control our emotions. We need to be able to regulate our negative emotions when they occur, as well as our positive, reinforcing emotions when they are challenged. Only if we can regulate such emotional processes in ourselves can we then engage in other critical thinking exercises, examining the possible biases in our thoughts, feelings, and actions and adjusting them accordingly. Without the ability to regulate emotions, such higher-order thought processes are impossible. We will discuss these processes in greater detail in the final chapter of this book.

Another type of intervention aimed at reducing prejudice and discrimination in young children is the work of Elliot Aronson (2002) and his "jigsaw classroom." In this type of classroom, students are each given different materials to learn, akin to each having a piece of a jigsaw puzzle, and they must cooperate and work together to learn and complete a task. Aronson's ideas are based on social identity theory and the importance of having common goals in reducing prejudice. Research on this technique demonstrates that students benefit from this type of cooperation as evidenced by higher levels of self-esteem, an increased liking for school and their classmates, and improved performance on tests.

Conclusion

Improving our understanding of ethnocentrism and stereotypes, and their contribution to prejudice and discrimination, is extremely important in today's world. Despite the steps we have taken in recent decades to close the gap between different groups of people, especially racial groups, the 1992 riots in Los Angeles, the recurring cries to "Buy American," and the Oklahoma City federal building bombing in 1995, in which Arabs were early on erroneously singled out as suspects, all speak to the strong and pervasive sentiments of group identification that can have negative or positive effects.

One of the first steps to improving our understanding of intergroup relations is improving our understanding of culture—notably, the influence of culture on basic psychological processes and the formation and maintenance of ethnocentrism and stereotypes. Improving our understanding of culture and its influences, however, is only one of many steps along the road. We need to search our own culture to discover the reasons these stereotypes have persisted and how our own culture may be fostered or facilitated by their maintenance. We need to recognize the existence of considerable individual variability within groups and cultures. We need to recognize the limitations of our own ethnocentrism and of vindictive, limited stereotyping. By recognizing group and individual differences and by acknowledging rather than ignoring their influences, we are free to allow ourselves to engage with people on a common ground rather than prejudging their actions, behaviors, and reasons via stereotypes based entirely on our ground or theirs.

The study of culture reveals the importance of cultural background, upbringing, and heritage and their impact on our behaviors. Many of our behaviors as adults are not only shaped by culture but also draw their meaning from culture. Recognizing the important contributions of culture to actions, behaviors, and the reasons behind them helps us to understand, respect, and appreciate those differences when we observe them in real life.

This material is presented early in the book to familiarize you with these processes before you engage with the material that follows. Undoubtedly, as you go on and engage with the rest of the book, you will discover many differences as well as similarities among people in their thoughts, feelings, actions, and behaviors. You will engage with that material with your ethnocentric cultural filters on, and through the lens of your stereotypic attitudes. Hopefully, because of the material presented in this chapter, you will be able to recognize your own ethnocentrism and stereotypic thinking as you engage with that material. Hopefully, you will be able to catch yourself if you start to cross the line from that ethnocentrism and those stereotypes to prejudice or discrimination. Hopefully, you will engage in critical thinking about some of the characteristics of those stereotypes, and regulate your emotional reactions.

Several studies over the years have highlighted the potential contribution of increased intercultural experiences to the reduction of inflexible ethnocentric attitudes, fixed stereotypes, prejudice, and discrimination (for example, Bochner & Perks, 1971; Vornberg & Grant, 1976). Many of these studies have focused on intercultural experiences gained by participants' traveling and living in cultures other than those in which they were enculturated. In that vein, it is our hope that you can engage with the rest of the material in this book as a sort of intercultural journey into the psychology of people of different cultural backgrounds. Hopefully, that experience can help increase your level of intercultural sensitivity.

And what are we to do if we are the victims of prejudice and discrimination? One of the first avenues of coping, based on the analyses presented in this chapter, is to recognize the limitations and origins of such thoughts, feelings, and actions in others. Unfortunately, in many instances we have little recourse concerning the limitations in others' thoughts or actions, as people will change only if they want to change. Recent research has also highlighted some attributional processes as well as psychological disengagement as important coping mechanisms for members of negatively stereotyped groups (Major, Spencer, Schmader, Wolfe, & Crocker, 1998; Moghaddam, Taylor, Lambert, & Schmidt, 1995).

The material in this chapter is some of the most difficult to write about because it is so emotionally charged. Almost everyone you talk with will have an opinion, sometimes a strong one, about these issues. These issues are so charged, in fact, that we become afraid to engage in what could be healthy discussion for fear of offending others or revealing supposed "biases" on our part. Although the material presented here is undoubtedly influenced by our own views, the most important point is that this presentation can serve as a springboard for healthy discussion about these most difficult topics. Whether you agree with the material presented here or not, we hope the interactions that result from the thoughts it stimulates will exhibit the type of tolerance for widely divergent opinions that the topic deserves.

 **Glossary**

appraisal   The process by which we evaluate the relevance of stimuli in terms of their meaning to our lives.

attribution   The process by which we infer the causes of our own and other people's behavior.

autostereotypes   Stereotypes you hold about your own group.

categorization   The process by which psychological concepts are grouped together.

concept   A mental category we use to classify events, objects, situations, behaviors, or even people with respect to what we perceive as common properties.

discrimination   The unfair treatment of others based on their group membership.

ethnocentrism   The tendency to view the world through one's own cultural filters.

flexible ethnocentrism   Ethnocentrism in which people can learn ways of putting on hold, however temporarily, their ethnocentrism and perceptions of and reactions to reality based on their cultural filters and interpret the behaviors of others from the others' perspective.

heterostereotypes   Stereotypes you hold about other groups.

inflexible ethnocentrism Ethnocentrism that is characterized by an inability to go outside one's own perspective and view the behavior of others from the others' cultural perspective.

institutional discrimination   Discrimination that occurs on the level of a large group, society, organization, or institution.

prejudice   The tendency to prejudge others on the basis of their group membership.

selective attention   The process by which we filter out many of the stimuli that bombard our senses, thus receiving a more meaningful, finite amount of information that we can then process.

semantic memory   A special type of long-term memory for rules, ideas, and general concepts about the world, including other people; it is usually based on generalizations or images about events, experiences, and learned knowledge.

stereotypes   Generalized images we have about groups of people, particularly about their underlying psychological characteristics or personality traits.

InfoTrac College Edition

Use InfoTrac College Edition to search for additional readings on topics of interest to you. For more information on topics in this chapter, use the following as search terms:

categorization	selective attention
discrimination	semantic memory
ethnocentrism	stereotype
prejudices	

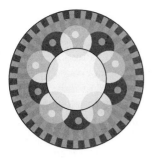

Culture and Basic Psychological Processes

Just as atoms and molecules serve as the building blocks of matter, some psychological processes serve as the building blocks of other psychological constructs. In this chapter, we begin our exploration of cultural similarities and differences in psychology by examining the nature of those psychological building blocks.

We begin by exploring how people of different cultures may differ in the biological bases of their behavior. Next, we examine the relationship between culture and perception, focusing on research that has examined cultural differences in visual perception using optical illusions. After that, we examine the relationship between culture and cognition, including memory, face recognition, categorization, problem solving, decision making, and creativity. Then, we discuss the relationship between culture and consciousness, examining cross-cultural research on dreams, time perspective and orientation, and the perception of pain. We conclude by looking at the important topic of intelligence and what recent cross-cultural research has to say about this highly charged topic, as well as the difficult issues surrounding the use of intelligence and aptitude tests in selection for employment and admission to schools.

Culture and the Biological Bases of Behavior

One of the first topics you learn about in introductory psychology is the various biological—anatomical and physiological—systems that underlie human behavior. Among these basic systems are the brain and central nervous system;

the structure of the eyes, ears, and other sensory systems; the autonomic nervous system, including the sympathetic and parasympathetic nervous systems; and the skeletal muscular systems, including striated and smooth muscles.

This information is important to our understanding of psychological phenomena for several reasons. First, it grounds us in our understanding of exactly how we process sensory information—for example, how stimuli are perceived on our retinas, and how that stimulation is converted to neural signals that travel along the optic nerve to our brains and become acted upon. Second, it helps us to understand how psychological phenomena may be represented in the body. What happens when we are stressed out? How does our brain tell us to move our hand when it touches a hot object? Finally, it helps us understand the bodily functions underlying movements and behaviors.

Like much information presented in mainstream psychology, much of this information is presented as if it were the same for all people of all cultures. In fact, there is very little research that speaks directly to this issue. Most scientists who are expert in the biological bases of behavior will attest to the fact that all people seem to have the same structural anatomy. Certainly, people are amazingly similar in their structural (anatomical) and functional (physiological) functions, regardless of culture, race, or ethnicity.

But evidence from a variety of sources points to differences as well. These are not necessarily differences in structural anatomy. All people have eyes, ears, nose, and mouth; all people have a stomach, intestines, and a heart; all people have a spinal column, brain, and neurons. Rather, evidence suggests that people may differ in the relative sizes of these anatomical structures as well as their functional, physiological relationships, thereby implying differences in psychological and behavioral functioning.

The field of medicine has long been aware of individual differences in biological function and process. Medication can have vastly different effects on two individuals, as can disease processes and health-promoting behaviors. What accounts for these differences? Surely some of them could be related to genetic or hereditary differences in precise biological composition. If so, these genetic differences may be related to selective evolutionary pressures that predisposed people to exhibit these biological characteristics. If such individual differences are not genetic in nature, they may have resulted from learning and environmental pressures early in life. In either scenario, learning and the environment play an important role in determining biological characteristics, highlighting the interaction between biology and lifestyle (see also Janicki & Krebs, 1998; Papousek & Papousek, 1997; Turner, 1993).

If the effects of learning and lifestyle exist on the group level, such effects may indeed be cultural. The field of anthropological medicine highlights these possible differences. For instance, we know that, at least in this country and culture, calcium plays an important role in the development of strong bones, and lack of calcium fosters the development of a potentially debilitating disease process known as osteoporosis. Osteoporosis, which can be detected by low levels of bone density measured in various areas of the body, increases the risk of fractures, especially among elderly women, which in turn can lead to major disruptions in lifestyle and even death. There are cultures in other parts of the world, however, where such relationships are not entirely true. Japanese women, for example, tend to have lower bone mineral densities, but have lower fracture rates than what would be expected based on baselines in this country. Mayan women of the Yucatan Peninsula also have low bone mineral densities, but low fracture rates. Such anecdotal evidence suggests that the functional relationships between minerals (calcium), bone density, and disease risk (fracture rates) may be mediated by lifestyle issues such as diet, exercise, social support, and other factors, all of which are important components of culture (see also work examining cultural differences in menopause by Weber, 1997).

Closer to home, psychologists are becoming increasingly aware of the reciprocal relationship between biology and psychology. Early work on the biological bases of behavior was colored by the bias of searching for how biology "caused" psychology—that is, the assumption that our biological composition "caused" predispositions for certain behaviors. Important new research, in such fields as the biobehavioral factors related to violent behaviors and aggression (APS Observer, 1997; Suomi, 2000), now shows that not only does physiology affect behavior, but experience alters physiology, even the very structure and function of the brain. This new research suggests that early learning experiences and environmental factors may modify the effects of predisposing physiological factors and may actually change neurophysiological functioning. These environmental factors may include diet, trauma, and even types of parenting (see also Repetti, Taylor, & Seeman, 2002, and Zahn-Waxler, Friedman, Cole, Mizuta, & Hiruma, 1996). If these effects are represented on the group level, as in most cultures, this opens the door to the possibility that cultural lifestyle practices influence biological composition, thereby affecting the biological bases of behavior.

A sample of male children studied for more than 20 years in England offers more evidence of the interaction between biology and psychology. Caspi and his colleagues (2002) were interested in the role of genotype in the cycle of violence in maltreated children. These researchers found that boys who were born with a genotype that did not express much of the enzyme monoamine oxidase A (MAOA) were significantly more likely to become antisocial and violent adults *if* they had experienced maltreatment when they were younger. Boys who had low levels of MAOA expression but did not experience maltreatment were much less likely to become violent adults. These findings underscore the interactive role that genes and environment play in the behaviors of individuals.

Theorists such as Sandra Scarr (1993; Scarr & McCartney, 1983) argue that both genetics and environment interact in several ways to make essential contributions to human development. Scarr distinguishes three kinds of gene–environment interactions. **Passive genotype–environment interactions** occur in biological families when parents provide both genes and environment for their children. For example, as a child, did your parents encourage you to draw by buying you drawing pencils and materials? Because they encouraged you in this way, you may have gravitated toward taking art classes in school, and now are studying to become an architect. Thus, your skill in drawing is a result of the stimulating environment your parents created for you, as well as the genes your parents passed on to you.

The second type of gene–environment interaction is **evocative genotype–environment interaction**. This occurs when the characteristics you inherited elicit or evoke certain responses from your environment. For example, if a child has physical characteristics that are particularly suitable for hunting, the child may elicit certain types of responses from others in their environment—for instance, from adults who may give them more opportunities to participate in a hunting expedition at an early age, which may then develop the child's hunting skills even more.

The third type of interaction is **active genotype–environment interaction**. This occurs when you actively seek out environments that support your genotype characteristics. For example, you might have asked for books from your parents at a young age because you were a good reader, or you may have decided to join the track team after school because you were a good runner. In sum, there are many ways that genes and environment interact with one another, resulting in a complex reciprocal relationship between biology and behavior.

Other areas of research also suggest such possibilities, as in the differential incidence of certain physical disease processes in people of different cultures, races, and ethnicities (see also the discussion of this topic in Chapter 8, Culture and Health). Some research has also documented racial differences in head size (to be discussed later in this chapter, along with the potential pitfalls of the methods and interpretations involved in that research). Research in the field of sports has documented racial differences in such variables as physique and stature, muscle size and length, and the speed of neural transmission. Cumulatively, all of these sources suggest that even though all humans may be born with the same anatomical structures, there may be differences as well as similarities in the functional and physiological relationships among those anatomical structures. And these similarities and differences, if they exist, may be related to culture as defined so far in this book.

We also need to acknowledge the potential political difficulties in conducting research in this area and reporting the findings. Examining cultural differences in many areas of psychology can be a very touchy issue, especially with regard to such topics as morality, intelligence, and cooperative behaviors. The political ramifications of such research are compounded when the biological bases of these phenomena are studied. We believe such research is made more difficult because of (1) people's assumption that biology "causes" the psychology, (2) the improper reliance on race as a measure of culture, and (3) biases in the interpretation of the findings from such research for personal or political agendas. As a result, many good researchers stay away from potentially "hot" topics. It is our hope, however, that such research will be conducted by competent scientists sensitive to these issues who can elucidate the nature of similarities and differences in biological bases of behavior and the possible causes of such similarities and differences that may be rooted in culture, as defined through functional issues such as lifestyle, diet, and exercise. At the same time, the general public needs to be educated about these issues and their potential pitfalls, so that the attitudes surrounding the receipt of such information can be constructive for knowledge, not destructive for people.

Culture and Perception

Perception and Experience

Perception is the process of gathering information about the world through our senses. Before considering how culture affects our perceptions, we must first realize that regardless of culture, our perceptions of the world do not necessarily match the physical realities of the world, or of our senses. Consider visual perception. All of us have a **blind spot** in each eye—a spot with no sensory receptors, where the optic nerve goes through the layer of receptor cells on its way back toward the brain. But if you close one eye, you probably won't experience a hole in the world. There is no blind spot in our conscious perception, even though we have no receptors receiving light from one area of the eye. Our brains fill it in so it looks as if we see everything. It is only when something comes at us out of this spot that we get some idea that something is wrong with our vision in this particular location. Many of you may have performed a brief experiment in an introductory psychology course that illustrates the existence of the blind spot. The point here is that our perception of the world as "complete" does not match the physical reality of the sensation we receive through our visual system.

Everyday experiences with temperature and touch illustrate similar distortions in perception. Fill three bowls with water—one with hot water, one with ice water, and one with lukewarm water. If you put your hand in the hot water for a few seconds and then in the lukewarm water, the lukewarm water will feel cold. If you wait a few minutes, then put your hand in the ice water and then the lukewarm water, the lukewarm water will feel warm. The lukewarm water will not have changed its temperature; rather, it is our perception of the water that has changed (compare Segall, 1979).

Once we begin to question our own senses, we want to know their limits. We want to know what influence our experiences and beliefs about the world have on what we perceive. We also want to know if other people perceive things the same as we do. If others do not see things as we do, what aspects of their experiences and backgrounds might explain those differences?

One thing we know about our perceptions is that they change. One way they change was noted in our perception of the temperature of the lukewarm water. Our perceptions also change when we know more about a particular thing. We all have experienced seeing something complex, such as a piece of machinery, for the first time. Can you remember the first few times you looked under the hood of a car? To those who don't now much about mechanics, the engine seems like one immense jumble. But for those who learn about the engine, it becomes familiar and differentiated into specific parts: a carburetor, an engine block, an alternator, and so forth. So, clearly, the way we "see" things changes with our experiences with them.

How might someone with a very different background "see" something that is very familiar to us? How might we "see" something that is very familiar to someone else and less so to us? An American teacher visiting in Australia related an interesting anecdote that highlights these cultural differences in perception. She was teaching at a school for Aborigine children in Australia and was trying to teach them to play a schoolyard game called "Who touched me?" In this game, everyone stands in a circle and the person who is "it" is blindfolded. Then another person from the circle quietly walks around the outside of the circle, touches the blindfolded person, and then returns to her or his place. The blindfold is removed, and the person who is "it" has to guess who touched him or her. The teacher found that the Aborigine children didn't really want to play, but they cooperated because she was the teacher. Later, in the classroom, she found the students to be uncooperative and reluctant to try anything she suggested. They refused to make any effort to learn the alphabet. She began to think they were being stupid or naughty. Later, to her surprise, she found out that the children thought she was the stupid one. Aborigine children can tell whose footprint is on the ground behind them with a casual glance. So the teacher had them playing a game that was completely silly to them; it was so easy as to make no sense at all as a game. When the children realized that the teacher couldn't tell people's footprints apart, they thought she was stupid and saw no point in paying attention to her. They just humored her so they wouldn't get into trouble, but they didn't take her or her ideas about what they should learn seriously.

Cultural Influences on Visual Perception

Most of what we know about cultural influences on perception comes from cross-cultural research on visual perception. Much of this excellent work has been based on testing differences in optical illusions by Segall, Campbell, and Hersokovits (1963, 1966). **Optical illusions** are perceptions that involve an apparent discrepancy between how an object looks and what it actually is. Optical illusions are often based on inappropriate assumptions about the stimulus characteristics of the object being perceived. One of the best-known optical illusions is the Mueller–Lyer illusion (see Figure 4.1). Research has shown that subjects viewing these two figures typically judge the line with the arrowheads pointing in as longer than the other line—even though the lines are actually the same length. Another well-known illusion is the horizontal–vertical illusion (see Figure 4.2). When subjects are asked to judge which line is longer, they typically respond that the vertical line is longer—when, again, they are the same length. A third well-known example is the Ponzo illusion (see Figure 4.3). When subjects view this image, they typically report that the horizontal line closer to the origin of the diagonals is longer than the one away from the origin. Of course, they are the same length.

Figure 4.1 The Mueller–Lyer illusion

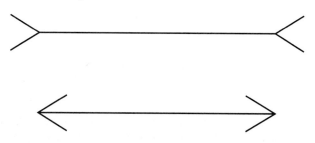

Which line is longer? To most people the top line appears longer than the bottom line. The lines are actually identical in length.

Figure 4.2 The horizontal–vertical illusion

Which line is longer? To most people the vertical line appears longer than the horizontal line, although both lines are the same length.

Figure 4.3 The Ponzo illusion

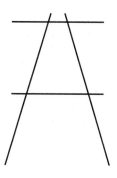

Which horizontal line is longer? To most people the upper line appears longer, although both are the same length.

Several important theories have been developed to explain why optical illusions occur. One of these is the **carpentered world theory,** which suggests that people (at least most Americans) are used to seeing things that are rectangular in shape and unconsciously come to expect things to have squared corners. If we see a house from an angle and the light reflected off it does not form a right angle on the eye, we still perceive it as a house with square corners. In the Mueller–Lyer illusion, we tend to see the figures as having square corners that project toward or away from us. We know that things that look the same size to our eyes but are at different distances are actually different in size.

The **front-horizontal foreshortening theory** suggests that we interpret vertical lines as horizontal lines extending into the distance. In the horizontal-vertical illusion, we interpret the vertical line as extending away from us, and we know that a line of set length that is farther away from us must be longer.

These two theories share some common characteristics. Both assume that the way we see the world is developed over time through our experiences. What we see is a combination of the way the object reflects light to our eyes and our learning about how to see things in general. Although learning helps us see well most of the time, it is the very thing that causes us to misjudge optical illusions. The second idea these theories share is that we live in a three-dimensional world that is projected onto our eyes in two dimensions. Our eyes are nearly flat, and light striking the eye in two places right next to each other may be coming from very different distances. Thus, we need to interpret distance and depth from cues other than where the light falls on the eye.

A number of cross-cultural studies challenge our traditional notions about optical illusions, as would be expected if experience contributes to our perceptions. As early as 1905, W. H. R. Rivers compared the responses to the Mueller–Lyer and horizontal–vertical illusions using groups in England, rural India, and New Guinea. He found that the English people saw the lines in the Mueller–Lyer illusion as being more different in length than did the two other groups. He also found that the Indians and New Guineans were more fooled by the horizontal–vertical illusion than were the English. These results surprised Rivers and many other people from Europe and the United States. They believed that the people of India and New Guinea were more primitive and would therefore be more readily fooled by the illusions than the more educated and "civilized" people of England. The results showed that the effect of the illusion differed by culture, but that something besides education was involved. The researchers concluded that culture must have some effect on the way the world is "seen." How this difference in perception comes about has been a source of curiosity ever since.

Both the carpentered world theory and the front-horizontal foreshortening theory can be used to explain Rivers's results. Whereas the English people in Rivers's study were used to seeing rectangular shapes, people in India and New Guinea were more accustomed to rounded and irregular environments. In the Mueller–Lyer illusion, therefore, English people would tend to see the figures as squared corners projecting toward or away from them, but Indians and New Guineans would have less tendency to make the same perceptual mistake. The front-horizontal foreshortening theory can also account for the cultural differences obtained in Rivers's study. With fewer buildings to block long-distance vistas in India or New Guinea, the Indians and New Guineans had learned to rely more on depth cues than did the English. As a result, they were more likely to see the horizontal–vertical figure as three-dimensional, and therefore to misjudge the line lengths.

A third theory has been offered to explain cultural differences in visual perception. The **symbolizing three dimensions in two** theory suggests that people in Western cultures focus more on representations on paper than do people in other cultures—and in particular, spend more time learning to interpret pictures. Thus, people in New Guinea and India are less likely to be fooled by the Mueller–Lyer illusion because it is more "foreign" to them. They are more fooled by the horizontal–vertical illusion, however, because it is more representative of their lifestyle (although in this example it is unclear whether the differentiation between the cultures is Western versus non-Western or industrialized versus nonindustrialized).

To ensure that Rivers's findings held for cultures in general, Segall and colleagues (1963, 1966) compared people from three industrialized groups to people from 14 nonindustrialized groups on the Mueller–Lyer and the horizontal–vertical illusions. They found that the effect of the Mueller–Lyer illusion was stronger for the industrialized groups, whereas the effect of the vertical–horizontal illusion was stronger for the nonindustrialized groups. Rivers's findings were supported.

Segall and colleagues (1963, 1966), however, also found some evidence that did not fit with any of the three theories—namely, that the effects of the illusions declined and nearly disappeared with older subjects. Based on the theories, we might expect the effects of the illusions to increase with age because older people have had more time to learn about their environments than younger people.

Wagner (1977) examined this problem using different versions of the Ponzo illusion and comparing the performance of people in both rural and urban environments, some of whom had continued their education and some of whom had not. One version of the Ponzo illusion looked like Figure 4.3; another showed the same configuration of lines embedded in a complete picture. Wagner found that with the simple line drawing, the effect of the illusion declined with age for all groups. With the illusion embedded in a picture, however, he found that the effect of the illusion increased with age, but only for urban people and people who continued their schooling. This study provides more direct evidence of the effects of urban environments and schooling on the Ponzo illusion.

There is also a physical theory that must be considered. Pollack and Silvar (1967) showed that the effects of the Mueller–Lyer illusion are related to the ability to detect contours, and this ability declines with age. They also noted that as people age and are more exposed to sunlight, less light enters the eye, and this may affect people's ability to perceive the lines in the illusion. In addition, they showed that retinal pigmentation is related to contour-detecting ability. Non-European people have more retinal pigmentation, and so are less able to detect contours. Thus, Pollack and Silvar (1967) suggested that the cultural differences could be explained by racial differences in retinal pigmentation (although how the researchers conceptually defined and actually measured race in their study may be problematic, given the ambiguity of that concept).

To test whether the racial or the environmental learning theory was more correct, Stewart (1973) noted that both race and environment need to be compared without being mixed together, as was done in the study by Segall and his colleagues. Stewart first tested the effects of the Mueller–Lyer illusion on both black and white children living in one American town (Evanston, Illinois). She found no differences between the two racial groups. She then compared groups of elementary school children in Zambia in environments that ranged from very urban and carpentered to very rural and uncarpentered. She found that the effects of the illusion depended on the degree to which the children lived in a carpentered environment. She also found that the effect declined with age, suggesting that both learning and physiology played roles in the observed cultural differences.

Hudson (1960) also conducted an interesting study that highlighted cultural differences in perception. He had an artist draw pictures, similar to those in the Thematic Apperception Test (TAT), that psychologists thought would evoke deep emotions in Bantu tribe members. They were surprised to find that the Bantu often saw the pictures in a very different way than anticipated; in particular, they often did not use relative size as a cue to depth. In Figure 4.4, for example, most Americans would see the hunter preparing to throw his spear at the gazelle in the foreground, while an elephant stands on a hill in the background. Many of the Bantu, however, thought the hunter in a similar picture was preparing to stab the baby elephant. In another picture, an orator, who

Figure 4.4 Hudson's (1960) picture of depth perception

What is the hunter's target? Americans and Europeans would say it is the gazelle in the foreground. The Bantu in Hudson's (1960) research, however, said it was the elephant.

we would see as waving his arms dramatically with a factory in the background, was seen as warming his hands over the tiny chimneys of the factory. Hudson (1960) found that these differences in depth perception were related to both education and exposure to European cultures. Bantu people who had been educated in European schools, or who had more experience with European culture, saw things as Europeans did. Bantu people who had no education and little exposure to Western culture saw the pictures differently.

Later work by McGurk and Jahoda (1975) found that children of different cultures, ranging in age from 4 to 10 years old, also saw things differently. For example, they found that Scottish children were more accurate than Ghanaian children in depicting spatial relationships in pictures where a woman and child stood in different positions relative to one another.

One might suppose that the cultural differences found in fundamental psychological processes of perception would have considerable implications for conflicts that may arise in intercultural interactions. If people from different cultures have learned different ways of perceiving and interpreting the world, what happens when they interact across cultures? Those learned patterns that each culture takes for granted may no longer be valid.

At the same time, however, one has to question the generalizability of these findings beyond the sorts of the tasks used in the studies. For example, in most research on visual perception and optical illusions, the stimuli are presented in two dimensions—either on a piece of paper or projected on a screen. Cultural differences in depth perception may certainly exist using these types of stimuli (as shown in the studies described here, as well as in drawing and other artwork). But to what extent do such effects actually exist in the three-dimensional world? Would Bantu tribespeople see the hunter ready to stab the elephant, and not the gazelle, if the same scene were portrayed out in the open space of their actual environment?

Motivation may be a factor as well. That is, people of different cultures may be differently motivated to perceive certain types of objects, or to perceive them in certain ways. In one study that demonstrated this effect (Broota & Ganguli, 1975), Hindu, Muslim, and American children in India perceived faces associated with either a reward or a punishment in a pretraining session. In the testing session, the participants viewed these and other faces, and judged their characteristics. Significant differences were found between the groups: The Hindu and Muslim children perceived more of the faces associated with punishment than reward, whereas the American children perceived more faces associated with reward rather than punishment.

Future research will need to address the question of the generalizability of previous findings to real-life scenarios, especially controlling for the motivational aspects of such perceptual processes. The literature to date is unclear on these practical issues (despite being quite convincingly clear on the cultural effects in the typical optical illusion paradigm), because there is little if any research that compares perceptual processes in real-life situations and on two-dimensional optical illusions across cultures. One way to address this issue would be to test for differences in perception using both types of stimuli, and to see whether the results using one type of test replicate the results using the other; such a study would also have to control for motivational level and prior experience with such stimuli. Hopefully, future research can address such issues, not only cross-culturally but within cultures as well.

Culture and Cognition

Just as culture influences the way we receive information about the world around us, culture also influences the way we process that information. Psychologists use the term **cognition** to denote all the mental processes we use to transform sensory input into knowledge. These processes include perception, rational thinking and reasoning, language, memory, problem solving, decision making, and the like. In this section, we will review cross-cultural research in six areas of cognition: categorization and concept formation, memory, face recognition, problem solving, decision making, and creativity.

Culture, Categorization, and Concept Formation

One basic mental process is the manner in which people group things together into categories. People **categorize** on the basis of similarities and attach labels (words) to groups of objects perceived to have something in common. In so doing, people create categories of objects that share certain characteristics. People often decide whether something belongs in a certain group by comparing it to the most common or representative member of that category. For instance, a beanbag chair, a straight-backed dining room chair, and a seat in a theater differ in appearance from one another, but all belong to the basic category *chair*. All these things can be grouped together under the label *chair*, because all share a common function. When we say "That thing is a chair," we mean that the item can and should be used as something for people to sit on (Rosch, 1978).

Some categories appear to be universal across cultures. Facial expressions that signal basic emotions—happiness, sadness, anger, fear, surprise, and disgust—are placed in the same categories across cultures (see Chapter 9). Likewise, there is widespread agreement across cultures about which colors are primary and which are secondary. The way people select and remember colors appears to be largely independent of both culture and language. Regardless of whether people speak a language that has dozens of words for colors or one that distinguishes colors only in terms of whether they are bright or dark, individuals universally group colors around the same primary hues. They also remember primary colors with greater ease when asked to compare and recall colors in an experimental setting. For example, an individual from a culture that has only one word for red/yellow/white will select the same kind of red as the best example of this category as graduate students at Harvard will. Also, both groups of people will remember this particular shade of red more easily than they will a shade like lilac or orange pink, despite having a very different set of names for colors (see Chapter 10 for a fuller discussion of color perception and the categorization of colors).

Culture and the process of categorization share an important and interesting relationship in other ways as well. In Chapter 3, for example, we discussed the process of stereotyping, which many people contend is a special form of categorization involving people. Culture plays a role in the process of stereotyping through the use of cultural filters, which color people's interpretations of the world around them. Culture also plays a role in the maintenance and reinforcement of stereotypes. As you will see in Chapter 6, some people believe that culture itself is represented in categories during the development of culture from childhood.

People across cultures tend to categorize shapes in terms of the best examples of basic forms (perfect circles, equilateral triangles, and squares) rather than forming categories for irregular geometrical shapes. These cross-cultural parallels suggest that physiological factors influence the way humans categorize certain basic stimuli. That is, humans seem to be predisposed to prefer certain shapes, colors, and facial expressions.

Research has also shown how cultures differ in categorization. For example, even though a particular category (for example, facial expressions or chairs) may be universal to all cultures, its exact prototype may differ across cultures. Because all people of the world have the same facial morphology (Oster & Ekman, 1979), facial prototypes of emotional expressions will not necessarily differ. However, because the materials used to construct furniture differ across cultures, the prototype of a chair is more likely to differ.

One common way to study cultural differences in categorization involves the use of sorting tasks. When presented with pictures that could be grouped in terms of either function, shape, or color, young children in Western cultures tend to group by color. As they grow older, they group by shape, and then by function (see Bruner, Oliver, & Greenfield, 1966). Western adults thus tend to put all the tools in one group and all the animals in another, rather than grouping all the red things or all the round things together. It had been assumed that this trend was a function of basic human maturation. But given similar sorting tasks, adult Africans showed a strong tendency to group objects by color rather than function (Greenfield, Reich, & Oliver, 1966; Suchman, 1966), suggesting that something besides simple maturation must be responsible for the category shifts.

These differences may be due to culture or education. Evans and Segall (1969) attempted to separate the effects of maturation from those of schooling by comparing children and adults in Uganda. Some of the subjects had received formal schooling; others had not. The researchers gave sorting tasks to all their subjects and found a preference for color grouping most common among people with little or no formal schooling. However, it is still not clear whether cultural differences in sorting tasks and categorization are best attributed to differences in cultural heritage or to differences in formal schooling. Future research on this topic is needed to sort out these influences and determine how culture and educational system jointly influence this cognitive process. Such research will also need to deal conceptually and empirically with the question of how culture, itself represented in categories, relates to the process, function, and development of other mental categories.

Culture and Memory

Another basic intellectual task we all share is remembering things. We have all agonized over the task of memorizing for tests and experienced the difficulty of memorizing lists of dates or names or scientific terms. Whenever we can, we use memory aids, such as shopping lists and calendars, to help us remember things we are likely to forget.

Many of us have heard the claim that individuals from nonliterate societies develop better memory skills because they don't have the ability to write things down to remember them (Bartlett, 1932). Is it true that our memories are not as good when we habitually use lists as aids in remembering? Ross and Millson (1970) suspected that reliance on an oral tradition might make people better at remembering. They compared the ability of American and Ghanaian college students to remember stories that were read aloud. They found that, generally, the Ghanaian students were better than the Americans at remembering the stories. Thus, it seemed that cultures with an oral tradition were better at remembering things. But Cole and his colleagues (Cole, Gay, Glick, & Sharp, 1971) found that nonliterate African subjects did not perform better when they were tested with lists of words instead of with stories. These findings suggest that cultural differences in memory as a function of oral tradition may be limited to meaningful material.

One of the best-known aspects of memory, established by research in the United States, is the **serial position effect**. This effect suggests that we remember things better if they are either the first (primacy effect) or last (recency effect) item in a list of things to remember. Interestingly, Cole and Scribner (1974) found no relation between serial position and the likelihood of being remembered in studying the memory of Kpelle tribespeople in Liberia.

Wagner (1980) hypothesized that the primacy effect depends on rehearsal—the silent repetition of things you are trying to remember—and that this memory strategy is related to schooling. Wagner compared groups of Moroccan children who had and had not gone to school and found that the primacy effect was much stronger in the children who had been to school. Wagner suggested that the process of memory has two parts: a "hardware" part, the basic limitation of memory, which does not change across cultures; and a "software" or programming part that has to do with how we go about trying to remember, which is learned. It is the software part that varies across cultures.

The ability to remember unconnected information appears to be influenced not so much by culture but by whether people have attended school. In a classroom setting, children are expected to memorize letters, multiplication tables, and other basic facts. Subjects who have been to school, therefore, have had more practice in memorizing than unschooled individuals. They are also able to apply these skills in test situations that resemble their school experience. A study by Scribner (1974) with educated and uneducated Africans supported this idea. Educated Africans were able to recall lists of words to a degree similar to that of American subjects, whereas uneducated Africans remembered fewer words. It is not clear whether culture or schooling or both contribute to the observed differences.

Memory has interesting implications for a wide range of psychological phenomena, including the production of stereotypes. In one study (Bigler & Liben, 1993), for example, European American children were asked to recall stories about European or African Americans that were either consistent or inconsistent with racial stereotypes. Negative traits were associated with either the European or African American child in the stories. The results indicated that children with better memory for counterstereotypic stories had lower degrees of racial stereotyping and greater ability to classify people along multiple dimensions. Memory, therefore, may affect stereotypes and the ways by which we understand people.

Despite cultural differences in memory ability (that may be mediated by exposure to formal educational systems), there may be some constants about memory across cultures as well, particularly in the relationship between memory and aging. Studies have shown that memory abilities tend to decrease as people get older (or at least people become more selective about what they remember!). One study showed that such memory decreases with age were consistent across cultures. In this study (Crook, Youngjohn, Larrabee, & Salama, 1992), Belgian and American participants, ranging in age from 14 to 88 years, were matched on gender and age and asked to perform computer-simulated everyday memory tasks. They found that age-related memory decline was consistent in the two groups.

The relationship between memory and oral traditions, and the possible influence of culture versus formal educational experiences on those traditions, raises some interesting questions for our understanding of the effects of culture on memory. Oral traditions are not necessarily limited to cultures with no formal educational systems; they are evident in epics, ballads, and rhymes in many cultures, including our own. Oral traditions can thus tell us something about the workings of memory in any culture (Rubin, 1995). To add to the complexity of these issues, some studies in the anthropology of language have indicated that linguistic structures in written language depend on the practice of orality in the development of writing (for example, Patel, 1996). Future research in this area, therefore, needs to control not only for the effects of education, but also for the cultural meanings of orality, written language, and the specific content of the thing being remembered. At this point, we know that culture influences memory, but we don't know what about culture influences what about memory for what kinds of events, and why.

Culture and Face Recognition

One area of research related to the issue of culture and memory that has received considerable attention in the past two decades is face recognition. Early research in this field showed the existence of a same-race bias in the ability to recognize faces. Malpass and Kravitz (1969), for example, showed photographs of either African American or European American individuals to observers in either a predominantly African American or European American university. The results indicated that observers recognized individuals of their own race better than they did people of the other race. These results have been replicated a number of times (for example, Malpass, 1974), using different methodologies (Wright, Bioyd, & Tredoux, 2001), and supported in meta-analyses examining findings across multiple samples and studies (for example, Bothwell, Brigham, & Malpass, 1989; Meissner & Brigham, 2001). Recent research has documented this effect for Asian faces as well, comparing European and Asian American judgments of European and Asian faces (O'Toole, Deffenbacher, Valentin, & Abdi, 1994). Other studies have also demonstrated a same-race bias in discriminating between male and female faces (O'Toole, Peterson, & Deffenbacher, 1996).

Over the years, a number of people have suggested some reasons as to why this bias in face recognition may occur. Brigham and Malpass (1985) and Meissner and Brigham (2001), for example, suggest that attitude toward people of same and other races, social orientation, task difficulty, and experience all contribute to this differential recognition ability. Meissner and Brigham's meta-analysis also suggests that the explanation provided by intergroup contact theories—that differential recognition stems from limited experience with members of other groups—has received only weak support in the research literature. Devine and Malpass (1985) showed that orienting strategies can affect differential face recognition. When observers in their study were told that they were participating in a reaction time experiment and would later be asked to make differential judgments about the people they observed, no difference in recognition rates occurred. A study by Levy, Lysne, and Underwood (1995) also established conditions in which same-sex, same-age, and same-race information was not associated with better memory recall. These researchers suggested that different self-schemas held by the observers accounted for the differences. Finally, some research suggests that same-race and other-race faces may actually be perceived and classified differently, with race features being coded differentially in same-race and other-race perceptions (Levin, 1996).

Regardless of the reason for this effect, these findings have important real-life implications, especially in the area of eyewitness testimony (for example, see Brigham & Malpass, 1985; Malpass, 1981; Wright et al., 2001; Meissner & Brigham, 2001). They suggest, for example, that cross-race face recognition of alleged criminals may be subject to a higher probability of error. These findings also have important implications for intergroup relations and stereotyping. For these reasons, future research should continue to examine the limitations of these findings, broadening its search for the parameters under which they do or do not hold. Future studies also need to examine more closely exactly what it is about culture—experience, motivation, meaningfulness, and the like—rather than race per se that influences the face recognition process, and why.

Culture and Problem Solving

Problem solving refers to the process by which we attempt to discover ways of achieving goals that do not seem readily attainable. Psychologists have tried to isolate the process of problem solving by asking people from different cultures to solve unfamiliar problems in artificial settings. One such experiment (Cole et al., 1971) presented American and Liberian subjects with an apparatus containing various buttons, panels, and slots. After basic instruction in how to work the apparatus, subjects were to figure out how to open the device and obtain a prize. The solution involved combining two different procedures—first pressing the correct button to release a marble, and then inserting the marble into the appropriate slot to open a panel. American subjects under the age of 10 were generally unable to obtain the prize, but older American subjects combined the two steps with ease. However, Liberian subjects of all ages and educational backgrounds experienced great difficulty solving the problem; less than a third of the adults were successful.

One might conclude from this experiment that Americans are better at advanced problem solving than Liberians and that the Liberian culture produces adults who lack a capacity for logical reasoning. Despite its apparent objectivity, however, this experiment may have been biased in favor of the Americans. That is, the Americans may have benefited from the hidden advantage of living in a technological society. Americans are accustomed to mechanical devices; buttons, levers, dials, and slots on machines are common in our daily environment. In some non-Western cultures, people seldom operate machines, and the unfamiliarity of the apparatus may have influenced the outcome by intimidating or bewildering the Liberian subjects. (Remember the first time you ever worked on a computer?)

Cole and his colleagues repeated their experiment with materials familiar to people in Liberia, using a locked box and keys instead of the mechanical contraption. In the new version of the two-step problem, the Liberian subjects had to remember which key opened the lock on the box and which matchbox container housed the correct key. Under these conditions, the great majority of Liberians solved the problem easily.

The success of the Liberians in solving a two-step problem with a familiar set of materials brings us back to the question of whether the experiment tested their ability to think logically or tested their previous knowledge and experience with locks and keys. In an attempt to clarify this issue, the researchers designed a third experiment, combining elements from both the first and second tests. Liberian and American subjects were again presented with a locked box, but the key that opened the box had to be obtained from the apparatus used in the first experiment. To the surprise of the researchers, the third test produced results similar to the first experiment. While Americans solved the problem with ease, most Liberians were not able to retrieve the key to open the box.

Cole and his colleagues concluded that the Liberians' ability to reason logically to solve problems depended on context. When presented with problems using materials and concepts already familiar to them, Liberians drew logical conclusions effortlessly. When the test situation was alien to them, however, they had difficulty knowing where to begin. In some cases, the problem went beyond confusion; uneducated Liberians appeared visibly frightened by the tests involving the strange apparatus and were reluctant to manipulate it. Although adult Americans did very well in these experiments in comparison to the Liberians, how might average Americans react if placed in a similar experimental situation that required the Americans to use wholly unfamiliar concepts and technology—for example, tracking animals by means of footprints and smells?

Another type of problem that has been studied cross-culturally involves syllogisms (for example: All children like candy. Mary is a child. Does Mary like candy?). In wide-ranging studies of tribal and nomadic peoples in East and Central Asia, Luria (1976) documented sharp differences in the way people approached these problems. As with other cultural differences in cognition and thought, the ability to provide the correct answer to verbal problems was found to be closely associated with school attendance. Individuals from traditional societies who were illiterate were generally unable to provide answers to syllogisms containing unfamiliar information. Individuals from the same culture and even from the same village who had received a single year of schooling could respond correctly.

Various explanations have been proposed to account for the inability of uneducated people to complete word problems. Luria (1976) concluded that illiterate people actually think differently from those who are educated. According to this hypothesis, logical reasoning is essentially artificial; it is a skill that must be learned in a Westernized school setting. Some studies lend support to this interpretation. Tulviste (1978) asked schoolchildren in Estonia ages 8 to 15 to solve verbal problems and explain their answers. Although the children were able to solve most of the problems correctly, they explained their answers by citing the logical premises of the problem only in areas where they did not have firsthand knowledge. Elsewhere, their answers were justified with appeals to common sense or statements about their personal observations.

Scribner (1979) questioned whether illiterate subjects are truly incapable of thinking logically and looked more closely into the reasons uneducated people fail to give correct responses to verbal problems. When uneducated peasants were asked to explain illogical answers to syllogism problems, they consistently cited evidence that was known to them personally or stated that they didn't know anything about the subject, ignoring the premises given to them. For example, in response to the word problem "All children like candy; Mary is a child; does Mary like candy?" subjects might shrug their shoulders and comment, "How would I know whether Mary likes candy? I don't even know the child!" or "Maybe she doesn't like candy; I've known children who didn't." These individuals appear to be unable or unwilling to apply concepts of scientific thinking to verbal problems. But this is not because they lack the capacity to reason logically; rather, they do not understand the hypothetical nature of verbal problems or view them with the same degree of importance. People who have been to school have had the experience of answering questions posed by an authority figure who already knows the correct answers. Uneducated people, however, have difficulty understanding the notion that questions need not be requests for information.

In summary, therefore, cross-cultural research on problem solving has documented a number of ways in which people of different cultures solve problems differently. Although many studies have shown that some people of some cultures are at a disadvantage in solving problems, many of these findings may be accounted for by such variables as experience with, meaningfulness of, and relevance of the problem to the participants' lives. It seems that all cultures foster the skills necessary for their members to solve problems that are appropriate and relevant in their lives within their cultural milieus. On this level, therefore, the process and goals of problem solving would be cross-cultural in nature. People's specific processes and abilities, however, would naturally differ across cultures because of differences in relevance, meaning, and experience with problems in different cultural milieus. This area of research may benefit from a combined effort of ethnographic and qualitative study, as well as traditional psychological research based in quantitative methods, to examine both similarities and differences in these abilities.

Culture and Decision Making

We make many decisions in our everyday lives. Research in the United States on decision-making processes has shown that we generally use certain strategies when we make decisions. We seek information to confirm a solution, make judgments about the representativeness of the event to a prototype, make judgments based on what comes to mind first, compare the information we have to a standard, and judge positive and negative outcomes of an event (Kahneman & Tversky, 1973; Tversky & Kahneman, 1981). Many people exhibit a confirmation bias—a tendency to commit to one type of judgment without adequately considering or testing other hypotheses.

Cross-cultural research on decision making suggests that people of many different cultural groups may use the same types of strategies. What may differ across cultures, however, is the relative weighting or importance of these various processes, and their precise manifestations. Americans, for example, may favor considering many possibilities, testing each as a hypothesis, and then choosing the best solution based on the available information. Tighter (more homogeneous) cultures or cultures high in uncertainty avoidance (those with many rituals to avoid anxiety about uncertainty) may have a greater tendency to make judgments based on representativeness.

Besides favoring certain types of strategies over others, people of different cultures manifest their use in different ways. For example, people of individualistic cultures are more likely to seek further information about an event themselves, whereas people of collectivistic cultures have a much greater tendency to involve others in their decision-making processes, asking opinions and advice from friends, families, and loved ones. People of collectivistic cultures are also more apt to adopt the advice of others, especially those in authority positions within that culture (such as parents or husband).

Research on decision making illustrates some of these concepts. For example, Keltikangas-Jaervinen and Terav (1996) showed cultural differences in social decision-making strategies between Finnish and Estonian adolescents. They interpreted their findings as indicative of individualistic versus collectivistic differences, and concluded that personal responsibility (a typically individualistic trait) may not develop if collective identity is expected to be present before personal identity has a chance to form. Another study by Yi and Park (2003), involving more than 800 college students from five countries—Korea, Japan, China, the United States, and Canada—also found cultural differences in different types of decision making. They hypothesized that students from more traditionally collectivistic countries (the three Asian countries) would show less competitive and more cooperative decision-making styles compared to students from North America. Their results only partially supported their hypotheses. Compared to American and Canadian students, Korean students exhibited higher levels of cooperative decision making. However, Japanese students exhibited the lowest levels of cooperative decision making, and students from the three Asian countries actually exhibited more competitive decision-making characteristics than the North American participants. The researchers suggest that their findings may reflect social changes in Asian societies concerning individualistic and collectivistic tendencies. Cultural differences have also been documented in relation to such topics as applying to college (Valadez, 1998), sex (Flores, Eyre, & Millstein, 1998), career choice (Martin & Farris, 1994), nursing home placements (Fitzgerald, Mullavey-O'Byrne, & Clemson, 2001), and organizational management (Walters, 1994).

However, cross-cultural research has been slow to map out exactly how different cultural tendencies may be related to what kinds of decision-making strategies, and how these strategies may differ according to context (Weber & Hsee, 2000). Such a line of research would require examining multiple decision-making processes in the same individuals across multiple contexts, and comparing individuals from different cultural milieus. Future studies will need to tackle this large but important task.

Culture and Creativity

Another aspect of cognition that has received attention in the literature is creativity. Research on creativity in the United States suggests that it depends on divergent thinking, rather than the convergent thinking that is typically assessed in measures of intelligence. Creative individuals have been shown to have a high capacity for hard work, a willingness to take risks, and a high tolerance for ambiguity and disorder (Sternberg & Lubart, 1995, 1999).

These same characteristics appear to be true of creative individuals in other cultures as well. For example, Khaleefa, Erdos, and Ashria (1996) highlighted these characteristics in their study of creativity in a conformist culture

(Sudanese); Simonton (1996) documented them in his study of creative individuals in Japanese history; and Satoh (1996) described their implementation in kindergarten programs in Japan to foster the development of creativity in children in that culture. All of these examples are consistent with Sternberg and Lubart's (1995, 1999) studies of the processes that creative individuals go through, particularly in overcoming obstacles presented to them by conformist-centered organizations.

Some important differences have been noted, however, in the specific ways in which creativity can be fostered in different cultures. Shane, Venkataraman, and MacMillan (1995), for example, studied innovative strategies among a sample of 1,228 individuals from 30 countries who were employees of four different work organizations. The authors characterized the countries in terms of Hofstede's dimensions of individualism, power distance, and uncertainty avoidance (see Chapter 2 for a review). They found that countries high on uncertainty avoidance prefer creative individuals to work through organizational norms, rules, and procedures. Countries higher on power distance preferred creative individuals to gain support from those in authority before action is taken, or to build a broad base of support among members for new ideas. Collectivistic countries preferred creative people to seek cross-functional support for their efforts.

Thus, although creative individuals may share some common core characteristics across cultures, they need to adapt their abilities to the specific cultural milieu within which they function, particularly in the implementation and adoption of their creative ideas (Csikszentmihalyi, 1999). Creativity requires people to "get outside of their own box" or framework; another area of cultural difference would be the degree to which this ability is fostered. Future research in this area will need to examine more formally the cross-cultural generalizability of the characteristics of creative individuals and thought processes, as well as the ways in which such processes can be engaged in different cultural milieus and the obstacles that these milieus may present. Future studies, and their authors, will need to be creative to achieve these goals!

Culture and Cognition: A Summary

The research on cognition highlights some interesting and important cultural differences in the ways people think. That research has shown differences in categorization, memory, face recognition, problem solving, decision making, and creativity. At the same time, however, there are important similarities across people of different cultures in each of these areas. In general, the processes and goals underlying many of these cognitive abilities may be similar across cultures, but the specific ways in which they are manifested and acted upon appear to differ substantially. Research has generally been preoccupied with the discovery of differences and has been slow to examine the simultaneous similar and different aspects of these cognitive abilities. Future research is also likely to uncover both similarities and differences in the same individuals across time.

Cross-cultural studies have been conducted in other cognitive areas of psychology as well, such as future-thinking and fantasies (Oettingen, 1997) and cognitive styles (Tullett, 1997). Another important area of cognitive skills that has received considerable attention in the cross-cultural literature is language and language processing (see Chapter 10 and Altarriba, 1993, for reviews). This ever-growing literature has important practical ramifications for all of us, especially those of us in the educational system and those of you contemplating becoming educators. How do people of different cultures learn? What are the similarities and differences across people and across cultures in the development of cognitive skills and abilities? How do context, culture, and social institutions interact to affect these skills and abilities? These are just a few of the questions we face today because of an increasing awareness of culture (see also Jacob, 1997). Hopefully, cross-cultural research in this area will lead us to develop new ways of understanding these complex processes, and engaging with them.

Culture and Consciousness

A topic of long-standing interest in culture and psychology is the relationship between culture and consciousness. In contemporary psychology, we generally define consciousness as a state of sensations, thoughts, and feelings. The content of this state, of course, may change from moment to moment, as exemplified in the difference between our waking and sleeping states.

People interested in the relationship between culture and consciousness have come at this problem from a variety of angles. Some authors, for example, have examined the content of dreams across cultures, noting that dream content may have different interpretations and meanings in different cultural contexts (for example, Tedlock, 1987). Others have examined psychopathologies and abnormal behaviors across cultures, including behaviors that appear to be dissociative from reality that are pathological in one culture and not so in another (for example, see the work by Bletzer, 1991). Much work has been done on time perspectives and orientations, and considerable cultural variations have been found. Still another line of inquiry in this area involves the perception of pain (for example, Morinis, 1985).

Some contemporary authors have suggested that consciousness itself is a cultural construction (for example, Lutz, 1992). That is, our states of feeling, perceiving, and sensing the world around us are as much a social and cultural construction as anything else. This logic suggests that just as there are differences in cultures across societies, there are necessarily differences in our states of consciousness as well. Another extension of this notion is that individual consciousness must differ from one person to another because of the differences inherent in personal experiences and development. The same viewpoint would suggest that there are also similarities in consciousness across individuals, to the degree that there are similarities in experience and development. If such similarities of learning experiences exist on the level of culture, the same viewpoint would suggest the existence of cross-cultural similarities in consciousness as well.

This section examines some of the cross-cultural and anthropological literature on the relationship between culture and consciousness through the study of dreams, time, and pain perception.

Culture and Dreams

Cross-cultural research on dreams has found considerable cultural differences in the manifest content of dreams. Punamaeki and Joustie (1998), for example, examined how culture, violence, and personal factors affected dream content among Palestinian children living in a violent environment (Gaza), Palestinian children living in a peaceful area, and Finnish children living in a peaceful area. Participants recorded the dreams they recalled every morning for seven days, and researchers coded their manifest contents. The results indicated that the dreams of the Palestinian children from Gaza incorporated more external scenes of anxiety, whereas the Finnish children's dreams had more "inner" anxiety scenes. Cultural differences in manifest dream content were also reported by Levine (1991) in her study of Irish, Israeli, and Bedouin children, and by Kane (1994) in her study of Anglo-American, Mexican American, and African American women.

The results of Punamaeki and Joustie's (1998) study, however, indicated that culture is not the only factor that influences dream content. That is, children living in the dangerous areas of Gaza had intensive and vivid dreams including themes related to persecution and aggression. These themes, of course, are present in these children's everyday lives, and affected the dreams considerably as well.

Some interesting research has also highlighted important differences in the role of dreams in different cultures. Tedlock (1992), for example, reported that dream sharing and interpretation was a common practice among Mayan Indians in Central America, regardless of the role or position of the person in the culture, and was important in the teaching of cultural folk wisdom. Thus, dreams were an important part of the cultural system, involving an organized, conventional set of signs. Likewise, Desjarlais (1991) examined dream usage among the Yolmo Sherpa of Nepal. Here, too, dreams constituted a local system of knowledge that helped in the assessment and communication of personal and social distress and conflict, and hence were an important vehicle for social understanding.

More recently, dream researchers have applied increasingly sophisticated technologies such as neuroimaging and electrophysiology to understanding dreams and their relationship to our psychology. Researchers such as Hobson (1999) have argued that Freud's (1900/1961) notion of dreams as reflecting unconscious motives (latent content) is outdated, with no empirical support. Hobson states that dreams, rather, may reveal emotionally salient concerns in an individual's life. Put another way, "In dreams we are often thinking about what we are already thinking about" (Flanagan, 2000, p. 190). Flanagan's work suggests that the content of our dreams is a reflection of our everyday experiences. Thus, it may not be the content of dreaming that is meaningful, but the emotions that it brings up, such as anxiety, which is "the leading emotion in all dreams and all dreamers" (Hobson, 1999, p. 170).

Dream content, the emotions associated with one's dreams, and dream usage may differ in important and interesting ways in different cultures. Because American culture does not place much emphasis on the importance of dreams as a symbol of individual and social concerns, American scientists have given relatively little consideration to the study of dreams as a way of understanding culture. Future studies will hopefully address this gap in our knowledge, and perhaps in our ways of understanding consciousness.

Culture and Time

People of different cultures experience time differently, even though time should be technically and objectively the same for everyone. Differences in time orientation and perspective are often a source of confusion and irritation for visitors to a new culture. Many visitors from cultures where time is respected and punctuality is cherished have difficulty adjusting to U.S. public transportation systems, which may not always be on time as scheduled! Visitors from other cultures, however, where time is not so much of the essence and queuing is commonplace, seem less affected by such deviations from schedule, viewing them as trivial and to be expected.

Time orientation can also be a source of pride for the people of a culture. Witness, for example, the clockwork precision of many of the rail systems of Europe and Japan. When one of us visited Moscow in the early 1990s, he was impressed by the efficiency of the Moscow subway system. His host observed that, given the upheaval that was occurring in the culture and society of the time, "the Moscow Metro is the only thing with any order that we can rely on anymore." In the early days of Perestroika, such reliance must have been a welcome relief for many.

Hall (1973) was one of the first to suggest that cultures differ in their time perspective and orientation. He analyzed differences among people of different cultures in their use of time, and how these differences manifested themselves in actual behavioral practices within such contexts as business. As you can imagine, cultural differences in the use and view of time can be especially agonizing in intercultural negotiation situations (see Chapter 15).

Since that early work, a number of studies have documented cultural differences in time orientation and perspective. Manrai and Manrai (1995), for example, classified individuals from cultures of Western Europe as low-context and individuals from Asia, Japan, the Middle East, and South America as high-context. They found that perceptions of work time were higher in the high-context cultures, whereas perceptions of leisure time were higher in low-context cultures. Levine (1988) studied perceptions of pace of life in Brazil, the United States, Taiwan, Japan, Indonesia, Italy, and England, and found not only that these cultures differed in their perceptions of pace of life, but also that these perceptions were related to well-being. Meade (1971) studied time perspective differences between students in the United States and India through the stories they generated on a semi-projective task, and found that Americans preferred future time orientations in their stories while Indians preferred past orientations. Time orientations can also vary individually within cultures, with some people more focused on the past, others on the present, and still others on the future. Zimbardo and Boyd (1999) argue that these different orientations toward time have large influences on our behaviors. For instance, an orientation toward the future has been linked to lower rates of risky health behavior (Strathman, Gleicher, Boninger, & Edwards, 1994).

These types of cultural and individual differences in time orientation and perspective have important implications for real-life situations, such as in business (negotiation), working in groups in school or at work, or just in everyday life (riding the bus or train, getting help at a store). Even though we may take such matters for granted within the cultural milieu in which we live, these differences can be a source of confusion, irritation, and conflict for many who travel across cultural boundaries. Future research will need to explore more fully the nature of the relationship between culture and time, identifying what it is about culture that affects the perception of time. With such knowledge, we can better anticipate conflicts before they arise, and deal with them when they do occur.

Culture and the Perception of Pain

Cross-cultural psychologists and anthropologists alike have long been interested in the relationship between culture and pain, mainly because of anecdotal reports and observations of considerable differences in pain management and tolerance in different cultures. More than 30 years ago, scientists began to formally recognize the influence of culture and attitudinal factors on the response to pain (Wolff & Langley,1968). Today, we know that culture influences the experience and perception of pain in several ways, including (1) the cultural construction of pain sensation, (2) the semiotics of pain expression, and (3) the structure of pain's causes and cures (Pugh, 1991). There is also a growing literature documenting the important implications and ramifications of cultural differences in the perception and management of pain, such as in doctor–patient interactions (Streltzer, 1997).

Although most cross-cultural research on pain has involved older children and adults, researchers are now recognizing that cultural differences in pain experiences, such as pain response, may occur quite early in life. For example, in a comparison of Chinese and non-Chinese Canadian 2-month-old infants, Chinese babies showed greater (more intense) response to pain as measured by facial expression and crying (Rosmus, Halifax, Johnston, Yip, & Yang, 2000).

One hypothesis concerning cultural differences in pain experience has to do with the effect of language on perception and cognition. The Sapir–Whorf hypothesis (discussed in Chapter 10) suggests that the structure of language, which is highly dependent on culture, affects our perceptions and cognitions of the world around us—including our pain experiences. Because the structure, content, and process of language differ across cultures, so does the experience of pain (Fabrega, 1989).

Another related topic is that of cultural display rules (discussed in Chapter 9, Culture and Emotion). Just as people of different cultures may have different rules for the appropriate expression of emotion, they may have similar rules governing the expression, perception, and feeling of pain. And just as the strength of people's emotional expressions are correlated with the intensity of their emotional experiences, so the rules governing the expression of pain will ultimately affect people's subjective experiences of pain. For example, a recent study of Indian and American college students shows that Indians were less accepting of overt pain expression and also had a higher level of pain tolerance than Americans (Nayak, Shiflett, Eshun, & Levin, 2000). Furthermore, level of pain tolerance and acceptance of overt pain expression were linked: The less acceptable overt pain expression was, the greater was the tolerance of pain.

The tolerance of pain may also be rooted in cultural values. Sargent (1984), for example, interviewed females of reproductive age and 18 indigenous midwives in the Bariba culture of Benin, West Africa. In this culture, stoicism in the face of pain was idealized, and the "appropriate" response to pain was considered intrinsic to Bariban identity. Features such as the tolerance of pain through circumcision or clitoridectomy signaled courage and honor, and were considered crucial values within the culture. In a qualitative study of Finnish women and their experiences of childbirth, the participants described labor pain as something natural that they should accept. One mother said, "It is God's will for women to feel pain when giving birth" (as reported in Callister, Vehvilainen-Julkunen, & Lauri, 2001, p. 30). Thus, cultural values shape one's experience and tolerance of pain.

Although we know that there are considerable cross-cultural differences in the perception of pain, research has not yet examined systematically exactly what aspects of culture produce those differences, and why. For instance, concerning childbirth specifically, one aspect may be local attitudes toward childbirth—for instance, whether childbirth is a community celebration or requires purification of the woman giving birth (Newton & Newton, 1972). Future studies need to take up this important topic, which is of considerable practical importance to real-life events. Cultural differences in pain management affect how many professionals in the health services—physicians, nurses, dentists, psychotherapists, counselors, and others—interact with clients and patients. Even outside the clinical setting, these issues are becoming more real and important for a growing number of people who deal with intercultural issues in their daily lives at home and at work. Future research needs to address these issues and their potential consequences.

Culture and Intelligence

Traditional Definitions of Intelligence in Mainstream American Psychology

The English word *intelligence* is derived from the Latin word *intelligentia,* coined 2,000 years ago by the Roman orator Cicero. In the United States, we use the term *intelligence* to refer to a number of different abilities, skills, talents, and knowledge, generally mental or cognitive in nature. Thus, we traditionally consider a number of processes to represent intelligence, such as memory (how well and how much we can remember for how long), vocabulary (how many words we know and can use properly), comprehension (how well we can understand a passage or a set of ideas or statements), mathematical abilities (addition, subtraction, and so forth), and logical reasoning (how well we can understand the underlying logic or sequence among events, things, or objects).

A number of theories have dominated our understanding of intelligence in psychology. Piaget's theory (described in Chapter 6) views intelligence as a reflection of cognitive development through a series of stages, with the highest stage corresponding to abstract reasoning and principles. Spearman (1927) and Thurstone (1938) developed what are known as factor theories of intelligence. These theories view intelligence as a general concept comprised of many subcomponents, or factors, including verbal or spatial comprehension, word fluency, perceptual speed, and others. Guilford (1985) built on factor theories to describe intelligence using three dimensions—operation, content, and product—each of which has separate components. Through various combinations of these three dimensions, Guilford suggests that intelligence is actually composed of more than 150 separate factors.

Spearman (1927) also proposed, along with the multiple factors of intelligence, a "general" intelligence representing overall mental ability. This factor, called *g,* is typically measured through a process of combining and summarizing the various component scores of a multiple-factor intelligence test. Although *g* may be a theoretically useful construct, its measurement and meaning have come under considerable scrutiny in the past several decades.

In short, intelligence in contemporary American psychology has generally been considered a conglomeration of numerous intellectual abilities centering around verbal and analytic tasks. Aside from pure knowledge, the ability to reason logically and deductively about hypothetical and abstract issues and events is generally considered a part of intelligence. This definition of intelligence has dominated its measurement and, consequently, the research in this area.

Cross-Cultural Research on Intelligence

Modern intelligence tests were first developed in the early 1900s for the purpose of identifying mentally retarded children. Intelligence tests provided a way to distinguish children in need of special education from those whose schoolwork suffered for other reasons. In the years that followed, intelligence tests came into widespread use in public schools and other government programs.

But not everyone benefited from the new tests of intelligence. Because such tests relied at least in part on verbal performance and cultural knowledge, immigrants who spoke English poorly and came from different cultural backgrounds were at a disadvantage. For example, when tests of intelligence were administered to immigrants at Ellis Island beginning in 1913, more than three-quarters of the Italian, Hungarian, and Jewish immigrants tested as mentally defective. Such low scores for certain immigrant groups provoked a storm of controversy. Some people defended the scientific nature of the new tests, charging that southern European immigrants were not fit to enter the country. Others responded that intelligence tests were biased and did not accurately measure the mental ability of people from different cultures. Thus, less than a decade after the invention of intelligence tests, using them with people from different cultures became a matter of political controversy.

At the end of the twentieth century, this controversy again resurfaced. The debate surrounding the interpretation of test scores of groups who do not belong to the dominant culture continues today, although the groups of people scoring low on standard tests have changed. The average scores of some minority groups in the United States are 12 to 15 percentage points lower than the average for European Americans. This does not mean that all the individuals in these groups test poorly—high-scoring individuals can also be found in minority subcultures—it simply means that larger percentages of the minority populations score low. In a controversy that has come to be known as the "nature versus nurture" debate, people have differed sharply in their interpretations of these scores. This debate is very important in psychology in general, and in cross-cultural psychology in particular.

Is IQ biologically predetermined?   The nature side of the debate argues that differences in IQ scores between different societies and ethnic groups are mainly heredity or innate. Arthur Jensen (1969, 1980, 1981) is one of the best known proponents of this position. He conducted many different studies on this topic, mostly examining differences between African and European Americans (for example, Jensen, 1968, 1969, 1971, 1973, 1977, 1980, 1981, 1983, 1984), and found that African Americans typically scored lower on IQ tests than European Americans. Jensen takes the position that about 80% of a person's intelligence is inherited and suggests that the gap between the scores of European Americans and ethnic minorities in the United States is due to biological differences. Based on the results of his studies, Jensen has argued that special educational programs for the underprivileged are a waste of money, time, and effort because inborn intellectual deficiencies of ethnic minorities are mostly responsible for their poorer performance on IQ tests. To support his claim, Jensen has also provided a substantial database examining the effectiveness of educational and remedial programs to bolster the intellectual capacity and abilities of ethnic minorities. When extraneous factors are controlled, he concludes, those programs have had little or no effect on improving intelligence in ethnic minority groups.

Studies of twins have also provided some evidence for the nature hypothesis. The most important of these studies compared identical twins who grew up in separate homes to fraternal twins raised together (Bouchard & McGue, 1981). If test scores are determined by heredity, identical twins raised apart should have very similar scores. But if environment is primary, the scores of the fraternal twins raised together should be more similar. These twin studies revealed that the scores of identical twins raised in different environments were significantly more alike than those of fraternal twins raised together. However, the scores of identical twins raised apart varied more than those of identical twins raised together.

Jensen himself earlier reviewed a number of twin studies (Jensen, 1970) and concluded that the correlation between twins on IQ was .824, which he interpreted as constituting an upper limit on the heritability of IQ. Environmental factors, however, were normally distributed, and IQ was not correlated with those factors. Jensen concluded that environmental factors could not have been systematically related to the intelligence levels of twin pairs.

Results from the twin studies have been used by both proponents and opponents of Jensen's views. Proponents interpret the results to support the claim that much of intelligence is genetic; opponents offer considerably lower estimates of the genetic component. There is widespread agreement, however, that at least 40% of intelligence can be attributed to heredity (Henderson, 1982; Jencks et al., 1972; Plomin, 1990). At the same time, one must keep in mind that heritability is a *population* statistic; it says nothing about IQ on an individual level. So, a heritability statistic of .40 for intelligence indicates that 40% of the variance in a population of IQ scores can be attributed to genetics, and the other 60% must be explained in some other way. It does not mean that 40% of an individual's IQ is determined by genetics.

Another important point to keep in mind is that differences between groups cannot necessarily be attributed to the same sources that contribute to within-group differences (Lewontin, 1976). For example, if genetics plays a role in determining IQ within a population of white children and within a population of black children, it does not follow that the differences *between* the two groups are necessarily also due to genetics.

Much of Jensen's research of the past two decades has involved studies that followed up his original thesis, in an attempt to uncover the biological bases underlying the ethnic and racial differences in IQ. For example, in some of his earlier research in this area, he documented differences in reaction and inspection times of different ethnic and racial groups of participants on a variety of cognitive tasks (for example, Jensen & Munro, 1979; Jensen & Reed, 1990; Jensen & Whang, 1993; Krantzler & Jensen, 1989). In subsequent research, he has examined the brain correlates of such reaction time measures and IQ, demonstrating a link between brain activity and processes on the one hand and reaction time and IQ on the other (for example, Reed & Jensen, 1992, 1993).

Some of his latest research has also documented a relationship among brain size, reaction times, and IQ (for example, Jensen & Johnson, 1994; Reed & Jensen, 1993).

The considerable amount of research generated by Jensen, his colleagues, and others in this area provides a substantial base of data suggesting that at least a large portion of intellectual capacity, as measured by typical IQ tests, is associated with biological characteristics, many of which are genetically heritable. These biological characteristics appear to be related to brain size and function, which in turn appear to be related to racial or ethnic differences.

Is IQ culturally or environmentally determined?   As you can imagine, such findings have stirred up considerable controversy. The findings originally reported by Jensen have been countered numerous times in the literature by proponents of the nurture side of the debate, who argue that culture and environment fully account for the difference in IQ scores between European Americans and minorities in the United States. Those who hold this position claim that minorities score lower because most subcultures in this country are economically deprived (Blau, 1981; Wolf, 1965). Advocates of this position have turned to studies showing that IQ scores are strongly related to social class. The average IQ score of poor whites, for instance, is 10 to 20 percentage points lower than the average score of the middle class. The effect of environment over race can be seen most clearly in studies showing that poor whites tested in Southern states scored lower than blacks who lived in Northern states. It is also possible that between-group differences in intelligence scores are the result of (1) different beliefs about what intelligence is or (2) culturally inappropriate measures of intelligence. What we do know is that intelligence tests are a good predictor of the verbal skills necessary for success in a culture associated with the formalized educational systems of modern industrial societies and increasingly adopted as a model throughout the world. However, such tests may not measure motivation, creativity, talent, or social skills, all of which are important factors in achievement.

A number of other authors and findings support this side of the debate. One recent theory that offers an alternative interpretation of the differences in IQ scores between African American and European American individuals is Claude Steele's work on **stereotype threat**—"the threat that others' judgments or their own actions will negatively stereotype them in the domain" (Steele, 1998, p. 613). In other words, he posits that societal stereotypes about a group— for instance, concerning academic or intellectual performance—can actually influence the performance of individuals from that group. In an interesting set of experiments with black and white college students at Stanford University, Steele and Aronson (1995) report that when black students were asked to record their race on a demographic questionnaire before taking a standardized test, they performed significantly worse compared to black students who were not primed to think about their race before taking the test. Furthermore, they also found that when the exam was presented as a measure of intellectual ability, black students performed worse than white students. However, when the same test was presented as unrelated to intellectual ability, the black students performed equally as well as the white students. His theory offers a social-cognitive perspective to understanding ethnic differences in intelligence tests.

Scarr and Weinberg (1976) also offer evidence for an environmental basis of intelligence. They showed that black and interracial children adopted by white families scored above the IQ and school achievement means for whites. Such a finding argues against biological predetermination and in favor of cultural and environmental factors. Greenfield (1997) has argued that intelligence tests can be understood in terms of symbolic culture, and therefore have little translatability (reliability or validity) when used with people of different cultural backgrounds—whether ethnic minorities within one country, or across countries. Such arguments have been proffered for decades now, and have led to the development of a number of "culture-free" or "culture-fair" tests of intelligence, such as the Cattell Culture Fair Intelligence Test.

Collectively speaking, there appears to be an equally large and strong literature base suggesting that IQ is at least malleable to cultural and environmental factors, and that previous findings indicating racial or ethnic differences in IQ are equivocal because of problems of validity in the tests used to measure intelligence in different cultural groups.

Reconciling the two positions. The origins of intelligence is a very involved debate, and we have outlined only some of the issues. The topic of intelligence is one that is emotionally charged for many people, scientists and laypersons alike. It has important practical ramifications as well, including the development of appropriate and effective educational programs, and selection of individuals for employment or admission to organizations. These issues have been so emotionally and politically charged, in fact, that many people have suggested that doing research on intelligence is unethical. Such sentiments have undoubtedly persuaded many researchers and other psychologists to stay away from discussions of this topic, let alone conduct research on it.

We prefer to take a more empirical and objective stance on the theoretical and empirical questions these issues raise. There are, in fact, problems on both sides of the issue. On the nature side, the use of race or ethnicity as a classifying variable is problematic because of the ambiguity of these concepts, which may not actually refer to anything meaningful about biology or psychology. As discussed in Chapter 3, these concepts are basically a social construction—categories that we create in our minds to help us classify people in the world around us. In actuality, whether there are truly distinct races of people is still an unanswered question; if anything, the literature suggests that those distinctions really do not exist. Although observable differences in "traditionally" racial characteristics such as skin color, face morphology, and the like surely exist, evidence is not conclusive that they are correlated with distinctive biological differences among reliable racial categories.

Given the problems with the concept of race, therefore, we need to recast the findings provided by Jensen and his colleagues concerning the relationship between race or ethnicity and IQ. The findings may indeed exist (data do not generally lie), and they may indeed be related to biological characteristics that have been examined until now, such as brain function, activity, and size. But should these findings be interpreted as indicative of a terminal, unchangeable biological condition? It is a fact that biology itself is influenced by cultural and environmental factors, not only over the long term through evolution, but also in the short term as a result of recent social history and even individual experience within the lifetime. Future research is needed to explore how these environmental and cultural factors may indeed affect brain structure and functioning, and how these components, in turn, are related to intellectual processes.

Some arguments on the nurture side of the controversy also have problems. If intelligence really is a cultural construct, then it would be impossible to construct a test that is indeed "culture-fair" or "culture-free" because any such test would, by definition, have to include specific items that are generated within a specific cultural milieu. Even culture-free tests and items would have the underlying bias of culture—a "culture of no culture." In fact, some studies have shown that such tests do suffer from the very biases they were designed to address. Nenty (1986), for example, administering the Cattell Culture Fair Intelligence Test to Americans, Indians, and Nigerians in order to test the validity of the scale, found that 27 of the 46 items administered were culturally biased, thus rendering scores for the three cultures incomparable to one another.

Proponents of the nurture side of the controversy raise many interesting and important issues concerning other possible influences of cultural and racial differences on intelligence, including motivational levels of the participants, experience with similar tests, and difficulty of the items. Such potential confounds raise issues and questions that can only be addressed empirically through research, not through argument and rationalizations. In fact, many of these issues were raised and addressed in Herrnstein and Murray's (1994) book, *The Bell Curve.* Although this book stirred up its own share of controversy and debate, it did review a number of studies that examined the potential influence of many of the possible confounding effects that critics of the Jensen studies have suggested. Rhetoric aside, the evidence should be examined objectively in its own right.

For example, Herrnstein and Murray reviewed studies that examined whether the intelligence tests used in previous research had different external validities for different groups—that is, whether those tests predicted performance for African Americans in the real world (jobs, schooling) in the same way that they did for European Americans. Their review of hundreds of studies found no evidence of differential external validity, ruling out this potential cause of differences. They also reviewed studies that examined evidence of bias in internal validity by comparing the difficulty of specific items for different groups. They reported that black/white differences were actually found on culturally neutral items, not culturally biased items, thus ruling out this potential cause of the differences. They examined studies investigating differences in students' motivation to try to do well on the intelligence tests, and found that lack of motivation could not explain the differences in scores. They also examined whether blacks and whites differed in the amount of coaching they received on similar tests, the amount of experience and exposure to such tests, English language fluency, and the racial congruence of the test administrators. They found no effect for any of these variables on the black/white differences, and thus ruled these potential effects out as well. They examined the potential effect of SES, and found that this variable did account for some of the differences between blacks and whites, but not all; in fact, black/white differences in intelligence actually increased with higher SES. Comparisons were also made with studies involving black participants in Africa, the rationale being that these individuals would not have been subjected to the same social legacies as blacks in America. The results across studies, however, showed that the same differences occurred.

The contribution of this work, as we see it, is its attempt to address the issues raised by many previous authors empirically, rather than through argument or rhetoric. And we believe that evidence should be examined objectively for whatever it may be worth. Because these are such highly politically and emotionally charged issues, it is easy to get wrapped up in the arguments of the debate, and relatively more difficult to extract oneself from the argument to lay out the questions that are raised by the arguments. These questions, in turn, form the bases of hypotheses that should be answered by research, not rhetoric or sweeping interpretations and generalizations that become ends in themselves.

Herrnstein and Murray (1994) themselves sum up these sentiments in the conclusion of their literature review:

> We cannot think of a legitimate argument why any encounter between individual whites and blacks need be affected by the knowledge that an aggregate ethnic difference in measured intelligence is genetic instead of environmental. . . . In sum: If tomorrow you knew beyond a shadow of a doubt that all the cognitive differences between races were 100 percent genetic in origin, nothing of any significance should change. The knowledge would give you no reason to treat individuals differently than if ethnic differences were 100 percent environmental. By the same token, knowing that the differences are 100 percent environmental in origin would not suggest a single program or policy that is not being tried. It would justify no optimism about the time it will take to narrow the existing gaps. It would not even justify confidence that genetically based differences will not be upon us within a few generations. The impulse to think that environmental sources of differences are less threatening than genetic ones is natural but illusory. (pp. 313–315)

Gaining some perspective on the research.   Sometimes we get so wrapped up in the literature concerning black/white differences in intelligence that we ignore the considerable literature on differences among other cultural groups. Studies have measured intelligence and its correlates in a wide variety of cultural groups, and compared them with one another. These groups have included Asian Americans (Herrnstein & Murray, 1994), Iranian children (Shahim, 1992), Bulgarians (Lynn, Paspalanova, Stetinsky, & Tzenova, 1998),

Chinese and Germans (Willmann, Feldt, & Amelang, 1997), Filipinos (Church & Katigbak, 1988), Chinese and Australians (Keats & Fang, 1987), Indians and Nigerians (Nenty, 1986), New Zealanders (Petrie, Dibble, Long-Taylor, & Ruthe, 1986), Hindu Indians (Ajwani, 1982), Nigerian high school students (Nenty & Dinero, 1981), Mexican Americans (Hays & Smith, 1980), Peruvians (Weiss, 1980), Costa Ricans (Fletcher, Todd, & Satz, 1975), Fijians (Chandra, 1975), Israelis (Miron, 1975), Irish (Hart, 1971), Metis and Eskimo schoolchildren (Rattan & MacArthur, 1968), Native Alaskans (Hanna, House, & Salisbury, 1968), Congolese (Claeys, 1967), Aborigines in central Australia (David & Bochner, 1967), secondary school pupils in Tanzania (Klingelhofer, 1967), and Guatemalan children (Johnson, Johnson, & Price-Williams, 1967).

Although most of this research has been concerned with documenting differences, we personally don't believe in the utility of testing for differences per se. Although it may have been important at one time to document such differences, we believe the field has evolved to the point where cross-cultural research of the future must try to specify what it is about culture that produces differences in what kinds of measurements of intelligence, and why. What learning processes, environmental factors, and developmental constituents influence the development of intelligence in different cultures? Is the contribution of these factors different for different methods of measuring intelligence? What is the contribution of biological endowment and genetic heredity to these correlations? These are the types of difficult questions that face the field. On the one hand, the breadth and scope of the research in this area around the world helps us keep a more healthy perspective on ethnic differences in intelligence within the United States. On the other hand, it highlights the important questions that still need to be asked and answered by future research.

Cultural Differences in the Meaning and Concept of Intelligence

The concept of intelligence in other cultures. One of the positive outcomes from so much research on the relationship between culture and intelligence is an expanded view of what intelligence may be, and how it may be conceptually related to culture. This issue is intricately intertwined with cross-cultural research on intelligence because one of the possible confounding factors in previous studies that documented cultural differences has been cultural differences in the very concept and meaning of intelligence.

Researchers in this area have discovered that many languages have no word that corresponds to our idea of intelligence. The closest Mandarin equivalent, for instance, is a Chinese character that means "good brain and talented." Chinese people often associate this concept with traits such as imitation, effort, and social responsibility (Keats, 1982). Such traits do not constitute important elements of the concept of intelligence for most Americans.

African cultures provide a number of examples. The Baganda of East Africa use the word *obugezi* to refer to a combination of mental and social skills that make a person steady, cautious, and friendly (Wober, 1974). The Djerma-Songhai in West Africa use the term *akkal,* which has an even broader meaning—a combination of intelligence, know-how, and social skills (Bissilat, Laya, Pierre, & Pidoux, 1967). Still another society, the Baoule, uses the term *n'glouele,* which describes children who are not only mentally alert but also willing to volunteer their services without being asked (Dasen et al., 1985).

Because of the enormous differences in the ways cultures define intelligence, it is difficult to make valid comparisons from one society to another. That is, different cultures value different traits (their definition of "intelligence") and have divergent views concerning which traits are useful in predicting future important behaviors (also culturally defined). People in different cultures not only disagree about what constitutes intelligence but also about the proper way to demonstrate those abilities. In mainstream North American society, individuals are typically rewarded for displaying knowledge and skills. This same behavior may be considered improper, arrogant, or rude in societies that stress personal relationships, cooperation, and modesty.

These differences are important to cross-cultural studies of intelligence because successful performance on a task of intelligence may require behavior that is considered immodest and arrogant in Culture A (and therefore only reluctantly displayed by members of Culture A) but desirable in Culture B (and therefore readily displayed by members of Culture B). Clearly, such different attitudes toward the same behavior could lead researchers to draw inaccurate conclusions about differences in intelligence between Culture A and Culture B.

Another reason it is difficult to compare intelligence cross-culturally is that tests of intelligence often rely on knowledge that is specific to a particular culture; investigators based in that culture may not even know what to test for in a different culture. For example, one U.S. intelligence test contains the following question: "How does a violin resemble a piano?" Clearly, this question assumes prior knowledge about violins and pianos—quite a reasonable expectation for middle-class Americans, but not for people from cultures that use different musical instruments.

Recent developments in theories about intelligence.

Our expanding knowledge about cultural differences in the concept of intelligence has had important ramifications for our theoretical understanding of intelligence in mainstream American psychology as well. Although traditional thinking and reasoning abilities have dominated views of intelligence in the past, in recent years psychologists have begun to turn their attention to other possible aspects of intelligence. Until very recently, for example, creativity was not considered a part of intelligence; now, however, psychologists are increasingly considering this important human ability as a type of intelligence. Other aspects of intelligence are also coming to the forefront. Gardner (1983) has suggested that there are really seven different types of intelligence: logical mathematical, linguistic, musical, spatial, bodily kinesthetic, interpersonal, and intrapersonal. According to this scheme, not only do the core components of each of these seven types of intelligence differ, but so do some sample end-states (such as mathematician versus dancer). His theory of multiple intelligences has broadened our understanding of intelligence to include other areas besides "book smarts."

Sternberg (1986) has proposed a theory of intelligence based on three separate "subtheories": contextual, experiential, and componential intelligence. Contextual intelligence refers to an individual's ability to adapt to the environment, solving problems in specific situations. Experiential intelligence refers to the ability to formulate new ideas and combine unrelated facts. Componential intelligence refers to the ability to think abstractly, process information, and determine what needs to be done. Sternberg's theory focuses more on the processes that underlie thought than on specific thought outcomes. Because this definition of intelligence focuses on process rather than outcome, it has the potential for application across cultures.

Perhaps the field is coming to realize that intelligence in its broadest sense may be more aptly defined as "the skills and abilities necessary to effectively accomplish cultural goals." If your culture's goals, for example, involve successfully pursuing a professional occupation with a good salary in order to support yourself and your family, that culture will foster a view of intelligence that incorporates cognitive and emotional skills and abilities that allow for pursuing such an occupation. Those skills and abilities may include deductive reasoning, logical thought, verbal and mathematical skills—the sorts of skills that are fostered in contemporary American culture. If your culture's goals, however, focus more on the development and maintenance of successful interpersonal relationships, working with nature, or hunting and gathering, intelligence will more aptly be viewed as the skills and abilities related to such activities. On one level, therefore, people of all cultures share a similar view of intelligence—a catchall concept that summarizes the skills and abilities necessary to live effectively in one's culture. At the same time, however, cultural differences naturally exist because of differences in how cultures define goals and the skills and abilities needed to achieve those goals. Future research will need to delve into these dual processes, searching for commonalities as well as differences across cultures and exploring what contextual variables affect intelligence-related behaviors, and why.

Culture, Intelligence, and Selection Issues

In the meantime, however, we are left with current ways of understanding and measuring intelligence, and the issues they raise when such tests are used for selection decisions for employment or admission to schools. Before leaving this section on intelligence, we would like to discuss briefly the important ramifications that potential cultural, racial, and ethnic differences have on such selection issues. When intelligence tests are used to predict performance (for example, in a job or at school), the validity of the criterion used to judge the outcome of the test becomes a practical issue. A test may be perceived as culturally "biased," yet still be the best predictor of performance at a certain task. Altering the test to reduce the cultural bias may actually weaken the ability of the test to predict performance. If people are admitted based on faulty data, their overall performance may not be as high as it could have been with the use of the better predictor, even though it is the more culturally biased test. If you were in an organization (or business) that needed to base selection on test scores, what would you do? This difficult issue has faced not only many business organizations, but many schools and universities around the country.

One response by some agencies to gender, race, and ethnic group differences in mean scores on tests for employment has been to convert applicants' scores to percentile scores adjusted for their racial, ethnic, or gender group. This procedure, known as within-group norming, was widely used by government, educational, and private organizations through the 1980s. The underlying rationale was that such norming would equalize differences among groups that may have resulted from prior social inequalities, cultural bias in the tests, or other such factors (Sackett & Wilk, 1994).

These procedures, however, have not been without their own set of philosophical and legal controversies. On one hand, the use of existing tests of intelligence and personnel selection leads to disparate impact, or racial imbalance, as long as racial or ethnic differences in test ability exist. Such disparate impact is generally considered evidence of unlawful discrimination (Gottfredson, 1994). On the other hand, employers can only avoid disparate impact if they engage in unlawful disparate treatment through racial preferences. As public attention was drawn to these difficult issues, it led to the Civil Rights Act of 1991, which prohibited within-group norming. The latest approach to this problem has been through a process known as banding—the grouping of individuals' test scores within ranges of scores. For example, all scores between 90 and 100 would be in Band 1, 80 and 89 in Band 2, 70 and 79 in Band 3, and so on. People whose scores fall in Band 1 would be selected before those in Band 2, and likewise down the line. All people within Band 1 would be treated as equals; individual differences within the band would be ignored.

Banding has many different manifestations, and entails numerous issues, including determination of bandwidth and movement of the band after selections are made. Like any procedure, it has both advantages and disadvantages. Future research will need to examine the pros and cons of this and other procedures in assessing the validity of tests of aptitude and intelligence for employment or admission to schools. In these studies, the biases and moral assumptions that inevitably underlie research procedures need to be made more explicit than they are now. The final issue, indeed, may not be the outcome of such research, but whether there is full disclosure of the moral decisions made by the researchers in the course of their research.

Conclusion

In this chapter, we have examined how culture influences the basic psychological processes of perception, cognition, consciousness, and intelligence. We have also speculated about the possible impact of culture on the biological bases of behavior. These influences have profound implications for our understanding of the impact of culture on people and behavior. I (the first author) remember fondly when I was first introduced to the material concerning cultural influences on visual perception and optical illusions. I had never thought that culture, and experience in general, could have the effect that it does on what I thought must be innate, basic properties. When I learned of cultural differences in optical illusions, it gave me a new perspective on the nature and pervasiveness of culture.

The issues discussed in this chapter serve as the basis for understanding findings from many cross-cultural studies to be discussed in subsequent chapters. Perception, cognition, and consciousness lie at the core of many psychological constructs, and cultural differences in these processes demonstrate the various levels of psychology that culture influences. As consciousness reflects our subjective experience of the world, we take for granted that our consciousness is shared by others; research in this area, however, has shown that there may be large cultural, as well as individual, differences in consciousness. And though we all share similar characteristics in our biological composition, there may also be important differences in the biology and physiology that underlie our psychological makeups.

These differences have important ramifications for intercultural interactions and applied settings. If people from different cultural backgrounds can view such things as optical illusions differently, it is no wonder they perceive so much of the rest of the world differently as well. When this information is coupled with information concerning other basic psychological processes such as attribution, emotion, and personality, the effect of culture on individual psychology is amazing.

Likewise, cultural differences and similarities in definitions and processes of intelligence have considerable relevance to various applied settings. Many current curriculum transformation movements in the United States, for example, are based on a particular view and definition of intelligence and cognitive development. It is not uncommon to hear allegations of cultural bias in these types of educational reforms. Indeed, if broad, sweeping educational changes are implemented in the United States without recognition and awareness of deeply embedded cultural differences in the nature and definition of intelligence, we may actually be broadening the gaps that already exist between groups and increasing, rather than decreasing, intergroup conflict in the name of "education."

Awareness of cultural differences in intelligence raises difficult questions concerning testing and the use of test scores. Should bias in testing be eliminated at the expense of the predictive validity of the test? Many educational institutions and business organizations today face this difficult question, which is compounded by legal ramifications and the constant threat of litigation. Perhaps we need to give consideration to yet another aspect of intelligence—that is, our attitudes regarding intelligence. A cross-cultural understanding of differences in the definitions and processes of intelligence should help to deepen our appreciation and respect for cultures different from our own, and help us to find similarities as well as differences among people.

Glossary

active genotype–environment interaction When a person actively seeks out environments that support his or her genotype characteristics.

blind spot A spot in our visual field where the optic nerve goes through the layer of receptor cells on its way back toward the brain, creating a lack of sensory receptors in the eye at that location.

carpentered world theory A theory of perception that suggests that people (at least most Americans) are used to seeing things that are rectangular in shape, and thus unconsciously expect things to have square corners.

categorize To classify objects on the basis of perceived similarities and attach labels (words) to those classifications.

cognition The way we process information in our minds, transforming sensory input into knowledge.

evocative genotype–environment interaction When a person's inherited characteristics elicit or evoke certain responses from his or her environment.

front-horizontal foreshortening theory A theory of perception that suggests that we interpret vertical lines as horizontal lines extending into the distance. Because we interpret the vertical line in the horizontal–vertical illusion as extending away from us, we see it as longer.

optical illusions Perceptions that involve an apparent discrepancy between how an object looks and what it actually is.

passive genotype–environment interactions This occurs in biological families when parents provide both genes and environment for their children.

perception The process of gathering information about the world through our senses.

problem solving The process by which we attempt to discover ways of achieving goals that do not seem readily attainable.

serial position effect The finding that people tend to remember something better if it is either the first or the last item in a list.

stereotype threat The threat that others' judgments or one's own actions will negatively stereotype one in the domain.

symbolizing three dimensions in two A theory of perception that suggests that people in Western cultures focus more on representations on paper than do people in other cultures, and in particular spend more time learning to interpret pictures.

InfoTrac College Edition

Use InfoTrac College Edition to search for additional readings on topics of interest to you. For more information on topics in this chapter, use the following as search terms:

carpentered world theory
culture and cognition
culture and decision making
culture and problem solving

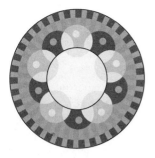

Enculturation

When the study of culture and psychology uncovers cultural differences, some natural questions are: How did these differences arise in the first place? What happens during development that makes people of different cultures different? What are the relative influences of parents, families, extended families, schools, and other social institutions? Are people born with inherent, biological predispositions to behavioral and cultural differences, or are such differences due entirely to environment and upbringing? What psychological differences are there in childhood and development when people are raised in different cultures? This chapter examines how the process of enculturation works. That is, how do people come to acquire their cultures? Research in this area has focused on parenting, peer groups, and institutions such as day care, the educational system, and religion, each of which will be discussed here. First, we'll define and compare two important terms in this area of study: enculturation and socialization.

Enculturation and Socialization

Childhood in any society is a period of considerable change and flux, subject to more cultural and environmental influences than any other in the life span. One aspect of childhood that is probably constant across cultures is that people emerge from this period with a wish to become happy, productive adults. Cultures differ, however, in exactly what they mean by "happy" and "productive."

Despite similarities in the overall goals of development, cultures exhibit a tremendous degree of variability in its content.

Each culture has some understanding of the adult competencies needed for adequate functioning (Ogbu, 1981; Kagitcibasi, 1996b), but these competencies differ by culture and environment. Children are socialized in ecologies that promote their specific competencies (Harrison, Wilson, Pine, Chan, & Buriel, 1990). For example, children who need a formal education to succeed in their culture are likely to be exposed to these values early in childhood; thus, they may receive books and instruction at a young age. Children in another culture may have to do spinning and weaving as part of their adult livelihood. These children are likely to receive early exposure to those crafts.

We are all truly integrated in our own societies and cultures. By the time we are adults, we have learned many cultural rules of behavior and have practiced those rules so much that they are second nature to us. Much of our behavior as adults is influenced by these learned patterns and rules, and we are so well practiced at them that we engage in these behaviors automatically and unconsciously without giving them much thought.

Still, at some time in our lives, we must have learned those rules and patterns of behavior. Culture, in its truest and broadest sense, involves so many different aspects of life that it is impossible to simply sit somewhere and read a book and learn about, let alone thoroughly master, a culture. Culture must be learned through a prolonged process, over a considerable period of time, with much practice. This learning involves all aspects of the learning processes that psychologists have identified over the years, including classical conditioning, operant conditioning, and social learning. In learning about culture, we make mistakes along the way, but people or groups or institutions are always around to help us, and in some cases force us, to correct those mistakes.

Socialization is the process by which we learn and internalize the rules and patterns of behavior that are affected by culture. This process, which occurs over a long period of time, involves learning and mastering societal and cultural norms, attitudes, values, and belief systems. The process of socialization starts early, probably from the very first day of life. Some people believe that the biological temperaments and predispositions we bring with us into the world at birth are actually part of the socialization process. Although this is an interesting and intriguing idea, most of what we know about the socialization process and the effects of socialization concern life after birth.

Closely related to the process of socialization is the process called **enculturation**. This is the process by which youngsters learn and adopt the ways and manners of their culture. There is very little difference, in fact, between the two terms. *Socialization* generally refers more to the actual process and mechanisms by which people learn the rules of society and culture—what is said to whom and in which contexts. *Enculturation* generally refers to the products of the socialization process—the subjective, underlying, psychological aspects of culture that become internalized through development. The similarities and differences between the terms *enculturation* and *socialization* are thus related to the similarities and differences between the terms *culture* and *society*.

Socialization (and enculturation) **agents** are the people, institutions, and organizations that exist to help ensure that socialization (or enculturation) occurs. The first and most important of these agents is parents. They help instill cultural mores and values in their children, reinforcing those mores and values when they are learned and practiced well and correcting mistakes in that learning.

Parents, however, are not the only socialization agents. Siblings, extended families, friends, and peers are important socialization and enculturation agents for many people. Organizations such as school, church, and social groups such as Boy or Girl Scouts also become important agents of these processes. In fact, as you learn more about the socialization process, you will find that culture is enforced and reinforced by so many people and institutions that it is no wonder we all emerge from the process as masters of our own culture.

In recent years, researchers have tried to examine the process of enculturation itself, looking at how people's interactions with the various socialization agents help to produce cultures, and how we develop cultural and ethnic identities. People are not passive recipients of cultural knowledge. Bronfenbrenner (1979) posits that human development is a dynamic, interactive process between individuals and their environments on several levels. These include the *microsystem* (the immediate surrounding such as the family, school, peer group, that children directly interact with), the *mesosystem* (the linkages between microsystems, such as between school and family), the *exosystem* (the context that indirectly affects children, such as parent's workplace), and the *macrosystem* (culture, religion, society). We are not simply socialized by our families, peer groups, and educational and religious institutions; we also contribute to our own development by affecting the people and contexts around us. In other words, we are also active producers of our own development. In the following sections, we will review research that includes several important contexts of enculturation: the family, peer groups, day care, and educational and religious institutions.

Culture, Child Rearing, Parenting, and Families

Parenting Goals and Beliefs

Clearly, our parents play an important, if not the most important, role in our development. Parenting has many dimensions: the goals and beliefs that parents hold for their children, the general style of parenting they exhibit, and the specific behaviors they use to realize their goals. The goals that parents have for their child's development are based on the caregiving context and the behaviors that each specific culture values (LeVine, 1977, 1997).

An example of how parenting goals may lead to variation in parenting behaviors across cultures is seen in the work of LeVine and his colleagues. These researchers (1996) have contrasted the parenting goals of Gusii mothers in Kenya with those of American mothers living in a Boston suburb. The Gusii are an agricultural people. Children are expected to help their mothers in the household and fields at a young age. In this environment, one goal Gusii mothers emphasize is protection of their infants. During infancy, soothing behaviors are emphasized to attain this goal. In Boston, however, one goal that mothers emphasize for their infants' development is active engagement and social exchange. Thus, these mothers emphasize stimulation and conversation with their infants.

Parents' beliefs concerning their role as caregivers also influence their behaviors. Parents in Western countries (especially in the United States) believe that they play a very active, goal-directed role in the development of their children (Coll, 1990; Goodnow, 1988). In India, however, parents do not believe they "direct" their children's development, but rather focus on enjoying the parent–child relationship (Kakar, 1978). Similarly, Kagitcibasi (1996b) describes traditional Turkish mothers as believing that their children "grow up" rather than are "brought up." This range of parenting beliefs will be reflected in the type and extent of involvement in children's upbringing, such as whether or not the mother will transmit cultural knowledge by verbalization or will expect her child to learn primarily by observation and imitation.

Parenting Styles

In addition to parental goals and beliefs, parenting styles are another important dimension of caregiving. Baumrind (1971) has identified three major patterns of parenting. **Authoritarian parents** expect unquestioned obedience and view the child as needing to be controlled. They have also been described as being low on warmth and responsiveness toward their children. **Permissive parents** are warm and nurturing to their children; however, they allow their children to regulate their own lives and provide few firm guidelines. **Authoritative parents** are sensitive to the child's maturity and are firm, fair, and reasonable. They also express a high degree of warmth and affection to their children. This is the most common type of parenting.

Other researchers (Maccoby & Martin, 1983) have identified a fourth type of parenting style, called uninvolved. **Uninvolved parents** are often too absorbed in their own lives to respond appropriately to their children and may seem indifferent to them. They do not seem committed to caregiving, beyond the minimum effort required to meet the physical needs of their child. An extreme form of this type of parenting is neglect.

Which of these parenting styles is optimal for a child's development? In general, research on American children indicates that children seem to do well with the authoritative parenting style. Compared to children of other parenting styles, children of authoritative parents demonstrate more positive mood, self-reliance, self-confidence, and higher emotional and social skills (Baumrind, 1967, 1971; Denham, Renwick, & Holt, 1997). This style is seen as promoting psychologically healthy, competent, independent children who are cooperative and at ease in social situations. Children of authoritarian parents are found to be more anxious and withdrawn, lacking spontaneity and intellectual curiosity.

Children of permissive parents tend to be immature; they have difficulty controlling their impulses and acting independently. Children of uninvolved parents fare the worst, being noncompliant and demanding. The benefits of authoritative parenting also extend to the later years. Teenagers with authoritative parents tend to have higher self-esteem, show higher achievement in school, and be more socially and morally mature (Lamborn, Mounts, Steinberg, & Dornbusch, 1991; Luster & McAdoo, 1996; Steinberg, Lamborn, Darling, Mounts, & Dornbusch, 1994; Steinberg, Lamborn, Dornbusch, & Darling, 1992; Steinberg, Mounts, Lamborn, & Dornbusch, 1991).

Because Baumrind's parenting styles were based on observations from a European American sample, Steinberg and his colleagues (1992) argued that the benefits of authoritative parenting may differ depending on the particular ethnic group. For example, when they compared several thousand U.S. adolescents from four ethnic groups (European American, African American, Asian American, and Hispanic American), they found that authoritative parenting significantly predicted higher school achievement for European American, African American, and Hispanic American adolescents, but not for Asian Americans. They also found that European American adolescents were the most likely, and Asian American adolescents the least likely, to report that their parents were authoritative.

Some researchers have conducted cross-cultural studies using the classifications of parenting derived from Baumrind's original research. For instance, a study with second-graders in China examined how children's school and social adjustment compared in authoritative versus authoritarian families (Chen, Dong, & Zhou, 1997). These researchers found that authoritarian parenting was related negatively, and authoritative parenting positively, to children's school and social adjustment. The researchers state that their findings are inconsistent with Steinberg et al.'s (1992) argument that the effects of authoritative parenting are less pronounced for Asian children. Still, further cross-cultural studies examining these parenting styles are needed before concluding that the authoritative style is optimal.

Some researchers argue that the conceptualization of these parenting styles itself may not be appropriate for parents of other cultures. For instance, Chinese parents have been thought to be more authoritarian. However, the significance and meaning attached to this parenting style may originate from a set of cultural beliefs that may differ greatly from the European American cultural belief system (Chao, 1994; Gorman, 1998). Chao advocates that researchers identify parenting styles that are specific to the culture by first understanding the values of the culture. For example, based on Confucian philosophy, Chinese parenting may be distinguished by the concept of *chiao shun*, or "training," in child rearing. She argues that this training aspect, which is not considered in Baumrind's styles of parenting, may be more useful in predicting Chinese children's outcomes. Research in Pakistan has also found this notion of training to be an important component of parenting (Stewart et al., 1999).

The specific dimensions of parenting styles, such as warmth and control, may have different meanings in different cultures. For example, in certain cultures such as the United States, control has a negative connotation, involving dominance and mistrust. In other cultures, however, "control" may connote something positive. Rohner and Pettengill (1985) report that Korean children's perception of parental control is positively associated with parental warmth and low neglect. Interestingly, Korean youth who undergo **acculturation** in a country that emphasizes different values (for example, independence versus interdependence) no longer view parental control positively. Kim (1992) reports that parental control is associated with less parental warmth and higher neglect in Korean Canadian and Korean American adolescents. These findings highlight the fact that perceptions of parenting are not static, but can be altered in a different social context.

Cross-Cultural Studies on Parenting Behaviors and Strategies

Over the past two or three decades, a considerable amount of cross-cultural research has examined differences in parenting behaviors across cultures and investigated the degree to which these parenting differences contribute to cultural differences on a variety of psychological constructs. Much of this research has centered on differences between American and Japanese parenting behaviors and strategies, mainly because Japanese culture seems to be very different from that of the United States yet is relatively accessible to American researchers. Studies of European cultures and Indian culture have been conducted as well, and also provide valuable information on this topic.

One interesting study investigated the strategies that Japanese and American mothers use to gain compliance from young children. In this study (Conroy, Hess, Azuma, & Kashiwagi, 1980), American and Japanese mothers and their firstborn children were interviewed about six hypothetical situations, each representing an action on the part of the child that the mother was likely to encounter in their daily interactions and that was likely to evoke an adult intervention. On the basis of the responses, the mothers' control strategies were then coded into categories such as appeals to authority, rules, feelings, consequences, or modeling. The Japanese mothers were more likely to engage in feeling-oriented appeals and demonstrated greater flexibility than the American mothers, who relied more extensively on their authority as mothers. The authors concluded that the findings reflected broad cultural differences in patterns of enculturation and socialization, with the focus in Japan on personal and interpersonal ties, in contrast to the American focus on direct instrumental processes with greater reliance on rewards and punishments.

Differences in child-rearing practices have also been found for other cultural groups. Kelley and Tseng (1992), for instance, compared European American and Chinese American mothers. They found that European American mothers scored higher on sensitivity, consistency, nonrestrictiveness, nurturance, and rule setting, whereas the Chinese American mothers scored higher on physical punishment and yelling. The authors related these results to the need for Chinese Americans to maintain their ties to their culture of origin. Also, Devereux,

Bronfenbrenner, and Suci (1962) reported that Germans engaged in more parenting behaviors related to affection, companionship, and direct punishment and control than did American parents.

Of the many different child-rearing behaviors people of different cultures engage in, one of the most representative of cultural differences concerns sleeping arrangements. One of the single greatest concerns of urban-dwelling Western parents, especially Americans, is getting their baby to sleep through the night, and to do so in a room separate from the parents'. Americans shun co-sleeping arrangements, with the underlying assumption that sleeping alone will help develop independence. Some assistance is offered to the child by way of "security objects" such as a special blanket or toy.

Many other cultures do not share this value. In rural areas of Europe, for example, infants sleep with their mothers for most, if not all, of their first year. This is true for many other cultures in the world, and comfort objects or bedtime rituals are not common in other cultures. Mayan mothers allow their children to sleep with them for several years because of a commitment to forming a very close bond with their children. When a new baby comes along, older children move to a bed in the same room or share a bed with another member of the family (Morelli, Oppenheim, Rogoff, & Goldsmith, 1992). The Mayan mothers in this study expressed shock and concern that American mothers would leave their babies alone at night. In traditional Japanese families, the child sleeps with the mother, either with the father on the other side or in a separate room. Again, these practices foster behaviors and values that are consonant with the developmental goals of the culture.

Cross-cultural research has also shown considerable differences in gender role differentiation between parents. Best, House, Barnard, and Spicker (1994), for instance, examined gender differences in parent–child interactions in France, Germany, and Italy. They found that French and Italian fathers engaged in more play than mothers, but the opposite was true in Germany. Devereux, Bronfenbrenner, and Suci (1962) found that the relative prominence of the mother is much more marked in American families than in German ones; that is, their American sample showed greater gender role differentiation than did their German sample. Bronstein (1984) studied parent–child dyads in Mexican families and found that fathers were more playful and companionable than mothers, whereas mothers were more nurturant in providing for immediate physical needs.

As stated earlier, many of these cultural differences in parenting behaviors may be related to expectations that parents have about child rearing and culture. Joshi and MacLean (1997), for example, investigated maternal expectations of child development in India, Japan, and England. In this study, mothers were asked to indicate the age at which they expected a child to achieve each of 45 developmental tasks. Japanese mothers had higher expectations than British mothers in the domains of education, self-care, and environmental independence. Indian mothers had lower expectations than the Japanese and British in all domains except environmental independence. Another study (Luthar & Quinlan, 1993) found that images about parental style in India and the United States were related to perceptions of care, ego resilience, and depressive tendencies.

Cross-cultural research has not only demonstrated cultural differences in parenting behaviors; it has documented numerous cultural similarities as well. Kelley and Tseng (1992), for example, found that both European American and Chinese American mothers place more emphasis on manners, school-related skills, and emotional adjustment when their children are 6–8 years of age than when they are 3–5. Solis-Camara and Fox (1995), using a 100-item rating scale called the Parent Behavior Checklist, found that Mexican and American mothers did not differ in their developmental expectations or in their parenting practices. Papps, Walker, Trimboli, and Trimboli (1995) found that mothers from Anglo-American, Greek, Lebanese, and Vietnamese ethnic groups all indicated that power assertion was their most frequently used disciplinary technique. And Keller, Chasiotis, and Runde (1992) reported cultural similarities among American, German, and Greek parents in the latencies of verbal and vocal behaviors toward children.

Thus, the available research evidence suggests both differences and similarities across cultures in parenting styles and child rearing. All of the studies have shown that parenting styles tend to be congruent with developmental goals dictated by culture; that is, cultural differences in specific values, beliefs, attitudes, and behaviors necessary for survival are associated with different developmental goals so that developing members of a society can carry on culture-relevant work related to survival. It seems that all people are similar in that their developmental processes are designed to meet cultural goals; people differ, however, in the specific nature of those goals.

Cultural differences in parenting reflect other social factors as well, such as the economic situation of the family, to which we now turn.

Diversity in Parenting as a Function of Economics

Parenting and child rearing often occur in very different economic conditions in different countries and cultures, and even within the United States. These diverse conditions produce socialization processes that vary widely from culture to culture. Child-rearing practices may differ not only because of difference in beliefs but also because of marked differences in standards of living. Applying U.S. standards to evaluate parenting in other countries and cultures can lead to harsh conclusions.

Consider the case of a slum-dwelling Brazilian mother who leaves her three children under the age of 5 locked in a bare, dark room for the day while she is out trying to meet their basic needs for food and clothing. We cannot judge the practices of others by the standards of the affluent and well-fed.

One recent study highlighted these issues. In this study, the reasons why mothers work and the number of hours they work were examined for mothers of firstborn children in the United States and Argentina (Pascual, Haynes,

Galperin, & Bornstein, 1995). In both countries, both length of marriage and whether a woman worked during pregnancy predicted whether she worked after giving birth. In the United States, however, better-educated women with higher-status occupations worked longer hours, whereas in Argentina, better-educated women with higher-status occupations worked shorter hours. Thus, different cultural and economic conditions mediated the women's decisions to work in these two countries.

It is common folklore that picking up a baby and bringing it to the shoulder reduces bouts of crying and that babies who are ignored and allowed to cry for fear of spoiling them actually cry more. However, in remote rural river regions of China, few-week-old infants are left for long periods of time while their mothers work in the fields. These babies are placed in large sacks of sand that support them upright and act as an absorbent diaper. These babies quickly cease crying because they learn early that it will not bring about any response at all.

If a society has a high rate of infant mortality, parenting efforts may concentrate on meeting basic physical needs. Parents may have little choice but to disregard other developmental demands. Sometimes the response to harsh and stressful conditions is parenting behavior that we might consider positive. In the Sudan, for example, the mother traditionally spends the first 40 days after delivery entirely with her baby. She rests while her relatives tend to her, and she focuses all her energy on her baby (Cederblad, 1988).

LeVine (1977) has theorized that the caregiving environment reflects a set of goals that are ordered in importance. First is physical health and survival. Next is the promotion of behaviors that will lead to self-sufficiency. Last are behaviors that promote other cultural values, such as morality and prestige.

Many families in the United States are fortunate in that they can turn their attention to meeting the second two goals. In many countries, the primary goal of survival is all-important and often overrides the other goals in the amount of parental effort exerted. Indeed, this is true in many areas of the United States as well.

Siblings

Siblings play an important role in the socialization of children (Dunn, 1988). Zukow-Goldring (1995) states that many of the behaviors and beliefs of the social group are transferred through siblings. For example, among the Kwara'ae infants in the Solomon Islands, siblings are highly involved as caregivers. In this culture, the responsibilities involved in caregiving are viewed as a training ground for siblings to become mutually dependent on one another in adulthood. For example, one sibling may be designated to go to school while the others combine their resources to support that sibling. In turn, this sibling will support the family financially once he has finishing his schooling and found a job (Watson-Gegeo, 1992). In agricultural societies especially, where there are usually a greater number of children in each family, siblings are often responsible for child care and thus influence one another in significant ways.

Extended Families

In many non–European American cultures, extended families are prevalent. In the United States in 1996, for example, 23% of African American, 24% of Asian and Pacific Islander, 24% of American Indian and Alaskan Native, and 22% of Hispanic children lived in extended families, compared with only 12% of European American children (Fields, 2001).

Extended families are a vital and important feature of child rearing, even when resources are not limited. Many cultures view extended-family child rearing as an integral and important part of their cultures. The extended family can provide a buffer to stresses of everyday living. It is also an important means of transmitting cultural heritage from generation to generation.

Extended families can support and facilitate child rearing in ways that are completely different from the European American nuclear family. Research on parenting style (authoritarian, permissive, authoritative, or neglectful) tends to assume a nuclear family structure. In the United States, ethnic minority families have been characterized as extended and generally more conservative than European American families. For example, Japanese American families have strict age and sex roles, and emphasize children's obedience to authority figures (Trankina, 1983; Yamamoto & Kubota, 1983). Arab American families are also characterized by an extended family system, where loyalty, emotional support, and financial assistance are emphasized (Nydell, 1998). Of course, not all ethnic minority families are extended, and caregiving between nuclear and extended families may differ. For instance, African American extended families tend to emphasize cooperation and moral and religious values more than African American nuclear families do (Tolson & Wilson, 1990).

In an extended family situation, even though mothers are still seen as the primary caregiver, children experience frequent interaction with fathers, grandparents, godparents, siblings, and cousins. Hispanic and Filipino families see godparents as important models for children, and as sources of support for the parents. Sharing households with relatives, characteristic of extended families, is seen as a good way of maximizing the family's resources for successful child rearing.

One need not look outside the United States to recognize the importance of extended families. One major difference, however, is that participation in child rearing via extended families in the United States is often seen as a consequence of poor economics rather than a desirable state of affairs. Limited resources are a reality, with 16.3% of children in the United States living in poverty in 2001 (U.S. Census Bureau, 2002). Many are born to single mothers, and here the extended family plays an important role in the child-rearing process. Grandmothers are more actively involved with their grandchildren when they live with their single adult daughters. These children experience a greater variety of principal caregivers and have different social interactions than their middle-class European American counterparts. Compounding this picture is the reality that ethnicity also confounds social class.

Teenage parenting also forces us to think differently about traditional notions of parenting. The presence of the maternal grandmother in these families has been found to cancel out some of the negative results associated with teen mothering (Garcia Coll, 1990). The grandmother often serves as a valuable source of information about child development. She also tends to be more responsive and less punitive with the child than the teen mother is. The grandmother in these three-generation households plays a very important role as teacher and role model to her daughter and can provide favorable, positive social interaction for her grandchild.

Extended families differ in their composition from one culture to another but have in common a sharing of resources, emotional support, and caregiving. The experiences of a child growing up in these situations can be quite different from those of a child in a European American nuclear family. In addition, we need to be aware that the traditional two-parent household is changing for many European Americans as well. Future studies will undoubtedly change the way we view parenting in this culture as well.

Culture and Peers

One's peer group is another critical context for enculturation. How much do your peers influence your development? It may depend on how rapidly your culture is changing. Margaret Mead (1928/1978) described three types of cultures with differing levels of peer influence on the socialization of its young people. In **postfigurative cultures,** where cultural change is slow, socialization occurs primarily by elders transferring their knowledge to their children. In this case, elders hold the knowledge necessary for becoming a successful and competent adult. In **cofigurative cultures,** where cultural change occurs more rapidly, adults continue to socialize their children, but peers play a greater role in socializing each other. Young people may have to turn to one another for advice and information. In **prefigurative cultures,** the culture is changing so rapidly that young people may be the ones to teach adults. The knowledge that adults hold may not be sufficient for the next generation, and adults may need to look to younger people to negotiate society.

Exposure to Peer Groups

Researchers have studied how cultures vary in the exposure that children have to their peer groups. In industrialized countries, children spend a significant amount of time with same-aged peers. Fuligni and Stevenson's (1995) comparison of the number of hours that teenagers spend with one another outside of school reveals that American teenagers spend more hours (18 hours) with their peers compared to Japanese (12) and Taiwanese (8). The nature and strength of peers as socializing agents in these highly industrialized cultures will differ from other cultures. For instance, children growing up in solitary farm settlements will have limited options to interact with a wide range of potential playmates. Or, children growing up in a hunting/gathering society may be socialized by their peers within the context of multi-age groups instead of the same-age groups that are characteristic of countries such as the United States, where age-stratified schooling is the norm (Krappmann, 1996). Thus, depending on the specific culture, the extent to which children interact with their peers may or may not be significant in terms of enculturation.

Friendships

The unique relationship called friendship is found in virtually all cultures (Krappmann, 1996), and these friendships are important vehicles for enculturation. Within the context of friendships, children learn cultural ways of negotiation, reciprocity, cooperation, and interpersonal sensitivity (Youniss & Smollar, 1989). Davis and Davis (1989) studied adolescent friendships in Zawiya, Morocco, and found that one of the main purposes of friendships in this culture is to learn about establishing one's "trustworthiness" in society—for instance, by building a good reputation. Toward this end, Moroccan teenagers emphasized that sharing, refraining from gossip, taking care of their reputation, and not being a bad influence on their friends were important concerns in their friendships. Davis and Davis write that "the core goal of Zawiya socialization is to produce a person worthy of trust and able to command respect, one who respects propriety, displays mature judgment, and stands by one's word. Interactions with friends help develop and hone this sense of how one comes across to people" (p. 89). This is a good illustration of how friendships are instrumental in helping children achieve culturally appropriate behaviors and values.

Culture and Day Care

Variations in Day Care

The differences we see across cultures in day care are a window into different cultural attitudes about children, parenting roles, and social organization. Variations in cultural attitudes concerning how children should be socialized affect the quality and availability of day care around the world. For instance, in the United States, there is a controversy regarding whether child care should be a public responsibility or a private, individual concern (Lamb & Sternberg, 1992). Perhaps because of this tension, there is no national day-care policy, and day-care facilities and practices vary greatly. Unfortunately, the quality of many day-care facilities in the United States appears inadequate. Many caregivers do not receive specialized training for teaching young children, and a majority of private day-care homes are unlicensed and therefore not subject to close monitoring to ensure that children are receiving high-quality care (Howes, Whitebrook, & Phillips, 1992; Kontos, Howes, Shinn, & Galinsky, 1995). In contrast, parents in other countries, such as Israel, take for granted that all citizens should share the responsibility of rearing and educating young children. Rosenthal (1992) points out that most Israeli parents believe it is appropriate and important for young children to interact in a group setting with their peers and not be kept at home. Cultural attitudes such as this contribute to the quality and availability of day care.

Day Care and Child Development

Whether day care is beneficial or detrimental to a child's development has been a hotly debated topic. The answer seems to lie in the quality of the day care. Studies in the United States demonstrate that low-quality day care can be detrimental to a child's social and intellectual development (Haskins, 1989; Howes, 1990). Conversely, high-quality day care can enhance children's development, especially for those from underprivileged, low-SES families (Phillips, Voran, Kisker, Howes, & Whitebrook, 1994). Studies of young children in Sweden, where day care is of uniformly high quality, show that those in day care seem to have slightly more advanced cognitive and social development compared to those cared for at home (Hwang & Broberg, 1992). Day care in all cultures can be an effective context in which children's development can be enriched, better preparing them to fill their societies' expected roles (Lamb & Sternberg, 1992).

Culture and Education

The single most important formalized mechanism of instruction in many societies and cultures today is the educational system. Most of us think of a country's educational system solely as an institution that teaches thinking skills and knowledge. But a society's educational system is probably the most important institution socializing its children and teaching and reinforcing its cultural values. Much of the cross-national and cross-cultural research in this area has focused on cross-national differences in math achievement.

Cross-National Differences in Math Achievement

Mathematics learning occupies a special place in our understanding of culture, socialization, and the educational system. Of course, learning math skills is crucial to the ultimate development of science in any society, which is probably why it has received so much research attention, as well as funding from government and private sources.

Still, math and culture have a very special relationship because, as Stigler and Baranes (1988) put it, math skills "are not logically constructed on the basis of abstract cognitive structures, but rather are forged out of a combination of previously acquired (or inherited) knowledge and skills, and new cultural input" (p. 258). Culture is not only a stimulator of math but is itself represented in math, and how a society teaches and learns it.

Cross-national research on math learning in schools has traditionally compared the math abilities of students around the world. An early study conducted by the International Association for the Evaluation of Education Achievement (IEA) (Husen, 1967), for example, measured math achievement scores in 12 different countries at the eighth and twelfth grades. The overall performance of the American eighth-graders was ranked 11th, and their mean scores were below the international mean in every area of math assessed. The performance of the American twelfth-graders was even worse. A later IEA study comparing 17 countries found that the performance of American students relative to the rest of the world had declined even further. According to Geary (1996), the top 5% of American elite math students (those enrolled in college-prep math courses) had average scores in relation to the international standard in algebra and calculus, and only slightly above average scores in geometry. American students who score at the 95th percentile in the United States would score at the 30th percentile in Japan and the 50th percentile in England.

These findings have been corroborated by other research involving primary school children (for example, Stevenson, Chen, & Lee, 1993). Even in first grade, the superiority of the Japanese and Chinese in math performance is already striking, reaching "dynamic" proportions by fifth grade (Stevenson, Lee, & Stigler, 1986; Stigler & Baranes, 1988, p. 291). The relatively poor performance of American children has also been documented in comparisons with Korean children (Song & Ginsburg, 1987). Moreover, the differences were observed not only in computational tests but in all math tests produced and administered by the researchers.

Of course, such findings have been alarming to educators at all levels in the United States for many years. The relatively poor performance of American youth in these skills is not only an important social concern; it is also of major concern for the future health of the U.S. economy, as more and more potentially unskilled or underskilled employees enter the workforce (Geary, 1996). Math abilities—and, more important, the logical reasoning skills underlying math and the mental discipline associated with math—are essential in many walks of life.

In searching for the possible causes of these differences, Geary (1996) has suggested a distinction between primary and secondary math abilities. Primary math abilities refer to natural abilities that are shaped by evolutionary processes that all people presumably share (for example, language, counting). Secondary abilities refer to unnatural abilities that are based in large part on primary systems. Whereas the motivation to acquire primary abilities is likely to be inherent, the motivation to acquire secondary abilities may be more strongly influenced by culture.

Are differences in math abilities biologically caused? If biological factors were responsible for cross-national differences in math ability, then cross-national differences in primary math abilities should exist. But, although the research is not definitive, indirect evidence indicates no cross-national differences in primary math abilities. Those cross-national differences that have been found appear to be related to secondary, not primary, math achievements

(Geary, 1996). Some people may suggest that research presented in the previous chapter on possible racial differences in IQ or head (brain) size may also be related to differences in math achievement and thus imply biological causes for those differences. Those IQ differences, however, tend to be small, and not robust enough to account for the rather large differences in math abilities. Moreover, comparisons of mean IQ scores of American, Japanese, and Chinese children (for example, Stevenson et al., 1985) have found no differences; thus, IQ cannot possibly account for cross-national differences among these children. As noted throughout this book, moreover, interpretation of biological differences based on classifications of race are always problematic.

Social and Cultural Factors That Influence Math Achievement

That cross-national differences in math achievement are related to secondary rather than primary math abilities implies that social and cultural factors play a major role in producing those differences. A number of possible contributing factors have been examined in the literature, including differences in language, school systems, parental and familial values, teaching styles and teacher–student relationships, and attitudes and appraisals of students. Work in each of these areas supports the contribution of each factor to cross-national differences in math achievement, and collectively constitutes a wealth of evidence concerning the relationship between culture and education.

Language. Research by Stigler, Lee, and Stevenson (1986) has shown that cross-national differences among Chinese, Japanese, and American children in counting and memory exercises may be largely a function of differences in the Chinese, Japanese, and English languages related to counting and numbers. The Japanese language, for example, has unique verbal labels only for the numbers 1 through 10. Number 11 is then "ten-one," 12 is "ten-two," 20 is "two-ten," 21 is "two-ten-one," and so forth. English, however, has unique labels for numbers 1 through 19 as well as all the decade numbers (20, 30, 40, and so forth). Research has shown that East Asian students make fewer errors than Americans in counting, and understand some basic math concepts related to counting and numbers better (Miura, Okamoto, Kim, Steere, & Fayol, 1993). These differences may account for some, but not all, of the cross-national differences in math abilities.

School systems. Research has shown that the educational system in which children take part plays an important role in producing cross-national differences in math abilities, while at the same time imparting cultural values. First of all, the content of what is taught in the schools reflects a priori choices by that culture or society regarding what it believes is important to learn. Different cultures believe different topics to be important for later success in that society. By teaching a certain type of content, the educational system reinforces a particular view of cognition and intelligence.

Another important factor to consider is the environmental setting in which education occurs. Many industrialized societies have a formal educational system, with identifiable areas and structures (schools) and identifiable education agents (teachers) to "do" education. In other cultures, formalized education may take place in small groups led by elders of the community. In yet other cultures, formalized education may be a family task (for example, the mother tutoring her own children in cognitive and other skills necessary for members of their community). Regardless of the environmental setting, the vehicle by which education occurs reinforces certain types of cultural values in its recipients.

The organization, planning, and implementation of lesson plans are other important cultural socializers. Some cultures encourage a didactic model of teaching, in which an expert teacher simply gives information to students, who are expected to listen and learn. Other cultures view teachers as leaders through a lesson plan, providing the overall structure and framework by which students discover principles and concepts. Some cultures view imparting of praise as an important process. Other cultures focus on mistakes made by students in the learning process. Some cultures have special classes and mechanisms to deal with many different types of students—for example, students with learning disabilities, physical handicaps, and special gifts or talents. Other cultures tend to downplay such differences among their students, treating them all as equals.

Once in school, children spend the majority of their waking hours away from their parents. The socialization process that began in the primary relationship with the parents continues with peers in play situations and in school. School institutionalizes cultural values and attitudes and is a significant contributor not only to the intellectual development of the child but, just as important, to the child's social and emotional development.

To highlight the role of the educational system as an enculturation agent, one need only recognize that not all cultures of the world rely solely on an institutionalized school setting to teach math. For example, important math skills are taught to Micronesian islanders in the Puluwat culture through navigation, to coastal Ghanaians by marketing fish, and even to bookies in Brazil (Acioly & Schliemann, 1986; Gladwin, 1970; Gladwin & Gladwin, 1971). Important math skills are imparted through nonschool activities not only in more "exotic" cultures, but also through activities such as dieting and athletic training in the United States (Stigler & Baranes, 1988).

Regardless of the way education occurs, the choices a society and culture make concerning its structure, organization, planning, and implementation all encourage and reinforce a certain view of culture. We are not always cognizant of our own cultural view because we are in the middle of it. To see our own biases and choices, we need to observe education in other cultures and compare what is done elsewhere to what we do. Through such comparisons, the differences and the similarities often become quite clear.

Parental and familial values.   Research has shown that a number of important differences in cultural values and belief systems among Americans, Japanese, and Chinese have an impact on education. For example, Japanese and

Chinese parents and teachers are more likely to consider all children as equal, with no differences between them. American parents and teachers are more likely to recognize differences and find reasons to treat their children as special. This difference is probably rooted in a cultural tension between individualism and collectivism among the three cultures.

American parents and teachers are more likely to consider innate ability more important than effort; for the Japanese and Chinese, however, effort is far more important than ability. This difference is also rooted in cultural differences among the three countries and has enormous implications for education.

American parents tend to be more easily satisfied at lower levels of competence than either the Japanese or the Chinese. Also, when problems arise, Americans are more likely to attribute the cause of the problem to something they cannot do anything about (such as ability). These cultural differences in attribution of causality are directly related to cultural differences in self-construals, discussed in Chapter 11.

Believing that ability is more important than effort has yet another side to it—a belief that each child is limited in his or her abilities. Once this belief becomes a cultural institution, it dictates how the educational system should respond. The resulting emphasis in the case of the American system is to seek unique, innate differences among the students, to generate separate special classes for these unique groups of students, and generally to individualize the process of education. As a result, more time is spent on individualized instruction and less on whole-group instruction.

Research has documented other interesting effects of parental and familial values related to achievement and academic success. Chao (1996), for example, found that Chinese mothers of preschoolers conveyed a high value on education, the high investment and sacrifice they themselves need to make in order for their children to succeed, their desire for direct intervention approaches to their children's schooling, and a belief that they play a major role in their children's success. American mothers of preschoolers in her study, however, conveyed a negation of the importance of academic skills, a desire for a less directive approach in instruction, and concern for building their children's self-esteem. Kush (1996) found that although European Americans and Mexican Americans differed in level of academic achievement, these differences disappeared when parental education was statistically controlled in the analysis.

Finally, Yao (1985) compared family characteristics of European American and Asian American high achievers. This study found that the family life of the European Americans was less structured and provided fewer formal educational experiences for children on weekends and after school. Asian families, in contrast, structured their children's lives more and actively sought more after-school and extracurricular programs to complement school learning. These findings suggest the importance of parental education in predicting and contributing toward cultural differences in academic achievement.

Attitudes and appraisals of students.   A number of studies have examined cultural differences between Asian or Asian American children and European

Americans. Pang (1991), for example, studied the relationships among test anxiety, self-concept, and student perceptions of parental support in Asian American and European American middle school students. This study found that Asian American students exhibited a stronger desire to please parents, greater parental pressure, but also higher levels of parental support, than did the European American students. Yan and Gaier (1994) looked at causal attributions for college success and failure in Asian and American college undergraduate and graduate students; they found that American students attributed academic achievement more often to ability than did Asian subjects. American students also believed that effort was more important for success than lack of effort was for failure, whereas Asian students considered effort equally important for success or failure. These results are consonant with similar tendencies in parental attitudes described earlier, and with attributional biases discussed elsewhere in this book. Similar findings were obtained with fourth-graders in Japan, China, and the United States (Tuss, Zimmer, & Ho, 1995).

Cross-national differences have been found in other samples as well. Little, Oettingen, Stetsenko, and Baltes (1995), for example, compared American, German, and Russian beliefs about school performance. They found that American children had the highest levels of personal agency and control expectancy, but the lowest belief–performance correlations. That is, Americans believed they had the most control over their academic outcomes, but this degree of perceived control was unrelated to their actual performance. Birenbaum and Kraemer (1995) also demonstrated differences in causal attributions in relation to academic success and failure in Arab and Jewish high school students.

Together, these findings suggest that students around the world approach their academic work with quite different worldviews, attitudes, and attributional styles; that these differences are related to parental differences found in other research; that they may account for cross-national differences in academic achievement; and that they are intimately related to culture.

Teaching styles and teacher–student relationships. Stigler and his colleagues have examined classrooms to find possible roots of the cross-national differences in math achievement reported earlier (for example, Stigler & Perry, 1988). Several major differences in the use of classroom time appear to underlie math performance differences. The Japanese and Chinese spend more days per year in school, more hours per day in school, a greater proportion of time in school devoted to purely academic subjects, and a greater proportion of time devoted to math. In addition, Japanese and Chinese teachers spend a greater proportion of time working with the whole class than do American teachers. This difference is even more dramatic because average class size is smaller in the United States than in Japan or China. As a result, American students spend less time working under the supervision and guidance of a teacher.

During class, it was observed, American teachers tend to use praise to reward correct responses. Teachers in Japan, however, tend to focus on incorrect answers, using them as examples to lead into discussion of the computational process and math concepts. Teachers in Taiwan tend to use a process more congruent with the Japanese approach. These teaching differences speak to the cultural emphasis in the United States on rewarding uniqueness and individualism and the emphasis in Japan and China on finding ways to engage in group process and sharing responsibility for mistakes with members of the group. Praise, while nice, often precludes such discussion.

Differences exist in other cultures as well. McCargar (1993), for example, documented differences among 10 cultural groups of students on 8 scales of student role expectations and 11 scales of teacher role expectations. Taken together, these studies highlight important differences that are present every day in the classroom in terms of teaching style, expectations, and actual behaviors that may account for cross-national differences in academic achievement.

Summary. We know that cross-national differences in academic achievement are not necessarily accounted for by biological differences between people of different cultures. And although differences in languages, especially related to counting systems, may be a factor, they cannot account for the size of the differences. Instead, research indicates that cross-national differences in academic achievement are the result of many social and cultural factors, some of which are institutionalized in educational systems, others found in parents and parental values, others in children's cognitive and attributional styles, and yet others in specific classroom practices. No research suggests that any single factor can fully account for cross-national differences in achievement; instead, it is a combination of these and other factors that leads to differences.

Nor are cross-national differences in academic performance, and the other cross-cultural differences that underlie them, solely products of culture. The performance of students of any culture, in any subject area, is the result of a complex interplay of economics, geography, resources, cultural values and beliefs, abilities, experiences, language, and family dynamics.

Research on differences in academic performance also highlights the role of the educational system as an important enculturation agent in any society. That is, not only do all of the differences discussed here contribute to cross-national differences in academic achievement; they also contribute to differences in culture itself. Parents' and children's attitudes, educational practices and curricula, teacher behaviors, and all other associated factors are important transmitters of culture. They impart important cultural knowledge to the students as members of a culture or society, and thus play a major role in the socialization and enculturation of the child members of many societies of the world. Differences in these institutions not only reflect but reinforce cultural differences in values, beliefs, attitudes, norms, and behaviors and help transmit this important cultural information from one generation to the next. The school-age period of life is indeed a critical time in any culture, when culture is strongly reinforced in children by society as a whole. This process is pervasive.

Religion

Religious institutions are another important vehicle of enculturation. In the United States, for most of the 20th century, psychologists neglected the role of religion in the development of individuals (Pargament & Maton, 2000). Religion, however, is an "ever present and extremely important aspect of the historical, cultural, social and psychological realities that humans confront in their daily lives" (Hood, Spilka, Hunsberger, & Gorsuch, 1996, p. 2). Religious institutions socialize children by setting rules for behavior, by preparing children for the roles they will play as men and women, and by helping individuals to create an identity (Arnett, 2001; Pargament & Maton, 2000). Furthermore, the religious community offers support to the developing child, a sense of belonging, and an affirmation of worthiness (Garcia Coll, Meyer, & Brillon, 1995). Whether it is Islam, Christianity, Judaism, Buddhism, or another religious system, religion is a part of the human experience that can provide individuals with guidance, structure, and appropriate ways of behaving and thinking in many aspects of life.

The importance and pervasiveness of religion, however, vary across cultures. Goossens (1994) reports that only 30% of Belgian adolescents believe in God, and only 10% regularly attend religious services. In contrast, 95% of American adolescents believe in God, and 32% attend weekly religious services (Gallup & Bezilla, 1992; Wallace & Williams, 1997). In Poland, 92% of youth are members of the Catholic church, and about 71% attend church regularly (Wlodarek, 1994). And in Korea, more than half of the adolescents report participating in some religion, ranging from Christianity to Buddhism to Catholicism (Choe, 1994).

Developmentally, religious ceremonies are an important part of child care and rites of passage in many cultures around the world. For instance, infants in India undergo a hair-shaving ceremony when they are born, and undergo a prayer and holy water ritual when they are named (Dosanjh & Ghuman, 1996). Some religious ceremonies mark the passage from childhood to adulthood, such as in Jewish culture, with the Bar (Bas) Mitzvah. In Islam, the beginning of adolescence is marked by participation in fasting during the holy month of Ramadan.

Dosanjh and Ghuman's (1997) study of Punjabi families living in England illustrates how parents use religion and religious practices in their daily lives to transmit the values and language of their culture to their children. A majority of the sample (87.5%) reported that religious education was "important" or "very important." They also reported discussing religion with their children, and actively encouraged them to attend religious services and engage in prayers at home. The authors note that for a majority of Punjabi families, religion plays a critical role in the development and maintenance of their personal identities.

Religious beliefs have been linked to the study of cognitive development in Jewish, Catholic, and Protestant children (Elkind, 1978); moral development in Africa (Okonkwo, 1997); attitudes toward sexuality in older adolescents in the United States (Fehring, Cheever, German, & Philpot, 1998); and attitudes toward suicide for Hindus and Muslims living in England (Kamal & Lowenthal, 2002). However, much still needs to be done to identify exactly what aspects of religion relate to what aspects of human development.

A major challenge for future cross-cultural researchers is to better understand the complex interplay between culture and religion and how they influence family beliefs and values, child-rearing goals and practices, and ultimately, the developing individual. In a world where religion is increasingly becoming a visible target of cross-cultural conflicts and misunderstandings, it is of utmost importance for us to continue exploring how religion defines and shapes an individual's personal experiences, belief systems, and identity.

Summary

The information presented so far speaks to just a few of the many ways in which enculturation occurs around the world. Differences in parenting styles and child rearing provide learning platforms for children that allow them to achieve developmental goals fostered by their particular cultures. Each culture's way of raising children—through parenting, sleeping arrangements, and other concrete mechanisms—represents that culture's way of ensuring that its values and norms are transmitted to those children. In all cultures, these practices are ritualized so that this transmission of information can occur generation after generation. Learning cultural values is as much a part of the process of socialization as it is an outcome of socialization.

What does contemporary cross-cultural research say about how all this occurs? According to Bornstein (1989), some early cross-cultural work in development (for example, Caudill & Frost, 1974; Caudill & Weinstein, 1969) focused primarily on the role of culture in "driving" parenting behaviors that resulted in changes in the infant and young child. This model suggests that culture unidirectionally provides the structure and environment for parents, particularly mothers, to affect their children in culturally appropriate ways: culture → mother → infant.

Others (for example, Shand & Kosawa, 1985) have focused on biology, proposing a developmental model that starts with the effects of genes, biology, and heredity on infant temperament, which then affects the mother's behaviors, which in turn produce cultural differences: genes → infant → mother → culture.

The available cross-cultural research provides support for both models of understanding. The work on parenting styles, for instance, supports the first model, while the work on temperament and attachment supports the second. Most recent work in this area (for example, Holloway & Minami, 1996) suggests a rapprochement between the two, conceptualizing both parents and children as interactive partners in the joint creation of cultural meanings. This view suggests that children's active processing of information results in the reproduction of culture, and the production of new elements of culture. The interaction of language between parent and child provides the platform on which divergent points of view construct new realities. These recent theories also attempt to discover cultural meanings held in common between parents and children, rather than assuming a common understanding "imposed" by an outside culture.

Additionally, the assumption in most of the literature on child rearing that the effect of caregiving flows from the caregiver to the child has been challenged (for example, Bell, 1968, Scarr, 1993). Is it really the case that authoritative parents produce more competent children, or is it that children who are easygoing, cooperative, and obedient elicit authoritative parenting? Characteristics of the child, such as temperament (discussed in detail in the next chapter), play an important role in the parenting the child receives. For instance, Ge et al. (1996) examined how an adolescent characterized by a difficult temperamental style might elicit negative parenting behaviors, leading to parent–adolescent conflict and subsequently to adolescent problem behavior. Ge et al. argue that the characteristics of both the adolescent and the parent must be considered in order to more fully understand how children and adolescents contribute to their own development in relation to their parents. Current theories on parenting emphasize this dynamic interaction between the child and his or her parent (Collins, Maccoby, Steinberg, Hetherington, & Bornstein, 2000). Whoever the caregiver may be—whether mother, father, sibling, or grandparent—there is a mutual exchange between the child and the caretaker(s) that drives a child's development (Tronick, 1989).

Future research in this area will hopefully bridge the gaps among all of these various components, assessing the interplay of temperament, attachment, parenting styles, and psychological culture in the milieu. Ideally, longitudinal studies will enable researchers to examine the interactions among these various components of the enculturation process in the same individuals across time.

Conclusion

This chapter has examined a multitude of factors that may influence how people become enculturated—parenting styles, child-rearing practices, peer groups, day care, the educational system, and religious institutions. Just how is it that all these processes are assembled in people's minds as enculturation occurs? Research that directly addresses this question is sorely lacking. Much of what we do know comes from theoretical and conceptual research in anthropology and cross-cultural psychology that attempts to aggregate the various pieces of evidence into a coherent whole.

Tomasello (1993), for example, has suggested that cultural learning manifests itself in three different ways in human development: imitation, instruction, and collaboration. These processes, in turn, are supposedly related to the development of social and cognitive concepts and processes that are necessary for enculturation to occur. Imitation relies on a concept of intentional agent and requires perspective taking. Instructional learning requires mental agents and involves interactive and coordinated perspective taking. Collaborative learning relies on the ability to reflect and involves integrated perspective taking.

Correlations between these aspects of social cognition and cultural learning in normal and autistic children, and in wild and enculturated chimpanzees, offer further support for these mechanisms. (The importance of imitation in cultural learning has drawn some criticism, however; see Heyes, 1993.) Some authors have suggested that culture can best be characterized as the conglomeration of situated context-related learning. Jacobsen (1996), for instance, suggests that contexts are inseparable from cognitive processes. As culture-appropriate learning occurs in multiple and different contexts, such culture-specific learning is joined together across contexts into a cohesive whole, on the level of either understanding, appreciation, or behavior. Likewise, Shore (1991) defines cultural cognition as the product of an organization of cultural texts and models, and the subjective processes of meaning construction through which we become aware of cultural symbols through subjective experience. Different cognitive processes and sensory experiences help to link schemas across contexts and provide cultural meaning that is constructed through that experience.

Super and Harkness (1986, 1994) suggest that enculturation occurs within what they term a developmental niche. This niche forms the structural and subjective framework within which children come to learn the cultural values and mores important to their society. According to these authors, this niche includes three major components: the physical and social setting, the customs of child care and child rearing, and the psychology of the caregivers. The developing child is influenced by all three components, or more precisely by their interaction, all of which occurs within a larger environmental and human ecology. In their niche, developing children are able to receive the influences of the various socialization agents and institutions around them, ensuring their enculturation, while at the same time the child also brings his or her temperamental disposition to the interaction.

The issue of enculturation is related to that of ethnic identity development, a topic that has received considerable attention in recent years. The concept of identity differs from that of enculturation in that identity typically refers to an awareness of one's culture or ethnicity. Certainly, people can become enculturated without having conscious awareness of that cultural learning. In fact, research has tended to show that the development of ethnic identity occurs in stages. In studying ethnic identity development in Mexican Americans, for example, Bernal (1993) has found that very young children (around 4 years of age) tend to have very limited knowledge of their ethnic identity. As they get older, however, their understanding of their heritage grows broader and more complex. Phinney's program of research has shown that ethnic identity continues to develop through adolescence and young adulthood, and is positively related to self-esteem (Phinney & Chavira, 1992; Phinney & Rosenthal, 1992; Phinney, Horenczyk, & Liebkind, 2001).

Thus, available studies suggest that culture may be learned through situated cognitive schemas and structures related to specific contexts, and that cultural meaning is constructed across these contexts as individuals develop social cognitive abilities that allow for such construction to occur. Awareness of the meanings associated with these cultural constructions leads to the development of cultural or ethnic identity, which appears to develop later than gender or racial identity. Future research will need to test these ideas directly and explore the degree to which these processes are similar or different in people of different cultures around the world.

 Glossary

acculturation The process of adapting to, and in many cases adopting, a different culture from the one in which a person was enculturated.

authoritarian parent A style of parenting in which the parent expects unquestioned obedience and views the child as needing to be controlled.

authoritative parent A style of parenting that is viewed as firm, fair, and reasonable. This style is seen as promoting psychologically healthy, competent, independent children who are cooperative and at ease in social situations.

cofigurative culture A culture in which change occurs rapidly. Both adults and peers socialize young people. Young people may have to turn to one another for advice and information in this type of culture.

enculturation The process by which individuals learn and adopt the ways and manners of their culture.

permissive parents A style of parenting in which parents allow children to regulate their own lives and provide few firm guidelines.

postfigurative culture A culture in which change is slow and socialization occurs primarily by elders transferring their knowledge to their children. Elders hold the knowledge necessary for becoming a successful and competent adult.

prefigurative culture A culture that is changing so rapidly that young people may be the ones to teach adults cultural knowledge.

socialization The process by which we learn and internalize the rules and patterns of behavior that are affected by culture. This process, which occurs over a long period of time, involves learning and mastering societal and cultural norms, attitudes, values, and belief systems.

socialization agents The people, institutions, and organizations that exist to help ensure that socialization occurs.

uninvolved parents A style of parenting in which parents are often too absorbed in their own lives to respond appropriately to their children and may seem indifferent to them.

InfoTrac College Edition

Use InfoTrac College Edition to search for additional readings on topics of interest to you. For more information on topics in this chapter, use the following as search terms:

acculturation
cross-cultural academic performance
cross-cultural parenting
socialization

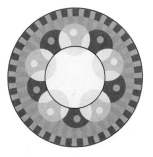

6

Culture and Developmental Processes

Are people born with inherent, biological predispositions to behavioral and cultural differences, or are such differences due entirely to environment and upbringing? What psychological differences are there in childhood and development when people are raised in different cultures? This chapter examines the main question of what kind of psychological differences appear to exist across cultures during infancy and childhood, and throughout development. A considerable amount of cross-cultural research has been conducted on topics such as temperament, attachment, and cognitive and moral development; in this chapter, we review that literature, comparing and contrasting what that literature says in relation to mainstream knowledge. The information presented complements that in the previous chapter; together they provide a comprehensive view of the influence of culture on developmental processes.

Culture and Temperament

As discussed in the previous chapter, the process of socialization starts early, probably from the very first day of life. Some people believe that the biological temperament and predispositions we bring with us into the world at birth are actually part of the socialization process. In other words, the characteristics we are born with determine, to some extent, how our caregivers react and interact with us, initiating the lifelong process of socialization. We begin this review by examining the possibility that children of different cultures are born with different biological predispositions to learn certain cultural practices—that is, the issue of **temperament**.

Traditional Knowledge

Any parent can tell you that no two babies are alike. It is not simply that they look different but that they differ from the very beginning in temperament. Each baby has its own way of being in the world—easygoing or fussy, active or quiet. These qualities of responsiveness to the environment exist from birth and evoke different reactions from people in the baby's world. Temperament is a biologically based style of interacting with the world that exists from birth.

Thomas and Chess (1977) have described three major categories of temperament: easy, difficult, and slow-to-warm-up. **Easy temperament** is defined by a very regular, adaptable, mildly intense style of behavior that is positive and responsive. **Difficult temperament** is an intense, irregular, withdrawing style generally marked by negative moods. **Slow-to-warm-up** infants need time to make transitions in activity and experiences. Though they may withdraw initially or respond negatively, given time and support they will adapt and react positively.

The interaction of a child's temperament with that of the parents, known as **goodness of fit,** seems to be a key to the development of personality. Parental reactions to a child's temperament can promote stability or instability in the child's temperamental responses to the environment. The parents' responses to the child's temperament may also affect subsequent attachment.

Cross-Cultural Studies on Temperament

Several studies have examined whether children of non-American cultures have general styles of temperament that differ from those described for American infants. The implications of differences in temperament, if they exist, are large. If children of other cultures have different temperaments at birth, they will respond to the environment differently. Moreover, they will evoke responses from the environment and caregivers that are different from what Americans would expect. These two fundamental differences—in temperament and environmental response—should produce a fundamental difference in the learning and social experiences of those children, and consequently in their worldview and culture as they grow older. Indeed, Freedman (1974) found that Chinese American babies were calmer and more placid than European American babies or African American babies. When a cloth was placed on their faces covering their noses, the Chinese American babies lay quietly and breathed through their mouths. The other babies turned their heads or tried to pull the cloth off with their hands. A more recent study supports similar cultural differences in temperament between Chinese and Anglo infants. It was found that Chinese infants were significantly less active, less irritable, and less vocal than American and Irish infants (Kagan, Snidman, Arcus, & Reznick, 1994).

Caudill (1988) found that Japanese infants cried less, vocalized less, and were less active than Anglo infants. Freedman (1974) also found similar differences with Japanese American and Navajo babies when compared to European Americans. Likewise, Chisholm (1983) extensively studied Navajo infants and found that they were much calmer than European American infants. Chisholm argues that there is a well-established connection between the condition of the mother during pregnancy (especially high blood pressure levels) and the irritability of the infant. This connection between maternal blood pressure and infant irritability has been found in Malaysian, Chinese, and Aboriginal and white Australian infants, as well as in Navajo infants (Garcia Coll, 1990). Garcia Coll, Sepkoski, and Lester (1981) found that differences in the health of Puerto Rican mothers during pregnancy were related to differences in their infants' temperaments when compared to European American or African American infants. The Puerto Rican babies were alert and did not cry easily. The African American babies scored higher on motor abilities—behaviors involving muscle movement and coordination.

Cross-cultural studies using the Neonatal Behavior Assessment Scale. Much cross-cultural research has been conducted using T. Berry Brazelton's Neonatal Behavior Assessment Scale (NBAS). This instrument, used to assess newborns' behaviors in the first 30 days of life, is thought to give an indication of temperamental characteristics of newborns. Studies all over the world have been conducted with the NBAS. For instance, Saco-Pollit (1989) investigated how altitude may relate to newborn behaviors. She compared Peruvian infants who were raised in high-altitude (in the Andes) and low-altitude (Lima) environments. She reports that in comparison to low-altitude infants, those raised in the Andes were less attentive, less responsive, and less active, and had a more difficult time quieting themselves. The harsh environment of living in the high Andes may have contributed to the newborns' differences. In a study of Nepalese infants, who by Western standards were undernourished, it was found that they were actually more alert and had better motor performance compared to a sample of U.S. infants (Walsh Escarce, 1989). The author hypothesizes that these results may reflect an adaptation on the part of the infant to years of poverty. She also noted that the cultural practice of daily massaging the infant, along with special rituals surrounding the baby, may have contributed to their higher performance on the NBAS.

Research conducted in the United States on Hmong infants in the Midwest, also using the NBAS, found that they were quieter and less irritable than Anglo infants (Muret-Wagstaff & Moore, 1989). These infant behaviors were also correlated with greater maternal sensitivity. The researchers raise an interesting question of how this culture in transition would be reflected in later infant–parent interactions. These studies with the NBAS illuminate how differences in temperament across cultures must not be considered in isolation from the cultural practices of infant caregiving, cultural goals for appropriate infant behaviors, and cultural ideas on the capabilities of infants. These studies also suggest that temperamental differences across cultures are indeed evident, even in infants only a few days after birth.

Temperament and learning culture. The interaction between parents' responses and infant temperament is certainly one of the keys to understanding the development of culture and socialization processes. The quiet temperament and placidity that are notable in infants from Asian and Native American backgrounds are probably further stabilized in later infancy and childhood by the response of the mothers. Navajo and Hopi babies spend long periods of time tightly wrapped in cradle boards; Chinese parents value the harmony that is maintained through emotional restraint (Bond & Wang, 1983). Thus, differences in infant temperament may make it easier for parents of different cultures to engage in parenting styles and behaviors that teach and reinforce their particular cultural practices. Temperament, therefore, may serve as a baseline biological predisposition of the infant that allows this type of learning to occur.

The cultural differences that we find concerning temperament, evident very early in life, may give us a clue to what kinds of personalities and behaviors are valued in a culture as an adult. For instance, in Japan, nonreactivity (which is related to a general suppression of emotionality) is more valued than in Western cultures, where higher levels of reactivity (expression of emotionality) are more acceptable. Thus, the differences in temperament we see in the first few days of life may be a reflection of what each culture values concerning appropriate ways of acting and being (Lewis, 1989). As stated earlier, a child's temperament and the environmental response to his or her temperamental style will most likely result in differences in the learning and social experiences of those children, and consequently in their behaviors, personalities, and worldviews as they become adults.

The goodness of fit between temperament and culture.   Research on Masai infants in Kenya has corroborated the importance of the goodness of fit between an infant's temperament and his or her environment. In other words, the adaptiveness of an infant's temperamental style to his or her development may be specific to the immediate environment. Based on Thomas and Chess's temperament classifications, deVries (1987, 1989) identified difficult and easy Masai infants and followed them for several years. What was considered a "difficult" temperament by Western standards became a protective factor against malnutrition during a time of drought. Those infants who were classified as difficult had a greater chance of survival compared to their easy counterparts. DeVries explains this surprising finding by suggesting that the difficult infants, who were very active and fussy, demanded and consequently received more feeding and caring from their mothers. In sum, a particular type of temperament may be adaptive in one culture and maladaptive in another. His findings highlight the need to consider the cultural context in analyzing the role of a child's characteristics in his or her development.

These findings also caution us about how we label the different temperamental styles. For instance, infants in the United States who have a "difficult" temperament have been found to be at risk for later behavior problems (Caspi, Henry, McGee, Moffitt, & Silva, 1995; Graham, Rutter, & George, 1973). However, having a "difficult" temperament in an extreme situation (as in the context of a life-threatening drought) may be protective, rather than a risk factor, improving the infant's chances of survival. We have to remember that the way we interpret an infant's dispositions and behaviors must be considered in relation to the specific culture; the same dispositions and behaviors may have different meanings when placed in a different cultural context.

Sources behind temperamental differences.   Why does temperament differ across cultures? It is possible that differences in temperament reflect differences in genetics and in reproductive histories. Thus, environmental and cultural pressures over generations may have helped to produce minor biological differences in infants through a functionally adaptive process. In addition, the cultural experiences of the mother during pregnancy, including diet and other culture-related practices, may contribute to a prenatal environment that modifies an infant's biological composition to correspond to those cultural practices. The fetal environment is one context where significant stimulation occurs; however, the nature and consequences of this stimulation are largely unknown (Emory & Toomey, 1991).

Whatever the causal mechanism, temperamental differences that are evident from birth contribute to the personality differences we observe in adults of different cultures. Therefore, it is important to understand the magnitude of their contributions as building blocks in the development of adult members of the cultures of the world. Future research in this area should focus on the cultural practices and actual behaviors of people of different cultural groups, and examine the relationship between those and infant temperament.

In sum, cross-cultural research suggests that there are group differences across cultures in infants' and children's temperaments. These differences may be due to multiple factors—what temperamental styles are valued in each culture, specific environmental demands (such as living in poverty or in a high-altitude environment), or physiological aspects of the mother (for example, higher blood pressure). Examining the interaction between the child's temperament and the caregiving environment into which he or she is born can help us understand the process of how we eventually learn to internalize the values, attitudes, and behaviors appropriate to our culture.

Culture and Attachment

Attachment refers to the special bond that develops between the infant and its primary caregiver. Many psychologists believe that the quality of attachment has lifelong effects on our relationships with loved ones. Attachment provides the child with emotional security. Once attached, babies are distressed by separation from their mothers (separation distress or anxiety). The studies on attachment in rhesus monkeys by the Harlows (Harlow & Harlow, 1969) highlighted the importance of contact and physical comfort in the development of attachment.

Bowlby's Theory of Attachment

Bowlby's (1969) evolutionary theory of attachment states that infants must have a preprogrammed, biological basis for becoming attached to their caregivers. This innate behavioral repertoire includes smiling and cooing to elicit physical attachment behaviors on the part of the mother. He argues that the attachment relationship between caregiver and child functioned as a survival strategy: Infants had a greater chance of survival if they remained close to the mother for comfort and protection.

Attachment as a survival strategy is illustrated in a study in Nigeria of Hausa infants and their caregivers (Marvin, VanDevender, Iwanaga, LeVine, & LeVine, 1977). The researchers report that the attachment relationship protected infants from the dangers of their environment, which included open fires and tools and utensils that were easily accessible. Infants explored their environment, but only when they were in close proximity to an attachment figure. Furthermore, True (1994) found that secure attachment functioned as a protective factor against infant malnutrition among the Dogon of Mali.

Ainsworth's Classification System of Attachment

Based on Bowlby's attachment theory, Mary Ainsworth's (1967, 1977) famous study in Uganda led to the tripartite classification system of attachment relationships between infants and their mothers. Based on her careful observations of 28 mother–infant pairs over a span of one year, she described three attachment styles: secure, ambivalent, and avoidant. The latter two attachment styles she labeled as "insecurely attached." She later replicated her results in a sample of Boston mothers and their infants. In her samples, she found that approximately 57% of mothers and infants were classified as securely attached, 25% as ambivalent, and 18% as avoidant.

Some studies from other cultures have found a similar distribution of attachment classifications; others have found considerable differences. Some attachment styles are not reported in certain cultures; for example, no avoidant infants were found in a sample of Dogon of Mali (True, 1994). In other countries (such as Israel), higher percentages of certain attachment styles (ambivalent) have been found (Sagi et al., 1994, 1997).

Cross-Cultural Studies on Attachment

Since Ainsworth's early studies, hundreds of studies of attachment have been conducted in cultures all over the world. Van IJzendoorn and Sagi (1999) outline some important cross-cultural issues that Ainsworth's Uganda study raised: the universality of the infant–mother attachment relationship and the tripartite classification system; whether maternal sensitivity is a necessary antecedent of attachment; and what aspects of attachment development are culture-specific.

Mothers of **securely attached** infants are described as sensitive, warm, and more positive in their emotional expression. Mothers of **avoidant** children, who shun their mothers, are suspected of being intrusive and overstimulating. **Ambivalent** children are uncertain in their response to their mothers, going back and forth between seeking and shunning her attention. These mothers have been characterized as insensitive and less involved. These mothers have also been characterized as being inconsistent in their responsiveness. In a review of 65 studies of attachment, parent sensitivity was related to security of attachment; however, this association was rather modest (DeWolff & van IJzendoorn, 1997). More cross-cultural studies on the antecedents of secure attachment are needed before definitive conclusions can be drawn.

Cross-Cultural Validity of Assessing Attachment

The cross-cultural validity of the methods of assessing attachment and the meaning of the attachment classifications themselves have been questioned. The meaning of the Strange Situation, a widely used measure of attachment, has been challenged. In the Strange Situation, infants are separated from their mothers for a brief period of time. The quality of attachment is derived partly from an assessment of the infant's reaction to the separation and subsequent reunion with the mother. However, the meaning of the separation may differ across cultures (Takahashi, 1990). As noted earlier, Japanese infants are rarely separated from their mothers, and the separation during the Strange Situation may represent a highly unusual situation that may mean something different for Japanese infants and their mothers than for U.S. infants and their mothers.

Other researchers studying Chinese infants and their mothers question the validity of the avoidant category as an indication of insecure attachment (Hu & Meng, 1996, cited in van IJzendoorn & Sagi, 1999). The researchers state that Chinese mothers emphasize early independence in their infants and, at the same time, stress their reliance on nonparental (usually the grandparent) caregivers. These factors, rather than an insecure relationship between the mother and her infant, may be responsible for findings of avoidant attachment. It may also be the case that subtle attachment behaviors (for instance, those that characterize avoidant relationships) are difficult even for well-trained coders to observe in infants from different cultures (Crittenden, 2000; van IJzendoorn & Sagi, 1999).

Is Secure Attachment a Universal Ideal?

In the United States, secure attachment is assumed to be the ideal. The very term that Ainsworth and colleagues chose to describe this type of attachment, and the negative terms used to describe others, reflects this underlying bias. Some research suggests that cultures may differ, however, in their notion of "ideal" attachment. For example, German mothers value and promote early independence and regard avoidant attachment as the ideal. German parents see the "securely" attached child as "spoiled" (Grossmann, Grossmann, Spangler, Suess, & Unzner, 1985). Of Israeli children who are raised on a kibbutz (collective farm), half display anxious ambivalent attachments, and only a third appear to be securely attached (Sagi et al., 1985). Children raised in traditional Japanese families are also characterized by a high rate of anxious ambivalent attachment, with practically no avoidant types (Miyake, Chen, & Campos, 1985). These traditional mothers seldom leave their children (such as with babysitters) and foster a strong sense of dependence in their children (which in itself is curious, because studies of U.S. culture have shown that ambivalent infants are generally associated with mothers who are less involved). This dependence supports the traditional cultural ideal of family loyalty. In nontraditional Japanese families, in which the mother may have a career, attachment patterns are similar to those in the United States (Durrett, Otaki, & Richards, 1984). Crittenden (2000) suggests that we should stop using value-laden terms such as "secure" and "insecure" in describing the attachment relationship. Instead, she proposes that it may be more useful to describe the attachment relationship as "adaptive" or "maladaptive" to the specific context, which would take into consideration how cultures differ in the particular attachment strategy that may be most appropriate for that culture.

However, other studies suggest that securely attached infants may indeed be the ideal across cultures. For instance, in a study involving experts (in the field of attachment) and mothers from China, Colombia, Germany, Israel, Japan, and the United States, Posada and his colleagues (1995) asked the experts to rate the characteristics of a securely attached child, and mothers to rate the characteristics of the ideal child. The researchers report that in each of the countries, the characteristics of the securely attached child were closely associated with the characteristics of the ideal child. Thus, even cultures that vary on the dimension of individualism and collectivism may have similar views on the importance of secure attachment.

A review of 14 studies on attachment from Africa, China, Israel, and Japan reports that in each of these samples the majority of infants and their mothers were classified as being securely attached (van IJzendoorn & Sagi, 1999). Furthermore, there is evidence that 7- to 9-month-old infants in every culture studied show distress when they are separated from their primary caregiver (Grossman & Grossman, 1990). Thus, attachment between infants and their mothers is considered a universal phenomenon. What may differ across cultures, however, is the specific attachment behaviors exhibited by the infant that indicate secure or insecure attachment (van IJzendoorn & Sagi, 1999).

In sum, the vast literature accumulated concerning attachment in different cultures suggests that attachment between infants and their caregivers is a universal phenomenon. There is also some evidence that the "secure" attachment relationship may be preferred in many different cultures. However, this is an ongoing debate. As stated earlier, researchers such as Crittenden (2000) argue that viewing attachment through the lens of being "adaptive" and "maladaptive" may be more useful than using the evaluative terms "secure" and "insecure." She defines adaptive attachments as relationships that promote the maximum level of safety for the child within a specific cultural context. This would then allow us to define an "optimal" relationship between infant and caregiver as one that may be achieved in different ways, under different circumstances, in different cultures.

Attachment and Child Development

Why is there such a keen interest in the development of a secure attachment to a parent? One reason is that attachment styles may predict child competence. Takahashi (1990) found that at 2 years old, securely attached Japanese infants, compared to resistantly attached infants, complied more with their mother's directions and demands, showed more curiosity about a new object, and demonstrated more social competence in how they related to unfamiliar peers. Security of attachment, however, did not predict infant competence in the third year of life. The long-term effects of the attachment relationship have been questioned. More longitudinal research that considers the stability of the caregiving environment (which is usually not measured), as well as the attachment relationship, is needed (van IJzendoorn, 1996).

Interestingly, the attachment relationship that an infant has with different caregivers may have implications for different areas of development. For instance, Gusii infants in Kenya who were securely attached to their *nonmaternal* caregivers scored higher on the Bayley Scales of Infant Development, which includes an assessment of cognitive development, than their insecurely attached counterparts. In this sample, an infant's security of attachment to his or her *mother* did not predict cognitive development. What the infant–mother attachment relationship did predict was the nutritional or health status of the infants: Infants who were securely attached to their mothers scored higher on nutritional status than insecurely attached infants. Thus, the various attachment relationships that infants experience may affect their development in different ways (Kermoian & Leiderman, 1986).

Studies involving an African tribe of forest-dwelling foragers known as the Efe show a very different pattern from the one psychologists have come to accept as necessary to healthy attachment (Tronick, Morelli, & Ivey, 1992). Efe infants are cared for by a variety of people in addition to their mothers; the time spent with caregivers other than their mothers increases from 39% at 3 weeks to 60% by 18 weeks. They are always within earshot and sight of about ten people. They have close emotional ties to many people other than their mothers and spend very little time with their fathers. However, when infants are 1 year old, they clearly show a preference for being cared for by their mothers and become upset when left by their mothers. At this age, then, mothers once again become the primary caretakers. Thus, there is evidence that attachment to a primary caregiver is still formed, and that children are emotionally healthy despite having multiple caregivers. The Efe have large extended families, and these families are permanent parts of the growing Efe children's lives.

Studies by Miyake (1993) and his colleagues on infant attachment patterns in Japan summarize and highlight many of these points. In numerous studies on this topic, Miyake has reported finding no avoidantly attached children. In contrast to the United States, where most attachments are characterized as secure, attachments in Japan are overwhelmingly characterized as ambivalent, indicating a strong desire to prevent separation (and thus to foster dependence between mother and infant). Some of their other studies, moreover, have demonstrated the close relationship between temperament and attachment. These researchers measured irritability in response to interruption of sucking—a common measure of temperament—during the 2nd and 5th days of life. They then classified the neonate's cries as either smooth (fast rise time, brief duration, quick quieting) or effortful (prone to interruption, raucous in quality, and with facial and vocal expressions disorganized). They found that the nature of these cries in the 2nd and 5th days of life predicted attachment one year later, with smooth criers being associated with secure attachments and effortful criers associated with ambivalent attachment (the Japanese mode). Other studies, however, do not find a relationship between temperament and attachment style (for example, Bates, Maslin, & Frankel, 1985; Vaughn, Lefever, Seifer, & Barglow, 1989). Thus, more work needs to be done before offering conclusive statements concerning the link between temperament and attachment.

Temperament and Attachment: A Summary

Much still needs to be done to understand the attachment patterns in other cultures and the relationship among cultural milieu, infant temperament, and attachment style. Notions about the quality of attachment and the processes by which it occurs are qualitative judgments made from the perspective of each culture. What is considered an optimal style of attachment may not necessarily be optimal across all cultures. Each culture has different but not necessarily better values than others. Furthermore, because nonparental caretaking is either the norm or a frequent form in most cultures (Weisner & Gallimore, 1977), examining the attachment "network" instead of focusing solely on dyads, as has traditionally been done, is of crucial importance (van IJzendoorn & Sagi, 1999).

The information presented so far concerning temperament and attachment relationships speaks to just a few of the many ways in which enculturation occurs around the world. Children may be born with differences in biological predispositions or temperament that may make it easier for them to engage in the cultural learning that occurs throughout socialization and enculturation. Differences in attachment provide learning platforms for children that allow them to achieve developmental goals fostered by their particular cultures. Thus, the temperamental characteristics that you were born with, your caregiver's responses to your temperamental style, and the resultant attachment relationship you develop with your caregiver together play important roles in how you come to acquire the aspects of your specific culture.

We turn now to examine cultural similarities and differences in two major developmental processes: cognitive and moral development. These topics are of great interest to developmental psychologists, both mainstream and cross-cultural, and speak to the pervasive influence of culture on developmental processes.

Cognitive Development

Piaget's Theory

Cognitive development is a specialty in psychology that studies how thinking skills develop over time. Theories of cognitive development have traditionally focused on the period from infancy to adulthood. The theory that has dominated this field for the past half-century is Piaget's stage theory of cognitive development.

Piaget based his theories on observations of Swiss children. He found that these children tended to solve problems quite differently at different ages. To explain these differences, Piaget (1952) proposed that children progress through four stages as they grow from infancy into adolescence.

1. **Sensorimotor stage.** This stage typically lasts from birth to about 2 years of age. In this stage, children understand the world through their sensory perceptions and motor behaviors. In other words, children understand by perceiving and doing. The most important achievement of this stage is the capability to use mental symbols to represent objects and events. The acquisition of object permanence—that is, knowing that objects exist even when they cannot be seen—illustrates this achievement. Early in this stage, children appear to assume that when a toy or other object is hidden (for example, when a ball rolls under a sofa), it ceases to exist. Later in this stage, children will search under the sofa for the lost ball, demonstrating that they have come to understand that objects exist continuously.

Other cognitive developments that also depend on the development of mental representation typical of this stage include deferred imitation and language acquisition. These developments have important implications for later cognitive development and enculturation. Imitation is an important cognitive component of observational learning, and language skills are necessary to ensure proper communication of verbal socialization processes.

2. **Preoperational stage.** This stage lasts from about 2 to 6 or 7 years of age. Piaget described children's thinking at this stage in terms of five characteristics: conservation, centration, irreversibility, egocentrism, and animism. **Conservation** is the awareness (or in this stage, the lack of awareness) that physical quantities remain the same even when they change shape or appearance. **Centration** is the tendency to focus on a single aspect of a problem. **Irreversibility** is the inability to imagine "undoing" a process. **Egocentrism** is the inability to step into another's shoes and understand the other person's point of view. **Animism**

is the belief that all things, including inanimate objects, are alive. For example, children in the preoperational stage may regard a book lying on its side as "tired" or "needing a rest," or they may think that the moon is following them. Children at this stage do not yet think in a logical and systematic manner.

3. **Concrete operations stage.** This stage lasts from about 6 or 7 years until about 11 years of age. During this stage, children acquire new thinking skills to work with actual objects and events. They are able to imagine undoing an action, and they can focus on more than one feature of a problem. Children also begin to understand that there are different points of view from their own. This new awareness helps children master the principle of conservation. A child in the concrete operations stage will understand that six apples are always six apples, regardless of how they are grouped or spaced, and that the amount of clay does not change as a lump is molded into different shapes. This ability is not present in the preoperational stage. However, instead of thinking a problem through, children in this stage tend to rely on trial-and-error strategies.

4. **Formal operations stage.** This stage extends from around 11 years of age through adulthood. During this stage, individuals develop the ability to think logically about abstract concepts, such as peace, freedom, and justice. Individuals also become more systematic and thoughtful in their approach to problem solving.

The transition from one stage to another is often gradual, as children develop new abilities alongside earlier ways of thinking. Thus, the behavior of some children may represent a "blend" of two stages when they are in a period of transition from one to the other.

Piaget hypothesized that two primary mechanisms are responsible for movement from one stage to the next: assimilation and accommodation. **Assimilation** is the process of fitting new ideas into a preexisting understanding of the world. **Accommodation** refers to the process of changing one's understanding of the world to accommodate ideas that conflict with existing concepts.

Piaget believed that the stages were universal, and that progression through these stages was invariant in order. According to Piaget, knowledge is constructed through the interactions between the biological maturation of the child and his or her actions and experiences with the physical and social environment. Because there are similarities across cultures in how individuals mature physically and in how they act on the physical world (for example, in every culture individuals ask questions, exchange information, and work together), the stages are thought to be universal. The richness of Piaget's theory has prompted a multitude of studies of cognitive development in cultures all over the world. One finds it difficult to think of another theorist who has sparked so much comparative cross-cultural research.

Piaget's Theory in Cross-Cultural Perspective

Cross-cultural research on Piaget's theory has focused on four central questions. The findings to date show an interesting blend of cultural similarities and differences in various aspects of cognitive development that parallel Piaget's stages.

Do Piaget's stages occur in the same order in different cultures?   Studies that have addressed this question have convincingly demonstrated that Piaget's stages occur in the same fixed order in other cultures. For instance, a large cross-cultural survey that tested children in Great Britain, Australia, Greece, and Pakistan (Shayer, Demetriou, & Perez, 1988) found that schoolchildren in these different societies performed Piagetian tasks within the same stage of concrete operations. We do not find cultures in which 4-year-olds typically lack an awareness of object permanency or 5-year-olds understand the principle of conservation. Thus, we know that children from very different cultures do indeed learn groups of Piagetian tasks in a similar order.

Are the ages that Piaget associated with each stage of development the same in all cultures?   Studies have found surprising cultural variations in the ages at which children in different societies typically reach the third and fourth Piagetian stages. In some cases, the difference may be as much as 5 or 6 years. However, it has often been overlooked that children may have the potential to solve tasks sooner than their answers would indicate. For example, a child in the concrete operations stage will typically give the first answer that comes to mind during a test. If the child comes from a culture in which he or she has had practice performing the task in question, this answer is likely to be correct. However, a child who has never thought about the concept before may well utter the wrong answer and only later realize the mistake. When researchers checked for this possibility by repeating tests a second time at the end of testing sessions, they found that many children corrected their previous answers on the second attempt (Dasen, 1982; Dasen, Lavallee, & Retschitzki, 1979; Dasen, Ngini, & Lavallee, 1979). Thus, it is important to remember that performance on a task may not reveal actual cognitive competence or ability.

Are there cultural variations within, rather than between, Piaget's stages?   There is considerable cultural variation in the order in which children acquire specific skills within Piaget's stages. In a comparative study of tribal children (the Inuit of Canada, the Baoul of Africa, and the Aranda of Australia), half of all Inuit children tested solved a spatial task at the age of 7 years, half of the Aranda solved it at 9 years, and the Baoul did not reach the halfway point until the age of 12 (Dasen, 1975). On a test of the conservation of liquids, however, the order changed dramatically: half of the Baoul children solved the problem when they were 8 years old, the Inuit at 9 years, and the Aranda at 12 years. Why did the ages at which these children could perform the same task vary so much? The Inuit and Aranda children live in nomadic societies, where children need to learn spatial skills early because their families are constantly moving. The Baoul children live in a settled society, where they seldom travel but often fetch water and store grain. The skills these children used in their everyday lives seem to have affected the order in which they were able to solve Piagetian tasks within the concrete operations stage.

Do non-Western cultures regard scientific reasoning as the ultimate developmental end point?   Piaget's theory assumes that the scientific reasoning associated with formal operations is the universal end point of cognitive development—that the thinking most valued in Swiss and other Western societies (formal operations) is the yardstick by which all cultures should be judged. Because Piaget considered scientific reasoning to be the ultimate human achievement, his stage theory is designed to trace the steps by which people arrive at scientific thinking. This perspective has been widely accepted within North American psychology, and generally by the North American public, at least until very recently.

Cross-cultural research indicates that this perspective is by no means universally shared. Different societies value and reward different skills and behaviors. For example, until recently, the most respected scholars in traditional Islamic societies were religious leaders and poets. Although the Islamic educational system included science and mathematics, its primary goal was not to train people in the scientific method but to transmit faith, general knowledge, and a deep appreciation for poetry and literature. People from such cultures could be expected to be at a disadvantage when confronted with advanced Piagetian tasks, which are drawn almost exclusively from Western physics, chemistry, and mathematics.

Many cultures around the world do not share the conviction that abstract, hypothetical thought processes are the ultimate or desired end point in the cognitive development process. Many cultures, for example, consider cognitive development to be more relational—involving the thinking skills and processes needed to engage successfully in interpersonal contexts. What North Americans refer to as "common sense," rather than cognitive development per se, is considered a much more desired outcome in many cultures. This value structure is especially apparent in more collectivistic and group-oriented cultures, in which high-level, individualistic, abstract thinking is often frowned upon.

Piaget's Theory: Summary and Discussion

Cross-cultural studies of Piaget's stage of formal operations have found that in some cultures, very few people are able to complete fourth-stage Piagetian tasks. Does this mean that entire cultures are suspended at a lower stage of cognitive development? To answer this question, we must first ask whether Piagetian tasks are a culturally appropriate way of measuring an advanced stage of cognitive development. In fact, those tasks may not be meaningful in other cultures. Besides the issue of cultural appropriateness, there is also the issue of what is being tested. Tests of formal operations may tell us whether people can solve a narrow range of scientific problems, but they do not tell us whether people in different cultures develop advanced cognitive skills in areas other than those selected by Piaget.

We can say with certainty, however, that people who have not attended high school or college in a Westernized school system perform very poorly on tests of formal operations (Laurendeau-Bendavid, 1977; Shea, 1985). These findings again raise the question of the degree to which Piagetian tasks depend on previous knowledge and cultural values rather than cognitive skills. It is also important to remember the wide range of differences in cognitive development within a given culture. These within-culture differences make it extremely difficult to draw valid conclusions or inferences about differences in cognitive development between cultures. For example, not only do members of non-Western cultures have difficulty with tests of formal operations, but many adults in North American society also have such difficulties. Scientific reasoning does not appear to be as common in Western societies as Piaget thought, and it is frequently limited to special activities. Individuals who apply scientific logic to a problem on the job may reason quite differently in other situations.

Because large numbers of people are unable to complete Piagetian tasks of formal operations, it has not been possible to demonstrate the universality of the fourth stage of Piaget's theory of cognitive development. It is possible that most adults do possess the ability to complete Piagetian tasks but lack either motivation or knowledge of how to demonstrate such ability. To demonstrate success on a task purporting to measure some aspect of cognitive ability or intelligence, it is crucial that the test-taker and the test-maker agree on what is being assessed. Cultural differences in the desired end point of cognitive development, as well as in definitions of intelligence (see Chapter 4), contribute to this dilemma.

Other Theories of Cognitive Development

Although Piaget's theory is the most influential theory in the United States, it is only one of many stage theories that have been proposed by Western social scientists. The 18th-century German philosopher Hegel, for example, ranked all societies on an evolutionary scale based on a classification of religious beliefs, with Christianity at the top. Stage theories multiplied in the 19th century after Darwin's theory of evolution became well known. Several writers (for example, Morgan, 1877; Spencer, 1876; Tylor, 1865) proposed that humanity had progressed from savagery to civilization in a series of stages.

One of the most influential stage theories of the early 20th century was proposed by the French philosopher Levy-Bruhl (1910, 1922, 1949). In common with earlier scholars, Levy-Bruhl drew most of his conclusions from material related to the mystical and religious beliefs of non-Western peoples. Levy-Bruhl put forth the **great divide theory,** separating the thought of Westerners from that of people who lived in primitive societies. He described non-Western peoples as having a distinct way of thinking, which he attributed to the effects of culture. According to Levy-Bruhl, non-Westerners were not bothered by logical contradictions, and they lacked a clear sense of individual identity.

More recently, some scientists (Goody, 1968, 1977; Hippler, 1980; Luria, 1976) have put forward new great divide theories. Although these researchers have various names for the two groups, their division of humanity breaks down along similar lines. In all these theories, the cultural development or thought of non-Westerners is usually judged as deficient or inferior to that of Europeans.

Several points need to be made about these theories. First, it is probably more than coincidence that stage theories produced by Westerners judge people from other cultures (and minorities within their own countries) in terms of how closely they resemble Westerners, thereby placing themselves at a relatively superior level of development. The popularity of stage theories in the 19th century, for example, coincided with the colonial imperialism of the period. Stage theories provided justification for imposing European rule around the world, based on the demonstrated superiority of European civilization.

Other problems also existed. Stage theorists persisted in evaluating the rationality of non-Westerners in terms of their magical and religious beliefs, while the rationality of Western beliefs was usually not questioned. Levy-Bruhl's theory has been fiercely attacked over the years by field anthropologists who have objected to both his methodology and his conclusions. Levy-Bruhl based his work on stories told by missionaries and travelers, many of whom could barely speak native languages.

But Westerners are not the only ones who have ethnocentric assumptions. Cross-cultural studies have shown that people from many cultures prefer their own groups and rate them more positively than they rate outsiders. For example, a study that compared what people in 30 different East African societies thought of themselves and others demonstrated that members of each society rated themselves highly and judged outsiders to be "advanced" when they were culturally similar to their own group (Brewer & Campbell, 1976).

This brings us back to Piaget's theory, which has several strong points. Piaget's theory is considerably more sophisticated than earlier theories. By devising tasks to measure concepts in an experimental setting, Piaget established a new standard by which to gauge cognitive development, one that appears to be less vulnerable to ethnocentric bias. Piaget's tests can be, and have been, administered cross-culturally, with clear-cut results that do not rest on the subjective beliefs of the researcher (although the choice of research instruments and the interpretation of data are still subject to researcher bias). Still, cognitive development is complicated, and it is unlikely that such tasks can capture all of its complexity.

Moral Reasoning

Another area of development crucial to our becoming functional adults in society and culture concerns moral judgments and reasoning. As they grow, children develop increasingly complex ways of understanding their world. These cognitive changes also bring about changes in their understanding of moral judgments. Why something is good or bad changes from the young child's interpretation of reward and punishment conditions to principles of right and wrong.

Morality and culture share a very close relationship. Moral principles and ethics provide guidelines for people's behaviors with regard to what is appropriate and what is not. These guidelines are products of a specific culture and society, handed down from one generation to the next. Morality is thus heavily influenced by the underlying, subjective, and implicit culture in which it is embedded. Morality also serves as the basis of laws, which are formalized guidelines for appropriate and inappropriate behavior. In this way, culture also affects the laws of a society. For these and other reasons, morality occupies a special place in our understanding of culture and cultural differences.

Our knowledge of the development of moral reasoning skills, at least in the United States, has been heavily influenced by the work of a psychologist named Lawrence Kohlberg. His model of moral reasoning and judgment is based in large part on Piaget's model of cognitive development.

Kohlberg's Theory of Morality

Kohlberg's theory of moral development (1976, 1984) proposes three general stages of development of moral reasoning skills. (Kohlberg further divided each of these three general stages into two stages, for a total of six substages of moral development.)

1. **Preconventional morality** involves compliance with rules to avoid punishment and gain rewards. A person operating at this level of morality would condemn stealing as bad because the thief might get caught and be thrown in jail or otherwise punished. The focus of the justification is on the punishment (or reward) associated with the action.
2. **Conventional morality** involves conformity to rules that are defined by others' approval or society's rules. A person operating at this level of morality would judge stealing as wrong because it is against the law and others in society generally disapprove of it.
3. **Postconventional morality** involves moral reasoning on the basis of individual principles and conscience. A person operating at this level of morality would judge stealing within the context either of societal or community needs or of his or her own personal moral beliefs and values, which supercede perceived societal and community needs.

Gilligan (1982) has challenged Kohlberg's theory by suggesting that its stages are biased toward the particular way in which males as opposed to females view relationships. She argues that male moral reasoning is based on abstract justice, whereas female moral reasoning is based on obligations and responsibilities. These two types of moral reasoning have been called "morality of justice" versus "morality of caring." Despite the fervor of the debate, however, reviews of the research seem to indicate few gender differences in moral reasoning (Walker, 1984, 1991). It appears that variations between males and females in moral reasoning can be explained by other variables, such as education, occupation, or types of issues under consideration. Cross-cultural research may shed more light on this issue.

Cross-Cultural Studies of Moral Reasoning

The universality or cultural specificity of moral principles and reasoning has been an area of interest for anthropologists and psychologists alike. A number of anthropological ethnographies have examined the moral principles and domains of different cultures (see review by Shweder, Mahapatra, & Miller, 1987). Many of these works have complemented and challenged traditional American views of morality, and for good reason. Culture, morality, ethics, and law share a close relationship.

The findings from a number of cross-cultural studies suggest that many aspects of Kohlberg's theory of morality are universal. Snarey (1985), for example, reviewed 45 studies involving participants in 27 countries and concluded that Kohlberg's first two stages could be regarded as universal. Others have reached similar conclusions, including Ma (1988), in a study involving Hong Kong and mainland Chinese as well as British participants; Ma and Cheung (1996), in a study involving Hong Kong, mainland Chinese, British, and Americans; and Hau and Lew (1989), in a study of Hong Kong Chinese participants.

However, a number of cross-cultural studies on moral reasoning raise questions about the universal generalizability of Kohlberg's higher stages. One of the underlying assumptions of Kohlberg's theory is that moral reasoning on the basis of individual principles and conscience, regardless of societal laws or cultural customs, represents the highest level of moral reasoning. This assumption is grounded in the cultural milieu in which Kohlberg developed his theory, which had its roots in studies involving American males in the midwestern United States in the 1950s and 1960s. Although democratic notions of individualism and unique, personal conscience may have been appropriate to describe his samples at that time and place, it is not clear whether those same notions represent universal moral principles applicable to all people of all cultures.

In fact, some researchers have criticized Kohlberg's theory for harboring such cultural biases (Bronstein & Paludi, 1988). Miller and Bersoff (1992) compared the responses to a moral judgment task by respondents in India and the United States. The Indian subjects, both children and adults, considered not helping someone a moral transgression more than did the American subjects, regardless of the life-threatening nature of the situation or whether the person in need was related. These researchers interpreted the cultural differences as having to do with values of affiliation and justice, suggesting that Indians are taught a broader sense of social responsibility—individual responsibility to help a needy person.

More recent evidence suggests that Chinese and Icelandic children differ in a way similar to the differences between Hindus and Americans concerning moral judgments (Keller, Edelstein, Schmid, Fang, & Fang, 1998). More specifically, Chinese children emphasized altruism and relationships when reasoning about moral dilemmas, whereas Icelandic children emphasized contractual and self-interest considerations. The issue of interpersonal responsiveness that

Miller and Bersoff (1992) and Keller et al. (1998) raised is related to Gilligan's (1982) claims of gender bias in U.S. studies. It is entirely possible that Gilligan's findings were influenced by cultural as well as gender differences.

Snarey's (1985) review mentioned earlier also concluded that moral reasoning at the higher stages is much more culture-specific than Kohlberg originally suggested. Other reviews of the cross-cultural literature by Bergling (1981) and Edwards (1981) reached similar conclusions. Kohlberg's theory, as well as the methodology for scoring moral stages according to verbal reasoning, may not recognize higher levels of morality as defined in other cultures. Should different cultures define those higher levels of morality along totally different dimensions, those differences would imply profound differences in people's judgments of moral and ethical appropriateness. Fundamental differences in the bases underlying morality and ethics across cultures are not at all impossible, given that they feed and are fed by subjective culture. Above all, those fundamental differences in morality as a function of culture form the basis for the possibility of major intercultural conflicts.

In order to better understand cultural differences in morality, researchers have highlighted the importance of the particular social structure and environment. For instance, Miller (2001) has argued that "the understanding of social structure entailed in Stage [substage] 4 and higher on the Kohlbergian scheme has relevance primarily in contexts that are closely tied to state or national governments, a finding that may explain, at least in part, the association observed cross-culturally between higher levels of Kohlbergian moral stage development and processes of modernization" (p. 159).

Miller (2001) also points out the need to consider other perspectives on morality that are overlooked in traditional theories of morality. She describes "moralities of community" that emphasize interpersonal relationships and community. For instance, in China, the concept of *jen*, which connotes love and filial piety, contributes to the way Chinese individuals view morality (Ma, 1997). In response to Kohlberg's moral dilemmas, Chinese individuals tend to emphasize the importance of filial piety—respecting and honoring parents and fulfilling their wishes—when judging what is right or wrong. Concerning Hindu Indians, Miller observes that "whereas European Americans tend to approach morality as freely given commitments or matters or personal choice . . . Hindu Indians tend to view interpersonal responsibilities as matters of moral duty that extend across a broader range of need and role situations" (p. 162). Miller also describes "moralities of divinity," in which religious beliefs and spirituality are central to moral development. For instance, Algerians' responses to Kohlberg's moral dilemmas are based on the belief that God is the creator and supreme authority of the universe (Bouhmama, 1984). In another example, fundamental Baptists in the United States consider divorce morally wrong based on their beliefs concerning the relationship between God, the church, and human relationships (Jensen, 1997).

One recent study exemplifies how the examination of morality at different levels of abstraction—from internalized ideals to actual behaviors—may be important to understanding cultural similarities and differences in moral judgment. In this study (Carlo, Koller, Eisenberg, DaSilva, & Frohlich, 1996), researchers examined prosocial moral reasoning in Brazilian and American adolescents. In addition, they assessed actual prosocial behaviors through peer ratings. In both cultures, age and gender differences in prosocial moral reasoning were the same, as was the relationship between prosocial moral reasoning and prosocial behaviors. There were, however, cultural differences in internalized moral reasoning, with American adolescents scoring higher than Brazilian adolescents. These findings suggest that cultural similarities and differences in moral reasoning and behavior may be explained by taking into account different levels of morality than are being examined. Future cross-cultural studies will need to incorporate such a multilevel view of morality to investigate similarities and differences in the same groups of participants across a broad range of morality-related psychological phenomena.

Other Developmental Processes

Cross-cultural research on psychological processes in development continues to be one of the most popular and thoroughly studied areas of the field, for good reason. This research offers important insights into the question of just how the differences observed in adults in many other studies over the years have come to be. In seeking to explain how and why cultural differences occur among adults, psychologists, mainstream and otherwise, have turned to developmental research to explicate the causes and contexts of the ontogenesis of cultural differences.

The past decade has witnessed a renewed interest in cross-cultural developmental research, no doubt due in large part to the increased interest in culture in all areas of psychology. This research has spanned many processes related to development, including future-oriented goals and commitments (Nurmi, Poole, & Seginer, 1995; Nurmi, Liiceanu, & Liberska, 1999), appraisal processes (Dalal, Sharma, & Bisht, 1983; DiMartino, 1994), social expectations (Rotherram-Borus & Petrie, 1996), affective and romantic relationships in adolescence (Takahashi, 1990; Takahashi & Majima, 1994; Coates, 1999), political formation in adolescence (ter Bogt, Meeus, Raaijmakers, & Vollebergh, 2001), task persistence (Blinco, 1992), preschoolers' responses to conflict and distress (Zahn-Waxler, Friedman, Cole, Mizuta, & Hiruma, 1996), children's social pretend play and social competence (Farver, Kim, & Lee-Shin, 2000; LaFreniere et al., 2002), coping (Olah, 1995; Seiffge-Krenke & Shulman, 1990), and social interaction (Farver & Howes, 1988). Other studies examining other developmental topics no doubt exist as well. Collectively, these studies highlight both similarities and differences in development across cultures, and pave the way for exciting new research in these areas in the future.

Conclusion

In this chapter, we have seen how culture produces similarities as well as differences in various areas of development, such as cognition and moral reasoning. The developmental research presented here provides a comprehensive view of how culture influences a number of developmental psychological processes. Still, much work remains to be done. In particular, cross-cultural developmental work has focused largely on infants and children, but mainstream psychology has come to recognize the importance of developmental processes throughout the life span, including adolescence, young, middle, and older adulthood, and old age.

The developmental differences discussed in this chapter all speak to how a sense of culture develops in each of us. As cultures exert their influence in their own special and unique ways, they produce specific tendencies, trends, and differences in their members when compared to others. When we are in the middle of a culture, as we all are, we cannot see those differences or how culture itself develops in us. Only when we look outside ourselves and examine the developmental and socialization processes of other cultures are we able to see what we are ourselves. Only then can we come to appreciate that those differences and similarities are our culture, or at least manifestations of our culture. Thus, while cultures produce differences in development that we observe in our research, these differences simultaneously contribute to the development of culture.

Glossary

accommodation The process of changing one's understanding of the world to accommodate ideas that conflict with existing concepts.

ambivalent attachment A style of attachment in which children are uncertain in their response to their mothers, going back and forth between seeking and shunning her attention. These mothers have been characterized as insensitive and less involved.

animism The belief that all things, including inanimate objects, are alive.

assimilation The process of fitting new ideas into a preexisting understanding of the world.

attachment The special bond that develops between the infant and its primary caregiver. The quality of attachment has lifelong effects on our relationships with loved ones.

avoidant attachment A style of attachment in which children shun their mothers, who are suspected of being intrusive and overstimulating.

centration The tendency to focus on a single aspect of a problem.

cognitive development A specialty in psychology that studies how thinking skills develop over time. The major theory of cognitive development is that of Piaget.

conservation An awareness that physical quantities remain the same even when they change shape or appearance.

conventional morality The second stage of Kohlberg's theory of moral development, emphasizing conformity to rules that are defined by others' approval or society's rules.

difficult temperament A type of temperament that is characterized by an intense, irregular, withdrawing style that is generally marked by negative moods.

easy temperament A type of temperament that is defined by a very regular, adaptable, mildly intense style of behavior that is positive and responsive.

egocentrism The inability to step into another's shoes and understand the other person's point of view.

goodness of fit The interaction of a child's temperament with that of the parents, considered a key to the development of personality.

great divide theories Theories of cognitive development that suggest that the thought of Westerners is superior to that of people who live in primitive societies.

irreversibility The inability to imagine "undoing" a process.

postconventional morality The third stage of Kohlberg's theory of moral development, emphasizing moral reasoning on the basis of individual principles and conscience.

preconventional morality The first stage of Kohlberg's theory of moral development, emphasizing compliance with rules to avoid punishment and gain rewards.

secure attachment A style of attachment in which babies are described as warm and responsive.

slow-to-warm-up A type of temperament in which infants need time to make transitions in activity and experiences. Though they may withdraw initially or respond negatively, given time and support they will adapt and react positively.

temperament Qualities of responsiveness to the environment that exist from birth and evoke different reactions from people in the baby's world. Temperament is generally considered to be a biologically based style of interacting with the world.

InfoTrac College Edition

Use InfoTrac College Edition to search for additional readings on topics of interest to you. For more information on topics in this chapter, use the following as search terms:

culture and attachment
cross-cultural temperament of infants
culture and moral development

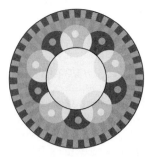

Culture and Gender

As with so many other aspects of our lives, culture influences the behaviors associated with being male or female. In the past 20 to 30 years, we have witnessed many changes in the behaviors Americans consider appropriate for males and females. Certainly, American culture is one of the most dynamic in the exploration of sex and gender differences (or similarities). This dynamism has led to a great deal of confusion and conflict, but it has also produced excitement about the changing nature of human relations and culture itself.

Recent events around the world have brought international attention to gender issues. From the Taliban in Afghanistan to the World Conference on Women held in Beijing, China, to global concern over female circumcision in Africa and Asia—gender roles, ideals, and expectations are heated topics widely discussed around the world. An example of a controversial cultural practice that is rooted in perceptions of gender and gender roles is female circumcision. It has been described as part of a female initiation ceremony and an important rite of passage marking the transition from childhood to adulthood (Lightfoot-Klein, 1989). Behind this practice lie many strongly held beliefs about women and the role of women. Those who defend the practice argue that it is a requirement for marriage and emphasize the importance of upholding tradition; those who condemn it emphasize the pain, suffering, and health risks involved. To understand this controversy, we need to first examine how our own cultural filters shape the way we view issues related to gender. If you find this practice abhorrent, why? How did you come to develop those beliefs? As discussed in Chapter 3, we perceive and make interpretations about others based on our cultural filters. When we encounter cultural practices that make us uncomfortable, we can engage in flexible ethnocentrism to attempt to understand the cultural viewpoint while not necessarily accepting or supporting it.

In this chapter, we will examine how culture influences behavior related to sex and gender. First, we will discuss some similarities between gender and culture concerns within mainstream psychology. Second, we will discuss some terminology and definitions concerning sex and gender that will help us understand what we are talking about and how to focus on cultural influences. Then, we will discuss cross-cultural research on gender differences, including gender stereotypes, sex roles and self-concepts, Hofstede's research, and other psychological constructs. We will discuss some theoretical notions of how psychologists believe gender differences come to exist, and why cultures seem to differ in these differences. We will also discuss ethnicity and gender-related issues in the United States. Throughout this discussion, we will see that the issues surrounding gender and gender differences, both pancultural and culture-specific, are complex as well as interesting.

The Relationship of Gender and Culture to Mainstream Psychology

Before turning to the cross-cultural literature on gender differences, it is interesting to note some parallels between the impact of gender and culture on mainstream psychology. Beginning 20 to 30 years ago, what is commonly known as the women's movement in the United States led American academic communities to evaluate the treatment and presentation of women in textbooks and research. They found that most research was conducted using men as subjects, and most information presented about "people" in academic textbooks and university courses was based on information gathered from men. This gender bias also affected what scholars considered important to study, the relative status of different studies and topics, and the probability and outlet for publication. Psychologists became increasingly aware of the possibility that men and women may differ psychologically, calling into question previous research findings and the theories based on them. Scholars, researchers, teachers, and students alike began to question whether knowledge based primarily on men was accurate for people in general.

One consequence of this growing awareness among researchers and scholars was a conscious effort to include women as research participants, to ensure that research findings would be applicable to women as well as men. At the same time, an increasing number of women became researchers and scholars, bringing different perspectives to the field, its theories, and its findings. Today, psychology enjoys more balanced contributions by both men and women, at least in the United States, and this combination of different perspectives and concerns makes for a dynamism that is rich, interesting, and important for the field.

As a result, we have come a long way toward improving our knowledge about both men and women in the social sciences. Although questioning the imbalance of research on men and women was difficult, many behavioral and social scientists have responded well to this inequity in our knowledge and practice. Today, studies of gender differences are commonplace in social science research, and textbooks routinely incorporate sex and gender differences when imparting knowledge about people (although the degree to which such material is presented and incorporated is still questioned and debated).

We have witnessed the same type of questioning with regard to cultural norms for women and men. Just as knowledge about women and women's concerns was missing from research and scholarship 30 years ago, so too was knowledge about cultural similarities and differences and cultural diversity. Much of this gap still exists today. Many of the same questions are still being raised concerning whether what we are learning in classes and in our laboratories is indeed true for people of all cultures and ethnicities. The answer so far has been "not necessarily." To address this gap, many researchers have made a conscious effort to study behaviors across cultures to learn what is similar across cultures and what is different. Academic institutions have also made a conscious effort to recruit and train people of diverse cultural backgrounds, so that they too can contribute to the research, teaching, and scholarship in psychology.

We interpret these changes as evidence of a continuing evolution in the field, similar to what has happened in relation to gender. That is, psychology is constantly changing and evolving, as the nature of the people it is supposed to be describing continues to change. As the United States and the entire world become increasingly diverse, the need for mainstream psychology to incorporate, explain, and describe that diversity increases. The field has become aware of this need only in the past decade or so (although cross-cultural psychology and cross-cultural research have a much longer history). Theories, research, and teaching are becoming more culturally sensitive, and this increasing awareness is bound to bring with it another evolution in the face and content of psychology. For this reason, it is an exciting time in both mainstream and cross-cultural psychology, as the gap between them narrows.

Some Definitions

Before examining cultural influences with regard to sex and gender, we first need to make clear what we mean by those terms. Social scientists have offered a variety of ideas to define and differentiate between sex and gender (for example, Prince, 1985).

The term **sex** generally refers to the biological and physiological differences between men and women, the most obvious being the anatomical differences in their reproductive systems. Other biological differences between the sexes include physiological, hormonal, and biochemical differences.

The term **sex roles** is used to describe the behaviors and patterns of activities men and women may engage in that are directly related to their biological differences and the process of reproduction. An example of a sex role for females is breastfeeding, a behavior that only women can engage in (Brislin, 1993). The term **sexual identity** is used to describe the degree of awareness and recognition of sex and sex roles an individual may have. Male sexual identity includes "his awareness that he has the potential to impregnate women and knows the necessary behaviors. Female sexual identity includes the woman's awareness of her reproductive potential and her knowledge about behaviors that lead to pregnancy" (p. 287).

In contrast, **gender** refers to the behaviors or patterns of activities that a society or culture deems appropriate for men and women. These behavior patterns may or may not be related to sex and sex roles, although they often are. For example, traditional gender roles that we all know about or have heard of suggest that males are aggressive and unemotional (with the exception of anger) and that the male should leave the home every day to make a living and be the principal wage earner. Traditional gender roles for females suggest that women are nurturant, caring, and highly emotional and that they should stay at home and take care of the home and children. **Gender role** refers to the degree to which a person adopts the gender-specific behaviors ascribed by his or her culture. **Gender identity** refers to the degree to which a person has awareness or recognition that he or she adopts a particular gender role. Finally, **gender stereotypes** refer to the psychological or behavioral characteristics typically associated with men and women.

Not everyone can be pigeonholed into stereotypes according to sex or gender roles, as there are considerable individual differences across people with regard to these roles. In addition, gender role stereotypes interact with other forms of group membership. African American women, for example, are generally not perceived in terms of the traditional gender roles just described (Binion, 1990), nor are women who are disabled or who have a different sexual orientation.

Separating the biological and physiological facts of sex from the behavioral aspects of gender is the first step in understanding differences between males and females. Indeed, it should become clear from this differentiation that we are mostly concerned with gender differences, not sex differences. Culture, as a macro construct, is likely to influence our perception of gender differences.

Cross-Cultural Research on Gender

Cross-cultural research on gender differences has spanned a considerable number of psychological themes and constructs that help us piece together how gender differences exist in different cultures, and help us speculate about the reasons for those differences. For the purposes of the presentation here, we have categorized the research into four areas: gender stereotypes, gender roles and self-concept, Hofstede's study, and psychological gender differences, which include perceptual/spatial/cognitive differences, conformity and obedience, aggression, and other psychological constructs. These classifications are, of course, entirely arbitrary; they are an attempt to provide some structure to the broad array of cross-cultural studies on gender differences. In addition, this review is not comprehensive, but only representative of the vast amount of research that exists on many different psychological topics examining gender differences across culture.

Culture and Gender Stereotypes

The number of roles available to males and females is limitless. Some cultures foster a certain gender distinction; other cultures foster other distinctions. We are all familiar with traditional gender role differentiations—the notion that males should be independent, self-reliant, strong, and emotionally detached, while women should be dependent, reliant, weak, nurturant, and emotional. To what degree is this an American or Western cultural phenomenon?

The Williams and Best studies.   The best-known study of gender stereotypes across cultures is one conducted by Williams and Best (1982). These researchers sampled people in 30 countries, 52–120 respondents per country, for a total of almost 3,000 individuals.

The study used a questionnaire known as the Adjective Check List (ACL). The ACL is a list of 300 adjectives. Respondents in each country were asked to decide whether each adjective was considered more descriptive of a male or of a female. Whether the subjects agreed with the assignment of an adjective to males or females was irrelevant; instead, they were asked merely to report the characteristics generally associated with males and females in their culture. The researchers tallied the data from all individuals. Looking at responses within each culture, Williams and Best (1982) established the criterion that if more than two-thirds of a sample from a country agreed on a particular term for either males or females, there was a consensus within that culture on that general characteristic. Then, looking at responses across the cultures, the researchers decided that if two-thirds of the cultures reached a consensus on the characteristic, there was a cross-cultural consensus on that characteristic as describing males or females. The results indicated a high degree of pancultural agreement across all the countries studied in the characteristics associated with men and women. Table 7.1 lists the 100 items of the pancultural adjective checklist reported by Williams and Best (1994) .

The degree of consensus these adjectives received in describing males and females is amazing. In fact, Berry and colleagues (1992) have suggested that "this degree of consensus is so large that it may be appropriate to suggest that the researchers have found a psychological universal when it comes to gender stereotypes" (p. 60)—while at the same time cautioning against such sweeping generalizations. But the possibility of a universally accepted gender stereotype has interesting ramifications for possible evolutionary similarities across cultures in division of labor between males and females and the psychological characteristics that result from that universal division of labor.

Williams and Best (1982) conducted a second type of analysis on their data in order to summarize their major findings. They scored the adjectives in each

Table 7.1 The 100 Items of the Pancultural Adjective Checklist

Male-Associated		Female-Associated	
Active	Loud	Affected	Modest
Adventurous	Obnoxious	Affectionate	Nervous
Aggressive	Opinionated	Appreciative	Patient
Arrogant	Opportunistic	Cautious	Pleasant
Autocratic	Pleasure-seeking	Changeable	Prudish
Bossy	Precise	Charming	Self-pitying
Capable	Progressive	Complaining	Sensitive
Conceited	Rational	Confused	Sexy
Confident	Realistic	Curious	Shy
Courageous	Reckless	Dependent	Softhearted
Cruel	Resourceful	Dreamy	Sophisticated
Cynical	Rigid	Emotional	Submissive
Determined	Robust	Excitable	Suggestible
Disorderly	Serious	Fault-finding	Superstitious
Enterprising	Sharp-witted	Fearful	Talkative
Greedy	Show-off	Fickle	Timid
Hardheaded	Steady	Foolish	Touchy
Humorous	Stern	Forgiving	Unambitious
Indifferent	Stingy	Frivolous	Understanding
Individualistic	Stolid	Fussy	Unintelligent
Initiative	Tough	Gentle	Unstable
Interests wide	Unfriendly	Imaginative	Warm
Inventive	Unscrupulous	Kind	Weak
Lazy	Witty	Mild	Worrying

Source: "Cross-Cultural Views of Women and Men," by J. E. Williams and D. L. Best. In W. J. Lonner & R. Malpass (Eds.), *Psychology and Culture,* 1994, p. 193. Published by Allyn & Bacon, Boston, MA. Copyright © 1994 by Pearson Education. Reprinted by permission of the publisher.

country in terms of favorability, strength, and activity to examine how the adjectives were distributed according to affective or emotional meaning. They found surprising congruence in these analyses: The characteristics associated with men were stronger and more active than those associated with women across all countries. On favorability, however, cultural differences emerged: Some countries (such as Japan and South Africa) rated the male characteristics as more favorable than the female, whereas other countries (for example, Italy and Peru) rated female characteristics as more favorable.

How are we to interpret these results? It could be that a division of labor for males and females according to reproductive processes produced differences in behaviors that, in turn, produced differences in psychological characteristics. It may be that these psychological characteristics had some evolutionary and adaptive advantages for males and females to fulfill their roles as prescribed by the division of labor. It could be that men and women in all cultures became locked into these set ways, accounting for universal consensus on these descriptors. It could be that men and women become locked into a particular mindset about cultural differences because of perceived social inequality or social forces and indirect communication via mass media and the like. Or these findings could all be a function of the way the research was conducted, using university students as participants, which would tend to make the entire sample more homogeneous than if people were sampled randomly from each culture.

Although it is impossible to disentangle these factors, it is important to note that Williams and Best themselves collected and analyzed data concerning gender stereotypes from young children and found a considerable degree of agreement between the findings for children and those for university students (Williams & Best, 1990). These results argue against (but do not entirely eliminate) the notion that the original findings were due to homogeneity among university students.

Williams and his colleagues have since extended their earlier work on gender stereotypes in important ways. Williams, Satterwhite, and Best (1999), for example, took the ACL data from 25 countries in their previous work and rescored them in terms of five personality dimensions known as the Big Five, or Five Factor Model of Personality. As you will see in Chapter 11, these terms refer to the five personality traits or dimensions that are considered universal or consistent around the world. They found that, overall, males were perceived to have significantly higher scores than females on all traits except agreeableness; females, however, were perceived to have significantly higher scores than males on this personality dimension.

In a subsequent follow-up study, Williams, Satterwhite, Best, and Inman (in press) took their ACL data from 27 countries and rescored these data according to the five-factor model of personality. They then examined male–female differences on the personality traits separately in each country. They found that the results they had obtained earlier were generally supported in all of the countries. In addition, they correlated the male–female differences with culture scores from two large value surveys (Hofstede, 1980, & Schwartz, 1994), some demographic variables, and gender ideology scores from a previous study (Williams & Best, 1990). They found that gender stereotype differentiation tended to be higher in countries that were conservative and hierarchical, with a lower level of socioeconomic development, a relatively low degree of Christian affiliation, and a relatively low proportion of women attending university. Countries that valued harmony and egalitarianism, had less traditional sex role orientations, and viewed male stereotypes as less favorable than female stereotypes were associated with less gender stereotype differentiation on the five factors.

In summary, this set of studies informs us that gender stereotypes around the world are rather stable, and are related to interesting and important psychological characteristics. Men are generally viewed as active, strong, critical, and adultlike, with psychological needs such as dominance, autonomy, aggression, exhibition, achievement, and endurance. Men are also associated more with the personality traits of conscientiousness, extroversion, and openness. Women are generally viewed as passive, weak, nurturing, and adaptive, with psychological needs such as abasement, deference, succorance, nurturance, affiliation, and heterosexuality. They are also associated with higher scores on the personality traits of agreeableness and neuroticism. As described earlier, the degree of stability of these findings across a wide range of countries and cultures provides a strong base of evidence for some pancultural universality in psychological attribution.

Other studies.   A number of other studies have also investigated gender and sex role stereotypes in different countries and cultures. Rao and Rao (1985), for example, examined sex role stereotypes in the United States and India; they found that Indians endorsed much more traditional stereotypes concerning mother, wife, and father roles than did the Americans. Trommsdorff and Iwawaki (1989) examined gender role differences between German and Japanese adolescents. They found that Japanese mothers were seen as more controlling than fathers, but German mothers were viewed as less controlling. The Japanese also had more traditional gender role orientations than did the Germans. In general, the results from these two studies support the overall findings of Williams and Best.

Perceiving gender differences in a stereotypical fashion is rather persistent. One reason for this persistence is that we tend to be more attuned to information that reinforces and supports our gender stereotypes. For instance, studies find that we tend to remember people and events better when they engage in gender-stereotyped rather than non-gender-stereotyped activities and behaviors (Furnham & Singh, 1986). Moreover, this tendency is greater for people who endorse stronger gender stereotypes.

Other studies have tried to shed light on how gender role stereotypes develop. Albert and Porter (1986), for example, reported that gender stereotypes increase with age, and that children are more likely to sex-type same-sex figures. Munroe, Shimmin, and Munroe (1984) found that children's understanding of gender and sex role preferences appear to be related to cognitive development. Other researchers have focused on the contribution of socializing agents, such as the media, to the development of gender role stereotypes. Fejes (1992) argues that the way the media have historically portrayed women parallels the way media have historically portrayed people of color. An analysis of images of women in television reveal that overly simplified, blatantly stereotypical images of women dominated the earlier years of mass media. Current portrayals of men and women are somewhat more diverse. Nonetheless, some stereotypes persist; for example, women are less likely than men to be in leading roles or portrayed as having a high-status job, and more likely than men to be shown in the home (Fejes, 1992).

Many questions remain unanswered in this important area of psychology. How congruent are people's behaviors with their stereotypes, and does this congruence differ across cultures and countries? Are stereotypes related to important psychological constructs or behaviors that affect everyday lives? How do we come to develop such stereotypes—what are the factors that produce them, and their boundaries? These and other questions provide the basis for important future research.

Culture, Gender Role Ideology, and Self-Concept

Another important topic that has been studied across cultures is **gender role ideology**—judgments about what males and females ought to be like or ought to do. To examine gender role ideologies, Williams and Best (1990) asked subjects in 14 countries to complete the ACL in relation to what they believe they are, and what they would like to be. The subjects also completed a sex role ideology scale that generated scores between two polar opposites, labeled "traditional" and "egalitarian." The traditional scores tended to describe gender roles that were consistent with the traditional or universal norms found in their earlier research; egalitarian scores reflected a tendency toward less differentiation between males and females on the various psychological characteristics.

The most egalitarian scores were found in the Netherlands, Germany, and Finland; the most traditional ideologies were found in Nigeria, Pakistan, and India. Women tended to have more egalitarian views than men. Gender differences within each country were relatively small compared to cross-country differences, which were considerable. In particular, countries with relatively high socioeconomic development, a high proportion of Protestant Christians, a low proportion of Muslims, a high percentage of women employed outside the home, a high proportion of women enrolled in universities, and a greater degree of individualism were associated with more egalitarian scores. These findings make sense, as greater affluence and individualistic tendencies tend to produce a culture that allows women increased access to jobs and education, thus blending traditional gender roles.

In addition to studying gender stereotypes and ideologies, Williams and Best (1990) also examined gender differences in self-concept. The same students in the same 14 countries rated each of the 300 adjectives of the ACL according to whether it was descriptive of themselves or their ideal self. Responses were scored according to masculinity/femininity as well as in terms of favorability, strength, and activity. When scored according to masculinity/femininity, both self and ideal-self ratings for men were more masculine than were women's ratings, and vice versa, across all countries. However, both men and women in all countries rated their ideal self as more masculine than their actual self. In effect, they were saying that they wanted to have more of the traits traditionally associated with males.

Gender role ideologies have also been studied in younger populations by Gibbons and her colleagues (Gibbons, Stiles, Schnellman, & Morales-Hidalgo, 1990; Gibbons, Bradford, & Stiles, 1989; Stiles, Gibbons, & Schnellman, 1990; de Silva, Stiles, & Gibbons, 1992). These researchers have conducted several cross-cultural studies involving almost 700 adolescents ranging in age from 11 to 17 years from Spain, Guatemala, and Sri Lanka. In their surveys, adolescents were asked to draw and describe characteristics of the ideal man or woman. Interestingly, the most important quality in these countries for both boys and girls was being "kind and honest," a characteristic that was not gender-specific. Some gender differences emerged, however, with being good-looking more often mentioned as an ideal for women and being employed in a job as more of an ideal for men.

Gibbons conducted another study on adolescents' attitudes toward gender roles that involved 265 international students, ages 11 to 17, who attended school in the Netherlands. Students filled out an Attitude Towards Women Scale for Adolescents (Galambos, Petersen, Richards, & Gitelson, 1985) that included 12 statements such as "Boys are better than girls" and "Girls should have the same freedom as boys." Adolescents were asked to report their level of agreement with these statements. Results indicated that girls were less traditional than boys, and that adolescents from wealthier and more individualistic countries were less traditional than adolescents from poorer and more collectivist countries (Gibbons, Stiles, & Shkodriani, 1991).

Gibbons's study of Sri Lankan adolescents (de Silva et al., 1992) indicates that gender role ideologies may be changing as societies undergo change. She found that more than half the girls in her study depicted the ideal woman as being employed outside the home, even though the traditional role of a Sri Lankan woman is that of homemaker. Mule and Barthel (1992) describe social change in Egypt, where there has been an increase in women's participation in the workforce and, to some extent, political life. Furthermore, globalization and exposure to Western culture have presented this traditionally Islamic country with alternative gender ideologies. Subsequently, gender role ideologies may undergo modification or redefinition in these countries.

Nonetheless, maintaining, not modifying, traditional gender roles in the face of modernization is also likely. For instance, a study of Palestinian women and their families found that one's level of education, participation in political activities, and employment are not major factors predicting more egalitarian family roles (Huntington, Fronk, & Chadwick, 2001). The authors were surprised by this finding, and argue that cultural values, defined by Islamic beliefs and practices, are resisting the forces of modernity. In other words, Islamic teachings on women, the family, and relationships between men and women may be a powerful influence in maintaining traditional family functioning, and especially traditional ideas of women's roles in family and society. These findings highlight the important role of religion in understanding how gender role ideologies are defined and preserved in different cultures.

Hofstede's Study

In Chapters 2 and 15, we discuss research by Hofstede, who studied work-related attitudes across 50 countries. Because his research is relevant to the issue of culture and gender, we will briefly review his study here.

Hofstede (1980) conducted a large-scale survey of work-related values in a major multinational corporation. Based on the data obtained, he generated four dimensions of differentiation among the cultures in his sample. One of these dimensions was called "masculinity" (MA). This dimension refers to the degree to which a culture will foster, encourage, or maintain differences between males and females. Cultures scoring high on MA tended to endorse items and values thought to be associated with masculinity and male gender roles in the workplace. Japan, Austria, Venezuela, and Italy had the highest MA scores. Cultures scoring low on MA minimized differences between the sexes and genders. Denmark, the Netherlands, Norway, and Sweden had the lowest scores.

Although Hofstede's study focused entirely on work-related values, his findings highlight a major point of this chapter—that cultures will arrive at different ways of dealing with differences between men and women. The behaviors men and women engage in produce different psychological outcomes that have direct ramifications for actual life behaviors (such as work-related behaviors). Cultures vary in how they act on these gender differences, with some cultures fostering and encouraging great differences between the genders and other cultures minimizing those differences. It is precisely these cultural differences in gender roles that Hofstede's data on MA address.

Psychological Gender Differences across Cultures

Culture, biology, gender roles, and gender role ideology all interact to produce differences between the genders on a variety of psychological and behavioral outcomes. That is, the division of labor and actual behaviors males and females engage in as a result of their biological and physiological differences help to produce a different psychology or mindset as well. These psychological differences between genders can be considered a product of the differences between males and females because of the division of labor and behaviors surrounding reproduction.

Just as there will be psychological differences between males and females in any one culture, psychological differences can also be found across cultures. And the degree, direction, or exact nature of those gender differences may differ across cultures. That is, one culture may foster a certain type of gender difference, but another culture may not foster that difference to the same degree. A third culture may foster that difference even more than the first two cultures. Psychological gender differences across cultures are not simply products of biology and culture; they are also important reinforcers of culture, feeding back onto the culture behaviors, gender roles, and gender role ideologies. In this cyclical fashion, the psychological products of gender differentiation also become a crucial aspect of the culture–behavior–psychology linkage that exists among a people and their rituals, traditions, and behaviors.

The cross-cultural literature on psychological differences between the genders highlights three general areas of difference: perceptual/spatial/cognitive abilities, conformity and obedience, and aggressiveness (Berry et al., 1992). Studies in each of these areas show that there are general differences between genders, but the degree of those differences is indeed different across cultures.

Perceptual/spatial/cognitive differences.   At least in American society, it is common folklore that males are better at mathematical and spatial reasoning tasks, whereas females are better at verbal comprehension tasks. An analysis of the scores for males and females on standardized tests in elementary school, college entrance examinations, or graduate school entrance examinations shows some degree of support for these notions, although the difference between males and females seems to have narrowed in recent years. In their review of the literature, Maccoby and Jacklin (1974) also concluded that males tend to do better on spatial tasks and other tasks having a spatial component.

Years ago, however, Berry (1966) pointed out that such differences do not appear to exist among males and females of the Inuit culture in Canada. Berry suggested that the gender difference did not exist because "spatial abilities are highly adaptive for both males and females in Inuit society, and both boys and girls have ample training and experience that promote the acquisition of spatial ability" (Berry et al., 1992, p. 65).

Following up on the possibility of cultural differences on this gender difference, Berry (1976) and his colleagues conducted a study in which a block design task was given to males and females in 17 different cultures. A stimulus card depicting a geometric representation of a set of blocks was presented, and the task was to manipulate an actual set of blocks to emulate the design provided. The results were interesting and provocative. In a number of cultures, males indeed did better than females on the task; however, in other cultures, females did better than males. In interpreting these data, Berry et al. (1992) suggested that male superiority on the task tended to be found in cultures that were tight (that is, relatively homogeneous), sedentary, and agriculturally based, but that female superiority was found in cultures that were loose, nomadic, and based on hunting and gathering. In these latter cultures, the roles ascribed to males and females are relatively flexible, with more members performing a variety of tasks related to the survival of the group. Further research is needed to follow up these interpretations as hypotheses and investigate the exact nature of and reasons for the differences.

A similar finding was reported in a meta-analysis of the research literature by Born, Bleichrodt, and Van der Flier (1987). They reported that although no gender differences in overall intelligence were found, gender differences on various subtests of intelligence did occur. Although their findings leave open the question of the exact role of culture in creating or maintaining the gender difference, they do show that the differences in the cognitive test scores between males and females are variable across cultures. In another study (Pontius, 1997), the male advantage in spatial abilities was not found on two spatial tasks in eastern Ecuador, a culture that emphasizes women's traditional tasks, such as sewing and needlework, that require spatial representation.

Thus, some cultures foster male superiority in these types of tasks, but others foster female superiority, and still others foster no differences. Although some suggestions have been made as to the nature and causes of these various gender differences, research has yet to pinpoint exactly what factors influence which types of differences, and why. Future research will need to explore these and other issues regarding perceptual/spatial/analytic abilities. With the increasing plurality of the world, this research will also need to be sensitive to the particular time period in which the research is conducted, as differences may be decreasing in many societies and cultures today.

Conformity and obedience.   One of the most common gender role stereotypes is that females are more conforming and obedient than males. This stereotype is no doubt related to the traditional gender roles females and males have occupied, with males traditionally being "head of the household," making primary decisions over big-ticket items that involve the family. In this traditional social arrangement, females were not to be concerned with authority and decision-making power; rather, the female role focused on caring for the children and managing the household affairs. In short, females were expected to conform to decisions imposed upon them by males or by society in general.

The degree to which this difference is enacted varies considerably from culture to culture. In Berry's (1976) study, the researchers also obtained an index of the degree to which each person conformed in the 17 cultures included in the sample. Across the 17 cultures, clear variations emerged; as with gender differences in spatial reasoning, these variations appeared to be related to the cultural concept of tightness. Cultures that were tighter appeared to foster a greater gender difference on conformity, with females more conformist than males; tight cultures may require a greater degree of conformity to traditional gender roles on the part of both males and females. In contrast, cultures that were looser fostered less gender difference on conformity, and in some of these cultures, males were found to be more conforming than females. Thus, traditional gender stereotypes of females as more conforming than males appear to have some validity, but considerable cross-cultural difference exists in the degree, and in some cases the direction, of this difference.

Future research needs to test these ideas further, examining the links between cultural variables such as tightness and psychological constructs such as conformity, and the degree to which gender differences on such constructs are fostered. Future research will also need to examine the degree to which gender differences on conformity are related to differences on perceptual, analytic, or spatial skills, or on other psychological traits and constructs such as aggressiveness.

Aggressiveness.   Another common gender stereotype is that males are more aggressive than females. Indeed, there is support for this stereotype in all cultures for which documentation exists (Block, 1983; Brislin, 1993). Males account for a disproportionate amount of violent crime in both industrialized and nonindustrialized societies. The focus in research on this topic has been adolescent males. Several researchers have searched for the biological correlates of aggression. In particular, some researchers have questioned whether increased levels of the hormone testosterone during male adolescence may account for or contribute to increased aggression in males. Increased testosterone levels have been associated with dominance hierarchies in some nonhuman primates, but the human analog is less clear. On the basis of the evidence available, it appears that hormones may contribute to some degree to aggressiveness, but culture and the environment can certainly act to encourage or discourage its emergence (Berry et al., 1992).

A study by Barry, Josephson, Lauer, and Marshall (1976) examined the degree to which cultures foster aggressive tendencies in the socialization of children. These researchers found a sex-related difference in the average amount of teaching about aggressiveness across 150 different cultures. Inspection of their data, however, reveals that this average difference was produced by a disproportionate number of high-scoring cultures in which teaching aggression actually occurs. In fact, a large majority of societies did not show a sex-related difference in teaching aggression.

Such interpretations have been bolstered by anthropological studies of some cultures known for their aggressive tendencies. Among these is the Yanomami culture of Venezuela and Brazil (for example, Sponsel, 1998), often referred to in anthropological circles as the "fierce people." Yet even with regard to these supposedly aggressive groups, more recent research and discussion have begun to call into question the potential bias in anthropological and comparative methods that may see only part of the culture (Sponsel, 1998). Such concerns affect cross-cultural research as well, bringing into question the specific definitions and measurements of aggressiveness and their degree of sensitivity to a variety of contexts.

Neither biology nor sex differences in teaching aggressive acts can account for gender differences in aggression observed across cultures. Some researchers (Berry et al., 1992; Segall, Dasen, Berry, & Poortinga, 1990) offer yet another possible explanation for gender differences in aggression across cultures. They suggest that male aggression may be a compensatory mechanism to offset the conflict produced by a young male's identification with a female care provider and his initiation into adulthood as a male. In this model, aggressiveness is viewed as "gender marking" behavior.

Regardless of the precise mechanisms that produce gender differences in aggression, it is clear that although the gender stereotype of aggressiveness may be generally true, considerable differences do exist across cultures. What is true for one culture may not be true for another. Future research needs to examine the exact mechanisms accounting for these differences, taking into account the complex interplay among biology, culture, and psychology. This research will need to be sensitive to the context specificity of aggressive acts, and the influence of the research methodology and data collection itself on the reporting or acting out of aggression.

Other psychological constructs.   Over the years, many other studies have documented culture and gender differences on a wide variety of psychological constructs. In the past five to ten years alone, research examining gender and cultural differences has addressed topics including gender identity (Harris, 1996), career plans (Morinaga, Frieze, & Ferlingoj, 1993), self-presentations (Reid & Trotter, 1993), dress (Reece, 1996), suicidal behavior (Wassenaar, van der Veen, & Pillay, 1998), dream content (Punamaeki & Joustie, 1998), personal relationships (Burleson, 1997), cognitive and coping styles related to sports (Anshel, Williams, & Hodge, 1997; Williams, Anshel, & Quek, 1997), self-esteem (Watkins, Akande, Cheng, & Regmi, 1996), conflict resolution (Itoi, Ohbuchi, & Fukuno, 1996), response styles (Watkins & Cheung, 1995), nonverbal behaviors (Remland, Jones, & Brinkman, 1995), attitudes toward marriage and sexual behaviors (Higgins, Zheng, Liu, & Sun, 2002), religious involvement (Loewenthal, MacLeod, & Cinnirella, 2002), and personal entitlements (Wainryb & Turiel, 1994). Cross-cultural work over the past few decades has uncovered culture and gender differences across other constructs as well.

There is little doubt, therefore, that gender differences exist on a wide variety of psychological constructs, and that cultures differ in the exact degree and nature of those gender differences. Some research has examined how such culture and gender differences come to manifest themselves. Dasgupta (1998), for example, examined the relationship between ethnic identity and two scales related to women and dating among Asian Indian immigrants in the United States, and found a strong similarity between parents and children on many target attitudes. This finding provides evidence for the important role parents play as enculturation agents in maintaining traditional cultural values, including gender differences.

How Does Culture Influence Gender?

The process of learning gender roles begins very early in life. The importance of gender in organizing our expectations and thinking is illustrated in the first question that we ask when a baby is born: "Is it a boy or a girl?" In American culture, we tend to give boys and girls different types of toys to play with and dress infants according to gender. If you look back to your baby pictures, you may find that you were often dressed in either blue or pink. One U.S. study reports that 90% of the infants observed at a shopping mall were dressed in gendered colors and/or styles (Shakin, Shakin, & Sternglanz, 1985). By the age of 3, children begin to accurately label people by sex (Fagot, Leinbach, & Hagen, 1986). Gender role socialization continues throughout life from various sources—expectations from parents, modeling of gender roles by peers, and images of males and females in the media, to name a few—that contribute to our ideas on what it means to be male or female.

How can we understand the influence of culture on gender? In terms of the definitions presented earlier, a newborn has sex but no gender. Gender is a construct that develops in children as they are socialized in their environments. As children grow older, they learn specific behaviors and patterns of activities appropriate and inappropriate for their sex, and they either adopt or reject those gender roles. Sandra Bem (1981), a prominent theorist on gender, argues that gender is one of the fundamental ways we organize information and understand experiences about the world. For instance, we learn what behaviors, attitudes, objects, and conventions are associated with being "male" and what are associated with being "female," and apply these gender schemas to understand the people around us as well as ourselves.

Ensuring that reproduction occurs fulfills men's and women's sex roles. But what happens before and after that depends on a host of variables. One of these variables is culture. The biological fact and necessity of reproduction, along with other biological and physiological differences between men and women, lead to behavioral differences between men and women. In earlier days, these behavioral differences were no doubt reinforced by a necessary division of labor. Someone had to look after children while someone else had to find food for the family; no one person could have done it all. Thus, the existence of reproductive differences led to a division of labor advantageous to the family as a unit. These differences, in turn, produced differences in a variety of psychological traits and characteristics, such as aggressiveness, nurturance, and achievement.

Berry and his colleagues (1992) have suggested that the model presented in Figure 1.2 in Chapter 1 describes how cultural practices can affect gender differences in psychological characteristics, and we think it is an excellent springboard for understanding the effects of culture on gender. However, it is important to remember that the factors involved in understanding culture and gender that are outlined in Figure 1.2 are not static or unidimensional. Indeed, the entire system is dynamic and interrelated and feeds back on and reinforces itself. As a result, this system is not a linear unit with influences going in a single direction; it acquires a life of its own. And the life of this system is reinforced by the glue we know as culture.

As different societies live in different environments, survival requires that they balance a number of factors, including natural resources, affluence, and population density. These external factors help to frame and mold specific behaviors that may affect the division of labor between men and women originally necessitated by biological differences. These differential behaviors that occur because of differences in external, environmental factors lead to patterns of behaviors across time that are associated with men and women. This pattern of behaviors across time, of course, is culture. In turn, it feeds back reciprocally onto the pattern of behaviors, reinforcing behaviors, beliefs, attitudes, and values. Thus, as different cultures must deal with different external factors, it is only natural that gender differences vary by culture. One culture may foster considerable equality between women and men and relatively few differences in their cultural practices and psychological characteristics. Another culture may foster considerable differences between the sexes, their cultural practices related to reproduction, and psychological characteristics associated with sex roles. Some cultures may foster differences between the sexes in one direction (for example, males as primary decision makers, females compliant and obedient); another culture may foster differences in the opposite direction. This type of explanatory model may account for the range of differences obtained in previous cross-cultural research on psychological constructs.

Yet the evidence also suggests that stereotypes and attitudes concerning gender differences are relatively constant across cultures, despite actual differences in psychological behaviors brought about by real differences in demands placed on cultures and societies by their environment. Some researchers, in fact, go as far as to say that the persistence of gender stereotypes across culture cannot be attributed to sociocultural factors and can only be explained by sociobiological models (Lueptow, Garovich, & Lueptow, 1995).

Future research will need to tackle the important questions posed by this theoretical understanding of cultural and gender differences, elucidating on the mechanisms and factors that help produce and maintain those differences in individual cultures, and then across cultures. In addition, future research will need to explore the relationship between differences in actual behaviors and psychological constructs and gender-related stereotypes, investigating whether these are two different psychological systems of the mind or whether they are linked in ways that are not yet apparent. Indeed, research to date is rather silent on the mechanisms that produce gender and cultural differences, and the interrelationship among different psychological processes. The important point to remember is that different cultures may arrive at different outcomes through the same process. Men and women will have gender-specific roles in any society or culture. All cultures encourage particular behavioral differences between the genders and help to define the roles, duties, and responsibilities appropriate for males and females.

Ethnicity and Gender in the United States

Among the most pressing issues and concerns facing the United States today are gender differences across different ethnicities and the continuing struggle for gender equity across all cultural and ethnic groups. Just as people in different cultures in faraway lands may have different gender roles and expectations, people of different ethnic backgrounds in the United States can have different gender role expectations as well. Many of these gender differences across ethnic lines are rooted in the cultures people of these ethnicities brought with them when they originally came to the United States. But gender differences in the United States today definitely reflect an "American" influence, making gender issues unique in American culture.

There is really very little research on gender differences between African American males and females. The research that exists typically compares African American males and females to European American males and females. African American males are more likely than European American males to live below the poverty line, die at an early age, make less money, be in jail, and be executed for a crime. With regard to psychological processes, African American males are especially adept at body language, nonverbal encoding and decoding, and improvised problem solving (Allen & Santrock, 1993).

Research on the concerns of African American females has painted a changing picture over the past 20 years (Hall, Evans, & Selice, 1989). Early research focused almost exclusively on generally negative characteristics and situations. Of late, however, an increasing amount of research has focused on many other psychological aspects of African American females, including self-esteem or achievement. For example, the number of PhDs awarded to African American women increased by 16% between 1977 and 1986 (Allen & Santrock, 1993), indicating some improvement in the accessibility of advanced graduate degrees for African American women and increased motivation to achieve those degrees. Other studies have found that compared to European American girls, African American girls report higher levels of self-esteem and are less concerned with their physical appearance (Basow & Rubin, 1999; Vasquez & de las Fuentes, 1999).

Some research has suggested that the gender identities of African Americans are more androgynous than those of European Americans. **Androgyny** refers to a gender identity that involves endorsement of both male and female characteristics. Harris (1996), for example, administered the Bem Sex Role Inventory, a scale that is widely used to measure gender identity, to African and European American males and females, and found that both African American males and females were more androgynous than European American males and females. In addition, he found that African American males and females have an equal propensity to endorse typically masculine traits, whereas European American males regard more masculine traits as self-descriptive than European American females do. Other studies conducted in the United States (Frome & Eccles, 1996), Israel (Orr & Ben-Eliahu, 1993), and Hong Kong (Lau, 1989) have found that adolescent girls who adopt an androgynous identity have higher levels of self-acceptance than either feminine or masculine girls. For boys, however, a masculine, not androgynous, identity is associated with the highest level of self-acceptance.

Many Asian American families have carried on traditional gender roles associated with males and females from their original culture. Asian females are often expected to bear the brunt of domestic duties, to raise children, and to be "good" daughters-in-law. Asian American males are often raised to remain aloof, unemotional, and authoritative, especially concerning familial issues (D. Sue, 1998). Some studies, however, have suggested a loosening of these rigid, traditional gender roles for Asian American males and females. Although Asian American males may still appear as figurative head of the family in public, in reality much decision-making power within the family in private is held by the Asian American female head of the household (Huang & Ying, 1989).

As with Asian American gender roles, the traditional role of the Mexican American female was to provide for the children and take care of the home (Comas-Diaz, 1992). Likewise, Mexican American males were traditionally expected to fill the role of provider for the family. These differences are related to the concept of **machismo**, which incorporates many traditional expectations of the male gender role, such as being unemotional, strong, authoritative, aggressive, and masculine (see Table 7.1 earlier in this chapter). However, recent research has shown that these gender differences for Mexican American males and females are also on the decrease. Mexican American women are increasingly sharing in decision making in the family, as well as taking on a more direct role as provider through work outside the home (Espin, 1993). Although adolescent Mexican American males are generally still given more freedom outside the home than are females, gender differences may be decreasing in the contemporary Mexican American family. This is likely to continue as increasing numbers of Latina women are employed and a Latina feminist movement has emerged (Espin, 1997). It is important to note, however, that this movement continues to place high value on the traditional emphasis of the role of wife and mother, yet offers a wider interpretation of roles acceptable for Latinas.

Gender role differentiation for Native Americans seems to depend heavily on the patriarchal or matriarchal nature of the tribal culture of origin. In patriarchal tribes, women assume primary responsibility for the welfare of the children and extended family members. But males of the Mescalero Apache tribe often take responsibility for children when they are with their families (Glover, 2001). As with other ethnic groups, the passage of time, increased interaction with people of other cultures and with mainstream American culture, and the movement toward urban areas seems to have effected changes in these traditional values and expectations for Native American males and females.

Certainly, the picture we have painted for these ethnic groups is not universally true or salient for all males and females within them. Instead, they serve as generalized descriptions of the gender roles males and females of these ethnic groups may have been socialized into in the past. Many of these cultural tendencies are rooted in the original cultures these peoples came from, and their intermixing and interaction in contemporary American society and culture make for an interesting blend of traditional values with contemporary equity. This balance, of course, produces tension. How well we can all negotiate this tension between ethnic and American cultures, with regard to gender and other psychological constructs, may be indicative of our effectiveness in this society.

Conclusion

Sex refers to the biological and physiological differences between males and females. *Sex roles* are behaviors expected of males and females in relation to their biological differences and reproduction. *Gender* refers to the psychological and behavioral traits and characteristics cultures carve out using sex differences as a base. *Gender roles* refer to the degree to which a person adopts the gender-specific behaviors ascribed by his or her culture. Gender and its permutations—roles, identities, stereotypes, and the like—share an important link with culture.

Gender roles are different for males and females in all cultures. Some stereotypic notions about gender differences seem to be universal across cultures, such as aggressiveness, strength, and lack of emotionality for males, and weakness, submissiveness, and emotionality for females. Other research, however, has shown that the degree, and in some case the direction, of these differences varies across cultures. That is, not every culture will necessarily harbor the same gender differences in the same way as other cultures. Further research is needed to gain a better understanding of culture-constant and culture-specific aspects of gender differences.

Examining gender differences in the United States is especially challenging because of the cultural and ethnic diversity within this single country and the influence of interactions with mainstream American culture. Each ethnic group has its own cultural preferences for gender differentiation, but some blending of the old with the new, the traditional with the modern, appears to be taking place. Without evidence to the contrary, it is probably best to consider this blending as an addition of different cultural repertoires concerning gender differences rather than a subtraction from the old ways.

As we meet people from different cultural backgrounds, we may encounter gender roles that are different from our own. Often, we feel strongly and negatively about these differences. Yet despite our own personal outlook, we must exercise considerable care and caution in imposing our preferences on others. In most cases, people of other cultures feel just as strongly about their own way of living. Many people of many other cultures, particularly women, still harbor many of the traditional values of their ancestral culture, and we have seen conflicts arise because Americans—men and women alike—look down on these traditional ways, criticize them, and attempt to force change. Many women in many cultures want to marry early, stay home, and take care of the family; many men want to adopt the traditional male roles as well. These tendencies are alive in many different people within the most egalitarian cultures and societies, including the United States. We need to respect these differences, rather than attempt to change them because they are not consonant with our own individual or cultural preferences. Still, this is a delicate balancing act for all of us, because there is a fine line between cultural relativity (a desired state of comprehension) and the unacceptable justification of oppression.

Glossary

androgyny A gender identity that involves endorsement of both male and female characteristics.

gender The behaviors or patterns of activities a society or culture deems appropriate for men and women. These behavioral patterns may or may not be related to sex and sex roles, although they often are.

gender identity The degree to which a person has awareness of or recognition that he or she has adopted a particular gender role.

gender role The degree to which a person adopts the gender-specific behaviors ascribed by his or her culture.

gender role ideology Judgments about what gender roles in a particular culture ought to be.

gender stereotype The psychological or behavioral characteristics typically associated with men and women.

machismo A concept related to Mexican American gender role differentiation that is characterized by many traditional expectations of the male gender role, such as being unemotional, strong, authoritative, aggressive, and masculine.

sex The biological and physiological differences between men and women, the most obvious being the anatomical differences in their reproductive systems.

sex roles The behaviors and patterns of activities men and women may engage in that are directly related to their biological differences and the process of reproduction.

sexual identity The degree of awareness and recognition by an individual of his or her sex and sex roles.

InfoTrac College Edition

Use InfoTrac College Edition to search for additional readings on topics of interest to you. For more information on topics in this chapter, use the following as search terms:

culture and sex roles
culture and gender identity
ethnicity and gender

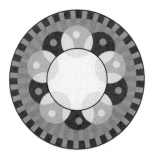

8

Culture and Health

One major role of education is to improve the lives of the people we touch. Whether through research, service, or provision of primary or secondary health care, we look forward to the day when we can adequately diagnose and treat medical diseases, prevent abnormal behavior, and foster positive states of being in balance with others and the environment. This is not an easy task; a multitude of forces influences our health and our ability to prevent and treat illness.

As we strive to meet this challenge, the important role of culture in contributing to the etiology, maintenance, and treatment of disease has become increasingly clear. Although our goals of prevention and treatment of disease and maintenance of health may be the same across cultures, cultures vary in their definitions of what is considered "healthy" or "mature" (Tseng & McDermott, 1981). Cultural differences also exist in perceptions of problems and in preferred strategies for coping with them (Terrell, 1992). Our job is made more difficult because cultural beliefs and practices influence treatment, and they shape both the therapist's and the client's definitions and understandings of the problem (Berry et al., 1992). Traditional approaches to treatment of abnormal behavior may prove insensitive or inappropriate when applied across cultures.

This chapter explores how cultural factors influence physical health and disease processes, and our attempts to treat them. We begin with an examination of cultural differences in the definition of health, and then explore cultural differences in conceptions of the body. We then review the considerable amount of research concerning the relationship between culture and heart disease, other physical disease processes, eating disorders, and suicide. We will also explore the way cultural differences influence help-seeking, treatment compliance, and issues of responsibility, trust, and self-control over personal health and disease processes. We will summarize the research in the form of a model, then use this information to consider ways of developing culturally relevant, sensitive, and effective treatment programs.

Cultural Differences in the Definition of Health

Before we look at how culture influences health and disease processes, we need to examine exactly what we mean by health. More than 50 years ago, the World Health Organization (WHO) developed a definition at the International Health Conference, with 61 countries represented. They defined health as "a state of complete physical, mental, and social well-being, and not merely the absence of disease or infirmity" (World Health Organization, 1948).

In the United States, our views of health have been heavily influenced by what many call the **biomedical model** of health and disease. This model views disease as resulting from a specific, identifiable cause originating inside the body. These causes, whether viral, bacterial, or other, are referred to as **pathogens** and are seen as the root of all physical and medical diseases. Cardiovascular disease, for example, has been linked to specific pathogens such as clotting from lipids and cholesterol. The biomedical model of disease has also influenced psychology's view of abnormal behavior and psychopathology. Traditional psychological approaches view the origin of abnormal behaviors as residing within the person. Such abnormalities may result from lack of gratification or overgratification of basic, instinctual processes (as suggested by Freudian psychoanalytic theory) or from learned responses (as suggested by classical or operant conditioning).

The traditional biomedical model of health in both medicine and psychology has had a profound influence on treatment approaches. If specific medical or psychobehavioral pathogens exist within a person's body, those pathogens must be dealt with when treating disease. Medical treatment and traditional psychological approaches focus on making an intervention within a person. In the traditional biomedical model, health is characterized as the lack of disease. If a person remains free of disease, the person is considered healthy.

Views of health from other cultures suggest different definitions of health. People of China and ancient Greece, for example, viewed health not only as the absence of negative states but also as the presence of positive ones. Balance between self and nature and across the individual's various roles in life is viewed as an integral part of health in many Asian cultures. This balance can produce a positive state—a synergy of the forces of self, nature, and others—that many call health. Alternative views of health that incorporate the presence of positive as well as the absence of negative states are important in many cultures today.

In China, the concept of health, based on Chinese religion and philosophy, focuses on the principles of *yin* and *yang*, which represent negative and positive energies, respectively. The Chinese believe that our bodies are made up of elements of *yin* and *yang*. Balance between these two forces results in good health; an imbalance—too much *yin* or too much *yang*—leads to poor health. Many things can disturb this balance, such as eating too many foods from one of the elements, a change in social relationships, the weather, the seasons, or even supernatural forces. Maintaining a balance involves not only the mind and body, but also the spirit and the natural environment. From the Chinese perspective, the concept of health is not confined to the individual but encompasses the surrounding relationships and environment (Yanchi, 1988).

Incorporating balance as a positive aspect of health is not foreign in the United States today. In the past decade or two, we have seen a rising frustration with defining health solely as the absence of disease. Americans have become much more aware of how lifestyle factors can contribute not only to the absence of negative states but also to the presence of positive ones. In particular, the concept of **hardiness** has been used in recent years in contemporary psychology to denote not only a lack of disease but the presence of positive health states. Biobehavioral medicine and health psychology, nonexistent even a few years ago, represent responses by the health care and academic professions to a growing interest in definitions of health different from those afforded by the traditional biomedical model. We now know that many of the leading causes of death are directly and indirectly attributable to lifestyle choices and unhealthy behaviors (Feist & Brannon, 1988), many of which will be explored in the remainder of this chapter. These findings contribute to our growing knowledge of the impact of behavior on health. And because behavior is heavily influenced by culture, an increased awareness of the links among health, lifestyle, and behavior can help us understand the sociocultural influences on health and disease.

Concepts of health may differ not only between cultures but also within a pluralistic culture such as the United States or Canada. Mulatu and Berry (2001) point out that health perspectives may differ between individuals from the dominant or mainstream culture and those of the nondominant social and ethnocultural group. They cite the example of Native Americans, who, based on their religion, have a holistic view of health and who consider good health to be living in harmony with oneself and one's environment. When one does not live in harmony and engages in negative behaviors such as "displeasing the holy people of the past or the present, disturbing animal and plant life, misuse of sacred religious ceremonies, strong and uncontrolled emotions, and breaking social rules and taboos" (p. 219), the result is ill health. This is in sharp contrast to the biomedical model, in which illnesses are thought to originate from viruses and bacteria.

Huff (1999) argues that the concepts of health held by various ethnic and immigrant groups within the United States may differ from and even contradict the health concepts of the mainstream society. This may create problems in the identification and treatment of illnesses, as discussed later in the chapter. However, mainstream culture is also adapting and incorporating ideas of health that immigrants have brought with them, as seen in the rising popularity and interest in alternative health practices such as acupuncture, homeopathy, herbal medicines, and spiritual healing (Eisenberg et al., 1998). Thus, our own views on health are changing as our culture becomes increasingly pluralistic.

Culture and Conceptions of the Body

Cultures differ in how they view the human body. These different conceptions of the human body influence how people of different cultures approach health and disease, treatment, and perhaps even the types of diseases that affect them.

MacLachlan (1997) has suggested that cultures have different metaphors for how they conceptualize the human body. The most widely held view, according to MacLachlan, involves the notion of balance and imbalance in the body: The various systems of the body produce harmony or health when in balance, illness and disease when in imbalance. A theory first developed by Hippocrates, which heavily influences views of the human body and disease in most industrialized countries and cultures today, suggests that the body is comprised of four humors: blood, phlegm, yellow bile, and black bile. Too much or too little of any of these throws the body out of balance, resulting in disease. Derivatives of these terms—such as sanguine, phlegmatic, and choleric—are widely used in health and medical circles today.

MacLachlan (1997) points out that common theories of disease in many Latin American cultures involve a balance between hot and cold. These terms do not refer to temperature, but to the intrinsic power of different substances in the body. Some illnesses or states are hot, others cold. A person who is in a hot condition is given cold foods to counteract the situation, and vice versa. The Chinese concept of *yin* and *yang* shows similarities to this concept.

Social and cultural factors play a major role in the perception of one's own and others' body shapes, and these perceptions influence the relationship between culture and health. For example, a number of studies have found an inverse relationship between social class and body weight in many American and European cultures; that is, individuals of higher social class generally have lower body weights than individuals of lower social class (reviewed in Furnham & Alibhai, 1983). The inverse, however, is true in many other cultures. And it has also been shown that the longer some immigrants have lived in traditionally Western cultures, the less obese they tend to be. Furnham and Alibhai (1983) examined how Kenyan Asian, British, and Kenyan British females perceived female body shapes. In their study, participants were shown drawings of women ranging from extremely anorexic to extremely obese, and were asked to rate each on a series of bipolar adjectives. The results indicated that the Kenyan Asians rated larger figures more favorably and smaller figures less favorably than did the British, as predicted. The Kenyan British were similar to the British group in their perceptions.

A later study by Furnham and Baguma (1994) also confirmed the role of culture in the perception of body shape. In this study, British and Ugandan students rated 24 drawings of male and female figures on 12 bipolar scales. Again, the figures ranged from extremely anorexic to extremely obese. The results showed cultural differences on the extreme pictures, with Ugandans rating the obese female and anorexic male figures as more attractive than British observers. Again, these findings point to the important role of culture and cultural stereotypes in the perception and evaluation of body shapes, which in turn has implications for health and disease processes. Other studies (for example, Henriques, Calhoun, & Cann, 1996) have documented similar differences among ethnic groups in the United States. Future research will need to establish the links between these types of perceptions and actual health-related behaviors, in order to document the degree to which these perceptions influence health and disease processes.

Sociocultural Influences on Physical Health and Medical Disease Processes

Psychosocial Determinants of Health and Disease

In the past few years, psychology as a whole has becoming increasingly aware of the important role that culture may play in the maintenance of health and the production of disease processes. This awareness can be seen on many levels, from more journal articles published on these topics to the establishment of new journals devoted to this area of research. This increased awareness is related to a growing concern with psychosocial determinants of health and illness in general.

Scholars have long been interested in the close relationship between mental and physical health. Research linking Type A personality patterns and cardiovascular disease is a good example of this area of study. As most people are aware, research originally conducted three decades ago showed that individuals who were pressed for time, always in a rush, agitated and irritable, and always on the go—characterized as Type A personality syndrome—appeared to be at greater risk for developing cardiovascular disease and heart attacks than non–Type A personalities. This linkage was important not only in informing us about the etiology and possible prevention of cardiovascular disease; it also opened the door to examining the close relationship between psychology and physiology—the field we now know as health psychology.

Over the past three decades, a number of important and interesting studies have continued to document the linkage between psychosocial factors and health/disease states. Steptoe and his colleagues (Steptoe, Sutcliffe, Allen, & Coombes, 1991; Steptoe & Wardle, 1994) have reviewed many of the previous studies, highlighting the links between unemployment and mortality, cardiovascular disease, and cancer; between goal frustration and negative life events and gastrointestinal disorders; between stress and myocardial ischemias and the common cold; between bereavement and lymphocyte functions; between pessimistic explanatory styles and physical illnesses; and between hardiness and physical illnesses, among others. Indeed, the field has come a long way beyond Type A personality patterns and cardiovascular disease in demonstrating the close relationship between psychosocial factors and health/disease outcomes.

Adler and her colleagues (1994) have reported that socioeconomic status (SES) is consistently associated with health outcomes, with people of higher SES enjoying better health than do people of lower SES. This relationship has been found not only for mortality rates, but for almost every disease and condition studied. Research, however, has not been able to identify the exact mechanisms that mediate the linkage between SES and health. Adler and colleagues suggest that health-related behaviors such as smoking, physical activity, and alcohol use may mediate that relationship, as these variables appear to be related to SES. In addition, psychological characteristics such as depression, hostility, stress, and social ordering—one's relative position in the SES hierarchy—may also mediate the relationship between SES and health, because each of these variables appears to be related to SES. Recent studies have proposed that other psychosocial factors such as perceived racism and discrimination contribute to negative health outcomes such as hypertension and cardiovascular disease (Brondolo, Rieppi, Kelly, & Gerin, 2003; Krieger, 1999).

Thus, research of the past two decades has demonstrated convincingly that psychosocial factors play an important role in maintaining and promoting health, and in the etiology and treatment of disease. Still, many avenues remain open for future research, including establishing direct links between particular psychosocial factors and specific disease outcomes, and identifying the specific mechanisms that mediate those relationships. Hopefully, research of the next two decades will be as fruitful as that of the past two decades in providing much-needed knowledge about these processes.

Beyond looking at psychosocial factors, many scholars and health care practitioners alike have long been interested in the contribution of sociocultural factors to health. In the past decade, a number of important studies have shown how culture may play a major role in the development and treatment of illness. These studies, to be reviewed in this chapter, destroy the common notion that physical illness has nothing to do with sociocultural or psychological factors, and vice versa. Indeed, they contribute to our combined knowledge of psychological factors in physical disease processes. Changes in lifestyle (for example, diet, smoking, exercise, and alcohol consumption) can be seen as our response to this increasing recognition of the complex interrelationship among culture, psychology, and medical processes.

Social Isolation and Mortality

Some of the earliest research on sociocultural factors in health and disease processes examined the relationship between social isolation or social support and death. Earlier research had highlighted the potential negative effects of social isolation and social disadvantage on health and disease (Feist & Brannon, 1988). One of the best-known studies in this area is the Alameda County study (Berkman & Syme, 1979), named after the county in California where the data were collected and the study conducted. Researchers interviewed almost 7,000 individuals to discover their degree of social contact; the final data set included approximately 4,725 people, as some people were dropped from the study. Following the initial assessment interview, deaths were monitored over a nine-year period. The results were clear for both men and women: Individuals with the fewest social ties suffered the highest mortality rate, and people with the most social ties had the lowest rate. These findings were valid even when other factors were statistically or methodologically controlled, including the level of physical health reported at the time of the initial questionnaire, the year of death, socioeconomic status, and a number of health-related behaviors (such as smoking and alcohol consumption). This study was one of the first to demonstrate clearly the enormous role that sociocultural factors may play in the maintenance of physical health and illness, and raised the awareness of scientists and theorists alike concerning the possible role of social factors in health/disease processes.

Individualism and Cardiovascular Disease

For many years now, researchers have examined how social and psychological factors influence the development and treatment of cardiovascular disease. Several factors have contributed to this focus on cardiovascular disease. One is the previous work identifying a number of psychological and behavioral factors that appear to influence cardiovascular disease—notably, the Type A personality profile (see Friedman & Rosenman, 1974). This profile, found across various cultures (del Pino Perez, Meizoso, & Gonzalez, 1999), is characterized by competitiveness, time urgency, anger, and hostility. Another is the relatively high incidence of cardiovascular disease in the United States, making it a major health concern for many Americans.

Although there has not been a lot of research on the role of social and cultural (as opposed to personality) factors, some studies indicate that they also contribute to cardiovascular disease. Marmot and Syme (1976), for example, studied Japanese Americans, classifying 3,809 subjects into groups according to how "traditionally Japanese" they were (spoke Japanese at home, retained traditional Japanese values and behaviors, and the like). They found that those who were the "most" Japanese had the lowest incidence of coronary heart disease—comparable to the incidence in Japan. The group that was the "least" Japanese had a three to five times higher incidence. Moreover, the differences between the groups could not be accounted for by other coronary risk factors. These findings point to the contribution of social and cultural lifestyles to the development of heart disease.

Triandis and his colleagues (1988) took this finding one step further, using the individualism–collectivism (IC) cultural dimension and examining its relationship to heart disease across eight different cultural groups. European Americans, the most individualistic of the eight groups, had the highest rate of heart attacks; Trappist monks, who were the least individualistic, had the lowest rate. Of course, this study is not conclusive, as many other variables confound comparisons between Americans and Trappist monks (such as industrialization, class, and lifestyle). Nevertheless, these findings again highlight the potential contribution of sociocultural factors to the development of heart disease.

Triandis and his colleagues (1988) suggested that social support or isolation was the most important factor that explained this relationship, a position congruent with the earlier research on social isolation. That is, people who live in more collectivistic cultures have stronger and deeper social ties with others than do people in individualistic cultures. These social relationships, in turn, are considered a "buffer" against the stress and strain of living, reducing the risk of cardiovascular disease. People who live in individualistic cultures do not have the same types or degrees of social relationships; therefore, they have less of a buffer against stress and are more susceptible to heart disease.

Other Dimensions of Culture and Other Diseases

The study by Triandis and his colleagues (1988) was especially important because it was the first to examine the relationship between cultural differences and the incidence of a particular disease state (heart disease). Research has also been done on other disease states and health-related behaviors, such as cancer, smoking, stress, and pain (see Feist & Brannon, 1988). Collectively, these studies suggest the important role of sociocultural factors—most notably, social support—in contributing to health and disease.

Still, these studies are limited in that they have focused on only one aspect of culture—individualism versus collectivism—with its mediating variable of social support. As discussed in Chapter 2 and elsewhere, however, culture encompasses many other important dimensions, including power distance, uncertainty avoidance, masculinity, tightness, and contextualization. Another limitation of the previous research is that it has looked almost exclusively at mortality rates or cardiovascular disease. Other dimensions of culture, however, may be associated with the incidence of other disease processes. If members of individualistic cultures are indeed at higher risk for heart disease, for example, perhaps they are at lower risk for other disease processes. Conversely, if collectivistic cultures are at lower risk for heart disease, they may be at higher risk for other diseases.

Matsumoto and Fletcher (1996) investigated this possibility by examining the relationship among multiple dimensions of culture and multiple disease processes, opening the door to this line of study. These researchers obtained the mortality rates for six different medical diseases: infections and parasitic diseases, malignant neoplasms (tumors), diseases of the circulatory system, heart diseases, cerebrovascular diseases, and respiratory system diseases. These epidemiological data, taken from the *World Health Statistics Quarterly* (World Health Organization, 1991), were compiled across 28 countries widely distributed around the globe, spanning five continents, and representing many different ethnic, cultural, and socioeconomic backgrounds. In addition, incidence rates for each of the diseases were available at five age points for each country: at birth and at ages 1, 15, 45, and 65. To get cultural data for each country, Matsumoto and Fletcher (1996) used cultural index scores previously obtained by Hofstede (1980, 1983), who analyzed questionnaire data about cultural values and practices from large samples in each of these countries and classified their responses according to four cultural tendencies: individualism versus collectivism (IC), power distance (PD), uncertainty avoidance (UA), and masculinity (MA).

Table 8.1 Summary of Findings on the Relationship between Four
Cultural Dimensions and Incidence of Diseases

Cultural Dimension	Rates of Disease
Higher Power Distance	▪ Higher rates of infections and parasitic diseases ▪ Lower rates of malignant neoplasm, circulatory disease, and heart disease
Higher Individualism	▪ Higher rates of malignant neoplasms and heart disease ▪ Lower rates of infections and parasitic diseases, cerebrovascular disease
Higher Uncertainty Avoidance	▪ Higher rates of heart disease ▪ Lower rates of cerebrovascular disease and respiratory disease
Higher Masculinity	▪ Higher cerebrovascular disease

Source: Matsumoto & Fletcher, 1996

Matsumoto and Fletcher then correlated these cultural index scores with the epidemiological data. The results were quite fascinating and pointed to the importance of culture in the development of these disease processes. See Table 8.1 for a summary of findings.

The countries in this study differ economically as well as culturally, and it may well be that these economic differences—particularly with regard to the availability of treatment, diet, and sanitation—also contribute to disease. To deal with this possibility, Matsumoto and Fletcher (1996) recomputed their correlations controlling for per capita gross domestic product (GDP) of each country. Even when the effects of per capita GDP were accounted for, the predictions for infections and parasitic diseases, circulatory diseases, and heart diseases all survived. The predictions for UA and cerebrovascular and respiratory diseases, and MA and cerebrovascular diseases, also survived. Thus, these cultural dimensions predicted disease above and beyond what is accounted for by economic differences among the countries. Only the prediction for malignant neoplasms was not supported, indicating that economic differences among the countries cannot be disentangled from cultural differences in predicting the incidence of neoplasms.

A study by Bond (1991) also looked at the influence of dimensions other than IC on health and disease processes other than heart disease. Bond surveyed the relationship between cultural values and the incidence of disease processes in 23 countries. The cultural values he measured were social integration, cultural inwardness, reputation, and morality. Social integration refers to the degree to which a culture fosters the coming together of people in an environment that nurtures social relationships. This dimension was statistically correlated with an increased incidence of cerebrovascular disease, ulcers of the stomach and duodenum, and neoplasms of the stomach, colon, rectum, rectosigmoid junction, and anus. Reputation was significantly correlated with acute myocardial infarction, other ischemic heart disease, neoplasms of the colon, rectum, rectosigmoid junction, and anus, and neoplasms of the trachea, bronchi, and lungs. Morality was significantly associated with cirrhosis of the liver.

How and why does culture affect medical disease processes? Triandis and colleagues (1988) suggested that culture—specifically, social support—plays an important role in mediating stress, which affects health. The findings of Matsumoto and Fletcher (1996) and Bond (1991), however, suggest a much more complex picture. Although collectivistic cultures were associated with lower rates of cardiovascular diseases, replicating the previous findings, they were also associated with death from infectious and parasitic diseases, and cerebrovascular diseases. Thus, although social support may be a buffer against life stress in the prevention of heart attacks, these data suggest that there is something else to collectivism that actually increases susceptibility to other disease processes. To be sure, these other factors may not be cultural per se. Collectivism, for example, is generally correlated with geographic location; countries nearer the equator tend to be more collectivistic. Countries nearer the equator also have hotter climates, which foster the spread of organisms responsible for infectious and parasitic diseases. The relationship between collectivism and death from these types of disease processes, therefore, may be related to geography rather than culture.

Still, these findings do suggest that individualism is not necessarily bad, and collectivism is not necessarily good, as earlier findings had suggested. The latest findings suggest, instead, that different societies and countries develop different cultural ways of dealing with the problem of living. Each way is associated with its own specific and different set of stressors, each of which may take its toll on the human body. Because different cultural ways of living take different tolls on the body, they are associated with different risk factors and rates for different disease processes. This view may be a more holistic account of how culture may influence health and disease processes.

Future research will need to investigate further the specific mechanisms that mediate these relationships. Some studies, for example, will need to examine more closely the relationship among culture, geography, and other noncultural factors in connection with disease incidence rates. Other studies will need to examine directly the relationship between culture and specific behavioral and psychological processes, to elucidate the possible mechanisms of health and disease. Matsumoto and Fletcher (1996), for example, suggested that culture influences human emotion and human physiology, particularly with respect to autonomic nervous system activity and the immune system. For example, the link between PD and circulatory and heart diseases may be explained by noting that cultures low on PD tend to minimize status differences among their members. As status and power differences diminish, people are freer to feel and express negative emotions, such as anger or hostility, to ingroup others. Containing negative emotions, as must be done in high-PD cultures, may have dramatic consequences for the cardiovascular system, resulting in a relatively higher incidence of circulatory and heart diseases in those cultures. A study by Ekman, Levenson, and Friesen (1983), documenting substantial increases in heart rate associated with angry expressions, lends further credence to this hypothesis. Hopefully, future research will be able to address these and other possibilities.

Cultural Discrepancies and Physical Health

Although the studies described so far suggest that culture influences physical health, more recent research suggests that culture per se is not the only culturally relevant variable. Indeed, the discrepancy between one's personal cultural values and those of society may play a large role in producing stress, which in turn leads to negative health outcomes. Matsumoto and colleagues (1999) tested this idea by asking university undergraduates to report what their personal cultural values were, as well as their perceptions of society's values and ideal values. Participants in this study also completed a scale assessing strategies for coping with stress; anxiety, depression, and other mood measures; and scales assessing physical health and psychological well-being. Discrepancy scores in cultural values were computed by taking the differences between self and society, and self and ideal, ratings. These discrepancy scores were then correlated with the scores on the eight coping strategies assessed. The results indicated that discrepancies between self and society's cultural values were significantly correlated with all eight coping strategies, indicating that greater cultural discrepancies were associated with greater needs for coping. These coping strategies were significantly correlated with depression and anxiety, which in turn were significantly correlated with scores on the physical health symptoms checklist scales. In particular, higher scores on anxiety were strongly correlated with greater health problems. The results of this study, therefore, suggest that greater discrepancy between self and societal cultural values may lead to greater psychological stress, which necessitates greater degrees of coping, which affects emotion and mood, which causes greater degrees of anxiety and depression, which then lead to more physical health problems.

Of course, this single study is not conclusive; future research will need to replicate these findings, and elaborate on them. They do suggest, however, the potential role of cultural discrepancies in mediating health outcomes, and open the door for new and exciting research in this area of psychology.

Culture and Eating Disorders

One health-related topic that has received considerable attention concerns eating disorders and obesity. As mentioned previously, a number of studies have reported a negative correlation between body weight and income in the United States: As people get wealthier, they tend to become thinner. In many other countries, the relationship is exactly the opposite: As people get wealthier, they tend to become larger; size is associated with wealth and abundance. A number of studies, in fact, have found considerable cultural differences in perceptions of and stereotypes about thinness and obesity. Cogan, Bhalla, Sefa-Dedeh, and Rothblum (1996), for example, asked university students in Ghana and the United States to complete questionnaires about their weight, frequency of dieting, social activities, perceptions of ideal bodies, disordered eating, and stereotypes of thin and heavy people. They found that the Ghanaians were more likely to rate larger body sizes as ideals in their society. Americans, especially females, were more likely to have dieted. American females also scored higher on dietary restraint, disordered eating behavior, and experiencing weight as a social interference.

Crandall and Martinez (1996) reported similar findings. These researchers compared attitudes about weight and fatness in American and Mexican students, by asking students to complete an anti-fat attitude scale and a scale on political ideologies and beliefs. The results indicated that Mexican students were less concerned about their own weight, and more accepting of fat people, than were the American students. Additionally, anti-fat attitudes in the United States appeared to be part of a social ideology that holds individuals responsible for their life outcomes. Attributions of controllability and responsibility were less important in predicting anti-fat attitudes in Mexico, where antipathy toward fat people did not appear related to any ideological framework.

Not only are such cultural differences in attitudes apparent across cultures outside the United States; a number of studies have recently documented similar findings across different cultural groups within the United States as well. Akan and Grilo (1995), for example, reported similar findings in comparing African, Asian, and European Americans. Harris and Koehler (1992) reported similar findings in comparing Anglo and Hispanic Americans in the southwestern United States. Abrams, Allen, and Gray (1993) reported similar findings comparing black and white female college students. And Hamilton, Brooks-Gunn, and Warren (1985) reported similar findings comparing black and white female professional ballet dancers.

Cultural differences in attitudes about fatness and thinness appear to be related to cultural differences in attitudes toward eating behaviors. In Akan and Grilo's (1995) study, for instance, European Americans reported greater levels of disordered eating and dieting behaviors, and greater body dissatisfaction, than did Asian and African Americans. Low self-esteem and high public self-consciousness were associated with greater levels of problematic eating behaviors, attitudes, and body dissatisfaction. In Abrams, Allen, and Gray's (1993) study, white females demonstrated significantly greater disordered eating attitudes and behaviors than black females. Disordered eating behaviors, in turn, were related to depression, anxiety, and low self-esteem. In Hamilton, Brooks-Gunn, and Warren's (1985) study, none of the black dancers reported anorexia or bulimia, compared with 15% and 19%, respectively, of the white dancers. Self-reported anorectics had higher disordered eating attitudes, exhibited more psychopathology, and had poorer body images than nonanorectics. The bulimics valued their career less, dieted more, and exercised less frequently than nonbulimics. Finally, a recent study of Pakistani females found that exposure to Western culture significantly predicted more disturbed eating attitudes (Suhail & Nisa, 2002).

Collectively, these studies demonstrate convincingly that attitudes toward body size and shape, and eating, are heavily influenced by culture. Cultural values, attitudes, beliefs, and opinions about wealth, abundance, beauty and attractiveness, power, and other such psychological characteristics likely play a major role in determining attitudes toward eating, thinness, and obesity. These latter attitudes, in turn, most likely directly affect health-related behaviors such as eating, diet, and exercise. The research also suggests that these tendencies may be especially prevalent in the United States, especially among European American females. Crandall and Martinez's (1996) study suggests that this tendency in the United States may be related to specific ideologies about people, power, and responsibility. However, such tendencies are not solely an American phenomenon. Cross-cultural research has pointed to similarities between Americans and members of other cultures in their attitudes toward eating and preoccupation with thinness—for example, the Japanese (Mukai & McCloskey, 1996).

Future research will need to tackle the difficult question of exactly what it is about culture that influences attitudes about eating and stereotypes about thinness and obesity, and where cultures draw the line between healthy patterns and disordered eating behaviors that have direct, negative impacts on health. Future research will also need to tie specific eating behaviors to specific health and disease outcomes, and attempt to link culture with these relationships.

Culture and Suicide

No other behavior has health consequences as final as suicide—the taking of one's own biological life. Psychologists, sociologists, and anthropologists have long been fascinated by suicide, and have studied this behavior across many cultures. The research to date suggests many interesting cross-cultural differences in the nature of suicidal behavior, all of which point to the different ways in which people of different cultures view not only death, but life itself.

One of the most glorified and curious cultures with regard to suicidal behavior is that of Japan. Tales of Japanese pilots who deliberately crashed their planes into enemy targets during World War II stunned and mystified many people of other cultures. These individuals clearly placed the welfare, spirit, and honor of their country above the value of their own lives. To be sure, such acts of self-sacrifice were not limited to the Japanese, as men and women on both sides of war reach into themselves in ways many of us cannot understand to sacrifice their lives for the sake of others. But the Japanese case seems to highlight the mysterious and glorified nature of some acts of suicide in that culture.

Among the most glorified acts of suicide in Japan (called *seppuku* or *hara-kiri*—the slitting of one's belly) were those of the masterless samurai swordsmen who served as the basis for the story known as *Chuushingura*. In this factual story, a lord of one clan of samurai was humiliated and lost face because of the acts of another lord. In disgrace, the humiliated lord committed *seppuku* to save the honor of himself, his family, and his clan. His now masterless samurai—known as *ronin*—plotted to avenge their master's death by killing the lord who had humiliated him in the first place. Forty-seven of them plotted their revenge and carried out their plans by killing the lord. Afterward, they turned themselves in to authorities, admitting to the plot of revenge and explaining the reasons for their actions. It was then decided that the only way to resolve the entire situation was to order the 47 *ronin* to commit *seppuku* themselves—which they did. In doing so, they laid down their lives, voluntarily and through this ritualistic method, to preserve the honor and dignity of their clan and families. Although these events occurred in the late 19th century, similar acts continue in Japan today. Some Japanese businessmen have committed suicide as a way of taking responsibility for the downturns in their companies resulting from the economic crisis in Japan and much of Asia.

Japan is by no means the only culture in which suicide has been examined psychologically and cross-culturally. Kazarian and Persad (2001) note that "suicide has been in evidence in every time period in recorded history and in almost every culture around the world. It is depicted, and reasons for its committal described, in tribal folklore, Greek tragedies, religious, philosophical, and historical writings, literature, modern soap operas, and rock music" (p. 275).

Many studies seem to point to profound cultural changes as a determinant of suicidal behavior. Leenaars, Anawak, and Taparti (1998), for example, suggest this factor as an important influence on suicide rates among Canadian Inuits, primarily among younger individuals. Sociocultural change has long been identified as a predictor of suicide among Native Americans, whose suicide rates are higher than those of other Americans (for example, EchoHawk, 1997; Bechtold, 1988; May & Dizmang, 1974; Resnik & Dizmang, 1971). Stresses associated with social and cultural changes have also been implicated in the suicide rates of many other cultural groups, including Native Hawaiians (Takeuchi et al., 1987), Greeks (Beratis, 1986), English (Robertson & Cochrane, 1976), Eskimos (Parkin, 1974), and many other groups.

Some researchers have attempted to identify other factors common to different cultures that may predict suicidal behavior. Literacy does not appear to affect suicide rates; one study comparing 54 cultural groups found no differences between literate and nonliterate cultures in those rates (Palmer, 1971). In another study, Boor (1976) compared suicide rates in ten countries—New Zealand, Israel, the United States, Canada, Italy, Australia, West Germany, France, Japan, and Sweden—and correlated those rates with mean scores on an internal–external control scale. The results indicated that cultures that foster high perceptions of external control are associated with higher suicide rates. Although this study was conducted more than 20 years ago, its findings are congruent with more contemporary analyses suggesting that suicide may be a product of the collectivity of ideas within a culture in relation to death and life (Kral, 1998). Concerning the cultural dimensions of individualism and collectivism, a study by Levine and Norenzayan (1999) reports that higher rates of suicide occur in individualistic than in collectivistic cultures.

Another factor that may be closely related to culture and suicide is religious beliefs. For instance, suicide is strictly forbidden in the Muslim and Jewish religions and was considered a mortal sin in the early history of Christianity (Kazarian & Persad, 2001). Kelleher, Chambers, Corcoran, Williamson, and Keeley (1998) examined data from suicide rates reported to the World Health Organization and found that countries with religions that strongly condemned the act of suicide had lower reported rates of suicide than countries without religions that strongly condemned suicide. However, the researchers also suggested that the reports may have been biased. Those countries with religious sanctions against suicide may have been less willing to report and record suicides.

There are also within-country differences in rates of suicide. For instance, Shiang (1998) found that in San Francisco, during the period between 1987 and 1996, African Americans, Latinos, and Native Americans had much lower suicide rates than European Americans and Asian Americans. Early and Akers (1993) suggested that having strong religious beliefs and the firm support of the religious community acts as a protective factor against suicide for the African American community. Nonetheless, the suicide rates among African Americans have been rising (Chance, Kaslow, Summerville, & Wood, 1998). In Canada, the rate of suicide among aborigines is two to four times the rate among the nonaboriginal population (Health Canada, 1995). Thus, we find varying suicide rates not only between but within countries.

Cross-cultural research over the past few decades has given us important glimpses into this difficult yet fascinating topic. Still, many questions remain unanswered. What is it about culture that produces differences in suicidal behaviors, and why? Why are there still considerable individual differences in attitudes toward suicide even in cultures where it is relatively more acceptable? Despite the glorified stories concerning suicide in Japan, for instance, there is still a relatively strong stigma against it and intense prejudice toward the mental disorders related to it, resulting in reluctance to seek help (Takahashi, 1997). When may suicide be an acceptable behavior in any culture? Given recent and ongoing advances in medical technology, such questions that run the borders of medicine, culture, and ethics are bound to increase in prominence. In the past decade, physician-assisted suicide, brought to national attention by Dr. Jack Kevorkian, has emerged as an issue in the United States. Future research within and between cultures may help to elucidate some of the important decision points as we approach these questions.

Summary

In this section, we have discussed a considerable amount of research concerning the influence of psychological, social, and cultural factors on health. We know that these factors can influence rates of mortality, heart disease, and several other disease processes. We also know that cultural discrepancies may be related to health, with greater discrepancies leading to greater stress and consequently more anxiety and greater health problems. We have seen how culture influences attitudes about body shape, eating, and eating disorders. And we have discussed how culture may play a role in suicidal behaviors. Future studies will begin to bridge the gap between culture as a macroconcept and specific medical disease processes in the body. Whatever the exact mechanisms, the contribution of culture to physical health and disease is clearer now than ever before. Future research will expand our understanding of how and why this relationship exists.

Cultural Influences on Attitudes and Beliefs Related to Health and Disease

Culture can influence health in many ways. Culture affects attitudes about health care and treatment, attributions about the causes of health and disease processes, the availability of health care and health care delivery systems, help-seeking behaviors, and many other aspects of disease and health care. We are only now becoming aware of the importance of sociocultural differences when developing treatment and intervention programs for medical and psychological problems.

In one study, Matsumoto and his colleagues (1995) recruited Japanese and Japanese American women over the age of 55 living in the San Francisco Bay Area to participate in a study of attitudes and values related to osteoporosis and its treatment. Osteoporosis is a medical disorder in which a decrease in bone density leads to a gradual weakening of the bones. It can be a particularly devastating disease for older women of European or Asian descent. The research included a complete medical history, an assessment of risk factors particular to osteoporosis, an attitudes survey about the disease, and a health care issues assessment. In addition, a subsample of the women were assessed for their bone mineral density (BMD) levels.

Among the most interesting results of this study were the cultural differences found in the attitudes survey and the health care issues assessment. The entire sample of women was divided into two groups: those born and raised in the United States who spoke English as their primary language, and those born and raised in Japan who spoke Japanese as their primary language. When asked about the types of problems they would have if they were diagnosed with osteoporosis, more Japanese than American women reported problems with finances and with finding help. The major concern for American women was "other" problems, including mobility. This finding is especially interesting because mobility is such a central element of individualism, which is more characteristic of the United States than Japan. When asked what kinds of problems they would have if they had to take care of someone with osteoporosis, more Japanese women mentioned not enough time. American women again mentioned "other" problems involving their physical abilities.

The researchers also asked about the types of support services the women would want to have available if they were diagnosed with osteoporosis. More Japanese women reported that they wanted institutions, temporary homes, rehabilitation centers, nursing homes, information services, social service organizations, and organizations to find help. More American women reported wanting "other" services such as medical care.

More American women knew what osteoporosis is. More Japanese women, however, reported that it was of major concern to them and that they would view it very negatively if diagnosed. Also, more American than Japanese women reported that people other than friends or family would care for them if diagnosed. If diagnosed with osteoporosis, Japanese women were more likely to attribute the cause of the illness to fate, chance, or luck; American women were more likely to attribute the illness to diet. Interestingly, there were no differences between the groups in degree of personal responsibility or control, nor in the number of women who specifically asked for osteoporosis examinations, nor in their feelings about estrogen therapy.

A final striking finding was that more Japanese women reported that they would comply with invasive treatment, even though fewer Japanese women had positive feelings about their physicians or reported that they trusted their physicians. This finding is related to the Japanese culture's emphasis on compliance with authority; it suggests that the relationship between interpersonal trust and compliance with authority figures in the Japanese culture is not the same as it is in the United States.

Many other studies also suggest the importance of culture in molding attitudes, beliefs, and values about illness and treatment. Domino and Lin (1993), for example, asked students in Taiwan and the United States to rate various metaphors related to cancer. The metaphors were then scored according to four different scales. The results indicated that the Taiwanese students had significantly higher scores than the Americans on both terminal pessimism and future optimism; that is, they appeared to be both more pessimistic and more optimistic than their American counterparts.

Cook (1994) also reported differences in beliefs about chronic illness and the role of social networks among Chinese, Indian, and Anglo-Celtic Canadians. In his study, Cook asked participants from all three cultural groups to respond to three scales designed to assess psychosocial, phenomenological, and social networking issues related to treatment options, illness, and social support. Data analyses indicated significant differences among the three cultural groups on ratings concerning the phenomenological causes of illness, the psychosocial and phenomenological results of illness, the psychosocial and phenomenological treatment aspects, and in social networks.

Other studies conducted in the past decade also suggest the importance of cultural influences on disease processes. Edman and Kameoka (1997), for example, documented cultural differences between Filipinos and Americans in illness schemas and attributions. Poole and Ting (1995) documented differences between Euro-Canadian and Indo-Canadian patients' attitudes toward maternity care. Mathews, Lannin, and Mitchell (1994) conducted interviews with African American women with advanced breast disease, and commented on the importance of multiple sources of knowledge in coming to terms with the diagnosis of breast cancer in this group of women. Jilek-Aall, Jilek, Kaaya,

Mkombachepa, and Hillary (1997) conducted a study on epilepsy in two iso-lated tribes in Africa; they reported significant differences in attitudes toward epilepsy, which influenced treatment approaches. Guinn (1998) reported data on Mexican American adolescents documenting the importance of psychologi-cal variables such as locus of control in influencing beliefs about health. Sun and Stewart (2000) found that internal locus of control was positively associ-ated with psychological adjustment in a sample of Hong Kong patients with cancer, even though beliefs about supernatural forces are prevalent in this cul-ture. Muela, Ribera, and Tanner (1998) reported on the influence of witchcraft on help-seeking behaviors of Tanzanians in regard to malaria. They found that such beliefs had consequences for noncompliance with treatment, and for de-lay in seeking diagnosis or treatment.

Other researchers have examined how perspectives on health may vary depending on level of acculturation. Quah and Bishop (1996) asked a group of Chinese Americans about their perceptions of health and also measured their level of acculturation by gathering information on generational status, language spoken, religious affiliation, and endorsement of traditional Chinese values. They found that those who rated themselves as being more Chinese believed that diseases were a result of imbalances in the body, such as exces-sive cold or excessive heat, in line with traditional Chinese views of illness. Those who rated themselves lower on being Chinese, in contrast, believed that diseases were a result of viruses, in line with the Western biomedical view of illness. The researchers also found that those who believed in the tra-ditional Chinese views of health and disease were more likely to turn to a practitioner of traditional Chinese medicine when seeking medical help. An-other study of acculturation and health involving Asian Canadians found that those with higher orientations toward Asian culture were more likely to en-dorse the traditional Chinese view of health than did those with higher orien-tations toward Western culture. Furthermore, those endorsing traditional Chi-nese medical beliefs also reported being less satisfied with Western medical care (Armstrong & Swartzmann, 1999).

Taken collectively, a growing literature in the field is showing an in-creased awareness of cultural influences on a host of psychological variables that ultimately have implications for health and disease. These findings sug-gest that health care providers need to deal not only with a patient's disease but also, and perhaps more important, with the psychological correlates of the disease. These may include such variables as attributions and beliefs about the causation of disease; attitudes about health, illness, and treatment; prefer-ences with regard to social support and networks; psychosocial needs with re-gard to autonomy versus reliance on others; and treatment compliance. Also, we cannot forget cultural differences in attitudes about body shapes and in definitions of health and disease, discussed earlier in this chapter. Contempo-rary health practitioners and the institutions in which they work—clinics, hospitals, laboratories—have become increasingly sensitized to these issues, and are now struggling with the best ways to understand and incorporate them for maximum effectiveness.

A Model of Cultural Influences on Physical Health

So far in this chapter, we have reviewed a considerable amount of literature concerning the influence of culture on health and disease processes. This research has begun to affect the ways in which we deliver treatment and other services to people of varying cultural backgrounds, and the type of health care systems we create. It has also made scholars in the field more sensitive to the need to incorporate culture as a major variable in their studies and theories.

So, just how does culture influence physical health and disease processes? Figure 8.1 summarizes what we know so far. We know from other research, not reviewed in this chapter, that culture affects rates of alcohol consumption, tobacco use, and exercise and activity levels. Each of these variables, in turn, has implications for health and disease. The research concerning the relationship between cultural dimensions and the incidence of various diseases also

Figure 8.1 A psychological model of cultural influences on physical health

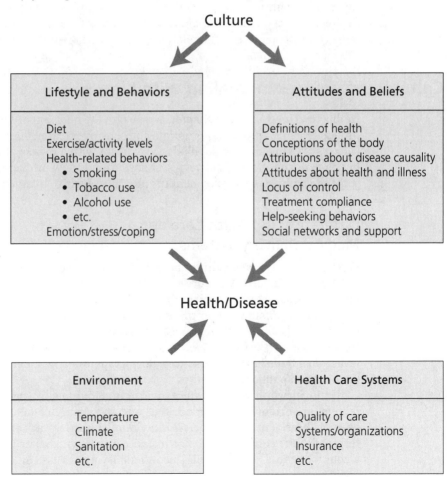

implicates lifestyles and behaviors as possible mediators. In particular, research seems to suggest that stress and emotion, and the ways we cope with them, are important determinants of health and well-being.

We have also discussed the contribution to health and disease of other psychological factors, most notably attitudes and beliefs about disease processes, causations, treatment, and help seeking. Finally, although this chapter has focused on the role of sociocultural factors in health and disease, we cannot ignore the contributory roles of the environment and available health care systems in promoting health and well-being.

Figure 8.1 is meant to provide a general overview of the role that culture and other social factors may play in the area of physical health. All of these factors will need to be fleshed out in greater detail, then tied together into a comprehensive and systematic whole to further our understanding of health and disease processes. Future research will also need to operationalize health according to dimensions other than mortality rates or incidence rates of various diseases. Incorporating cultural, environmental, social, and psychological factors in determining multiple definitions of health is an enormous job for the future, but it is one that we must work toward if we are to get a clearer and more complete picture of the relative contribution of all these factors.

Cultural Differences in Dealing with Illness

In this final section of the chapter, we turn to the question of how health care professionals can provide appropriate and sensitive treatment and other health care services to a diverse population. We begin with a review of differences in health care and medical delivery systems around the world, and then look at some research on the development of culturally sensitive treatment approaches.

Differences in Health Care and Medical Delivery Systems

Different countries and cultures have developed their own unique ways of dealing with health care. A country's health care delivery system is a product of many factors, including social and economic development, technological advances and availability, and the influence of neighboring and collaborating countries. Also affecting health care delivery services are a number of social trends, including urbanization, industrialization, governmental structure, international trade laws and practices, demographic changes, demands for privatization, and public expenditures.

National health systems can be divided into four major types: entrepreneurial, welfare-oriented, comprehensive, and socialist (Roemer, 1991). Within each of these general categories, individual countries vary tremendously in terms of their economic level. For instance, the United States is an example of a country with a relatively high economic level that uses an entrepreneurial system of health care, characterized by a substantial private industry covering individuals as well as groups. The Philippines and Ghana also use an entrepreneurial system of health care, but have moderate and low economic levels, respectively. France, Brazil, and Burma are examples of high-, moderate-, and low-income countries with welfare-oriented health systems. Likewise, Sweden, Costa Rica, and Sri Lanka have comprehensive health care, and the former Soviet Union, Cuba, and China have socialist health systems.

A quick review of the countries listed here suggests that cultural differences are related to the type of national health system a country is likely to adopt. It makes sense that an entrepreneurial system is used in the United States, for example, because of the highly individualistic nature of American culture. Likewise, it makes sense that socialist systems of health care are used in China and Cuba, given their collectivistic, communal nature. However, cultural influences cannot be separated from the other factors that contribute to national health care systems. In the complex interactions among culture, economy, technology, and government, social aspects of culture are inseparable from social institutions.

The Development of Culturally Sensitive Treatment Approaches

In the past decade, a number of important studies have examined the issue of culturally sensitive treatment approaches for people of diverse cultural backgrounds. In the past, at least in the United States, health professionals and medical communities tended to approach health and the treatment of physical diseases in all people similarly, with the underlying assumption that people's bodies are all the same. As the American population has diversified, however, and as research continues to uncover more ways in which people of different cultural backgrounds differ from one another, the health professions are slowly becoming aware of the need to develop culturally sensitive and appropriate treatment approaches.

The need for such approaches is borne out in the literature. Ponchilla (1993), for example, reports that cultural beliefs among Native Americans, Mexican Americans, and Pacific Islanders affect the success of health-related services to native peoples who are suffering vision loss as a result of diabetes. These cultural beliefs include the circle of life, identification with persons with disabilities, the value of silence, and even the healing power of blindness itself. Ponchilla also suggests that the increase in the incidence of diabetes among these cultural groups is due to their adoption of Western diets and lifestyles.

Other findings also suggest the influence of culture on treatment success.

Wing, Crow, and Thompson (1995) examined barriers to seeking treatment for alcoholism among Muscogee Indians, and found that this group traditionally perceives alcoholism to be caused by a lack of spirituality. Admission of alcohol abuse thus causes embarrassment and shame, and the practice of humility in Western-oriented alcoholism programs hinders treatment. Talamantes,

Lawler, and Espino (1995) examined issues related to caregiving and the use of hospice services by Hispanic American elderly, who are less likely to use such long-term care services. They found that factors affecting level of use included alienation; language barriers; availability of culture-sensitive services; beliefs regarding illness, suffering, coping, and death; socioeconomic and demographic factors; acculturation; and the availability of informal care, most notably via extended family and community support. Delgado (1995) also pointed out the importance of such natural support systems among the Hispanic cultures in the treatment of alcoholism.

Studies of other cultural groups also highlight the importance of families and communities in the treatment of health-related problems. Nemoto and colleagues (1998), for example, examined cultural factors such as family support in the treatment and prevention of drug abuse in Filipino and Chinese individuals. More specifically, they examined factors that prevent drug abuse and the escalation of drug use in these groups, including family support, cultural competence, religious beliefs, and life satisfaction. One of the interesting findings of this study was that some drug users received financial support from family members who knew the recipients' drug habits. Family members tried not to talk about the problems in the family, yet continued to provide financial support to the user. The authors concluded that culturally sensitive and appropriate treatment needs to involve the immediate family and extended family members if the treatment is to be effective. These and other findings suggest that health problems arise as much from a collective system of individuals and social agents as from a single individual. This collective system, therefore, must be engaged if treatment is to be relevant and effective.

Armstrong and Swartzman (2001) also point out the need to understand how different cultures speak and communicate about illnesses. For instance, people from a collectivistic culture may not directly tell a doctor what is bothering them, but may be much more circumspect in describing their illness. If the doctor has an individualistic orientation and is much more direct in trying to find out what is ailing the patient by asking pointed, direct questions and expecting direct answers, this may cause distress for the patient and may hinder both the patient and the health care provider in dealing with the illness.

It is extremely difficult to grasp the complexity that culture brings to the development of successful and effective treatment approaches. Besides family issues, a host of variables may include religion and spirituality, social support networks, beliefs and attitudes about causes and treatments, socioeconomic factors, language barriers, shame, face, and many others. Although some culturally relevant programs have been shown to be successful (for example, Uziel-Miller, Lyons, Kissiel, & Love, 1998; Damond, Breuer, & Pharr, 1993), others have not (for example, Rossiter, 1994). Thus, it is not clear what the exact ingredients for successful treatment interventions are, and whether these ingredients differ depending on the cultural group or individual that is seeking help. Basic educational programs about health and disease prevention that tap cultural groups in relevant ways may be a relatively easy way to access many individuals. One such program (Hiatt et al., 1996) investigated knowledge, practices, and attitudes of 4,228 women from five ethnic groups in the San Francisco Bay Area with regard to barriers to using breast and cervical cancer screening tests. Latina, white, and black women had screening levels that were higher than national averages; Chinese and Vietnamese women, however, did not. The data underscored the importance of basic educational programs that may help make it easier for more women to obtain such screenings at earlier ages, thus increasing the potential for effective treatment if and when problems are found.

Clearly, the field is still struggling to discover what the most important culturally relevant variables are and whether these variables are similar or different across cultural groups. Our guess would be that there are some culture-constant needs that need to be addressed, but that these needs are manifested in different ways in different attitudes, values, beliefs, social support, extended families, and the like. Future research has a large job in evaluating the host of potentially important variables to distill a set of guidelines that can be useful for health care professionals in their attempts to improve people's lives.

❀ Conclusion

Many factors contribute to health and disease processes. Besides effects of the environment, diet, directly health-related behaviors (smoking, alcohol consumption), and health care availability, culture is also a major factor. Understanding the role that culture plays in the development of disease, whether medical or psychological, will take us a long way toward developing ways of preventing disease in the future. As research uncovers the possible negative consequences of cultural tendencies, we can also look to an understanding of cultural influences to help us treat people of different cultures better than we have in the past.

In this chapter, we have examined how cross-cultural research has attempted to explore the influence of culture on physical health. We have seen how different cultures have different definitions of health and disease, and different conceptions of the body. We have reviewed a considerable amount of research that shows how culture appears to be related to a number of different disease processes around the world. This literature complements the already large literature that highlights the importance of other psychosocial determinants of health and disease, such as personality and socioeconomic status. We have also seen how individual cultural discrepancies may be related to health, and how culture influences specific behaviors such as eating and suicide. We have explored the nature of culturally relevant and sensitive treatment approaches, including the importance of family and community in some cultural groups.

Still, much remains to be learned, and many questions remain unanswered. What is the relative contribution of cultural variables to the development of disease or the maintenance of health, in relation to other determinants such as psychological, social, demographic, economic, and environmental factors? What is it about culture that influences health and disease, and why? What are the basic ingredients of a culturally relevant and effective treatment approach, and to what degree are these ingredients constant across cultures and individuals?

Recognition of the role of culture in influencing the definition and expression of health suggests that we must modify our methods of assessing and treating disease. Developing adequate assessment strategies requires that culturally based definitions of health and disease be taken into account. Awareness of culture-specific systems of healing is also necessary to develop effective methods of both assessment and treatment. Culturally sensitive assessment and treatment methods are vital to improving our ability to meet the health needs of culturally diverse populations, both in the United States and globally.

Glossary

biomedical model A model of health that views disease as resulting from a specific, identifiable cause originating inside the body.

hardiness A positive state of health that goes beyond the absence of disease.

pathogen In the biomedical model, a cause of disease, whether viral, bacterial, or other; the root of all physical and medical diseases.

InfoTrac College Edition

Use InfoTrac College Edition to search for additional readings on topics of interest to you. For more information on topics in this chapter, use the following as search terms:

culture and disease
culture and suicide
culture and eating disorders
individualism and health aspects
social isolation

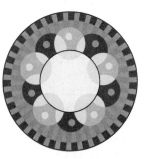

Culture and Emotion

The Importance of Emotion in Our Lives

It is difficult to imagine life without emotion, devoid of feeling. We treasure our feelings—the joy we feel at a ball game, the pleasure of the touch of a loved one, the fun we have with our friends on a night out, seeing a movie, or visiting a nightclub. Even our negative or unpleasant feelings are important: the sadness when we are apart from our loved ones, the death of a family member, the anger we feel when violated, the fear that overcomes us in a scary or unknown situation, and the guilt or shame we feel toward others when our sins are made public. Emotions color our life experiences. They inform us of who we are, what our relationships with others are like, and how to behave. Emotions give meaning to events. Without emotions, those events would be mere facts of our lives.

Emotions separate us from computers and other machines. Technological advances have brought machines that are increasingly capable of recreating many of our complex thought processes. Computers now handle much of our work more efficiently than humans can. But no matter how much a computer can accomplish, no technology can make a computer feel as we feel. (Not yet, anyway!)

Feelings and emotions may be the most important aspect of our lives. All people of all cultures have them, and all must learn to deal with them, to attribute some degree of value and worth to them. Life around us may appear to be focused on developing technological capabilities for artificial intelligence and critical thinking and reasoning skills. But our emotions hold the key to make it all happen.

The world of emotion underscores the great diversity among people. How we package emotion, what we call it, how much importance we give it, how we express and perceive it, and how we feel it—these are questions that all people and all cultures answer differently. These differences among individuals and among cultures contribute substantially to the great diversity that we see and, more important, feel among people of different lands and nations.

This chapter explores the nature of those differences, as well as similarities, in human emotion across cultures. We begin by exploring how some emotions may be universal in their expression, regardless of culture, whereas others may differ in their expression across cultures. We then discuss both pancultural and culture-specific aspects of emotion perception, the experience of emotion, emotion antecedents (the events that elicit emotion), the process of appraising or evaluating emotions, and finally, the concept and language of emotion. We will find that at least a small set of emotions share a universal base across all human cultures, and that they provide a base of similarity in all aspects of emotion—expression, perception, experience, antecedents, appraisal, and concept. Building on this common base, culture exerts its influence in molding our emotional worlds, resulting in cultural differences as well as similarities. The integration of both universality and cultural differences is the challenge that faces cross-cultural work on human emotion.

Culture and Emotion Expression

Our examination of the influence of culture on human emotion begins with the topic of emotional expression for several reasons. First, cross-cultural work on emotional expressions, especially facial expressions, laid much of the groundwork for contemporary research on emotion, both cross-cultural and mainstream. Thus, the cross-cultural study of facial expressions of emotion has an important historical significance to this area of psychology. Second, cross-cultural research on facial expressions of emotion has demonstrated convincingly that certain facial expressions appear to be universal across all human cultures. Other studies have suggested their biological innateness. Therefore, it is important to have a firm grasp of the biological substrates of emotion that may exist for all humans regardless of culture before considering cultural influences on emotional processes above and beyond what may be inborn. Thus, we begin by looking at the universality of facial expressions of emotion.

The Universality of Facial Expressions of Emotion

Although philosophers have argued and discussed the possible universal basis of facial expressions of emotion for centuries (see Russell, 1995, for a review), much of the impetus for contemporary cross-cultural research on facial expressions of emotion stems from the writing of Charles Darwin. Many people are familiar with Darwin's theory of evolution, outlined in his work *On the Origin of Species* (1859). Darwin suggested that humans had evolved from other, more primitive animals, such as apes and chimpanzees, and that our behaviors exist today because they were selected through a process of evolutionary adaptation. In a subsequent volume, *The Expression of Emotion in Man and Animals* (1872; see also the new 1998 edition), Darwin suggested that facial expressions of emotion, like other behaviors, are biologically innate and evolutionarily adaptive. Humans, Darwin argued, express emotions in their faces in exactly the same ways around the world, regardless of race or culture. Moreover, those facial expressions can also be seen across species, such as in gorillas. According to Darwin, facial expressions of emotion have both communicative and adaptive value. They ensure the survival of the species by providing both intrapsychic information to the individual, about well-being and person–environment relationships, and social information for others in the community.

During the early to mid-1900s, several studies were conducted to test Darwin's ideas concerning the universality of emotional expressions (for example, Triandis & Lambert, 1958; Vinacke, 1949; Vinacke & Fong, 1955). Unfortunately, many of them had methodological problems that made drawing conclusions based on them difficult (see Ekman, Friesen, & Ellsworth, 1972, for a review). At the same time, prominent anthropologists such as Margaret Mead and Ray Birdwhistell argued that facial expressions of emotion could not be universal; instead, they suggested that facial expressions of emotion had to be learned, much like a language (Ekman, Friesen, & Ellsworth, 1972). Just as different cultures had different languages, they also had different facial expressions of emotion.

It was not until the 1960s, when psychologists Paul Ekman and Wallace Friesen (Ekman, 1972) and, independently, Carroll Izard (1971) conducted the first set of methodologically sound studies that this debate was laid to rest. Spurred on by the work of Sylvan Tomkins (1962, 1963), these researchers conducted a series of studies now called the **universality studies**. Four different types of studies were originally included in the series. In the first of these studies, Ekman, Friesen, and Tomkins selected photographs of facial expressions of emotion they thought portrayed universally recognizable emotions (Ekman, 1972). The researchers showed these photographs to observers in five different countries (the United States, Argentina, Brazil, Chile, and Japan) and asked the observers to label each expression. If the expressions were universal, the researchers reasoned, judges in all cultures would agree in what emotion was being portrayed; if the expressions were culturally specific, the judges from different cultures should disagree. The data revealed a very high level of agreement across all observers in all five cultures in the interpretation of six emotions: anger, disgust, fear, happiness, sadness, and surprise. Izard (1971) conducted a similar study in other cultures and obtained similar results.

One problem with these studies was that all of the cultures included in the research were literate, industrialized, and relatively modern. It was possible, therefore, that the observers in those cultures could have learned how to interpret the facial expressions in the photographs. The fact that these cultures shared mass media—television, movies, magazines, and so forth—reinforced this possibility. The research was criticized, therefore, on the basis of shared visual input across the cultures studied.

To address this concern, Ekman, Sorenson, and Friesen (1969) conducted similar studies in two preliterate tribes of New Guinea. Because of the nature of the participants in these studies, Ekman and his colleagues were forced to change the nature of the experiment, allowing participants to select a story that best described a facial expression instead of using emotion words. When these participants were asked to identify the emotions in the photographs, the data were amazingly similar to those obtained in literate, industrialized societies. Thus, judgments of posed expressions by preliterate cultures constituted a second source of evidence in support of universality.

Ekman and his colleagues took their research in New Guinea a step further, asking different tribe members to show on their faces what they would look like if they experienced the different emotions. Photographs of these expressions were brought back to the United States and shown to American observers, none of whom had ever seen the tribe members from New Guinea. When asked to label the emotions shown on the tribe members' faces, the data were again similar to those found in previous studies. Judgments of expressions posed by preliterate tribes thus constituted a third source of evidence for universality.

All of the research conducted so far had involved judgments of facial expressions of emotion, and were based on the researchers' assumption that people of different cultures would agree on what emotion is being portrayed in a face if the expression were universal. Still, a question remained as to whether people actually, spontaneously display those expressions on their faces when they experience emotion. To address this question, Ekman (1972) and Friesen (1972) conducted a study in the United States and Japan, asking American and Japanese subjects to view highly stressful stimuli as their facial reactions were videotaped without their awareness. Later analysis of the video records indicated that Americans and Japanese did indeed show exactly the same types of facial expressions at the same points in time, and these expressions corresponded to the same expressions that were considered universal in the judgment research. Data from spontaneous facial expressions of emotion, therefore, constituted the fourth line of evidence in the original set of universality studies. Figure 9.1 shows the original six emotional expressions—anger, disgust, fear, happiness, sadness, and surprise—that were found to be universally expressed and recognized across cultures. (The seventh expression, contempt, will be discussed in connection with more recent studies.)

Although these four sets of findings constitute the bulk of the evidence traditionally considered to comprise the universality studies, it is not the entire evidentiary basis of support for the universality thesis. Important studies involving nonhuman primates and congenitally blind infants (reviewed in Ekman, 1973) also support the universality contention. Studies involving nonhuman primates lend support to Darwin's original thesis concerning the evolutionary basis of facial expressions of emotion. Research involving congenitally blind infants shows that visual learning cannot account for the fact that

Figure 9.1 The seven universal expressions of facial emotion

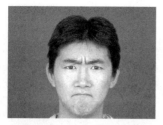

anger

disgust

fear

happiness

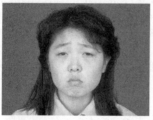

sadness

surprise

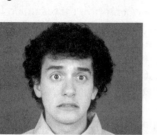

contempt

Source: Courtesy, David Matsumoto

humans within or across cultures share the same set of facial expressions. Additionally, many of Ekman and Friesen's original findings have been replicated in numerous studies in many different countries and cultures by other investigators, ensuring the robustness of their work (see Matsumoto, 2001, for a review). Collectively, these studies constitute a considerable body of evidence demonstrating quite convincingly that facial expressions of emotion are universal and biologically innate.

If these conclusions are correct, they have far-reaching implications. They suggest that all humans are born with the capacity to express the same set of emotions in the same ways. Moreover, they imply similarities in other aspects of emotion. They suggest that all humans have the capacity to experience these same emotions in basically the same ways, and that many of the same kinds of events or psychological themes evoke the same types of emotions in all people across cultures. In short, they suggest that we are all born with the capacity to experience, express, and perceive the same basic set of emotions.

Of course, we experience a range of emotion that is much broader than the set of emotions considered to be universally expressed—love, hate, jealousy, pride, and many others. The existence of basic emotions, however, suggests that these emotions blend with our experiences, personality, and sociocultural milieu to create an infinite degree of shading, blends, and coloring in our emotional world. Much like colors on a color wheel, the existence of basic emotions suggests that cultures shape, mold, and color our emotional lives by using the set of basic emotions as a starting point to create other emotions.

At the same time, the existence of basic, universal emotions does not imply that cultures cannot differ in the ways they express, perceive, or experience emotion. Indeed, much of the research reviewed in this chapter indicates that cultures exert a considerable influence on all these facets of emotion. What the universality of emotion does suggest is that basic emotions provide cultures with a base from which the molding and shaping can start. This perspective is important to keep in mind as we examine the research on cultural differences in emotion.

Cultural Differences in Facial Expressions: Display Rules

Despite the fact that facial expressions of emotion may be universal, many of us have experienced uncertainty about how to interpret the expressions of someone from a different cultural background. We may also wonder whether our own expressions are being interpreted in the way we intend. Although we see emotional expressions that are similar to ours in people from very diverse backgrounds, more often than not we see many differences as well. These experiences run counter to what scholars typically believed about facial expressions until only a few decades ago. How is it that our everyday experiences, and the experiences of well-known scholars such as Margaret Mead, can lead us to believe that people's emotional expressions differ from one culture to another, when the findings from so many studies say otherwise?

Ekman and Friesen (1969) pondered this question many years ago and came up with the concept of **cultural display rules** to account for the discrepancy. Cultures differ, they reasoned, in the rules governing how universal emotions can be expressed. These rules center on the appropriateness of displaying each of the emotions in particular social circumstances. These rules are learned early, and they dictate how the universal emotional expressions should be modified according to the social situation. By adulthood, these rules are automatic, having been very well practiced.

Ekman (1972) and Friesen (1972) designed a study to document the existence of these cultural display rules and their role in producing cultural differences in emotional expressions. In the study described earlier, American and Japanese subjects were asked to view highly stressful films while their facial reactions were videotaped. That experiment actually had two conditions. In the first condition, subjects viewed the stimuli by themselves. In a second condition, an older, higher-status experimenter came into the room and asked the subjects to watch the films again, with the experimenter observing them. Their facial reactions were again videotaped. Analyses showed that the Americans in general continued to show negative feelings of disgust, fear, sadness, and anger. The Japanese, however, invariably smiled in these instances. These findings show how universal, biologically innate emotional expressions can interact with culturally defined rules of display to produce appropriate emotional expressions. In the first condition, when display rules did not operate, the Americans and the Japanese exhibited the same expressions. In the second condition, display rules were operative, forcing the Japanese to smile in order not to offend the experimenter, despite their obvious negative feelings. These findings are especially impressive because the subjects in the second condition that produced differences were the same individuals as in the first condition that produced similarities.

Thus, facial expressions of emotion are under the dual influence of universal, biologically innate factors and culturally specific, learned display rules (see Figure 9.2). When an emotion is triggered, a message is sent to the facial affect program (Ekman, 1972), which stores the prototypic facial configuration information for each of the universal emotions. This prototypic configuration is what constitutes the universal aspect of emotional expression, and is biologically innate. At the same time, however, a message is sent to the area of the brain storing learned cultural display rules. The resulting expression represents the joint influence of both factors. When display rules do not modify an expression, the universal facial expression of emotion will be displayed. Depending on social circumstances, however, display rules may act to neutralize, amplify, deamplify, qualify, or mask the universal expression. This mechanism explains how and why people can differ in their emotional expressions despite the fact that we all share the same expression base.

Recent Cross-Cultural Research on Emotional Expression and Display Rules

In recent years, a number of cross-cultural studies have extended our knowledge of the influence of culture on expression and display rules. For example, Stephan, Stephan, and de Vargas (1996) compared expressions of Americans

Figure 9.2 The neurocultural theory of emotional expression

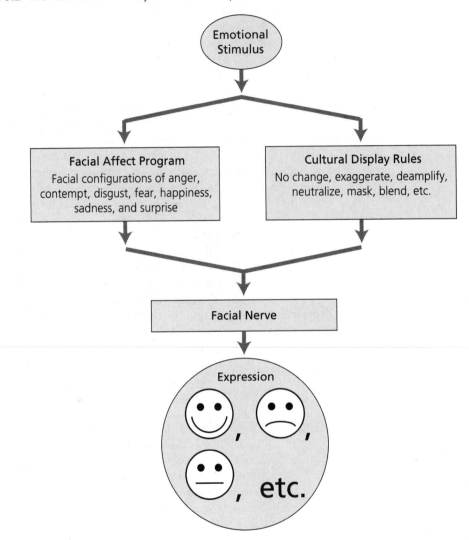

Source: Adapted from P. Ekman, "Universals and Cultural Differences in Facial Expression of Emotion," in J. Cole (ed.), *Nebraska Symposium of Motivation, 1971,* vol. 19 (Lincoln: University of Nebraska Press, 1972).

and Costa Ricans by asking participants in both countries to rate 38 emotions in terms of how comfortable they would feel expressing them toward their family and to strangers. They also completed a self-concept scale of independence versus interdependence (see Chapter 11) and rated the emotions as to whether they were positive or negative, and independent or interdependent. The results indicated that Americans were more comfortable than Costa Ricans in expressing both independent and interdependent emotions. Costa Ricans were significantly less comfortable in expressing negative emotions.

Research has also documented the existence of cultural differences in emotional expression among ethnic groups in the United States. In one study (Matsumoto, 1993), Caucasian, black, Asian, and Latino American participants viewed the universal facial expressions of emotion and rated the appropriateness of displaying them in different social situations. The findings showed that Caucasians rated contempt as more appropriate than Asians, disgust as more appropriate than blacks and Latinos, fear as more appropriate than Latinos, and sadness as more appropriate than blacks and Asians. In addition, Caucasians rated the expression of emotions in public and with children as more appropriate than Latinos, with casual acquaintances as more appropriate than blacks, Asians, and Latinos, and with lower-status others as more appropriate than blacks or Latinos. Interestingly, however, blacks reported expressing anger more often than Caucasians, Asians, and Latinos. In another study, Aune and Aune (1995) found that Filipino Americans expressed emotions more intensely than did Japanese Americans when positive and negative emotions were aroused in a romantic relationship.

Other studies also demonstrate the existence of cultural differences in stereotypes about emotional expression. In one study (Pittam, Gallois, Iwawaki, & Kroonenberg, 1995), participants in Australia and Japan rated how they expressed eight emotions through 12 behaviors, and how they thought a person of the other country expressed them. Both groups rated Australians as more expressive than the Japanese on positive emotions. But both groups rated the other group as more expressive than themselves on negative emotions. In a much larger study involving more than 2,900 college students in 26 countries, Pennebaker, Rime, and Blankenship (1996) found that people from warmer, southern climates were perceived as more expressive than people from northern areas.

Although the studies reviewed so far point to many ways in which cultures differ in their expressivity, it is not exactly clear how expressions are controlled when display rules are enacted. Two studies have shed some light on these processes. In the first, McConatha, Lightner, and Deaner (1994) compared American and British participants on emotional control. They found that American males exhibited more rehearsal and inhibition than did British males. American females also engaged in more inhibition than did British females. British females, however, engaged in more aggression control and benign control than did American females.

In the second study, Matsumoto, Takeuchi, Andayani, Koutnetsouva, and Krupp (1998) surveyed participants in the United States, Japan, Russia, and South Korea and asked them to select what they would do if they felt one of 14 emotions in four different social situations. The seven response alternatives were as follows:

1. Express the feeling with no modification
2. Deamplify or reduce the expression

3. Amplify or exaggerate the expression
4. Mask or conceal your feelings by showing something else
5. Qualify your expression with a smile
6. Neutralize your expression
7. Something else

The results indicated that, although cultural differences did exist, participants from all cultures selected all of the alternatives, indicating that these alternatives are a fair representation of the response repertoires available to people as they modify their emotional expressions in social contexts.

Finally, research of the past decade has gone beyond documenting differences in emotional expression to develop a theoretical framework of how and why cultures produce these differences. Matsumoto (1991), for example, has used the concept of ingroups and outgroups (see Chapter 14) to suggest that cultural differences in the meaning of self–ingroup and self–outgroup relationships have particular meaning for the emotions expressed in social interactions. In general, the familiarity and intimacy of self–ingroup relations in all cultures provide the safety and comfort to express emotions freely, along with tolerance for a broad spectrum of emotional behaviors. Part of emotional socialization involves learning who are ingroup and outgroup members and the appropriate behaviors associated with them. In Matsumoto's framework, collectivistic cultures foster more positive and fewer negative emotions toward ingroups because ingroup harmony is more important to them. Positive emotions ensure maintenance of this harmony; negative emotions threaten it. Individualistic cultures, however, foster more negative emotions and fewer positive emotions toward ingroups; because harmony and cohesion are less important to these cultures, it is considered appropriate to display emotions that may threaten group cohesion. Individualistic cultures foster more positive and less negative emotions toward outgroups, because it is less important in individualistic cultures to differentiate between ingroups and outgroups; thus, they allow expression of positive feelings and suppression of negative ones toward outgroup members. Collectivistic cultures, however, foster more negative expressions toward outgroups to distinguish more clearly between ingroups and outgroups and to strengthen ingroup relations (via the collective expression of negative feelings toward outgroups). These variations in the expressions of personal emotions are summarized in Table 9.1.

Two studies have confirmed many of these hypotheses. One study, conducted by Matsumoto and Hearn in 1991 (reported in Biehl, Matsumoto, & Kasri, in press) examined cultural display rules in the United States, Poland, and Hungary. Poles and Hungarians reported that it was less appropriate to display negative emotions in ingroups (such as family and close friends) and more appropriate to display positive emotions; they also reported that it was more appropriate to display negative emotions to outgroups (for example, in public). Americans, in contrast, were more likely to display negative emotions to ingroup members and positive emotions to outgroup members. Compared to

Table 9.1 Expression of Personal Emotions in Self–Ingroup and Self–Outgroup Relationships in Individualistic and Collectivistic Cultures

	Type of Culture	
	Individualistic	Collectivistic
Self–Ingroup Relations	Okay to express negative feelings; less need to display positive feelings	Suppress expressions of negative feelings; more pressure to display positive feelings
Self–Outgroup Relations	Suppress negative feelings; okay to express positive feelings as would toward ingroups	Encouraged to express negative feelings; suppress display of positive feelings reserved for ingroups

Americans, Poles also reported that the display of negative emotions was less appropriate even when they were alone. Matsumoto and Hearn interpreted these results as supportive of Matsumoto's (1991) theoretical predictions. The findings from a United States–Japan comparison also supported these predictions (Matsumoto, 1990). A third study (Matsumoto et al., 1998) demonstrated that many of the cultural differences in such findings were accounted for by cultural differences in dimensions such as individualism versus collectivism or status differentiation.

Thus, research of the past decade has gone well beyond the original documentation of universality of facial expressions and the existence of cultural display rules conducted by Ekman and his colleagues. The available research shows that culture exerts considerable influence over our emotional expressions via culturally learned display rules, and gives us an idea of what those rules are like. Recent research also suggests what it is about cultures that produces cultural differences in emotional expressions, and why. Given that most interactions among people are social by definition, we should expect that cultural differences via display rules are operative most, if not all, of the time.

To understand the emotional expressions of people of different cultures, then, we must understand, first, what universal bases underlie those expressions and, second, what kinds of cultural display rules are operating when we interact with them. Still, many gaps in our knowledge remain to be filled. For example, future research will need to examine how people of different cultures learn their various display rules, and what those display rules are. Future studies will also need to examine further how and why cultures produce differences in emotional behavior, incorporating dimensions other than individualism versus collectivism, such as power or status differentiation.

Culture and Emotion Perception

The Universality of Emotion Recognition

Many of the judgment studies documenting the universal expression of emotion also tell us that facial expressions of emotion can be universally recognized. When shown photographs of the universal facial emotions, observers in all countries and cultures studied agreed on what emotion was being portrayed in the expressions, at quite high levels across cultures (Ekman, 1972; Ekman & Friesen, 1971; Ekman, Sorenson, & Friesen, 1969; Izard, 1971). As you will remember, these studies involved posed expressions not only judged by people in both literate and preliterate cultures, but posed by people in both literate and preliterate cultures. Another study (reported in Ekman, 1972) also found universality in the judgment of spontaneous facial expressions of emotion.

Numerous studies conducted since the original universality research have replicated the original findings (for example, Boucher & Carlson, 1980; Markham & Wang, 1996; see Ekman, 1982, and Matsumoto, Wallbott, & Scherer, 1987, for reviews). For example, Ekman and colleagues (1987) asked observers in ten different cultures to view photographs depicting each of the six universal emotions. The judges not only labeled each emotion by selecting an emotion word from a predetermined list but also rated how intensely they perceived the emotion to be expressed. The judges in all ten cultures agreed on what emotion was being displayed, highlighting the universality of recognition. In addition, observers in each culture gave the strongest intensity ratings to the emotions that corresponded with the facial expressions they were judging.

The findings from these numerous studies have shown unequivocally that people of all cultures can recognize the universal facial expressions of emotion depicted in Figure 9.1. Recent research suggests that, like emotional expression, the perception of emotion has both universal, pancultural elements and culturally specific aspects.

Evidence for More Cross-Cultural Similarities in Emotional Perception

A universal contempt expression. Since the original university studies, a number of studies have reported the universality of a seventh facial expression of emotion, contempt. Initial evidence was collected from ten cultures, including West Sumatra (Ekman & Friesen, 1986; Ekman & Heider, 1988). These findings were later replicated by Matsumoto (1992b) in four cultures, three of which were different from Ekman and Friesen's original ten cultures. This seventh universal expression has received considerable attention and criticism (Izard & Haynes, 1988; Russell, 1994a, 1994b). Russell, for example, suggests that the context in which the expression was shown influenced the results in favor of universality. In his study, the contempt expression was more often labeled as either disgust or sadness when shown either alone or after showing a disgust or sadness picture (Russell, 1991). Ekman, O'Sullivan, and Matsumoto

(1991a, 1991b), however, reanalyzed their data to address this criticism and found no effect of context. Biehl and associates (1997) also found no effects for other possible methodological confounds. An example of the contempt expression is included in Figure 9.1.

Relative intensity ratings.   Cultures agree on the relative intensity they attribute to facial expressions. That is, when comparing two expressions, all cultures generally agree on which is more strongly expressed. When Ekman and colleagues (1987) presented paired expressions of the same emotion, they found that 92% of the time the ten cultures in their study agreed on which was more intense. Matsumoto and Ekman (1989) extended this finding by including comparisons across different poser types, including Caucasian and Japanese posers. Looking separately at each emotion, first within culture across gender and then within gender across culture, they found that Americans and Japanese agreed on which photo was more intense in 24 out of 30 comparisons. These findings suggest that cultures judge emotions on a similar basis, despite differences in facial physiognomy, morphology, race, and sex of the posers, and culturally prescribed rules governing the expression and perception of faces.

The association between perceived expression intensity and inferences about subjective experience.   When people see a strong emotional expression, they will infer that the poser is actually feeling the emotion strongly. When they see a weaker expression, they will infer a less emotional experience. Matsumoto, Kasri, and Kooken (1999) demonstrated this effect by obtaining Japanese and American judgments of 56 expressions posed by Japanese and Caucasians. The observers judged what emotion the poser was expressing, and then the strength of both the external display and the internal, **subjective experience of emotion.** Data analyses indicated that observers from both cultures associated the strength of the external display with the presumed strength of the internal experience for all expressions, suggesting commonality in that linkage across culture. The link between the presence or absence of an expression and the underlying experience, and the intensity of both, is a topic of considerable importance in contemporary theories of emotion. Some authors have claimed that the linkage between expression and experience is unfounded (for example, Russell, 1997; Fernandez-Dols, Sanchez, & Carrera, 1997); others have argued that expressions and experience are intimately linked (but need not always be coupled) (Rosenberg & Ekman, 1994; see also the literature on the facial feedback hypothesis, reviewed by Matsumoto, 1987; Winton, 1986). The data from Matsumoto and colleagues (1999) clearly support notions of linkage.

Second mode of response in emotion recognition.   Cultures are also similar in the second most salient emotion they perceive in some emotional expressions. Observers in Ekman et al.'s (1987) study judged not only which emotion was portrayed in the faces, but also the intensity of each of seven emotion categories. This task allowed observers to report multiple emotions, or no emotion, instead of being forced to select an emotion to describe the face. Although previous studies had shown universality in the first mode of response, cultures might have differed in which emotion is next most prevalent. Analyses, however, supported cultural agreement. For every culture in Ekman et al.'s (1987) study, the secondary emotion for the disgust expressions was contempt, and for fear expressions surprise. For anger, the second mode varied depending on the photo, with disgust, surprise, or contempt as the second response. These findings have been replicated by Matsumoto and Ekman (1989) and Biehl and colleagues (1997), suggesting pancultural agreement on the multiple meanings derived from universal faces. This agreement may exist because of overlap in the semantics of the emotion categories, in the antecedents and elicitors of emotion, or in the facial configurations themselves.

Evidence for Cross-Cultural Differences in Emotional Perception

Emotion recognition.   Although the original universality research showed that subjects recognized emotions at well over chance rates, no study has ever reported perfect cross-cultural agreement (100% of the judges in any or all of the cultures agreeing on what emotion is portrayed in an expression). Matsumoto's (1992a) comparison of Japanese and American judgments found that recognition rates ranged from 64% to 99%, which were consistent with earlier universality studies. Americans were better at recognizing anger, disgust, fear, and sadness than the Japanese, but accuracy rates did not differ for happiness or surprise. These results were interpreted as supportive of the universality of facial expressions of emotion because the agreement was consistently high (in most cases, well above 70%) and statistically significant.

Some new research has also shown that although people of different cultures agree reliably on the most salient emotion message conveyed in universal facial expressions, cross-cultural differences emerge in the perception of other emotions in the same expression. For example, Yrizarry, Matsumoto, and Wilson-Cohn (1998) report that when judging anger expressions, Americans and Japanese agreed that anger was the most salient emotion portrayed in the expression. However, Americans saw more disgust and contempt in those same expressions than did the Japanese, whereas the Japanese saw more sadness in the anger expressions. Although previous research (reviewed in Yrizarry et al., 1998) has consistently shown that judges see multiple emotions when viewing universal faces, this was the first study to document cultural differences in multiple emotion judgments of the same expressions.

Emotion recognition and dimensions of culture.   Given at least some cultural differences in rates of emotion recognition, several researchers have attempted to identify the causes of such differences. Russell (1994a), for example, has argued for a Western/non-Western distinction, suggesting that the methodologies that have been used to test emotion recognition across cultures have been biased in favor of Western—that is, North American and European—

judges (see also rebuttals by Ekman, 1994, and Izard, 1994). Biehl and associates (1997), however, comparing emotion recognition across six cultures, demonstrated that a Western/non-Western dichotomy is not statistically supported to explain cross-national variation. Instead, Biehl and associates suggest that underlying sociopsychological variables or cultural dimensions (as postulated by Hofstede 1980, 1983) influence the emotion judgment process. As an example of the use of such dimensions to explain cultural differences in emotion recognition rates, Matsumoto (1989) selected recognition data from 15 cultures reported in four studies and correlated these with Hofstede's (1980, 1983) four cultural dimensions—power distance (PD), uncertainty avoidance (UA), individualism (IN), and masculinity (MA)—for each culture. (See Chapter 2 for a review of these dimensions.) Matsumoto found that individualism was positively correlated with mean intensity ratings for anger and fear, supporting the claim that Americans (individualistic culture) are better at recognizing negative emotions than Japanese (collectivistic culture). A meta-analysis by Schimmack (1996) also found differences in emotion perception as a function of culture. Individualism was a better predictor of recognition of happiness than ethnicity (operationalized as Caucasian/non-Caucasian), supporting the notion that sociocultural dimensions account for differences in the perception of emotion. Together, these studies demonstrate the promise of using such dimensions to examine cultural influences on emotion perception, releasing researchers from an unhealthy reliance on archaic distinctions such as the Western/non-Western dichotomy.

Attributions of expression intensity.   People of different cultures differ in how strongly they perceive emotions in others. Ekman et al.'s (1987) study of ten cultures was the first to document this effect. Although overall recognition data supported universality, Asians gave significantly lower intensity ratings on happiness, surprise, and fear. These data suggested that the judges were acting according to culturally learned **decoding rules** about how to perceive expressions, especially given the fact that all posers were Caucasian. That is, it was possible that the Asians rated the Caucasian posers less intensely out of politeness or ignorance. To examine this notion, Matsumoto and Ekman developed a stimulus set comprised of Asian and Caucasian posers (the Japanese and Caucasian Facial Expressions of Emotion set, or JACFEE), and presented it to judges in the United States and Japan (Matsumoto & Ekman, 1989). For all but one emotion, Americans rated the expressions more intensely than the Japanese, regardless of the race of the person being judged. Because the differences were not specific to the poser, Matsumoto and Ekman (1989) interpreted the differences as a function of rules that the cultures may have for interpreting the expressions of others. Differences in attribution of expression intensity have also been documented among ethnic groups within the United States (Matsumoto, 1993).

Matsumoto's (1989) study described earlier also investigated the relationship between Hofstede's dimensions of culture and emotion intensity ratings.

Two important findings emerged. First, there was a negative correlation between power distance and intensity ratings of anger, fear, and sadness, suggesting that cultures that emphasize status differences rate these emotions less intensely. Perhaps these emotions threaten status relationships, and thus are downplayed in emotional perception. Second, individualism was positively correlated with intensity ratings of anger and fear, suggesting that people of individualistic cultures see more intensity in these expressions. Not only can these findings be interpreted in relation to the behavioral tendencies we would expect as a result of high individualism or power distance; they also suggest that understanding dimensions of culture may be the key to explaining cultural differences in the perception of negative emotions.

Inferences about emotional experiences underlying facial expressions of emotion. Although cultures differed in their judgments of external display, it was unclear whether cultures also differed in their inferences about underlying experience, and if so, whether these differences were similar to those with regard to external display. Matsumoto et al. (1999) tested this notion by comparing American and Japanese judgments when separate ratings were obtained for expression intensity and subjective experience. Americans rated external display more intensely than the Japanese, replicating previous findings. The Japanese, however, rated internal experience more intensely than the Americans. Within-culture analyses indicated no significant differences between the two ratings for the Japanese. Significant differences were found, however, for the Americans, who consistently rated external display more intensely than subjective experience. Although the researchers had previously suggested that American–Japanese differences occurred because the Japanese suppressed their intensity ratings, these findings indicated that in fact it was the Americans who exaggerated their external display ratings relative to subjective experience, not the Japanese who suppressed. Not only are such findings wake-up calls to experienced cross-cultural researchers; they also force us to consider how culture produces these tendencies, and why.

Attributions of personality based on smiles. The smile is a common sign of greeting, acknowledgment, or acceptance. It is also used to mask emotions, and cultures may differ in the use of smiles for this purpose. In Friesen's (1972) study, for example, when Japanese and American men watched disgusting video clips with an experimenter in the room, the Japanese men used smiles to cover up their negative expressions much more often than the American men (Ekman, 1972; Friesen, 1972). To further investigate the meaning of those differences, Matsumoto and Kudoh (1993) obtained ratings from Japanese and Americans on smiling versus nonsmiling (neutral) faces with regard to intelligence, attractiveness, and sociability. Americans rated smiling faces as more intelligent than neutral faces; the Japanese, however, did not. Americans and Japanese both found smiling faces more sociable than neutral faces, but the difference was greater for Americans. These differences suggest that cultural display rules cause Japanese and Americans to attribute different meanings to the smile, and serve as a good explanation for perceived major differences in communication styles across cultures.

Culture and the Experience of Emotion

When people of different cultures feel an emotion, do they experience it in the same or different ways? Do they experience the same types of emotions? Do they experience some emotions more frequently, or more strongly, than others? Do they have the same types of nonverbal reactions, or physiological and bodily symptoms and sensations?

These questions are important both theoretically and practically, in terms of our everyday lives. Theoretically, the work serving as the basis for the universality of emotion expression and perception suggests that all humans may also share the same experiential base of emotion—at least for those emotions that have a pancultural signal in the face. That is, however, an empirical question; it is at least hypothetically possible, though not very likely, that our emotional experiences are not necessarily associated with pancultural signals of emotion. On the practical side, knowing that we share the same experiential base of emotion is important in having empathy for other people's experiences; empathy (discussed in Chapters 10 and 16) is important for the development of intercultural sensitivity and for successful interpersonal and intercultural experiences.

In the past few years, several major research programs have examined the degree to which emotional experience is universal (common to all people of all cultures) and culturally specific (different for people of different cultures). Two major lines of research—one led by Klaus Scherer and Harald Wallbott in Europe, the other represented by a host of independent researchers—have addressed these questions. Together, they suggest that many aspects of our emotional experiences are indeed universal, whereas other aspects of our emotional lives are culture-specific.

Universality of Emotional Experiences

Scherer and his colleagues have conducted a number of studies using questionnaires designed to assess the quality and nature of emotional experiences in many different cultures. An initial study (Scherer, Summerfield, & Wallbott, 1983) involved about 600 participants in five European countries. In a second study (Scherer, Wallbott, & Summerfield, 1986), they collected additional data from three more European countries, raising the total to eight countries. A third study (Scherer, Matsumoto, Wallbott, & Kudoh, 1988) then compared a weighted sample of the European participants to samples from the United States and Japan, to test whether the pattern of results obtained in Europe would be the same when comparing European to non-European cultures.

The methodology was basically the same in all cultures. Participants completed an open-ended questionnaire about four basic emotions: joy/happiness, sadness/grief, fear/anxiety, and anger/rage. They described a situation in which they felt that emotion and then provided information concerning their nonverbal reactions, physiological sensations, and verbal utterances. The results from the first two studies indicated a surprising degree of similarity in the emotional experiences of the European respondents. Although their responses did vary according to culture, the effect of culture was rather small, especially in comparison to the differences among the emotions themselves. That is, the differences among the four emotions tested were much larger than the differences among the cultures. The researchers concluded that at least the emotions tested seem to share a universal experiential base across humans.

Moreover, when the European data were compared to the American and Japanese data, Scherer and his colleagues found that although the effect of culture was slightly larger, it was still very small relative to the differences found among the emotions. Across all three studies, therefore, the researchers concluded that culture can and does influence the experience of these emotions, but this influence is considerably smaller than the basic differences among the emotions themselves. More plainly, cultures show much more similarity than difference.

The differences among the emotions that seem to be universal across cultures are summarized in Table 9.2. For example, joy and anger generally occur more frequently than sadness and fear. Joy and sadness are experienced more intensely than anger and fear, and for longer durations. Anger and fear are associated with more ergotropic arousal (muscle symptoms and perspiration)

Table 9.2 Summary of the Differences among Emotions Reported in the First Set of Studies by Scherer and Colleagues

Domain	Variable	Finding
Subjective feeling	Time distance (long ago to recently)	Sadness = fear < joy = anger
	Intensity (weaker to stronger)	Anger = fear < sadness = joy
	Duration (shorter to longer)	Fear < anger < joy = sadness
	Control (weaker to stronger)	Joy < fear = sadness = anger
Physiological symptoms	Ergotropic arousal (weaker to stronger)	Sadness = joy < anger < fear
	Trophotropic arousal (weaker to stronger)	Joy < fear = anger < sadness
	Temperature (colder to warmer)	Fear < sadness < joy < anger
Behavioral reactions	Approach/withdrawal (away to toward)	Fear = sadness = anger < joy
	Nonverbal behavior (little to much)	Fear < sadness < joy = anger
	Verbal behavior (little to much)	Fear = sadness < joy = anger

Source: Based on Scherer, Summerfield, & Wallbott, 1983.

than sadness and joy, whereas sadness is associated with more trophotropic arousal (such as stomach symptoms, lump in the throat, crying). Joy and anger are also experienced with higher temperature than fear and sadness. Joy is associated with approach behavior, and joy and anger are associated with more verbal and nonverbal reactions.

The second set of studies conducted by Scherer and his colleagues involved 2,921 participants in 37 countries on five continents (see Wallbott & Scherer, 1986, for a first report; Scherer & Wallbott, 1994, for a complete report). The original questionnaire was modified to include three more emotions—shame, guilt, and disgust—for a total of seven emotions. Analysis of the data led to the following conclusion:

> For all response domains—subjective feelings, physiological symptoms, and motor expression patterns—the seven emotions differed significantly and strongly (in terms of relative effect sizes) among each other. Geographical and sociocultural factors, as reflected in country effect sizes, also affected emotional experience, but the effects were much smaller than those for differences among the emotions. Significant interaction effects indicate that geographical and sociocultural factors can have differential effects on specific emotions, but that the size of these effects is relatively small. These results warrant the conclusion that there are strong and consistent differences between the reaction patterns for the seven emotions and that these are independent of the country studied. It could be argued that these universal differences in self-reports of emotional reactions are evidence for psychobiological emotional patterning. (Scherer & Wallbott, 1994, p. 317)

These findings indicate once again that the experience of these emotions is universal—that regardless of culture, people share the same basic emotional experiences. Although culture does influence the experience of these emotions, this influence is not nearly as large as the seemingly innate differences among the emotions themselves. Again, emotional experience is much more similar than different. The universal differences among emotions reported in this second, broader set of studies are summarized in Table 9.3. Another study, involving participants from the United States, Japan, Hong Kong, and the People's Republic of China, and conducted by a separate team of researchers (Mauro, Sato, & Tucker, 1992), produced similar results concerning the universality of emotional experience.

Cultural Differences in Emotional Experiences

Although cultural differences found in the studies just described were considerably smaller than differences among the emotions, they nevertheless existed. For example, Scherer and colleagues found that Japanese reported experiencing all emotions—joy, sadness, fear, and anger—more often than either the Americans or the Europeans. The Americans, in turn, reported experiencing joy and anger more often than the Europeans. Americans reported feeling their emotions for longer durations and at greater intensities than did the Europeans or

Table 9.3 Summary of Differences among Emotions Reported in the Second Set of Studies by Scherer and Wallbott

Domain	Variable	Finding
Subjective feeling	Duration (from shorter to longer)	Fear = disgust = shame ≤ anger < guilt < joy < sadness
	Intensity (from weaker to stronger)	Shame = guilt = disgust < anger = fear ≤ joy = sadness
	Control (from low to high)	Joy < anger < disgust < sadness = fear < guilt < shame
Physiological symptoms	Ergotropic arousal (from weak to strong)	Disgust = joy = guilt = sadness ≤ shame < anger < fear
	Trophotropic arousal (from weak to strong)	Joy < shame = anger – disgust ≤ guilt ≤ fear < sadness
	Temperature (from cold to warm/hot)	Fear = sadness < disgust < guilt < anger < shame < joy
Behavioral reactions	Approach/withdrawal behavior (from withdrawal to approach)	Shame = guilt = disgust = sadness < fear < anger < joy
	Nonverbal reactions (from little to much)	Guilt < disgust = shame = fear < sadness ≤ anger < joy
	Paralinguistic behavior (from little to much)	Disgust = guilt ≤ shame ≤ sadness < fear < joy < anger
	Verbal behavior (from little to much)	Fear = sadness = shame = guilt < disgust < anger = joy

Source: Adapted from Scherer & Wallbott, 1994.

the Japanese. Japanese respondents on the whole reported fewer hand and arm gestures, whole body movements, and vocal and facial reactions to the emotions than did Americans or Europeans. Americans reported the highest degree of expressivity in both facial and vocal reactions. Americans and Europeans also reported many more physiological sensations than did the Japanese. These sensations included changes in temperature (becoming flushed, hot), cardiovascular changes (heart racing, pulse changing), and gastric disturbances (stomach problems).

How and why do cultural differences in emotional experience exist? Researchers have tried to account for cultural differences among the countries in their emotional experiences in two ways. In one (Wallbott & Scherer, 1995), they examined the relationship between the experience of shame and guilt and Hofstede's four dimensions of culture: individualism (IN), power distance (PD), uncertainty avoidance (UA), and masculinity (MA). Their results were fascinating. Shame, for example, was experienced with relatively shorter duration, as less immoral, and more often accompanied by laughter and smiles in collectivistic cultures than in individualistic cultures. Shame in collectivistic cultures was also characterized by high felt temperature and low trophotropic arousal. The same findings were also obtained for cultures high in PD and low in UA. These findings are interesting indeed because they are contrary to what one would predict based on previous writings (for example, Piers & Singer, 1971) that have characterized collectivistic cultures as "shame cultures."

In another attempt to uncover possible bases of cultural differences in emotional experience, Wallbott and Scherer (1988) correlated their data with the gross national product (GNP) of each of the countries in their studies. They found that the poorer the country is, the longer-lasting, more intense, and further in the past the emotions are. Subjects from poorer countries seem to report "'more important and more severe' emotional incidents" (Wallbott & Scherer, 1988, p. 271).

A host of other researchers, led by Kitayama and Markus (1991, 1994, 1995), Wierzbicka (1994), and Shweder (1994), have taken a different approach in describing cultural influences on emotional experiences. Using a "functionalist" approach, these researchers view emotion as a set of "socially shared scripts" composed of physiological, behavioral, and subjective components. They suggest that these scripts develop as individuals are enculturated into their culture, and that they are inextricably linked to the culture in which they are produced and with which they interact. Emotion, therefore, reflects the cultural environment in which individuals develop and live, and are as integral a part of culture as morality and ethics are. Markus and Kitayama (1991b; see also Chapter 11 for a review) cite evidence from a variety of sources to support this view, including studies that demonstrate a difference between cultures in the experience of socially engaged versus disengaged emotions, and in cultural patterns of feeling good and happiness.

In this view, culture shapes emotion. Because different cultures have different realities and ideals that produce different psychological needs and goals, they produce differences in habitual emotional tendencies. This model of the "cultural construction of emotion" is summarized in Figure 9.3.

Many writers who take this functionalist approach challenge the universal and possibly biologically innate aspects of emotion. Basically, their argument is that precisely because of the inextricably intertwined relationship between culture and emotion, emotion could not possibly be biologically "fixed" for all people. They suggest that the universality of emotion is a misnomer, and that supportive findings derive from the experimental and theoretical biases of the researchers that have reported them.

Personally, we do not believe that the functionalist approach to emotion is necessarily antithetical or antagonistic to the universality of emotion. For one thing, these researchers have studied different emotions. The universality position is limited to a small set of discrete emotions that have a corresponding unique facial expression. Studies conducted by the functionalists have incorporated a broad range of emotional experience that goes well beyond this limited

Figure 9.3 The cultural shaping of emotion

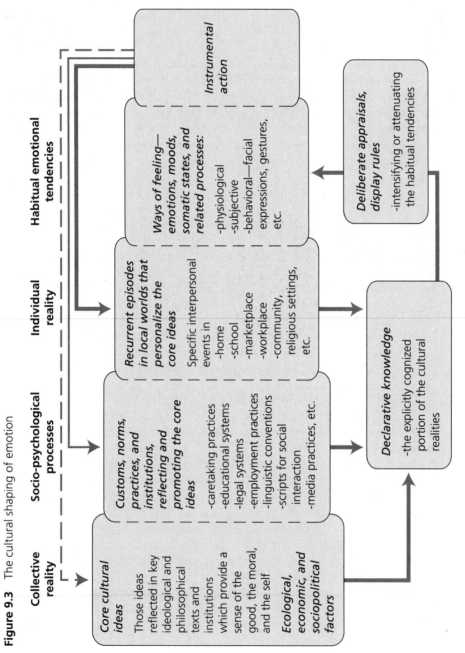

Source: Markus and Kitayama, *Emotion and Culture: Empirical Studies of Mutual Influence*, 1994, p. 342. Copyright © 1994 by the American Psychological Association. Reprinted with permission.

set of universal emotions. Also, these researchers have studied different aspects of emotion. The universality of emotion is based on the existence of pan-cultural signals of emotional expression in the face. Much of the research on the cultural construction of emotion is based on the subjective experience of emotion, and the emotion lexicons in language that are used to describe and represent those experiences. It is not inconceivable that one component of emotion may be universal while the other is culturally relative. Finally, the existence of universals and innate biological substrates of emotion does not preclude the possibility that cultures can also construct much of their experience. As mentioned earlier, the universal bases of emotion may provide a standard platform upon which such construction may take place. It seems, therefore, that cultural construction of emotional experience can occur above and beyond the baseline that is provided by basic emotions with universal expressions. Future research in this area may be guided by such complementary viewpoints rather than driven by arbitrarily antagonistic positions.

Culture and the Antecedents of Emotion

Emotion antecedents are the events or situations that trigger or elicit an emotion. For example, losing a loved one may be an antecedent of sadness; getting an "A" in a class in which you wanted to do well may elicit happiness or joy. In the scientific literature, emotion antecedents are also known as emotion elicitors.

For many years, scholars have debated whether emotion antecedents are similar or different across cultures. On the one hand, a number of scientists have argued that emotion antecedents must be similar across cultures, at least for the universal emotions, because these emotions are panculturally similar and all humans share their experiential and expression base. The results from cross-cultural studies reviewed earlier on emotion expression, perception, and experience all tend to support such a view. On the other hand, many writers have argued that cultures must differ in their emotion antecedents; that is, the same events in different cultures can and do trigger entirely different emotions in those cultures. Sadness is not necessarily elicited in all cultures at funerals, for example, and getting an A in a class may not always elicit joy. There are many other examples of such cross-cultural differences in emotion elicitors, and research has provided considerable support for this viewpoint as well.

Cultural Similarities in Emotion Antecedents

A considerable number of studies have supported the universality of emotion antecedents. Boucher and Brandt (1981), for example, asked participants in the United States and Malaysia to describe situations in which someone caused someone else to feel anger, disgust, fear, happiness, sadness, or surprise. Their selection of the emotions to study was guided by the previous universality research. A total of 96 antecedents to the various emotions were generated. A separate group of American participants then rated the antecedents, attempting to identify which emotion each elicited. The results indicated that the Americans correctly classified the antecedents equally well regardless of whether they were originally generated by Americans or by Malaysians; that is, culture of origin did not affect the classification. Subsequently, Brandt and Boucher (1985) replicated these findings using American, Korean, and Samoan participants. Taken together, the results suggest that the antecedents shared a common base cross-culturally, supporting views of pancultural similarity in emotion antecedents.

The largest concerted effort to study emotion antecedents across cultures was the work by Scherer and his colleagues described earlier. In their studies, respondents were asked to describe a situation or event in which they experienced various emotions. Trained coders then coded the situations described by participants into general categories such as good news and bad news, temporary and permanent separation, and success and failure in achievement situations. No culture-specific antecedent category was necessary to code the data, indicating that all categories of events generally occurred in all cultures to produce each of the seven emotions studied.

In addition, Scherer and his colleagues found many similarities across cultures in the relative frequency with which each of the antecedent events elicited emotions. For example, the most frequent elicitors of happiness across cultures were "relationships with friends," "temporary meetings with friends," and "achievement situations." The most frequent elicitors of anger were "relationships" and "injustice." The most frequent elicitors of sadness were "relationships" and "death." These findings also supported the view that emotion antecedents are similar across cultures.

A small number of other studies have also reported similarities across cultures in emotion antecedents. Galati and Sciaky (1995), for example, found that antecedents for anger, disgust, fear, happiness, sadness, and surprise were similar in northern and southern Italy. Buunk and Hupka (1987) reported that flirtatious behaviors were considered elicitors of jealousy in all seven cultures they studied. Levy (1973) concluded that many situations that give rise to emotions in Tahiti would give rise to the same emotions elsewhere.

Cultural Differences in Emotion Antecedents

Research has also provided considerable support for cultural differences in emotion antecedents. Scherer and associates, for example, found many cultural differences (as well as similarities) in the relative frequencies of the various antecedent events reported by their respondents. Cultural events, the birth of a new family member, body-centered "basic pleasures," and achievement-related situations were more important antecedents of joy for Europeans and Americans than for the Japanese. Death of family members or close friends, physical separation from loved ones, and world news were more frequent triggers of sadness for Europeans and Americans than for the Japanese. Problems in relationships, however, produced more sadness for the Japanese than for Americans or Europeans. Strangers and achievement-related situations elicited more fear for Americans, whereas novel situations, traffic, and relationships were more frequent elicitors of fear for the Japanese. Finally, situations involving strangers were more frequent elicitors of anger for the Japanese than for the Americans or Europeans. Situations involving relationships brought about more anger for Americans than for Japanese. These findings make it clear that the same type of situation or event will not necessarily trigger the same emotion in people across cultures.

Several other studies have provided similar or comparable results (for example, see review by Mesquita & Frijda, 1992). Collectively, they suggest considerable differences among cultures in the antecedents to emotion.

Coexistence of Similarities and Differences in Emotion Antecedents

Given that cross-cultural research has found both similarities and differences in emotion antecedents across cultures, how can we reconcile these findings? Matsumoto (1996) has suggested that one useful way to interpret cross-cultural findings on emotion antecedents is to make a distinction between latent and manifest content in events and situations that produce emotions. Manifest content is the actual event or situation, such as spending time with friends, attending a funeral, or having someone cut in front of you in line. Latent content is the psychological meanings associated with the manifest content that underlie the situation or event. For example, the latent content underlying spending time with friends may be the achievement of psychological goals of warmth and intimacy with others. The latent content underlying attending a funeral may be the loss of a loved object. The latent content underlying someone cutting in front of you in line may be a perception of injustice or obstruction of a goal.

A review of the cross-cultural research suggests universality in the latent content of emotion antecedents. That is, certain psychological themes produce the same emotions for most people in most cultures. The latent content underlying sadness is inevitably loss of a loved object. The latent content underlying happiness is inevitably achievement of some goal that is important to the person. The latent content underlying anger is often injustice or goal obstruction. Similarly, a few core latent-content constructs underlie each of the universal emotions that are found consistently across cultures. These core constructs, summarized in Table 9.4, appear to allow these emotions to share some universal basis across all cultures.

At the same time, cultures differ in the exact situations, events, or occurrences that are associated with the latent content. That is, there is not always a one-to-one correspondence between latent and manifest content across cultures. Whereas death may produce sadness in one culture, for example, it may produce another emotion in another culture. In one culture, the manifest content of death may be associated with the latent content of loss of loved object,

Table 9.4 Latent Content of Emotions

Emotion	Universal Underlying Psychological Theme
Happiness	Accomplishing a goal
Anger	Being prevented from accomplishing a goal
Sadness	Being kept from something you desire or want
Disgust	Being sickened or repulsed by something
Fear	Sensing danger caused by unexpected, novel events and being completely helpless to do something about it
Surprise	Acknowledging something new or novel
Contempt	Feeling morally superior over someone else
Shame and guilt	Feeling a high level of responsibility for one's own behaviors, which conflict with one's own standards

producing sadness; in another culture, the manifest content of death may be associated with a different latent content, such as achievement of a higher spiritual goal, producing a different emotion, happiness. Thus, the same manifest event may be associated with different underlying psychological themes, which give rise to different emotions.

Also, the same latent themes may be associated with different manifest content across cultures. For example, threats to one's personal well-being may be a psychological theme underlying emotions of fear. In one culture, this theme may be associated with being out alone late at night in a large city. In another culture, this theme may be associated with traffic rather than being out late. Despite the differences in manifest content, both situations may result in fear in the respective cultures because of the similarity in latent content.

People of different cultures learn to associate culture-specific events, situations, and occurrences (manifest content) with a limited set of core psychological themes (latent content) that produce emotions. Although there is high agreement across cultures on the nature of that latent content, manifest content is more variable across cultures. This distinction explains why cross-cultural research has found both similarities and differences in emotion antecedents. This concept of latent content is also useful in connection with another emotion-related process: appraisal.

Culture and Emotion Appraisal

Cultural Similarities in Emotion Appraisal

Emotion appraisal can be loosely defined as the process by which people evaluate the events, situations, or occurrences that lead to their having emotions. This aspect of the study of human emotion has a long and complex history, yet basic questions about the nature of the appraisal process in relation to culture remain. How do people of different cultures think about or evaluate the events that trigger their emotions? Do emotions and their eliciting situations show commonalities across cultures? Or do people of different cultures think about emotion antecedents differently?

In the past decade, a number of important and interesting studies have found that many appraisal processes appear to be consistent across cultures, suggesting the possible universality of these processes in eliciting emotions. Mauro, Sato, and Tucker (1992), for example, asked participants in the United States, Hong Kong, Japan, and the People's Republic of China to complete an extensive questionnaire requiring them to describe a situation that elicited one of 16 different emotions. The researchers found few, if any, cultural differences on primitive dimensions of cognitive appraisal: pleasantness, attention, certainty, coping, and goal/need conduciveness. In addition, they found only a few cultural differences on two dimensions: legitimacy and norm/self compatibility. They interpreted these findings as evidence of universality in emotion appraisal processes.

Although the selection of the appraisal dimensions included in this study was driven by theoretical considerations, Mauro and associates (1992) also tested empirically to discover the smallest number of dimensions necessary to describe the differences among the emotions. They used a statistical technique called a principal components analysis, which groups variables into a smaller number of factors based on the interrelationships among the original set of variables in the analysis. The results of this analysis indicated that only seven dimensions were necessary to explain emotion elicitation: pleasantness, certainty, effort, attention, perceived control of others, appropriateness, and control of the circumstances. When cultural differences were tested on these dimensions, they found that there were no cultural differences on the more primitive dimensions, and only a few on the more complex ones. Again, these results suggest that these dimensions of emotion appraisal are universal, at least for the emotions included in their study.

Roseman, Dhawan, Rettek, Nadidu, and Thapa (1995) used a different methodology to study the appraisal processes of sadness, anger, and fear in American and Indian participants. They showed respondents a facial expression corresponding with one of these emotions and asked them to label the emotion portrayed, describe what had happened to cause the person to feel that emotion, and evaluate that event. They found that, for both Americans and Indians, appraisals of powerlessness characterized incidents eliciting anger and fear, whereas appraisals of relative power differences brought forth anger. Also, in both cultures, appraisals that an event was caused by someone else elicited anger but not sadness or fear, whereas events caused by circumstances elicited sadness or fear but not anger. These findings provide further support for cultural similarities in emotion appraisal processes.

Perhaps the largest cross-cultural study on emotion appraisal processes is Scherer's, described earlier, involving 2,921 participants in 37 countries. In that study, respondents were asked to describe an event or situation in which they experienced one of seven emotions: anger, disgust, fear, happiness, sadness, shame, and guilt. Scherer (1997a, 1997b) found that emotion appraisal processes were more similar than different across cultures. The appraisal processes found to be associated with the seven emotions studied were as follows:

- Happiness—high goal conduciveness and high coping potential
- Fear—sudden, novel events caused by others or by circumstances, obstructive to needs, where one feels powerless
- Anger—goal obstruction, immorality, but one has sufficient coping potential to deal with
- Sadness—low goal conduciveness and low coping potential
- Disgust—strong immorality and unfairness
- Shame and guilt—high self-attribution of responsibility for an action, high inconsistency of this action with one's internal standards

Again, these findings indicate a high degree of cross-cultural similarity in emotion appraisal processes and are clearly associated with the universal psychological themes underlying the emotion antecedents discussed above. They support the notion that emotions are a universal phenomenon with psychobiological similarities across all humans regardless of culture, a position that is consistent with previous findings regarding the universality of many of these emotions.

Cultural Differences in Emotion Appraisal

Despite the strong evidence for cross-cultural consistency in emotion appraisal processes, each of the studies just reviewed reported a number of cultural differences as well. In all the studies, the cultural differences were relatively small compared to differences attributed to emotions regardless of culture, which is why all of the authors argued for at least some degree of universality in emotion appraisal processes. Nevertheless, the cultural differences that were obtained need to be accounted for.

For example, one early study comparing American and Japanese responses showed considerable cultural differences in the ways people in different cultures evaluate emotion-eliciting situations (Matsumoto, Kudoh, Scherer, & Wallbott, 1988). Emotions had a more positive effect on self-esteem and self-confidence for Americans than they did for the Japanese. Attributions of causality of emotions also varied by culture: Americans attribute the cause of sadness-producing events to others, whereas Japanese attribute the cause of sadness to themselves. Americans are also more likely to attribute the causes of joy, fear, and shame to other people, whereas the Japanese tend to attribute the causes of these emotions to chance or fate. Japanese believe more than Americans do that no action or behavior is necessary after an emotion is elicited. For emotions such as fear, more Americans than Japanese believe they can do something to influence the situation positively. For anger and disgust, more Americans believe they are powerless and dominated by the event and its consequences. For shame and guilt, more Japanese than Americans pretended that nothing had happened and tried to think of something else.

Other cultural differences have also been reported. In Roseman et al.'s (1995) study, for example, compared with Americans, Indians appraised sadness-, fear-, and anger-eliciting events as more consistent with their motives. In other words, Indians were more likely to report that the emotions triggered by the events were conducive to their particular motivations, such as accomplishing a goal. They also appraised their power to change those events to be less, and the probability of those events to be lower. Mauro and associates (1992) reported differences among the four cultures in their study on dimensions of control, responsibility, and anticipated effort. They suggested that these cultural differences were related to differences on individualism versus collectivism, because differences on this dimension would be associated with differences in perceived control over events. Indeed, they found that the Americans generally had higher control scores than did respondents in the other three countries.

In both of his studies, Scherer (1997a, 1997b) reported cultural differences in emotion appraisal. In the first, Scherer (1997a) classified each of the 37 countries into one of six geopolitical regions: North/Central Europe, Mediterranean Basin, New World, Latin America, Asia, and Africa. Correlations among the appraisal dimensions across regions indicated great similarities across regions in appraisal processes, but Latin America and Africa seemed to differ slightly from the other regions. Scherer's further analyses (1997b) indicate that for all emotions except happiness, participants from African countries appraised the emotion-eliciting events as higher on unfairness, external causation, and immorality than did people from other regions. Respondents from Latin America had lower scores on perceptions of immorality than did people from other regions. Analyses involving climate, cultural values, and socioeconomic and demographic factors did not account for these differences. Still, Scherer suggested that a general factor of urbanism may account for both sets of findings (Africa and Latin America).

Collectively, these studies suggest that although many appraisal processes appear to be universal across humans, there is room for some cultural differences, especially in appraisal dimensions that require judgments relative to cultural or social norms such as fairness and morality. It would appear, therefore, that cultural differences may occur on these more "complex" appraisal dimensions, but not on more "primitive" dimensions, as suggested by Roseman and associates (1995). There appears to be something inherent to all humans that allows for the elicitation of a set of universal emotional experiences, but a role for culture in complex cognitive processes that allow for finer distinctions among emotions.

These findings and interpretations are entirely congruent with the findings reported throughout this chapter on the universal and culturally relative aspects of emotion. Cross-cultural research on emotion appraisals has generally involved only a small set of emotions that are considered universal. Future studies can expand on these findings by including a broader range of emotions to flesh out possible greater cultural differences in appraisal processes for more culturally relative emotions.

Culture and the Concept and Language of Emotion

In the final section of the chapter, we examine how culture influences the concept of emotion itself, and the languages used to represent it around the world. Indeed, throughout this chapter, we have been discussing emotion as if it means the same thing to all people. Researchers who study emotion also fall into that same trap. And certainly, the studies documenting the universality of emotional expression, recognition, experience, antecedents, and appraisals would argue for similarity in the concept, understanding, and language of at least that small set of emotions. But what about other terms and phenomena we call "emotion"? Let's begin our examination by looking at emotions as we understand them in the United States.

Emotions in Everyday American Life

In the United States, we place a premium on feelings. We all recognize that each of us is unique and that we have our own individual feelings about the things, events, situations, and people around us. We consciously try to be aware of our feelings, to be "in touch" with them, as we say. To be in touch with our feelings and to understand the world around us emotionally is to be a mature adult in our society.

We place importance and value on feelings and emotions throughout the life span. We cherish our feelings as adults, and we actively try to recognize the feelings of our children and of other young ones around us. It is not uncommon for parents to ask their young children how they feel about their swimming lessons, their piano lessons, their teachers at school, or the broccoli on their plates. Parents often give considerable weight to the feelings of their children in making decisions that affect them. "If Johnny doesn't want to do it, we shouldn't make him do it" is a common sentiment among parents in the United States. Indeed, children's emotions are afforded almost the same status as the emotions of adults and the older generations.

Much therapeutic work in psychology centers around human emotions. The goal of individual psychotherapy systems is often to get people to become more aware of their feelings and emotions and to accept them. Much psychotherapeutic work is focused on helping individuals freely express the feelings and emotions they may have bottled up inside. In group therapy, the emphasis is on communicating feelings toward others in the group and listening to and accepting the expressions of feelings by others. This emphasis is also prevalent in workgroups. Industrial and organizational interventions are common, and much time, effort, and energy are spent establishing better lines of communication among employees and recognizing the feelings and emotions of individuals.

How American society values and structures people's feelings and emotions is directly related to the values that the American culture fosters. In the United States, rugged individualism has been a cornerstone of the dominant culture, and part of that rugged individualism means that we recognize and value the unique aspects of each and every person. Diversity of feelings and emotions is part of this package; in fact, it may be the most important part in identifying individuals because emotions themselves are highly personalized and individual. Children are valued as separate entities, and their feelings are valued.

Cultural Similarities and Differences in the Concept of Emotion

Many studies have been conducted in the fields of anthropology and psychology to address this important issue. Ethnographic approaches—the in-depth immersion and study of single cultures on their own merits that originates from anthropology—are especially useful in helping to uncover how different cultures define and understand the concept we call emotion. A few years ago, Russell (1991) reviewed much of the cross-cultural and anthropological literature on emotion concepts and pointed out many ways in which cultures differ, sometimes considerably, in their definitions and understanding of emotion. His review provides a strong basis for discussion of this topic.

The concept and definition of emotion.   First of all, Russell (1991) points out, not all cultures have a word that corresponds to our word *emotion*. Levy (1973, 1983) reports that Tahitians do not have a word for emotion; nor, according to Lutz (1980, as reported in Russell, 1991; Lutz, 1983), do the Ifaluks of Micronesia. The fact that some cultures do not even have a word that corresponds to our word *emotion* is important; clearly, in these cultures, the concept of emotion is different from ours. Perhaps it is not as important to these cultures as it is to ours. Or perhaps what we know as emotion is labeled differently, in an untranslatable way, and refers to something other than internal, subjective feelings. In this case, too, their concept of emotion would be quite different from ours.

But most cultures of the world do have a word or concept for what we call emotion. Brandt and Boucher (1986) examined the concepts of depression in eight different cultures, whose languages included Indonesian, Japanese, Korean, Malaysian, Spanish, and Sinhalese. Each of the languages had a word for emotion, suggesting the cross-cultural existence of this concept. But even if a culture has a word for emotion, that culture's word may have different connotations, and thus different meanings, than our English word *emotion*. For example, Matsuyama, Hama, Kawamura, and Mine (1978) analyzed emotional words from the Japanese language, which included some words that are typically considered emotions (for example, *angry*, *sad*) but also some words that Americans would not consider to be emotions (for example, *considerate*, *lucky*). Samoans do not have a word for emotion but do have a word (*lagona*) that refers to feelings and sensations (Gerber, 1975, as reported in Russell, 1991).

In summary, not all cultures of the world have a word or concept for what we label *emotion* in English, and even among those that do, it may not mean the same thing as the English word *emotion*. These studies suggest that the class of events—expressions, perceptions, feelings, situations—that we call emotion does not necessarily represent the same class of phenomena in other cultures.

Categorization or labeling of emotion.
People in different cultures also categorize or label emotions differently. Some English words, such as *anger, joy, sadness, liking*, and *loving*, have equivalents in different languages and cultures. But many English words have no equivalent in another culture, and emotion words in other languages may have no exact English equivalent.

The German language, for example, contains the word *Schadenfreude*, which refers to pleasure derived from another's misfortunes. There is no exact English translation for this word. The Japanese language contains words such as *itoshii* (longing for an absent loved one), *ijirashii* (a feeling associated with seeing someone praiseworthy overcoming an obstacle), and *amae* (dependence), which also have no exact English translation. Conversely, some African languages have a word that covers what English suggests are two emotions: anger and sadness (Leff, 1973). Likewise, Lutz (1980) suggests that the Ifaluk word *song* can be described sometimes as anger and sometimes as sadness. And some English words have no equivalents in other languages. The English words *terror, horror, dread, apprehension,* and *timidity* are all referred to by the single word *gurakadj* in Gidjingali, an Australian aboriginal language (Hiatt, 1978). This aboriginal word also refers to the English concepts of shame and fear. *Frustration* may be a word with no exact equivalent in Arabic languages (Russell, 1991).

Just because a culture does not have a word for something that we consider an emotion certainly does not mean that people of that culture do not have those feelings. The fact that there is no exact equivalent in some Arabic languages for our word *frustration* does not mean that people of these cultures never feel frustrated. Similarly, just because our English language does not have a translation equivalent for the German word *Schadenfreude* does not mean that people in the United States do not sometimes derive pleasure from someone else's misfortunes. Certainly, in the world of subjective, emotional feeling, there must be considerable overlap in the emotions we feel, regardless of whether different cultures and languages have translation equivalents for those feeling states.

The fact that translation differences exist in the exact meaning and labeling of different emotional states across languages and cultures does suggest, however, that different cultures divide their world of emotion differently. The fact that German culture, for example, contains the word *Schadenfreude* must mean that identification of that feeling state or situation has some importance in that language and culture that it does not have in American culture or the English language. The same can be said of English words that find no exact translation equivalent in other languages. The types of words that different cultures use to identify and label the emotion worlds of their members give us yet another clue about the way different cultures structure and mold the emotional experiences of their people. Not only are the concepts of emotion culture-bound, but so also are the ways each culture attempts to frame and label its emotion world.

The location of emotion.   To Americans, perhaps the single most important aspect of emotion is the inner, subjective experience. In the United States, it seems most natural that our feelings take precedence over all other aspects of emotion. But the importance we place on inner feelings and the importance of **introspection** (looking inside yourself) may be culture-bound in American psychology. Other cultures can and do view emotions as originating or residing elsewhere.

Emotion words in the languages of several Oceanic peoples, such as the Samoans (Gerber, 1975), Pintupi aborigines (Myers, 1979), and Solomon Islanders (White, 1980), are statements about relationships among people or between people and events. Likewise, Riesman (1977) suggests that the African Fulani concept *semteende*, which is commonly translated as shame or embarrassment, refers more to a situation than to a feeling. That is, if the situation is appropriate to *semteende*, then someone is feeling it, regardless of what any one individual actually feels (Russell, 1991).

In the United States, we place emotion and inner feelings in the heart. Even cultures that locate emotions within the body differ in that exact location. The Japanese identify many of their emotions in the *hara*—the gut or abdomen. The Chewong of Malay group feelings and thoughts in the liver (Howell, 1981). Levy (1984) reports that Tahitians locate emotions as arising from the intestines. Lutz (1982) suggests that the closest Ifaluk word to the English word *emotion* is *niferash*, which she translates as "our insides."

That different cultures locate emotions in different places informs us that emotions are understood differently and have different meanings for different peoples. Locating emotions in the heart is convenient and important for American culture, as it speaks to the importance of feelings as something unique to oneself, that no one else can share. By identifying emotion with the heart, Americans identify it with the most important biological organ necessary for survival. The fact that other cultures identify and locate emotions outside the body, such as in social relationships with others, speaks to the importance of relationships in those cultures, in contrast to the individualism of American culture.

The meaning of emotions to people and to behavior.   All the differences we have discussed in the concept and meaning of emotion point to differences in the ways different cultures attribute meanings to emotional experiences. In the United States, emotions have enormous personal meaning, perhaps because Americans typically view inner, subjective feelings as the major defining characteristic of emotion. Once emotions are defined in such a way, a major role of emotion is to inform oneself about the self. Our self-definitions are informed by our emotions, which are personal, private, inner experiences.

Cultures differ in the role or meaning of emotions. Many cultures, for example, consider emotions as statements of the relationship between people and their environment, be it objects in the environment or social relationships with other people. Emotions for both the Ifaluks of Micronesia (Lutz, 1982) and the

Tahitians (Levy, 1984) denote statements of relationships with others and with the physical environment. The Japanese concept *amae*, a central emotion in Japanese culture, specifies an interdependent relationship between two people. Thus, the very concept, definition, understanding, and meaning of emotion can differ across cultures. Therefore, when talking to others about our feelings, we cannot simply assume that they will understand us in the way we expect, even though we are speaking of something as "basic" as human emotion. And we certainly cannot assume that we know what someone else is feeling, and what it means, just on the basis of knowing about emotions from our own limited perspective.

Views of emotion as social constructions with social meaning have not been totally absent in American psychology (for example, Averill, 1980; Kemper, 1978), but they have received considerably less attention in mainstream academic psychology than views that center on the introspection of subjective feeling states. As Americans are increasingly exposed to cultural diversity, perhaps American social science will come to embrace thoughts, ideas, and research on emotions from a social and cultural perspective.

Summary.   Although there are many similarities in the concept and language of emotion around the world, across culture and language, there are many interesting differences as well. Do these differences suggest that emotions are fundamentally and inherently incomparable across cultures? Some scientists have suggested as much, most notably those who subscribe to a "functionalist" approach. Personally, we do not believe that this is an either/or question. We believe that both universal and culturally relative aspects of emotion exist in all cultures. What the studies in this section do imply, however, is the need for scientists to integrate assessments of the concept of emotion in the cultures in which they work, along with whatever other aspects of emotion they are studying. That is, scientists interested in studying emotional expression across cultures should assess concepts related to emotion in the cultures they study in addition to their behavioral expressions, in order to examine the degree to which cultural similarities or differences in expression are linked with differences and similarities in emotion concept. The same is true for all aspects or components of emotion.

Conclusion

Emotions—the most private, personal, and arguably the most important aspects of our lives—give life events meaning. They tell us what we like and what we don't, what is good and bad for us. They enrich our lives, giving color and meaning to events and the world around us. They tell us who we are and how we are faring with others. Emotion is the invisible glue that binds us with the rest of the world, whether it be events around us or people.

Emotions play such a central role in our lives that it is no wonder culture, that invisible shaper of experiences, shapes and molds our emotional world. Although we may be born with certain innate abilities, such as the capacity to express and perceive emotions in our faces and to feel emotions, culture helps to shape when, where, and how we can express, perceive, and feel those emotions. Culture creates the meaning of emotions for us, whether we understand emotion as a totally personal, private, and individual experience or as an interpersonal, public, collective experience with others.

In this chapter, we have seen the universality of a small set of facial expressions of emotion that are most likely evolutionarily adaptive and biologically innate. We have seen evidence of universal recognition of this set of facial expressions around the world, as well as universal ways of experiencing them when they occur. We have also seen universality in the nature of the antecedents that elicit these emotions, and in the ways these antecedents are appraised in bringing forth emotion. Yet we have also seen that cultures can differ in their emotional expressions through cultural display rules, and in their emotional perceptions via cultural decoding rules. People differ across cultures in the ways in which they experience emotion, and in the specific antecedent events that elicit it. Some aspects of emotion appraisal, and even the concept and language of emotion, can also differ across cultures.

The coexistence of universal and culture-specific aspects of emotion has been a source of debate for many years. We believe that these are not necessarily mutually exclusive positions; that is, universality and cultural relativity can indeed coexist. It appears that universality may be limited to a rather small set of basic emotions, which serve as a platform for interactions with learned rules, social mores, and shared social scripts, resulting in a myriad of more complex culture-specific emotions and emotional meanings. The mere fact that universality exists does not negate the potential for cultural differences. Likewise, the mere fact that cultural differences exist does not negate the potential for universality. They are two sides of the same coin, and both need to be incorporated into future theories and research on emotion, whether within or across cultures.

Indeed, the incorporation of underlying, universal, psychobiological processes into a model of cultural construction of emotion is a challenge that lies ahead in this area of research. Scientists in this area of psychology will need to take up the greater challenge of how biology interacts with culture to produce the individual and group psychologies we see around the world. If nothing else, at least our recognition of emotions as a universal process can help bring people together, regardless of culture, race, ethnicity, or gender. As we continue our study of human feelings and emotions across cultures, perhaps it is most important to recognize how these boundaries mold our emotions. Although we all have emotions, they mean different things to different people and are experienced, expressed, and perceived in different ways. One of our first tasks in learning about emotions across cultures is to recognize and respect those differences. But an equally important task is to recognize our similarities as well.

 Glossary

cultural display rules   Culturally prescribed rules that govern how universal emotions can be expressed. These rules center on the appropriateness of displaying emotion, depending on social circumstances. Learned by people early in their lives, they dictate how the universal emotional expressions should be modified according to social situation. By adulthood, these rules are quite automatic, having been very well practiced.

decoding rules   Rules that govern the interpretation and perception of emotion. These are learned, culturally based rules that shape how people of each culture view and interpret the emotional expressions of others.

emotion antecedents   The events or situations that elicit an emotion.

emotion appraisal   The process by which people evaluate the events, situations, or occurrences that lead to their having emotions.

introspection   The process of looking inside yourself.

subjective experience of emotion   An individual's inner feelings or experiences of an emotion.

universality studies   A series of studies conducted by Ekman and Friesen and by Izard that demonstrated the pancultural universality of facial expressions of emotion.

InfoTrac College Edition

Use InfoTrac College Edition to search for additional readings on topics of interest to you. For more information on topics in this chapter, use the following as search terms:

culture and emotion
introspection
display rules
emotion appraisal

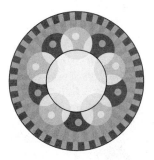

Culture, Language, and Communication

10

Communication is one of the most important aspects of our lives. It is a process that ties us all together; it helps us get work done, have relationships, and accomplish goals. It is also important for developing, maintaining, and transmitting culture from one generation to the next, and in reinforcing cultural goals and values within generations. Thus, communication plays a special role in our understanding of culture and cultural influences on behavior.

When we think of communication, the first and perhaps most salient aspect that comes to mind is verbal language. Words and language play a major role in our communication processes, and are uniquely human. Our verbal language—whether English, French, Arabic, Chinese, or Indonesian—is extremely important to our ability to communicate. People place great emphasis on the words we use and how we use them. Mastery of verbal language is an important part of any successful communication, and we all tend to make judgments of people based on their level of mastery of their particular language. Of course, verbal language is not the only aspect of communication. Another large and important component is nonverbal communication, including facial expressions, tone of voice, posture, dress, distance, and the like.

In the first part of this chapter, we begin by exploring the components of language thought to be applicable to all languages of the world, and discuss language differences across cultures, including differences in language lexicons as well as pragmatics. Next, we examine the relationship between language and cognition, focusing on the Sapir–Whorf hypothesis. This hypothesis suggests that language helps to structure our worldview and is crucial to the culture-language relationship. We will also look at the special case of bilingualism as it affects behavior and personality, and dispel some common misperceptions about bilingual individuals. In the second part of the chapter, we focus on the relationship between culture and nonverbal behaviors, the area of nonverbal communication that has received the most attention in cross-cultural research. We will begin by reviewing the various functions of nonverbal behaviors. Then, we will discuss how verbal and nonverbal behaviors combine in communication, examining the relative contribution of each to overall communication processes and content. Finally, in the last part of the chapter, we will compare intracultural communication with intercultural communication, and discuss the latter's unique aspects. We will also discuss strategies for building effective intercultural communication, focusing on emotions, conflict management, and the development of intercultural sensitivity. But first, we start off with language.

The Structure of Language

Before examining the relationship between culture and language, it is useful first to identify the basic structure and features of language. Understanding the various components of language will enable us to consider exactly what it is about language that is influenced by, and influences, culture. It also provides a basis for reviewing research examining the relationship between culture and language, which often focuses on specific components of language.

Linguists typically describe language using the following five critical features, which appear to apply to all languages in all cultures:

1. The **lexicon**, or vocabulary, refers to the words contained in a language. For example, the words *tree, eat, how,* and *slowly* are each part of the English lexicon.
2. The **syntax and grammar** of a language refer to the system of rules governing word forms and how words should be strung together to form meaningful utterances. For example, English has a grammatical rule that says we add *s* to the end of many words to indicate plurality (*cat* becomes *cats*). English also has a syntactic rule that we generally place adjectives before nouns, not after (for example, *small dog,* not *dog small*).
3. **Phonology** refers to the system of rules governing how words should sound (pronunciation) in a given language. For instance, in English, we don't pronounce *new* the same as *sew*.
4. **Semantics** refers to what words mean. For example, *table* refers to a physical object that has four legs and a flat horizontal surface.
5. **Pragmatics** refers to the system of rules governing how language is used and understood in given social contexts. For example, the statement "It is cold" could be interpreted as a request to close a window or as a statement of fact about the temperature. How it's interpreted depends on the social and environmental context.

Linguists use two other concepts to help explain the structure of language. **Phonemes** are the smallest and most basic units of sound in a language, and

morphemes are the smallest and most basic units of meaning in a language. Phonemes thus form the base of a language hierarchy in which language gains in complexity as sounds gain meaning, which in turn produces words, which are strung together in phrases and, finally, sentences.

Language Differences across Cultures

The Relationship between Culture and Language

Culture and language are intimately related. Culture influences the structure and functional use of language, and language can be thought of as the result or manifestation of culture. American English, its words and how we use them, is a reflection of American culture. Language also influences and reinforces our cultural values and worldview, thus feeding back onto them. The cyclical nature of the relationship between culture and language suggests that no culture can be fully understood without understanding its language, and vice versa. And because language influences our thinking and worldview, understanding cultural influences on language has important implications for understanding cultural differences in worldview perspectives. One way to observe the relationship between language and culture is by noting the association between different cultures' languages and their lexicons, or vocabulary.

Culture and Lexicons

Self/other referents. In American English, we generally use one of two words, and their derivatives, to describe ourselves when talking to others: *I* and *we*. We use these words irrespective of whom we are talking to or what we are talking about. If we are talking to a university professor, we use the word *I* to refer to ourselves. If we are talking to our parents, we use the same word *I*. And we use the same word *I* when referring to ourselves with friends, family, neighbors, acquaintances, bosses, or subordinates. Likewise, we generally use a single word in English to refer to another person or group of people: *you*. In conversation with our parents, bosses, friends, lovers, strangers, children, and just about anyone, we use *you* or one of its derivatives to refer to the other person or persons.

Many languages in the world, however, have much more elaborate systems of reference that depend on the nature of the relationship between people. The Japanese language provides one of the most extreme examples. Japanese does have translation equivalents of the English words *I*, *we*, and *you*, but these words are used much less frequently in Japanese than in English. In Japanese, what you call yourself and others is totally dependent on the relationship between you and the other person. Often, the decision about what is appropriate to call yourself and another person depends on the status differential between the two people. For example, if you are of a higher status than the other person, in Japan you would refer to yourself by position or role rather than by the English equivalent of *I*. In Japan, teachers use the word *teacher* to refer to themselves when talking to students. Doctors may use the term *doctor*, and parents use the word *mother* or *father* when speaking to their children.

In the Japanese language, if you are of a lower status than the person to whom you are speaking, you refer to yourself using one of several pronoun equivalents of *I*, such as *watashi, watakushi, boku,* or *ore.* The use of these different terms for *I* depends on your sex (women cannot say *boku* or *ore*), degree of politeness, and degree of familiarity with the other person. When speaking to someone of higher status, for example, people generally use *watashi* to refer to themselves. When speaking to friends or colleagues, men usually refer to themselves as *boku* or *ore.*

Likewise, if you are speaking to someone of higher status, you generally refer to that person by role or title. When speaking to your teachers, you refer to them as *teacher,* even when addressing them directly. You would call your boss by his or her title, such as *section chief* or *president.* You would definitely not use a personal pronoun such as our English *you* in addressing a person of higher status. When speaking to a person of lower status, you would generally use a personal pronoun or the person's actual name. As with personal pronouns for *I,* the Japanese language contains several pronouns for *you*—among them, *anata, omae,* and *kimi.* Again, the appropriate use of each depends on the relationship; generally, *omae* and *kimi* are used when speaking to someone of lower status than you or to someone very familiar and intimate with you. Indeed, the Japanese language system of self- and other-referents is very complicated, especially when compared to American English (see Figure 10.1).

These differences between the English and Japanese languages reflect important cultural differences. In the Japanese culture, language, mannerisms, and other aspects of behavior must be modified according to the relationship and context under which the communication is occurring. The most important dimensions along which behavior and language are differentiated in Japan are status and group orientation. All aspects of behavior differ depending on whether one person is higher or lower in status than the other person in the conversation. Also, behavior and language differ depending on whether the other person is a member of your ingroup or not. Thus, the choice of appropriate self- and other-referents in the Japanese language reflects important aspects of Japanese culture.

Counting systems. Counting systems provide yet another example of how culture influences the structure of a language. In the Japanese language, for example, different words are used to denote different things being counted. Round, cylindrical objects are counted by the suffix *hon* (*ippon, nihon, sanbon,* and so on); flat objects are counted by *mai* (*ichimai, nimai, sanmai,* and so on). Japanese has many such counters, as do many other languages. In English, however, all objects are simply counted by the number, with no such prefix or suffix to denote the type of object being counted.

In addition, the Japanese language, like many other languages, bases all numbers on the words for one through ten. Eleven is literally ten-one (*ju-ichi*),

Figure 10.1 Japanese words for self and other

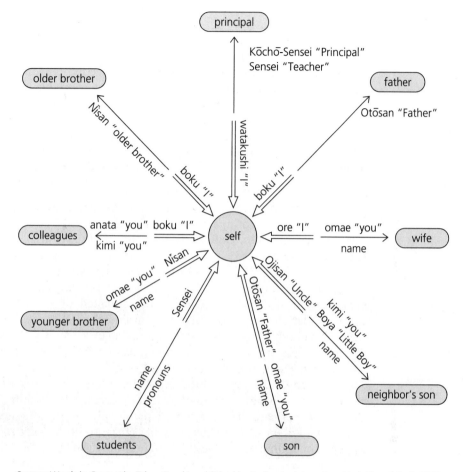

12 is ten-two (*ju-ni*), 20 is two-ten (*ni-ju*). In English, however, numbers 1 through 19 are unique, and an additive system similar to Japanese numbers starts at 20. These linguistic differences are thought to contribute to differences in math achievement between the United States and Japan (see Stigler & Baranes, 1988).

Culture and Pragmatics

Culture affects not only the language lexicons, but also pragmatics—that is, the rules governing how language is used and understood in different social contexts.

Pronoun use.   Kashima and Kashima (1998), for example, examined 39 languages used in 71 countries, obtaining both cultural and linguistic data from each country. The cultural scores included Hofstede's (1980, 1983) four dimensions—individualism, power distance, uncertainty avoidance, and masculinity—and 15 other culture-related dimensions. The linguistic data included an analysis of the use of first- and second-person pronouns, and whether the language permitted dropping these pronouns in conversation. The correlations between these two sets of data were analyzed in two separate ways to examine the relationship between culture and pronoun usage. Kashima and Kashima (1998) found that cultures whose languages allowed pronouns to be dropped tended to be less individualistic, which they interpreted as reflecting different cultural conceptualizations of self and others.

Communication styles.   Gudykunst and his colleagues have also done a number of studies that demonstrate cultural variability in language use and communication styles. Gudykunst and Nishida (1986b), for example, asked participants in the United States and Japan to make intimacy ratings of 30 relationship terms (such as brother, employer, stranger) and, in another study, to rate communication styles in six relationships on personalization, synchrony, and difficulty. The results indicated that the Japanese rated ingroup relationships—coworkers and university colleagues—as more intimate than did the Americans, and that the Japanese perceived more personalization but less synchrony across relationship terms. In a subsequent study, Gudykunst, Yoon, and Nishida (1987) tested participants from the United States, Japan, and Korea, asking them to rate the same three dimensions of communicative behavior in ingroup and outgroup relationships. They found that the Americans had the lowest personalization and synchronization scores, the Koreans the highest, and the Japanese in the middle, but only for ingroup communication. These researchers suggested that members of collectivistic cultures use a principle of equity involving greater social penetration when communicating with ingroup members than do members of individualistic cultures.

Communication topics.   Cultural differences have also been documented in a number of other communication areas, such as apologies (Barnlund & Yoshioka, 1990), children's personal narratives (Minami & McCabe, 1995), self-disclosure (Chen, 1995), compliments (Barnlund & Araki, 1985), and interpersonal criticism (Nomura & Barnlund, 1983). Chen, for example, asked American and Taiwanese participants to complete a measure of self-disclosure in relation to four target persons and six different conversational topics. The results indicated that Americans had a significantly higher level of self-disclosure than did the Taiwanese Chinese across all topics and target persons. Barnlund and Yoshioka reported that Japanese participants preferred more direct, extreme forms of apology, while Americans preferred indirect, less extreme forms. Also, Americans tended to favor explanation as a form of apology, whereas the Japanese preferred compensation.

Recent research has extended these findings of cultural differences by showing how such differences are mediated by self-construals and values held on the individual level, and by some personality dimensions. The addition of such mediator variables is an example of research involving context variables, discussed in Chapter 2. Kim and associates (1996), for example, asked participants in Korea, Japan, Hawaii, and mainland United States to rate the importance of five different conversational constraints (for example, clarity, concern for the other's feelings) in relation to six vignettes. Participants also completed a scale measuring their self-construals as either independent or interdependent (see Chapter 11). These researchers found that culture affected the self-construals, which, in turn, affected the ratings of the conversational constraints. In a similar fashion, Gudykunst and colleagues (1996) reported that self-construals and individual values mediate the use of context-dependent communication styles; Gudykunst and colleagues (1992) reported that two variables, self-monitoring and predicted outcome value of the relationship, mediated cultural differences in communication styles in ingroup and outgroup relationships.

Summary

Collectively, the work cited in this section paints a rather complete picture of the profound influence of culture not only on language lexicons, but also on the use and function of language. Language differences reflect important differences between cultures, and they also help to reinforce culture. For example, as a result of using the complex system of self- and other-referents in the Japanese language, a person's system of thought and behavior becomes structured over time to reflect the culture. Through the use of language, an individual is transformed into an agent of the culture. Thus, the feelings, associations, connotations, and nuances of language both influence and are influenced by the culture. Over time, an individual embodies the very essence of culture via language, and in using the language, he or she reinforces that language's concepts of culture. This same relationship holds true for Japanese, American English, and all other languages and cultures (see Figure 10.2).

These observations make it clear that people of different cultures structure the world around them differently, at least in the language they use to describe that world. But are these differences so pervasive that people actually see the same things differently? For instance, do Americans and Japanese actually see, think, and feel differently about objects they are counting? And are these differences related to differences in their language? Or do they see exactly the same things but just categorize them differently? Studies examining these and related questions suggest that such language differences are not just a matter of categorization, but reflect genuine differences in worldview.

Figure 10.2 The reciprocal relation between culture and language

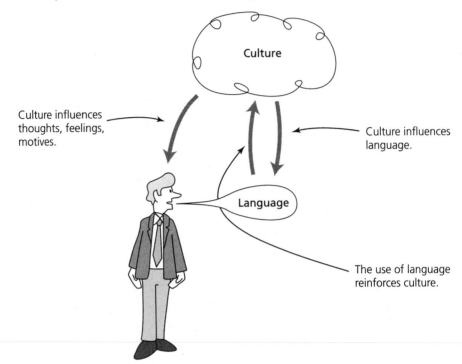

Culture influences thoughts, feelings, motives.

Culture influences language.

The use of language reinforces culture.

Culture, Language, and Cognition: The Sapir–Whorf Hypothesis

One of the most important and long-standing debates in studies of language and behavior involves the relationship between language and thought processes. This relationship is particularly important to the cross-cultural study of language because each culture is associated with a given language as a vehicle for its expression. How does culture influence language? And how does language influence culture?

The Sapir–Whorf Hypothesis

The **Sapir–Whorf hypothesis,** also referred to as *linguistic relativity,* suggests that speakers of different languages think differently, and that they do so because of the differences in their languages. Because different cultures typically have different languages, the Sapir–Whorf hypothesis is especially important for understanding cultural differences (and similarities) in thought and behavior as a function of language.

If the Sapir–Whorf hypothesis is correct, it suggests that people of different cultures think differently, just by the very nature, structure, and function of their language. Their thought processes, their associations, their ways of interpreting the world—even the same events we perceive—may be different because they speak a different language and this language has helped shape their thought patterns. This hypothesis also suggests that people who speak more than one language may actually have different thought patterns when speaking different languages.

Support for Sapir–Whorf

Many studies have looked at language–cognition issues since Edward Sapir and Benjamin Whorf first proposed their hypothesis in the 1950s. In one of the earliest language studies, Carroll and Casagrande (1958) compared Navajo and English speakers. They examined the relationship between the system of shape classification in the Navajo language and the amount of attention children pay to shape when classifying objects. Similar to the Japanese language described earlier in this chapter, the Navajo language has the interesting grammatical feature that certain verbs of handling (for example, "to pick up," "to drop") require special linguistic forms depending on what kind of object is being handled. A total of 11 such linguistic forms describe different shapes—round spherical objects, round thin objects, long flexible things, and so forth. Noting how much more complex this linguistic feature is in Navajo than in English, Carroll and Casagrande (1958) suggested that such linguistic features might play a role in influencing cognitive processes. In their experiment, they compared Navajo- and English-dominant children to see how often they used shape, form, or type of material to categorize objects. The Navajo-dominant children were significantly more likely to categorize by shape than were the English-dominant children. In the same study, Carroll and Casagrande (1958) also reported that the performance of low-income African American English-speaking children was similar to that of European American children. This finding is particularly important because the African American children, unlike the European Americans, were not accustomed to blocks and form-board toys. The results of this study—along with the observations concerning the relationship between culture and language lexicons, and culture and pragmatics reviewed earlier—provided early support for the idea that the language we speak influences the kind of thoughts we have. Language, that is, may act in a mediating role, helping to determine the ways in which children conceive of some aspects of their world.

Later studies also provided support for linguistic relativity. For instance, Kay and Kempton (1984) compared the thought processes of speakers of English with those of speakers of Tarahumara, a language indigenous to the Yucatán peninsula in Mexico that does not distinguish between blue and green. They had subjects complete two nonlinguistic tasks, both of which involved choosing from a number of color chips the color that was the "most different" from the others. They found that color discrimination was better when subjects could use a naming strategy, demonstrating that linguistic differences can affect the performance of a nonlinguistic task.

A study by Bloom (1981) reported that Chinese speakers are less likely than English speakers to give hypothetical interpretations to a hypothetical story. He interpreted these results as constituting strong evidence for the structure of language as a mediator of cognitive processes because English and Chinese differ in how they convey hypothetical meaning. In English, we use the subjunctive ("if I were you," not "if I am you"). Chinese has no subjunctive in the sense of a mandatory marking in each verb (the grammatical Chinese equivalent of "if I were you" would be roughly translated "be if I am you").

A number of other studies have also supported linguistic relativity. Lucy (1992), comparing American English with the language of the Yucatec Maya in southeastern Mexico, identified distinctive patterns of thought relating to differences in the two languages. Hoosain (1986, 1991) has shown how unique aspects of the Chinese language influence the ease of processing information. Garro (1986), comparing American English and Mexican Spanish, demonstrated that language influenced memory for colors. Santa and Baker (1975) provided evidence in favor of Sapir–Whorf in their study of language effects on the quality and order of visual reproduction of figures. Lin and Schwanenflugel (1995), comparing English and Taiwanese Chinese, demonstrated that language structure was related to the structure of category knowledge in American and Chinese speakers. Collectively, these studies provide support for the Sapir–Whorf hypothesis.

Challenges to Sapir–Whorf

However, findings from other studies challenge the Sapir–Whorf hypothesis. For instance, Berlin and Kay (1969) tested Gleason's (1961) earlier claims that "The continuous gradation of color which exists in nature is represented in language by a series of discrete categories. . . . There is nothing inherent either in the spectrum or the human perception of it which would compel its division in this way. The specific method of division is part of the structure of English" (p. 4). To test this claim, Berlin and Kay (1969) undertook a study of the distribution of color terms in 20 languages. They asked international university students in the United States to list the "basic" color terms in each of their native languages. They then asked these foreign students to identify from an array of glass color chips the most typical or best examples of a basic color term the researchers specified. Berlin and Kay (1969) found a limited number of basic color terms in any language. They also found that the color chips chosen as best examples of these basic terms tended to fall in clusters they termed focal points. In languages that had a basic term for bluish colors, the best example of the color was found to be the same "focal blue" for speakers of all the languages. These findings suggested that people in different cultures perceive colors in much the same way despite radical differences in their languages.

Berlin and Kay's findings were later confirmed by a series of experiments conducted by Rosch. In her experiments, Rosch (for example, 1973) set out to test just how culturally universal these focal points were. She compared two languages that differ markedly in the number of basic color terms: English, with multiple color terms, and Dani, which has only two color terms. Dani is the language spoken by a Stone Age tribe living in the highlands of Irian Jaya, Indonesian New Guinea. One color term, *mili*, was found to include both "dark" and "cold" colors (for example, black, green, and blue), while the second color term, *mola*, included both "light" and "warm" colors (for example, white, red, and yellow). Rosch also explored the relationship between language and memory. She argued that if the Whorfian position were correct, Dani's lack of a rich color lexicon would inhibit Dani speakers' ability to discriminate and remember colors. As it happened, Heider and Oliver (1972) found that Dani speakers did not confuse color categories any more than did speakers of English. Nor did Dani speakers perform differently from English speakers on memory tasks.

Berlin and Kay (1969) also examined 78 languages and found that 11 basic color terms form a universal hierarchy. Some languages, such as English and German, use all 11 terms; others, such as Dani (New Guinea), use as few as two. Further, they noticed an evolutionary order in which languages encode these universal categories. For example, if a language has three color terms, those three terms describe black, white, and red. This hierarchy of color names in human language is as follows:

1. All languages contain terms for white and black.
2. If a language contains three terms, it also contains a term for red.
3. If a language contains four terms, it also contains a term for either green or yellow (but not both).
4. If a language contains five terms, it contains terms for both green and yellow.
5. If a language contains six terms, it also contains a term for blue.
6. If a language contains seven terms, it also contains a term for brown.
7. If a language contains eight or more terms, it also contains a term for purple, pink, orange, gray, or some combination of these.

Studies have also challenged Bloom's (1981) earlier claim of linguistic relativity with Chinese and English speakers. Au (1983), for example, reported five studies intending to replicate Bloom's (1981) study, using Chinese and English versions of stories used by Bloom. Au concluded that the use of hypothetical interpretations was probably not related to the use of the subjunctive, or to counterfactual reasoning in the Chinese (see also critique of Au's study by Bloom, 1984). Liu (1985) also failed to replicate Bloom's study. Takano (1989) discussed both conceptual and methodological problems with Bloom's study, and suggested that the positive findings obtained by Bloom may have been an artifact of methodological flaws. He conducted three studies investigating the nature of those flaws, and concluded that differences in the amount of mathematical training, not linguistic differences, may have produced the differences Bloom originally reported.

In a recent overview of the debate concerning the Sapir–Whorf hypothesis, Pinker (1995) concludes that many of the earlier studies claiming linguistic relativity are severely flawed (such as Bloom's). He then points to the fact that we can think *without* words and language, suggesting that language does not necessarily determine our thoughts. He cites evidence of deaf children who clearly think while lacking a language, but soon invent one; of isolated adults who grew up without language but still could engage in abstract thinking; how babies, who have no words, can still do very simple forms of arithmetic (Wynn, 1992); and how thought is not just made up of words and language, but is also visual and nonverbal. Other studies conducted over the years also provide evidence challenging the validity of Sapir–Whorf (for example, Davies, Sowden, Jerrett, Jerrett, & Corbett, 1998). Recently, a number of scholars have offered alternative models of the relationship between language and thought (for example, Gumperz & Levinson, 1996; Hadley, 1997; Lucy, 1992).

Sapir–Whorf: The Bottom Line

Perhaps the best way to make sense of this area of study comes from an analysis of the basic Sapir–Whorf hypothesis published many years earlier. Many studies of the Sapir–Whorf hypothesis read as if it were only one hypothesis; actually, there are several different Sapir–Whorf hypotheses. In 1960, Joshua Fishman published a comprehensive breakdown of the most important ways the Sapir–Whorf hypothesis has been discussed (see Table 10.1). In his description, these different approaches are ordered in increasing levels of complexity. Two factors determine the level at which a given version of the hypothesis might fall. The first factor relates to the particular aspect of language that is of interest—for example, the lexicon or the grammar. The second factor relates to the cognitive behavior of the speakers of a given language—for example, cultural themes or nonlinguistic data such as a decision-making task. Of the four levels, Level 1 is the least complex; Level 4 is the most complex. Levels 3 and 4 are actually closer to Whorf's original ideas in that they concern the grammar or syntax of language as opposed to its lexicon.

Table 10.1 Fishman's Sapir–Whorf Hypothesis Schema

Data of Language Characteristics	Data of Cognitive Behavior	
	Linguistic Data	Nonlinguistic Data
Lexical/Semantic	Level 1*	Level 2
Grammatical	Level 3	Level 4**

*Least sophisticated
**Most sophisticated

In reviewing the literature on the Sapir–Whorf hypothesis, it is important to keep in mind exactly which level of the hypothesis is being tested. Few research studies test the Sapir-Whorf hypothesis at Fishman's Level 3 or 4. A considerable amount of research compares lexical differences and linguistic behavior (Fishman's Level 1) or nonlinguistic behavior (Fishman's Level 2). Most of this research is at Level 2, comparing lexical differences with nonlinguistic behaviors. When such comparisons have shown differences, language is assumed to have caused these differences.

Viewed according to Fishman's classifications, the best-studied area is lexical differences between languages, which provides some of the weaker support for the hypothesis. This makes sense, because the lexicon seems to be only minimally related to thought processes, which may account for some skepticism about the Sapir–Whorf hypothesis. A less-studied area, however—that of syntactic and grammatical differences between languages—provides evidence for the claim that language influences cognition. Perhaps stronger evidence will be found in future studies of how the pragmatic systems of different languages influence speakers' thought processes.

Bilingualism and Culture

Bilingualism and Sapir–Whorf

To this point, we have assumed monolingualism—that each person speaks only one language; in fact, most, if not all, of the research on language and culture has been limited to a comparison of monolingual populations. But what about people who are fluent in more than one language? What might the Sapir–Whorf hypothesis imply about the behavior of bilingual or multilingual populations?

One implication might be that the thoughts, feelings, and behaviors of bilingual individuals would depend on which language they are using. A Mexican American or Mexican immigrant bilingual in English and Spanish, for example, may think a certain way when speaking American English and a different way when speaking Spanish. In fact, many bilinguals report that they think, feel, and act differently depending on the language they are using at the time. Such anecdotal evidence would certainly argue in favor of linguistic relativity.

Or would it? Actually, such a phenomenon may not be strictly a "Whorfian" issue, because it does not necessarily imply that any aspect of the two languages (such as their lexical or grammatical systems) causes the language-related changes in behavior. It may simply be that when we learn a language, we learn it in the context of a culture. When bilinguals learn two languages, they often do so in the context of two different cultures. Each language may simply access a different set of cultural values. Thus, bilinguals may think differently when using two languages, but the languages per se may not cause the thinking differences.

At this point, it may be advantageous to make a further distinction between "strong" and "weak" versions of the Sapir–Whorf hypothesis. A strong version would suggest that language causes differences in thinking. A weak version, however, might suggest that language is simply associated with differences in thinking, without necessarily causing them. The cause, in fact, may be found in a mediating variable, such as culture or cultural values, that is associated both with language and with differences in thinking, feeling, and acting.

Putting aside the question of whether or not language causes changes in thinking, feeling, and acting, the study of bilinguals seems a perfect complement to the research described earlier in assessing the validity of at least a weak version of the Sapir–Whorf hypothesis. Conceptually, differences in thinking or behavior in bilinguals as a function of language in use at the time of testing would certainly support at least the weak version of the Sapir–Whorf hypothesis, even though it could not be proven that different language use caused the differences in thinking. Although any correlation would not warrant inferences about causation, it would not rule them out either. It is certainly possible that language may cause differences in thinking and behavior, either directly or indirectly (via common cultural values).

Along with the potential advantages to our conceptual understanding of linguistic relativity, the study of bilinguals also offers considerable methodological advantages. When language effects on behaviors, cognitions, or emotions are tested in bilinguals, differences among individual participants in the study cannot possibly confound the results because the same individuals are in both language conditions of the study. When comparisons are made between groups of monolingual participants—for example, Chinese-speaking Taiwanese and English-speaking Americans—not only does language differ between the groups, but so do the individuals. If differences are found between these groups, we cannot be sure that the differences are due to language (which is the thrust of the Sapir–Whorf argument) rather than to differences between individuals. With bilinguals serving as research participants, the inherent confound of individual differences is eliminated.

One of the crucial issues in research using bilinguals is establishing the degree of equivalence between the languages being compared. For many bilinguals, one of the languages is a first, native language, whereas the second is learned later in life. And many bilinguals are more proficient or fluent in one language or the other. Such differences may preclude conclusive comparisons in research on bilinguals, because differences between languages may actually reflect differences in degree of proficiency rather than linguistic relativity. Thus, researchers who study bilinguals need to take special care in recruiting and screening participants to establish equivalency in language proficiency.

Bilingualism and Psychological Differences

Can we assume that bilinguals have access, through their two languages, to two culturally different modes of thought? If so, does this imply the existence of two different personalities within the same individual, each associated with one of the bilingual's two languages? Ervin (1964) compared responses from a sample of English/French bilinguals to pictures from the Thematic Apperception Test (a common test used in many cross-cultural studies). The subjects told their stories in response to the pictures once in English and then another time in French. Ervin found that subjects demonstrated more aggression, autonomy, and withdrawal in French than they did in English, and that females demonstrated a greater need for achievement in English than in French. Ervin attributed these differences to the higher value French culture places on verbal prowess and to greater sex role differences.

How might the issue of bilingualism and personality be important for immigrants to the United States? Consider, for example, a Chinese/English bilingual raised in a monolingual Chinese-speaking home who learned English naturalistically only after migrating to the United States from China at age 8. She is now a 20-year-old college student, living with her parents. She uses Chinese as the only language in the home, but English at school and with most of her peers. We might predict that when using Chinese she would be likely to behave in ways appropriate to Chinese cultural norms in the home. In English, however, she might be more likely to behave in ways that are closer to European American norms. A "Whorfian" view might account for such language-related behavioral differences in terms of the pragmatic systems of Chinese and English (as well as other linguistic differences). However, at least two other explanations have been offered for the mechanisms that underlie such language-related shifts in personality. They are known as the culture-affiliation hypothesis and the minority group–affiliation hypothesis.

The **culture-affiliation hypothesis** is simply that immigrant bilinguals will tend to affiliate themselves with the values and beliefs of the culture associated with the language in which they are currently operating. When the language is switched, so are the cultural values with which they affiliate. The **minority group–affiliation hypothesis**, in contrast, suggests that immigrant bilinguals will tend to self-identify as members of an ethnic minority group and adopt the behavioral stereotypes of the majority culture about their minority as their own when they are operating in the language associated with their minority group. To the extent that such stereotypes are accurate, the minority group–affiliation hypothesis will make the same predictions as does the culture-affiliation hypothesis; that is, when interacting in their first language, people will behave in ways more typical of their ancestral culture, which may also be consistent with majority culture stereotypes of that culture. Language context would predict differences in behavior, and also in personality.

Hull (1987) and Dinges and Hull (1992) have reported studies in which this prediction was tested. They reasoned that if any such differences were to be found, they would be most evident among a population of immigrant bilinguals. Such bilinguals are believed to have two clearly distinct cultural affiliations, accessible through the language in which much of this cultural knowledge was learned or is associated. In these studies, Chinese/English and Korean/English immigrant bilinguals were given the California Psychological Inventory (CPI), a widely used personality test. The immigrant bilinguals completed the CPI twice—once in their native language and once in English. The central question was, would a dual self or dual personality emerge, showing up as between-language, within-group differences in CPI scores? The answer was a resounding yes. In other words, these bilinguals presented different personalities depending on whether they were responding in their first language (Chinese or Korean) or in English (their second language). In a second study, Hull (1990a, 1990b) confirmed these earlier findings using a different measure of personality.

Some evidence also suggests that our perceptions of others are dependent on the language we speak when making those judgments. Matsumoto and Assar (1992) asked bilingual observers in India (Hindi and English) to view a set of 40 different facial expressions of emotion. The observers were asked to judge which emotion was being portrayed in the faces, and how intensely. The observers made these judgments twice, a week apart, the first time in English, and the second time in Hindi. The results showed that judgments of which emotion was being portrayed were more accurate when the judgments were made in English. But the emotions were perceived more intensely when the ratings were made in Hindi. The same people, viewing the same facial expressions, made different judgments of those expressions depending on which language they used to make those judgments.

The research described here demonstrates how closely language and culture are intertwined. It also demonstrates the importance of language in everyday experience. In addition, these findings help to dispel the misconception that the existence of two personalities within an individual means that the individual is suffering from a mental disorder. Such a situation is clearly a natural and healthy part of the bilingual/bicultural experience.

Other misconceptions persist, however. For example, negative impressions and stereotypes, particularly about intelligence, can occur when communicating with people in their second language because they may take more time in responding and appear to have cognitive difficulties while processing information. These difficulties, known as **foreign language processing difficulties**, arise because of nonfamiliarity or lack of fluency in speaking a language, and because of uncertainty or ambiguity about the intended meaning of messages when received in a foreign language. These difficulties are a normal part of learning a language, and should not be used as a basis for negative inferences about intelligence or other dispositional characteristics of individuals who may be communicating in a second (or third) language.

Bilinguals may also experience difficulties in nonlinguistic thinking tasks; such difficulties are known as the **foreign language effect** (Takano & Noda, 1993). This term refers to a temporary decline in the thinking ability of people who are using a foreign language in which they are less proficient than their native language. The foreign language effect, seen in nonlinguistic thinking tasks, is a by-product of the foreign language processing difficulty seen in linguistic tasks. Takano and Noda (1993) demonstrated the existence of this effect in two studies involving Japanese/English bilinguals. In the first study, Japanese Japanese/English and American English/Japanese bilinguals performed a calculation task and responded to a question-and-answer task in either their first (native) or second (foreign) language. Performance for both groups of participants was lower when the question-and-answer task was in the foreign language. In the second study, basically the same methods were used with a different thinking task (nonverbal spatial reasoning tasks) and a different linguistic task (sentence verification), producing the same results.

Takano and Noda (1995) reported two additional studies that showed the foreign language effect was larger when the discrepancy between the native and foreign languages was greater, and smaller when the difference between the native and foreign languages was smaller. Their first study used the same methods as the first study in Takano and Noda (1993), using native speakers of German and Japanese with English as a common foreign language. They found that the foreign language effect was larger for the Japanese. They explained this finding in terms of the greater difference between Japanese and English than between German and English. Their second study replicated the findings from the first, this time using native Korean and English speakers, with Japanese as the common foreign language.

Collectively, these studies indicate that interference in both linguistic (foreign language processing difficulty) and nonlinguistic (foreign language effect) tasks is a normal and expected occurrence in bilinguals. These interferences occur in the same way as interferences between any two cognitive tasks asked of the same person. Seen as normal cognitive interferences, these difficulties should not be used as a basis to form negative impressions or stereotypes of bilinguals. As discussed earlier in this book (see Chapter 3), it is easy to fall into this trap, allowing our perceptions to be driven by ethnocentrism and, in some cases, an unconscious wish to validate preexisting stereotypes. The research clearly shows, however, that such perceptions have little basis in fact.

Monolingualism and Ethnocentrism

For much of its history and even today, the United States has remained largely monolingual. In fact, earlier in this century, many Americans thought that knowledge of more than one language should be avoided. It was commonly believed that humans have limited "room" to store language—that learning "too much" language takes "space" away from other functions such as intelligence. We now know that such notions are wrong; there is no evidence that bilinguals do worse on intellectual (or other) tasks. On the contrary, there is evidence that knowledge of more than one language may improve cognitive flexibility (for example, see Price-Williams & Ramirez, 1977).

On a global level, in fact, most people speak more than one language; monolinguals, including most Americans, are in the minority. And although English is the most widely used language in the world, Americans also constitute a minority of the world's English speakers. These linguistic facts should help Americans place themselves in a more global context with regard not only to multiple language fluency, but also to related topics such as cognitive flexibility, potential for empathy, and ethnocentrism.

Recognition of the special relationship between language, culture, and behavior is especially important for students in the United States. Americans are notoriously ignorant of languages other than English, and this ignorance is often accompanied by an ethnocentric view rejecting the need to learn, understand, and appreciate other languages, customs, and cultures. Given that Americans are the most monolingual of all peoples of the world, that language is intimately tied to culture, and that multilingualism is associated with an appreciation of different cultures, it may be that Americans are actually the most ethnocentric of all people. Our ignorance of languages other than English, and the unfortunate ethnocentrism that often accompanies this ignorance, may be the root of our future downfall. For many of us who have little exposure to these issues in our everyday lives, now is the time to begin our study of language and culture for a better understanding of the partners in our global village.

Summary

Language is the principal means by which we communicate with one another and store information. Language is also the principal means by which each generation receives its cultural inheritance from the previous generation. Indeed, without language, culture as we know it would not exist at all. So it should come as no surprise that language is of particular interest to cross-cultural researchers.

Languages differ enormously from one another, and these differences are related to important differences in the customs and behaviors of the cultures in which those languages reside. As we have seen, culture is intimately related to both language lexicons and pragmatics. Language also plays an important predictive role in the personalities of multilingual individuals.

Understanding the relationship between culture and language is important in understanding and becoming proficient in the process of **intercultural communication.** As we will see later in the chapter, because culture and language are intimately intertwined, intercultural communication processes differ from those involved in communicating with members of one's own culture (**intracultural communication**). Understanding the extent and pervasiveness of this relationship is integral to gaining an appreciation of these differences. Research on foreign language processing difficulty and the foreign language effect reviewed earlier also helps in understanding and engaging in such interactions.

The Components of Communication

Communication does not occur in a vacuum; it occurs in a specific context. People have certain biases, and words are couched in a particular framework, coupled with facial expressions, gestures, postures, and other behaviors. When we interact with others, the amount of information transmitted from one person to the next is unbelievably large. We may think that the only part, or the main part, of communication is the words being spoken. Indeed, we attend to the words and the language that people use. Our formal educational experi-

Figure 10.3 These American servicemen were taken captive when North Korea seized the U.S. ship *Pueblo* in 1968. Can you find the nonverbal behavior displayed by some of these men, sending a message that their captors were unaware of? (Look at the position of their fingers.)

Source: Courtesy, AP/Wide World Photos

ences, from elementary school on up, center around language—words, grammar, spelling, and punctuation. We spend much of our time thinking about just the right words to use to express ourselves—our ideas, our thoughts, our opinions. We think about just the right thing to say to our boyfriends and girlfriends, business associates, acquaintances, work colleagues, or the police. We concentrate on the words and language when we speak.

But the words we use are only one part of the entire communication process. Our verbal language channel is just one of many channels activated when we communicate. All our behaviors and **gestures**—in short, our nonverbal behaviors—form important channels of communication as well (see Figure 10.3). The only difference is that, usually, we do not think about them as much or as consciously as we think about the words we use or the language we speak. And we do not think about them as much when we listen to others speak. But even if we do not attend to them consciously, these nonverbal behaviors are very important in conveying meaning. The words coming out of someone's mouth may tell you one thing, but the person's nonverbal behaviors (tone of voice, gaze) may tell you something else. Someone may say "I love you" in words but communicate "not really" with nonverbal behaviors.

Nonverbal Communication

Nonverbal communication can be classified in two general categories: nonverbal behaviors and nonbehaviors. **Nonverbal behaviors** are all the behaviors, other than words, that occur during communication. Such nonverbal behaviors include:

- Facial expressions
- Movements and gestures of the hands, arms, and legs
- Posture, lean, and body orientation
- Tone of voice and other vocal characteristics, including pitch, rate, intonation, and silence
- Interpersonal space
- Touching behaviors
- Gaze and visual attention

Nonverbal behaviors thus include behaviors that we typically associate with active expressivity and others that are more subtle.

Nonbehavioral nonverbal communication involves a host of other sources of messages and signals that carry meaning in human communication, but that are not produced directly by specific behaviors. These more subtle forms of communication include the use of time, the type of clothing we wear, the type of architectural structures we live and work in, and the cosmetic changes we make to our appearance. These nonbehaviors convey messages during communication just as verbal language and nonverbal behaviors do, and are an integral part of the entire communication package.

Both behaviors and nonbehaviors fall under the general category of nonverbal communication. When you stop to think of all the different things that are actually occurring when people communicate with each other—that is, all the different channels of signals and messages that are being sent and received at any one time—it is pretty mind-boggling. People come to an interaction in a certain place that is bounded by how they have structured it physically. They come to that interaction with a certain appearance. They space themselves from one another at certain distances. They adopt certain postures when interacting. They gesture and use hand movements to illustrate what they are saying. Their faces may become animated or reserved. Their voices may become excited or suppressed. Indeed, when communication is occurring, the actual words and verbal language used are only a small part of the entire package of events and behaviors that constitute communication. In a sense, there are two languages involved when people communicate—one verbal, and the other nonverbal.

The Relative Contribution of Verbal and Nonverbal Messages

Many studies have reported that only a small fraction of the meaning people get in an interaction derives from the words that are spoken; most of the messages conveyed and perceived in interactions are nonverbal (for example, Mehrabian,

1981). Research demonstrating the dominance of nonverbal over verbal communication has included studies on the communication of friendly and hostile attitudes (Argyle, Alkema, & Gilmour, 1978); inferior and superior attitudes (Argyle, Salter, Nicholson, Williams, & Burgess, 1970); friendliness, approval, and consideration (Bugental, Kaswan, & Love, 1970); positivity and dominance (DePaulo, Rosenthal, Eisenstat, Rogers, & Susan, 1978; Friedman, 1978); positive, negative, and neutral evaluations (Mehrabian & Wiener, 1967); perceptions of leadership (Gitter, Black, & Fishman, 1975); honesty and deceit (Stiff, Hale, Garlick, & Rogan, 1990); and confidence (Walker, 1977).

In all these studies, the degree to which nonverbal behaviors contributed to the messages received by judges was quite large. Recently, one of your authors (Matsumoto) conducted an effect size analysis of the nonverbal dominance reported in these studies, in order to investigate exactly how large the effect is. The effect size estimate, R^2, corresponds to the degree of variability in the entire data set that is accounted for by the difference between nonverbal and verbal stimuli. Across all studies examined, the average effect size was .56 (average r = .75). An effect size of this magnitude is considered huge; many effect size estimates in contemporary psychology experiments are about .09 (corresponding to an r of about .30).

Moreover, the contribution of nonverbal behaviors is larger when discrepant messages are transmitted. That is, when faced with ambiguous messages posed by discrepant signals in the verbal and nonverbal channels, people generally derive more meaning from nonverbal behaviors. Friedman (1978), for example, showed participants combinations of facial expressions portraying one of four emotions along with positive and negative verbal content. Judges were asked to rate the positivity in the combined stimuli. The results indicated that the nonverbal stimuli (faces) had a much stronger influence on the judgments than did the verbal stimuli. Likewise, Mehrabian and Wiener (1967) created audio stimuli that consisted of positive, neutral, and negative words spoken in a positive, neutral, or negative tone of voice. Once again, the findings indicated that tone influenced the rating of positivity much more strongly than did the actual words.

Although research examining the relative contribution of verbal and nonverbal behaviors have been common in studies conducted in the United States, we know of only a few cross-cultural studies conducted on the same topic. Those few, however, also confirm the dominance of nonverbal behaviors over verbal language in influencing messages decoded during communication. Kudoh and Kaji (1988), for example, provided Japanese participants with either verbal descriptions of behaviors, stick figure drawings, or combinations of both. The verbal and nonverbal stimuli were classified as either positive or negative, depending on the participants' ratings on three semantic differential scales assessing positivity, arousal, and dominance. Combinations of the stimuli included both congruent and discrepant combinations. The findings indicated that when participants viewed discrepant stimuli, their ratings were more highly correlated with ratings for the nonverbal stimuli than for the verbal stimuli. Kudoh and Tamie (1991) replicated and extended this study by including two levels of discrepant verbal and nonverbal combinations (high and low), and by using more sophisticated multiple regression analyses to assess the independent degrees of contribution of verbal and nonverbal behaviors to the messages decoded. The results again indicated a strong dominance of nonverbal over verbal channels in the overall message perceived by the judges.

In short, communication is an intricate, complicated process with many different channels available for message transmission and many different messages being transmitted. During interaction, we all do amazing things. We take all the information we are receiving and synthesize it somehow to make sense out of it. Although much conscious energy is spent understanding and interpreting the words and the language we and others use in interaction, most of how we learn to read and interpret the important nonverbal dimension is unconscious and automatic. No one ever taught us how to do this; we don't attend classes in nonverbal behavior. All of our education about nonverbal behaviors is informal, in our homes and on the streets. Yet all of us learn the rules by which members of our society and culture engage in nonverbal behaviors and interpret them. We receive nonverbal messages, process them, make sense out of it all, and put that information together with the verbal messages we receive via language. And, based on limited cross-cultural evidence, it seems that this process may be pancultural.

Encoding and Decoding

Another way of looking at the communication process is in terms of encoding and decoding. **Encoding** refers to the process by which people select, consciously or unconsciously, a particular modality and method by which to create and send a message to someone else. Although we don't think about this process all the time as adults, as children we had to learn the rules of syntax, grammar, pragmatics, and phonology in order to encode competently. We also had to learn rules of appropriateness governing messages sent nonverbally. In the research literature, the person who encodes and transmits messages and meanings is often called an *encoder* or *sender*.

Decoding refers to the process by which a person receives signals from an encoder and translates those signals into meaningful messages. Just as "proper" encoding depends on understanding and applying the rules of verbal and nonverbal behaviors, "proper" decoding depends on those rules in order for messages to be interpreted in the manner in which they were meant to be conveyed. In the scientific literature, the person who decodes messages is often called the *decoder* or the *receiver*.

Of course, communication is not a one-way street, with one person encoding and sending a message and another person decoding it. Communication is a vastly complex process of encoding and decoding in rapid succession, overlapping in time so as to occur almost simultaneously. It is this rapid give and take, back and forth, of the encoding and decoding process that makes the study of communication challenging, but also rewarding. During this process, individuals switch roles from moment to moment, from encoder to decoder and back again.

Channels, Signals, and Messages

Along with the two major modes of verbal language and nonverbal behaviors, and the two major processes of encoding and decoding, communication has a number of other components. **Signals** are the specific words and behaviors that are sent during communication—that is, the specific verbal language and nonverbal behaviors that are encoded when a message is sent. A facial expression, for example, may be a signal that is encoded with a particular message. Other signals might include specific words or phrases, body posture, or tone of voice.

Messages are the meanings that are intended or received with the signals. They are the knowledge, ideas, concepts, thoughts, or emotions that encoders intend to convey and decoders interpret. Signals are observable behaviors that do not necessarily have inherent meaning; messages are the meanings that we attribute to those behavioral signals.

Finally, **channels** refer to the specific sensory modalities by which signals are sent and messages are retrieved, such as sight or sound. The most widely used channels of communication are visual—seeing facial expressions, body postures, gestures, and the like—and auditory—hearing words, tone of voice, and so on. However, all the other senses are used in communication, including touch, smell, and taste.

The process of communication can thus be described as one in which a sender encodes a message into a set of signals. These signals are conveyed through a variety of channels that are open and operating in the receiver. The receiver decodes the signals to interpret the message. Once a message is interpreted, the decoder then becomes the encoder, relaying back his or her own messages via the same process. The original encoder then becomes the decoder. This complex process of exchange, with switching roles and encoding and decoding of messages, constitutes the process of communication.

The Role of Culture in the Communication Process

Culture has a pervasive and profound influence on verbal and nonverbal encoding and decoding processes. We have already discussed many of these influences. Here, we bring together these various pieces of information, summarizing what has been discussed previously. Although we discuss these influences on the communication process as if they were separate, in reality they are interrelated in a complex system in which each affects, and is affected by, the others.

Cultural Influences on Verbal Language and Nonverbal Behaviors (Encoding)

As we saw earlier in the chapter, culture exerts considerable influence over the verbal languages that we speak. In that domain, culture influences the language lexicons and vocabulary, and the rules by which words are put together to form meaningful phrases and sentences. Culture also influences our thoughts, feelings, and actions via language.

Just as spoken languages differ from one culture to the next, so do unspoken, nonverbal behaviors. That is, just as culture influences our verbal languages, culture also exerts considerable influence over our nonverbal languages. People of all cultures learn to use nonverbal behaviors—facial expressions, gestures, distance, gaze, and postures—as part of their communication repertoire, but people in each culture learn to use them in very specific ways. All humans are born with the capacity to form all types of sounds; culture dictates how we shape and mold those sounds into particular languages. In the same way, culture shapes and molds nonverbal behaviors into each culture's nonverbal language.

Consider, for example, American culture. When we speak to people, we look them straight in the eye. Our faces and gestures often become animated, highlighting specific, important parts of our speech. We learn to sit or stand at a certain distance when we interact, depending on whom we are interacting with and the specific context or situation in which that interaction is occurring. We learn how to signal when we are finished speaking and when we want to continue speaking. In short, we learn a very specific, American system of nonverbal behaviors to aid in our communication process, just as we have learned American English as a verbal language.

When we interact with people from our own culture, they have generally learned the same system or language of nonverbal behaviors as we have. They will most likely follow the same rules of distance, tone of voice, facial expressions, gestures, and postures. When we interact with longtime friends, for example, we know what that system is, even though we may not be able to verbalize it. We can interact with them successfully, with no ambiguity regarding the content of the message or its intent.

Now consider a situation in which you are interacting with someone from a different culture. People from another culture bring with them their own verbal language. A person from Israel, for example, will bring the ability to speak Hebrew. A person from India will bring the ability to speak Hindi or a provincial dialect of India. But beyond the culture-specific verbal language that people bring with them, they also bring a culture-specific nonverbal language. Thus, people from Israel will bring with them the Israeli- or Jewish-specific language of nonverbal behaviors; people from India will bring with them the India-specific (or Hindu- or Muslim- or Brahmin-specific) language of nonverbal behaviors. Any type of interaction always involves two languages—one verbal and the other nonverbal.

Some kinds of nonverbal behaviors are common to many cultures, such as greeting behaviors (for example, the eyebrow raise), whereas others differ radically (for example, touching behaviors) (Keating, 1976). In general, however, people from different cultures generate their own rules for engaging in nonverbal behaviors. These rules may be quite different from the rules you or we may be fluent in. These rules may dictate that different behaviors are enacted to get a certain point across or to accent a specific point. These rules may mean that the same behavior can actually carry quite different meanings. Developmental research has suggested that these rules are as old as verbal languages, and that children learn their culture's rules governing nonverbal behaviors as they learn the rules of vocal expression and acquire verbal language (Von Raffler-Engel, 1981). If this is the case, it is no wonder that the cultural rules of nonverbal behavior are well ingrained in us by the time we are adults, and that we use them without much second thought.

When we interact with people from a different culture, we generally attend closely to the verbal language. But nonverbal language is also occurring, even if we don't consciously attend to it. The unconscious filters and processes through which we automatically interpret the nonverbal behaviors of others are also in active use, whether or not we are aware of them.

The problem in intercultural communication is that nonverbal language is silent, and interpretational processes are unconscious and automatic. Whether or not we attend to them, messages are being transmitted. More often than not, the nonverbal language of people of a different culture is different from what we are accustomed to. After interacting with someone from another culture, it is not uncommon to wonder whether we really "got" what was meant. Often we leave these situations feeling as though we may have missed something. These feelings arise because our unconscious system of nonverbal communication is having difficulty interpreting the nonverbal behaviors of someone from a different culture. Something just doesn't "feel" right.

Problems can occur in positive as well as negative directions. People often interpret certain types of behaviors positively when, in fact, they are not meant to be positive at all. Consider, for example, the Japanese head nodding and use of the word *hai*. The best translation of this word in English is "yes." But in Japanese, this word does not necessarily mean yes. It may mean yes, but it can also mean maybe, or even no. It is often used as a speech **regulator,** informing the speaker that the listener is listening. It can be a signal of deference to authority. This word and the nonverbal behaviors associated with it (head nod) most definitely do not have the same meaning in Japanese as they do in English. Yet many business and government negotiations have faltered on the interpretation of exactly this behavior, with Americans believing that the Japanese have agreed to something and that the deal is closed. The Japanese, however, may merely be signaling that they are listening. This type of cultural difference is the source of many interpersonal conflicts between spouses and lovers as well.

When we interact with people who have different nonverbal languages, we often form negative impressions of them. In the United States, for example, we learn to interact with people at a certain distance. When you interact with someone you do not know very well and this person places himself so close to you that you feel his breath when he speaks, you will probably feel quite uncomfortable and try to adjust the distance. He will follow. You will adjust again. He will follow again. You will probably want to get out of that interaction as soon as possible. You may consider the person rude or without manners. Many Arab and Middle Eastern cultures foster what Americans would consider too close interpersonal spacing during interactions, and this can be unsettling.

We make these interpretations because we are trying to match observed behavior with our own rules for what those behaviors should mean. If the person you are interacting with is indeed from your own culture and operating according to the same rules, you will probably be correct in your interpretations. But what if the person is from a different culture, operating under different rules? Then your negative impressions and interpretations may be totally off base. Nonetheless, you leave feeling bad about the interaction, probably not wanting to interact again. The other person probably feels the same.

Nonverbal behaviors are just like a second language, albeit a silent, unspoken one. Just as cultures develop spoken, verbal languages, they also develop unspoken, nonverbal languages. Culture, along with biology, gender, and personality, is one of the most important influences on the interpretation of nonverbal behaviors; in conjunction with the social environment and other cognitive and affective mediators, it plays an important role in overall person perception (Patterson, 1995). If we are to get a handle on cultural similarities and differences in communication, we obviously need to pay more attention to cultural differences in these silent, nonverbal languages.

Cultural Influences on Decoding

Culture affects the decoding process in several ways. As with cultural decoding rules regarding the perception and interpretation of emotion, discussed in Chapter 9, we learn rules from early childhood on that aid us in deciphering the cultural codes inherent in speech and all other aspects of interaction. These decoding rules develop in conjunction with display or encoding rules, and are a natural part of the development of communication skills.

Culture influences the decoding process in other ways as well. By way of summary, we would like to review three of these processes that have been discussed before.

Cultural filters, ethnocentrism, emotions, and value judgments. In Chapter 3, we defined ethnocentrism as the tendency to view the world through one's own cultural filters. These ethnocentric filters are one mechanism through which culture affects communication.

As we grow up, we learn cultural rules of appropriate communicative encoding with respect to both verbal and nonverbal behaviors. When we are little, these rules are constantly reinforced by parents, friends, teachers, and other enculturation agents . Many rules are also transmitted and reinforced by organizations and institutions (as in our study of language through the school system). As we get older, we need to be reminded less about these rules, and their use requires less conscious effort. The inevitable result is unique, culture-specific ways in which communication—verbal and nonverbal—occurs.

As we grow, we also learn how to perceive signals and interpret messages; that is, we learn cultural rules of appropriate decoding as well. Because we share a set of encoding and decoding rules with people of our culture, we develop a set of expectations about communication. These rules and expectations form a basis of tacit understanding that need not be spoken each time we, as adult members of the same culture, communicate with one another.

Not only do we have certain expectations about the communication process; we have also learned emotional reactions associated with those expectations. These reactions can range from acceptance and pleasure to outrage, hostility, and frustration. Our emotions, in turn, are intimately tied to value judgments, which we often make without a second thought. These judgments seem only natural because they are rooted in our upbringing; they are the only types of judgments we have learned to make. Emotions and values serve as guidelines in helping us form opinions about others and ourselves.

Thus, decoding rules, and their associated emotions and value judgments, form the basis of the "filters" that we use in seeing the world. As we become more enculturated, we add more layers to those filters. These filters are like lenses that allow us to perceive the world in a certain way. By the time we are adults, we share the same filters with others in our cultural group. They become part of our self, inseparable and invisible, and are a normal part of our psychological composition because of the way we have been enculturated.

Culture and stereotypes. As defined in Chapter 3, stereotypes are generalizations about people, particularly about their underlying psychological characteristics or personality traits. Stereotypes are inevitable products of normal psychological processes, including selective attention, appraisal, concept formation and categorization, attributions, emotion, and memory. Stereotypes are invaluable mental aids, helping us organize information about the world. As a special type of category having to do with people, they are important in helping us interact with others in our world, and are especially important in communication. Stereotypes are easily reinforced. Stereotypes prime our expectations. We may selectively attend to events that support our stereotypes, and ignore, albeit unconsciously, events and situations that challenge them. Negative attributions may reinforce negative stereotypes. Even when we perceive events contrary to stereotype, we may convince ourselves that the stereotype is correct. Such dismissals can occur quickly, without much conscious thought or effort, and are resilient to emotion.

These psychological processes—including selective attention, attribution, and emotion—are all part of our self-concept. These processes reinforce the cultural knowledge we have learned from many years of enculturation, and thereby reinforce our sense of self. As we confirm our stereotypes, therefore, we reinforce our self-concept. Stereotypes are thus an integral part of the package of psychological processes, and are intimately tied to our emotions, values, and core self.

Culture and social cognition. As we will see in greater detail in Chapter 11, culture influences how we interpret the actions of others—that is, our attributions regarding others. Americans, for example, tend to draw inferences about other people's internal states or dispositions that supposedly underlie or even cause their behavior. This bias is known as *fundamental attribution error* (Ross, 1977). Cross-cultural research has shown that this bias may not exist in other cultures. Miller (1984), for example, comparing Americans' and Hindu Indians' explanations for another person's actions, found that dispositional explanations were common for Americans but much less so for the Hindus. Instead, the Hindus provided explanations in terms of the actor's duties, social roles, and other situation-specific characteristics (see also Shweder & Bourne, 1984). Other attributional tendencies, such as self-serving bias and defensive attributions, are also manifested differently in different cultures.

In summary, culture plays a large role in decoding signals during communication episodes—first because of the close relationship between cultural rules governing encoding and decoding, and second because of cultural influences in the development of ethnocentrism, stereotyping, and social cognition. Cultural decoding rules are intimately associated with emotions and value judgments, which collectively form our self-concepts. Because communication involves moment-to-moment switching from encoder to decoder and back, understanding the role of culture in this process is challenging—whether the communication is intracultural or intercultural. One way to highlight the unique circumstances under which intercultural communication occurs, however, is to compare these two types of communication.

Intracultural versus Intercultural Communication

Intracultural Communication

During intracultural communication, interactants implicitly share the same ground rules. When people communicate within the boundaries of accepted ground rules, they can focus on the content of the messages that are being exchanged. They encode and decode messages using the same cultural codes. When we communicate within the shared boundaries of culture, we make an implicit judgment that the other person is a member of our culture or is engaging in socially appropriate behavior. We may consider the individual to have been socialized "well" into our culture, and we make value judgments about the process and the person's ability to engage in that accepted process.

When we communicate with others within our own culture, this process "works" because we share the same codes and rules of encoding and decoding. Thus, the coded "packages" we send when we are encoders, and those that we receive and open when we are decoders, are familiar to us because we generally share the same type of wrapping and box.

Even in intracultural situations, when we interact with people who transgress what we view as "normal" or "socially appropriate," we often have negative reactions. We have trouble interpreting the signals they are trying to send because they don't conform to the cultural rules of "packaging" that we expect of members of our culture. We react negatively because we have learned that such transgressions are not appropriate, and we may make negative dispositional attributions such as "bad," "stupid," "had a bad upbringing," or "has no common sense."

Even in intracultural communication situations, negative stereotypes can easily develop. Because our cultural filters and ethnocentrism create a set of expectations about others, communicating with people whose behaviors do not match our expectations often leads to negative attributions. Such unanticipated events require substantive processing (Forgas, 1994), which is most affected by induced emotion. If the emotion induced is negative, then it will contribute to negatively valenced attributions about others. These attributions form the core of a stereotype of such people, and reinforce the value and expectation system originally held. These processes are common even within intracultural communication episodes.

Intercultural Communication

When we examine intercultural communication in micromomentary detail, we find much the same process as with intracultural communication. During intercultural communication, interactants do not necessarily share the same ground rules. It becomes more difficult to focus on the content of the messages that are being exchanged, as people may be encoding and decoding messages using different cultural codes. If this happens, if communication does not proceed smoothly and misunderstandings occur, we may tend to make implicit judgment that the other person does not know how to act appropriately, is rude, or not a good person.

The message that one person wants to send is packaged in this person's cultural code. The packaged signals are received by the other person, and the second person has trouble opening up the package because his or her cultural codes differ from the first. As a result, the message may be unclear, distorted, or ambiguous.

Because intercultural communication occurs under these circumstances, it is associated with a host of additional psychological issues that do not normally occur in intracultural communication. Here we will discuss two issues that have gained widespread attention in the intercultural research literature: uncertainty and ambiguity, and conflict.

Uncertainty and ambiguity. One characteristic that sets intercultural communication apart from intracultural communication is uncertainty or ambiguity concerning the ground rules by which the interaction will occur. Because of the widespread and pervasive influence of culture on all aspects of the communication process, we cannot be sure that the rules by which two people from different cultures operate are similar. This uncertainty is inherent in both verbal and nonverbal behaviors, in both coding and decoding modes: how to package messages into signals that will be interpreted according to one's intentions, and how to open packages according to the sender's original intentions.

Intercultural interactants often engage with each other in a verbal language that is not a native language for at least one of them, and sometimes both. Thus, there is inherent uncertainty in the meaning of the words. Cultural differences in the use of all nonverbal channels add to the uncertainty. Decoders can never be as sure as they are in intracultural situations that they are interpreting signals and messages as originally intended by encoders.

Gudykunst and his colleagues have documented how interactants work to reduce uncertainty in intercultural interactions, at least in initial encounters. Their work is based on Berger (1979) and Berger and Calabrese (1975), who suggested that a primary concern of strangers in initial encounters is to reduce uncertainty and increase predictability in themselves and others. Gudykunst and Nishida (1984) tested 100 American and 100 Japanese participants, assigning them to one of four experimental conditions: cultural similarity (intracultural communication) and attitude similarity, cultural dissimilarity (intercultural communication) and attitude similarity, cultural similarity and attitude dissimilarity, and cultural dissimilarity and attitude dissimilarity. Cultural similarity or dissimilarity was manipulated by having participants interact with a stranger from either their own culture or the other culture. Attitude similarity or dissimilarity was manipulated through a description of similar or dissimilar attitudes when introducing the stranger. For each participant, the researchers assessed intent to self-disclose, intent to interrogate, nonverbal affiliative expressions, attributional confidence, and interpersonal attraction. The results indicated that intent to interrogate, intent to self-disclose, and nonverbal affiliative expressiveness were all higher in the cultural dissimilarity condition than in the cultural similarity condition. Uncertainty reduction theory predicts that these strategies would be used more extensively in communication contexts with higher levels of uncertainty. Gudykunst, Sodetani, and Sonoda (1987) extended these findings to include members of different ethnic groups as well, demonstrating that differences in ethnicity and stage of relationship are also related to differences in communicative behaviors designed to reduce uncertainty.

In a more recent study, Gudykunst and Shapiro (1996) asked students at a large university to record their perceptions of communication episodes with other students. The researchers found that students rated intracultural episodes higher than intercultural episodes in quality of communication and positive expectations, but rated intercultural episodes higher in anxiety, uncertainty, and social identity. Likewise, students rated intraethnic encounters as higher in quality and satisfaction, and interethnic encounters as higher in anxiety and uncertainty. These data support the notion that intercultural communication episodes are marked by greater uncertainty than intracultural encounters.

Conflict. A second characteristic of intercultural communication is the inevitability of conflict and misunderstandings. During intercultural encounters, chances are great that people's behaviors will not conform to our expectations. We often interpret those behaviors as transgressions against our value system and morality. They produce negative emotions, which are upsetting to our self-concepts. These conflicts arise in intercultural episodes not only with people but also with other agents of a cultural system (such as public transportation, the post office, shops, businesses). These interactions are bound to accentuate differences in process, which inevitably lead to conflict or misunderstanding.

Figure 10.4 illustrates why this conflict is inevitable. Because interactants cannot send or receive signals unambiguously, as they are accustomed to in

Figure 10.4 A micromomentary analysis of intercultural communication

intracultural situations, the intercultural communication episode can be frustrating and patience-testing. Tempers are quick to flare in such situations, and people can easily become distraught or turned off by the extra effort such interactions require. Even if interactants are somewhat successful in unpackaging signals, the messages interpreted may be partial, ambiguous, or misunderstood. Messages may not be deciphered according to the sender's original intent, leading to miscommunication gaffes and problems later on.

Of course, uncertainty contributes to this conflict. People may become impatient with or intolerant of the ambiguity, leading to anger, frustration, or resentment. Even after uncertainty is reduced, however, conflict is inevitable because of the differences in meaning of verbal language and nonverbal behaviors across cultures, and the associated emotions and values inherent in the cultural system. The result is often differences in the interpretation of underlying intent among interactants—which can sometimes occur in intracultural communication as well.

Together, uncertainty and conflict make intercultural communication a complex yet fascinating process that challenges even the most practiced and interculturally sensitive of people. Given these challenges, how can we develop our skills at intercultural communication and improve intercultural relationships?

Improving Intercultural Communication

Barriers to Effective Communication

Barna (1996) has outlined six major obstacles or "stumbling blocks" to effective intercultural communication.

Assumptions of similarities.   One reason why misunderstandings occur in intercultural communication episodes is that people naively assume that all people are the same, or at least similar enough to make communication easy. Certainly, all humans share a number of basic similarities in biological and social needs. Communication, however, is a uniquely human trait that is shaped by specific cultures and societies. Indeed, communication itself is a product of culture. Furthermore, people of some cultures make more assumptions of similarity than others; that is, the degree to which people assume that others are similar varies across cultures. Thus, the assumption of similarities is itself a cultural variable.

Language differences.   When people are trying to communicate in a language in which they are not entirely fluent, they often think that a word, phrase, or sentence has one and only one meaning—the meaning they intend to convey. To make this assumption is to ignore all the other possible sources of signals and messages discussed in the previous two chapters, including nonverbal expressions, tone of voice, body orientation, and many other behaviors. To the extent that people cling rigidly to single, simple interpretations of what is really a complex process, problems in communication are bound to arise.

Nonverbal misinterpretations.   As we have seen, nonverbal behaviors comprise the bulk of communication messages in any culture. But it is very difficult to be totally fluent in the nonverbal language of a culture that is not one's own. Misunderstandings in relation to the interpretation of nonverbal behaviors can easily lead to conflicts or confrontations that break down the communication process.

Preconceptions and stereotypes. As discussed previously, stereotypes and preconceptions about people are natural and inevitable psychological processes that influence all of our perceptions and communications. Overreliance on stereotypes can prevent us from viewing others and their communications objectively, and from searching for cues that may help us interpret their communications in the way they were intended. Stereotypes are sustained by a host of psychological processes, including selective attention, that may influence communication in negative ways.

Tendency to evaluate. Cultural values also influence our attributions about others and the world around us. Different values may generate negative evaluations of others, which become yet another stumbling block to effective intercultural communication.

High anxiety or tension. Intercultural communication episodes are often associated with greater anxiety and stress than are more familiar intracultural communication situations. In many cases, some degree of anxiety and tension is necessary for optimal "performance," whether in intercultural communication or in other arenas of life (such as taking a test or competing in sports). Too much anxiety and stress, however, can lead to dysfunctional thought processes and behaviors. Stress and anxiety can exaggerate all of the other stumbling blocks, making it more likely that people will cling dogmatically to rigid interpretations, hold onto stereotypes despite objective evidence to the contrary, and make negative evaluations of others. Thus, too much anxiety or stress is not at all functional for intercultural communication.

Given these stumbling blocks, as presented by Barna (1996) and throughout this chapter, how can we overcome them to engage in effective intercultural communication?

Concepts to Improve Communication

Several concepts can help us improve our communication abilities when we encounter difficulties or conflicts—namely, mindfulness and uncertainty reduction, face, and emotional regulation.

Mindfulness and uncertainty reduction. Ting-Toomey (1996) suggests that effective conflict management requires knowledge of and respect for cultural differences in worldviews and behaviors, as well as sensitivity to differences between high- and low-context communication patterns and differences in cultural perceptions of time. She stresses the importance of **mindfulness** in dealing with conflict in intercultural communication. According to Langer

(1989; cited in Ting-Toomey, 1996), mindfulness allows people to be conscious of their own habits, mental scripts, and cultural expectations concerning communication. Mindfulness allows one to continually create new mental categories, remain open to new information, and be aware of multiple perspectives. In short, mindfulness allows one to be conscious and conscientious about the various characteristics that are associated with ethnorelativism.

Gudykunst (1993) also suggests ways to improve intercultural communication that include mindfulness. His model of intercultural competence has three main components: motivational factors, knowledge factors, and skill factors. Motivational factors include the specific needs of the interactants, attraction between the interactants, social bonds, self-conceptions, and openness to new information. Knowledge factors include expectations, shared networks, knowledge of more than one perspective, knowledge of alternative interpretations, and knowledge of similarities and differences. Skill factors include the ability to empathize, tolerate ambiguity, adapt communication, create new categories, accommodate behavior, and gather appropriate information. Gudykunst suggests that these three types of factors influence the amount of uncertainty in a situation and the degree of anxiety or stress interactants actually feel. Finally, these components influence the degree to which interactants are "mindful" of the communication episode—that is, the degree to which they take conscious and deliberate steps to think through their own and others' behaviors, and to plan and interpret the interaction appropriately as it unfolds. According to this model, a high degree of mindfulness offsets uncertainty and anxiety, resulting in effective communication.

Thus, **uncertainty reduction** is one of the major goals of initial intercultural encounters. Without uncertainty reduction, it is impossible for interactants to begin processing the content of signals and interpreting messages properly, because uncertainty renders messages inherently ambiguous. If uncertainty is reduced, interactants can then focus on the content of the signals and messages that are being exchanged. Intercultural communication is like deciphering coded language: The first step is to decipher the code (reduce uncertainty); the second is to interpret and respond to the content, once deciphered.

Face. Ting-Toomey (1996) offers separate suggestions for effective conflict management for people of individualistic tendencies as opposed to people with collectivistic tendencies. People of individualistic cultural tendencies who have to deal with conflicts in a collectivistic culture should be mindful of the importance of "face" and the maintenance of face in the collectivistic culture; be proactive in dealing with low-grade conflict situations; not be pushy; be sensitive to the importance of quiet, mindful observation; practice attentive listening skills, especially in relation to the feelings of others; discard the model of dealing with problems directly; and let go of conflict situations if the other party does not want to deal with them directly. Collectivistic people who must deal with conflicts in an individualistic context should be mindful of individualistic problem-solving assumptions; focus on resolving major issues and expressing their feelings and opinions openly; engage in assertive conflict behavior;

take individual responsibility for dealing with conflict; provide verbal feedback; use direct verbal messages; and commit to working out the problem directly with the other person.

In sum, according to Ting-Toomey (1996), people from both individualistic and collectivistic cultures need to be mindful of the cognitive, affective, and behavioral biases and framework within which they normally operate, and of the blinders that they often bring to communication and conflict-mediation situations. They need to be open to learning and trying new communication skills, and to create new mental categories to build more successful intercultural relationships. Finally, they need to be conscious of important cultural concepts such as "face" in order to communicate effectively.

The Role of Emotional Regulation, Openness, Flexibility, and Critical Thinking

One of the messages you are probably getting from this chapter is that effective intercultural communication is not always easy! Conflict and misunderstandings are inevitable, and our normal ethnocentric and stereotypic ways of thinking often lead us to make negative value judgments about those differences, conflicts, and misunderstandings. Negative emotions are often associated with these judgments. These negative reactions make it difficult for us to engage in more constructive methods of interacting; they keep us from appreciating differences and integrating with people who are different. As conflict is inevitable in intercultural communication, it becomes extremely important to be able to control our negative emotional reactions. Those who can control their emotions will be able to engage in a more constructive intercultural process, opening the door to more successful intercultural interactions. Those who cannot will have that door closed to them. Emotions, therefore, hold the key to successful intercultural experiences.

The ability to regulate or control our emotions, in fact, is a key to personal growth. Many of us who have experience dealing with children know that, despite their often altruistic nature, when something happens to hurt or upset them, their thinking and worldview revert to a more primitive way of dealing with their world. It becomes impossible for them to engage in altruistic acts, because they are locked into a more infantile mode of operation. This concept, known as *regression,* is not limited to children and adolescents; adults regress at times as well. In such situations, people are overcome by negative feelings, which "take over" their way of being. Even the most altruistic or critically minded person may not be able to think or act constructively when overcome by such negative emotions.

When faced with cultural differences and conflict in intercultural communication, individuals who can somehow control their negative feelings—putting them on hold and not acting directly upon them or allowing them to overcome their thinking, acting, and feeling—will be able to engage in other processes that will help them broaden their appraisal and attribution of the causes of those differences. Once emotions are held in check, individuals can then engage in critical thinking about the origins of those differences, hopefully going beyond their own cultural framework to consider causes they may not have even been aware of. If this type of critical thinking can occur, individuals can be open to alternative hypotheses concerning the causes of those differences, and have the flexibility to accept or reject them.

Regulating or controlling negative emotions, therefore, is a gatekeeper ability that allows us to become more mindful of our communication and style and to engage in more constructive and open creation of new mental categories. Having the most complex mental model of effective intercultural communication will not help us one bit unless we are able to deal with the negative emotions that are bound to occur in intercultural communication episodes—to put them aside for the time being so that we can engage in more constructive thought processes that involve the creation of new mental categories via critical thinking. Regulating emotions is the key that allows us to open the door to these more advanced complex processes.

In addition to emotional regulation, being a critical thinker when confronted with cultural differences and being open to new ideas and perspectives are also key ingredients to becoming an effective intercultural communicator. Critical thinking requires an understanding of your own cultural filters and ethnocentrism and a recognition that cultural differences are legitimate. Being open and flexible to accept, or at least attempt to understand, cultural differences is also necessary. In general, the literature suggests that knowledge and skills are necessary components of effective intercultural communication, but that they are not sufficient. Knowledge and skills must be combined with openness and flexibility in one's thinking and interpretations, and with the motivation to communicate effectively and build a successful relationship.

Conclusion

Language is the primary way we communicate with one another. It plays a critical role in the transmission, maintenance, and expression of our culture. In turn, culture has a pervasive influence on language, and language symbolizes what a culture deems important in our world. Both culture and language affect the structure of our thought processes. Thus, understanding the culture–language relationship is an important step in becoming skillful intercultural communicators.

But language is just one part of communication—and perhaps not the most important part. We use many other vehicles of expression to communicate our thoughts, feelings, desires, and wishes to others. These other means of communication are not verbal, but nonverbal.

Communication in its broadest sense occurs both verbally (via language) and nonverbally. We have discussed how nonverbal behaviors contribute the bulk of the messages received and interpreted in communication, and that this effect appears to be pancultural. Despite the importance of nonverbal behaviors, however, we often take them for granted. Although we receive no formal training in how to send or receive nonverbal messages and signals, by adulthood we have become so skilled at it that we do so unconsciously and automatically. Nonverbal behaviors are just as much a language as any other. Just as verbal languages differ from culture to culture, so do nonverbal languages. Because we are aware of the differences between verbal languages, we do not hesitate to use dictionaries and other resources to help us understand different languages. But when it comes to nonverbal language, we often mistakenly assume that our systems of communicating nonverbally are all the same.

Understanding cultural differences in nonverbal behavior is the first step in the process of truly appreciating cultural differences in communication. We must learn to recognize the central role that nonverbal behaviors play in the communication process and then realize how our own cultural background influences the ways we engage and interpret the nonverbal world around us. Although these processes are usually unconscious and automatic, we can work consciously to make them more flexible and inclusive of different cultural systems.

Finally, we have seen that communication is a rich and complex process that involves multiple messages sent via multiple signal systems. Culture has a pervasive influence on the encoding of both verbal and nonverbal signals, and the decoding of those signals. Because of this influence, conflict and misunderstanding are inevitable in intercultural communication. To overcome these obstacles, scholars have proposed a personal growth model focusing on emotion regulation and mindfulness. Individuals who can engage in these processes can enhance their intercultural sensitivity, creating new mental categories, being respectful and open to cultural differences, and empathizing with others. Research on intercultural communication has made considerable progress in specifying the unique components of the intercultural communication process.

It is our hope that the information presented in this chapter has allowed you to sit back and examine what kinds of blinders and cultural scripts you have when communicating and interacting with others, and has given you an idea of how to move from an ethnocentric base of interaction to an ethnorelative one.

Glossary

channels The specific sensory modalities by which signals are sent and messages are retrieved.

culture-affiliation hypothesis The hypothesis that immigrant bilinguals will tend to affiliate themselves with the values and beliefs of the culture associated with the language in which they are currently operating. When the language is switched, so are the cultural values with which they affiliate.

decoding The process by which a person receives signals from an encoder and translates these signals into meaningful messages.

encoding The process by which people select, consciously or unconsciously, a particular modality and method by which to create and send a message to someone else.

foreign language effect A temporary decline in the thinking ability of people who are using a foreign language in which they are less proficient than their native tongue.

foreign language processing difficulties Problems associated with learning a foreign language, such as taking more time to respond and experiencing cognitive difficulties while processing information.

gestures Movements of the body, usually the hands, that are generally reflective of thought or feeling.

intercultural communication The exchange of knowledge, ideas, thoughts, concepts, and emotions among people of different cultural backgrounds.

intracultural communication Communication that occurs among people of the same cultural background.

lexicon The words contained in a language, the vocabulary.

messages The meanings that encoders intend to convey and decoders interpret.

mindfulness A strategy to improve intercultural communication that allows people to be conscious of their own habits, mental scripts, and cultural expectations concerning communication.

minority group–affiliation hypothesis The hypothesis that immigrant bilinguals will tend to self-identify as members of an ethnic minority group and adopt the behavioral stereotypes of the majority culture about their minority as their own when they are operating in the language associated with their minority group.

morphemes The smallest and most basic units of meaning in a language.

nonverbal behaviors All the behaviors, other than words, that occur during communication, including facial expressions; movements and gestures of hands, arms, and legs; posture; vocal characteristics such as pitch, rate, intonation, and silence; interpersonal space; touching behaviors; and gaze and visual attention.

phonemes The smallest and most basic units of sound in a language.

phonology The system of rules governing how words should sound (pronunciation, "accent") in a given language.

pragmatics The system of rules governing how language is used and understood in given social contexts.

regulators Nonverbal behaviors we engage in to regulate the flow of speech during a conversation.

Sapir–Whorf hypothesis The proposition that speakers of different languages think differently, and that they do so because of the differences in their languages. Also referred to as *linguistic relativity*.

semantics What words mean.

signals The specific words and behaviors that are sent during communication.

syntax and grammar The system of rules governing word forms and how words should be strung together to form meaningful utterances.

uncertainty reduction One of the major goals of initial intercultural encounters—to reduce the level of uncertainty and anxiety that one feels when attempting to decode intercultural messages.

InfoTrac College Edition

Use InfoTrac College Edition to search for additional readings on topics of interest to you. For more information on topics in this chapter, use the following as search terms:

communication and culture
culture and bilingualism
intercultural communication
language and culture

monolingualism
nonverbal communication and language
Sapir–Whorf

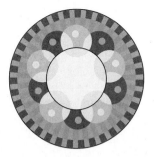

Culture, Self, and Personality

Although culture is generally considered a macrolevel construct, it operates both on the social level and on the personal and individual level, as discussed in Chapter 1. All of us operate in our worlds as individual agents of culture, bringing our implicit, underlying psychological culture to every situation, context, and interaction. We bring this culture to school, work, and meetings with our friends and family. It is a basic part of our selves.

Because culture plays such a major role in shaping our sense of self and identity, it has a pervasive influence on all our behaviors across all contexts. It is imperative that we go beyond the material presented in Chapter 1 that defined culture and examine how culture comes to play such a dominant role in shaping our core sense of self. Then we can explore how that sense of self, fundamentally interrelated with culture, affects our feelings, our thinking, and our motivations. Our sense of self, also known as *self-concept* or *self-construal,* is an important guide to understanding our own behavior as well as understanding and predicting the behavior of others.

In the first part of this chapter, we examine the importance of the concept of self in explaining cultural differences in behaviors and psychological traits. We will explore some examples of different cultural conceptualizations of self, uncovering the consequences of these different conceptualizations for different aspects of behavior. We will also review some of the most recent work on culture and self that challenges previous assumptions about their relationship. We will also discuss the relevant and timely topic of bicultural identity, a topic that has gained importance because of the increasing number of people in all societies who are multicultural. In the second part of the chapter, we will examine a concept closely related to the self—namely, personality. This is one of the most important and widely studied areas in cross-cultural psychology. Our initial review of how culture contributes to our concepts of self will provide a foundation for understanding the relationship between culture and personality.

Culture and Concepts of Self

One of the most powerful and pervasive concepts in the social sciences is the **self-concept**. Scholars have wondered and written about the "self" for many years. We may not consciously think about our self very much, yet how we understand or construe our sense of self is intimately and fundamentally tied to how we understand the world around us and our relationships with others in that world. Whether conscious or not, our concept of self is an integral and important part of our lives.

Think about some descriptions of yourself. You may believe you are an optimist or a pessimist, extroverted or introverted. We use these labels as shorthand descriptions to characterize ourselves. Suppose a young woman tells you she is "sociable." An array of underlying meanings is attached to this one-word description. Descriptive labels such as this usually imply (1) that we have this attribute within us, just as we possess other attributes such as abilities, rights, or interests; (2) that our past actions, feelings, or thoughts have close connections with this attribute; and (3) that our future actions, plans, feelings, or thoughts will be controlled or guided by this attribute and can be predicted more or less accurately by it. In short, if someone describes herself as "sociable," we know that her concept of self is rooted in, and supported and reinforced by, a rich repertoire of specific information concerning her own actions, thoughts, feelings, motives, and plans. The concept of her self as "sociable" may be central to her self-definition, enjoying a special status as a salient identity (Stryker, 1986) or self-schema (Markus, 1977).

A sense of self is critically important and integral to determining our own thoughts, feelings, and actions, and to how we view the world and ourselves and others in that world, including our relationships with other people, places, things, and events. In short, our sense of self is at the core of our being, unconsciously and automatically influencing our every thought, action, and feeling. Each individual carries and uses these internal attributes to guide his or her thoughts and actions in different social situations. A noted anthropologist, Clifford Geertz (1975), described the self as "a bounded, unique, more or less integrated motivational and cognitive universe, a dynamic center of awareness, emotion, judgment, and action organized into a distinctive whole and set contrastively both against other such wholes and against a social and natural background" (p. 48).

These assumptions about the meaning and importance of self are especially relevant within an American psychological framework that is rooted in an individualistic way of thinking. In an individualistic culture, the self is seen as a bounded entity consisting of a number of internal attributes, including needs, abilities, motives, and rights. As people grow up within a certain cultural milieu, that cultural milieu shapes, bounds, and molds their sense of self so that the self-concept "makes sense" within that cultural milieu. If self-concepts are important integrators and organizers of all our psychological traits, characteristics, and behaviors, and if culture shapes and molds our sense of self, then we can conclude that culture shapes and molds our behaviors, thoughts, and feelings indirectly via our self-concepts.

Because cultures differ, it follows that different cultures produce different self-concepts in their members, and these different self-concepts, in turn, influence all other aspects of individual behaviors. That is, what people actually mean and understand as the self differs dramatically from one culture to another. The sense of self we define in a predominantly individualistic American culture is not necessarily the same sense of self as that defined by other cultures, especially collectivistic ones. These differences in self-concepts occur because different cultures are associated with different systems of rules of living, and exist within different social and economic environments and natural habitats. The different demands that cultures place on individual members mean that individuals integrate, synthesize, and coordinate their worlds differently. In short, they have fundamentally different self-concepts.

Just as our own sense of self has a powerful influence on our lives, so the sense of self of people in other cultures influences their lives just as profoundly. Our self-concepts may be totally different from those of another culture. Yet we do not often think about these differences because we are not very aware of our own sense of self and how much it influences our behavior. "Self" is an important, abstract concept that helps us understand much of our psychological composition. But because it is an abstract concept, we are not always cognizant of its influence on ourselves, let alone on others. We only see these differences in the clashes that occur when people with different senses of self interact.

By raising the possibility that your own concept of self may not make much intuitive sense to people of other cultures, we don't want to imply that students or experts in social psychology from other cultures fail to understand the notion of self as a theoretical concept in social psychology. To the contrary, they certainly can and do understand "self" as a theoretical construct. Yet the nature of their understanding is very different from that of Americans. People from other cultural backgrounds may understand Western concepts of self in the same way many Americans understand four-dimensional space. That is, they may understand the concept on a theoretical or cognitive level but have almost no experiential basis for that understanding. They don't feel that understanding emotionally.

Markus and Kitayama (1991b) used these notions to describe two fundamentally different senses of self, contrasting the Western or individualistic construal of self as an independent, separate entity with a composite construal of self more common in many non-Western, collectivistic cultures, in which the individual is viewed as inherently connected or interdependent with others and inseparable from a social context. They illustrated how these divergent forms of self are tied to differences in what people notice and think about, what they feel, and what motivates them (Markus & Kitayama, 1991b). Of course, all cultures cannot be pigeonholed into one of these two categories, but we can use these categories by way of example to highlight the relationship among culture, self, and psychology. However, we need to apply them flexibly if we are to understand different cultures and, more important, different people on their own bases rather than forcing them into conceptual categories based on theory alone.

An Example of Different Cultural Conceptualizations of Self: Independent and Interdependent Selves

An Independent Construal of Self

In the United States, standing out and asserting yourself is a virtue: "The squeaky wheel gets the grease." American politicians routinely credit their success to self-confidence, trusting their instincts, and the ability to make decisions and stick by them. In many individualistic cultures like ours, there is a strong belief in the separateness of individuals. The normative task in these cultures is to maintain the independence of the individual as a separate, self-contained entity.

In American society, many of us have been socialized to be unique, to express ourselves, to realize and actualize the inner self, and to promote our personal goals. These are the tasks the culture provides for its members. These cultural tasks have been designed and selected throughout history to encourage the independence of each separate self. With this set of cultural tasks, our sense of self-worth or self-esteem takes on a particular form. When individuals successfully carry out these cultural tasks, they feel satisfied with themselves, and self-esteem increases accordingly. Under this **independent construal of self**, individuals focus on personal, internal attributes—individual ability, intelligence, personality traits, goals, or preferences—expressing them in public and verifying and confirming them in private through social comparison. This independent construal of self is illustrated graphically in Figure 11.1a. Self is a bounded entity, clearly separated from relevant others. Note that there is no overlap between the self and others. Furthermore, the most salient self-relevant information (indicated by bold Xs) relates to attributes thought to be stable, constant, and intrinsic to the self, such as abilities, goals, and rights.

An Interdependent Construal of Self

Many non-Western, collectivistic cultures neither assume nor value overt separateness. Instead, these cultures emphasize what may be called the "fundamental connectedness of human beings." The primary normative task is to fit in and maintain the interdependence among individuals. Individuals in these cultures are socialized to adjust themselves to an attendant relationship or a group to which they belong, to read one another's minds, to be sympathetic, to occupy and play their assigned roles, and to engage in appropriate actions. These cul-

Figure 11.1 **(a)** Independent construal of self; **(b)** interdependent construal of self

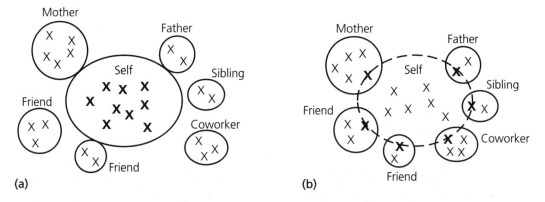

(a)

(b)

Source: "Culture and the Self: Implications for Cognition, Emotion, and Motivation," by H. Markus and S. Kitayama, 1991. *Psychological Review, 98,* pp. 224–253. Copyright © 1991 American Psychological Association. Reprinted by permission of the authors.

tural tasks have been designed and selected throughout history to encourage the interdependence of the self with others.

Given this construal of the self, self-worth, satisfaction, and self-esteem can have very different characteristics from those familiar to us. The self-esteem of those with interdependent construals of the self may depend primarily on whether they can fit in and be part of a relevant ongoing relationship. Under this construal of self, individuals focus on their interdependent status with other people and strive to meet or even create duties, obligations, and social responsibilities. The most salient aspect of conscious experience is intersubjective, rooted in finely tuned interpersonal relationships. The **interdependent construal of self** is illustrated graphically in Figure 11.1b. The self is unbounded, flexible, and contingent on context. Note the substantial overlapping between the self and relevant others. The most salient aspects of the self (shown by bold Xs) are defined in relationships—that is, those features of the self related to and inseparable from specific social contexts. This does not mean that those with interdependent selves do not have any knowledge of their internal attributes, such as personality traits, abilities, and attitudes. They clearly do. However, these internal attributes are relatively less salient in consciousness and thus are unlikely to be the primary concerns in thinking, feeling, and acting.

Because of their collectivistic nature, many Asian cultures foster interdependent construals of self. In these cultures, if you stand out, you will most likely be punished: "The nail that sticks up shall get pounded down." In Japan, for example, political rhetoric sounds very different from that in the United States. A former vice prime minister of Japan once said that in his 30-year career in national politics, he had given the most importance and priority to interpersonal relations. Similarly, "politics of harmony" was the sound bite a former Japanese prime minister used to characterize his regime in the 1980s.

Of course, considerable variations on independent versus interdependent construals of the self can occur within a single culture. People of different ethnicities within a culture, for example, may have different tendencies with regard to independent versus interdependent self-construals. Men and women may have different self-construals. Even within ethnic and gender groups, considerable variation in self-construals may, and often does, occur (Gilligan, 1982; Joseph, Markus, & Tafarodi, 1992). These intracultural differences are also important when considering cultural differences. In this chapter, we will describe general tendencies associated with independent and interdependent self-construals, acknowledging the limitations in representation within groups.

Consequences for Cognition, Motivation, and Emotion

Different concepts of self between cultures contribute to substantial cross-cultural differences in a variety of areas and behaviors. In this section, we will show how the two construals of the self affect our thinking, our feelings, and our behaviors. Cognitive, emotional, and motivational processes can vary dramatically with the construal of the self shared by a cultural group, and these variations have major implications for behavior. ▪

Consequences for self-perception. Different construals of self have different consequences for how we perceive ourselves. With an independent construal of self, one's internal attributes such as abilities or personality traits are the most salient self-relevant information. These internal attributes should be relatively less salient for those with interdependent selves, who are more likely to think about the self in particular social relationships (for example, "me" with family members, "me" with my boyfriend) or in specific contexts ("me" in school, "me" at work).

Several studies (Bond & Tak-Sing, 1983; Shweder & Bourne, 1984) have supported these notions. In these studies, subjects wrote down as many of their own characteristics as possible. Subjects typically generated several types of responses. One response type was the abstract, personality-trait description of the self, such as "I am sociable." Another response type was the situation-specific self-description, such as "I am usually sociable with my close friends." Consistent with our knowledge of independent and interdependent selves, these studies show that American subjects tend to generate a greater number of abstract traits than do Asian subjects. These findings confirm that people with an independent construal of self view their own internal attributes, such as abilities or personality traits, as the most salient self-relevant information. Internal attributes are relatively less salient for those with interdependent selves, who are more likely to think about the self in particular social relationships or contexts.

These findings, of course, do not mean that Americans have more knowledge about themselves than Asians do, or vice versa. Because the most salient information about self for the interdependent selves is context-specific, these individuals generally find it difficult or unnatural to state anything in abstract, noncontextual terms. Instead, those with interdependent selves are culture bound to define themselves in relation to context.

Consistent with this analysis, Triandis and colleagues (see Triandis, 1989, for a review) have shown that individuals from interdependent cultures (for example, China, Japan, and Korea) generate many more social categories, relationships, and groups to which they belong. Indeed, in a study done in the People's Republic of China, as many as 80% of all the responses given to the self-description task were about their memberships in a variety of different groups. Dhawan, Roseman, Naidu, Komilla, and Rettek (1995) reported similar tendencies in self-perception in a study comparing American and North Indian participants.

Another study by Bochner (1994) compared self-perception statements made by Malaysian, Australian, and British participants. The responses were coded according to whether they were idiocentric (individualistic), allocentric (collectivistic), or group self-references, and weighted according to the order in which they were reported. As predicted, Malaysians produced more group and fewer idiocentric references. This is a strong indication that specific relationships are very important for self-definition in this culture. The data also indicated that cultural variations in self-concept are not categorically different across cultures; that is, all people seem to identify themselves according to both personal attributes and group membership. Rather, what differentiates among people in different cultures is the relative salience of either type of self-reference when describing oneself.

The studies cited so far suggest that interdependent selves find it difficult to describe themselves in terms of abstract internal attributes; that is, they find it artificial and unnatural to make abstract statements such as "I am sociable" without specifying a relevant context. Whether a person is sociable or not depends on the specific situation. If this interpretation is correct, then interdependent people should be comfortable describing themselves in terms of abstract internal attributes once a context has been specified.

Cousins (1989) has provided evidence to support this analysis. He used the Twenty Statements Test to ask American and Japanese respondents to write down who they were in various specific social situations (for example, at home, in school, or at work). This instruction supposedly helped respondents to picture a concrete social situation, including who was there and what was being done to whom. Once the context was specified, the Japanese respondents actually generated a greater number of abstract internal attributes (for example, I am hardworking, I am trustworthy, I am lazy) than did the Americans. American respondents tended to qualify their descriptions (I am more or less sociable at work, I am sometimes optimistic at home). It was as if they were saying "This is how I am at work, but don't assume that this is the way I am everywhere." With this more contextualized task, the Americans may have felt awkward providing self-descriptions because their self-definitions typically are not qualified by specific situations.

Consequences for social explanation. Self-construals also serve as a **cognitive template** for interpreting the behaviors of other people. (This process is related to the material on cultural differences in attributions in Chapter 14.) Those with independent selves assume that other people will also have a set of relatively stable internal attributes such as personality traits, attitudes, or abilities. As a result, when they observe another person's behavior, they draw inferences about the actor's internal state or disposition that supposedly underlies and even caused that behavior.

Research done primarily in the United States supports these claims. For example, when subjects read an essay supporting Fidel Castro in Cuba (Jones & Harris, 1967), they inferred that the author must have a favorable attitude toward Castro. Furthermore, such dispositional inferences occur even when obvious situational constraints are present. The subjects in this study inferred a pro-Castro attitude even when they were explicitly told that the person was assigned to write a pro-Castro essay and no choice was given. The subjects ignored these situational constraints and erroneously drew inferences about the author's disposition. This bias toward inference about the actor's disposition even in the presence of very obvious situational constraints has been termed **fundamental attribution error** (Ross, 1977).

Fundamental attribution error may not be as robust or pervasive, however, among people of interdependent cultures, who share assumptions about the self that are very different from those in Western cultures. This self-construal includes the recognition that what an individual does is contingent on and guided by situational factors. These individuals are more inclined to explain another's behavior in terms of the situational forces impinging on the person rather than internal predispositions.

J. G. Miller (1984) examined patterns of social explanation in Americans and Hindu Indians. Both Hindu and American respondents were asked to describe someone they knew well who either did something good for another person or did something bad to another person. After describing such a person, the respondents were asked to explain why the person committed that good or bad act. American respondents typically explained the person's behavior in terms of general dispositions (for example, "She is very irresponsible"). The Hindus, however, were much less likely to offer dispositional explanations. Instead, they tended to provide explanations in terms of the actor's duties, social roles, and other situation-specific factors (see also Shweder & Bourne, 1984).

Fortunately, Miller (1984) collected data from people of different social classes and educational attainment and showed that the Indian tendency toward situation-specific explanations did not depend on these factors. Thus, it is very unlikely that the situational, context-specific thinking common among Indians was due to an inability to reason abstractly. Instead, the context-specific reasoning common in India seems to be due primarily to the cultural assumption of interdependence that is very salient in the Hindu culture. Given the interdependent construal of self, the most reasonable assumption to be made in explaining another's behavior is that this behavior is very much constrained and directed by situation-specific factors. A later study by Miller

(1994) found that these differences in self-construals were linked to cultural differences in duty-centered (Hindu culture) versus individual-centered (American culture) moral codes.

Consequences for achievement motivation.

Western literature on motivation has long assumed that motivations are internal to the actor. A person's motives to achieve, affiliate, or dominate are salient and important features of the internal self—features that direct and energize overt behaviors. With an alternative, interdependent self-construal, however, social behaviors are guided by expectations of relevant others, felt obligations to others, or the sense of duty to an important group to which one belongs. This point is best illustrated by achievement motivation.

Achievement motivation refers to a desire for excellence. Such a desire, in this broad sense, is found quite widely across cultures (Maehr & Nicholls, 1980). In the current literature, however, desire for excellence has been conceptualized in a somewhat more specific manner—as individually or personally based rather than socially or interpersonally rooted. In two classic works in this area (Atkinson, 1964; McClelland, 1961), the desire for excellence is closely linked with an individual's tendency to push him- or herself ahead and actively strive for and seek individual successes. This notion of achievement, in fact, is congruent with the independent construal of the self widely shared in Western culture.

From an alternative, interdependent frame of reference, however, excellence may be sought to achieve broader social goals. These social forms of achievement motivation are more prevalent among those with an interdependent construal of the self. Interdependent selves have ever-important concerns that revolve around fully realizing the individual's connectedness with others. Thus, the nature of achievement motivation in these groups is quite different from that among those with independent construals of the self.

Yang (1982) distinguished between two forms of achievement motivation: individually oriented and socially oriented (compare Maehr & Nicholls, 1980). Individually oriented achievement is commonly found in Western cultures such as the United States. It is for the sake of "me" personally that the individual strives to achieve. In Chinese society, however, socially oriented achievement is much more common. According to this form of achievement, the individual strives to achieve for the sake of relevant others such as family members. A Chinese student, for example, may work hard to gain admission to a prestigious university and then eventually to a top company. Behaviorally, there may be no difference between this Chinese individual and an American who also strives to succeed both in school and at work. In the Chinese case, however, the ultimate goal may not be advancement of his or her personal career but rather a goal that is more collective or interdependent in character. Interdependent goals may include enhancing his or her family's social standing, meeting a felt expectation of family members, or satisfying his or her sense of obligation or indebtedness to the parents who have made enormous sacrifices to raise and support the student. In other words, the Chinese student's desire to achieve is much more socially rooted and does not necessarily reflect his or her desire to advance the quality or standing of "me" personally.

Supporting this notion, Bond (1986) assessed levels of various motivations among Chinese individuals and found that the Chinese show higher levels of socially oriented rather than individually oriented achievement motivation. Yu (1974) reported that the strength of the achievement motive in China is positively related to familism and **filial piety**. In fact, filial piety is a major social construct in many cultures influenced by Confucian and Buddhist teachings and philosophy, which tend to be more collectivistic than individualistic. In such cultures, those most strongly motivated to excel also take most seriously their duties and obligations to family members, especially to parents.

A similar observation has been reported in Japan. K. Doi (1982, 1985) asked Japanese college students 30 questions measuring tendencies to persevere and pursue excellence (achievement tendency). An additional 30 questions measured desires to care for and be cared for by others (affiliation tendency). The results suggested a very close association between achievement motivation and affiliation, with those high in achievement also high in affiliation. These findings are in stark contrast to many Western findings, which indicate that these two dimensions of motivation are typically unrelated (for example, Atkinson, 1964). Both the Chinese study and the Japanese study indicate that achievement in those cultures is closely related to people's social orientation of being connected and interdependent with important others in their lives. Other researchers report that the motivation to achieve includes a combination of *both* social (loyalty to family and larger society) and self (self-realization) factors in other cultures, such as Turkey (Phalet & Claeys, 1993). Thus, the roots of achievement motivation—predominantly self, predominantly social, or a combination of self and social factors—may differ dramatically across cultures.

Consequences for self-enhancement.

One of the main ways in which people maintain their self-esteem is through **self-enhancement**. Self-enhancement refers to a collection of psychological processes by which individuals reinforce or enhance their self-esteem. People all over the world, regardless of culture or gender, are motivated to positively affirm themselves; however, the way they do so varies, depending on the specific cultural background and context within which they live. For example, at least in the United States, people tend to exhibit a **self-serving bias:** They attribute good deeds and successes to their own internal attributes, but attribute bad deeds or failures to external factors (Bradley, 1978). For example, if you receive a good grade in class, you are more inclined to say that you earned that good grade because of hard work or because you are intelligent. In other words, you attribute the cause of the good grade to something internal to you. If you receive a bad grade, however, you are more inclined to say that the teacher didn't do a good job teaching the material, or there were too many things going on in your life during the semester that prevented you from putting enough effort into the class. In other words, you attribute the cause of the bad grade to something external to you.

Another method for enhancing self-esteem, in the United States, is the **false uniqueness effect.** Wylie (1979) found that American adults typically consider themselves to be more intelligent and more attractive than average. This effect appears to be stronger for males than for females in the United States (Joseph et al., 1992). In a national survey of American students, Myers (1987) found that 70% of the students thought they were above average in leadership ability; with respect to the ability to get along with others, 0% thought they were below average, and 60% thought they were in the top 10%. These type of studies clearly show that there is a tendency to view oneself and one's ability and traits more positively in comparison to others, at least in the United States.

Early studies of the self-serving bias and the false uniqueness effect in countries and cultures outside the United States demonstrated that these biases did not exist. For example, when Japanese students were asked to rate themselves in comparison to others on a number of abilities and traits, they claimed that about 50% of students would be better than they are (see Figure 11.2; Markus & Kitayama, 1991a; Markus, Mullally, & Kitayama, 1997). In other words, the false uniqueness effect was nonexistent in this sample. Furthermore, Japanese

Figure 11.2 Estimates of the percentage of people who are better than oneself in three categories of behavior

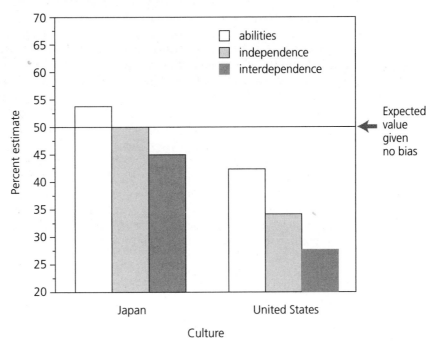

Source: Data from H. R. Markus and S. Kitayama, "Cultural Variation in Self-Concept." In G. R. Goethals and J. Strauss (Eds.), *Multidisciplinary Perspectives on the Self* (New York: Springer-Verlag, 1991).

participants are more likely to say that successful things have occurred because of good luck or effort; and failures have occurred because of insufficient abilities (Shikanai, 1978).

Similar results have been found in many other cross-cultural studies (see review in Matsumoto, 2001). Subsequently, many psychologists came to believe that people of other cultures did not engage in self-enhancement to boost their self-esteem. But more recent evidence has clearly demonstrated that people of other cultures do indeed enhance their self-esteem; they just do it differently. For example, Japanese participants who don't exhibit self-serving bias or false uniqueness effect still show evidence of engaging in self-enhancement processes, at least implicitly. For example, when asked to select a letter from a pair of letters that they like better, they almost always choose the letter that is in their names (Kitayama & Karasawa, 1997). People from many other countries and cultures also show this partiality to letters that are in their name, suggesting an implicit, less obvious method of self-enhancement. Finally, although self-enhancement may not occur in other cultures when people are asked to focus on their own individual traits and attributes, when people are asked about relational and community-related traits, self-enhancement does indeed take place (Kurman, 2001). Thus, it appears that people of all cultures engage in self-enhancement in order to bolster, enhance, or maintain their self-esteem, but that the manner and form in which this is accomplished varies greatly across different cultures. The underlying psychological need or motive to enhance one's sense of self, therefore, is probably a universal process; the ways in which it occurs, however, depends on the specific culture.

Consequences for the social connotation of emotion.   Emotions can be classified into those that encourage independence of the self from others and those that encourage interdependence with others (Kitayama, Markus, & Matsumoto, 1995). Some emotions, such as pride or feelings of superiority, occur when you have accomplished your own goals or desires or have confirmed desirable inner attributes, such as intelligence and wealth. The experience of these emotions tends to verify those inner attributes. Similarly, some negative emotions, such as anger or frustration, result primarily when your own internal attributes, such as goals or desires, are blocked or interfered with. In both cases, your inner attributes are made salient and contrasted against the relevant social context. These emotions tend to separate or disengage the self from social relationships and to promote the perceived independence of the self from those relationships. Kitayama et al. have called these types of emotions **socially disengaged emotions.**

Other positive emotions, such as friendly feelings and feelings of respect, result from being part of a close, more or less communal, relationship. Once experienced, they further encourage this interpersonal bond. Some types of negative emotions, such as feelings of indebtedness or guilt, act in a similar manner. These emotions typically result from failure to participate successfully in an interdependent relationship or from doing some harm to the relationship.

They motivate the individual to restore harmony in the relationship by compensating for the harm done or repaying the debt. These behaviors further engage and assimilate the self in the relationship and enhance the perceived interdependence of the self with relevant others. These emotions can be called **socially engaged emotions.**

All people experience both types of emotions, but people with interdependent self-construals may experience them differently from people with independent self-construals. Socially engaged emotions may be more intense and internalized for interdependent selves, whereas those with independent self-construals may experience socially disengaged emotions more intensely and internally.

Consequences of social connotation and indigenous emotions. Although many emotions are common across cultures, others are unique to particular cultures (Russell, 1991). Such culture-specific emotions are called **indigenous emotions.** Several anthropological studies have suggested that the socially engaged emotions just described are salient in some non-Western cultures to a degree that is unheard of in the West. Lutz (1988), who studied the emotions of people in the Micronesian atoll of Ifaluk, found that an emotion known as *fago* is central to this culture. According to Lutz, *fago* can be roughly described as a combination of compassion, love, and sadness. This emotion is likely to motivate helping behaviors and to create and enhance close interpersonal relationships. In our terminology, *fago* is a highly socially engaged emotion. A contrasting emotion, *ker*, described as a combination of happiness and excitement, is perceived as "dangerous, socially disruptive" (p. 145). Ifaluk people regard *ker* as a highly socially disengaged emotion.

A similar analysis has been applied to another non-Western culture. T. Doi (1973) has suggested that the emotion *amae* is pivotal in understanding the Japanese culture. *Amae* refers to a desire or expectation for others' indulgence, benevolence, or favor. According to Doi, its prototypic form can be found in the mother–infant relationship, whereby the infant feels a desire for "dependency" on the mother and the mother provides unconditional care and love to the infant. This prototype is subsequently elaborated to an adult form of *amae*, which is much more differentiated and sophisticated and is applicable to nonkin relationships, such as work relationships between a supervisor and his or her subordinates. Subordinates may feel *amae* toward the supervisor for his or her favor and benevolence. Reciprocal feelings on the part of the supervisor increase and consolidate the affectionate bond between them. A lack of reciprocation can lead to negative emotions on both sides. As in the Ifaluk concept of *fago*, social engagement seems to define this emotion for the Japanese culture.

These anthropological studies fit well with the two construals of the self described here. For people with interdependent self-construals, public and intersubjective aspects of the self are elaborated in conscious experience; for those with independent selves, private and more subjective aspects are highlighted.

Compare Figures 11.1 and 11.2. Because social connotation is a relatively public and intersubjective aspect of emotion, it is especially salient in the emotional experience of non-Western, interdependent people in collectivistic cultures. By contrast, in Western, individualistic cultures that foster an independent sense of self, the more internal, private aspects of emotion, such as good and bad feelings or moods, may be more salient (Kleinman, 1988). This is true even though people of individualistic cultures recognize the social connotations of different emotions.

Consequences for happiness. *Happiness* refers to the most generic, unqualified state of feeling good. Terms such as *relaxed, elated,* and *calm* are used to describe this generic positive state. People across cultures share the general notion of happiness as defined in this way (Wierzbicka, 1986). However, the specific circumstances of happiness, and the meanings attached to it, depend crucially on the construal of the self as independent or as interdependent. Evidence suggests that people experience this unqualified good feeling when they have successfully accomplished the cultural task of either independence or interdependence.

Kitayama, Markus, Kurokawa, and Negishi (1993) asked both Japanese and American college undergraduates to report how frequently they experienced different emotions, including three types of positive emotions. Some terms used to describe the emotions were generic, such as *relaxed, elated,* and *calm.* Others had more specific social connotations, either socially engaged (such as *friendly feelings, feelings of respect*) or disengaged (*pride, feelings of superiority*). An interesting cross-cultural difference emerged when correlations among these three types of emotions were examined (see Figure 11.3). For the American students, generic positive emotions were associated primarily with the socially disengaged emotions. That is, those who experienced the emotions that signal success in cultural tasks of *independence* (socially disengaged emotions such as pride) were most likely to feel "generally good." This pattern was completely reversed among the Japanese students. Those who experienced the emotions that signal success in cultural tasks of *interdependence* (socially engaged emotions such as friendly feelings) were most likely to feel "generally good."

A more recent study by the same authors (Kitayama, Markus, & Kurokawa, 2000) has replicated these results, with "good feelings" associated with a higher frequency of socially engaged positive emotions in Japan, but a higher frequency of socially disengaged positive emotions in the United States. Furthermore, they found that Americans reported a significantly higher frequency of experiencing positive emotions than negative emotions, and that Japanese reported a higher frequency of experiencing socially engaged emotions than socially disengaged emotions. The exact meanings or connotations of "feeling good" are shaped through culture and are linked very closely with the cultural imperatives of independence (in the United States) and interdependence (in Japan).

Figure 11.3 Cultural differences in the correlation between general positive feelings and socially engaged versus disengaged emotions in the United States and Japan

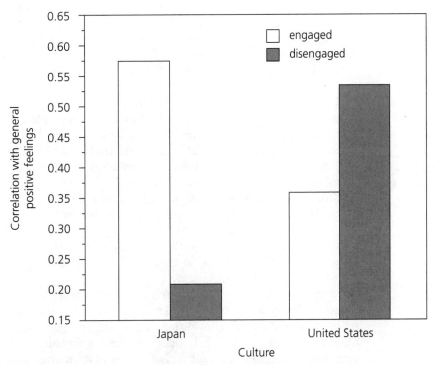

Source: Data from S. Kitayama, H. R. Markus, M. Kurokawa, and K. Negishi, *Social Orientation of Emotions: Cross-Cultural Evidence and Implications* (unpublished manuscript, University of Oregon, 1993).

Critical Evaluation of the Analysis of Independent and Interdependent Selves

As described earlier in this chapter, there is little doubt that culture influences our sense of self which, in turn, affects many other aspects of our psychological characteristics and behaviors. The work of Markus and Kitayama (1991b) reviewed here has been very influential in the field. It offers a prime example of how self-concepts may differ across cultures and provides a conceptual framework within which to understand the influence of culture on self. Their approach has the additional advantage of synthesizing and integrating a wide variety of cross-cultural research findings related to self-perceptions, social explanations, motivation, and emotion. The notions of independent versus interdependent self-construals make intuitive sense, permitting their easy acceptance in cross-cultural as well as mainstream psychology.

A scholarly evaluation of their theory, however—or any theory, for that matter—must go beyond merely asking whether or not it "makes sense" and whether or not the outcomes predicted by the theory occur. A more difficult, and more needed, level of analysis is to examine the assumptions underlying the theory and provide direct evidence in support of those assumptions. Without such support, it cannot be known in any true sense whether the predicted outcomes (as in self-perception) are occurring because of the theoretical framework (independent versus interdependent selves) or because of some other factors. That is, the framework needs to be supported in and of itself, rather than through its predicted outcomes.

For example, studies comparing Asians and Americans were used to support the notion of independent versus interdependent self-construals. However, when differences between these groups are attributed to different self-construals, and these self-construals are related to individualism and collectivism, at least two major assumptions are being made: (1) that Asians have interdependent self-construals, whereas Americans have independent self-construals; and (2) that Asians are collectivistic and Americans are individualistic. Without ascertaining empirically that these two assumptions are valid, it is impossible to assert that the observed differences are due to cultural differences of self-construals, and not to other differences such as geography, social class, or diet. The only way to address these concerns is to examine them empirically.

One of the hindrances to research examining the first assumption has been the lack of a psychometrically valid and reliable way to measure self-construals on the individual level. However, Singelis and his colleagues (Singelis, 1994; Singelis & Sharkey, 1995) have developed such a measure, and have used it in two studies testing self-construals of people of different ethnic groups at the University of Hawaii. In both studies, they found that Asian Americans were more interdependent than European Americans, and European Americans were more independent than Asian Americans. These findings are consistent with Markus and Kitayama's claims concerning Asian and non-Asian differences in self-construal, albeit among ethnic groups within the United States. However, in another study using the same scale with American and Japanese nationals (Carter & Dinnel, 1997), the Japanese were found to be more independent than the Americans. Studies on other cultural groups report no differences in independent versus interdependent self-responses (Watkins & Regmi, 1996), questioning the generalizability of that assumption.

A recent study by Dabul, Bernal, and Knight (1995) provides another interesting twist on these findings. These researchers conducted open-ended interviews calling for self-descriptors from Mexican and Anglo American adolescents. When total scores derived from coding were used, they found that Mexican Americans described themselves more allocentrically than did Anglo Americans, whereas idiocentric self-descriptors were more important for Anglo Americans. When these scores were corrected for frequency of usage, however, the differences disappeared. Not only do these findings raise further questions about the validity of the assumption, they also highlight the possible influence of different methods of research and data analysis on the findings.

The second assumption—that Asians are collectivistic and Americans are individualistic—also has major problems. As described in Chapter 1, a host of measurement techniques are now available to assess individualistic and collectivistic tendencies on the individual level. These measures have been used quite extensively over the past few years, and their results generally do not support the stereotype of Asian, and particularly Japanese, collectivism. For example, when Matsumoto, Weissman, and colleagues (1997) measured IC tendencies using their IC Interpersonal Assessment Inventory, they found that Americans were more collectivistic than Japanese. In a follow-up study, Matsumoto, Kudoh, and Takeuchi (1996) showed that within Japan, older working adults (average age 40) were more collectivistic than Japanese university undergraduates, suggesting that the stereotype of Japanese collectivism may have been appropriate in the past but is questionable today (see Matsumoto, 2002).

Carter and Dinnel (1997) have reported similar findings. They administered Yamaguchi's (1994) collectivism scale, Triandis's collectivistic values index (Triandis et al., 1990), Singelis's (1994) self-construal scale, and a host of individual and collective self-esteem measures to American and Japanese participants. Contrary to their expectations, they found that collectivism was more characteristic of Americans than Japanese, and that independent self-construals were more characteristic of Japanese than Americans (contrary to Singelis's findings on Asian Americans versus European Americans). Carter and Dinnel (1997) found no difference between the Americans and Japanese on collective self-esteem.

In yet another study, Kashima and colleagues (1995) administered a number of collectivism and allocentrism scales to participants in Australia, mainland United States, Hawaii, Japan, and Korea. Koreans and Japanese did score higher than mainland Americans and Australians on collectivism, whereas the latter scored higher on scales related to agency and assertiveness. These findings are consistent with previous notions of cultural differences among these groups. However, on a scale measuring interpersonal relatedness, mainland American women scored highest, followed by Australian women, Hawaiian women, Korean men, Hawaiian men, Australian men, and mainland American men. Unexpectedly, Japanese men and women scored lowest on this scale.

Recently, Takano and Osaka (1997) reviewed ten other studies comparing Americans and Japanese on individualism–collectivism measures. They reported that two studies on conformity and five questionnaire studies found no differences between samples from the two countries. Two experimental studies on cooperation and one questionnaire study found that Japanese were more individualistic than Americans. The only study that found Japanese respondents to be more collectivistic than Americans was Hofstede's (1980) original study (described in Chapter 1), in which individualism was defined without a collectivistic component.

Oyserman, Coon, and Kemmelmeier's (2002) recent meta-analysis of 83 empirical studies of individualism and collectivism tested whether European Americans (U.S. and Canadian) were indeed more individualistic and less collectivistic compared to individuals from other countries and within the United States. Their results demonstrated that European Americans were, in general, more individualistic and less collectivistic than, for instance, Chinese, Taiwanese, Indians, and Asian Americans. However, European Americans were not more individualistic than African Americans or Latinos, and not less collectivistic than Japanese or Koreans.

Taken together, these studies highlight the difficulty of accepting the validity of the two assumptions underlying Markus and Kitayama's (1991b) conceptual framework regarding independent versus interdependent self-construals. Matsumoto's (1999) critique of Markus and Kitayama's (1991b) assumptions of East–West differences points out that most studies concerning self-construals are flawed because the nature of the self-construals is not measured directly but simply presumed (see also Bond & Tedeschi, 2001), and those studies that have included measures of independent and interdependent self-construals or individualism–collectivism do not actually provide support for hypothesized cultural differences on these dimensions. Aside from the studies cited in this section, the most crucial test of these assumptions would be a simultaneous assessment of IC tendencies on the group level and self-construals on the individual level within the same participants in the same study. Without such an assessment, we cannot assert with any confidence that these proposed factors, and no others, influenced the data outcome. This study, unfortunately, does not exist.

Where does this leave us? We believe that Markus and Kitayama's (1991b) original conception of independent versus interdependent self-construals is an important one that has made a major contribution to the field, increasing our awareness of the influence of culture on self and thus on individual behaviors. We agree with the notion of independent versus interdependent self-construals, but strongly believe that it is incumbent on its proponents to test the crucial underlying assumptions. It may be that these types of self-construals do exist but their underlying bases are related to something other than individualism and collectivism. Future research needs to elucidate this matter more directly.

Beyond Independent and Interdependent Self-Construals: Interrelated and Isolated Self-Concepts

Actually, the concept of independent versus interdependent selves is not unlike other dualities of self and human nature proposed throughout the history of psychology, including Freud's (1930/1961) union with others versus egoistic happiness, Angyal's (1951) surrender and autonomy, Balint's (1959) ocnophilic and philobatic tendencies, Bakan's (1966) communion and agency, Bowen's (1966) togetherness and individuality, Bowlby's (1969) attachment and separation, Franz and White's (1985) individuation and attachment, Stewart and Malley's (1987) interpersonal relatedness and self-definition, and Slavin and Kriegman's (1992) mutualistic and individualistic urges (all cited in Guisinger & Blatt, 1994). Many theorists, including Doi (1973), Kim and Berry (1993), Heelas and Lock (1981) and, more recently, Singelis (2000), have noted the difference between conceptualization of self in mainstream American psychology and in other cultures. Sampson (1988) has referred to the sense of self in mainstream approaches as *self-contained individualism,* contrasting it with what he termed *ensembled individualism,* in which the boundary between self and others is less sharply drawn and others are part of oneself.

Guisinger and Blatt (1994) suggest that mainstream American psychology has traditionally emphasized self-development, stressing autonomy, independence, and identity over the development of interpersonal relatedness. They also suggest, however, that evolutionary pressures of natural selection have fostered two basic developmental approaches—one involving self-definition as described in mainstream psychology, the other focusing on the development of interpersonal relatedness. They cite evidence from observational research as well as social biology to support their claims that cooperation, altruism, and reciprocation are aspects of self-development equally as important as autonomy and individual definition. Moreover, they suggest that these dual developmental processes are not mutually exclusive, as they are often depicted. Rather, they are fundamentally and basically intertwined, with the development of a mature sense of self in one aspect depending, in part, on the development of a mature self in the other.

More recently, Niedenthal and Beike (1997) have carried these concepts a step further, proposing the existence of both interrelated and isolated self-concepts. Whereas previous theories of self distinguished different types of self on the level of personality, motivation, and culture, their view focuses on the level of cognitive representation. Specifically, they suggest that "some concepts derive their meaning through mental links to concepts of other people, whereas other concepts of self have an intrinsic or cognitively isolated characterization" (p. 108). Like Guisinger and Blatt (1994), they suggest that these concepts exist not as dichotomies, but rather as interrelated dualities. Referring mainly to the cognitive structures characteristic of these two tendencies, Niedenthal and Beike (1997) suggest that individuals represent the self with a variety of more or less interrelated structures at the same time, and that one person can have separate interrelated and isolated self-concepts in the same domain. Likewise, Kagitcibasi (1996a, 1996b) proposes an integrative synthesis of the self that is both individuated and, at the same time, relational.

These recent developments in notions of self, incorporating issues of relatedness into mainstream conceptions of autonomy and individuality in a coherent system of dualism, have many far-reaching implications for our understanding of culture and self. If these dualities coexist, cultures may emphasize both types of self-construal rather than only one. Moreover, the relative importance of one sense of self may differ in different contexts, and cultures may influence these relativities as well. Future research needs to examine the simultaneous duality of these aspects of self across contexts and cultures to create a clearer picture of the relationship between culture and self, and of how culture influences individual behaviors via self.

Multicultural Identities

The term *cultural identity* refers to individuals' psychological membership in a distinct culture. As culture is a psychological construct—a shared system of rules—it is conceivable that people have not just a single cultural identity but, in some circumstances, two or more such identities. These multicultural identities are becoming increasingly commonplace in today's world, with borders between cultural groups becoming less rigid, increased communication and interaction among people of different cultural groups, and more intercultural marriages. If culture is defined as a psychological construct, the existence of multicultural identities suggests the existence of multiple psychocultural systems of representations in the minds of multicultural individuals.

In fact, a small but important number of studies have begun to document the existence of such multiple psychological systems in multicultural individuals. Oyserman (1993), for example, conducted four studies testing Arab and Jewish Israeli students in Israel. Although social, collectivistic types of identities had long been considered central to many cultures of that region, Oyserman suggested that these cultures would include considerable individualistic aspects as well, given the history of the region and the influence of the British. In her studies, participants completed a battery of tests, including assessments of individualism, collectivism, public and private self-focus, and intergroup conflicts. Across all four studies, the results indicated that individualism as a worldview was related to private aspects of the self and to distinguishing between self and others, while collectivism was related to social identities, public aspects of the self, and increased awareness of intergroup conflict. Both cultural groups endorsed both types of cultural tendencies, suggesting that members of these groups use both individualistic and collectivistic worldviews in organizing perceptions of self and others.

Another study by Oyserman and her colleagues (Oyserman, Gant, & Ager, 1995) also supported the existence of multiple concepts of self. In this study, the researchers examined the effects of multiple, contextualized concepts of the self on school persistence in European American and African American youths. They found that different self-concepts were predictive of achievement-related strategies for European Americans and African Americans. More important, balance between different achievement-related self-construals predicted school achievement, especially for African American males.

Other studies have documented a *cultural reaffirmation* effect among multicultural individuals living in multicultural societies. For example, Kosmitzki (1996) examined monocultural and bicultural Germans and Americans, who made trait-attribute ratings of themselves, their native cultural group, and their adoptive cultural group. Compared with monoculturals, bicultural individuals identified more closely with their native culture, evaluated it more positively, and evaluated the two cultures as less similar to each other. In short, the bicultural individuals appeared to endorse even more traditional values associated with their native culture than did native monocultural individuals in those native cultures.

This curious finding is well supported in other studies. For example, Matsumoto, Weissman, and colleagues (1997) compared ratings of collectivistic tendencies in interpersonal interactions of Japanese Americans with those of Japanese nationals in Japan. They found that the Japanese Americans were more collectivistic than the Japanese nationals in the native culture. A study comparing Korean Americans and Korean nationals on the same measure (Lee, 1995) found similar results. Sociological studies involving immigrants to the United States, including China, Japan, Korea, and the Philippines, also suggest that the immigrant groups in the United States from other Asia–Pacific countries appear to be more traditional than the native cultures from which they came (for example, Takaki, 1998). Anecdotally, strong cultural traditions, customs, heritage, and language seem to continue among Chinese American immigrant populations throughout the United States.

What may account for such findings? We would speculate that when immigrant groups arrive in the United States, they bring with them the culture of their native group at that time. As they are immersed within a multicultural society, the stress of multicultural life in a different world contributes to the cultural reaffirmation effect, as documented by Kosmitzki (1996) and others. The immigrant group thus crystallizes its sense of culture—the one they brought with them at the time—and it is this psychological culture that is communicated across generations of immigrant groups. As time passes, the native culture itself may undergo change, but the immigrant group continues to transmit the original cultural system they brought with them. After some time, if you compare the immigrant group with the native cultural group, you will find that the immigrant group actually conforms more to the original cultural stereotype than does the native group, because the immigrant culture has crystallized while the native culture has changed. Thus, while individual members of immigrant groups often grow up with multicultural identities, the identity of their native culture is often one of long-standing tradition and heritage.

Summary

Culture is a macrolevel social construct that identifies the characteristics and attributes we share with others. But culture also influences the very core nature of our beings as individuals. Because culture shapes and colors our experiences, behaviors, attitudes, and feelings, it helps mold our fundamental sense of self—our self-concept, self-construals, and self-identities. Culture influences these core aspects of our sense of self, and we carry these self-construals with us in all aspects of life. Whether at work, at school, having fun, or interacting with other people, we take our culture and our culture-bound sense of self with us. These self-construals help us understand the world around us and others in it, and guide us and our behaviors in ways we are not always aware of. Because culture influences core aspects of the self, we need to understand its importance and pervasiveness. An awareness of how our fundamental concepts of self may contrast sharply with other cultures' concept of self will help us appreciate and understand why people from other cultures may be motivated to feel, think, and behave in ways that may differ from ours.

We now turn to a topic that is closely related to the self—studies on the relationship between culture and personality.

Culture and Personality

One of the most important and widely studied areas in cross-cultural psychology is personality. Anthropologists, psychologists, and other social scientists have long been interested in the "national character" of people of different cultures, and the extent to which personality as we know it in North American psychology is similar or different in other cultures. Indeed, the search for the underlying bases of individual differences, which serve as the backbone of understanding personality, shares a close conceptual and empirical connection with culture in any cultural milieu.

In this section, we first discuss the various approaches that scholars have used to understand the relationship between culture and personality. Then, we review major cross-cultural research on personality over the past few decades, highlighting important similarities and differences in those findings. In particular, we will review research on the Five Factor Model (FFM), which suggests that five personality dimensions are universal to all humans. We discuss the measurement of personality across cultures, as well as the use of some personality scales to assess psychopathology across cultures. We also discuss indigenous approaches to personality, and some of the research that has been conducted in this area. Although culture-specific aspects of personality and universal notions of personality may seem contradictory, we will seek ways of understanding their mutual coexistence and conceptualizing and studying their duality.

Defining Personality

The first thing we need to do is define what we mean by personality. In psychology, **personality** is generally considered to be a set of relatively enduring behavioral and cognitive characteristics, traits, or predispositions that people take with them to different situations, contexts, and interactions with others, and that contribute to differences among individuals.

In North American psychology, personality is generally based on stability and consistency across contexts, situations, and interactions. This notion of personality has a long tradition in European and North American psychology. The psychoanalytic work of Freud and the neoanalytic approaches of Jung and Adler share this definition of personality. The humanistic approach of Maslow and Rogers, the trait approach of Allport, the behavioral approach of Skinner, and the cognitive approach of Rotter, Bandura, and Mischel also share this notion. Although these approaches differ in their conceptions of how personality develops, they are consistent in their basic notion of personality as stable and enduring across contexts and situations. Most scholars, even in cross-cultural psychology, adopt this or similar definitions of personality when studying it across cultures.

Cross-Cultural Approaches to the Study and Understanding of Personality

Over the course of the 20th century, several different approaches and methods have been used to elucidate the relationship between culture and personality. Some of the earliest contributions to our understanding of this relationship came from anthropologists who were interested in human psychology within their anthropological discipline. Through mostly ethnographic fieldwork, these individuals—such as Margaret Mead, Edward Sapir, Weston Labarre, and Ruth Benedict—developed ideas and theories about culture and personality that served as a basis for cross-cultural comparison of personalities and today's cultural psychology (see review in Piker, 1998). Although many cultural and psychological anthropologists recognize the important contributions of biologically innate factors to personality and psychology, the main thrust of the anthropological contribution is its view of personality as culturally specific, formed by the unique forces each culture deals with in its milieu. The anthropological view of personality, therefore, attributes more importance to the learning of psychological mechanisms and personality in the environment through cultural practices than to biological and evolutionary factors.

Whereas psychological anthropology made major contributions in the first half of the 20th century, the second half was dominated by the cross-cultural psychological approach (see review by Church & Lonner, 1998). This approach generally views personality as something discrete and separate from culture, and as a dependent variable in research. Thus, two or more cultures are treated as independent variables, and they are compared on some personality traits or dimensions. In contrast to the cultural or psychological anthropological approach, the cross-cultural approach tends to see personality as an etic or universal phenomenon that is equivalently relevant and meaningful in the cultures being compared. To the extent that personality does exhibit universal aspects, how did they originate? Two separate but not mutually exclusive possibilities are (1) the existence of biologically innate and evolutionarily adaptive factors that create genetic predispositions to certain types of personality traits and (2) the possibility of culture-constant learning principles and processes (see also the discussion by MacDonald, 1998).

Cross-cultural research on personality, however, has also been concerned with the discovery of culture-specific personality traits, characteristics, and patterns. Cross-cultural psychologists describe culture-specific **indigenous personalities** as constellations of personality traits and characteristics found only in a specific culture (for more information, see reviews by Ho, 1998, and

Diaz-Loving, 1998). These types of studies, though psychological in nature, are heavily influenced in approach and understanding by the anthropological view of culture and personality.

Another approach to understanding the relationship between culture and personality that has emerged in recent years is known as *cultural psychology* (for example, Shweder, 1979a, 1979b, 1980, 1991, 2000; Markus & Kitayama, 1998). This approach sees culture and personality not as separate entities, but as a mutually constituted system in which each creates and maintains the other.

> The cultural perspective assumes that psychological processes, in this case the nature of functioning of personality, are not just influenced by culture but are thoroughly culturally constituted. In turn, the cultural perspective assumes that personalities behaving in concert create the culture. Culture and personality are most productively analyzed together as a dynamic of mutual constitution . . . ; one cannot be reduced to the other. . . . A cultural psychological approach does not automatically assume that all behavior can be explained with the same set of categories and dimensions and first asks whether a given dimension, concept, or category is meaningful and how it is used in a given cultural context. (Markus & Kitayama, 1998, p. 66)

The cultural psychological viewpoint has been heavily influenced by the cultural anthropologists, as well as by the cross-cultural work on indigenous psychologies (see Kim, 2001) and personalities. It is inherently antithetical to the cross-cultural psychological search for universals and rejects the possibility of biological and genetic mechanisms underlying universality. Instead, it suggests that just as no two cultures are alike, the personalities that comprise those cultures should be fundamentally different because of the mutual constitution of culture and personality within each cultural milieu.

The tension between the cross-cultural psychology school and the cultural psychology school, in terms of universality versus culture-specificity in personality, can be seen in the literature reviewed in this chapter. Although considerable evidence points to the universality of some aspects of personality, a considerable amount of evidence also documents the existence of indigenous personalities, as well as cultural differences in supposedly etic personality domains. How to make sense of this all is perhaps the greatest challenge facing this area of cross-cultural psychology in the near future. Some theorists, such as Church (2000), have taken up this challenge by arguing for an integrated *cultural trait psychology* that incorporates both cross-cultural psychology and cultural psychology in studies of personality.

Cross-Cultural Research on Personality

For many years, one of the most common and popular methods of examining the relationship between culture and personality has been cross-cultural research.

In this approach, researchers take samples of individuals from two or more cultures, administer a personality scale, and compare the responses between groups. Cross-cultural differences in the personality measure are then interpreted with respect to differences in the values, behaviors, and practices observed in the cultures being compared.

This approach, though simple in concept, has provided a wealth of useful and interesting information about cultural similarities and differences in personality. In this section, we will review and discuss some of the major findings.

Locus of Control

One of the most widely studied personality concepts across cultures is **locus of control.** This concept was developed by Rotter (1954, 1966), who suggested that people differ in how much control they believe they have over their behavior and their relationship with their environment and with others. According to this schema, locus of control can be perceived as either internal or external to the individual. People with an internal locus of control see their behavior and relationships with others as dependent on their own behavior. Believing that your grades are mostly dependent on how much effort you put into study is an example of internal locus of control. People with an external locus of control see their behavior and relationships with the environment and others as contingent upon forces outside themselves and beyond their control. If you believed your grades were mostly dependent on luck, the teacher's benevolence, or the ease of the tests, you would be exemplifying an external locus of control.

Research examining locus of control has shown both similarities and differences across cultures. In general, Americans often appear to have higher internal locus of control scores, whereas non-Americans tend to have higher external locus of control scores. A number of studies have found this pattern in comparisons of Americans with Asians, especially Chinese and Japanese (for example, Hamid, 1994; see also, however, Spadone, 1992, for a nonfinding in an American–Thai comparison). Lee and Dengerink (1992) found higher internal locus of control scores among Americans than Swedes, and Munro (1979) found that Americans had higher internal locus of control scores than participants in Zambia and Zimbabwe (then Rhodesia). In a review of cross-cultural studies on locus of control, Dyal (1984) concluded that European Americans appear to be characterized by a more internal locus of control than African Americans. Locus of control differences have also been documented in children; Paguio, Robinson, Skeen, and Deal (1987), for example, showed that American children had higher internal locus of control scores than Filipino and Brazilian children.

These findings have often been interpreted as reflecting the American culture's focus on individuality, separateness, and uniqueness, in contrast to a more balanced view of interdependence among individuals and between individuals and natural and supernatural forces found in many other cultures. People of non-American cultures may be more likely to see the causes of events and behaviors in sources that are external to themselves, such as fate, luck, supernatural forces, or relationships with others. Americans, however, prefer to take more personal responsibility for events and situations, and view themselves as having more personal control over such events.

Although such interpretations are interesting and provocative, they still leave some gaps to be filled. For example, they do not account for such phenomena as self-serving bias or defensive attributions, in which Americans tend to place the responsibility for negative events on others, not themselves (see the earlier section in this chapter on self-enhancement). Also, some researchers have suggested that locus of control is really a multifaceted construct spanning many different domains—academic achievement, work, interpersonal relationships, and so on—and that separate assessments of each of these domains are necessary to make meaningful comparisons on this construct. Finally, Smith, Dugan, and Trompenaars (1997), in their 14-country study of locus of control and affectivity, found some cross-national differences in locus of control, but larger differences by gender and status across countries. Thus, the search for cross-cultural differences may obscure larger differences based on other social constructs. Future research needs to address all these concerns to further elucidate the nature of cultural influences on locus of control.

Self-Esteem

A number of studies have examined the construct of self-esteem and the related construct of self-worth. Research in the United States has repeatedly shown that European Americans have a pervasive tendency to maintain their feelings of self-esteem and self-worth. Concepts such as self-serving bias, defensive attributions, and illusory optimism have been invoked as mechanisms of self-enhancement among European Americans. These particular self-enhancing mechanisms are not generally found in other groups, especially Asians (see review by Diener & Diener, 1995). Some researchers even suggest that Asians, such as Chinese and particularly Japanese, are more attuned to negative than positive self-evaluations, in both private and public settings (Kitayama, Matsumoto, Markus, & Norasakkunkit, 1997; Leung, 1996).

Cross-cultural studies lend support to these differences in self-esteem across cultures. Wood, Hillman, and Sawilowsky (1995), for example, found that American adolescents had significantly higher self-esteem scores than their Indian counterparts. Americans also report higher self-esteem scores than Japanese or Chinese (Heine, Lehman, Markus, & Kitayama, 1999). Studies with children have also found differences in Asian versus European countries on individual self-esteem. Chan's (2000) study of 1,303 children compared Anglo and Chinese children in Britain and Chinese children in Hong Kong. As predicted, he found that Hong Kong Chinese children reported significantly lower levels of self-esteem than did Anglo British children. Interestingly, Chinese British children reported higher levels of self-esteem than did those in Hong Kong, and did not significantly differ on levels of self-esteem from their Anglo British peers, suggesting acculturation to the host society's more individualistic norms. In contrast, several studies in North America have found that Asian Americans still report lower self-esteem scores than European Americans (Crocker & Lawrence, 1999; Mintz & Kashubeck, 1999; Porter & Washington, 1993). Radford, Mann, Ohta, and Nakane (1993), comparing self-esteem related to decision making in Australian and Japanese students, found that Australians had higher self-esteem scores than did the Japanese.

The higher self-esteem scores of British children compared to Hong Kong children and Australians compared to Japanese suggests that self-esteem may be related to individualism, rather than specific to American culture. If self-esteem is related to individualism and collectivism, then perhaps individualism fosters a certain type of self-esteem—one that is often measured in psychological research—whereas collectivism fosters a different type of self-esteem. Tafarodi and Swann (1996) tested this "cultural trade-off" hypothesis in a study of Chinese and American college students. They hypothesized that highly collectivistic cultures promote the development of global self-esteem, which is reflected in generalized self-liking, while at the same time challenging the development of another dimension of self-esteem, reflected in generalized self-competence; individualistic cultures, they hypothesized, foster the opposite tendencies. As predicted, they found that the Chinese were lower in self-competence but higher in self-liking than the Americans. These findings support the notion that self-esteem may have multiple facets, and that different cultural milieus either support or challenge the development of different facets.

This notion also received some support in a recent study by Kitayama and Karasawa (1997). This study examined implicit rather than explicit self-esteem in a sample of Japanese individuals by examining their preference for certain Japanese alphabetical letters and numbers over others. The results indicated that letters included in one's own name and numbers corresponding to the month and day of one's birth were significantly better liked than other letters and numbers. The authors interpreted these findings to suggest a dimension of self-esteem that may be fostered in a collectivistic cultural milieu, but not necessarily within an individualistic one.

These recent studies suggest the importance of delineating different aspects of self-esteem and then investigating how different cultural frameworks encourage or discourage those various aspects. This line of research raises the possibility that the need for self-esteem is a universal one across humans, but that its exact behavioral and psychological manifestations may differ depending on cultural context. Future research has a rather large job in documenting and elaborating on these ideas.

The Eysenck Personality Scales

One of the most commonly used personality scales in the cross-cultural literature is the Eysenck Personality Questionnaire (EPQ). It measures three different personality traits: tough-mindedness (known in the EPQ as Psychoticism), emotionality (known in the EPQ as Neuroticism), and Extroversion. It also contains a Lying or Social Desirability Scale designed to determine the degree to which respondents may be providing false or inaccurate responses. Over the past few decades, the EPQ has been standardized and used in cross-cultural research in a number of different countries, including Nigeria, Japan, Greece, Yugoslavia, Brazil, France, and others (see review in Eysenck & Chan, 1982). A junior version, developed for use with children, has been used in Spain, New Zealand, Hungary, Japan, and other countries.

The numerous cross-cultural studies involving the EPQ have produced a number of interesting cross-cultural findings. Eysenck and Chan (1982), for example, administered the adult and junior versions of the EPQ to adults and children in Hong Kong and England. They found that adults in Hong Kong scored higher on Psychoticism and Social Desirability and lower on Extroversion than did British adults. Children in Hong Kong scored higher on Social Desirability and lower on Extroversion and Neuroticism than British children. Eysenck and colleagues have found various other differences in comparisons of Romanian and English adults (Eysenck, Baban, Derevenco, & Pitariu, 1989), Danish and English children (Nyborg, Eysenck, & Kroll, 1982), Iranian and English children (Eysenck, Makaremi, & Barrett, 1994), and Egyptian and English children (Eysenck & Abdel-Khalek, 1989).

The goal of most of the published studies involving the EPQ has been validation of the measure for use in cross-cultural research in the countries and cultures in which the tests have been administered. These studies have provided the field with a measure that apparently "works" in a variety of cross-cultural contexts, measuring aspects of personality that are generally considered universal to all humans. However, these studies lack a consistent interpretation of the nature and causes of cultural differences when they occur. While providing a wealth of findings documenting cross-cultural differences, they tell us little about what cultural factors contribute to these differences. Are cross-cultural differences related to stable dimensions of cultural variation, such as individualism versus collectivism, or status/power differentiation? We don't know. A major goal of future research in this area, therefore, should be the generation and testing of viable hypotheses concerning the reasons and processes behind these differences and similarities.

Other Miscellaneous Studies

A number of other studies provide interesting glimpses into the nature of cultural influences on other aspects of personality. Several studies, for example, have reported cultural differences in the personality construct known as *self-monitoring*. This construct has been described as "self-observation and self-control guided by situational cues to social appropriateness" (Snyder, 1974, p. 526). People of individualistic cultures tend to have higher scores on self-monitoring than do people of collectivistic cultures (for example, Gudykunst, Gao, Nishida, Bond, et al., 1989; Gudykunst, Yang, & Nishida, 1987).

In another interesting study, Yamaguchi, Kuhlman, and Sugimori (1995) examined the personality correlates of allocentric (collectivistic) tendencies in individualistic and collectivistic cultures. These researchers administered a collectivism scale to participants in the United States, Korea, and Japan, and measured individual differences in the degree to which the participants exhibited allocentrism—that is, personally held collectivistic values (see Chapter 1). They also measured affiliative tendency, sensitivity to rejection, and need for uniqueness. The results indicated that individuals who scored higher on allocentrism also scored higher on affiliation and sensitivity to rejection, but lower on need for uniqueness; these relationships held in all three countries. The researchers explained their findings by suggesting that allocentric individuals are more concerned with rewards and punishments from ingroup members, and thus have less need to be unique, than those with greater idiocentric tendencies.

Cross-cultural differences have also been reported in studies on authoritarianism and rigidity involving Iranian respondents (Mehryar, 1970); on Cattell's 16 Personality Factors (PF) with Amish respondents (Wittmer, 1971); on the Maudsley Personality Inventory and the Manifest Anxiety Scale with Hindu Indians (De & Singh, 1972); on value systems among Australians and Chinese (Feather, 1986); on cognitive styles and field dependence in Mexican, African, and European American children (Figueroa, 1980); on spirituality (from a motivational/trait perspective) in Christian, Hindu, and Muslim Indians (Piedmont & Leach, 2002); and on authoritarianism in German and American adolescents (Lederer, 1982).

Summary and Evaluation

Although the bulk of the research documents cross-cultural differences in the various domains of personality that have been tested, the very fact that these personality dimensions have been measured across cultures could be taken as some kind of evidence for their universality. That is, the cultures studied are similar in that they share the same personality dimensions, even though they differ in where they fall along these dimensions.

To be sure, the mere fact that personality scales have been translated and used in cross-cultural research is not sufficient evidence that the personality domains they measure are indeed equivalent in those cultures. In fact, when this type of research is conducted, one of the researchers' primary concerns is whether the personality scales used in the study can validly and reliably measure meaningful dimensions of personality in all the cultures studied. As discussed in Chapter 2, the equivalence of a measure in terms of its meaning to all cultures concerned, as well as its psychometric validity and reliability, is of prime concern in cross-cultural research if the results are to be considered valid, meaningful, and useful.

Indeed, a common practice in many of the earlier cross-cultural studies on personality was to take a personality scale that had been developed in one country or culture—most often the United States—and simply translate it and use it in another culture. In effect, the researchers simply assumed that the personality dimension measured by that scale was equivalent between the two cultures, and that the method of measuring that dimension was psychometrically valid and reliable. Thus, many studies imposed an assumed etic construct upon the cultures studied (Church & Lonner, 1998). Realistically, however, one cannot safely conclude that the personality dimensions represented by an imposed etic are equivalently and meaningfully represented in all cultures included in a study.

Many of the more recent studies in this area have been sensitive to this issue, and researchers have taken steps to assure some degree of psychometric equivalence across cultures in their measures of personality. In their study of the EPQ in Hong Kong and England, for example, Eysenck and Chan (1982) included only those items that were common to scoring keys derived separately in both cultures, thus ensuring some comparability in the scale scores used in their comparison. Likewise, Tafarodi and Swann (1996) tested the cross-cultural equivalence in their measure of self-esteem by conducting a confirmatory factor analysis on the items measured in their scales in both cultures before testing for differences. In testing for cultural differences in locus of control, Hamid (1994) back-translated his measures, administered both original and translated measures to bilinguals, and assessed the parallel forms correlation of the two questionnaires before using them in the main study. Munro (1979) established equivalence in the factor structures of his locus of control questionnaires before testing for cultural differences between blacks and whites in Africa, and Smith, Dugan, and Trompenaars (1997) conducted a pancultural factor analysis on their locus of control measure before testing for differences. This procedure allowed them to derive scale scores after eliminating individual and cultural differences in the ratings of the individual items included in the scale.

Support for the notion that cross-cultural comparisons of personality are meaningful comes from other sources as well. First, the findings derived from many of these studies "make sense"; that is, they are interpretable to a large degree and match predictions based on what we might reasonably expect based on our knowledge of culture and its probable influence on personality. Findings that were uninterpretable based on available knowledge of the cultures tested would raise questions about the psychometric validity of the scales being used. That many studies provide interpretable findings, however, suggests that the scales do measure something that is meaningful.

Another source of support comes from the data analyses used to compare cultures. Although significant differences in mean values reflect between-culture differences in averages, they do not necessarily reflect the degree of overlap among individuals within the samples comprising the various cultures in the comparison. In most cases, the degree of individual variation is many times larger than the degree of difference between cultures. Analysis of such effects would surely lead one to suspect a considerable degree of individual similarity in the personality constructs being measured (see Matsumoto, 2001, for a critique and discussion of the usefulness of cultural differences on mean scores and effect sizes).

A final source of support for the notion that many of the personality scales used in previous cross-cultural studies are valid comes from recent studies investigating the possible link between genetics and personality. Indeed, an increasing number of studies in recent years have begun to show that personality has some direct relationship to genes (for example, Berman, Ozkaragoz, Young,

& Noble, 2002; Brummett et al., 2003; Eley, 1997; Jang, McCrae, Angleitner, Riemann, & Livesley, 1998; Joensson et al., 2003; Riemann, Angleitner, & Strelau, 1997; Saudino, 1997). To the extent that genetic and biological factors contribute to personality, they provide the basis on which stability in personality can be conceptualized, measured, and studied not only across individuals within a culture, but across cultures as well. Should such stability exist, and if this stability is related to biological factors that are in turn related to evolutionary factors and adaptive functions, it supports the argument that some aspects of personality may indeed be universal. This argument does not preclude the possibility of cultural specificity in some aspects of personality, in the manifestations of personality, or even in the emergence and existence of indigenous personalities; it merely suggests that some aspects of personality may be universal to all humans.

Culture and the Five Factor Model of Personality

The Five Factor Model (FFM) of personality is a conceptual model built around five distinct and basic personality dimensions that appear to be universal for all humans. The five dimensions are Extroversion, Neuroticism, Agreeableness, Conscientiousness, and Openness.

The FFM was conceived after a number of writers noticed the similarities in the personality dimensions that had emerged across many studies, both within and between cultures. Most notably, support for the FFM arose out of factor analyses of trait adjectives from the English lexicon that were descriptive of self and others (Juni, 1996). The factors that emerged from these types of analyses were similar to dimensions found in the analysis of questionnaire scales operationalizing personality. Further inquiry across cultures, using both factor analysis of descriptive trait adjectives in different languages and personality dimensions measured by different personality questionnaires, lent further support to the FFM. Eysenck's (1983) many studies using the EPQ, for example, provided much support for Extroversion and Neuroticism as stable, universal personality scales. In early studies of the FFM, those factors were reported in German (Amelang & Borkenau, 1982), Dutch (De Raad, Hendriks, & Hofstee, 1992), French (Rolland, 1993), Japanese, Chinese, and Filipino samples (Bond, 1979; Bond, Nakazato, & Shiraishi, 1975; Guthrie & Bennett, 1971; all cited in McCrae, Costa, Del-Pilar, & Rolland, 1998).

Cross-cultural research of the past decade on the validity of the FFM in different countries and cultures has continued to support claims of universality. De Fruyt and Mervielde (1998), for example, confirmed the validity of the FFM in the Dutch language, Trull and Geary (1997) confirmed its validity in Chinese, and Benet-Martinez and John (2000) in Castilian Spanish. De Raad, Perugini, and Szirmak (1997) reported support for the FFM in Dutch, Italian, Hungarian, American English, and German; Hofstee, Kiers, De Raad, Goldberg et al. (1997) also provided support for the FFM in Dutch, American English, and German. McCrae, Costa, and Yik (1996) provided support for the FFM in the Chinese personality structure, and Digman and Shmelyov (1996) documented its utility in Russia. Other studies have documented its validity in other countries and cultures, including Italy (Caprara, Barbaranelli, & Comrey, 1995; Caprara & Perugini, 1994); Australia and South Africa (Heaven, Connors, & Stones, 1994); Hong Kong (Ng, Cooper, & Chandler, 1998); Canada, Finland, Poland, and Germany (Paunonen, Jackson, Trzebinski, & Forsterling, 1992); Germany, Portugal, Israel, China, Korea, and Japan (McCrae & Costa, 1997); the Philippines (Katigbak, Church, Guanzon-Lapena, Carlota, & Del Pilar, 2002); Muslim Malaysia (Mastor, Jin, & Cooper, 2000) and others (McCrae, 2001; also see review in McCrae et al., 1998). Collectively, these studies provide convincing and substantial evidence to support the claim that the FFM—consisting of Extroversion, Neuroticism, Openness, Conscientiousness, and Agreeableness—represents a universal taxonomy of personality that is applicable to all humans.

The universality of the FFM suggests that all humans share a similar personality structure that can be characterized by the five traits or dimensions that comprise the FFM. To explain this universality, some writers (for example, MacDonald, 1998) have suggested an evolutionary approach. This approach posits a universality both of human interests and in the neurophysiological mechanisms underlying trait variation. Personality structure is viewed as a universal psychological mechanism, a product of natural selection that serves both social and nonsocial functions in problem solving and environmental adaptation. Based on this theory, one would expect to find similar systems in animals that serve similar adaptive functions, and one would expect personality systems to be organized within the brain as discrete neurophysiological systems.

In this view, traits such as Conscientiousness (emotional stability), Neuroticism (affect intensity), and the other components of the FFM are considered to reflect stable variations in systems that serve critical adaptive functions. Conscientiousness, for example, may help individuals to monitor the environment for dangers and impending punishments, and to persevere in tasks that are not intrinsically rewarding (MacDonald, 1998). Affect intensity, measured by Neuroticism, is adaptive in that it helps mobilize behavioral resources by moderating arousal in situations requiring approach or avoidance.

According to MacDonald (1991, 1998), this evolutionary approach suggests a hierarchical model in which "behavior related to personality occurs at several levels based ultimately on the motivating aspects of evolved personality systems" (p. 130). In this model, humans possess evolved motive dispositions—for example, intimacy, safety—which are serviced by a universal set of personality dispositions that help individuals achieve their affective goals by managing personal and environmental resources. This resource management leads to concerns, projects, and tasks, which in turn lead to specific action units or behaviors through which the individual achieves the goals specified by the evolved motive dispositions (see Figure 11.4).

Note that this model—and the assumptions about universality of the FFM made by McCrae and Costa and others (for example, McCrae & Costa, 1997)—does not minimize the importance of cultural and individual variability. Cul-

Figure 11.4 Hierarchical model of motivation showing relationships between domain-specific and domain-general mechanisms

Level 1	EVOLVED MOTIVE DISPOSITIONS	(Domain-Specific Mechanisms)
Level 2	PERSONAL STRIVINGS	(Direct Psychological Effects of Domain-Specific Mechanisms)
Level 3	CONCERNS, PROJECTS, TASKS	(Utilize Domain-General Mechanisms)
Level 4	SPECIFIC ACTION UNITS	(Utilize Domain-General Mechanisms)

EXAMPLE:

Evolved Motive Disposition	INTIMACY
Personal Striving	INTIMATE RELATIONSHIP WITH A PARTICULAR PERSON
Concern, Project, Task	Arrange meeting Improve appearance Get promotion
Action Units	Find phone number Begin dieting Work on weekends

Source: From L. Pervin (Ed.), *Goal Concepts in Personality and Social Psychology,* 1989. Reprinted by permission of Lawrence Erlbaum Associates, Inc.

ture can substantially influence personality through the resources, social structures, and social systems available in a specific environment to help achieve goals. Culture can therefore influence mean levels of personality, and values about the various personality traits. Culture is "undeniably relevant in the development of characteristics and adaptations that guide the expression of personality in thoughts, feelings, and behaviors" (McCrae et al., 1998). Culture defines context and provides differential meaning to the components of context, including who is involved, what is happening, where it is occurring, and the like. Culture, therefore, plays a substantial role in producing the specific behavioral manifestations—the specific action units—that individuals will engage in to achieve what may be universal affective goals. A universal personality structure, however, is considered to be the mechanism by which such goals are achieved through a balance and interaction with culture.

The utility of the approach offered by the FFM, along with its underlying concept of a universal personality structure, continues to receive considerable support in the literature. Recent research has shown that the FFM can predict variations in behavior within individuals in longitudinal studies (Borkenau & Ostendorf, 1998) and is stable across different instruments and observers (McCrae & Costa, 1987). Some recent evidence even suggests that the FFM may apply to nonhuman primates as well. King and Figueredo (1997) presented 43 trait adjectives with representative items from the FFM to zoo trainers who work with chimpanzees in 12 different zoos. The trainers were asked to describe the chimpanzees in terms of the adjectives provided. The results showed no differences between the zoos, and the interrater reliability among the raters was high. Factor analysis of the ratings produced six factors, five of which corresponded to the FFM; the sixth corresponded to dominance. Of course, the findings from this study are not conclusive. A conservative interpretation would be that they merely indicate that human raters use their implicit theories of personality to rate nonhumans. Taken in conjunction with the growing literature concerning the relationship between biological and genetic factors and personality, however, they suggest that the FFM may be indicative of a universal personality structure that may be applicable not only to humans but also to nonhuman primates and perhaps other mammals as well (McCrae et al., 1998).

The Measurement of Personality across Cultures

One of the most serious issues in all cross-cultural research on personality is whether or not personality can be measured reliably and validly across different cultures. If methods of assessing personality are not reliable or valid across cultures, then the results of research using these methods cannot be trusted to give accurate portrayals of personality similarities or differences across cultures.

Most personality measures used in cross-cultural research were originally developed in a single language and single culture, and validated in that language and culture. The psychometric evidence typically used to demonstrate a measure's reliability and validity in a single culture involves examination of internal, test–retest, and parallel forms reliabilities, convergent and predictive validities, and replicability of the factor structures that comprise the various scales of the test. To obtain all these types of psychometric evidence for the reliability and validity of a test, researchers must literally spend years conducting countless studies addressing each of these specific concerns. The best measures of personality—as well as all other psychological constructs—have this degree of psychometric evidence backing them.

To validate personality measures cross-culturally requires similar psychometric evidence from all cultures in which the test is to be used. In the strictest sense, therefore, researchers interested in cross-cultural studies on personality should select instruments that have been demonstrated to have acceptable psychometric properties. This is a far cry from merely selecting a test that seems to be interesting and translating it for use in another culture. At the very least, equivalence of its psychometric properties should be established empirically, not assumed or ignored.

Data addressing the psychometric evidence necessary to validate a test in a target culture would provide the safest avenue by which such equivalence can be demonstrated. If such data exist, they can be used to support contentions concerning psychometric equivalence. Even if those data do not offer a high degree of support (reliability coefficients are lower, or factor structures are not exactly equivalent), that does not necessarily mean that the test as a whole is not equivalent. There are, in fact, multiple alternative explanations of why such data may not be as strong in the target culture as in the culture in which the test was originally developed. Paunonen and Ashton (1998) outline and describe ten such possible interpretations, ranging from poor test translation and response style issues to different analytic methods. Thus, if a test is examined in another culture for its psychometric properties and the data are not as strong as they were in the original culture, each of these possibilities should be examined before concluding that the test is not psychometrically valid or reliable. In many cases, the problem may be minor and fixable.

Given these criteria, how have the various personality tests used in cross-cultural research fared? Paunonen and Ashton (1998) have reviewed the data concerning the California Psychological Inventory, the Comrey Personality Scales, the 16 Personality Factors Questionnaire, the Pavlovian Temperament Survey, the Personality Research Form, and the Nonverbal Personality Questionnaire. After reviewing each test's reliability, convergent validity, predictive validity, and factor structure invariance, these writers conclude that "(a) structured tests of personality can readily be adapted for use in a wide variety of cultures, and (b) there is an organization to many Western-derived personality traits that appears to be universal, or at least general to many of the world's cultures" (p. 165). Clearly, this conclusion is consonant with the notion of personality structure as universal in humans. Other recent studies (for example, Benet-Martinez & John, 1998) have also provided evidence for the psychometric equivalence of measures of the Five Factor Model. These data provide some degree of reassurance that the cross-cultural studies reviewed in this chapter have measured personality in psychometrically acceptable ways.

Culture and Indigenous Personalities

As stated earlier in the chapter, indigenous personalities are conceptualizations of personality developed in a particular culture that are specific and relevant only to that culture. In general, not only are the concepts of personality rooted in and derived from the particular cultural group under question, but the methodologies used to test and examine those concepts are also particular to that culture. Thus, in contrast to much of the research described so far, in which standardized personality measures are used to assess personality dimensions, studies of indigenous personalities often use their own nonstandardized methodologies.

Over the years, many scientists have been interested in indigenous conceptions of personality, and have described many different personality constructs considered to exist only in specific cultures. Berry and colleagues (1992) examined three such indigenous personality concepts, each of which is fundamentally different from American or Western concepts. The African model of personality, for example, views personality as consisting of three layers, each representing a different aspect of the person. The first layer, found at the core of the person and personality, embodies a spiritual principle; the second layer involves a psychological vitality principle; the third layer involves a physiological vitality principle. The body forms the outer framework that houses all these layers of the person. In addition, family lineage and community affect different core aspects of the African personality (Sow, 1977, 1978, cited in Berry et al., 1992; see also Vontress, 1991).

Doi (1973) has postulated *amae* as a core concept of the Japanese personality. The root of this word means "sweet," and loosely translated, *amae* refers to the passive, childlike dependence of one person on another. It is said to be rooted in mother–child relationships. According to Doi, all Japanese relationships can be characterized by *amae*, which serves as a fundamental building block of Japanese culture and personality. This fundamental interrelationship between higher- and lower-status people in Japan serves as a major component not only of individual psychology but of interpersonal relationships, and it does so in ways that are difficult to grasp from a North American individualistic point of view.

Early work in this area produced findings of many other personality constructs thought to be culture-specific. Such constructs have included the national character or personality of Arab culture (Beit-Hallahmi, 1972), North Alaskan Eskimos (Hippler, 1974), the Japanese (Sakamoto & Miura, 1976), the Fulani of Nigeria (Lott & Hart, 1977), the Irulas of Palamalai (Narayanan & Ganesan, 1978), Samoans (Holmes, Tallman, & Jantz, 1978), South African Indians (Heaven & Rajab, 1983), and the Ibo of Nigeria (Akin-Ogundeji, 1988). Researchers using standardized personality tests have found that scales derived from such tests are not fully adequate to describe personality in some cultures, such as India (Narayanan, Menon, & Levine, 1995) and the Philippines (Church, Katigbak, & Reyes, 1996; Church, Reyes, Katigbak, & Grimm, 1997).

Indigenous personality measures—that is, measures developed for use in a particular culture—give us further ideas and insights about the nature of indigenous psychologies and personalities. Cheung and Leung (1998), for example, reviewed three measures of personality developed for use in Chinese cultures. Of them, the Chinese Personality Assessment Inventory (CPAI) most resembles the standardized personality measures familiar to Americans and Europeans. Factor analyses of its items, however, produced four major scales: Dependability, Chinese Tradition, Social Potency, and Individualism. Although there is some overlap between the concepts underlying these scales and the FFM, there are also clear discrepancies (such as Chinese Tradition). It seems that some aspects of personality that are relevant and important to Chinese culture are probably not captured in traditional personality measures that assess the Big Five.

Other indigenous personality descriptions from various cultures include the Korean concept of *cheong* (human affection; Choi, Kim, & Choi, 1993); the Indian concept of *hishkama karma* (detachment; Sinha, 1993); the Chinese concept of *ren qin* (relationship orientation; Cheung et al., 1996); the Mexican concept of *simpatia* (avoidance of conflict; Triandis, Marin, Lisansky, & Betancourt, 1984); and the Filipino concepts of *pagkikipagkapwa* (shared identity), *pakikiramdam* (sensitivity, empathy), and *pakikisama* (going along with others; Enriquez, 1992) (all cited in Church, 2000, p. 654).

Clearly, this line of research suggests that not all aspects of personality in the various cultures of the world can be adequately defined and measured by concepts and traits such as those described in the FFM. Indeed, much of the work on indigenous psychology and personality has provided fuel for those who subscribe to the cultural psychology school—the view that culture and personality are mutually constituted. In this view, it makes no sense to consider personality as a universal construct; instead, it makes more sense to understand each culture's personalities as they exist and have developed within that culture.

The cultural psychology viewpoint rejects the notion of a universal organization to personality that may have genetic, biological, and evolutionary components. Its proponents argue that the research supporting universality and its possible biological substrates may be contaminated by the methods used. These methods, the argument goes, have been developed in American or European research laboratories by American or European researchers; because of this cultural bias, the findings support the FFM as a default by-product of the methods. Indigenous approaches, it is claimed, are immune from such bias because their methods are centered around concepts and practices that are local to the culture being studied (see, however, the replication of the FFM using nontraditional methods of assessing taxonomies of trait adjectives in multiple languages; De Raad, Perugini, Hrebickova, & Szarota, 1998).

Is there a middle ground? We believe there is. In the past, scientists interested in cross-cultural psychology have tended to think about universal and culture-specific aspects of psychological phenomena—personality, emotion, language, and the like—as mutually exclusive, dichotomous categories. Thus, personality is either universal or indigenous. A better and more fruitful approach might be to consider the question not of whether personality is universal or indigenous, but rather how personality is both universal and culture-specific. It is entirely possible that some aspects of personality may be organized in a universal fashion, either because of biological or genetic factors or because of culture-constant learning and responses to the environment. The fact that some aspects of personality may be organized universally, however, does not necessarily argue against the possibility that other aspects of personality may be culturally unique. It may be these culturally unique aspects that give personality its own special flavor in each specific cultural milieu, and allow researchers the possibility of studying aspects of personality that they might not observe in other cultures. Thus, a more beneficial way of understanding the relationship between culture and personality may be to see indigenous and universal aspects of personality as two sides of the same coin, rather than as mutually exclusive. If we come to understand the relationship between culture and personality (and biology, for that matter) in ways that allow for the coexistence of universality and indigenization, then we can tackle the problem of exactly how to conceptualize and study this coexistence.

 **Conclusion**

In this chapter, we have discussed the major approaches to understanding and studying the relationship between culture, self, and personality, and have examined many different types of studies on this topic. Cross-cultural studies have shown that cultures differ considerably in their conceptualizations of the self. It has been argued that people from Western, individualistic cultures tend to view and value the self from an independent perspective in which self is a separate entity, not bound to the specific context. In contrast, those from non-Western, collectivistic cultures view and value the self from a more interdependent perspective, in which self is connected to and inseparable from the specific context and relationship. Research has shown that adopting these different senses of self has consequences for our cognitions, motivations, and emotions—affecting, for instance, our self-perceptions, achievement motivations, and feelings of happiness. Future research needs to investigate how different construals of self can exist simultaneously across contexts and cultures to clarify the relationship between culture and self, and how culture influences individual characteristics and behaviors via self.

Cross-cultural studies of personality dimensions have shown many ways in which cultures may differ in mean levels of personality. More recent research on the organization of personality, however, suggests that the Five Factor Model—a constellation of personality traits comprising Neuroticism, Extroversion, Openness, Conscientiousness, and Agreeableness—may be universal to all humans. Some research has also provided support for the existence of these factors in nonhuman primates. Research on indigenous approaches to personality, however, have demonstrated culturally specific aspects of personality that cannot be accounted for by the FFM. These two seemingly disparate sets of findings suggest a conflict in our understanding of the relationship between culture and personality, represented by the cross-cultural psychology versus cultural psychology schools of thought. We have suggested that these two seemingly opposing viewpoints need not be seen as mutually exclusive; rather, it may be more beneficial to view them as different, coexisting aspects of personality. The challenge for future research is to capture this coexistence, examining the relative degree of contribution of biological and cultural factors in the development and organization of personality.

In our quest to understand the relationship among culture, self, and personality, one of the biggest issues we will need to tackle concerns the influence of context, and the effects of context on that understanding. As we have seen, context is a major dimension of culture (Hall, 1966). High-context cultures place little value on cross-context consistency, allowing (and necessitating) behaviors and cognitions that differ according to context or situation. Low-context cultures, in contrast, discourage cross-context differences, emphasizing instead consistency and stability across contexts. American culture is relatively low-context, emphasizing stability. It is only within this type of cultural context that we can even conceive of personality as a set of enduring characteristics with stability and consistency across cultures. Thus, a person in this cultural context should exhibit similar personality characteristics despite considerable differences in context.

It is relatively easy to demonstrate the existence of context specificity effects in assessments of personality. In one study, participants were randomly assigned to fill out a personality test under several conditions (Schmit, Ryan, Stierwalt, & Powell, 1995). The personality test was the NEO Five Factor Inventory (Costa & McCrae, 1989). One group completed the measure in the usual way with general directions. Another group completed the measure as if they were applying for a customer service representative job in a department store, a job they really wanted. Even with this simple context manipulation, an analysis of the data indicated that students' responses differed substantially under the two conditions. Compared to students in the general condition, participants in the work-related condition gave significantly lower ratings on neuroticism and significantly higher ratings on extroversion, agreeableness, and conscientiousness. Thus, context specificity in personality assessment can be obtained with American participants as well, further challenging our traditional notions of personality, and the very definition of personality. Ultimately, these concerns need to be addressed in future work as well.

Glossary

achievement motivation   A desire for excellence.

cognitive template   A logical framework that serves as the basis for understanding ourselves and others.

false uniqueness effect   The tendency for individuals to underestimate the commonality of desirable traits and to overestimate their uniqueness.

filial piety   A sense of duty and obligation to family members, especially parents. This sense is especially strong in Asian and other collectivistic cultures.

fundamental attribution error   A tendency to explain the behaviors of others using internal attributions but to explain one's own behaviors using external attributions.

independent construal of self   A sense of self that views the self as a bounded entity, clearly separated from relevant others.

indigenous emotions   Emotions relatively specific to particular cultures.

indigenous personalities   Conceptualizations of personality developed in a particular culture

that are specific and relevant only to that culture.

interdependent construal of self   A sense of self that views the self as unbounded, flexible, and contingent on context. This sense of self is based on a principle of the fundamental connectedness among people.

locus of control   People's attributions of control over their behaviors and relationships as internal or external to themselves. People with an internal locus of control see their behavior and relationships with others as dependent on their own behavior. People with an external locus of control see their behavior and relationships as contingent upon forces outside themselves and beyond their control.

personality   A set of relatively enduring behavioral and cognitive characteristics, traits, or predispositions that people take with them to different situations, contexts, and interactions with others, and that contribute to differences among individuals.

self-concept   The way in which we understand or construe our sense of self or being.

self-enhancement A collection of psychological processes by which individuals maintain or enhance their self-esteem.

self-serving bias A bias in which people tend to attribute good deeds and successes to their own internal attributes but attribute bad deeds or failures to external factors.

socially disengaged emotions Emotions that tend to separate or disengage the self from so-cial relationships and to promote the perceived independence of the self from those relationships.

socially engaged emotions Emotions that lead to behaviors that engage and assimilate the self in social relationships and enhance the perceived interdependence of the self with others.

InfoTrac College Edition

Use InfoTrac College Edition to search for additional readings on topics of interest to you. For more information on topics in this chapter, use the following as search terms:

culture and the self
interdependent self
multicultural identity
culture and personality
culture and the Big Five
indigenous personality

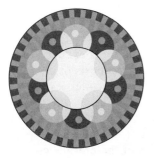

12

Culture and Abnormal Psychology

One important goal of psychology is to use the knowledge gained through research to help people suffering from psychological disorders to rid themselves of symptomatology and lead more effective, productive, and happy lives. Several themes have guided research and practice in this area of psychology. First and foremost are questions concerning definitions of abnormality—what is abnormal behavior? A second set of questions relates to the expression of abnormal behavior and our ability to detect it and classify it when it is expressed (assessment and diagnosis). A third question concerns how we should treat abnormal behavior when it is detected. This chapter will address the first two of the questions, and the next chapter will address the treatment of abnormal behavior.

Culture adds an important dimension to these basic questions. Incorporating culture into our psychological theories and concepts raises a number of important issues with regard to abnormal behaviors (Marsella, 1979):

- Do definitions of normality and abnormality vary across cultures, or are there universal standards of abnormality?
- Do cultures vary in rates of abnormal behavior?
- Is abnormal behavior expressed in the same way across cultures, or can we identify culturally distinct patterns of abnormal behavior?
- Can the field develop cross-culturally reliable and valid ways of measuring, classifying, and diagnosing abnormal behaviors?
- How do psychotherapeutic approaches need to be modified in order to deal effectively with cultural influences on abnormality?

The answers to these questions have important implications for how we identify abnormal behavior and intervene to effect change. A poor understanding of the ways in which abnormal behavior is bound within the context of culture may lead to overdiagnosis, underdiagnosis, and/or misdiagnosis of distress symptoms (Paniagua, 2000), with potentially harmful consequences to the individual.

This chapter is devoted to the considerable amount of research and writing that seeks to address these questions and concerns. First, we will discuss the role of culture in defining abnormality, review studies of the prevalence and course of schizophrenia and depression across cultures, and describe a number of culture-specific psychological disorders. As you will see, culture plays a major role in shaping people's experience of psychological disorder. Second, we will discuss the role of culture in the assessment of abnormal behaviors, examine the classification schemes currently in use, and explore some issues surrounding the actual measurement of abnormality. Third, we will look at how the measurement of personality has been used in assessing psychopathology across cultures. Finally, we'll cover a topic of increasing interest in the field of culture and mental health: the potentially psychologically stressful experiences of migrant populations.

Defining Abnormality: Some Core Issues

Psychologists and other social scientists have long been interested in the influence of culture on psychopathology, or abnormal behaviors. Historically, the literature has been somewhat divided between two points of view (for a more detailed review, see Draguns, 1997). One view suggests that culture and psychopathology are inextricably intertwined, and that abnormal behaviors can only be understood within the cultural framework within which they occur. This perspective is known as **cultural relativism.** The contrasting view suggests that although culture plays a role in determining the exact behavioral and contextual manifestations of abnormal behavior, there are cross-cultural similarities, even universalities, in the underlying psychological mechanisms and subjective experiences of many psychological disorders.

Consider, for example, the following scenario:

> A woman is in the midst of a group of people but seems totally unaware of her surroundings. She is talking loudly to no one in particular, often using words and sounds the people around her find unintelligible. When questioned later about her behavior, she reports that she had been possessed by the spirit of an animal and was talking with a man who had recently died.

Is this woman's behavior abnormal?

In defining abnormal behavior, American psychologists often use a statistical approach or apply criteria of impairment or inefficiency, deviance, or subjective distress. Using a statistical approach, for example, we could define the woman's behavior as abnormal because its occurrence is rare or infrequent. Being out of touch with your surroundings, having delusions (mistaken beliefs) that you are an animal, and talking with the dead are not common experiences.

One problem with this approach to abnormality, however, is that not all rare behavior is disordered. Nor is all disordered behavior rare! Composing a concerto and speaking four languages are uncommon behaviors, yet we generally view them as highly desirable. Conversely, drinking to the point of drunkenness occurs quite frequently in the United States (and in many other countries of the world). Nevertheless, drunkenness is widely recognized as a sign of a possible substance abuse disorder.

Another traditional approach to defining abnormality focuses on whether an individual's behavior is associated with impairment or inefficiency when carrying out customary roles. It is hard to imagine the woman described here carrying out normal day-to-day functions, such as caring for herself and working, while she believes herself to be an animal. In many instances, psychological disorders do involve serious impairments or a reduction in an individual's overall functioning. However, this is not always the case. Some people suffering from bipolar disorder (manic-depression), for example, report enhanced productivity during manic episodes.

If we examine the woman's behavior in terms of deviance, we might also conclude that it is abnormal, because it seems to go against social norms. But not all behavior that is socially deviant can be considered abnormal or psychologically disordered. For example, many people continue to believe that homosexuality is deviant, although it is no longer classified as a mental disorder in the United States (American Psychiatric Association, 1987). Although some Americans may view homosexuality as abnormal, in other cultures and at various periods in history homosexuality has been widely practiced. Lee (2001) reports that homosexuality is still considered pathological in China, partly because homosexuals are not so organized as they are in the United States and thus do not have the power and influence to challenge social norms on this issue. He believes that with time, however, homosexuality will no longer be classified as a mental disorder. Thus, using societal norms as a criterion for abnormality is difficult not only because norms change over time but because they are subjective. What one member of a society or culture considers deviant, another may accept as normal.

Reliance on reports of subjective distress to define abnormal behavior is also problematic. Whether a person experiences distress as a consequence of abnormal behavior may depend on how others treat him or her. For example, if the woman just described is ridiculed, shunned, and viewed as "sick" because of her behavior, she may well experience distress. Conversely, if she is seen as having special powers and is part of an accepting circle, she may not be distressed at all.

Each of these more or less traditional ways of defining abnormality has advantages as well as disadvantages. These issues become even more complex when culture is considered. Definitions of abnormality may vary both within and across cultures.

As an alternative to these traditional approaches, many cross-cultural scholars argue that we can understand and identify abnormal behavior only if we take the cultural context into account. This viewpoint suggests that we must apply the principle of cultural relativism to abnormality. For example, the woman's behavior might appear disordered if it occurred on a street corner in a large city in the United States. It could, however, appear appropriate and understandable if it occurred in a shamanistic ceremony in which she was serving as healer. Cultures that believe in supernatural interventions are able to clearly distinguish when trance states and talking with spirits are an acceptable part of a healer's behavioral repertoire and when the same behaviors would be considered a sign of disorder (Murphy, 1976). Examples of such cultures include the Yoruba in Africa and some Eskimo tribes in Alaska. Along the same lines, behaviors associated with some religions (for example, revivalist Christian groups in the United States), such as speaking in tongues (glossolalia) and seeing visions, are widely practiced and accepted and may not necessarily indicate a mental disorder (Loewenthal, 1995).

Some behaviors, particularly those associated with psychosis (for example, delusions, hallucinations), are universally recognized as abnormal (Murphy, 1976). However, some investigators (for example, Kleinman, 1988; Marsella, 1979, 1980) argue that abnormality and normality are culturally determined concepts. These investigators point to the fact that cultures differ in their beliefs and attitudes about abnormal behavior. Others argue that seemingly abnormal behavior may be viewed through an entirely different lens, not as detrimental to one's mental health but as a positive and significant part of one's life experiences. For instance, against the backdrop of certain religions or spiritual beliefs, suffering and "abnormal" behaviors may be considered a normal part of life. The individual may not need to be "cured" from his or her disorder, but rather experience it as it is and accept it (Rhi, 2000).

Reliance on reports of subjective distress to define abnormal behavior is also problematic when considering abnormality across cultures. There is some indication that cultural groups vary in the degree of distress they report experiencing in association with psychological disorders. Kleinman (1988) describes research indicating that depressed Chinese and African samples report less guilt and shame than do depressed European American and European samples. The Chinese and African samples, however, report more somatic complaints. These findings may reflect a cultural response bias (see Chapter 2). Some cultural groups may have values that prohibit reporting or focusing on subjective distress, in contrast to Western notions of the importance of self-disclosure.

Whether to accept universal or culturally relative definitions of abnormality is a source of continuing controversy in psychology. Examination of the cross-cultural literature may help provide clues on how to understand the role of culture in contributing to abnormality.

Cross-Cultural Research on Abnormal Behaviors

Cross-cultural research over the years has provided a wealth of evidence suggesting that abnormal behaviors and psychopathology have both universal and culture-specific aspects. In this section, we will look at schizophrenia, depression, somatization, and a number of apparently culture-specific disorders.

Schizophrenia

Schizophrenia is part of a "group of psychotic disorders characterized by gross distortions of reality; withdrawal from social interaction; and disorganization of perception, thought, and emotion" (Carson, Butcher, & Coleman, 1988, p. 322). The prevalence rate has been estimated to be 1.3% in the general U.S. population (Keith, Regier, & Rae, 1991). Some theories concerning the etiology (causes) of schizophrenia give primacy to biological factors (for example, excess dopamine or other biochemical imbalances). Other theories emphasize family dynamics (for example, expression of hostility to the ill person). The diathesis–stress model of schizophrenia suggests that individuals with a biological predisposition to the disorder (diathesis) may develop the disorder following exposure to environmental stressors.

The World Health Organization (WHO, 1973, 1979, 1981) sponsored the International Pilot Study of Schizophrenia (IPSS) to compare the prevalence and course of the disorder of 1,202 patients in several countries: Colombia, Czechoslovakia, Denmark, England, India, Nigeria, the Soviet Union, Taiwan, and the United States. Following rigorous training in using the research assessment tool, psychiatrists in each of the countries achieved good reliability in diagnosing schizophrenia in patients included in the study. As a result, WHO investigators were able to identify a set of symptoms present across all cultures in the schizophrenic samples. These symptoms include lack of insight, auditory and verbal hallucinations, and ideas of reference (assuming one is the center of attention) (Leff, 1977). The WHO studies are widely cited to bolster arguments for the universality of schizophrenia.

But some important cross-cultural differences emerged as well. In a finding that took the investigators by surprise, the course of the illness was shown to be easier for patients in developing countries compared to those in highly industrialized countries. Patients in Colombia, India, and Nigeria recovered at faster rates than did those in England, the Soviet Union, or the United States. These differences were attributed to cultural factors such as the presence of extended kin networks, community support, and the tendency to return to work in developing countries.

The researchers also noted differences in symptom expression across cultures. Patients in the United States were less likely to demonstrate lack of insight and auditory hallucinations than were Danish or Nigerian patients. These findings may be related to cultural differences in values associated with insight and self-awareness, which are highly regarded in the United States but less well regarded in the other countries. Also, cultures may differ in their tolerance for particular symptoms; the Nigerian culture as a whole is more accepting of the presence of voices. Nigerian and Danish patients, however, were more likely to demonstrate catatonia (extreme withdrawal or agitation).

Kleinman (1988) and Leff (1981) have discussed some of the methodological problems that plagued the WHO studies—among them, an assessment tool that failed to tap culturally unique experiences and expressions of disorder. Kleinman also noted that the samples were made artificially homogeneous because of the selection criteria. He argued that the findings of cross-cultural differences might have been greater still had not the heterogeneity of the sample been reduced. Because the conclusions of the study emphasized the similarities and not the differences of schizophrenia across the various cultures, Kleinman (1995) states, "There is, then, a tacit professional ideology that exaggerates what is universal in psychiatric disorder and de-emphasizes what is culturally particular" (p. 636). Thus, the biases of the investigators may have led them to search for cultural commonalities while overlooking important cultural differences.

Other cross-cultural comparisons of schizophrenia (Leff, 1977; Murphy, 1982) have found evidence of cultural variations in rates and symptomatology. Murphy found that rates of admissions for schizophrenia are four times higher in Ireland than in England and Wales, suggesting that some features of Irish culture (for example, sharp wit, ambivalence toward individuality) may affect the incidence of schizophrenia. In an early study of New York psychiatric cases, Opler and Singer (1959) found that Irish American schizophrenic patients were more likely to experience paranoid delusions than were Italian American patients. The authors cited cultural differences in parenting to account for the difference. A study of Japanese schizophrenics (Sue & Morishima, 1982) indicated that they are more likely than their European American counterparts to be withdrawn and passive, conforming to cultural values.

Recent studies of schizophrenics have tested the theory that expressed emotion—family communication characterized by hostility and overinvolvement—increases the risk of relapse. The expressed emotion construct is important because it suggests that family and social interactions influence the course of schizophrenia. These interactions are influenced, in turn, by cultural values. Research indicates that expressed emotion predicts relapse in Western samples (Mintz, Mintz, & Goldstein, 1987). Kleinman (1988), however, notes the difficulties in using this construct in other cultures, particularly those that emphasize nonverbal communication. Karno and associates (1987) reported that expressed emotion also predicts relapse in Mexican Americans, but Kleinman questions whether measures of expressed emotion developed in one cultural context have validity in another. Paniagua (2000) states that cultural variations in language, style of emotional expressions, body language, and eye contact should all be considered when diagnosing schizophrenia.

Reports of cultural differences in diagnosis have also raised questions about the validity of assessment techniques used in cross-cultural comparisons of schizophrenia and other disorders (Kleinman, 1988; Leff, 1977). In a reanalysis of some of the early WHO data, Leff found that U.S. psychiatrists were more likely to give diagnoses of schizophrenia than were psychiatrists in England, and less likely to give diagnoses of depression. Abebimpe (1981) and Thomas and Sillen (1972) have documented that African Americans are more likely than European Americans to receive diagnoses of schizophrenia rather than depression, even when the symptom picture is the same. Racial bias seems to account for some of the differential pattern (Thomas & Sillen, 1972), and cultural differences in expression of symptomatology may also be important.

In summary, the WHO studies provide ample evidence of a universal set of core symptoms that may be related to schizophrenia. Other studies, however, help to temper this interpretation by documenting specific cultural differences in the exact manifestations, experience, and diagnosis of schizophrenia in different cultural contexts.

Depression

All of us have experienced moods of depression, sadness, or the blues in our lives. We may have these feelings in response to a death in the family, the breakup of a relationship, falling short of a goal, and other stresses or disappointments. The presence of a depressive disorder, however, involves symptoms of "intense sadness, feelings of futility and worthlessness, and withdrawal from others" (Sue, Sue, & Sue, 1990, p. 325). Depression is often characterized by physical changes (such as sleep and appetite disturbances) and motivational changes (such as apathy and boredom), as well as emotional and behavioral changes (such as feelings of sadness, hopelessness, and loss of energy) (Berry et al., 1992).

Depression is one of the most common psychological disorders in the United States. In a large-scale study, Myers and associates (1984) found that 3% and 7% of the adult male and female population, respectively, had experienced a depressive disorder in the previous six-month period. Lifetime prevalence rates for depression may be as high as 26% for women and 12% for men (Sue et al., 1990). There is also some evidence to suggest that the incidence of depression has risen over the past few decades (Robins et al., 1984), especially among adolescents (Lewinsohn, Rohde, Seeley, & Fischer, 1993). Developmentally, the incidence of depression increases dramatically around the time of puberty, at least in the United States, and more so for females than for males (Compas, Ey, & Grant, 1993). This gender difference remains throughout adulthood.

A study by WHO (1983) investigated the symptoms of depression in four countries—Canada, Switzerland, Iran, and Japan—and found that the great majority (76% of the 573 cases) reported cross-culturally constant symptoms, including "sadness, joylessness, anxiety, tension, lack of energy, loss of interest, loss of ability to concentrate, and ideas of insufficiency" (p. 61). More than half of this group (56%) also reported suicidal ideation. Based on these findings, Marsella (1980; Marsella, Sartorius, Jablensky, & Fenton, 1985) suggested that vegetative symptoms such as loss of enjoyment, appetite, or sleep are cross-culturally constant ways in which people experience depression. Other studies—for example, comparing Hungarians with Americans and Canadians (Keitner et al., 1991); of Iranians (Haghighatgou & Peterson, 1995); and of children in six countries (Yamamoto, Soliman, Parsons, & Davies, 1987)—have tended to support this viewpoint.

Other cross-cultural studies of depression, however, document wide variations in expression of symptomatology of this disorder. Some cultural groups (for example, Nigerians) are less likely to report extreme feelings of worthlessness and guilt-related symptoms. Others (for example, Chinese) are more likely to report somatic complaints (Kleinman, 1988). Indigenous expressions of depression for Hopi Indians include worry sickness and heartbrokenness (Manson, Shore, & Bloom, 1985). As with schizophrenia, rates of depression also vary from culture to culture (Marsella, 1980), ranging from 3.3% in South Korea to 6.24% in Iran to 12.6% in New Zealand (Hwu & Compton, 1994; Mehrabi et al., 2000). However, different assessments and manifestations of the disorder render it difficult to obtain comparable prevalence rates.

Leff (1977) argues that cultures vary in terms of their differentiation and communication of emotional terminology and, hence, in how they experience and express depression. Some cultures have few words to convey emotions such as sadness or anger (see Chapter 9). Also, cultures locate feeling states in different parts of the body. For instance, consider these lines from a tenth-century Beijing opera:

> Missing my dear mother, as a son
>   my liver and intestines are painfully broken!
> Crying for my old mother, as a son
>   my tears pour onto my chest! (quoted in Young, 1997, p. 43)

This may explain why some cultural groups emphasize somatic complaints in the expression of depression.

Kleinman (1978) takes the position that depressive disease reflects a biologically based disorder, whereas depressive illness refers to the personal and social experience of depression. In arguing for a culturally relative definition of depression, Kleinman (1988) writes that

> depression experienced entirely as low back pain and depression experienced entirely as guilt-ridden existential despair are such substantially different forms of illness behavior with distinctive symptoms, patterns of help seeking, and treatment responses that although the disease in each instance may be the same, the illness, not the disease, becomes the determinative factor. And one might well ask, is the disease even the same? (p. 25)

Although Kleinman accepts the idea that depressive disease is universal, he argues that the expression and course of the illness are culturally determined.

Marsella (1979, 1980) also argues for a culturally relative view of depression, saying that depression takes a primarily affective form in cultures with strong objective orientations (that is, individualistic cultures). In these cultures, feelings of loneliness and isolation dominate the symptom picture. In subjective cultures (those having a more communal structure), somatic symptoms such as headaches are dominant. Marsella (1979) has also proposed that depressive symptom patterns differ across cultures because of cultural variations in sources of stress as well as in resources for coping with the stress.

Other researchers also highlight the need to consider the current social and cultural environment of the disorder. For instance, the criteria for major depression in earlier editions of the *Chinese Classification of Mental Disorders* (CCMD) included a duration of symptoms for 4 weeks (in the most recent edition, it is 2 weeks). Earlier editions used 4 weeks because mental health professionals in China argued that "2 weeks of depressive symptoms could be difficult to distinguish from social suffering, which was common in China's history of wars, turmoil, and rapid social change" (Lee, 2001, p. 423). Thus, taking into account the broader social and historical context is important in defining disorders.

Thus, as with the cross-cultural work on schizophrenia, the literature on depression points to both universal and culture-specific ways in which the disorder may occur and be experienced across cultures.

Somatization

Many cross-cultural psychologists, psychotherapists, and counselors are sensitive to the issue of **somatization**—essentially, bodily complaints as expressions of psychological distress. Some studies have suggested that members of certain cultural groups, such as Hispanics (Koss, 1990), Japanese (Radford, 1989), Chinese (Kleinman, 1982), and Arabs (El-Islam, 1982) tend to somaticize more than Europeans or Americans. In fact, it has been commonly thought that such somatic complaints (for example, low back pain or intestinal problems) are just a code or camouflage for psychological symptoms.

Recent cross-cultural studies, however, challenge this viewpoint. Kirmayer (2001), for example, reviewed the available evidence and concluded that there was not much support for the notion that the degree and amount of somatization vary across cultures. Moreover, although Kleinman (1982) concluded that Chinese diagnoses of neurasthenia were really cases of depression, this view was not shared by the mainland Chinese psychiatrists (reported in Draguns, 1997). According to Lee (2001), Chinese psychiatrists believe that Chinese people do not camouflage but readily reveal psychological symptoms within the context of a trusting doctor–patient relationship and that "the coexistence of psychologic symptoms with the presenting physical symptoms is consonant with Chinese philosophy. This is because the development of the somatoform category is grounded in the Western intellectual legacy of mind–body dichotomy, which differs from the Oriental notions of balance of holism" (p. 423). Not only Chinese but Japanese psychiatrists also disagree with the concept of somatization (Yamashita & Koyama, 1994). Isaac, Janca, and Orley (1996) have reported that somatic expression of psychological distress is a universal phenomenon and that the presence of large numbers of somatic symptoms is strongly related to the overt expression of psychological distress in European and American cultures, too. Finally, Cheng, Leong, and Geist (1993) have shown that although Asian American students more often present academic and career issues when seeking counseling, these issues are actually associated with greater personal and emotional problems than they are for European American students.

Thus, the available research tends to suggest that, although previously considered a culture-specific phenomenon, somatization may be a universal phenomenon with culture-specific meanings and expression modes.

Culture-Bound Syndromes

The approach used in cross-cultural studies of depression and schizophrenia can be characterized as etic; that is, it assumes universally accepted definitions of abnormality and methodology (review Chapter 1 for definitions of *etic* and *emic*). In contrast to this etic approach are various ethnographic reports of culture-bound syndromes—forms of abnormal behavior observed only in certain sociocultural milieus. Findings concerning differential rates and courses of a disorder across cultures, and of culturally distinct forms of the disorder, suggest the importance of culture in shaping the expression of abnormal behavior. In fact, ethnographic reports of **culture-bound syndromes** provide perhaps the strongest support for cultural relativism in understanding and dealing with abnormality.

Using primarily emic (culture-specific) approaches involving ethnographic examinations of behavior within a specific cultural context, anthropologists and psychiatrists have identified several apparently unique forms of psychological disorder. Some similarities between symptoms of these culture-specific disorders and those recognized across cultures have been observed. The particular pattern of symptoms, however, typically does not fit the diagnostic criteria of psychological disorders recognized in Western classification schemes. A case study of a Korean woman (P. M.) reported by a Korean anthropologist (Harvey, 1979) illustrates the kinds of symptoms that are attributed to *sinbyong* (spirit sickness), which occurs when a woman is believed to be recruited to become a shaman.

> She was not only hearing things but seeing things as well. Her ears rang a lot and she could hear voices whispering in them; and when she yielded to the urge to talk she uttered prophetic statements. Neighbors and relatives began to speculate that she had been "caught by the spirit" and was possessed. She suffered from terrible palpitations of the heart, indigestion, and dizzy spells, sometimes alternately and sometimes in combinations. She was constantly afraid of being caught hallucinating by her husband or his family. She was determined to overcome these symptoms and began to read a lot of novels as a way of fighting off the hallucinations. (p. 105)

However, after experiencing several more episodes of *sinbyong*, Harvey reports that P. M. ultimately decided to accept her calling as a shaman, became quite successful, and made a good living.

Other culture-bound disorders have been documented by various writers. *Amok*, the most widely observed culture-bound syndrome, has been identified in several countries in Asia (Malaysia, Philippines, Thailand). The disorder is characterized by sudden rage and homicidal aggression. It is thought to be brought on by stress, sleep deprivation, and alcohol consumption (Carson et al., 1988) and has been observed primarily in males. Several stages of the disorder have been identified, ranging from extreme withdrawal prior to the assaultive behavior to exhaustion and amnesia for the rage. The term *running amok* derives from observations of this disorder.

Witiko (also known as *windigo*) is a disorder that has been identified in Algonquin Indians in Canada. It involves the belief that the individual has been possessed by the witiko spirit—a man-eating monster. Cannibalistic behavior may result, along with suicidal ideation to avoid acting on the cannibalistic urges (Carson et al., 1988).

Anorexia nervosa is a disorder identified in the West but not at first observed in Third World countries (Swartz, 1985). The disorder is characterized by a distorted body image, fear of becoming fat, and a serious loss of weight associated with food restraining or purging. Several factors have been cited as possible causes of this disorder, including a cultural emphasis on thinness as an ideal for women, constricted sex roles, and an individual's fear of being out of control or of taking on adult responsibilities. In countries where attention is not drawn to the female figure and the female body is usually entirely covered, such as in Saudi Arabia, eating disorders have not been mentioned in psychiatric literature until recently (Al-Subaie & Alhamad, 2000). Recent research has suggested that anorexia nervosa is no longer limited to Europe and North America, but may now be found in many urbanized parts of the world such as Hong Kong, Korea, Singapore, and China (for example, Gordon, 2001; Hoek, van Harten, van Hoeken, & Susser, 1998; Lee, 1995; Goh, Ong, & Subramaniam, 1993). However, the particular criteria for being anorexic may differ slightly among different cultural groups. For instance, distinctive reasons for forced starvation in China is not a fear of getting fat, but having an "extreme distaste for food" or being "intolerably full" (Lee-Sing, Leung, Wing, & Chiu, 1991).

Ataque de nervios is observed in Latin American groups (Guarnaccia, Rivera, Franco, & Neighbors, 1996). Symptoms include trembling, uncontrollable shouting, intense crying, heat in the chest rising to the head, and dizziness. This disorder tends to surface during stressful family events, such as funerals, divorce or separation, or witnessing an accident including a family member.

Zar is an altered state of consciousness observed among Ethiopian immigrants to Israel (Grisaru, Budowski, & Witztum, 1997). The belief in possession by Zar spirits, common in Africa, is expressed by involuntary movements, mutism, and incomprehensible language.

Whakama is a New Zealand Maori construct that includes shame, self-abasement, feelings of inferiority, inadequacy, self-doubt, shyness, excessive modesty, and withdrawal (Sachdev, 1990). It does not have an exact equivalent in European or American societies.

"Sinking heart" is a condition of distress in the Punjabi culture (Krause, 1989). It is experienced as physical sensations in the heart or chest, and is thought to be caused by excessive heat, exhaustion, worry, or social failure. It has some characteristics of depression but also resembles a cardiovascular disorder.

Avanga is actually a constellation of other, more specific forms of disorder, all of which include a vivid, imaginary companionship with a single external spirit. Originating in Tongan culture, its incidence is on the rise as people move toward cities and urbanization (Puloka, 1997).

Qigong-induced mental disorder is a condition induced by overengaging in a trance-based form of a traditional Chinese healing system that includes meditation and exercise movements (Lee, 2001). A specific form of *qigong, falungong,* may be familiar to the reader. The symptoms include somatic discomforts, motor overactivity, anxiety, weepiness, irritability, delusions, and bizarre and violent behavior.

Other culture-bound syndromes, cited in literature reviews by Kiev (1972) and Yap (1974), include *latah* (characterized by hysteria and echolalia, observed primarily in women in Malaysia); *koro* (extreme fear that the penis is shrinking or retracting, observed in Southeast Asian men, or extreme fear that the nipples are retracting, observed in Southeast Asian women); and *susto* (characterized by depression and apathy thought to reflect "soul loss," observed in Indians of the Andean highlands). Other writers have suggested that some conditions found in American society, such as premenstrual syndrome, are culture-bound syndromes (for example, Hill & Fortenberry, 1992; Johnson, 1987). Many other such culture-bound syndromes have been documented around the world.

Yap (1974) has attempted to organize information concerning culture-bound syndromes into a classification scheme that parallels Western diagnostic schemes. In this scheme, for example, *latah* and *susto* are viewed as unique cultural expressions of universal primary fear reactions, and *amok* is seen as a unique cultural expression of a universal rage reaction. Yap recognizes that his attempt to subsume culture-bound syndromes into a universal classification scheme may be premature, particularly since Western clinical tools and methods of research may make it difficult to assess culturally diverse expressions of abnormal behavior.

Pfeiffer (1982) has identified four dimensions for understanding culture-bound syndromes. First, he cites culture-specific areas of stress, including family and societal structure and ecological conditions. For example, *koro* might be best understood as resulting from the unique emphasis on potency in certain cultures that emphasize paternal authority. Then, culture-specific shaping of conduct and interpretations of conduct may mean that certain cultures implicitly approve patterns of exceptional behavior. An example is amok, in which aggression against others "broadly follows the patterns of societal expectations" (p. 206). Finally, Pfeiffer argues that how a culture interprets exceptional behavior will be linked to culture-specific interventions. For example, interventions to heal the soul loss associated with *susto* will involve sacrifices carried out by a native healer to appease the earth so that it will return the soul.

Some scholars (for example, Kleinman, 1988; Marsella, 1979; Pfeiffer, 1982) argue that current Western classification schemes cannot be used to understand culture-bound syndromes because they are experienced from a qualitatively different point of view. They argue that culture shapes the experience of psychological disorder, both in determining the expression of symptoms of universal disorders and in contributing to the emergence of culture-specific disorders. Recognizing the role of culture in shaping abnormal behavior requires that we reexamine the way we assess and treat individuals with psychological disorders.

Paniagua (1998, 2000) offers four assessment guidelines for practitioners to distinguish psychopathology and culture-related conditions: (1) They should familiarize themselves with the cultural background of the client by consulting with family members, peers, and folk healers (such as medicine men and women for Native Americans). For example, "if an American Indian client reports that 'I believe that my weakness, loss of appetite, fainting are the result of the action of witches and evil supernatural forces,' this statement would be an example of schizophrenia in the case of a clinician unfamiliar with the effect of 'ghost sickness' among American Indians" (2000, p. 158). (2) Practitioners should check their own cultural biases and prejudice before attempting to evaluate clients who are culturally different. (3) Practitioners should not immediately jump to the conclusion that the client's symptoms are manifestations of a culture-bound syndrome simply because the client is of that culture. (4) Practitioners should ask culturally appropriate questions that would allow the client and family members to elaborate on possible cultural factors that may help explain the disorder under consideration. Paniagua suggests, for example, that it is inappropriate to ask very traditional Latino parents a question such as "Do you really think *susto* can explain what is going on with your daughter?" It may appear that the practitioner is questioning what may be a deep-seated belief in *susto* as a possible cause of mental illness.

Summary

The material reviewed in this section suggests that there are universal aspects of symptomatology and disease expression for at least some of the major psychopathologies such as depression and schizophrenia. At the same time, however, it also suggests that psychopathologies are heavily influenced by culture, especially in terms of the specific behavioral and contextual manifestations of the abnormal behavior, and the meaning of the behavior to the lifestyles and lives of individuals. The existence of culture-bound syndromes—disorders that appear to occur only in specific cultural milieus—reinforces the position of the cultural relativists.

We began this section by positing two viewpoints about the relationship between culture and abnormal behavior: the universalist position and the cultural-relativist position. The research reviewed here provides ample evidence for both positions, indicating that psychopathology across cultures contains both universal and culturally specific components. Other writers who have reviewed the field in far more depth—including Al-Issa (1995), Draguns (1997), Pfeiffer (1994), and Tanaka-Matsumi and Draguns (1997)—have reached the same conclusion. Draguns, for example, concludes that "neither [position] should be disregarded or exaggerated and both should be sensitively and realistically blended in providing service across cultural lines" (p. 230). We still have a long way to go in infusing both etic and emic perspectives on mental disorders.

Culture and the Assessment of Abnormal Behavior

Assessment of abnormal behavior involves identifying and describing an individual's symptoms "within the context of his or her overall level of functioning and environment" (Carson et al., 1988, p. 531). The tools and methods of assessment should be sensitive to cultural and other environmental influences on behavior and functioning. Although the field has made considerable progress over the years, the literature on standard assessment techniques indicates that there may be problems of bias or insensitivity when psychological tests and methods developed in one cultural context are used to assess behavior in a different context.

Culture and Psychiatric Diagnoses

In assessing abnormal behavior, psychologists seek to classify abnormal behaviors into categories—diagnoses—that are both reliable and valid. Reliability, as you will recall, has to do with the degree to which the same diagnoses would be made consistently over time and by different clinicians; validity refers to the degree to which the diagnosis accurately portrays the clinical disorder it is supposed to describe.

Because culture exerts some degree of influence on the creation, maintenance, and definition of abnormal behaviors, cross-cultural issues arise concerning the reliability and validity of diagnoses, and even of the diagnostic categories used. If all abnormal behaviors were entirely etic in their expression and presentation—that is, entirely the same across cultures—then creating reliable and valid diagnostic categories would not be a problem. But just as individuals differ in their presentation of abnormality, cultures also vary; indeed, some culture-bound syndromes appear to be limited to only one or a few cultures. Thus, developing diagnostic systems and classifications that can be reliably and validly used across cultures around the world, or across different cultural groups within a single country, becomes a challenge.

One of the most widely used systems of classification is the American Psychiatric Association's *Diagnostic and Statistical Manual of Mental Disorders* (DSM). The DSM, originally published in 1952, has undergone several major revisions and is now in its fourth edition (DSM-IV). Some of the changes from DSM-III to DSM-IV represent the field's response to heavy criticism by cross-cultural psychiatrists.

> A large number of disorders described in the manual were different or simply did not exist in societies and cultures beyond the Western world. It was repeatedly noted that, after all, 80% of the world population does not belong to the Western cultural sphere, and that the manual could lose credibility, its international popularity notwithstanding.
>
> . . .
>
> Diagnosis does not mean to drive an individual into a particular slot; ethnicity, diversity, and pluralism should be duly recognized as politically important. . . .

For culture to be built into the DSM-IV, diagnosticians always should be reminded that their task is essentially cultural: The patient and the clinician each brings his or her own culture, and the clinician–patient encounter realizes culture. (Alarcon, 1995, pp. 452, 455)

To address these criticisms, several modifications were made to the DSM-IV to increase its cultural sensitivity: (1) incorporating information on how the clinical manifestations of the disorders can vary by culture; (2) including 25 culture-bound syndromes in an appendix (some of which have been mentioned in this chapter); and (3) adding guidelines for in-depth assessment of the individual's cultural background, including cultural expressions of the individual's disorder, cultural factors related to psychosocial functioning in the individual's specific cultural context, and cultural differences between the clinician and the individual (American Psychiatric Association, 1994). Thus, the DSM-IV has taken considerable steps to incorporate the role of culture in the expression and reliable classification of psychological disorders. However, the DSM-IV does not go so far as to *require* an assessment of cultural elements that may be necessary to recognize and classify a culture-bound syndrome (Paniagua, 2000). Thus, challenges to the DSM-IV remain, especially concerning its difficulty in classifying culture-bound syndromes.

Another well-known and often used classification system is the *International Classification of Diseases*, Tenth Edition (ICD-10). Its section on mental health includes 100 major diagnostic categories encompassing 329 individual clinical classifications. It is intended to be descriptive and atheoretical. Unfortunately, reviews of ICD-10 (for example, Alarcon, 1995) have suggested that it fails to recognize the importance of culture in influencing the expression and presentation of disorder.

To address the problem of the lack of cultural considerations in the assessment of mental disorders, local diagnostic systems have been created. The *Chinese Classification of Mental Disorders* (CCMD), for example, has been heavily influenced by the DSM-IV and ICD-10 but has culture-specific features that do not exist in the international systems. The most recent edition, the CCMD-3, was revised in 2001. This manual includes disorders distinctive to Chinese culture (such as the *qigong*-induced mental disorder) and excludes irrelevant disorders (such as sibling rivalry, because of the one-child policy). In the mid-1980s, three African psychiatrists developed a handbook for North African practitioners (Douki, Moussaoui, & Kacha, 1987). Surely, we will see more and more indigenously created manuals to classify mental disorders across cultures.

Having a reliable and valid classification system of diagnoses would be a major plus for all health professionals and the people they seek to help. The DSM-IV seems to have made major strides toward creating such a system. Still, work in this area is continually evolving, and we are sure to see future changes in this and other classification systems. Hopefully, those changes will be informed by meaningful and relevant cross-cultural research. One such attempt to develop more culturally sensitive, valid, and reliable diagnoses can be found in the research journal *Culture, Medicine and Psychiatry*, which devotes a special "Clinical Cases Section" to case studies of individuals within their specific cultural context (Tanaka-Matsumi, 2001). The case narratives include a clinical case history, cultural formulation, cultural identity, cultural explanation of the illness, cultural factors related to psychosocial environment and levels of functioning, cultural elements of the clinician–patient relationship, and overall cultural assessment. Attempts such as this should benefit the development of more culturally valid classification manuals of disorders.

Cross-Cultural Assessment of Abnormal Behavior

Not only is it important to have a reliable and valid system of classification of abnormal behaviors; it is also important to have a set of tools that can reliably and validly measure behaviors, feelings, and other psychological parameters related to mental illness. Those tools may include questionnaires, interview protocols, or standardized tasks that require some sort of behavior on the part of the test taker.

Needless to say, many of the issues that concern the valid and reliable measurement of any psychological variable cross-culturally for research purposes are also relevant to discussions of measurement tools for abnormality. For instance, it may be difficult to adequately transfer and use a psychological assessment that has been developed in one culture to another because of cultural-specific expressions of distress. Kleinman (1995) points out that many items of an assessment instrument may use wordings that are so culture-specific (for example, "feeling blue") that directly translating them to another culture would be nonsensical. Draguns (1997) recently reviewed a number of issues in this area of psychological measurement, including stimulus equivalence, sample characteristics, comparability of constructs, structured self-reports, personal interviews, experimental apparatuses, and the impact of the examiner. These issues, and others, make valid and reliable measurement of pathology across cultures very difficult and complex.

A critical examination of how the tools in use fare across cultures provides a stark glimpse of reality. Traditional tools of clinical assessment in psychology are generally based on a standard definition of abnormality and use a standard set of classification criteria for evaluating problematic behavior. Therefore, the tools may have little meaning in cultures with varying definitions, however well translated into the native language; and they may mask or fail to capture culturally specific expressions of disorder (Marsella, 1979). The assessment problems encountered in studying schizophrenia and depression across cultures illustrate the limitations of traditional assessment methods.

The WHO studies described earlier, for example, used the Present State Examination (PSE) to diagnose schizophrenia. Leff (1986) has commented on the ethnocentric bias of procedures such as the PSE and the Cornell Medical Index. In a psychiatric survey of the Yoruba in Nigeria, investigators had to supplement the PSE to include culture-specific complaints such as feeling "an expanded head and goose flesh."

Standard diagnostic instruments to measure depressive disorder may also miss important cultural expressions of the disorder in Africans (Beiser, 1985) and Native Americans (Manson, Shore, & Bloom, 1985). In an extensive study of depression among Native Americans (Manson & Shore, 1981; Manson et al., 1985), the American Indian Depression Schedule (AIDS) was developed to assess and diagnose depressive illness. The investigators found that depression among the Hopi includes symptoms not measured by standard measures of depression such as the Diagnostic Interview Schedule (DIS) and the Schedule for Affective Disorders and Schizophrenia (SADS). These measures, based on diagnostic criteria found in the DSM-III (American Psychiatric Association, 1987), failed to capture the short but acute dysphoric moods sometimes reported by the Hopi (Manson et al., 1985).

Concerning children, the Child Behavior Checklist (CBCL; Achenbach, 2001) has been used to assess emotional and behavioral problems of children in various parts of the world, including Thailand, Kenya, and the United States (Weisz, Sigman, Weiss, & Mosk, 1993; Weisz et al., 1988); China (Su, Yang, Wan, Luo, & Li, 1999); Israel and Palestine (Auerbach, Yirmiya, & Kamel, 1996); and Australia, Jamaica, Greece, and nine other countries (Crijnen, Achenbach, & Verhulst, 1999). Generally, studies have found that U.S. children tend to exhibit higher levels of undercontrolled behaviors ("externalizing behaviors" such as acting out and aggression) and lower levels of overcontrolled behaviors ("internalizing" behaviors such as fearfulness and somaticizing) compared to children of other, particularly collectivistic, cultures. Thus, the CBCL (sometimes slightly modified) has been widely used in many cultures to assess problematic behaviors. However, a study that recruited American Indian (Dakota/Lakotan) parents to assess the acceptability and appropriateness of using the CBCL in their culture found that some questions were difficult for the parents to answer because the questions did not take into account Dakotan/Lakotan cultural values or traditions, and because the parents believed their responses would be misinterpreted by members of the dominant culture who did not have a good understanding of the Dakotan/Lakotan culture (Oesterheld, 1997). This underscores again the importance of critically examining assessment tools for use cross-culturally.

Several researchers (Higginbotham, 1979; Lonner & Ibrahim, 1989; Marsella, 1979) have offered guidelines for developing measures to use in cross-cultural assessment of abnormal behavior. They suggest that sensitive assessment methods examine sociocultural norms of healthy adjustment as well as culturally based definitions of abnormality. Higginbotham also suggests the importance of examining culturally sanctioned systems of healing and their influence on abnormal behavior. There is evidence that people whose problems match cultural categories of abnormality are more likely to seek folk healers (Leff, 1986). Failure to examine **indigenous healing systems** thus overlooks some expressions of disorder. Assessment of culturally sanctioned systems of cure should also enhance planning for treatment strategies, one of the primary goals of traditional assessment (Carson et al., 1988).

Other research has found that the cultural backgrounds of therapist and client may contribute to the perception and assessment of mental health. For instance, Li-Repac (1980) conducted a study to evaluate the role of culture in the diagnostic approach of therapists. In this study, Chinese American and European American male clients were interviewed and videotaped, then rated by Chinese American and European American male therapists on their level of psychological functioning. The results showed an interaction effect between the cultural backgrounds of therapist and client on the therapists' judgment of the clients. The Chinese American clients were rated as awkward, confused, and nervous by the European American therapists, but the same clients were rated as adaptable, honest, and friendly by the Chinese American therapists. In contrast, European American clients were rated as sincere and easygoing by European American therapists, but aggressive and rebellious by the Chinese American therapists. Furthermore, Chinese American clients were judged to be more depressed and less socially capable by the European American therapists, and European American clients were judged to be more severely disturbed by the Chinese American therapists. These findings illustrate how judgments of appropriate, healthy psychological functioning may differ depending on the cultural background and notions of normality of the person making the assessment.

Lopez (1989) has described two types of errors in making clinical assessments: overpathologizing and underpathologizing. **Overpathologizing** may occur when the clinician, unfamiliar with the client's cultural background, incorrectly judges the client's behavior as pathological when in fact the behaviors are normal variations to that individual's culture. For instance, in some cultures, hearing voices from a deceased relative is considered normal. A clinician unaware of this feature of his or her client's culture may overpathologize and mistakenly attribute this behavior to a manifestation of a psychotic disorder. **Underpathologizing** may occur when a clinician indiscriminantly explains the client's behaviors as cultural—for example, attributing a withdrawn and flat emotional expression to a normal cultural communication style when in fact this behavior may be a symptom of depression.

Finally, one interesting topic in recent literature concerns language issues in psychological testing. In more and more cases today, test takers (such as patients or clients) have a first language and culture that differ from the diagnostician's or clinician's. Some writers (for example, Oquendo, 1996a, 1996b) have suggested that evaluation of such bilingual patients should really be done in both languages, preferably by a bilingual clinician or with the help of an interpreter trained in mental health issues. The reason, as was discussed in Chapter 10, is that cultural nuances may be encoded in language in ways that are not readily conveyed in translation. That is, translations of key psychological phrases and constructs from one language to another may give the closest semantic equivalent, but may not have exactly the same nuances, contextualized meanings, and associations. Also, Oquendo (1996a) suggests that patients may use their second language as a form of resistance to avoid intense emotions. Administration of tests and therapy bilingually may help to bridge this gap.

The Measurement of Personality to Assess Psychopathology across Cultures

One of the interesting ways in which personality tests are used cross-culturally involves the assessment not only of personality but also of clinical states and psychopathology. The most widely used scale in such cross-cultural assessments is the Minnesota Multiphasic Personality Inventory (MMPI). Recently, Butcher, Lim, and Nezami (1998) reviewed the use of the MMPI in various countries and cultures, including six Asian cultures, six Spanish-speaking cultures, eight European cultures, and three cultures in the Middle East. They reported on the procedures most researchers used in adapting the MMPI for use in their particular cultural milieu, including translation and back-translation, bilingual test–retest evaluation, study of equivalency, and the like. They concluded:

> Clinical case studies involving the assessment of patients from different cultures have shown that MMPI-2 interpretations drawn from an American perspective generally produce congruent conclusions about clinical patients tested in other countries. . . . Computer-based MMPI-2 interpretations appear to have a high degree of accuracy when applied to patients from other countries. Computer-based reports derived on interpretive strategies developed for the United States were rated as highly accurate by clinicians when they were applied in Norway, Australia, and France. (p. 207)

Thus, clinical studies across cultures involving personality scales such as the MMPI have been shown to be quite reliable and valid in assessing psychopathology and abnormal behavior in other cultures as well. This finding is once again consistent with the premise of a universal underlying personality structure that can be reliably and validly assessed by methods typically developed and refined in the United States or Europe. If such a universal personality structure exists and can be measured by some means, then deviations from that personality structure in the form of psychopathology should also be measurable using those same means.

However, others argue that some of the items of the MMPI simply do not mean the same thing in other cultures. For instance, answering "yes" to items such as "Evil spirits possess me at times" may not be a marker of pathology for Puerto Rican individuals, as spiritism is widely practiced in that culture (Rogler, Malgady, & Rodriguez, 1989). To address these problems, there have been recent attempts at developing culture-specific measures of personality, such as the Chinese Personality Assessment Inventory (CPAI) by Cheung, Kwong, and Zhang (2003). Based on a combined etic–emic approach that included indigenous concepts from Chinese culture, this personality measure was created for use specifically with Chinese individuals. The CPAI measure may be more valid and useful in assessing mental health with this population than purely imported assessments.

Mental Health of Ethnic Minorities and Migrants

Currently, we have an inadequate understanding of the prevalence of mental disorders among ethnic minority groups in the United States. One reason is that in the past, institutional populations, in which minority groups are disproportionately represented, were overlooked in national studies on the epidemiology of mental disorders (U.S. Department of Health and Human Services, 1999). More recently, efforts have been made to address this gap in knowledge. In this final section of the chapter, we will first discuss rates of psychopathology among four ethnic groups that have been a focus of recent research: African Americans, Asian Americans, Latino Americans, and Native Americans. Because most research has focused on primarily European American samples, prevalence rates are usually compared to this group. Second, we will discuss the mental health of immigrants and refugees both within and outside the United States.

African Americans

A study by Regier and colleagues (1993a), involving 18,571 adults from five U.S. cities, examined the prevalence of a variety of mental disorders (including schizophrenia, depression, anxiety disorders, somatization disorders, and antisocial personality disorders) and found that the prevalence of mental disorders was higher among African Americans than among European Americans. Similarly, Lindsey and Paul (1989) report that African Americans are more often diagnosed with schizophrenia than European Americans. However, these differences in prevalence may be due not to inherent cultural differences but rather, to some extent, to socioeconomic (SES) disparities. For instance, when Regier et al. took socioeconomic factors into account, the prevalence differences between African Americans and European Americans disappeared. Regier and colleagues argue that the enormous SES disparities among different ethnic groups in the United States may place those at the lower SES level at higher risk for mental disorders. Other researchers argue that ethnic minorities may also be more likely to be misdiagnosed with disorders such as schizophrenia as a result of bias and stereotyping (Lewis, Croft-Jeffreys, & Anthony, 1990). Goater, King, & Cole's (1999) five-year study of schizophrenia in London found that although the nature and outcome of schizophrenia were similar across whites, blacks, and Asians, black patients were more likely to be detained, taken to the hospital by the police, and given emergency injections.

Asian Americans

It is difficult to paint an accurate picture of the prevalence of mental illness in Asian Americans because for many years they have not been included in epidemiological studies (U.S. Department of Health and Human Services, 1999). Furthermore, being stereotyped as the "model minority" masks the fact that

Asian Americans may also be at risk for poor mental health (Uba, 1994). Some studies indicate that Asian Americans report higher rates of mental illness than European Americans (Takeuchi & Uehara, 1996; Uba, 1994). Nonetheless, studies also show great variation within the Asian American population depending on the specific ethnic background, generational status, and immigrant or refugee status. For instance, Kuo's (1984) study found that Korean Americans had higher incidences of depression, followed by Filipino Americans, Japanese Americans, and Chinese Americans. Kuo argued that part of the reason may be that Korean immigrants have been in the United States for shorter periods of time and have lower-status jobs and more difficulty adjusting to the United States. Among Southeast Asians, Hmongs are more likely to report depression than are Laotians, Cambodians, Vietnamese, and Chinese Vietnamese (Ying, Akutsu, Zhang, & Huang, 1997). Southeast Asians may also be more likely to show lower levels of functioning than Chinese Americans (Uehara, Takeuchi, & Smukler, 1994). Clearly, the wide variation within an ethnic group demonstrates that sweeping generalizations in discussions of possible ethnic groups differences in mental health are not possible nor accurate.

Latino Americans

Several epidemiological studies report few differences between Latino Americans and European Americans in lifetime rates of psychiatric disorders (Robins & Regier, 1991). Canino et al.'s (1987) study of 1,513 Puerto Ricans reported similar lifetime and 6-month prevalence rates of psychiatric disorders compared with three U.S. communities (in Missouri, Connecticut, and Maryland). As with Asian Americans, there are also significant within-group differences in rates of psychopathologies depending on the specific Latino group and generational status. For instance, one study found that Puerto Ricans have higher rates of major depression than Cuban and Mexican Americans (Cho et al., 1993). Furthermore, recent studies involving Mexican Americans in California found that U.S.-born Mexican Americans showed rates of mental disorders similar to the U.S. national population, whereas foreign-born Mexican Americans reported lower rates of psychiatric disorders (Alderete, Vega, & Kolody, 2000; Vega et al., 1998).

Native Americans

The lives of some Native Americans are characterized by socioeconomic difficulties, segregation and marginalization, which may translate into greater risk for mental health problems (Organista, Organista, & Kurasaki, 2003). Very few epidemiological surveys of mental health and mental disorders have included this ethnic group. However, the few studies that have included this population suggest that depression is a significant problem in many Native American communities (Kinzie et al., 1992; Nelson, McCoy, Stetter, & Vanderwagen, 1992).

Moreover, alcohol abuse and rates of suicide among Native Americans are significantly higher than U.S. national statistics (Boehnlein, Kinzie, & Leung, 1992; Indian Health Service, 1997).

Migrants

There has been an increased interest in the mental health of migrants (Tanaka-Matsumi, 2001). Migrants adapting to a new cultural environment are confronted with many challenges, such as learning the customs and language of the host culture while at the same time maintaining aspects of their traditional culture (Berry & Kim, 1988). Berry and Sam (Berry, 1997; Berry & Sam, 1997) report that depression, anxiety, and psychosomatic problems are common among individuals undergoing acculturation to a new culture. Thus, Berry and others have hypothesized that experiencing stresses associated with acculturation may lead to poorer mental health.

Interestingly, some studies report that immigrants in the United States (such as Mexican Americans) actually report fewer mental health problems than their U.S.-born counterparts (Alderete et al., 2000; Escobar, 1998; Vega, et al., 1998). Sam (1994) has also reported that acute psychiatric disorders are less prevalent in immigrant children in Norway. Concerning the acculturation process related to immigration, some studies have found that psychopathology is predicted by low assimilation to the host culture (Padilla, Wagatsuma, & Lindholm, 1985; Szapocznik, Scopetta, & Tillman, 1979), whereas others have found psychopathology to be predicted by high assimilation to the host culture (for example, Burnam, Hough, Karno, Escobar, & Telles, 1987; Sodowsky & Carey, 1987). Furthermore, a study by Nguyen, Messe, and Stollack (1999) of Vietnamese immigrant adolescents living in a midwestern U.S. city found that those reporting themselves to be more Vietnamese in their attitudes and behaviors also reported higher levels of behavioral symptoms and depression. In sum, findings are inconsistent concerning whether immigrants are indeed at higher risk for mental health problems as a result of undergoing the acculturation process.

To reconcile these divergent findings regarding acculturation's link to mental health, an ecological perspective on acculturation has been proposed. In other words, taking into account important aspects of the community, societal, and cultural contexts—such as the tolerance for and acceptance of cultural diversity, policies that may prevent the acculturating group from participating fully in the larger society, and the existence of a network of supports—may help clarify how acculturation relates to the mental health of immigrants and their children (Berry, Kim, Minde, & Mok, 1987; Bourhis, Moise, Perreault, & Senecal, 1997; Nguyen et al., 1999). For example, Nguyen et al.'s study suggests that Vietnamese teenagers living in a culturally unsupportive environment were at greater risk for emotional and behavioral distress if they were highly involved in Vietnamese culture. However, in a culturally diverse environment such as the city of San Francisco, where many cultural traditions are supported, encouraged, and even celebrated, Vietnamese teenagers who strongly maintained the attitudes, values, and behaviors of their traditional culture may be less at risk for emotional and behavioral distress.

In addition to relating to levels of distress, an individual's level of acculturation may also contribute to the content and expression of his or her distress, with implications for the assessment, diagnosis, and treatment of acculturating individuals at risk for mental disorders.

> If it is assumed that highly acculturated individuals are culturally similar to members of the dominant society, then they may also be similar in the way they express psychological distress. However, psychological symptomatology among less acculturated individuals may not follow this pattern. By definition, less acculturated individuals are culturally different from the groups for whom conventional symptomatology scales have been developed. Thus, the question of whether standard measures of psychological symptomatology fit the realities of ethnic minority groups remains unanswered. (Cortes, 2003, p. 208)

Refugees

The acculturation, adaptation, and mental health of refugees—migrants who are forced to flee from their countries because of political violence, social unrest, war, or civil conflicts—has also been studied. Sadly, the number of refugees worldwide is increasing for the first time in several years (U.S. Committee for Refugees, 2000). Not surprisingly, because of their traumatic experiences marked by profound losses and upheavals, refugees tend to show higher rates of posttraumatic stress disorder (PTSD), depression, and anxiety (Boehnlein & Kinzie, 1995; Kinzie & Sack, 2002; Liebkind, 1996; van Ommeren et al., 2002) than those who migrated voluntarily. Recent work with Vietnamese refugees in Finland (Leibkind, 1996) and Bosnian refugees living in Chicago (Miller, Worthington, Muzurovic, Tipping, & Goldman, 2002) suggests, however, that postmigration factors are just as important (if not more) in predicting a refugee's emotional distress and psychopathology as the premigration traumatic experiences. For example, based on intensive, in-depth narrative interviews with Bosnian refugees, Miller et al. found that postmigration factors such as social isolation and loss of community, the loss of life projects such as building a home or running a business, and the loss of social roles and meaningful activity all contributed to refugees' posttraumatic stress reactions and emotional and physical distress.

Summary

Recent studies have finally included ethnic minority and immigrant groups in studying the prevalence of mental illness in the United States. To understand ethnic differences in rates of mental disorders, contextual factors such as poverty, discrimination, and stresses associated with immigrating to a new country need to be taken into account. For example, people in the lowest level of SES are about two and a half times more likely than those in the highest SES to experience a mental disorder (Regier et al., 1993b). Because ethnic minorities in the United States are disproportionately exposed to poverty and the stresses associated with it, they may be more at risk for poor mental health (Miranda & Green, 1999). However, it must also be emphasized that there is great diversity among and within ethnic groups in the prevalence of mental disorders. The strong ties to family and community that characterize African, Latino, Asian, and Native American communities is an asset that can contribute to the development of positive mental health. Future research should not only continue to examine the prevalence of mental illnesses in more diverse populations, but also move beyond adopting a merely comparative approach to explore which protective factors, such close family ties, may help prevent these illnesses.

 ## Conclusion

Psychiatric diagnoses, classification schemes, and measurement of abnormality are complex and difficult issues. To the extent that there are both etic and emic aspects of psychopathology, classification systems and assessment methods need to contain both etic and emic elements. Where to draw the lines, and how to measure psychological traits and characteristics within this fluid, dynamic, and ever-changing system, is the challenge that faces this area of psychology today. Although the field has made vast improvements in this area in the past few years, future research will need to elaborate even further on these issues so that classification and measurement can be made more precise, meaningful, and relevant. Inclusion of more diverse populations in pluralistic countries such as the United States is also needed in this area of research. The significance of this is not trivial, as the proper understanding, assessment, and diagnosis of mental disorders is a necessary step to develop effective preventions and treatments that improve and enhance people's lives.

 ## Glossary

cultural relativism   A viewpoint that suggests that the unique aspects of a particular culture need to be considered when understanding and identifying behavior.

culture-bound syndromes   Forms of abnormal behavior observed only in certain sociocultural milieus.

indigenous healing systems   Systems of cure, such as folk healers, particular to a certain culture.

overpathologizing   Misinterpreting culturally sanctioned behavior as expressions of pathological symptoms.

somatization   Bodily complaints as expressions of psychological distress.

underpathologizing   Attributing pathological symptoms to normative cultural differences.

InfoTrac College Edition

Use InfoTrac College Edition to search for additional readings on topics of interest to you. For more information on topics in this chapter, use the following as search terms:

culture and depression
culture and somatization
culture-bound mental health syndromes
African Americans and mental health
Asian Americans and mental health
Latino Americans and mental health
Native Americans and mental health

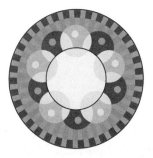

Culture and the Treatment of Abnormal Behavior

One of the primary goals of psychology is to use the knowledge generated by research to help people improve their lives. In the previous chapter, we discussed the important role that culture plays in defining abnormality, influencing its expression and presentation in individuals and our ability to reliably and validly assess and diagnose it. The proper assessment and diagnosis of psychopathology is a necessary step toward helping people with mental disorders improve their lives. In this chapter, we discuss issues related to the treatment of abnormal behavior. We begin our discussion by reviewing a common approach to addressing psychopathology—namely, psychotherapy. In doing so, we will address the question of whether or not psychotherapy, which emerged from Western European culture, is applicable and useful in other cultures. Next, we discuss treatment across diverse cultures within the United States and talk about various issues, such as why some ethnic minorities are less likely to seek treatment and more likely to end treatment prematurely. Then, we discuss treatment in other cultures outside the United States and talk about the relatively new field of community-clinical psychology, which offers an alternative approach to treatment. Finally, we end with a discussion of culture and clinical training.

Culture and Psychotherapy

Among the many ways in which practicing or applied psychologists pursue the goal of improving people's lives is through psychological interventions with people who have abnormal behavior disorders, and whose lives are dysfunctional because of those disorders. The primary vehicle for delivering such intervention is psychotherapy.

Traditional Psychotherapy

Traditional psychotherapy has its origins in Western Europe and can be traced to Sigmund Freud, the father of psychoanalysis. In Vienna, Freud discovered that patients under the influence of hypnosis would talk more freely and emotionally about their problems, conflicts, and fears. Moreover, recalling and reliving earlier traumatic experiences appeared to alleviate some of the patients' symptoms. Through individual therapy sessions, he encouraged his patients to explore their memories and unconscious thoughts, much as an archaeologist explores a buried city (Hothersall, 1990). His observations led him to develop the psychoanalytic model, a comprehensive theory on the structure of personality that contributes to our knowledge about the origins of psychopathology.

Freud's theory caught the attention of American psychologists, and psychotherapy was introduced to the United States in the early 1900s. Carl Rogers (1942), an American psychologist, later modified Freud's psychoanalysis techniques and developed a client-centered approach to psychotherapy. Rogers moved away from the role of the therapist as the interpreter of the patient's troubles to emphasize the client's self-propelled growth while the therapist remained empathically sensitive to the feelings and emotions of the client. Despite these modifications, traditional psychotherapy clearly stems from and is bounded by a uniquely Western cultural perspective on the understanding and treatment of individuals.

Contemporary Psychotherapy

Over the course of the past century, traditional psychoanalytic psychotherapy has been transformed and evolved into many different forms and types of psychotherapeutic approaches. These approaches may differ in their theoretical perspective, activity/passivity of the therapist, guidance, focus of treatment on actual behaviors or underlying psychology, and a host of other factors. They are all similar, however, in their goal of improving the patient/client's life, their one-on-one approach, and the use of psychological principles to effect behavioral change.

Modified psychotherapeutic approaches that have developed since Freud's time include cognitive and cognitive-behavioral therapies (Beck, 1967, 1976; Ellis, 1962). In these therapies, what a person believes is more important than what a person thinks or sees. One difference between cognitive and cognitive-behavioral therapy is that cognitive interventions have traditionally focused on examining the rationality or validity of one's beliefs, whereas cognitive-behavioral interventions emphasize the development of strategies for teaching cognitive skills (Hollon & Beck, 1994). Underlying these types of therapy is an assumption that by changing our thinking, we can change our behaviors, and vice versa. These therapeutic approaches originated in the treatment of depression, in which depressed individuals presumably maintain negative thoughts and evaluations of themselves, the world, and the future. Helping such individuals to understand and control their thought patterns and emotions, and changing their maladaptive views to become more adaptive, can help them to recover.

Again, these contemporary psychotherapeutic techniques are infused with cultural assumptions, such as the inherent separation of thoughts and behaviors. The recognition that psychotherapy, the most widely used form of treatment for psychopathology in the United States, is a distinctively Western approach, has led some psychologists to challenge the use of psychotherapy with individuals of non-Western backgrounds. In the next section, we will discuss some of the cultural limitations of psychotherapy.

Cultural Limitations of Psychotherapy

In a diverse world, many psychologists have come to see these "traditional" psychotherapeutic approaches as effective for some people, but less so for others, particularly those of non-European descent. Some authors (for example, Wohl, 1989) have proposed that psychotherapy itself is inescapably bound to a particular cultural framework (see also Alarcon & Leetz, 1998). This notion may make sense for several reasons. First, as we have seen, expressions of abnormality, and their underlying psychological causes, are at least partly bound to culture. Second, the ability of the therapist or clinician to assess and deal with such behaviors is intimately related to his or her knowledge, understanding, and appreciation of the cultural context within which the behaviors occur. Third, if the goal of psychotherapy is to help people to become more functional within their society, then functionality itself is culturally determined; that is, different cultures and societies would necessitate different outcomes.

In examining the roots and history of the development of psychotherapy, some writers have suggested that psychoanalysis—the basis for contemporary psychotherapy—was developed specifically within a Jewish cultural framework, and that it shares features with Jewish mysticism (Langman, 1997). In fact, the development of other psychotherapeutic approaches, such as behavioral or humanistic approaches, could be considered a "culturalization" of traditional psychoanalysis to American culture and society. Viewed in this fashion, psychotherapy can be considered a cultural product, reflecting and reproducing a cultural context. Because cultural context is in part composed of moral traditions embedded in political structures, psychotherapy is itself unavoidably a moral practice with political consequences embedded within a cultural framework. In this sense, there can be no value-free psychotherapy, because all psychotherapy is bound to a particular cultural framework, and cultures are inextricably tied to moral values and systems. It is useful to take a step back and examine how our approaches to treatment are bound to our cultural norms, values, and beliefs (Sue & Sue, 1999).

In traditional and contemporary psychotherapy, for instance, the focus is on the individual. The individual is expected to express verbally his or her emotions, thoughts, and feelings and to engage in self-reflection and self-disclosure in order to arrive at insights into the individual's own behavioral and thought patterns underlying the mental illness. Thus, for Western psychologists, focusing on yourself, talking about your feelings, openly expressing your emotions, and being in touch with your inner self are important ways to understanding and treating distressed individuals. In other cultures, however, this approach may run exactly counter to what is considered constructive for treating a mental disorder. In some Asian cultures, for example, dwelling on one's thoughts, especially if they are painful, unpleasant, or upsetting, is strongly avoided and believed to exacerbate the existing problem. Furthermore, persons from collectivistic cultures might find this focus on the self unusual and uncomfortable. Consequently, using this type of therapy may not be appropriate. Nonetheless, the use of psychotherapy has been, and continues to be, implemented with culturally diverse populations within the United States, as well as in other countries.

Summary

Psychotherapy is widely used within the United States and, to a (much) lesser extent, in other parts of the world. Because of its roots in Western notions of the self, distress, and healing, the usefulness of treating with psychotherapy individuals who do not originate from this cultural group is, to date, not well established. Although practitioners working with diverse cultures in the United States, as well as in other parts of the world, use modified versions of psychotherapy in their mental health services, very few studies provide empirical support for the effectiveness of this approach. Recently, some clinical psychologists have been advocating strongly for studies of empirically supported treatments (EST)—treatments that have been shown, through empirical studies, to be effective (for a review on conducting EST research with ethnic minority populations, see Bernal & Scharrón-Del-Río, 2001). Only by evaluating the efficacy of our treatments can we determine whether we are truly helping, and not harming, individuals by importing culturally bound psychotherapeutic interventions.

Treatment of Abnormal Behavior across Diverse Cultures in the United States

Psychotherapy with Diverse Cultures in the United States

As stated previously, there is a paucity of research addressing whether psychotherapy is effective with people of diverse cultural backgrounds within the United States. Several recent reviews have found that rigorous research (in which participants are randomly assigned to control and treatment groups, outcomes are assessed over time, and findings are replicated) involving culturally diverse groups is practically nonexistent (Chambless et al., 1996; Sue, Zane, & Young, 1994). Most research on treatments and their outcomes can only be generalized to European American, middle-class, English-speaking females (Rosselló & Bernal, 1999). More studies that rigorously test psychotherapy effectiveness in diverse samples should include using within- as well as between-ethnic group comparisons, adequate sample sizes, and various cross-culturally valid outcome measures (Kurasaki, Sue, Chun, & Gee, 2000).

To date, the handful of studies that have been conducted with diverse groups have focused on four major ethnic groups in the United States, with a notable lack of studies involving Arab Americans. These few studies report conflicting results for some cultural groups. For instance, earlier studies with African Americans found no differences in outcomes compared to other ethnic groups (Jones & Matsumoto, 1982; Lerner, 1972), but more recent studies have found treatment outcomes to be poorer (Sue, Fujino, Hu, Takeuchi, & Zane, 1991; Sue, Zane, & Young, 1994). Outcomes for Asian Americans have found that psychotherapy can be used successfully, for instance, with Southeast Asian Americans dealing with posttraumatic distress disorder or depression (Kinzie, Leung, & Bui, 1988). In a large-scale study in the Los Angeles area, Sue et al. (1991) found that, compared to other ethnic groups, Latinos were most likely to improve after treatment. However, it is still premature to arrive at definitive conclusions about the effectiveness of psychotherapy with culturally diverse populations. Systematic studies are needed to identify which elements of psychotherapy may be universally effective, and which elements may be culture-specific.

With increasing recognition that our current approaches must include a cultural understanding of how clients respond to this type of treatment, researchers and practitioners have advocated for the infusion of cultural elements to promote successful treatment. For example, the American Psychological Association (2002) has created guidelines for providing mental health services to ethnic minority groups. Others researchers and clinicians are developing culturally driven theoretical approaches to treatment, such as the theory of multicultural counseling and therapy (Sue, Ivey, & Pedersen, 1996).

Seeking Treatment

In a pioneering study of ethnic differences in response to standard mental health services in the Seattle area, Sue (1977) found lower rates of utilization of services by Asian Americans and Native Americans than by European Americans and African Americans. More dramatically, he found that relative to European Americans, all other groups had higher dropout rates and poorer treatment outcomes. A later study in the Los Angeles area produced similar findings (Sue, 1991).

More recent studies have found similar utilization patterns with adolescents. For instance, in a study of utilization rates of mental health services of 853 African American, 704 Asian American, 964 Latino American, and 670

European American adolescents (ages 13–17) in Los Angeles over a five-year period, patterns of utilization reflected earlier studies involving adults. Namely, after controlling for sex, age, and poverty status, results showed that African American adolescents used services more than European American and Asian American adolescents, and that Latino American adolescents used these services less than European Americans (Bui & Takeuchi, 1992). Unlike studies with adult populations, Bui and Takeuchi did not find ethnic differences in dropout rates. However, they did find that Asian American adolescents were more likely to remain in treatment longer than European American adolescents, and that African American adolescents remained in treatment for the shortest time period. Length of treatment is a critical variable to look at because studies have shown that the more time spent in treatment, the more likely change occurs (Orlinsky, Grawe, & Parks, 1994).

Asian Americans are distinguished by extremely low levels of soliciting treatment for mental health problems (Leong & Lau, 2001). However, we must also keep in mind there is much variation within this ethnic group (as with others). Findings from studies with Southeast Asians in particular have been mixed, with some suggesting higher rates of utilization (Ying & Hu, 1994) and others finding lower rates (Zane, Hatanaka, Park, & Akutsu, 1994) compared to the Asian American population as a whole. One consistent finding, however, is that Southeast Asian groups do not seem to improve with treatment as much as other Asian groups (Ying & Hu, 1994). As Southeast Asians are more likely to be refugees who have been exposed to war trauma and more likely to fall into lower socioeconomic categories, which may exacerbate the severity of a mental illness, success in treatment may be more difficult to achieve.

Researchers have found that characteristics of mental health services, such as whether they are ethnic-specific (defined as having more than 50% of clients from a specific minority group) or mainstream, may contribute to variation in utilization rates. Yeh, Takeuchi, and Sue's (1994) study over a five-year period of Asian American adolescents and their use of mental health services in the Los Angeles area found that ethnic-specific mental health services were more successful in providing services to Asian American youth. More specifically, Asian American adolescents who received treatment from ethnic-specific centers were less likely to terminate services prematurely, used the services more, and were assessed to be higher functioning at the end of services than Asian Americans who sought treatment at mainstream facilities.

Takeuchi, Sue, and Yeh (1995) have expanded these findings to include African American, Asian American, and Mexican American adults. After controlling for age, sex, SES, and whether they had a serious or nonserious mental illness, the results revealed that over a six-year period, those using ethnic-specific mental health services were more likely to return for treatment, and stayed in treatment for a longer period of time, than those using mainstream services. Thus, having access to ethnic-specific services may encourage more ethnic minorities to seek out and utilize these treatment centers.

In sum, members of various ethnic groups in the United States who suffer from psychological distress are not accessing available treatment services to the extent that mainstream populations are. In the next section, we explore possible reasons why.

Barriers to Seeking Treatment

One of the pioneers of research in multicultural mental health is Stanley Sue, who directs the National Research Center for Asian American Mental Health. Sue suggests that some of the reasons why Asian Americans underutilize mental health services include shame, loss of face, active avoidance of morbid thoughts, attributions of causes of mental illness to biological factors, willpower, and fear of a system not set up to deal well with cultural differences. Sue (1994) also suggests that these reasons are more pronounced for recent immigrants. Cheng and colleagues (Cheng, Leong, & Geist, 1993) report that some Asian Americans believe that dwelling on upsetting thoughts or events will only exacerbate the problem. If this is the case, it makes sense that seeking help that requires talking and dwelling on the problem is avoided.

For other groups, such as African Americans, individuals may be encouraged to rely on their own willpower to confront problems, to be self-reliant, and to "tough out" difficult situations (Broman, 1996; Snowden, 2001). Tolman and Reedy (1998) suggest that reduced utilization of services by Native Americans may be the result of cultural beliefs that sickness comes from disharmony with oneself, one's community, and nature. Thus, seeking help from formal mental health services, which traditionally do not focus on such a holistic view of mental health, may not be desirable. Some research indicates that Chicanos associate seeking help outside the family for treatment of mental disturbances with shame, weakness of character, and disgrace (Leong, Wagner, & Tata, 1995). As with Asian Americans, the primary source of support and help during times of difficulty are the extended family and folk healers (Koss-Chioino, 2000). Hence, formal mental health professionals such as clinicians or psychiatrists may be a last resort, at least for very traditional Chicanos.

In Latino communities, the cause of mental disturbances may be attributed to evil spirits; consequently, it is believed that the power to cure problems lies within the church and not with mental health professionals (Paniagua, 1998). Prayers are an important aspect of psychological and physical healing for this community, and it may be the case that only when religious and folk healers cannot help are mental health professionals acknowledged. Likewise, in Arab American families, individuals may first seek help from informal systems of support, such as the extended family or traditional healers, before turning to more conventional mental health services (Al-Krenawi & Graham, 2000). As a result, it may be wise for mental health professionals to collaborate with churches and religious organizations to provide information about services and to think about incorporating religious and spiritual values and practices into providing treatment.

Other more general reasons that ethnic minorities may underutilize mental health services are mistrust and stigma. Sussman, Robins, and Earl's (1987) study found that African Americans were more likely than European Americans to voice mistrust toward formal mental health services, fearing hospitalization and fearing treatment. A study by Takeuchi, Bui, and Kim (1993) found that African American parents fear that coming into contact with professional help may lead to the institutionalization of their child. Mistrust among African Americans may stem from their history and experiences of segregation, racism, and discrimination (Primm, Lima, & Rowe, 1996; Priest, 1991). Similarly, the history and experiences of Native Americans may also leave them feeling mistrustful of formal mental health services.

Uba's (1994) study of Asian Americans identified stigma, suspiciousness, and a lack of awareness about the availability of services as barriers to seeking treatment. For Arab Americans, utilizing mental health services may also be stigmatizing, especially for women. For women, being involved with conventional mental health services could damage their marriageability or increase the likelihood of separation or divorce (Al-Krenawi & Graham, 2000).

In sum, reasons such as mistrust and stigma are likely explanations as to why some ethnic minority groups in the United States do not seek treatment. Other cultural groups in the United States that underutilize mental health services no doubt have their own sets of culture-specific reasons that discourage and prevent them from utilizing available resources. Future research should continue to identify these reasons and to evaluate empirically the contribution of these reasons to help-seeking behavior.

Treatment Issues

In one recent study (Lee & Mixson, 1995), Asian and Caucasian clients at a university counseling center were asked to rate counseling helpfulness, counselor characteristics, and other aspects of their counseling experiences. The Asians tended to rate counseling as less helpful for personal and emotional concerns and to rate their counselors as less competent than did the Caucasians. To the extent that such perceptions are generalizable to larger populations of ethnically and culturally diverse peoples, they do not bode well for the ability of some contemporary mental health services to deal effectively with the emotional concerns of a wide variety of people. This section highlights some of the issues and challenges that may arise during treatment when the clinician and patient differ with respect to their cultural backgrounds.

One issue, especially relevant when treating recent immigrants, is understanding culturally different ways of thinking about illness and expressing thoughts about illness. Moreover, when language difficulties and culturally different ways of communicating are thrown into the picture, it can be a challenge for the clinician and patient to communicate effectively. Consequently, treatment may be compromised. The following exchange between a Pakistani immigrant receiving services in Britain and a British psychiatrist illustrates some of these difficulties (Rack, 1982, p. 110):

Psychiatrist (English-speaking): "How is your wife getting on now?"

Husband: "She is very well now, doctor. She is fine. She is looking after the house. She is cooking the food, she is caring for the baby. Thank you, so much. . . ."

Psychiatrist: "Good, I am glad she is able to do those things: and is she feeling well herself?"

(Brief conversation between the husband and wife)

Husband: "She is very well now, doctor, she is able to look after the family, she is cooking the food, I am able to go back to work now. . . ."

Psychiatrist: "Yes, yes, but please ask her how does she feel in herself? Is she happy? Is her mind clear? Is the *feeling* alright?"

(A further lengthy conversation. Husband and wife both evidently perplexed, but wanting to answer the question helpfully.)

Husband: "She is very happy now, doctor, because she is able to do the cooking, she is able to look after the family, she is able to care for the baby, she is able to clean the house. Thank you very much. . . ."

This exchange illustrates the potential difficulty for the clinician and patient to communicate properly when, for example, cultural differences in the meaning of the word "feeling" are coupled with language difficulties. In addition to being sensitive to aspects of verbal communication, interpreting nonverbal aspects of communication correctly is also important. In some cultures, making direct eye contact is disrespectful, such as in traditional Native American (Everett, Proctor, & Cartmell, 1983) or Arab cultures (Al-Krenawi & Graham, 2000). Thus, if the therapist is not familiar with this cultural norm, he or she might falsely assume that the client is showing a lack of interest, resisting treatment, or even rude.

Taking into account how cultures vary on the importance of hierarchy in interpersonal relationships is also important. Wilson, Kohn, and Lee (2000) highlight the importance of showing respect for traditional family roles with Asian families, for instance by initially reinforcing the father's role as head of the family. This is also true for many Arab families. Jalali (1982) writes that the patriarchal organization of the family in Arab cultures should be recognized and respected, by addressing the father first and as the head of the family. If the therapist tries to alter power hierarchies or role patterns, this may well alienate the family (Jalali, 1982). Likewise, if a child is brought in for help and the therapist treats the child and his or her parents similarly, in an egalitarian way, this may be upsetting for families from cultures where hierarchy, respect, and obedience are highly valued. Parents may feel that the therapist is undermining their authority.

Treatment expectations may also differ across cultures. For instance, in many cultures, the therapist is the authority and is expected to be directive, to make suggestions, and to give reassurance. For instance, a study of Puerto Rican patients found that they expected their doctor to be active and concrete, dispensing advice or prescribing medication. Following a traditional psychological approach, in which the client is expected to discuss and reflect on problems while the therapist assumes a more passive role, may result in the Puerto Rican client's prematurely terminating treatment (Abad, Ramos, & Boyce, 1974). Similarly, insight-oriented therapies, in which clients engage in deep self-reflection, may not work with traditional Native American clients (Atkinson, Morten, & Sue, 1989). LaFromboise, Trimble, and Mohatt (1990) report that for Native Americans, more directive and strategic interventions are preferred over client-centered or reflective therapy. The introspective approach may lead to impatience and dropping out of therapy. Other studies have also found that Latino and Asian Americans (Atkinson, Maruyama, & Matsui,1978; Ponce & Atkinson, 1989) and Arab Americans (Al-Krenawi & Graham, 2000) prefer directive over nondirective therapists.

Asian families may tend to wait a long time to seek formal treatment because of their reluctance to call for help outside the family. When they do finally reach out to more formal mental health services, it may be their last resort because the problem has reached a crisis level (Lin, Inui, Kleinman, & Womack, 1992). Consequently, more directive and solution-oriented approaches to treatment may be more appropriate than insight- and growth-oriented approaches (Wang, 1994). In sum, a large body of research on preferences for therapeutic approaches in ethnically different populations in the United States indicates that non–European American clients tend to prefer action-oriented therapy to nondirective approaches such as psychoanalytic or humanistic therapy (Sue & Zane, 1987).

Finally, in many cultures, the extended family is a primary source of support in times of distress. Recognizing and involving members of the extended family instead of focusing on the individual and nuclear family may be useful and may present a more familiar approach to problem solving. It is also important to note that with many ethnic families, nonblood kin may also be considered family, such as neighbors and ministers in African American families, godparents in Latino families, and elders in Asian communities (Porter, 2000).

We have highlighted just some of the many issues that come into play when counseling clients from diverse cultural origins. Hopefully, this brief discussion has illustrated how assumptions about what may work best in treating one population may not necessarily be true for another. Developing responses to psychological distress that are sensitive to each individual's cultural outlook, beliefs, and practices is the goal for many psychologists working with diverse populations. There is much to be done to improve on our services to these culturally diverse groups (Sue et al., 1994). In the next section, we discuss some ways that researchers and mental health professionals are promoting more culturally appropriate treatment and services.

Culturally Competent Services

A growing body of literature by researchers and practitioners has prompted mental health professionals to stress the need for culturally competent services in order to improve utilization and effectiveness of treatment for individuals from diverse cultural backgrounds. Understanding and respecting the histories, traditions, beliefs, and value systems of various cultural groups underlies culturally competent services.

To fashion more culturally sensitive services, Sue and others (Sue & Zane, 1987; Comas-Diaz & Jacobsen, 1991; Higginbotham, 1979; Tseng & McDermott, 1981) suggest that treatment methods should be modified to improve their fit with the worldviews and experiences of culturally diverse clients. For example, psychoanalytic approaches are derived from a worldview that assumes that unconscious conflicts (probably sexual) give rise to abnormal behavior. This worldview may reflect the experience of the well-to-do Austrian women Freud treated and based many of his theoretical assumptions on. However, a therapeutic approach based on such a worldview may prove inappropriate for cultures that attribute abnormality either to natural factors (for example, physical problems or being out of harmony with the environment) or supernatural causes (for example, spirit possession). Cultural systems of cure and healing may be effective precisely because they operate within a particular culture's worldview (Tseng & McDermott, 1981). For example, a spiritual ceremony performed by a native shaman (priest or healer) may prove to be a more effective treatment of the culture-bound syndrome *susto* than the cognitive behavioral approach typically used in the United States.

There is also some indication that culturally diverse clients prefer to see therapists who are similar to them in cultural background and gender. But more recent research indicates that similarity of worldviews and attitudes to treatment between client and therapist may be more important than ethnic similarity (Atkinson, Ponce, & Martinez, 1984). For instance, matching a Korean American client who does not consider herself to be very Korean (she does not speak Korean and does not identify herself with Korean values and attitudes) with a Korean therapist may not make much difference compared to pairing her with a therapist of another ethnicity. Thus, acculturation status and ethnic identity may be more important determinants of client responses to treatment (Atkinson, Casa, & Abreu, 1992). Indeed, a study with African Americans found that those who identified strongly with African American culture preferred an ethnically similar therapist, compared to those who did not identify strongly with African American culture (Ponterotto, Alexander, & Hinkston, 1988). In a study with Chicano college students, only those who expressed a strong commitment to Chicano culture desired an ethnically matched counselor. Chicano students who primarily identified themselves with the majority culture were not concerned that their counselor be of the same ethnicity (Sanchez & Atkinson, 1983).

Thus, although such matching may be beneficial in the therapy process, it may not be essential for effective counseling. A recent meta-analysis of seven studies conducted in the past two decades on ethnic matching found that the effect sizes were very small (ranging from $r = .01$ to $r = .04$) for outcomes such as dropout, number of treatment sessions, and assessment of client functioning at the end of treatment (Maramba & Hall, 2002). Other factors such as cultural matching (as in worldviews, cognitive styles, and language) and the level of cultural sensitivity of the therapist may be more crucial (S. Sue, 1998).

Thus, clinicians who are sensitive to the client's cultural background and who take the time and effort to understand the client within his or her cultural context can be more beneficial than simply matching ethnicities. Culture-sensitive counselors have been rated as being more credible and competent to conduct treatment across cultures by African Americans (Atkinson, Furlong, & Poston, 1986), Asian Americans (Gim, Atkinson, & Kim, 1991), and Mexican Americans (Atkinson et al., 1992).

Not only do client views of the therapist differ depending on the match between therapist and client; therapist views of the client also differ. In one study (Russell, Fujino, Sue, Cheung, & Snowden, 1996), for example, the records of thousands of African, Asian, Mexican, and European American outpatient clients in the Los Angeles County mental health system were examined for ethnic match with their therapist. In this study, a black therapist–black client dyad or Chinese therapist–Chinese client dyad was considered an ethnic match. However, for Asian Americans, a Chinese therapist–Japanese client was not a match. Results indicated that ethnically matched therapists tended to judge clients to have higher mental functioning than did mismatched therapists. This finding held even after controlling for variables such as age, gender, marital status, and referral source. Thus, how the therapist perceived the client differed according to whether the therapist was of the client's ethnic group or not.

Several authors (for example, Higginbotham, 1979; Sue, Akutsu, & Higashi, 1985; Sue & Zane, 1987; Tseng & McDermott, 1981) have outlined the competencies and knowledge base necessary for therapists to conduct sensitive and effective treatment across cultures. Sue and associates (1985) suggest that the culturally sensitive therapist will have acquired (1) knowledge of diverse cultures and lifestyles, (2) skill and comfort in using innovative treatment methods, and (3) actual experience working with culturally diverse clients. It is also critically important that the therapist be aware of his or her own cultural background and its influences on definitions and perceptions of abnormal behavior. Furthermore, the therapist must be aware of how cultural beliefs and experiences influence the course of treatment. Comas-Diaz and Jacobsen (1991) have outlined several ways in which ethnocultural factors may shape therapy, including the elicitation of strong transference reactions on the part of the client (unconscious projections onto the therapist) and barriers to empathy on the part of the therapist (understanding of another's experience). Only with a deep understanding of how people's conceptions of the cause and course of illness are embedded and shaped by their cultural upbringing and outlook can we begin to offer ways to alleviate and improve their situation.

Examples of Blending Traditional Western-Based Treatment Approaches with Indigenous Healing Practices

Vang was a Hmong refugee who resettled in Chicago with his family. On the first several nights in Chicago, he reported severe sleep disturbances, including a severe shortness of breath and extreme panic. He reported that he was pinned down and rendered immobile the first night by a cat sitting on his chest, the second night by a figure like a large black dog, and the third night by a tall, white-skinned spirit. He awoke screaming, out of breath, and feared he was going to die during the night, or that the spirit would make his wife infertile (Tobin & Friedman, 1983). As Vang explains it:

> The most recent attack in Chicago was not the first encounter my family and I have had with this type of spirit, a spirit we call Chia. . . . We are susceptible to such attacks because we didn't follow all of the mourning rituals we should have when our parents died. Because we didn't properly honor their memories we have lost contact with their spirits, and thus we are left with no one to protect us from evil spirits. (p. 444)

From a Western perspective, Vang's symptoms of sleeplessness, extreme anxiety, and depression could be seen as a result of the trauma and stress of his experiences as a refugee, perhaps leading to a diagnosis of posttraumatic distress disorder. Therapists in the United States most likely would not attribute his disturbances to spirits, as Vang does. Considering these two perspectives, what kind of treatment would be effective in this case? Would traditional psychotherapy be effective? Or would an indigenous healing method be more effective? In this particular case, the mental health workers treating Vang were sensitive to his cultural background and to his beliefs as to the origins of his extreme distress. Both Western (psychotherapeutic counseling) and non-Western healing methods indigenous to the Hmong culture (involving a shaman to perform a spirit cleansing ritual) were used to treat him, with success.

Another case study is described by Zuniga (1997, cited in Sue & Sue, 1999, p. 149):

> Mrs. Lopez, age 70, and her 30-year-old daughter, sought counseling because they had a very conflictual relationship. The mother was not accustomed to a counseling format. At a pivotal point in one session, she found talking about emotional themes overwhelming and embarrassing. In order to reengage her, the counselor asked what resources she used when she and her daughter quarreled. She prayed to Our Lady of Guadalupe.

The counselor consequently used a culturally sensitive strategy of having Mrs. Lopez use prayer to understand her daughter and to find solutions for the conflicting relationship that they could discuss in the counseling sessions. Acknowledging and incorporating religion, a central guiding element in Mrs. Lopez's life, into the treatment allowed Mrs. Lopez to discuss spiritual guidance and possible solutions to the problems.

Other researchers have advocated treatment that combines and integrates traditional cultural healing practices (Kurasaki et al., 2000; Sue & Sue, 1999). In the United States, some Native American communities recognize and fund traditional healing in mental health services. However, little is known regarding how the individual or family connects indigenous approaches with conventional mental health services (Tata & Leong, 1994). Better research is needed to uncover the effectiveness of a combination of indigenous and conventional treatments (Cauce et al., 2002).

Treatment of Abnormal Behavior in Other Cultures

Psychotherapy in Cultures Outside the United States

Psychotherapy has been exported to other parts of the world such as Singapore (Devan, 2001), Malaysia (Azhar & Varma, 2000), India (Prasadaro & Matam, 2001), and China (Zhang, Young, & Lee, 2002). Psychologists in these cultures have attempted to incorporate essential elements of their culture to make psychotherapy useful. In Malaysia, for example, religion has been incorporated into psychotherapy (Azhar & Varma, 2000). Integrating religious beliefs and behaviors, such as prayer and focusing on verses of the Koran that address "worry," are some techniques to make psychotherapy more culturally relevant. Studies comparing patients with a variety of disorders, including anxiety disorder and depression, suggest that religious psychotherapy is more effective and encourages more rapid improvement compared to supportive psychotherapy (Azhar, & Varma, 1995; Azhar, Varma, & Dharap, 1994). In China, Taoist and Confucian principles are embedded in psychotherapy techniques. For instance, verses from Taoist writings that highlight main principles, such as restricting selfish desires, learning how to be content, and learning to let go, are read and reflected on by the patient. A recent study found that this approach, called Chinese Taoist cognitive psychotherapy, was more effective in the long term in reducing anxiety disorders than treating the patient with medications (Zhang et al., 2002).

In addition to one-on-one psychotherapy, group psychotherapy has been exported to countries outside the United States and Europe, including countries in the Middle East. Al-Mutlaq and Chaleby (1995), however, identified several problems when conducting group therapy in Arab cultures. They discovered that the Arabs in their groups had a difficult time viewing the group as therapeutic and not just as a social activity; that because of the strict gender roles in Arab society, mixed-sex group therapy was highly criticized; and that differences in tribal status made it difficult for some individuals to communicate with others in the group who were from a different tribal status. Thus, understanding the usefulness of psychotherapy in treating people with mental illnesses in different cultures is still in its infancy.

Indigenous Healing

A focus in recent discussions of cross-cultural treatment of abnormal behavior has been culture-specific interventions, or **indigenous healing.** Indigenous healing encompasses therapeutic beliefs and practices that are rooted within a given culture. In other words, these beliefs and practices are not imported from outside cultures but are indigenously developed to treat the native population (Sue & Sue, 1999).

Many indigenous methods of healing differ widely from Western notions of healing. For instance, many indigenous treatments are rooted in religion and spirituality, not biomedical science (Sue & Sue, 1999). A study of indigenous healing in 16 non-Western countries identified several commonalities among indigenous practices (Lee, Oh, & Mountcastle, 1992). One was the heavy reliance on family and community networks as both the context and instrument for treatment. For instance, family and community were used in Saudi Arabia to protect the disturbed individual, in Korea to reconnect and reintegrate the individual with members of the family, and in Nigeria to solve problems in the context of a group. Another commonality was the incorporation of traditional, spiritual, and religious beliefs as part of the treatment—for instance, reading verses from the Koran, opening treatment with a prayer, or conducting treatment in religious houses or churches. Finally, another commonality was the use of shamans in treatment.

Several culture-specific forms of treatment have been identified in the literature, including *naikan* and *morita* therapy in Japan and *espiritismo* practiced among some Puerto Ricans. These approaches are generally very "foreign" to many Americans. *Naikan* therapy, for example, involves a "process of continuous meditation based upon highly structured instruction in self-observation and self-reflection" (Murase, 1986, p. 389). Patients are usually placed in a small sitting area and practice their meditations from early in the morning (5:30 A.M. or so) until the evening (9:00 P.M. or so). Interviewers come every 90 minutes to discuss progress, usually for about 5 minutes. Patients are instructed to examine themselves severely, much as a prosecutor would examine an accused prisoner. The patient is asked to meditate on several aspects of their relationships with others: (a) what other people have done for them, (b) what they have done for others, and (c) how they cause difficulties to others (Reynolds, 1980).

Psychological interventions in other cultures, however, are not limited to culture-specific interventions. In fact, there is a considerable movement in many other countries and cultures to merge aspects of traditional psychotherapy with culture-specific methods and beliefs to produce unique systems of healing. For example, Sato (1998) suggests that culturally indigenous therapies such as *naikan* and *morita* can be augmented successfully with aspects of contemporary cognitive and behavioral therapies. Writers have pointed to a variety of ways in which traditional methods of psychotherapy need to blend with and accommodate culture-specific issues, such as the discouragement of egoistic and individualistic strivings, and the doctrine of karma and reincarnation in India (Hoch, 1990); issues of deculturation, outmigration, alienation, distrust, and despair among Native American and Alaska Native cultures (Rodenhauser, 1994); issues of guardianship, social network, and social support in Shanghai (Zhang, Yan, & Phillips, 1994); and the interaction of spiritual, emotional/mental, physical, and family health in Maori New Zealand (Durie, 1997).

Prince (1980) argues that what is common to treatment across cultures is the mobilization of healing forces within the client. If, for example, Native Americans believe that illness results from disharmony among self, community, and nature, treatment should revolve around resolving the disharmony and restoring a state of balance and integration (Tolman & Reedy, 1998). Several others (for example, Torrey, 1972; Tseng & McDermott, 1981) have also attempted to determine universal features of culture-specific systems of treatment. Viewed in this fashion, culture-specific systems of treatment share the common characteristic of mobilizing healing forces within the client, but cultures (and psychotherapeutic approaches) differ in the exact ways in which the mobilization of healing forces occurs. Although selecting an approach may be as much an art as it is a science, cross-cultural research in the future should play an important role in evaluating the effectiveness of different approaches to mobilizing those healing forces within the client, and hence the overall effectiveness and outcomes of treatment.

An Alternative Approach to Treatment

Much of our discussion in this chapter has focused on a particular treatment based on a medical model—namely, psychotherapy. Even with modifications to traditional psychotherapy, this type of treatment may still not be wholly appropriate with people of many cultures. In the medical model, treatment is designed and directed at the individual. Some assumptions of this model are that the problem resides in the individual and that highly trained professionals such as clinicians should provide the treatment. Recognizing the limitations of the medical model, the field of community psychology, led by researchers such as Kelly (1990) and Trickett (1996), combines traditional principles of clinical psychology with an emphasis on the multiple and diverse ecologies of individuals to create alternative conceptual frameworks for understanding abnormal behavior. Community psychologists go beyond the traditional focus of responding to a person's distress on an individual level to include an analysis of mental health at the community level. In other words, understanding how to treat individuals successfully requires a recognition of the relationship between the individual and his or her daily interactions within diverse social settings and contexts in the community.

Based on these considerations, some community-oriented psychologists describe an entirely different approach to the treatment of emotional distress. For example, Miller (1999) proposes a community-based treatment to complement traditional psychotherapy:

> In contrast to the medical model, which focuses on the individual as the unit of analysis and intervention, and which emphasizes the treatment of pathology by highly trained experts, the ecological model emphasizes the relationships between people and the settings they live in; the identification of naturally occurring resources within communities that can promote healing and healthy adaptation; the enhancement of coping and adaptational strategies that enable individuals and communities to respond effectively to stressful events and circumstances; and the development of collaborative, culturally grounded community interventions that actively involve community members in the process of solving their own problems. (p. 288)

Community-based treatments may be especially relevant for helping populations such as immigrants and refugees, who are unfamiliar with the host culture, who tend not to seek out professional help, and who tend to underutilize mental health services. Such approaches can also be a useful alternative in developing countries, where access to professional mental health services and resources are scarce. Successful community interventions have been developed in diverse parts of the world, including Angola (Wessells & Monteiro, 2001), Sri Lanka (Tribe & DeSilva, 1999), and Mozambique (Boothby, 1994).

In sum, researchers and clinicians are learning how various cultural communities can use cultural informants and community structure to provide mental health services in ways that differ from traditional psychotherapy. We see this as an evolution in psychotherapeutic method in which healing, drawing on and utilizing the strengths and resources of the community, is aimed not only at individuals but toward the health of the community as a whole. This offers a promising and potentially powerful alternative to the medical model of clinical psychology for understanding and responding to psychological distress in culturally diverse populations.

Culture and Clinical Training

Because of all the issues discussed in this chapter, and throughout the book, all accredited programs of clinical training in the United States have, for some time now, been mandated to incorporate culture and diversity in their training programs. Clinical psychologists who will be in the field actually applying psychological knowledge and principles to people who seek help need to have a base for understanding the role of culture in the expression and presentation of mental illness, the difficulties and complexities involved in psychological assessment, and the issues regarding culturally sensitive yet effective treatment. Beyond these factors, however, contemporary clinicians and therapists receive training in the broad base of culture's influence on all aspects of psychology, from perception and sensation through development to social behavior and personality. It is only with this broad base of training that contemporary psychologists can gain the perspective necessary to work effectively with their clients and patients to help them improve their lives. Of course, this need for a broad understanding of the influence of culture on psychology applies to the training and practice of psychologists outside the United States as well. Moreover, the implications of psychologists' training in other cultures, learning culturally bound methods of treatment, and then returning home to practice has not been studied.

Issues regarding culture and diversity also arise in areas outside of traditional one-on-one psychotherapy—for example, the role of culture in the development and treatment of children (Tharp, 1991) and ethnic and cultural diversity in group therapy (Brook, Gordon, & Meadow, 1998). Finally, the increasing number of bilingual/bicultural individuals seeking help raises its own set of special issues, including the language and cultural framework within which psychotherapy and healing will occur. A number of writers have suggested that language proficiency, level of acculturation, and the degree to which cultural expressions represent symptomatology should be considered in the development of an effective treatment plan (for example, Altarriba & Santiago-Rivera, 1994; Ben-David, 1996; Santiago-Rivera & Azara, 1995). The need for multiple language and cultural fluency adds to the growing list of requirements for culturally competent therapists.

These issues are not only relevant to people of different ethnicities, races, or nationality. Given that psychotherapy is inescapably bound to a particular cultural framework, perhaps *all* psychotherapy can be seen as essentially cross-cultural, in that no two people have internalized identical constructions of their cultural worlds (Wohl, 1989); this view is consistent with the emphasis in this book on culture as a psychological phenomenon. Perhaps sound principles and concepts of psychotherapy can be applied cross-culturally as long as cultural differences are taken into account; this notion is consistent with the view that cross-cultural research methods are nothing more than good traditional research methods applied cross-culturally. Although some issues (such as language) are specific to applying research methods or therapeutic approaches across cultural lines, the coming together of traditional and cross-cultural approaches could provide the basis for a fundamental revision in the training of psychotherapists and clinicians in the future.

Conclusion

In this chapter, we have discussed the important role culture plays in attempting to help people with mental disorders improve their lives. The material in this chapter is not only relevant on its own, but is informed by material in the entire book showing the pervasive influence of culture on all aspects of our psychological composition. It is only within this larger perspective of the influence of culture that we can begin to truly grasp and appreciate the difficulties and complexities of diagnosing and treating abnormal behavior in a diverse world.

The difficulties presented, however, should be viewed as challenges, not obstacles. Through the study of culture, psychopathology, assessment, and psychotherapy, we are afforded the chance to expand our theoretical and conceptual horizons regarding abnormality and treatment, and to help our treatment systems evolve into bigger and better systems effectively serving larger and larger groups of people. We are currently engaged in the search for principles and knowledge that will help us achieve those goals.

Continued cross-cultural research on clinical issues—defining and assessing abnormality, designing treatment approaches that effectively mobilize healing forces within clients—is a must. But research on these major issues of definition, assessment, and treatment should proceed cautiously and systematically.

Future research will need to explore the efficacy of different treatment approaches that address both etic and emic concerns, blending traditional and culture-specific modalities in an overall, comprehensive fashion.

 ## Glossary

indigenous healing   Helping beliefs and practices that originate within a given culture or society, are not transported to or from other regions, and are designed for treating the inhabitants of the given group.

InfoTrac College Edition

Use InfoTrac College Edition to search for additional readings on topics of interest to you. For more information on topics in this chapter, use the following as search terms:

culture and psychotherapy
indigenous healing
psychotherapy

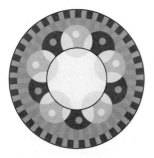

14

Culture and Social Behavior

Humans are social animals, and much of our everyday lives involves interactions with and influences of others. Especially in North America, we struggle with the tension between being unique, separate individuals ("Every man for himself") and being fundamentally connected to one another ("No man is an island").

Culture exerts considerable influence in the social arena. How we interact with others, perceive others, and work with others—all are influenced by the culture in which we live. We have all learned particular ways of behaving, perceiving, and working based on our own cultural upbringing and milieu. We may believe our way is the way people of all cultures should behave and interact, but what is true for us is often not true for people of other cultural groups.

This chapter will review some of these cultural differences in social behavior, including ingroup and outgroup relationships; interpersonal attraction, love, and intercultural marriage; attributions; aggression; and conformity, compliance, obedience, and cooperation. The goal of this chapter is to highlight the many and profound ways in which people of different cultures behave differently in social contexts. At the same time, we will see cross-cultural similarities.

Culture and Ingroup/Outgroup Relationships

Culture influences social behavior in many different ways. We all live with others, forming attachments, bonds, and relationships. We are close to some people and distant from others. We make friends, acquaintances, and even enemies.

Some of the people we see every day we know well, yet other people we see every day we don't know at all. Strangers, family members, friends, coworkers, acquaintances—the list of people in our everyday world is long.

One way social scientists have learned to understand our relationships with different people is by classifying them into categories that approximate the psychological categories we create. Especially important to understanding self–other relationships and pertinent to understanding cultural differences in social behavior is the category of ingroups versus outgroups.

Ingroups and Outgroups

The ingroups–outgroups classification is one of the oldest and best studied social classifications in social psychology and sociology (see Brewer & Kramer, 1985; Messick & Mackie, 1989; and Tajfel, 1982, for reviews and more complete descriptions of this distinction). Most of us intuitively know the difference between ingroups and outgroups. **Ingroup relationships** are relationships characterized by some degree of familiarity, intimacy, and trust. We feel close to the people around us we consider in our ingroup. Self–ingroup relationships develop through bonds that tie the ingroup together through common friendship or relationships or goals.

Outgroup relationships are just the opposite. Outgroup relationships lack the familiarity, intimacy, and trust characteristic of relationships with ingroup others. Ingroup relationships may be associated with feelings of closeness, but outgroup relationships may lack such feelings altogether and may even involve negative feelings of hostility, aggression, aloofness, or superiority. A bond exists that binds ingroup relationships together, but no such bond exists for relationships with people on the outside. These people simply exist and are barely in our consciousness. They do not have any special relationship with us.

The ingroup–outgroup distinction is dichotomous, allowing us to characterize or classify everyone in our world into one of these two categories. But social scientists know the world is not that simple. Our social relationships cannot be neatly classified into two categories. There are differing degrees of intimacy, familiarity, and closeness even within one category. Classification schemes like ingroups–outgroups are simply aids that help us understand our behavior with others while acknowledging that greater complexity exists in those relationships.

Much of socialization and enculturation—the time of growing and learning about the rules and standards of our society and culture—is spent learning which people constitute our ingroup and outgroup. From birth (and arguably before), we are busy building relationships with the people around us. As we go to school, make friends, find jobs, fall in love, and generally go through life, we develop relationships with many different people. Explicitly or implicitly, we categorize those relationships in our own minds according to the dimensions that define our ingroups and outgroups.

The ingroup–outgroup distinction is applicable to all cultures and societies of the world. People of all cultures must learn to differentiate among the people they have relationships with. However, people of different cultures differ in exactly how these relationships develop, and with whom. The people we generally consider to belong to our ingroup may not be the same people that members of another culture consider to be in their ingroup. The same is true for outgroups. And even when the same people can be classified as ingroup or outgroup across cultures, the particular shapes, forms, and meanings of those relationships may be entirely different. Recognizing these similarities and differences forms the basis for understanding how culture can influence ingroup and outgroup relationships and guide our social behaviors.

Cultural Differences in Ingroup/Outgroup Relationships

Structure and format of ingroup/outgroup relationships. We have already touched on how people of different cultures can differ in their self–ingroup and –outgroup relationships. Our own observations suggest that people of different cultures may not consider the same types of people and relationships when defining ingroups and outgroups. Just because we consider a certain type of person (a friend at school, a work colleague) an ingroup (or outgroup) member, we cannot assume that people from another culture will interpret and act on those relationships in exactly the same way.

Cultures differ in the formation and structure of self–ingroup and self–outgroup relationships in other ways as well. In North American culture, ingroup and outgroup membership is stable, no matter what we are talking about, to whom we are talking, or where we are talking. Our friends are our friends no matter what. But to someone in another culture, some people may constitute an ingroup in one circumstance or situation, but the same people may constitute an outgroup in another. It is not uncommon for businesspeople in many Asian cultures, for example, to consider each other outgroups and competitors when talking about domestic business issues. But when the discussion turns to international business competition, those same outgroup competitors may band together to form an ingroup. This type of switching of ingroups and outgroups is not limited to Asian or collectivistic cultures; it is present in many, if not all, cultures. When former President Bush visited Japan in 1991 with the chief executive officers of many different American companies, they all represented ingroup "Americans," even though those companies and officers would consider each other outgroup rivals in relation to domestic issues. As with many cultural differences, cultures differ in terms of degree but not necessarily presence or absence of this switching phenomenon.

Cross-cultural research has amply demonstrated that people of different cultures perceive relationships differently. Forgas and Bond (1985), for example, asked participants in Hong Kong and Australia about 27 social episodes related to university student life. They asked participants to group the episodes into categories based on their perceived similarity, to label their groupings, and to identify subgroups of the most similar episodes within those groups. They then subjected the data to a statistical technique known as multidimensional scaling, which identifies the kinds of dimensions that best underlie the groupings made by each group of participants. Four dimensions best described how the Hong Kong Chinese participants cognitively represented the episodes: (1) power distance, (2) task versus social orientation, (3) evaluation, and (4) involvement. For the Australian sample, however, a different set of four dimensions emerged: (1) competitiveness, (2) social versus task orientation, (3) involvement, and (4) self-confidence. These differences are clearly related to differences in the cultural values of the two societies. The Hong Kong Chinese cultural values of strong communal feelings, collectivism, and social usefulness, together with an acceptance of authority, influence their perceptions of the social events. For the Australians, competitiveness, self-confidence, freedom, and hedonistically based evaluations dominate their perceptions. These data demonstrate clearly how the same social episodes can be perceived very differently in different cultures.

Another recent study also demonstrated interesting psychological differences in how people perceive their ingroups. In this study (Harrison, Stewart, Myambo, & Teveraishe, 1995), adolescents in Zimbabwe and the United States completed a 33-item test that measured six aspects of social relationships: (1) reliable alliance, (2) enhancement or worth, (3) affection, (4) instrumental help and guidance, (5) companionship and social integration, and (6) intimacy. The researchers added three other dimensions: (7) conflict, (8) satisfaction, and (9) discipline. The participants completed this test about their relationship with six target individuals: mother, father, favorite relative, teacher, best friend, and favorite sibling. The results indicated that the Zimbabweans perceived social support as being provided by a variety of persons in their social network. The Americans, however, perceived social support as being provided primarily by parents and best friends. Also, the Zimbabweans perceived their social support network as providing them with intimacy; the Americans, on the other hand, perceived their social support network as basically providing them with affection. Again, these differences highlight the different ways in which people of different cultures can perceive ingroups and outgroups, and the different psychological meanings attributed to them. These differences are related to differences in cultural values: Zimbabwean culture places a higher value on relationships, whereas American culture places a higher value on individuality and uniqueness.

The meaning of ingroup/outgroup relationships.

Some scientists have done a considerable amount of work on cultural differences in self–ingroup and –outgroup relationships. Triandis and his colleagues (1988) have done an especially nice job of elucidating how self–ingroup and self–outgroup relationships differ across cultures by using the cultural dimension of individualism versus collectivism to understand cultural differences in social behavior.

As we have seen throughout this book, individualism–collectivism (IC) is one of the most important social psychological dimensions of culture. Many writers across the social science disciplines have used this dimension to understand differences in social behaviors across the cultures they have studied (for example, Hofstede, 1980, 1983; Kluckholn & Strodtbeck, 1961; Mead, 1961; Triandis, 1972). IC refers to the degree to which a culture promotes individual needs, wishes, desires, and values over group and collective ones. Individualistic cultures encourage their members to become unique individuals; hierarchical power and status differences are minimized, and equality is emphasized. Collectivistic cultures stress the needs of a group; individuals are identified more through their group affiliation than by individual position or attributes. Hierarchical differences and vertical relationships are emphasized, and role, status, and appropriate behaviors are more clearly defined by position.

Self–ingroup and self–outgroup relationships differ in individualistic and collectivistic cultures, and these differences in the meaning of ingroup and outgroup relationships produce differences in the types of behaviors people engage in when interacting with others. In individualistic cultures, such as the United States, people often belong to multiple ingroups. Many Americans belong to several ingroups—music groups, sports groups, church groups, social groups, and so forth. Children may belong to football teams during football season, basketball teams during basketball season, and baseball teams during baseball season. They may take swimming lessons, take piano or violin lessons, belong to Boy or Girl Scouts, and generally just be the busiest people around. In contrast, members of collectivistic cultures, including many Asian and South American cultures, belong to fewer ingroups. They do not belong to all the different sports, music, and social groups that people in individualistic cultures do.

This difference between individualistic and collectivistic cultures in ingroup membership has important consequences for the degree of commitment people have to different groups. In general, in exchange for belonging to fewer groups, people in collectivistic cultures have greater commitments to the groups to which they belong. They also identify more with the groups to which they belong; that is, the groups themselves become an integral part of each individual's self-concept and identity. This makes sense because, by definition, collectivistic cultures depend on groups to a much greater degree, and subjugating personal goals in favor of collective goals is a necessity.

Members of individualistic cultures do not necessarily collapse their sense of self-identity and self-concept into the groups to which they belong. They have fewer commitments to their ingroups and move much more easily from ingroup to ingroup. Groups take on special importance in collectivistic cultures, but the same degree of importance does not attach to group membership in individualistic cultures.

It follows that collectivistic cultures require a greater degree of harmony, cohesion, and cooperation within their ingroups and place greater burdens on individuals to identify with the group and conform to group norms. Sanctions usually exist for nonconformity. Individualistic cultures depend less on groups and more on the uniqueness of their individuals. The pursuit of personal goals rather than collective ones is of primary importance. As a result, individualistic cultures require less harmony and cohesion within groups and place less importance on conformity of individuals to group norms.

These differences in the meaning of self–ingroup relationships between individualistic and collectivistic cultures have consequences for behavior. In collectivistic cultures, for example, we would expect people to make more individual sacrifices for their ingroups in pursuit of group goals. We would expect to see people trying harder to cooperate with one another, even if it means that the individual must suppress his or her own feelings, thoughts, behaviors, or goals to maintain harmony and cohesion. We would expect people to try to find ways of agreeing with each other, downplaying and minimizing interpersonal differences for the sake of harmony.

Self–ingroup relationships in individualistic cultures have different consequences for behavior. In these cultures, we would expect people to make fewer sacrifices of their own individual goals, needs, and desires for the sake of a common good. We would expect people to be more expressive of their own feelings, attitudes, and opinions, without as much fear or worry about the consequences for group harmony or cohesion. We would expect people to bring up interpersonal concerns, problems, and conflicts more freely.

Not only do self–ingroup relationships differ between individualistic and collectivistic cultures, but self–outgroup relationships also differ. In collectivistic cultures, the primary focus of attention is on ingroup relationships. For that reason, relationships with outgroup people are marked by a relative lack of concern. To the degree that members of collectivistic cultures focus on harmony, cohesion, and cooperation in ingroup relations, they tend to exhibit distancing, aloofness, and even discrimination with regard to self–outgroup relationships. The opposite is true in individualistic cultures. People of individualistic cultures are more likely to treat outgroup persons more equally, with relatively less distinction between ingroups and outgroups. Members of individualistic cultures engage in positive, relationship-building behaviors with outgroup others that members of collectivistic cultures would reserve only for ingroup others. These concepts are summarized in Table 14.1.

Recent cross-cultural research on ingroup and outgroup relationships.

Recent research continues to support many of these notions originally proposed by Triandis and his colleagues (1988). In Chapter 9, for example, we discussed two studies that found differences in emotional expressions among the United States, Japan, Poland, and Hungary that supported these ideas concerning cultural differences in self–ingroup and self–outgroup relationships. In another study, Goodwin and Lee (1994) asked British and Singapore Chinese university students to complete a questionnaire designed to assess the degree to which they would discuss or do 35 behaviors that are typically considered taboo. The items ranged from discussion of sexual fantasies to crying in front of friends. Participants answered these items in relation to interactions with close friends of both sexes. The results indicated that the British participants were more likely than the Chinese participants to discuss taboo subjects with their close friends. These findings are consistent with the greater maintenance of harmony and cohesion in ingroup relationships in more collectivistic cultures.

Table 14.1 Self–Ingroup and Self–Outgroup Relationship Differences as a Function of Individualism and Collectivism

Type of Culture	Characteristics
In individualistic cultures . . .	1. People have more ingroups. 2. People are not as attached to any single ingroup, because there are numerous ingroups to which they can be attached. 3. Survival of the individuals and the society is more dependent on the successful and effective functioning of individuals rather than groups. 4. People make relatively fewer distinctions between ingroups and outgroups.
In collectivistic cultures . . .	1. People have fewer ingroups. 2. People are very attached to the ingroups to which they belong. 3. Survival of the individuals and the society is more dependent on the successful and effective functioning of the groups rather than individuals. 4. People make greater distinctions between ingroup and outgroup others.

Source: Adapted from Triandis et al., 1988.

In another study, Wheeler, Reis, and Bond (1989) asked participants in the United States and Hong Kong to complete the Rochester Interaction Record (RIR) for a period of two weeks. The RIR involves the self-description of every interaction that lasts for more than 10 minutes in which interactants attended to and adjusted their behavior between each other. Each interaction is described in terms of when it occurred, its length, who the interactants were, their sex breakdown, and eight scales involving ratings of disclosure, quality, satisfaction, and the nature of the interaction. The results indicated that the Hong Kong Chinese students had longer but fewer interactions, with fewer people, than did the American students. The Chinese students also reported a higher percentage of group and task interactions, and indicated great self- and other-disclosure. These findings are certainly consonant with the previous discussion concerning the type, number, and quality of self–ingroup interactions in collectivistic versus individualistic cultures.

Summary

People in all cultures and societies grow up learning to make distinctions among others in terms of ingroups and outgroups. Culture exerts considerable influence not only over the structure and format of those self–ingroup and self–outgroup relationships but also over the very meaning of those relationships. And cultural differences in the meaning of those relationships produces real, observable differences in the behaviors, thoughts, and feelings of the individual when interacting with ingroup and outgroup others.

How we conceptualize and act on our relationships with others can differ dramatically from culture to culture. Therefore, in interacting with others, if we try to interpret their social behaviors within our own limited cultural framework, it is very possible that we will misunderstand and misinterpret those behaviors. Good intentions may be seen as bad; innocuous behaviors may be seen as threatening or aggressive.

Culture, Person Perception, and Attractiveness

Person perception refers to the process of forming impressions of others. Social scientists have long realized the influence of impressions and perceptions of others on our interactions. Questions concerning the degree to which impressions influence actual behaviors and the extent to which people's expectations color their impressions of others fall within the purview of person perception. Social scientists are also interested in whether bad first impressions can be overcome. Research on person perception has outlined several key factors that contribute to the formation of our impressions of others, including appearance, schemas, stereotypes, and selectivity in person perception.

Knowledge Based on U.S. Research

Appearance, especially physical attractiveness, influences judgments of personality. Research with American subjects has consistently shown that people tend to ascribe desirable personality characteristics to those who are good-looking, seeing them as more sensitive, kind, sociable, pleasant, likable, and interesting than those who are unattractive (Dion, 1986; Patzer, 1985). Attractive people are also judged to be more competent and intelligent (Ross & Ferris, 1981).

In the past few years, two meta-analytic studies of the correlates of attractiveness have been conducted, aggregating data involving judges in the United States and Canada. In one (Eagly, Ashmore, Makhijani, & Longo, 1991), attractiveness ratings were shown to be strongly correlated with social competence, adjustment, potency, and intellectual competence, and negatively with modesty. In the other (Feingold, 1992), attractiveness was correlated with social skills, sociability, mental health, dominance, intelligence, and sexual warmth, and again negatively with modesty. These meta-analyses, which were conducted and reported independently, demonstrated quite consistent agreement in findings involving North American participants with regard to the psychological meanings attributed to attractive faces.

Other aspects of appearance also influence our perceptions of others. For example, greater height, which is generally considered attractive, has been associated with leadership ability, competence, and high salary (Deck, 1968;

Patzer, 1985). Adults with baby-face features tend to be judged as warm, kind, naive, and submissive; adults with more mature facial features tend to be judged as strong, worldly, and dominant (Berry & McArthur, 1985, 1986). People who are neat dressers are thought to be conscientious (Albright, Kenny, & Malloy, 1988). People with poor eye contact are often judged as dishonest (DePaulo, Stone, & Lassiter, 1985).

Research on person perception in the United States has also focused on the ways impressions are formed and the way information about others is stored. Much attention has been given to the study of **cognitive schemas** as organizational tools. A schema is a conceptual framework that people use to make sense of the world and people around them. **Social schemas** are organized clusters of ideas about categories of social events and people that have been shown to influence person perceptions (Markus & Zajonc, 1985). Much attention has also been given to the study of stereotypes—widely held beliefs about people's underlying psychological characteristics or personality traits—and their influence on our impressions of others (see Chapter 3). Finally, social psychologists have studied the influence of selectivity on our perceptions of others to either confirm or disconfirm beliefs and stereotypes.

Cross-Cultural Studies on Attractiveness

Although the effects of attractiveness and physical appearance on the formation of positive impressions is well documented in the mainstream psychological literature, cultures clearly differ on the meaning and definition of attractiveness. Beauty is a relative judgment, and people of different cultures can have quite different concepts of what is beautiful and what is not. Cultural differences in the definition of attractiveness, in turn, can influence the formation of impressions. Daibo, Murasawa, and Chou (1994), for example, compared judgments of physical attractiveness made by Japanese and Koreans. They showed male and female university students in both countries slides of Japanese and Korean females and asked them to rate the attractiveness and likability of each person using 13 bipolar adjective scales. Three poses of each person were shown: front view, profile, and three-quarter view. Facial physiognomy—that is, the anatomical characteristics of the face—were also measured separately by an anatomist, and these measurements were correlated with the psychological judgments provided by the respondents. In Japan, attractiveness ratings were positively correlated with large eyes, small mouths, and small chins. In Korea, however, attractiveness ratings were correlated with large eyes, small and high noses, and thin and small faces. Koreans tended to attach other affective and psychological judgments, such as maturity and likability, to judgments of attractiveness. The Japanese, however, did not. These findings show not only that the two cultures have different standards for beauty, but that beauty has culturally specific psychological meanings.

A study by Wheeler and Kim (1997) demonstrated similar effects. These researchers showed photos of Korean males and females to Korean university students, who made judgments of social competence, intellectual competence, concern for others, integrity, adjustment, potency, sexual interest/warmth, and modesty. Consistent with research involving North American judges, this study found that Korean students rated attractive faces as more socially and intellectually competent, better adjusted, more sexually interesting, and less modest. Contrary to previous research with North Americans, however, the Koreans did not rate attractive faces as more potent. They did rate them as having more integrity and concern for others, which was not found in previous mainstream studies. Wheeler and Kim concluded that, while all cultures appear to stereotype on the basis of physical attractiveness, the contents of the stereotypes probably depend on cultural values.

Another study also demonstrated cultural differences in the psychological meaning derived from attractive faces. Matsumoto and Kudoh (1993) asked American and Japanese subjects to judge Caucasian and Japanese faces that were either smiling or neutral on three dimensions: attractiveness, intelligence, and sociability. The Americans consistently rated the smiling faces higher on all three dimensions, congruent with our traditional notions of person perception and impression formation. The Japanese, however, only rated the smiling faces as more sociable. There was no difference in their ratings of attractiveness between smiles and neutrals, and they rated the neutral faces as more intelligent.

Despite the abundance of cross-cultural research demonstrating cultural differences in judgments of attractiveness and its inferred psychological meaning, at least one convincing study has reported judgments of attractiveness that are consistent across cultures. Cunningham, Roberts, Barbee, Druen, and Wu (1995) conducted a series of three studies, all using basically the same methodology. In the first study, European Americans and Asian and Hispanic immigrants judged faces of Asian, Hispanic, African American, and European American women. In the second study, Taiwanese respondents rated the same stimuli. In the third study, African and European Americans rated African American female faces. The stimuli were photographs whose subjects ranged from college students to contestants in beauty contests in other cultures. In all three studies, the researchers obtained attractiveness ratings from the judges, as well as 28 separate measurements of facial features. The results across all three studies indicated extremely high correlations among the judge groups in their attractiveness ratings. Moreover, the attractiveness ratings by all groups correlated with the same facial characteristics, which included the nature of the eyes, nose, cheeks, chins, and smiles.

There is no clear-cut answer as to why some studies have found differences across cultures and others have found cross-cultural similarity. Clearly, methodological differences across the studies need to be ruled out before making any definitive statements concerning the possible influence of culture on ratings of attractiveness. For example, the differences in the results across studies may be attributable to the nature of the samples tested, or the nature of the stimuli used. Also, differences in the findings across cultures may be associated with degree of exposure to other cultures' standards of beauty via mass media (magazines, movies, television), and these effects are not handled consistently in all cross-cultural research. Regardless of the research findings, however, we know from personal experience that there are enough individual differences within any culture in judgments of attractiveness to suggest that beauty really is in the eye of the beholder.

Cross-Cultural Research on Other Aspects of Person Perception

Many cross-cultural studies challenge our traditional notions of person perception in North American psychology. For example, cross-cultural studies of nonverbal behavior—gaze, proximity, touching behaviors, verbal utterances, facial expressions—all speak to the impact of culture on communication. Differences in these behaviors arising from differences in cultural upbringing undoubtedly influence our perception of people of different cultures. We are often unaware of or unprepared to deal with cultural differences, and it is easy to form negative perceptions of others because of cultural differences in these nonverbal behaviors.

The recognition of faces is yet another area of research related to person perception. Numerous studies have amply demonstrated that people tend to recognize others of their own perceived race more accurately than the faces of other perceived races. Most studies examining and demonstrating this effect have involved comparisons of European and African Americans (for example, Bothwell, Brigham, & Malpass, 1989; Brigham & Malpass, 1985; Shapiro & Penrod, 1986), but this finding has also been replicated using Asian faces and respondents (Ng & Lindsay, 1994). A number of hypotheses have been offered to explain such effects. For example, differences in facial anatomical features may make certain types of faces more easily recognizable than others. The contact hypothesis suggests that recognition accuracy is directly related to the amount of contact one has with others; as people generally have more contact with others of their same perceived race, this exposure leads to higher recognition rates. Another hypothesis suggests that nonfamiliar faces, especially of other perceived races, all "look alike" and thus are less discernible than own-race faces. Another hypothesis suggests that racial attitudes, including prejudice against others, may cause individuals to process faces of other races differently than own-race faces. Although cross-cultural research has amply demonstrated own-race superiority in facial recognition, research is far behind in examining which of these hypotheses, or others, either singly or in combination, may account for this phenomenon.

Even when different cultures agree on overall dimensional judgments of others, they may disagree on the behavioral consequences of those judgments. For example, Bond and Forgas (1984) presented Chinese and Australian subjects with a description of a target person varying across the dimensions of extroversion, agreeableness, conscientiousness, and emotional stability. Across both cultures, conscientiousness was linked with intentions of trust, while extroversion and agreeableness were linked to intentions of association. However, the Chinese subjects were much more likely than the Australians to form behavioral intentions of trust and to form behavioral associations based on agreeableness.

Certainly, as the research on attractiveness suggests, there are similarities as well as differences in person perception processes across cultures. Bernieri and Gillis (1995), for example, reported striking similarities between American and Greek participants' judgments of rapport when viewing 50 video-recorded dyadic interactions. Thus, ample evidence exists to suggest that cultures are both similar and different in both the process and the meaning of person perception and impression formation. This area of social psychology is indeed germane to our understanding of cultures, stereotypes, and ethnocentrism because it forms the basis for such intergroup and interpersonal processes. Future research has the daunting task of trying to unravel how similarities and differences in these processes coexist, and why.

Culture and Interpersonal Attraction: Love, Intimacy, and Intercultural Marriages

As our world gets smaller and smaller, the frequency of interacting with people of ethnic and cultural backgrounds different from our own increases. As these intercultural interactions increase, so does the likelihood that people will become attracted to each other, fall in love, get married, and have families. Indeed, whereas intercultural and interracial relationships were a rarity in the past, they are now more and more frequent. With this increase in intercultural and interracial relationships come increased tensions, frustrations, worries, and joys.

Driven by new concerns arising from our increasingly intercultural world, the amount of cross-cultural research on this topic has also increased. Psychologists use the term **interpersonal attraction** to encompass a variety of experiences, including liking, friendship, admiration, lust, and love. U.S. research on interpersonal attraction and love has produced a number of interesting findings, mainly focusing on the factors that contribute to attraction. At the same time, cross-cultural research gives us important clues to cultural differences in attraction and love, and an increasing number of studies on intercultural relationships point to the pitfalls and possible solutions.

Interpersonal Attraction and Love in the United States

About 90% of people in most societies get married (Carroll & Wolpe, 1996). What attracts people in selecting another as a mate and marriage partner? Studies conducted by psychologists as early as the 1950s (for example, Festinger, Schachter, & Back, 1950) showed that proximity influences attraction: People who live close to each other are more likely to like one another. Findings from more recent studies support these early findings. In the late 1970s, for instance, Ineichen (1979) showed that people who live close together are more likely to get married.

In the United States, physical attractiveness is an important ingredient of interpersonal relationships (Patzer, 1985), but attractiveness may be more important in male preference for females than the reverse (Buss, 1988). Most people surveyed in the United States prefer physically attractive partners in romantic relationships. But a **matching hypothesis** also suggests that people of approximately equal physical characteristics are likely to select each other as partners. Likewise, a **similarity hypothesis** suggests that people similar in age, race, religion, social class, education, intelligence, attitudes, and physical attractiveness tend to form intimate relationships (Brehm, 1985; Hendrick & Hendrick, 1983). Certainly, there is something safe about similarities in a relationship that make similar partners particularly attractive for romance and love. A glance at the wedding announcement section in the Sunday edition of *The New York Times* certainly seems to support the similarity hypothesis. Finally, a **reciprocity hypothesis** suggests that people tend to like others who like them (Byrne & Murnen, 1988).

Few people in the United States would discount the importance of love in the development and maintenance of long-term relationships such as friendship and marriage, and love has been a particularly well studied topic in American psychology. Hatfield and Berscheid's (Berscheid, 1988; Hatfield, 1988) theory of love and attachment proposes that romantic relationships are characterized by two kinds of love. One is **passionate love**, involving absorption of another that includes sexual feelings and intense emotion. The second is **companionate love**, involving warm, trusting, and tolerant affection for another whose life is deeply intertwined with one's own. Sternberg's (1988) theory is similar to Hatfield and Berscheid's but divides companionate love into two separate components: intimacy and commitment. Intimacy refers to warmth, closeness, and sharing in a relationship. Commitment refers to an intention to maintain a relationship in spite of the difficulties that arise. In Sternberg's theory, seven different forms of love can exist, depending on the presence or absence of each of the three factors: passionate love, intimacy, and commitment. For instance, **infatuation** is passion alone, without intimacy or commitment; **romantic love** is a combination of passion and intimacy, but without commitment. When all three factors are present, Sternberg calls that relationship **consummate love**.

Another well-studied area of interpersonal attraction is intimacy. In research conducted in the United States, intimacy is closely associated with self-disclosure—the degree to which people will disclose information about themselves to others (for example, Adamopoulos, 1991; Altman & Taylor, 1973; Helgeson, Shaver, & Dyer, 1987). In the United States, high levels of self-disclosure characterize intimate relationships. According to social penetration theory, relationship development is based on four stages of increasing disclosure, with partners able to describe themselves fully in the final stage.

Interpersonal Attraction, Love, and Intimacy across Cultures

Cross-cultural studies have amply demonstrated cultural differences in attitudes about love and romance around the world. For example, Ting-Toomey (1991) compared ratings of love commitment, disclosure maintenance, ambivalence, and conflict expression by 781 participants from France, Japan, and the

United States. Love commitment was measured by ratings of feelings of attachment, belongingness, and commitment to the partner and the relationship; disclosure maintenance by ratings of feelings concerning the private self in the relationship; ambivalence by ratings of feelings of confusion or uncertainty regarding the partner or the relationship; and conflict expression by ratings of frequency of overt arguments and seriousness of problems. The French and the Americans had significantly higher ratings than the Japanese on love commitment and disclosure maintenance. The Americans also had significantly higher ratings than the Japanese on relational ambivalence. The Japanese and the Americans, however, had significantly higher ratings than the French on conflict expression.

Simmons, vom Kolke, and Shimizu (1986) examined attitudes toward love and romance among American, German, and Japanese students. The results indicated that romantic love was valued more in the United States and Germany than in Japan. These researchers explained this cultural difference by suggesting that romantic love is more highly valued in less traditional cultures with few strong, extended family ties, and less valued in cultures where kinship networks influence and reinforce the relationship between marriage partners.

Many other studies document cultural differences in attitudes about love and romance. Furnham (1984), for instance, administered the Rokeach Value Survey to groups of South Africans, Indians, and Europeans. The Europeans valued love more than did the South Africans and the Indians. The South Africans, however, placed a higher value on equality and peace. Murstein, Merighi, and Vyse (1991) compared American and French college students' attitudes about love. They found that Americans tended to prefer friendships that slowly evolve into love, as well as relationships in which the lovers are caught up in an excited, panicky state; the French rated higher on love as characterized by altruistic generosity. Wang (1994) found that contrary to popular stereotypes, Italian males report less passionate love feelings in their relationships than American males.

Landis and O'Shea's (2000) examination of multiple dimensions of passionate love included 1,709 participants from Denmark, England, Israel, Canada, and five cities in the United States. Using a form of factor analysis, they found that the specific structure of passionate love varies across countries. For example, some aspects of passionate love were unique to a specific country, such as a factor encompassing protective intimacy ("I would get jealous if I thought he/she were falling in love with someone else") and tender intimacy ("I will love him/her forever") for Indiana and Houston males and females, and realistic closeness ("If she/he were going through a difficult time, I would put away my concerns to help him/her out") and idealistic closeness ("No one else could love her/him like I do") for Danish males and females.

Dion and Dion (1993a) tested respondents who were classified into one of four ethnocultural groups—Anglo-Celtic, Chinese, Other Asian, and European—on a 54-item love attitude scale. The results indicated that the Chinese and Other Asian respondents were more friendship oriented in their love relationships than were respondents of the other two groups. Asian women also expressed more altruism than did Anglo-Celtic women. Ellis, Kimmel, Diaz-Guerrero, Canas, and Bajo (1994) used a semantic differential technique to examine the subjective meaning of love and power in Spaniards, Mexicans, Hispanic Americans, and Anglo-Americans. This technique involves multiple-item ratings on three scales: evaluation (positive–negative), potency (strong–weak), and activity (active–passive). The results indicated that the Mexicans rated love as less positive and less potent than the other three groups. They also found that the psychological judgments of love and power along the three dimensions were correlated for Spaniards, but not for the other three groups. Finally, Elbedour, Shulman, and Kedem (1997) examined and compared perceptions of intimacy in friendships among Israeli Jewish and Bedouin adolescents. Overall, the data indicated that intimacy was perceived to reflect a balance between closeness and individuality. But Jewish adolescents reported less of a need to control or to be similar to each other in friendships, whereas Bedouin adolescents reported more emphasis on control and conformity to friends.

Despite differences in the definitions and importance of attraction, love, and romance, however, some research suggests amazing cross-cultural similarity in sex differences with regard to mate selection. In one of the best-known studies on this topic (Buss, 1989, 1994), more than 10,000 respondents in 37 different cultures drawn from 33 countries completed two questionnaires, one dealing with factors in choosing a mate and the second dealing with preferences concerning potential mates. In 36 of the 37 cultures, females rated financial prospects as more important than did males; in 29 of those 36 cultures, females also rated ambition and industriousness as more important than did males. In all 37 cultures, males preferred younger mates and females preferred older mates; in 34 of the cultures, males rated good looks as more important than did females; and in 23 of the cultures, males rated chastity as more important than did females. Buss (1989) concluded that females value cues related to resource acquisition in potential mates more highly than males do, whereas males value reproductive capacity more highly than do females. These findings were predicted, in fact, on the basis of an evolutionary-based framework that generated hypotheses related to evolutionary concepts of parental involvement, sexual selection, reproductive capacity, and certainty of paternity or maternity. The degree of agreement in sex differences across cultures has led Buss (1989) and his colleagues to view these mate selection preferences as universal, arising from different evolutionary selection pressures on males and females.

A more recent study by Hatfield and Sprecher (1995) has replicated and extended the findings by Buss and his colleagues. In this study, male and female students in the United States, Russia, and Japan were surveyed concerning their preferences in a marital partner, using a 12-item scale. The items all referred to positive traits: physically attractive, intelligent, athletic, ambitious, good conversationalist, outgoing and sociable, status or money, skill as a lover, kind and understanding, potential for success, expressive and open, and sense of humor. Across all three cultures, the data indicated that the only scale on which men gave higher ratings than women was physical attractiveness.

Women gave higher ratings than men on all the other scales except good conversationalist. There were also some interesting cultural differences. For example, Americans preferred expressivity, openness, and sense of humor more than did the Russians, who in turn preferred these traits more than did the Japanese. Russians desired skill as a lover most, while Japanese preferred it least. The Japanese gave lower ratings than the other two cultures on kind and understanding, good conversationalist, physical attractiveness, and status. In this study, however, no mention was made of the possibility of cultural response sets, which may render the cultural differences reported ambiguous.

Other researchers offer an alternative explanation for interpersonal attraction based on a social construction perspective (for example, Beall & Sternberg, 1995). This perspective highlights the importance of individual and cultural, as opposed to evolutionary, factors in understanding interpersonal attraction. Indeed, social constructionists argue that there are more gender similarities than differences when it comes to choosing mates. For instance, a U.S. study of the most important traits reported by both men and women when looking for a partner are kindness, consideration, honesty, and a sense of humor (Goodwin, 1990).

A recent study by Pines (2001) provides evidence for both the evolutionary theory and the social construction theory of mate selection. In this study, American and Israeli students were extensively interviewed about their romantic relationships. As evolutionary theory would predict, more men than women mentioned physical appearance as a reason for attraction to their partner. However, as social construction theory would predict, culture also played an important role in determining what was considered attractive. For example, Americans were attracted to the status of their partners more than Israelis were. Also, closeness and similarity were more important factors for Americans than for Israelis.

There may also be developmentally different preferences in what one considers attractive in a partner. For instance, a study involving Dutch and German participants reports that as people get older, the stereotypical male preference for appearance and female preference for financial prospects give way to a preference for a steady relationship, home, and children (de Raad & Boddema-Winesemius, 1992).

A recent study highlights cross-cultural similarity in another important aspect of intimate relationships: anger expressions and possible conflict resolutions. In this study (Kubany et al., 1995), 160 Filipino college students rated their feelings and reactions to four different types of statements: self-attributed distress ("I feel anxious"), self-attributed anger ("I'm getting angry"), partner attributed distress ("You've been making me feel upset all week"), and partner attributed anger ("You're getting me angry"). The results indicated that "You" messages were rated as more aversive, more likely to evoke animosity, less likely to evoke compassion, more like to evoke antagonistic behavior, and less likely to evoke conciliatory behavior. Also, compared to statements of distress, anger statements were rated as more aversive, more likely to evoke animosity, less likely to evoke compassion, more likely to evoke antagonistic behavior, and less likely to evoke conciliatory behavior. According to Kubany and colleagues, these findings replicate similar studies conducted in the United States, suggesting that

> explicitly communicated anger and blame may operate similarly as instigators of animosity and antagonism—across cultures and across languages. It may be that words of anger generally tend to evoke animosity and antagonism because words of anger, by definition and from experience with "angry" people, connote or communicate unfriendliness and adversarial antagonism. Similarly, the experience of being blamed may tend to instigate animosity and antagonistic inclinations in people everywhere. On intuitive grounds alone, it seems unlikely that many people like to be blamed for negative outcomes, and the experience of being blamed may generally tend to instigate a hostile counterresponse. (pp. 76–77)

Thus, although there may be cross-cultural differences in views about love and intimacy, there may be something universal about how we express ourselves, particularly our anger, that can help resolve or perpetuate conflicts in those types of relationships.

Intercultural Marriages

Given the cultural differences in attitudes toward love, interpersonal attraction, and marriage, it is no wonder that intercultural and interracial marriages and relationships bring with them their own special problems and issues. As the frequency of interacting with people from many diverse cultures and ethnicities increases in our everyday lives, so too will the number of such relationships.

Although theories about love and attraction are prevalent and popular in American psychology, we know of no research across cultures that directly tests their validity. That is, are the components and psychological meanings of love the same or different across cultures? There is sufficient information from cross-cultural research, however, to suggest how the concepts of attraction, love, and intimacy differ across cultures.

It is important to consider first how different cultures may view love. In the United States, people generally feel that love is a necessary and sometimes sufficient ingredient for long-term romantic relationships and marriage. "Love conquers all," as the saying goes. But love does not enjoy the same consideration for long-term relationships and marriage in many cultures as it does in the United States. Matsumoto remembers talking to a person from another culture about the "divorce rate problem" of the United States. We were discussing sociological data indicating that the frequency of divorce is higher than it has ever been in American history and that it continues to rise. He commented to me that there is no such problem in his country. "The reason for this difference," he said, "is quite clear. You Americans marry the person you love; we love the person we marry."

These types of differences were exemplified in a recent study by Levine, Sato, Hashimoto, and Verma (1995). These researchers asked students in 11 different countries to rate the importance of love for both the establishment and maintenance of a marriage. The countries included were India, Pakistan, Thailand, Mexico, Brazil, Japan, Hong Kong, the Philippines, Australia, England, and the United States. The responses of the participants were correlated with indices of individualism versus collectivism, gross domestic product and living costs, marriage rates, fertility rates, and divorce rates. The results indicated that the individualistic countries were more likely to rate love as essential to the establishment of a marriage, and to agree that the disappearance of love is a sufficient reason to end a marriage. Countries with large GDPs also showed this tendency—not surprising, given the high correlation between affluence and individualism. Also, countries with high marriage and divorce rates, and low fertility rates, assigned greater importance to romantic love. Divorce rates were highly correlated with the belief that the disappearance of love warranted the dissolution of a marriage.

Using data collected by anthropologists that compared 186 traditional cultures on love, Jankowiak and Fischer (1992) showed that in every single culture but one, young people reported falling passionately in love, experienced the euphoria and despair of passionate love, knew of poems, stories, and legends about famous lovers, and sang love songs. Nonetheless, this did not mean that the young people from these cultures could pursue these feelings of love and marry the person they fell in love with. Instead, in these cultures, arranged marriages were the norm.

Arranged marriages are quite common in many cultures of the world, including Japan, China, Egypt, and India. In India, arranged marriages date back 6,000 years (Saraswathi, 1999). Sometimes marriages are arranged by parents far before the age at which the couple can even consider marriage. In other cases, marriage meetings are held between prospective couples, who may then date for a while to decide whether to get married or not. In these cultures, marriage is seen as more than just the union of two individuals, but rather as a union and alliance between two entire families (Dion & Dion, 1993b; Stone, 1990). Love between the two individuals is often not part of this equation but is something that should grow in the marriage relationship. Hatfield and Rapson (1996) report that getting married based on romantic love is a relatively new concept, about 300 years old in the West and much newer in non-Western cultures. With globalization, however, young people from these countries are opting for selecting their own mates. For instance, 40% of young people in India intend to find a marriage partner on their own (Sprecher & Chandak, 1992). This trend is currently reflected in other countries as well, such as Japan, China, Egypt, and Turkey (Arnett, 2001).

When any two people get married, conflict is inevitable, because any two people come from two different worldviews and perspectives. This situation is exacerbated in intercultural marriages, because the two people bring not only their individual differences but also their cultural differences and values (see Kiev, 1973). Studies of intercultural marriages (see Cottrell, 1990, for a review) have generally shown that conflicts in intercultural marriages arise in several major areas, including the expression of love and intimacy, the nature of commitment and attitudes toward the marriage itself, and approaches to child rearing when couples have children. Other potential sources of conflict include differences in perceptions of male–female roles (McGoldrick & Preto, 1984; Romano, 1988), differences in domestic money management (Ho, 1984; Hsu, 1977; Kiev, 1973; McGoldrick & Preto, 1984), differences in perceptions of relationships with extended family (Cohen, 1982; Markoff, 1977), and differences in the definitions of marriage itself (Markoff, 1977).

It is no wonder that couples in intercultural marriages experience conflicts around intimacy and love expression. As described in Chapter 9, people of different cultures vary considerably in their expression of basic emotions such as anger, frustration, or happiness. And as we have seen, cultures differ on the degree to which emotions such as love and intimacy are seen as important ingredients of a successful marriage. These differences arise from a fundamental difference in attitudes toward marriage. Americans tend to view marriage as a lifetime companionship between two individuals in love. People of many other cultures view marriage more as a partnership formed for succession (that is, for producing offspring) and for economic and social bonding. Love rarely enters the equation in the beginning for people in these cultures, although they usually tend to develop a love relationship with the marriage partner over time. With such fundamental differences in the nature of marriage across cultures, it is no wonder that intercultural marriages are often among the most difficult of relationships.

Sometimes the differences between two people involved in an intercultural marriage do not arise until they have children. Often, major cultural differences emerge around issues of child rearing. This is no surprise, either, because of the enormous differences in socialization practices and the role of parenting in the development of culture, as was discussed in Chapter 5. Although it has been a common belief that children of intracultural marriages have stronger ethnic identities than children of intercultural marriages, recent research does not tend to support this claim (for example, Parsonson, 1987). Children tend to develop strong or weak ethnic identities based not on their parents' similarity or difference, but on their upbringing, especially with regard to attitudes, values, and behaviors regarding their single or dual cultures. Children with stronger ethnic identities, however, are more likely to want to marry within their own ethnic group (Parsonson, 1987).

How can intercultural couples overcome these additional obstacles in their relationships to build successful marriages? Of course, communication is important in any relationship, and such communication is especially important in intercultural relationships (Atkeson, 1970). Many of the skills discussed in Chapter 10 come into play here. Couples involved in an intercultural relationship need to develop intercultural sensitivity and a constructive method of dealing with conflict to make their relationships successful.

Ho (1984) has suggested that three types of adjustments help to resolve differences: capitulation, compromise, and coexistence. Capitulation refers to the ability and willingness to give up one's own cultural behaviors and accept the other's position occasionally. Compromise refers to finding a mutual point, with both partners partially giving up their positions and partially accepting each other's. Coexistence refers to the process by which both partners live with their respective differences by accepting each other "as they are" in their marriage.

Tseng (1977) offers some additional ways of dealing with intercultural relationships. Tseng's "alternating way" is one in which partners take turns in adapting their cultural behaviors. A "mixing way" is one in which partners take some behaviors and customs from both cultures and randomly introduce them into their marriage. "Creative adjustment" is when partners invent a completely new set of behavior patterns after deciding to give up their respective cultural norms.

It seems to us that there is yet another way of negotiating the trials and tribulations of intercultural marriage, which we will call the "context constructionistic" way. Cultural differences between two people will manifest themselves in specific contexts. One way for two people from different cultures to deal with these differences is to discuss the perspectives of both cultures in relation to each context in which there is a conflict or difference. The couple can then discuss the pros and cons of both perspectives in relation to their lives as a whole—work, family, children, and cultural and ethnic "balance"—and make functional decisions based on these discussions. In some cases, a couple may choose to go with one cultural perspective, in other cases, with the other perspective. The couple may choose to alternate perspectives, or to be creative and establish their own unique perspective on the situation, blending their cultural knowledge. In this fashion, the everyday negotiation of intercultural marriage is an interesting and exciting journey in which the couple as a unit must engage, rather than a "problem" to be dealt with.

In many ways, intercultural marriages are the prime example of intercultural relationships. For them to be successful, both partners need to be flexible, compromising, and committed to the relationship. If these three ingredients are in the pot, couples will often find ways to make their relationships work. Despite the difficulties, anecdotal evidence suggests intercultural marriages are not necessarily associated with higher divorce rates than intracultural marriages. Perhaps it all comes down to how much both spouses are willing to work to negotiate differences, compromise, and stay together.

Culture and Attributions

Attributions are the inferences people make about the causes of events and their own and others' behaviors. Attributions represent the ways we understand the world around us and the behavior of others. You might attribute a friend's failure to show up for a date to irresponsibility, too much traffic, or just forgetting. You might attribute your success on an exam to your effort or to luck. Attributions allow us to examine the biases people have when explaining others' behavior, which in turn affect their own behavior.

The study of attributions has a rich history in social psychology. Researchers have studied the types of attributions people make, especially in relation to the locus of causality. An important concept in attribution research is the distinction between internal and external attributions. Internal attributions specify the cause of behavior within a person; external attributions locate the cause of behavior outside a person. Researchers have also studied the causal properties of attributions, including locus, stability, controllability, and globality. Attributions have been widely studied in achievement situations, ranging from academic settings to sports and occupational contexts. These studies have led to the development of several major theories of attribution. And research on attribution bias has led to several popular concepts in American social psychology, including fundamental attribution error, defensive attributions, and self-serving bias.

Traditional American Patterns of Attributions

One of the most popular models of attribution in American psychology is Kelley's (1967, 1973) covariation model. This model assumes that people attribute behavior to causes that are present when the behavior occurs and absent when the behavior does not occur. According to this theory, people consider three types of information when making attributions: consistency, distinctiveness, and consensus. **Consistency** refers to whether a person's behavior in a situation is the same over time. **Distinctiveness** refers to whether a person's behavior is unique to the specific target of the behavior. **Consensus** refers to whether other people in the same situation tend to respond in the same manner. Behaviors that have high consistency but low distinctiveness or consensus produce internal attributions. Behaviors that have high consistency, high distinctiveness, and high consensus produce external attributions.

Another major theory of attribution in American psychology is Weiner's (1974; Weiner et al., 1987) theory, which focuses on the concept of stability. According to Weiner, stability cuts across the internal–external dimension, creating four types of attributions for success and failure (stable and unstable, internal and external). For example, if you failed to get a job you wanted, you might attribute your failure to stable internal factors (lack of ability or initiative), stable external factors (too much competition), unstable internal factors (lack of effort), or unstable external factors (bad luck). Using Weiner's model of attribution, the types of emotions and behaviors that will probably occur as a consequence of these attribution types can be predicted.

Studies conducted on attributional styles of people in the United States have shown a number of different ways we may be biased in interpreting the world around us and the behavior of others. **Fundamental attribution error** refers to a bias toward explaining the behavior of others using internal attributions but explaining our own behaviors using external attributions (Jones & Nisbett, 1971; Watson, 1982). It is not uncommon to hear students attribute a friend's bad grade to low intelligence or ability (internal). At the same time, however, they may attribute their own bad grades to a teacher's choice of test questions or to bad luck (external).

Self-serving bias is the tendency to attribute one's successes to personal factors and one's failures to situational factors (Bradley, 1978). If you fail an exam, for instance, you may attribute your failure to a poorly constructed test, lousy teaching, distractions, or a bad week at home (external). If you ace an exam, however, you are more likely to attribute your success to effort, intelligence, or ability (internal).

Defensive attributions refer to the tendency to blame victims for their misfortune. Some scientists have suggested that we engage in defensive attributions because they make us feel less likely to be victimized in a similar way (Thornton, 1984). If you attribute others' misfortunes (for example, burglary, rape, loss of a job) to the victim rather than to circumstance, it is easier to believe that the same misfortunes will not happen to you.

These attributional styles and theories have an impact both on our own behavior and on our understanding of the behavior of others; many of you can probably recognize some of these attributional tendencies in your own behavior. However, these attributional styles and biases have been documented in research conducted almost exclusively in the United States with American participants. Cross-cultural research suggests that attributional styles and biases may be culture-bound.

Attributional Styles across Cultures

Attributions about academic achievement. Much of the early cross-cultural research on attributions focused on attributions concerning success and failure in academic achievement situations, for several reasons. The participants in most studies are students, and academic achievement is a relevant and meaningful topic on which to obtain data. Such data are also relevant and meaningful across cultures, as many people in many cultures go to school. All students have experience with similar situations, unlike other types of success and performance. And obtaining attributional data from students is relatively easy.

Many studies have found considerable differences across cultures in the nature of attributions about academic performance, and these findings often differ from what has typically been found to be true of Americans. Table 14.2 summarizes a selective representation of these studies. Hau and Salili (1991), for example, asked junior and senior high school students in Hong Kong to rate the importance and meaning of 13 specific causes of academic performance. Effort, interest, and ability—all internal attributions—were rated the most important causes, regardless of success or failure. Research from the United States would have predicted that these dimensions would be important in making attributions of success but not failure, because of self-serving bias.

Two studies with Taiwanese subjects also challenge our notions about self-serving attributions. Crittenden (1991) found that Taiwanese women used more external and self-effacing attributions about themselves than did

Table 14.2 Selected Cross-Cultural Studies Examining Attributions Regarding Academic Achievement

Citation	Participants	Attributions about . . .	Major Findings
Hau and Salili, 1991	Hong Kong Chinese	Perceived performance in an examination taken the previous week	Most important causal attributions were effort, interest in study, study skill, and ability in study.
Hall et al., 1986	Black and white U.S. junior high school students	Test performance	Attributions of success or failure did not predict active or nonattending behaviors.
Graham and Long, 1986	Black and white U.S. junior high school students	Hypothetical and actual performance in an exam	Blacks did not revise their expectancies downward as much as whites when the causes of success were perceived as unstable. Blacks were less certain that failure would occur again. Blacks anticipated relatively higher praise when success was due to external uncontrollable causes. Middle-SES white children attributed high exam performance to good luck less than did low-SES white and middle-SES black children. Middle-SES white children attributed poor performance to difficulty of the exam, whereas middle-SES black children perceived poor instruction from their teacher as a dominant cause of failure.
Graham, 1984	Black and white U.S. sixth graders	Induced failure performance on a puzzle	Black children attributed their failure more to insufficient effort, reported higher expectancies, perceived themselves as more competent, and persisted longer at the task.

(continued on next page)

Table 14.2 Selected Cross-Cultural Studies Examining Attributions Regarding Academic Achievement *(continued)*

Citation	Participants	Attributions about . . .	Major Findings
Crittenden, 1991	Taiwanese and American university students	Hypothetical situations that may happen to a college student involving relationships and achievement events	Taiwanese students saw likability as less highly correlated with productivity traits than Americans. Students in both cultures expressed preference for internal rather than external attributions, and for self-effacing rather than self-enhancing patterns. Taiwanese liked the external and self-effacing patterns slightly more than internal and self-enhancing patterns.
Bong, Leung, and Wan, 1982	Hong Kong Chinese students	Confederate's competent or incompetent performance on an intellectual task	Self-effacing confederate was better liked but rated less competent than a self-enhancing confederate. Incompetent confederates who made self-enhancing attributions were perceived as more anxious than other confederates.
Mizokawa and Ryckman, 1990	Six groups of Asian Americans—Chinese, Japanese, Korean, Filipino, Vietnamese, and other Southeast Asian—in 4th through 11th grades	Success and failure in school achievement situations	Koreans had the highest effort attribution scores, and Southeast Asians the lowest. Japanese and Korean students attributed more success than failure to ability. Chinese and Vietnamese students evenly attributed success and failure to ability. Southeast Asians attributed failures to lack of ability. Koreans attributed successes to ability, but failures to other factors.
Yan and Geier, 1994	American, Chinese, Japanese, Korean, and Southeast Asian university undergraduates	School-related successes and failures	Americans attributed academic achievement more often to ability than did Asians; they also attributed success more to effort than they attributed failure to lack of effort. Asians attributed effort equally for success and failure; students in the four Asian groups appeared more similar than different in their attributions.

Study	Sample	Task	Results
Ng, McClure, Walkey, and Hunt, 1995	New Zealand and Singapore university students	Success and failure in examinations	The most frequent attribution for both success and failure was effort for both groups; the second most frequent attribution for New Zealanders was ability, for Singaporeans luck. Singaporeans gave higher attributional importance ratings than New Zealanders to mood, study technique, examination skill, luck, God and supernatural factors, and family; the New Zealanders gave higher ratings to effort.
Wong, Derlega, and Colson, 1988	White and black U.S. university undergraduates	Performance of either a white or black 4-year-old being taught a lesson on home and family safety	Both white and black participants generated more attributional questions and provided more causal explanations to account for the performance of a black than a white target person, reflecting greater concern for causal understanding of performance by minority children. Both black and white participants expected the white student to do better than the black student in three different achievement situations.
Kashima and Triandis, 1986	Japanese and American university students in the United States	Success or failure in a memory task	Japanese attributed failure more to themselves and success less to themselves than did Americans.
Salili, 1994	British and Chinese children in Hong Kong, and Chinese undergraduates and adults	Importance ratings of success or failure in participant-generated situations	British females considered success in personal social life significantly more important than did British males and Chinese. Chinese students considered success in academic work and outstanding achievement significantly more important than did Britons. Chinese men rated success in extracurricular activities more important than did Chinese women and all Britons.

American women. Crittenden suggested that the Taiwanese women did this to enhance their public and private self-esteem by using an attributional approach that conformed to a feminine gender role. Earlier, Bond, Leung, and Wan (1982) found that self-effacing Chinese students were better liked by their peers than those who adopted this attributional style less often.

Other cross-cultural studies on attributions concerning academic performance pepper the literature with findings that challenge American notions of attribution. Kashima and Triandis (1986) showed that Japanese people use a much more group-oriented, collective approach to attribution with regard to attention and memory achievement tasks. Compared to their American counterparts, Japanese subjects attributed failure to themselves more and attributed success to themselves less. Kashima and Triandis interpreted this finding as suggestive of American and Japanese cultural differences in degree of responsibility taking.

Research has gone beyond the mere documentation of cultural differences in attributional styles to suggest several possible negative consequences. Wong, Derlaga, and Colson (1988), for example, asked 40 white and 40 black undergraduates to read stories about the performance of either a black or a white child. The students were then asked to (1) explain why the child failed or succeeded, (2) describe questions in their mind concerning the child's performance, and (3) predict the child's performance on other tasks. All subjects, regardless of race, generated more questions and causal explanations for the performance of a black than a white child. And all subjects expected the white child to do better than the black child on other tasks.

In the same vein, Tom and Cooper (1986) examined the attributions of 25 white elementary school teachers for the performance of students varying in social class, race, and gender. The results indicated that the teachers were more likely to take account of the successes of middle-class white students and discount their failures, relative to students of other social classes or race.

However, the consequences of cultural differences in attributional style are not entirely negative. Hall, Howe, Merkel, and Lederman (1986) asked teachers to make causal attributions about the performance of black and white students. They found that the teachers believed that black females exerted the greatest amount of effort (and that black males exerted the least). Sandra Graham and her colleagues (for example, Graham, 1984; Graham & Long, 1986) have reported considerable overlap in the attributions of the black and white subjects in their studies and that these attributions are often equally adaptive. They have also found that attributions are influenced by social factors such as class as well as race and culture.

Collectively, these studies paint a rather consistent and persuasive picture about the nature of attributional processes with regard to academic performance and achievement. More recent research has gone beyond academic performance to assess attributions with regard to a wide range of other topics.

Attributions in nonacademic areas. Are the data presented so far limited to attributions concerning academic achievement, or are they representative of more global ways in which people around the world interpret the events around them? Cross-cultural research in the past decade has demonstrated that cultural differences in attributional styles are not limited to academic achievement and performance, but exist in relation to a wide range of life situations.

Table 14.3 provides a brief summary of selected cross-cultural studies examining attributional processes in relation to nonacademic achievement and performance. A perusal of these studies also indicates widespread differences in the nature of attributions around the world. For example, Moghaddam, Ditto, and Taylor (1990) examined the attributional processes of high- and low-distressed Indian female immigrants to Canada in relation to the degree to which they have adjusted to life in Canada. They found that the Indian women were more likely to attribute both successes and failures to internal causes. American research would have hypothesized that the subjects would attribute only successes to internal causes and attribute failures to external causes, again because of self-serving bias.

Forgas, Furnham, and Frey (1989) documented broad cross-national differences in the importance of different types of specific attributions for wealth. Their study included 558 subjects from the United Kingdom, Australia, and the Federal Republic of Germany. The British considered family background and luck the most important determinants of wealth. The Germans also considered family background the most important determinant. The Australians, however, rated individual qualities the most important determinant of wealth. Romero and Garza (1986) reported differences between Hispanic and Anglo women in their attributions concerning occupational success and failure. In their study, Chicana and Anglo-American female university students provided data concerning their attributions about an Anglo, African American, or Chicana female's success or failure in a teaching job. They found that Chicanas tended to make more attributions on the basis of luck, ethnicity, or gender. In making attributions about failure, Anglo females tended to attribute less competence to the actor than did the Chicana females.

Several studies have examined newspaper articles to investigate whether attributions about certain "real-life" behaviors (as opposed to filling out a questionnaire about imaginary behaviors in someone's research lab) may differ across cultures. For example, Morris & Peng (1994) found that U.S. newspaper articles were more likely to attribute the cause of a murder to an individual's personality traits, attitudes, and beliefs (such as "bad temper," "psychologically disturbed"), but Chinese newspapers were more likely to attribute the cause to situational factors (such as "didn't get along with his advisor," "isolated from his community"). Lee, Hallahan, and Herzog (1996) coded Hong Kong and U.S. newspaper articles concerning sporting events for attributional style and judged the extent to which events were attributed to personal or situational factors. As hypothesized, they found that attributions by Hong Kong reporters were more situational and less dispositional than those of U.S. resporters.

As Table 14.3 indicates, cultural differences in the nature of attributional processes exist across a wide range of events, including occupational performance, wealth and economic success, crime, physical and psychological

Table 14.3 Selected Cross-Cultural Studies Examining Attributions Regarding Nonacademic Topics

Citation	Participants	Attributions about . . .	Major Findings
Schuster, Forsterlung, and Weiner, 1989	Taxi drivers and civil servants in Germany, Belgium, India, South Korea, and England	An unsuccessful attempt to find employment	Indian respondents rated all causes as more external, variable, and uncontrollable than did participants in other countries.
Romero and Garza, 1986	Chicana and Anglo female university students	A description of occupational success or failure of an Anglo, Black, or Chicana female	Chicanas showed greater tendency to attribute the actor's occupational outcome to luck, ethnicity, or gender. In the failure condition, the Anglo females attributed less competence to the actor than did the Chicana females.
Forgas, Furnham, and Frey, 1989	Individuals in Britain, Australia, and Germany	Wealth and economic success	British considered family background, individual effort, exploitation, and luck the most important. Germans considered family background, exploitation, individual ability, and effort as most important. Australians considered individual effort and ability, family background, social rewards, and membership in special trades or professions the most important.
Na and Loftus, 1998	Korean and American law students and undergraduates	Law, prisoners, and crimes	Korean undergraduates had less positive attitudes toward law than did American undergraduates. Koreans were more lenient toward criminals and made more external attributions of crimes than did Americans.

Furnham and Akande, 1997	Underlying factors for overcoming cognitive disorders (dyslexia, fear of flying, amnesia, and "learning difficulties")	South Africans endorsed self-reliance, external control, and professional help more than Britons as methods of overcoming cognitive disorders.
British and South Africans		
Edman and Kameoka, 1997	Physical illness	Filipino women attributed the cause of illnesses to spiritual-social explanations more frequently than did Americans.
Filipino and American women		
McGowan, McGowan, and Omifade, 1997	Ruminations of success and failure	African Americans tended to attribute failure to factors that were more internal, stable, and personally controllable than did West Africans.
West African and African American athletes		
Lee, Hallahan, and Herzog, 1996	Events described in articles	Attributions from Hong Kong were more situational and less dispositional than those from the United States.
Sports articles and editorials of newspapers in Hong Kong and the United States		
Si, Rethorst, and Willimczkik, 1995	Achievement outcomes in sports	Chinese participants perceived the causes for subjective success and failure as more internal and more controllable than did the Germans.
Chinese and German individuals		
Kawanishi, 1995	Stress and coping	Japanese were more likely to attribute successful coping with stress to luck, and to see the cause of stress as their own responsibility.
Anglo-Americans and Japanese		

(continued on next page)

Table 14.3 Selected Cross-Cultural Studies Examining Attributions Regarding Nonacademic Topics (*continued*)

Citation	Participants	Attributions about . . .	Major Findings
Morris and Peng, 1994	American and Chinese students	Social and physical events	Causal perceptions of social but not physical events differed between the two groups. English-language newspapers were more dispositional and Chinese-language newspapers more situational in explanations of the same crimes. Chinese survey respondents differed in weightings of personal disposition and situational factors as causes of recent murders and in counterfactual judgments about how murders might have been averted by changed situations.
Al-Zharany and Kaplowitz, 1993	American and Saudi university students	Moral or immoral behaviors associated with success or failure	Americans favored internal attributions. Saudis showed more outgroup derogatory bias and intergroup bias.
Moghaddam, Ditto, and Taylor, 1990	Indian immigrant women in Canada	Adjustment to life in Canada	Indian women were likely to attribute both successes and failure to internal causes.

disorders, sports, and moral and immoral behaviors. Collectively, these studies indicate quite convincingly that attributional styles differ substantially across cultures, and that they do not conform to the attributional biases we are familiar with from research involving Americans.

Summary

As these studies exemplify, attributional styles are quite different across cultures. But we need to go beyond the mere documentation of differences to discover why those differences occur. It may be that the way Americans conceptualize attributions, success, and failure has a lot to do with the differences found in cross-cultural research. Duda and Allison (1989) have suggested that our definitions of success and failure are ethnocentrically biased. How Americans view success and failure—that is, in terms of personal achievement on the basis of competition with others—is different from how people of other cultures define them. They also suggest that the meanings of the specific elements in theories and research on attribution may differ among cultures (for example, effort, work, luck). Different meanings assigned to these elements have implications for the meanings of the attributions associated with them. Finally, Duda and Allison suggest that the use of bipolar dimensions in research may be extremely limited. Cultural differences in the dimensions that are important for understanding and predicting attributions may lead to entirely different expectations of attribution styles.

As some of the research reviewed here involving children indicates, cultural differences in attributional styles appear quite early in life. Culture-specific attributional styles may be a natural part of enculturation and socialization, as children are exposed to these cultural styles from an early age. Bornstein and associates (1998), for example, examined attributions of mothers of 20-month-olds in Argentina, Belgium, France, Israel, Italy, Japan, and the United States with regard to success and failure in seven parenting tasks. They found only a few cross-cultural similarities, but many differences, especially with regard to degree of competence and satisfaction in parenting. Child age could not be a factor, as it was controlled in the study, and child gender was found not to influence the data either. These types of findings provide us with ideas about how and why parents transmit valuable cultural information to their children, resulting in specific styles of attribution (among many other psychological effects).

In another study, Chandler and Spies (1996) examined cultural differences in ratings of 11 attributes of achievement in seven countries. The attributes rated were bias, help, luck, ability, competence, effort, task, chance, knowledge, skills, and mood; the dimensions they were rated on were internal–external, global–specific, controllable–uncontrollable, stable–unstable, and predictable–unpredictable. The results indicated cultural differences on 9 of the 11 attributes across the seven countries, suggesting that different cultures attribute different psychological meanings to the various attributional components. Such data, in turn, help us understand how and why certain attributions may be used in certain countries and cultures, depending on the particular cultural values and mores in those countries. The results from this study suggest one of the reasons why many of the attributional styles that have been consistently found in research with Americans are not necessarily true for people in other parts of the world: Even though the components of the attribution process may be the same across cultures, the way in which these components are used differs across cultures.

As stated earlier, future research needs to go beyond merely documenting differences to exploring how and why these differences occur. More research is needed to explore the developmental processes associated with cultural differences in attributions; other studies will need to investigate the possible mediators of cultural differences in attributional styles. Research will also need to examine the linkage between culture as measured on the individual level and attributional styles, reducing the reliance on the use of countries as culture, with its inherent stereotypic description of culture underlying country.

At the same time, more theoretical work is needed on the nature of the attributional process itself, and its meaning to individuals and cultures. For example, although the research reviewed here is quite convincing in documenting cultural differences in attributional styles, it seems to us that there may be a basic commonality across cultures in the core values underlying the attributional differences. That is, all cultures may encourage an attributional style that has at its core "enhancement of the self" as an underlying value. Yet because people of different cultures come to define the self in different ways (see Chapter 11), the specific nature of the attributions that a person learns and uses will be different, reflecting these differences in the definition of self, despite commonality in the core theme or value. If, for example, bolstering one's self-impression about one's abilities and efforts enhances the self, as traditional American research has documented in relation to successful events, then this attributional style may operationalize the core value of "self-enhancement."

But in another culture, bolstering one's self-worth in the way that Americans do may actually be detrimental to the core self; in such a culture, restraint in such attributions may actually be operationalizing the core value of "self-enhancement," even though the outward manifestation of the attribution does not reflect such enhancement. Thus, people of different cultures may appear to differ in their attributional styles on one level, yet on another level may be entirely similar in their core values and principles. Future research needs to take into account such possibilities and delve more deeply into the nature of attributions, especially with regard to the meaning of attributional styles to the individual and culture.

Nevertheless, cultural differences in attributions are especially important in furthering our understanding of intercultural interactions. The consequences of incorrect attributions are potentially severe. Interpreting the causes of behavior accurately, especially with regard to intentions and good will, is important to the success of any type of social interaction. Intercultural interactions are no exception. We should not be too quick to attribute another person's behavior to ill will or negative feelings, when that behavior may actually be rooted in a cultural dynamic that fosters that behavior with no ill will. If we leave room for the influence of cultural factors in our attributions of others' behavior as well as our own, we will have taken an important step toward improving intercultural understanding and relationships.

Culture and Aggression

Aggression may be defined as any act or behavior that hurts another person, either physically or psychologically. Although some research suggests that the tendency to be aggressive is biologically and perhaps even genetically based, most psychologists would agree that there is a large learning and environmental component to aggression. That is, the tendency to be aggressive appears to be learned as one is socialized and enculturated into society and culture. The most prevalent models of aggression suggest that aggression occurs when provocation of some sort leads to some kind of negative emotions, which prime a person to either fight or flee. Which response the individual chooses depends on genetics and biological predispositions, previously learned response patterns, and the specific characteristics of the context and situation (Geen, 1994).

That culture may influence group-level tendencies toward aggression is well documented in the literature. Many cross-cultural psychologists and anthropologists have examined cultures such as the Yanomami of Venezuela and Brazil (for example, Sponsel, 1998)—a cultural group well known for its aggressive tendencies, both within the group and toward outsiders, and often referred to as the "fierce people." Landau (1984) compared levels of stress, social support systems, and the rates of murder and other crimes in 13 countries and found a correlation among these variables. Robbins, DeWalt, and Pelto (1972) showed that countries with hotter and more humid climates are associated with higher murder rates, and this tendency has also been documented for the states of the United States (Anderson & Anderson, 1996).

Indeed, many studies document cross-cultural differences in aggression. For example, Terav and Keltikangas (1998) examined justifications for aggression and withdrawal in Finland and Estonia. Participants were presented with a description of two everyday social problems and a list of problem-solving strategies, and were asked to provide a justification for each strategy. The results indicated that the Estonian participants more often chose instrumental justifications for their aggressive behavior, suggesting that aggression was a means to an end. The Finnish participants, however, more often reported that aggression was fun. The authors concluded that aggression is considered more deviant in Finland than in Estonia.

Bond, Wan, Leong, and Giacalone (1985) studied aggressive insults and criticisms in Hong Kong and the United States. They hypothesized that such insults and criticisms by a boss of a subordinate would be perceived as less aggressive in Hong Kong, because this culture is relatively higher on Hofstede's (1980) dimension of power distance than the United States. Therefore, aggressive behaviors would be more acceptable in relationships where status and power are unequal. Their data did indicate that the Chinese perceived such insults as less illegitimate, and saw less reason to dislike the superior who delivered them.

Richardson and Huguet (2001) asked American and French university students to fill out a questionnaire concerning their attitudes toward aggressive actions and the acceptability of these actions. They found that American university students were significantly more likely than French students to support items that referred to aggression as a means of maintaining a tough public image ("I am more likely to hit out physically when someone shows me up in public") and items that were consistent with a need to justify aggressive behaviors ("I believe that physical aggression is necessary to get through to people"). The researchers argued that Americans have more exposure and experience with aggression in their everyday lives, and therefore need to be able to justify their aggressive behaviors.

Cultural differences in aggression appear not only across countries, but within countries as well. Cohen, Nisbett, Bowdle, and Schwartz (1996), for example, conducted three experiments comparing European American males who were born in either the northern or southern part of the United States. A confederate in the experiment insulted the participants, whose reactions were recorded. The northerners appeared relatively unaffected by the insult. The southerners, however, perceived more threat to their masculine reputation; they were more upset, more physiologically and cognitively primed for aggression, and more likely to engage in aggressive and dominant behavior. Cortisol and testosterone levels were measured, and both were found to be elevated in the southern sample. The authors attributed these findings to the southern culture of "honor" that manifested itself in cognitions, emotions, and behaviors among southerners but not northerners.

Some studies have suggested that groups tend to be more aggressive than individuals. Jaffe and Yinon (1983), for example, showed that groups of Israeli participants were more willing to administer shocks to subjects in an experiment than were individuals. Other studies, however, have suggested that being in groups does not necessarily lead to more aggression. Rather, people are more sure of themselves in groups. If the group's cultural norms favor aggression, then aggressive behaviors are more likely to occur. However, if the group's cultural norms favor nonaggression, then behaviors are more likely to be restrained (Rabbie & Horwitz, 1982).

Not only are there cultural differences in instigation of aggression; there appear to be such differences in being the target of aggression. Harris (1996), for example, assessed experiences as both target and instigator of aggression in Anglo and Hispanic university students. The Anglo students reported experiencing significantly more lifetime aggression as both target and aggressor than did the Hispanic participants.

A number of studies indicate that cultural differences in aggression appear early in life. Osterman, Bjorkquist, and Lagerspetz (1994), for example, documented differences in perceptions of aggression among 8-year-olds in two samples from Finland, two from the United States, and one from Poland. Another study (Farver, Welles-Nystroem, Frosch, Wimbarti, & Hoppe-Graff, 1997) documented differences in 4-year-old children in the United States, Sweden, Germany, and Indonesia. In this study, children told two stories using toys with aggressive and neutral cues. American children's narratives had significantly more aggressive content, aggressive words, unfriendly characters, and mastery of situations with aggression than did those of the other three cultures. Zahn-Waxler and associates (1996) documented similar tendencies in a comparison of 4-year-old American and Japanese children. They found that American children showed more anger, more aggressive behavior and language, and greater underregulation of emotion than did Japanese children across different contexts of assessment.

Some studies have searched for some of the learning and environmental sources of cultural differences in aggression. Yamauchi and Li (1995), for example, examined the relationship between aggressive motives and child-rearing conditions in Japanese and Chinese college students. They found that child-rearing practices were indeed related to aggression, albeit in different ways for the two samples. In another study, Osterweil and Nagano-Nakamura (1992) asked Japanese and Israeli mothers of kindergarten children about their children's fights and quarrels. They reported considerable differences in the mothers' perceptions, which surely must affect the children's attitudes toward aggression through socialization and enculturation. The Japanese mothers saw aggression as natural—a fact of life with both positive and negative elements, but that should be kept under control so as not to harm others. The Israeli mothers saw aggression as dangerous to both aggressor and aggressee. Thus, the Japanese viewed aggression as a natural and necessary aspect of development, whereas the Israelis perceived it as justified mainly as self-defense and as expressing negative emotional states.

However, not all cross-cultural studies document differences in tendencies or attitudes toward aggression. A few studies have reported cultural similarities as well. Tomada and Schneider (1997), for example, examined elementary school children in Italy, and compared their results with previous findings in the United States. American studies had shown that overt physical and verbal aggression is more prevalent among boys, whereas covert aggression within interpersonal relationships is more prevalent among girls. Although the data did not perfectly support this difference in the Italian sample, the authors concluded that the distinction between overt and covert aggression is useful in describing sex differences in aggression across cultures.

In a different vein, a study by Ramirez (1993) examined the degree of acceptance of various forms of aggressive behavior in four regions in Spain. Not only were these four regions surprisingly similar in their attitudes regarding acceptance of aggression, but these data were related to similar data collected in Finland and Poland. Ramirez recently extended this study to include participants in South Africa, the United States, Japan, and Iran, and again found more cultural similarities than differences concerning the moral approval of certain types and circumstances of aggression (Ramirez et al., 2001). These findings suggest a possible cross-cultural or universal aspect to attitudes about aggression.

Thus, some cross-cultural research has shown that aggressive tendencies, attitudes, and norms differ across cultures, and that these differences are firmly established at a relatively early age. The available evidence also points to aspects of child rearing and maternal values and attitudes as possible sources of cultural differences in aggression. At the same time, some studies have shown that at least some aspects of aggression, such as sex differences and attitudes concerning acceptance, may be similar across cultures. What we do not know at this point is which specific aspects of aggression are similar across cultures, and which are different. Nor do we know what specific sources of learning—child rearing, parental views on aggression, or others—contribute to aggressive behavior, or the relative contribution of psychological as opposed to biological or genetic factors. Future research will need to address these issues, going beyond documenting cultural similarities and differences in aggression to delve into the more difficult questions of how and why these similarities and differences occur.

Culture and Conformity, Compliance, Obedience, and Cooperation

Few words and concepts are associated with such negative connotations in American social psychology and social behavior as conformity, compliance, and obedience to the group. These words often stir up forceful images of robots and automatons lacking any individuality. Without doubt, these images strike at the heart of the "rugged individualism" that is not only central but vital to American culture and sense of self. **Conformity** means yielding to real or imagined social pressure. **Compliance** is generally defined as yielding to social pressure in one's public behavior, even though one's private beliefs may not have changed. **Obedience** is a form of compliance that occurs when people follow direct commands, usually from someone in a position of authority. Whether we like it or not, these issues are very real in all of our lives. Research on these topics in the United States has shown that not only do conformity, compliance, and obedience exist, but their effects are pervasive.

In contrast to the often negative connotations of conformity, compliance, and obedience, cooperation is a construct with generally positive connotations. **Cooperation** refers to people's ability to work together toward common goals. It is a hallmark value of many cultures, especially collectivistic cultures, as it is necessary for the successful functioning of ingroups.

Research on these topics has been conducted quite extensively around the world. In the United States, several studies serve as landmark classics in this area of social psychology, including those by Asch and Milgram.

Research in the United States

Two of the best-known studies on conformity, compliance, and obedience are the Asch and Milgram studies. In his earliest experiments, Asch (1951, 1955, 1956) examined a subject's response to a simple judgment task after other "subjects" (actually experimental confederates) had all given the same incorrect response. For example, a subject would be placed in a room with others, shown objects (lines, balls, and so forth), and asked to make a judgment about the objects (such as relative sizes). The answer was often obvious, but subjects were asked to give their answers only after a number of experimental confederates had given theirs. The basic finding from these simple experiments was that, more often than not, subjects would give the wrong answer, even though it was obviously wrong, if the people answering before them had given that same wrong answer. Across studies and trials, group size and group unanimity were major influencing factors. Conformity peaked when the group contained seven people and was unanimous in its judgments (even though the judgments were clearly wrong).

In Asch's studies, compliance resulted from subtle, implied pressure. But in the real world, compliance can occur in response to explicit rules, requests, and commands. We can only imagine how forceful and pervasive group pressure to conform and comply are in the real world if they can operate in a simple laboratory environment among people unknown to the subject on a task that has relatively little meaning.

In Milgram's (1974) famous study, subjects were brought into a laboratory ostensibly to study the effects of punishment on learning. Subjects were instructed to administer shocks to another subject (actually an experimental confederate) when the latter gave the wrong response or no response. The shock meter was labeled from "Slight Shock" to "DANGER: Severe Shock," and the confederate's behaviors ranged from simple utterances of pain through pounding on the walls, pleas to stop, and then deathly silence. (No shock was actually administered.) Milgram reported that 65% of the subjects obeyed the commands of the experimenter and administered the most severe levels of shock.

The Asch experiments were rather innocuous in the actual content of the compliance (for example, judgments of the length of lines). The Milgram studies, however, clearly highlighted the potential negative and harmful effects of compliance and obedience. To this day, it stands as one of the best-known studies in American social psychology. Replication is unlikely to be attempted today because of restrictions based on ethics and university standards of conduct, but its findings speak for themselves on the power of group influence.

Cross-Cultural Research on Conformity and Compliance

In thinking about cultural differences in conformity, compliance, and obedience, we need to be aware of the American cultural bias against these terms.

We need to understand that our negative feelings are firmly rooted in our own individualistic culture. If we can see that these feelings are rooted in our cultural upbringing, it then follows that different cultures may have different feelings about conformity, obedience, and compliance. Whereas these behaviors are viewed negatively in American culture, they may very well be positively valued social behaviors in other cultures.

A number of cross-cultural studies do indeed show that people of other cultures view conformity, obedience, and compliance differently than Americans. Some studies have shown that Asian cultures in particular not only engage in conforming, compliant, and obedient behaviors to a greater degree than Americans, but also value conformity to a greater degree. For example, Punetha, Giles, and Young (1987) administered an extended Rokeach Value Survey to three groups of Asian subjects and one group of British subjects. The British subjects clearly valued individualistic items, such as independence and freedom, whereas the Asian subjects endorsed societal values including conformity and obedience.

Studies involving other Asian and American comparisons have generally produced the same results. Hadiyono and Hahn (1985) reported that Indonesians endorsed conformity more than Americans did. Argyle, Henderson, Bond, Iizuka, and Contarello (1986) found that Japanese and Hong Kong Chinese endorsed obedience more than did British and Italian subjects. Buck, Newton, and Muramatsu (1984) found that Japanese were more conforming than Americans. Nor is valuing conformity and obedience limited to Asian cultures. Cashmore and Goodnow (1986) demonstrated that Italians were more conforming than Anglo-Australians, and El-Islam (1983) documented cultural differences in conformity in an Arabian sample.

Two cross-cultural studies on child-rearing values speak to the strength of these values in socialization and enculturation. Not only Asian but also Puerto Rican subjects were found to value conformity and obedience in child rearing (Burgos & Dias-Perez, 1986; Stropes-Roe & Cochrane, 1990). A number of anthropological works on Japanese culture (for example, Benedict, 1946; Doi, 1985) confirm the importance of obedience and compliance in Japanese child rearing.

Recently, Bond and Smith (1996) conducted a meta-analysis of studies examining the effects of conformity across studies involving the types of tasks originally used by Asch. Analyzing 133 studies conducted in 17 different countries, they found that the magnitude of the effect of conformity was very large in some countries and very small in others, with a mean effect of moderate value. When they analyzed the relationship between the magnitude of the effect and characteristics of the studies, they found that conformity was higher when the majority that tried to influence the conforming participant was larger, and when there was a greater proportion of female participants. Conformity was also greater when the majority did not consist of outgroup members, and when the stimuli were more ambiguous. Of particular note was the finding that effect size was significantly related to individualism–collectivism, with conformity higher in collectivistic countries than in individualistic ones.

That conformity is related to cultural values of individualism or collectivism makes sense. Traditional American culture fosters individualistic values, endorsing behaviors and beliefs contrary to conformity. To conform in American culture is to be "weak" or somehow deficient. But many other cultures foster more collectivistic, group-oriented values; in those cultures, concepts of conformity, obedience, and compliance enjoy much higher status and a positive orientation. In these cultures, conformity is viewed not only as "good" but as necessary for the successful functioning of the culture, its groups, and the interpersonal relationships of its members.

Culture and Obedience

Like conformity, obedience is a value that has different connotations and meanings in different cultures. In Milgram's (1974) study, you will recall, about 65% of the participants obeyed the instructions of the experimenter and administered a high level of shock to a confederate (who in reality received no shock). Smith and Bond (1999) reviewed nine other studies that used the Milgram paradigm, conducted in the United States and eight other countries. The results of these studies indicated a broad range in the percentage of participants obeying the experimenter, ranging from a low of 16% among female students in Australia to a high of 92% in the Netherlands. These differences may reflect real cultural differences in obedience, but they may also reflect other types of differences, including differences in the meaning of the particular tasks used in the studies, the specific instructions given to the participants, and the nature of the confederate who supposedly received the shocks.

We need to ask ourselves why the best-known studies of conformity and obedience conducted in the United States are so negative in their orientation. Although the Asch studies are rather innocuous, the Milgram studies are clearly a powerful indictment of the potential negative consequences of obedience. Have any studies been conducted by American social psychologists that might show positive outcomes of conformity, compliance, or obedience? If not, perhaps we need to examine the possible biases of American social scientists in approaching these topics.

Culture and Cooperation

A number of studies in the cross-cultural literature highlight the important differences between cultures in their values and attitudes about cooperation, and in their cooperative behaviors. Domino (1992), for example, compared children from the People's Republic of China with children from the United States on a social values task. The task required the child to decide between two alternatives offering tokens to the child and an unspecified classmate. Basically, the choices involved receiving more tokens for oneself or receiving fewer tokens and allowing the classmate to receive more. Six different types of outcome preferences were distinguished: individualism, competition, equality, group enhancement or cooperation, competition and individualism, and equality and individualism. Across a series of trials, the most common preferences of American children were individualism (receiving many tokens for oneself) and competition (receiving as many more tokens than the other as possible). In contrast, the most common preferences of Chinese children were equality (equal division of tokens) and group enhancement (most number of tokens collectively for both individuals, irrespective of division). Domino interpreted these findings as supportive of the notion that the process of socialization in China is geared to promoting group solidarity and group consciousness.

In another study, Mann, Mitsui, Beswick, and Harmoni (1994) compared 11- and 12-year-old Australian and Japanese children on their endorsement of rules governing respect for others. The children completed two questionnaires about their endorsement of seven rules in relation to six target persons: father, mother, best friend, teacher, adult neighbor, and same-age neighbor. The results indicated that Japanese children showed greater correspondence between endorsed and self-reported respect than did Australian children. The Japanese also differentiated more than the Australians did in their respect for parents and teacher versus friends and neighbors. These findings indicate that Japanese social rules governing respect are highly person- and situation-related, consistent with the strong distinction between ingroups and outgroups in collectivistic cultures, and consistent with Hall's (1976) analysis of Japan as a high-context culture.

Cultural differences are apparent not only in the levels of respect and cooperation afforded others, but also in the process of engaging in cooperative tasks. Filardo (1996), for example, videotaped European American and African American eighth-graders participating in a cooperative, problem-solving board game that involved group decision making. Transcripts of these videotapes were coded by research assistants in terms of the activities that occurred as well as the ways in which participants interacted. The results indicated that, overall, African Americans were more active than their European American counterparts and engaged in more performance outputs that expressed "a lack of consideration for the point of view of the listener or a view of the parties as having asymmetrical rights with respect to one another or as expecting compliance" (p. 75). European Americans engaged in more brief, unelaborated expressions of agreement with another group member's previous utterance or action.

While research seems to indicate that collectivistic cultures are more conforming and obedient, they also seem to be more cooperative. The onus is on future cross-cultural research to examine the ways in which conformity and obedience, on the one hand, and cooperation, on the other, coexist in a delicate balance within a culture and society, as well as the specific contexts in which these behaviors occur. It seems that conforming or cooperating occurs within a context of recognizing the possible ramifications and consequences of nonconforming or noncooperating, and future studies should take into account what these ramifications are. It may be that, given equivalent consequences, people's conformity or cooperation will be more similar than different across cultures.

Conclusion

Humans are social animals. By nature, we bond with others, live with others, work and play with others. Our whole lives are spent in some kind of interaction or relationship with other people. No matter how we look at it, we cannot ignore the fact that we are fundamentally connected with other people in our world. Our behaviors, thoughts, and feelings are all influenced by others, and we in turn influence those around us.

As we grow in our own cultures and societies, we learn certain ways of behaving, interacting, feeling, and interpreting in relation to the world around us. By the time we are adults, we are so well practiced at these ways that we often don't think about how or why we do the things we do. Our attributions, interpersonal and romantic relationships, and group behaviors are all strongly influenced by the culture in which we live. The research reviewed in this chapter—on ingroup/outgroup behaviors, person perception, intimate relationships, attributions, and conformity and obedience—underscores the profound and pervasive impact of culture.

We need to recognize that culture plays a major role in shaping our behaviors with others. And we need to recognize that what is true for us in our own social behavior may not be true for other people from other cultures. We may frown on conformity to group norms or obedience to authority, but many cultures view them as positive aspects of social behavior. We may believe that our successes are due to internal attributes and our failures to external ones, but people from other cultures may attribute successes and failures to themselves equally. We may accept or even encourage expressing negative feelings toward ingroup others, but people from other cultures may find such expressions reprehensible or even dangerous.

These are a few examples of how culture can influence social behavior. Just as how we think and feel and act is valid for us within our culture, how people from other cultures think and feel and act is equally valid for them based on their cultural background, no matter how different their behaviors are from ours. Validity, of course, is a different question from acceptance or liking, but it is the first step toward those goals as well.

As we close this chapter, we cannot help feeling that, despite the great differences across cultures in people's social behaviors, there are considerable underlying similarities as well. As we suggested at the end of the section on attributions, there must be some kind of underlying core value or psychological principle operating in all of us that helps us enhance our sense of self, or foster our psychological and cultural goals. Culture produces differences in how we define those goals, and in their behavioral manifestations. Yet, at the core of it all, perhaps there is some culture-constant belief or value that we all operate on as human beings. The seminal review by Amir and Sharon (1988) on the cross-cultural validity of social psychological laws speaks to this point. Their review of studies examining social psychological principles across cultures indicated that original findings are often replicated across studies in statistical main effects—that is, in broad ways transcending culture. Somehow, cross-cultural psychology and research should attempt to engage this core, seeking similarities as well as differences at various levels of our psychological lives.

Glossary

aggression Any act or behavior that hurts another person, either physically or psychologically.

attributions The inferences people make about the causes of events and of their own and others' behaviors.

cognitive schemas Conceptual frameworks that people use to make sense of the world and people around them.

companionate love Love that involves warm, trusting, and tolerant affection for another whose life is deeply intertwined with one's own.

compliance Yielding to social pressure in one's public behavior, even though one's private beliefs may not have changed.

conformity Yielding to real or imagined social pressure.

consensus One of the dimensions thought to influence the nature of attributions; it refers to whether other people in the same situation tend to respond in the same manner.

consistency One of the dimensions thought to influence the nature of attributions; it refers to whether a person's behavior in a situation is the same over time.

consummate love Love that is characterized by passionate love, intimacy, and commitment.

cooperation People's ability to work together toward common goals.

defensive attributions The tendency to blame victims for their misfortune.

distinctiveness One of the dimensions thought to influence the nature of attributions; it refers to whether a person's behavior is unique to the specific target of the behavior.

fundamental attribution error An attributional bias to explain the behavior of others using internal attributions but explain our own behaviors using external attributions.

infatuation According to Sternberg, love that is passion alone, without intimacy or commitment.

ingroup relationships Relationships characterized by some degree of familiarity, intimacy, and trust. We feel close to people around us we consider to be in our ingroup. Self–ingroup relationships develop through bonds that tie the ingroup together through common friendship or relationships or goals.

interpersonal attraction Attraction that encompasses a variety of experiences, including liking, friendship, admiration, lust, and love.

matching hypothesis A hypothesis about love relationships that suggests that people of approximately equal physical characteristics are likely to select each other as partners.

obedience A form of compliance that occurs when people follow direct commands, usually from someone in a position of authority.

outgroup relationships Relationships that lack the familiarity, intimacy, and trust characteristic of relationships with ingroup others.

passionate love Love that involves absorption of another and includes sexual feelings and intense emotion.

person perception The process of forming impressions of others.

reciprocity hypothesis A hypothesis about love relationships that suggests that people tend to like others who like them.

romantic love According to Sternberg, love that involves a combination of passion and intimacy, but without commitment.

self-serving bias The tendency to attribute our successes to personal factors and our failures to situational factors.

similarity hypothesis   A hypothesis about love relationships that suggests that people similar in age, race, religion, social class, education, intelligence, attitudes, and physical attractiveness tend to form intimate relationships.

social schemas   Organized clusters of ideas about categories of social events and people that have been shown to influence person perceptions.

InfoTrac College Edition

Use InfoTrac College Edition to search for additional readings on topics of interest to you. For more information on topics in this chapter, use the following as search terms:

ingroups
outgroups
person perception
culture and attractiveness
culture and romantic love
culture and intimacy

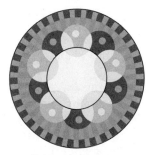

Culture and Organizations

We all spend a major portion of our lives in organizations. In fact, most of you reading this book are probably doing so within the educational system—an organization that plays an important part in many people's lives and is an important agent of socialization in the development and maintenance of culture. The companies that we work for are also organizations. And many of the extracurricular activities we engage in are supported by organizations, such as the YMCA, churches, sport clubs, and the like. Other organizations provide structure and services, such as government and hospitals.

In the past, it was probably easier than it is now to study organizations in relative isolation from issues of culture. Previously, the American workforce was less racially, ethnically, and culturally diverse than it is today. With less cultural diversity, the expectations of the members of any work organization were generally similar. Communication, lines of authority, and hierarchical structure were established with less conscious awareness of differences among people. Members of organizations had implicit, tacit knowledge about how to behave around one another and how to work together, because they all started with relatively similar cultural backgrounds.

Organizations were more isolated from issues of culture in yet another way, as many companies in the past were entirely or primarily domestic. Most of the work-related issues companies dealt with were confined to the United States and its culture. And most of the companies that competed or cooperated with one another were based in the same country and culture. This national work environment has now become a thing of the past. Not only is the American workforce culturally diverse, but many companies today operate in an international arena.

The American workplace now includes unprecedented numbers of **multinational and international corporations**—work organizations that have subsidiaries, satellite offices, and work units in more than one country. These companies need to deal increasingly with people of diverse and varied backgrounds. Today, transfers from one business unit to another within the same company can mean a transfer from one country to another. Clearly, this internationalization of business brings with it more intercultural issues and challenges.

Even domestic companies that are not multinational in their structure must face the challenge of internationalization, with its associated intercultural issues. New trade laws and treaties (such as the North American Free Trade Agreement, or NAFTA) have brought more business competitors from distant cultures, as well as increased opportunities for opening markets in other countries and cultures. Advances in communication and transportation allow companies and individuals to work more easily today than ever before over vast physical and cultural distances.

Technological changes in communication—telephones, facsimile machines, videoteleconferencing, and electronic mail—have forced the issue of culture to the forefront of our work lives. The business world has become a global village, in which the exchange of goods, services, and resources knows few boundaries. This global village raises issues within our borders as well as across borders. Many of these issues are cultural. Our ability to deal with these issues in an ever-changing business world will determine our success or failure.

Although there are many different types of organizations in the world, this chapter will focus on one particular type—work organizations—because they have been the topic of many intercultural studies and provide the context for our knowledge of the effects of culture on organizations. The information gained in understanding the relationship between culture and work organizations can be useful in understanding other organizations as well.

In this chapter, we begin by defining organizational culture and distinguishing it from organizational climate. We examine cross-cultural research analyzing organizational culture first through organizational structure and then through work-related values, using Hofstede's four major dimensions of culture. Finally, we examine cross-cultural research on a variety of work-related behaviors, including motivation and productivity, leadership and management, decision making, and intercultural issues related to business.

Organizational Culture and Organizational Climate

An organization is a structure created by people to achieve certain objectives. Organizations are generally composed of people who work collectively to address the overall goals of the organization. Different people or groups may have different specific goals within the organization, but theoretically they should collectively address a common goal (for example, building a car, selling groceries). Different people or groups may be specialized according to role, objective, or task, and rank or status within a hierarchy may differentiate them from one another.

Like people, each organization is unique; like groups of people and cultures, groups of organizations have similarities we may characterize as culture. In recent years, it has become fashionable to refer to this aspect of organizations as "organizational culture" or "corporate culture" (O'Reilly, 1989; O'Reilly, Chatman, & Caldwell, 1991). It is important to define *organizational culture* and to distinguish it from another widely used term, *organizational climate.*

Although various definitions of organizational culture have been offered, most are comparable to the definition of culture presented earlier in this book (Chapter 1), but applied to an organization instead of a social group or society. As you will recall, we have defined culture as a dynamic system of rules—explicit and implicit—established by groups in order to ensure their survival, involving attitudes, values, beliefs, norms, and behaviors, shared by a group but harbored differently by each specific unit within the group, communicated across generations, relatively stable but with the potential to change across time. **Organizational culture**, therefore, refers to a dynamic system of rules that are shared among members of an organization. The rules involve various psychological constructs, such as attitudes, values, beliefs, norms, and behaviors. Organizational culture is thus larger than the behavioral practices we observe in everyday work. It refers to deeper-seated values and beliefs held to be important not only by individual employees, but by the organization itself.

This definition of organizational culture allows us to define, analyze, and understand organizational culture not as a single, unitary construct, but rather as a dynamic, multifaceted construct that exists on many different levels. This is important because, as you will see in the remainder of this chapter, most writers talk about organizational culture as if there were only one such entity in an organization. In our work on this topic (for example, Colvin, Matsumoto, Taylor, & Grogan, 1998), we have differentiated three levels of organizational culture: individual, intraorganizational, and interorganizational.

On the *individual* level, culture is manifested in the cultures that individuals bring with them to the workplace, based on the cultural milieu in which they were raised and socialized. At the *intraorganizational* level, culture exists within an organization—that is, among people within departments and units, and among departments and units within a company. This level is most congruent with contemporary views of organizational culture. It includes the explicit and implicit rules governing shared daily practices, such as human resource policies regarding pay, raises, promotion, and termination, as well as unspoken rules of how to deal with your manager. Finally, the *interorganizational* level recognizes that companies do not exist in a vacuum. Instead, they coexist with other companies, both within a country and across countries, on which they depend for survival and existence. Culture at this level includes many explicit (in the form of domestic and international business laws) and implicit (informal dos and don'ts) rules that govern how companies deal with one another and coexist for mutual prosperity and wealth.

Organizational climate refers to a shared perception of "the way things are around here" (Reichers & Schneider, 1990)—a shared perception of organizational policies, practices, and procedures. In addition, the term contains nuances of an emotional climate—that is, how people generally feel in their normal, everyday business practices. Climate can probably be best understood as a manifestation of organizational culture (Reichers & Schneider, 1990; Schein, 1985), which generally refers to a deeper, less consciously held set of values, attitudes, and meanings.

The concept of organizational climate is a long-standing one in the field of industrial and organizational psychology. Reichers and Schneider (1990), in their review of these two constructs, point out that writing appeared as early as 1939 on organizational climate and its relationship to work behaviors. Organizational culture, on the other hand, is a relatively new concept. It first appeared in the literature in 1979 and has become an important catchphrase for the 1980s and 1990s. Most of the cross-cultural research on organizations has focused on culture, not climate, and that will be our focus in this chapter. Hopefully, future research will begin to examine in more detail how organizational climate is related to culture, and how it differs across national and social cultures.

Culture and Organizational Structure

One way in which scientists have traditionally tried to understand organizational culture is by analyzing organizational structures. The assumption is that differences in underlying values, beliefs, norms, and behaviors between organizations should manifest themselves in observable differences in how companies structure and organize themselves to do their work. Thus, by examining differences in structure, we should be able to gain an understanding of the organizational cultures underlying those structures.

This approach has not been without merit. Some writers, for example, have suggested that organizations differ along certain stable dimensions. Robbins (1987) suggests that organizations differ in complexity, formalization, and centralization. **Complexity** refers to the degree to which organizations foster differentiation of tasks and activities within themselves. **Formalization** refers to the degree to which organizations provide structure and rules for their operations. **Centralization** refers to the degree to which organizations concentrate their operations and decision-making capabilities in a limited number of business units or people.

Berry and associates (1992) point out that a number of factors determine how organizations deal with these three dimensions. These factors include the size of the organization, the technology available to it, its resources, and its history. In addition, we need to take into account the culture of the people comprising the organization—its employees—and their worldview or ways of understanding and interacting with the world and with other people.

Given all these factors, it is no wonder that organizations differ on these dimensions according to the national culture in which they exist. Several writers have used these differences to describe the "national character" of organizations, clearly referring to what we would call organizational culture. Lammers and Hickson (1979), for example, suggest three different types of national character in organizations: the Latin type, the Anglo-Saxon type, and the Third World type. The **Latin type** is characterized as a classic bureaucracy, with centralized power and decision making and many hierarchical levels. The **Anglo-Saxon type** is more or less the opposite, with less centralization, more diffusion of power and decision making, and less hierarchy in the bureaucracy. The **Third World type** is characterized by greater centralization of decision making, less formalization of rules, and a more paternalistic or traditional family orientation.

Lammers and Hickson's (1979) study is but one attempt to examine cultural differences in organizational structure. All the different types of organizations of the world cannot be pigeonholed into three (or any number of) limited classifications, just as it would be impossible to pigeonhole all people into neat categories of classification (no matter how hard psychologists and the Census Bureau may try!). But general tendencies toward differences in organizational structure can be observed across countries, and these differences are most likely related to cultural differences in the people comprising the organizations and the countries in which they exist. As with people, each organization needs to be understood on its own terms. Many other countries, not only the United States, are dealing with increasing diversity in their populations. This diversity challenges us to begin questioning the validity of broad generalizations about people and organizations based solely on structure.

Cultural Differences in Work-Related Values

Another way in which scientists have tried to understand organizational culture is through research on employees' work-related values. This approach represents an evolution in the field's understanding of organization culture, from conceptualizing it in terms of structural components to describing culture in terms of its functional components. Much of how we understand corporate culture today is based on this functional approach, which has its roots in assessing corporate culture by examining the work-related values of company employees.

People of different cultural backgrounds come to work with different values related to their work. These values include individual orientation and attitudes toward work itself, toward the organization and company loyalty, toward personal relationships with other members of the company, and so forth. Cultural similarities and differences in value orientations related to work can be a source of overall growth and financial gain or of conflict, frustration, and organizational stumbling.

The best-known study of work-related values was conducted by Hofstede (1980, 1984) in the 1960s and 1970s. His study involved employees at International Business Machines (IBM), a multinational corporation with branch offices and subsidiaries in many different countries. In his original study (1980), Hofstede reported data collected from workers in 40 different countries. In a later study (1984), he reported data from an additional 10 countries. Altogether, more than 116,000 questionnaires were distributed to workers in these various countries, spanning upwards of 20 different languages and including a total of seven different occupational levels.

The questionnaire itself contained approximately 160 items, of which 63 were related to work values. The questions clustered around four major themes: satisfaction, perception, personal goals and beliefs, and demographics. Hofstede identified four major dimensions of work-related values and computed overall scores for each country on each of these four dimensions. This approach allowed him to order the countries according to their score on each dimension. This ecological approach, using country or group scores as the units of analysis, is useful for identifying and characterizing national tendencies; however, a one-to-one correspondence with those same tendencies does not necessarily exist on the individual level within a country.

Hofstede called the four major dimensions in his study power distance (PD), uncertainty avoidance (UA), individualism (IN), and masculinity (MA). IN was introduced in Chapter 2 as the construct individualism versus collectivism (IC), and all four dimensions have been referred to frequently throughout this book. Indeed, Hofstede's study was a major impetus to viewing and understanding cultures using a dimensional approach. Moreover, the findings of this study have served as the foundation for much of the work that has been done since on culture and organizations. Each of the dimensions he identified is related to concrete differences in attitudes, opinions, beliefs, and behaviors within work organizations, and each forms the basis for understanding certain societal norms in each of the countries in Hofstede's studies. These dimensions also have consequences for organizational structure and interorganizational behavior.

Power Distance

Status and power are sociological concepts associated with groups of individuals. In companies and organizations, vertical or hierarchical relationships based on status and power differences are common. Indeed, differentiating people according to their roles, functions, and positions is vital to the successful operation of an organization. The various statuses afforded different individuals within a hierarchy come with certain benefits, rights, privileges, and power not afforded others. The "chain of command" within a company identifies the players and their roles.

The basic hierarchical relationship is that between a boss and his or her immediate subordinate. In most cases, an employee is involved in a hierarchical relationship both with someone of higher status and with others of lower status. People within each culture develop ways of interacting with others according to the status differential that exists between the individual and the person with whom he or she is interacting. Power distance (PD) refers to the degree to which different cultures encourage or maintain power and status differences between interactants. Cultures high on PD develop rules, mechanisms, and rituals that serve to maintain and strengthen the status relationships among their members. Cultures low on PD minimize those rules and customs, ignoring if not eliminating the status differences between people.

In Hofstede's original study (1980), the Philippines, Mexico, Venezuela, and India had the highest scores on this dimension. These findings suggest that the cultures underlying these countries maintained strong status differences. New Zealand, Denmark, Israel, and Austria had the lowest scores on PD, suggesting that the cultures underlying these countries did the most to minimize status and power differentials. Spain, Pakistan, Japan, and Italy were right in the middle of the scores. The United States had slightly lower scores, reflecting some degree of minimizing of power differences.

According to Hofstede, cultural differences on PD are related to individual differences in behaviors that have consequences for their work. Table 15.1 summarizes PD-related characteristics Hofstede gleaned from his own research and that of others. For example, managers in organizations in high-PD cultures are seen as making decisions autocratically and paternalistically, whereas managers in low-PD cultures are seen as making decisions only after more extensive consultation with their subordinates.

The concrete behaviors listed in Table 15.1 are related to societal norms, which in turn have important consequences for organizational structure. In general, cultures high on PD foster organizations with greater centralization of organization and process, taller organizational pyramids, larger proportions of supervisory personnel, larger wage differentials, lower qualifications for lower strata of employees, and greater valuation of white-collar as opposed to blue-collar jobs. All these characteristics of work organizations and of interpersonal relationships within companies can be considered as natural consequences of social and cultural differences on power distance.

Uncertainty Avoidance

Uncertainty is a fact of life. No one can predict with 100% accuracy what the future holds for any of us. While this is true for individuals, it is especially true for companies. Today's profits can easily turn into tomorrow's losses, and vice versa. How a market will react to a new product, revisions in old products, corporate restructuring, mergers and acquisitions, and all the other changes that occur within organizations and in the business world is a major source of uncertainty. With this uncertainty can come confusion, stress, and anxiety.

Every society and every organization develops its own ways of dealing with the anxiety and stress associated with uncertainty. Often, these ways involve development of rituals, informal or written, concerning a code of conduct among employees, as in intracompany policies regarding communication or

Table 15.1 Summary of Connotations of Power Distance (PD) Differences Found in Survey Research

Low-PD Countries	High-PD Countries
Parents put less value on children's obedience.	Parents put high value on children's obedience.
Students put high value on independence.	Students put high value on conformity.
Authoritarian attitudes in students are a matter of personality.	Students show authoritarian attitudes as a social norm.
Managers seen as making decisions after consulting with subordinates.	Managers seen as making decisions autocratically and paternalistically.
Close supervision negatively evaluated by subordinates.	Close supervision positively evaluated by subordinates.
Stronger perceived work ethic: strong disbelief that people dislike work.	Weaker perceived work ethic: more frequent belief that people dislike work.
Managers more satisfied with participative superior.	Managers more satisfied with directive or persuasive superior.
Subordinates' preference for manager's decision-making style clearly centered on consultative, give-and-take style.	Subordinates' preference for manager's decision-making style polarized between autocratic-paternalistic and majority rule.
Managers like seeing themselves as practical and systematic; they admit a need for support.	Managers like seeing themselves as benevolent decision makers.
Employees less afraid of disagreeing with their boss.	Employees fear to disagree with their boss.
Employees show more cooperativeness.	Employees reluctant to trust each other.
Managers seen as showing more consideration.	Managers seen as showing less consideration.
Students have positive associations with "power" and "wealth."	Students have negative associations with "power" and "wealth."
Mixed feeling about employees' participation in management.	Ideological support for employees' participation in management.
Mixed feelings among managers about the distribution of capacity for leadership and initiative.	Ideological support among managers for a wide distribution of capacity for leadership and initiative.
Informal employee consultation possible without formal participation.	Formal employee participation possible without informal consultation.
Higher-educated employees hold much less authoritarian values than lower-educated ones.	Higher- and lower-educated employees show similar values about authority.

Source: Geert Hofstede, *Culture's Consequences: Comparing Values, Behaviors, Institutions, and Organizations across Nations,* 2nd ed., 2001. Used by permission of the author.

interpersonal relationships. These rules may also govern behavior between companies within a society, or across cultures, as in domestic and international laws governing business and interbusiness relationships.

Uncertainty avoidance (UA) describes the degree to which different societies and different cultures develop ways to deal with the anxiety and stress of uncertainty. Cultures high on UA develop highly refined rules and rituals that are mandated and become part of the company rubric and normal way of operation. Companies in these cultures may be considered rule-oriented. In Hofstede's survey, Greece, Portugal, Belgium, and Japan were the four countries with the highest scores on this dimension. Cultures low on UA are less concerned with rules and rituals to deal with the stress and anxiety of uncertainty. Companies in these cultures have a more relaxed attitude concerning uncertainty and ambiguity and mandate fewer rules and rituals for their employees. In Hofstede's study, Sweden, Denmark, and Singapore had the lowest scores on UA.

Cultural differences on UA are directly related to concrete differences in jobs and work-related behaviors. Table 15.2 lists the characteristics of people associated with cultures high or low on UA. For example, cultures high on UA tend to be associated with greater job stress than cultures low on UA. This finding is ironic, given that cultures high on UA place greater emphasis on developing ways of dealing with the stress and anxiety produced by uncertainty. Perhaps the ways that are developed are so complex that they produce increased stress in the workers who have to abide by those rules and rituals!

Individualism–Collectivism

Individualism–collectivism (IC) has been used to explain, understand, and predict cultural differences in a variety of contexts. IC refers to the degree to which a culture fosters individualistic tendencies as opposed to group or collectivistic tendencies. Individualistic cultures tend to foster development of autonomous, unique, and separate individuals. In these cultures, the needs, wishes, desires, and goals of individuals take precedence over group or collective goals. Collectivistic cultures foster interdependence of individuals within groups. In these cultures, individuals sacrifice their own personal needs and goals for the sake of a common good.

IC is a very important dimension in relation to work organizations. Collectivistic cultural values foster more compliance with company policies and more conformity in group, section, or unit behavior. Collectivism also fosters a greater degree of reliance on group work and group orientation to company and organizational tasks. Harmony within groups, sections, or business units is valued more in collectivistic cultures; members are more likely to engage in behaviors that ensure harmony and to refrain from behaviors that threaten harmony.

In Hofstede's study, the United States, Australia, Great Britain, and Canada had the highest scores on IC. Workers in these countries were characterized as being the most individualistic of all workers in the study. It is interesting to

Table 15.2 Summary of Connotations of Uncertainty Avoidance (UA) Differences Found in Survey Research

Low-UA Countries	High-UA Countries
Lower anxiety level in population.	Higher anxiety level in population.
Greater readiness to live by the day.	More worry about the future.
Lower job stress.	Higher job stress.
Less emotional resistance to change.	More emotional resistance to change.
Less hesitation to change employers.	Tendency to stay with the same employer.
Loyalty to employer is not seen as a virtue.	Loyalty to employer is seen as a virtue.
Preference for smaller organizations as employers.	Preference for larger organizations as employers.
Smaller generation gap.	Greater generation gap.
Lower average age in higher-level jobs.	Higher average age in higher-level jobs: gerontocracy.
Managers should be selected on criteria other than seniority.	Managers should be selected on the basis of seniority.
Stronger achievement motivation.	Less achievement motivation.
Hope of success.	Fear of failure.
More risk-taking.	Less risk-taking.
Stronger ambition for individual advancement.	Lower ambition for individual advancement.
Prefers manager career over specialist career.	Prefers specialist career over manager career.
A manager need not be an expert in the field he/she manages.	A manager must be an expert in the field he/she manages.
Hierarchical structures of organizations can be by-passed for pragmatic reasons.	Hierarchical structures of organizations should be clear and respected.
Preference for broad guidelines.*	Preference for clear requirements and instructions.
Rules may be broken for pragmatic reasons.	Company rules should not be broken.
Conflict in organizations is natural.*	Conflict in organizations is undesirable.
Competition between employees can be fair and right.	Competition between employees is emotionally disapproved of.
More sympathy for individual and authoritative decisions.	Ideological appeal of consensus and of consultative leadership.
Delegation to subordinates can be complete.*	Initiative of subordinates should be kept under control.
Higher tolerance for ambiguity in perceiving others (higher LPC).	Lower tolerance for ambiguity in perceiving others (lower LPC).
More prepared to compromise with opponents.	Lower readiness to compromise with opponents.

*Based on studies by Laurent (1978).

Table 15.2 Summary of Connotations of Uncertainty Avoidance (UA) Differences Found in Survey Research (*continued*)

Low-UA Countries	High-UA Countries
Acceptance of foreigners as managers.	Suspicion toward foreigners as managers.
Larger fractions prepared to live abroad.	Fewer people prepared to live abroad.
Higher tolerance for ambiguity in looking at own job (lower satisfaction scores).	Lower tolerance for ambiguity in looking at own job (higher satisfaction scores).
Citizen optimism about ability to control politicians' decisions.	Citizen pessimism about ability to control politicians' decisions.
Employee optimism about the motives behind company activities.	Employee pessimism about the motives behind company activities.
Optimism about people's amount of initiative, ambition, and leadership skills.	Pessimism about people's amount of initiative, ambition, and leadership skills.

Source: Geert Hofstede, *Culture's Consequences: Comparing Values, Behaviors, Institutions, and Organizations across Nations,* 2nd ed., 2001. Used by permission of the author.

note that each of these countries has a strong historical link to Great Britain. Peru, Pakistan, Colombia, and Venezuela had the lowest scores on IC and were the most collectivistic.

IC differences between countries and cultures are associated with concrete differences in worker attitudes, values, beliefs, and behaviors about work and their companies. Table 15.3 summarizes the differences Hofstede gleaned from his and other people's studies. For example, people in individualistic cultures tend to regard their personal time as important and to make clear distinctions between their time and company time. People in individualistic cultures place more importance on freedom and challenge in their jobs, and initiative is generally encouraged on the job. In collectivistic cultures, freedom, independence, and initiative are normally frowned upon.

Masculinity

Biological differences between men and women are a given. The question that every society, culture, and individual has to deal with is the degree to which the biological differences translate, or should translate, to practical differences in social roles, functions, or positions. Traditionally, American culture has expected men to be more assertive, dominant, and the primary wage earner and women to be more nurturing, caring, and primarily concerned with family and child care issues (see also Chapter 7). This picture has been changing rapidly in the United States and continues to be a source of conflict, controversy, and confusion. Values concerning equity and equality have infused the workplace, and many American companies are still in transition toward providing gender equity in the workplace.

Table 15.3 Summary of Connotations of Individualism (IC) Differences Found in Survey and Related Research

Low-IC Countries	High-IC Countries
Importance of provisions by company (training, physical conditions).	Importance of employees' personal life (time).
Emotional dependence on company.	Emotional independence from company.
Large company attractive.	Small company attractive.
Moral involvement with company.	Calculative involvement with company.
Moral importance attached to training and use of skills in jobs.	More importance attached to freedom and challenge in jobs.
Students consider it less socially acceptable to claim pursuing their own ends without minding others.	Students consider it socially acceptable to claim pursuing their own ends without minding others.
Managers aspire to conformity and orderliness.	Managers aspire to leadership and variety.
Managers rate having security in their position more important.	Managers rate having autonomy more important.
Managers endorse "traditional" points of view, not supporting employee initiative and group activity.	Managers endorse "modern" points of view on stimulating employee initiative and group activity.
Group decisions are considered better than individual decisions.	Individual decisions are considered better than group decisions.
Duty in life appeals to students.	Enjoyment in life appeals to students.
Managers choose duty, expertness, and prestige as life goals.	Managers choose pleasure, affections, and security as life goals.
Individual initiative is socially frowned upon: fatalism.	Individual initiative is socially encouraged.
More acquiescence in responses to "importance" questions.	Less acquiescence in responses to "importance" questions.
People thought of in terms of ingroups and outgroups; particularism.	People thought of in general terms; universalism.
Social relations predetermined in terms of ingroups.	Need to make specific friendships.
More years of schooling needed to do a given job.	Fewer years of schooling needed to do a given job.
More traffic accidents per 1000 vehicles.	Fewer traffic accidents per 1000 vehicles.
More traditional time use pattern.	More modern time use pattern.

Source: Geert Hofstede, *Culture's Consequences: Comparing Values, Behaviors, Institutions, and Organizations across Nations,* 2nd ed., 2001. Used by permission of the author.

Each culture and society must deal with the issue of sex roles and gender differences. A fourth dimension emerged in Hofstede's study, which he labeled masculinity (MA). This label is somewhat misleading because almost all the employees who completed the questionnaire were male. Many of the items identified with this dimension, in fact, had more to do with materialism than relationships, and Hofstede interpreted this factor as associated with masculinity. Still, this dimension can be conceptually useful in understanding gender differences in the workplace. According to Hofstede, MA refers to the degree to which cultures foster or maintain differences between the sexes in work-related values. Cultures high on MA—such as Japan, Austria, Venezuela, and Italy—were associated with the greatest degree of sex differences in work-related values. Cultures low on MA—such as Denmark, Netherlands, Norway, and Sweden—had the fewest differences between the sexes.

As with each of the other dimensions Hofstede generated, cultural differences on MA were associated with very concrete differences between workers and organizations. Table 15.4 summarizes these differences. For example, managers in cultures high on MA valued leadership, independence, and self-realization; cultures low on MA placed less importance on these constructs. Employees in high-MA cultures regarded earnings, recognition, advancement, and challenge as relatively more important than did employees in low-MA cultures. And fewer women were in mixed-sex jobs in organizations in high-MA cultures than in low-MA cultures.

Cultural differences on MA have interesting consequences for both organizational structure and employee relationships (Hofstede, 1980). For example, young men in high-MA cultures generally expect to make a career in their jobs, and those who don't see themselves as failures. In high-MA cultures, organizational interests, needs, and goals are viewed as a legitimate reason to interfere in the personal and private lives of employees. High-MA cultures generally have fewer women in more qualified and better-paid jobs, and those women who are in more qualified jobs tend to be very assertive. Job stress is generally higher in organizations located in high-MA cultures.

Recent Research on Organizational Culture

Hofstede's original research described above was an important catalyst for the field, redefining corporate culture in terms of culture as cross-cultural psychologists and anthropologists have typically defined it, and allowing for measurement-driven assessments of it in actual work settings. Not only did this work have far-reaching consequences in the area of organizational psychology; the specification and quantification of the four dimensions of culture was a major plus for many other areas of psychology as well. Harry Triandis (1998), for example, attributes much of his initial interest in and attention to the concept of individualism–collectivism to Hofstede's work, and by now we are well

Table 15.4 Summary of Connotations of Masculinity (MA) Differences
Found in Survey and Related Research

Low-MA Countries	High-MA Countries
Relationship with manager, cooperation, friendly atmosphere, living in a desirable area, and employment security relatively more important to employees.	Earnings, recognition, advancement, and challenge relatively more important to employees.
Managers relatively less interested in leadership, independence, and self-realization.	Managers have leadership, independence, and self-realization ideal.
Belief in group decisions.	Belief in the independent decision maker.
Students less interested in recognition.	Students aspire to recognition (admiration for the strong).
Weaker achievement motivation.	Stronger achievement motivation.
Achievement defined in terms of human contacts and living environment.	Achievement defined in terms of recognition and wealth.
Work less central in people's lives.	Greater work centrality.
People prefer shorter working hours to more salary.	People prefer more salary to shorter working hours.
Company's interference in private life rejected.	Company's interference in private life accepted.
Greater social role attributed to other institutions than corporation.	Greater social role attributed to corporation.
Employees like small companies.	Employees like large corporations.
Entire population more attracted to smaller organizations.	Entire population more attracted to larger organization.
Lower job stress.	Higher job stress.
Less skepticism as to factors leading to getting ahead.	Skepticism as to factors leading to getting ahead.
Students more benevolent (sympathy for the weak).	Students less benevolent.
Managers have more of a service ideal.	Managers relatively less attracted by service role.
"Theory X" (employees dislike work) strongly rejected.	"Theory X" gets some support.
More women in jobs with mixed sex composition.	Fewer women in jobs with mixed sex composition.
Smaller or no value differences between men and women in the same jobs.	Greater value differences between men and women in the same jobs.
Sex role equality in children's books.	More sex role differentiation in children's books.

Source: Geert Hofstede, *Culture's Consequences: Comparing Values, Behaviors, Institutions, and Organizations across Nations,* 2nd ed., 2001. Used by permission of the author.

familiar with the major contributions Triandis has made to all areas of cross-cultural and mainstream psychology from this perspective.

Subsequent research on organizational culture has focused, to a large extent, on the deep-seated values that employees may have. These values are generally assumed to occur as a result of the employees' relationship with their companies, or because of the particular sociocultural milieu within which the employees and the companies exist. Research in this area in the past two decades has expanded our knowledge of dimensions of corporate culture in several ways.

Bond and Hofstede's Confucian Dynamism

Although the four dimensions Hofstede originally described seemed applicable to companies and cultures around the world, some scientists raised questions about their adequacy in the Asian business world. Although dimensions such as IC, PD, UA, and MA are indeed important markers of culture in Asia, other values seem to be at work in Asian companies that are not fully described by Hofstede's original four dimensions. To investigate this possibility further, Michael Bond and his colleagues, in collaboration with Hofstede (Chinese Culture Connection, 1987; Hofstede & Bond, 1988), have studied the work-related values and psychological characteristics of workers and organizations in Asian countries. No doubt, much of the impetus for this line of research has been the surge in industry and business success of the "five dragons" of Asia: Japan, Hong Kong, Korea, Taiwan, and China.

Through their work, these researchers have identified a fifth important dimension of work-related values: **Confucian dynamism**. Many of the principles and values found to be important to Asian companies are thought to be rooted in Confucian thought and principles, including:

■ Unequal status relationships lead to a stable society.
■ The family is typical of all social organizations.
■ Virtue in life consists of working hard, acquiring useful skills and as much education as possible, not being a spendthrift, and persevering when faced with difficult tasks.

These principles translate to abstract values that play an important role not only in interpersonal relationships in business but also as organizational goals and principles. These values include persistence and perseverance, relationships ordered by status, preservation of this order, thrift, and a sense of shame. Also important are values that enforce personal steadiness and stability; protection of face and outward stance; respect for tradition, custom, history, and heritage; and reciprocation of favors, greetings, and gifts. Many writers have suggested that these values stand at the core of many Asian cultures, permeating work and organizational life as an important cultural dimension above and beyond those originally identified by Hofstede.

Other Research on Organizational Culture

Since the original publication of Hofstede's work, a number of scientists have taken up the call to study in more depth corporate culture from the standpoint of work-related values. In general, these studies not only confirm the importance of Hofstede's original work, but expand and improve our knowledge in this area.

Hofstede (1996a) himself, since his original study, has gone on to collect more data from IBM subsidiaries around the world, expanding on the original database that served as the foundation for the first set of findings. In addition, he has linked the four dimensions of culture with characteristics of the countries to which they are related, such as geography, climate, educational levels, and the like. He has analyzed specific companies in terms of the kinds of cultural values they harbor, and has conducted many case studies analyzing the success and failure of organizational development activities in these companies. In many of these cases, he has shown how developmental or training activities that are not congruent with the underlying cultural values of the organization face a difficult path at best, and at worst are doomed to fail. His point is that understanding the psychological dimensions underlying companies is a necessary component of successful plan development for training and other organizational activities.

Research by other scholars has shed additional light on the nature of cultural differences in work-related values around the world. Trompenaars (1993), for example, reported data from about 15,000 respondents, ranging across 30 companies in 50 different countries. Analysis of the data indicated that seven factors were particularly relevant to predicting intercultural differences among the countries, and to the conduct of international business. These factors are universalism versus particularism, individualism versus collectivism, neutral versus emotional, specific versus diffuse, achievement versus ascription, time orientation, and attitude toward the environment. Universalism versus particularism refers to the degree to which people emphasize relationships with others (particularism) as opposed to using standards that are independent of specific social relationships. Achievement versus ascription refers to the characteristics that determine a person's status. Status afforded because of an accomplishment (such as academic or athletic achievement) is achieved status. Status afforded because of a nonaccomplishment characteristic (such as a hereditary title) is ascribed status.

Smith, Dugan, and Trompenaars (1996), following up on these ideas, sampled 8,841 employees from 43 different countries on these dimensions and others. They submitted their data to a statistical technique known as multidimensional scaling, which identifies dimensions that may underlie the ratings provided by the participants and reduces the data to a smaller set of dimensions that seem to account for the data. Three dimensions were found to be important in differentiating among the cultures in this study: achievement versus ascription, individualism–collectivism, and a combination dimension that included elements of the first two along with elements of power distance, Confucian dynamism, egalitarianism, and integration. These authors argued that Hofstede's original IC and PD dimensions may be better described as representing different orientations to continuity in group membership (loyal versus utilitarian involvement) and toward obligations in social relationships (conservative versus egalitarian commitment).

Hofstede (1996b), however, reanalyzed Trompenaars's (1993) data on the country or ecological level rather than the individual level. Using factor analyses and correlational techniques, he found that only two of Trompenaars' seven dimensions could be confirmed statistically: individualism/achievement and universalism/diffuse. Moreover, Hofstede reported that both these dimensions were correlated with his own Individualism index. Thus, it is possible that the set of dimensions on the individual employee level may differ slightly from the dimensions found on the ecological or country level.

Some research has been conducted on dimensions other than those proposed by Hofstede. Furnham, Bond, Heaven, and Hilton (1993), for example, had 1,688 participants from 13 countries complete seven scales designed to measure Protestant work ethic. The results indicated highly significant differences between countries, and these differences were consistent across measures. Participants from industrialized countries tended to have lower scores than those from Third World countries. In addition, scores for the countries were highly positively correlated with Hofstede's dimension of power distance, and negatively correlated with individualism.

Collectively, the findings from recent research suggest that many of Hofstede's original cultural dimensions may be appropriate for describing ecological-level differences in cultural values across countries. In addition, a fifth dimension—Confucian dynamism—may be especially important for Asian companies and cultures. Other dimensions may be important for understanding cultural differences on the individual, rather than the ecological, level.

Measuring Organizational Culture

Although the research on organizational culture has been influential in all fields of cross-cultural psychology, its practical applications have been especially apparent in actual work settings. Much of the emphasis on corporate culture in the fields of business and management today is based on this research. Many people quickly realized the relevance of the topic to their everyday work lives, and the importance of understanding organizational culture from a business standpoint. For this reason, researchers of the past 10 to 15 years have been hard at work developing methods of assessing organizational culture that can be directly applied to the corporate business world.

A number of applied scales assessing organizational culture have been developed over the past decade. Rousseau (1990) reviewed seven such scales: the Norms Diagnostic Index (Allen & Dyer, 1980), the Kilmann–Saxton Culture-Gap Survey (Kilmann & Saxton, 1983), the Organizational Culture Inventory (Human Synergistics, 1986), the Organizational Value Congruence Scale (Enz,

1986), the Organizational Culture Profile (O'Reilly, Chatman, & Caldwell, 1988), the Organizational Beliefs Questionnaire (Sashkin & Fulmer, 1985), and the Corporate Culture Survey (Glaser, 1983). Other scales have been developed since the time of this review, including Beach's (1993) Organizational Culture Survey. Like much of the research on work-related values, all of these scales focus on cultural norms, attitudes, or values held by employees.

One limitation of these approaches is that they are focused almost exclusively on the level of the individual. As discussed earlier in this chapter, organizational culture is a dynamic, multilevel construct that exists not only at the level of individual employees, but also across departments and business units within an organization and among organizations in a larger national and international business milieu. Thus, although it is important to capture individual-level culture, a complete picture of organizational culture needs to address the intra- and interorganizational levels as well.

For example, companies generally develop their own sets of rules, attitudes, values, beliefs, and attitudes regarding intraorganization functioning. Rules exist for communication and interaction among department units within companies. Policies exist for human resources, promotion, raises, pay, training, length of employment, and many other intraorganizational factors. Laws exist that govern how businesses can work with one another, and international business laws exist to dictate how corporations can interact across national borders. All of these constitute levels of corporate culture above and beyond the culture that individuals bring with them to work.

Some Practical Implications of Organizational Culture

Our increased awareness of the nature and function of organizational culture has brought about a growing interest in the practical implications of organizational culture in business and places of work. An increasing number of studies have examined these implications in the past ten years, and they provide important information concerning real-life issues involving organizational culture. Some studies, for example, have examined the role of organizational culture in producing or mitigating stress perceived by employees (for example, Peterson, 1997; Peterson & Smith, 1997; Thompson, Stradling, Murphy, & O'Neill, 1996). Peterson suggests that not only does the specific work that people do create stress, but so does the culture in which they work. Some organizational cultures may produce stress by their very nature (Thompson et al., 1996) or through the historical evolution of cultural values in the company (Peterson & Smith, 1997).

One topic that has gained prominence not only in the scientific literature but also in applied work is the issue of cultural fit between person and company. Given the work conducted in the past two decades on organizational culture, and the work that has been done for years on individual culture, a logical question concerns the match between employees and the cultures they come from, on the one hand, and a company and its organizational culture, on the other. Do "mismatches" create conflicts? Do successful "matches" lead to more productive companies?

To address these types of questions, Bochner and Hesketh (1994) examined Hostede's dimensions of power distance (PD) and individualism (IN) in 263 employees of a multinational company, representing 28 different countries. Participants completed a questionnaire that measured more concrete work-related attitudes, such as superior–subordinate relationships, decision-making styles, work ethic, task orientation, psychological contracts, and individual-versus group-level achievements. The researchers classified respondents according to their country's rankings on PD and IN in Hofstede's previous data, and examined differences between high- and low-PD and high- and low-IN countries. They found that respondents in high-PD cultures were less open with their superiors, had more contact with them, and described supervision as being more close and direct. These respondents were also more task-oriented, and showed a greater tendency to believe that some people are inherently lazy and find work noxious. The results for IN indicated that collectivists had more informal contact with fellow workers, knew staff better, and were more likely to work on a team than alone. The researchers also classified respondents in terms of ingroups or outgroups, and found that when people of opposing work-related values interact daily and cooperatively, difficulties still arise, even though the interactions occur on an equitable basis. In particular, there were major differences between these two groups in perceived discrimination, attitudes toward multiculturalism, and counternormative behavior.

Abrams, Ando, and Hinkle (1998) examined cross-cultural differences in organizational identification and subjective norms as predictors of workers' turnover intentions. In their study, employees of companies in Great Britain and Japan completed questionnaires related to turnover intentions, attitudes toward leaving the organization, subjective norms regarding perceived approval for leaving, and organizational identification. In the British sample, turnover intentions were predicted by organizational identification; workers with stronger identifications with the company had lower turnover intentions. In the Japanese sample, however, turnover intentions were associated with both organizational identification and subjective norms. These findings suggest that although social identity is strongly associated with employee turnover in both cultures, subjective normative aspects of group membership play a larger role in predicting turnover in Japan than they do in Great Britain.

Research has also documented positive aspects of employee–company cultural congruence. Meglino, Ravlin, and Adkins (1989), for example, questioned 191 production workers, 17 supervisors, and 13 managers on job satisfaction and organization commitment; they also collected objective data concerning attendance, performance, and efficiency. Two measures of employees' values congruence were computed and correlated with all psychological and behavioral data. Correlational analyses indicated that workers who were more satisfied and committed had values that were congruent with those of their supervisor.

These findings raise important questions concerning the nature of personnel selection in all companies and cultures today, especially in the United States with its diverse workforce population. Adding to the complexity of these issues are the cultural and ethnic differences in career choices of today's young adults (Kim, 1993) and perceived past and future barriers to career development (Luzzo, 1993). Finding an appropriate match between employer and employee is a daunting task for both individuals and organizations, as neither side profits from an unsuitable relationship or unhappy employees.

The literature of the past few years includes a number of approaches to personnel selection and training, all of which demonstrate an increasing sensitivity to cultural issues. For example, Love, Bishop, Heinish, and Montei (1994) have described the adaptations and modifications they made to a selection system for hiring American workers in a Japanese–American joint venture assembly plant. During the 1980s, the number of such joint ventures between the United States and Japan increased dramatically, particularly in the automotive industry. Today, there are many such ventures, not only with Japanese companies but with companies from many different cultures. In addition, an increasing number of American companies are establishing themselves in other countries and cultures, raising the same issues overseas. In their work, Love and colleagues modified job analysis procedures and traditional selection systems to accommodate Japanese culture and management philosophy. They then engaged in a series of steps to validate their system cross-culturally to ensure compatibility with Japanese management demands regarding productivity, team orientation, quality standards, and formal employee performance evaluations. It is particularly interesting to note the reason why the selection system could not be compared with performance criteria data on individuals:

> After submitting a formal proposal to develop a performance appraisal system, in part for validation purposes, and meeting with management, it quickly became obvious that Japanese management philosophy prohibits such a practice. Differentiating between employees on the basis of job performance is an affront to Japanese cultural beliefs which prefer a homogeneous workforce (Maher & Wong, 1994). In particular, Japanese managers suggested that individual performance appraisals would damage the "team" concept, held in high esteem throughout the plant. (Love et al., 1994, p. 843)

Thus, organizational culture and the fit between employee and company are real-life issues that have important implications in our everyday lives. Organizations have begun to struggle with the issue of cultural match between employee and company, and new ways of assimilating newcomers into organizations are constantly being developed from a cultural perspective (see, for example, Hess, 1993). Although most research approaches this issue from the organization's point of view, some writing has also addressed efforts by employees to assess the fit between themselves and the culture of the organization to which they are applying (for example, Pratt, 1993). Systematic research on these issues is still young, and we have much to learn. What constitutes a "successful" or "unsuccessful" match? How do we make these assessments? In some cultures, as Love et al. discovered, making such assessments may be counter to the prevailing cultural norms. And how valid is the suggestion that all personnel selection decisions should be informed by matches? Are there optimal levels of mismatches that may spur on maximal performance? For example, although individualism is usually associated with creativity and initiative, at least one study has shown that innovation and entrepreneurship is highest under conditions of balanced individualism and collectivism, and lowest in either highly individualistic or highly collectivistic corporations (Morris, Avila, & Allen, 1993). Could such an effect exist within organizations as well?

Summary

Clearly, the research indicates that culture plays an important role in influencing work organizations as a whole, as well as their individual members. Culture influences organizational goals, structures, and functions. Culture also influences employee attitudes, values, behaviors, and interpersonal dynamics. The dimensions that Hofstede, Bond, and others have identified are extremely useful in helping us understand how and why these cultural differences exist. Researchers have developed a number of ways of measuring organizational culture, and we know that differences in organizational culture have many important ramifications on our work lives.

As we leave this section on organizational culture, we would like to comment on the widespread perception that individuals may lose a part of themselves and a part of their individual culture when they become employees of an organization with its own culture. Certainly, many people approach this topic with considerable fear and apprehension. Research on organizational climate or corporate culture, however, has not provided support for such a loss of cultural identity or values. Berry and associates (1992) reviewed several studies that examined correlations between organizational climate and actual employee attitudes and productivity. In general, these studies found very little correlation.

Undoubtedly, employees need to learn organizational rules concerning proper behavior, but these rules are learned relatively late in their personal development. After all, people have been learning the rules of their culture since birth. Organizational culture may refer more to "values related shared daily practices in the workplace" (Berry et al., 1992, p. 322) than to shared values of life, which is more akin to our understanding of culture. Thus, it may be more accurate to suggest that employees of an organization all learn to engage temporarily in the organizational culture while they are within the organization. That is, they learn to work and function within a "temporary culture" that is added to the cultural milieu within which they normally operate. This temporary culture exists as an entity separate from more basic cultural values and does not necessarily change the fundamental self outside of the work environment. Thus, although a tangible climate exists within corporations and organizations, it does not replace or detract from our individual cultures.

Culture and the Meaning of Work

In the rest of this chapter, we turn our attention from cultural influences on organizations to the ways in which culture influences specific work-related behaviors in individuals. We begin by examining how people of different cultures define work differently, or derive different meanings from work.

People construe themselves and their existence in relation to work differently across cultures, and these differences are related to meaningful dimensions of cultural variability. As discussed in Chapter 11, people who are members of collectivistic cultures tend to have interdependent construals of self; that is, they tend to see people around them as fundamentally interrelated with themselves and as integral parts of their self-identity. Thus, people of collectivistic cultures may view their work groups and the work organizations (companies) to which they belong as a fundamental part of themselves. Work, work colleagues, and the company become synonymous with the self. The bonds between these people and their work colleagues, and between themselves and their company, are stronger and qualitatively different from those of people in individualistic cultures.

Individualistic cultures, by contrast, tend to foster a view of self as independent, unique, and autonomous from others. People in individualistic cultures thus have an easier time separating themselves from their jobs. They make greater distinctions between "work time" and "personal time," and between company-based expense accounts and personal expenses. They also make greater distinctions between social and work activities, with regard to both their work colleagues and their business associates (potential clients, customers, and so forth).

Cultural differences in the meaning of work can manifest themselves in other aspects of work as well. For example, in American culture, it is easy to think of work simply as a means to accumulate money (pay or salary) and make a living. In other cultures, especially collectivistic ones, work may be seen more as fulfilling an obligation to a larger group. In this situation, we would expect to find less movement of individuals from one job to another because of the individual's social obligations toward the work organization to which he or she belongs and to the people comprising that organization. In individualistic cultures, it is easier to consider leaving one job and going to another because it is easier to separate jobs from the self. A different job will just as easily accomplish the same goals.

Of course, the fact that people come from different cultures does not necessarily mean that they think about work entirely differently. For example, in a study involving British and Japanese employees (Abrams et al., 1998), we saw that organizational identification was an important predictor of turnover attitudes in both cultures. Thus, people of different cultures exhibit important similarities as well as differences. Nonetheless, cultural differences in the meaning of work appear to be related to cultural differences in a number of work-related behaviors, including motivation and productivity, leadership and management styles, and decision-making processes.

Culture, Motivation, and Productivity

One important issue all companies, work organizations, and businesses must address is the degree to which their employees will be productive in various types of work settings. All companies want to maximize productivity while minimizing personnel costs and the expenditure of other resources, thereby ensuring the greatest profit margins. This concern has led to an important area of research on productivity as a function of group size.

Early research on group productivity in the United States typically showed that individual productivity tends to decline in larger groups (Latané, Williams, & Harkins, 1979). These findings contributed to the coining of the term **social loafing**. Two factors appear to contribute to this phenomenon. One is reduced efficiency resulting from a lack of coordination among workers' efforts, resulting in lack of activity or duplicate activity. The second factor is a reduction in effort by individuals when they work in groups as compared to when they work by themselves. Latané (1981) and his colleagues (Latané et al., 1979) conducted a number of studies investigating group size, coordination, and effort. They found that in larger groups, both lack of coordination and reduced effort resulted in decreased productivity. Latané (1981) attributed these findings to a diffusion of responsibility in groups. As group size increases, the responsibility for getting a job done is divided among more people, and group members ease up because their individual contribution is less recognizable.

Early cross-cultural research on groups and their productivity, however, found exactly the opposite phenomenon in other cultures. Earley (1989) examined social loafing in an organizational setting among managerial trainees in the United States and in the People's Republic of China. Subjects in both cultures worked on a task under conditions of low or high accountability and low or high shared responsibility. The results clearly indicated social loafing for the American subjects, whose individual performances in a group were less than when working alone, but not for the Chinese.

Shirakashi (1985) and Yamaguchi, Okamoto, and Oka (1985) conducted studies involving Japanese participants in several tasks. They found that not only did social loafing not occur, but exactly the opposite occurred. Working in a group enhanced individual performance rather than diminished it. Gabrenya, Wang, and Latané (1985) also demonstrated this **social striving** in a sample of Chinese schoolchildren.

Several authors have speculated as to why social striving is observed in other cultures. These explanations center around the culture's degree of collectivism or group orientation. Cultures that are more collectivistic (such as China and Japan) foster interpersonal interdependence and group collective functioning more than does the individualistic American culture. Groups tend to be more productive in these cultures precisely because they foster coordination among ingroup members. These cultures also place higher values on individual contributions in group settings.

Interestingly, this trend may also be occurring in the United States, at least partially as a result of the influence of Asian, especially Japanese, business practices that focus on teamwork, cooperation, and quality (see Ebrahimpour & Johnson, 1992; Hodgetts, Luthans, & Lee, 1994). As a result of studying successful business practices overseas, many American companies have tried to adapt and adopt some of these practices, including increasing teamwork, in their daily work behaviors. Indeed, several studies involving American participants have begun to challenge the traditional notion of social loafing (for example, Harkins, 1987; Harkins & Petty, 1982; Shepperd & Wright, 1989; Weldon & Gargano, 1988; Zaccaro, 1984). Jackson and Williams (1985), for instance, reported that Americans working collectively improved performance and productivity. In a more recent study, Westaby (1995) asked participants in the United States and Japan to complete a paper-and-pen tracing task, either individually or in the presence of a group. Although the author expected that the Japanese would perform better in the group situation, the effect of group presence was actually the same for Americans and Japanese. Participants of both cultures had higher productivity and job quality in the presence of a group than when working alone. Further analyses indicated that although Japanese participants had higher productivity than American participants in general (regardless of social context), there was no difference in the quality of the work. Thus, our notions of social loafing and group productivity are now being challenged not only cross-culturally but also within American culture.

Other recent research continues to complement our knowledge of cultural influences on social loafing, social striving, and group-related work behaviors. Wagner (1995), for example, had 492 students complete questionnaires assessing the degree to which they perceived a shared responsibility with others, identifiability with others, individualism and collectivism, and cooperation. They produced a group report that required cooperation among group members. The results indicated that individualists who felt independent and less reliant were less apt to engage in cooperative behavior, whereas collectivists who felt interdependent and reliant on groups were more likely to behave cooperatively. These findings suggest that there may be a relationship between individualistic cooperation and social loafing, but that the same relationship cannot explain cooperation in collectivists.

Finally, as more recent research has uncovered social striving effects among work groups with American participants, an increasing number of scientists are examining the mechanisms underlying such social striving in an individualistic culture. Some scholars have suggested that one way in which work groups and teams can become more productive in an individualistic culture is through the use of constructive thought patterns that help to transform self-managing teams into self-leading teams (for example, Manz, 1992; Neck & Manz, 1994). The idea is that employees become empowered to influence strategic issues concerning what they do and why, in addition to how they do their work. Again, these suggestions highlight the notion that different bases may underlie productivity or nonproductivity in different cultural groups.

With increased American interest in the organizational and management styles of other countries, this topic is sure to receive even more attention in the future. A central question revolves around the best combination of ingredients (such as group size, nature of the individuals, nature of the tasks) to maximize social striving among all participants and to minimize social loafing. Recent economic necessities have forced many companies and organizations to spend less on personnel, resulting in "downsizing" or, more recently, "rightsizing." With fewer people doing more work, people in successful business organizations have been forced to reevaluate and redefine their own identities within their work groups in a more collectivistic way, for the success of the business unit and their own survival. The research conducted to date suggests that groups from all types of cultures may experience social striving or social loafing. Which outcome occurs depends on a host of factors, including group size, identifiability, shared responsibility, and culture. Exactly which factors influence which outcomes in what ways is not yet clear, and more research is clearly needed. The picture that emerges so far is that the specific ingredients that result in striving or loafing are different in different cultural milieus.

Culture, Leadership, and Management Styles

Given that organizations and the people who are members of them differ so much across cultures, it is no surprise that leadership and management styles of people in power in those organizations also differ. But before we can understand these differences, we need to realize that the definition of leadership and management differs across cultures.

Cultural Differences in the Definition of Leadership and Management

In many industrialized cultures, **leadership** can be defined as the "process of influence between a leader and followers to attain group, organizational, or societal goals" (Hollander, 1985, p. 486). Leaders may be autocratic, dictatorial, democratic, and so on. In common language, we speak of "strong" and "effective" leaders as opposed to "weak" and "ineffective" ones. In many work situations, especially in the United States, we expect leaders to have vision, authority, and power and to give subordinates tasks that have meaning in a larger picture. In American culture, leaders are expected to be decision makers, "movers and shakers" of organizations and people.

In other cultures, leaders may share many of these same traits, but their leadership and managerial styles are not necessarily seen as dynamic or action-oriented. For example, some of the most effective leaders and managers in organizations in India are seen as much more nurturing, taking on a parental role within the company and in relation to their subordinates (Sinha, 1979). These leaders are seen as much more participative, guiding and directing their subordinates' tasks and behaviors as opposed to merely giving directives. Still, leaders and managers in India need to be flexible, at times becoming very authoritative in their work roles. Thus, the optimal leadership style in India, according to Sinha, is somewhere between a totally participative and totally authoritative style.

Another way leadership and managerial styles differ across cultures is in the boundaries of that leadership. In American culture, for example, workers make a clear distinction between work and personal life. When 5:00 P.M. arrives and the bell to end work rings, many American workers consider themselves "off" from work and on their personal time. The boundary between work and their personal lives is very clear. Leaders, bosses, and others in the company should have nothing to say about how members of the company live their personal lives (for example, where they should live or whom they should marry). In other cultures, however, the boundaries between work and personal life are less clear. In many countries, the individual's existence at work becomes an integral part of the self. Thus, the distinction between work and company, on the one hand, and one's personal life, on the other, is fuzzy and blurred. Needless to say, leaders in such cultures can request overtime work from their subordinates and expect to receive it with much less griping than in American culture.

As the distinction between work and self becomes blurred, so do the boundaries of jurisdiction for leaders. For example, leaders and managers in India and Japan are expected to look after their subordinates in terms of their work and existence within the company; but it is not uncommon for leaders to be concerned with their subordinates' personal, private lives as well. Subordinates in these cultures will not hesitate to consult with their bosses about problems at home and to seek advice and help from them about those problems. Leaders, more often than not, will see helping their subordinates with this part of their lives as an integral and important part of their jobs. In India and Japan, it is not uncommon for bosses to find marriage partners for their subordinates and to look after them inside as well as outside the company. The bond between them extends well beyond the company.

As with many other cultural differences, differences in the definition and boundaries of leaders and managers are related to individualism–collectivism (IC). As we have seen, people in collectivistic cultures identify themselves more with their work organizations and companies; they see their work and their company as an integral part of themselves. People in individualistic cultures see themselves as unique and autonomous beings; the distinction between themselves and their company is clear-cut. Thus, leaders and managers in collectivistic cultures see their responsibilities as extending beyond the work environment to a much greater extent than do managers in individualistic cultures.

Cross-Cultural Research on Leadership and Management

Given these cross-cultural differences in the definition of leadership, it is not surprising that many cross-cultural studies report differences in specific leadership behaviors (see, for example, Black & Porter, 1991, on managerial differences in the United States and Hong Kong; Okechuku, 1994, on managers' ratings of subordinates in Canada, Hong Kong, and China; Smith, Peterson, & Schwartz, 2002, on sources of guidance of managers in 47 nations). Smith, Peterson, and Misumi (1994), for instance, obtained effectiveness ratings of work teams in electronics assembly plants in Japan, Great Britain, and the United States, as well as ratings of ten event management processes used by superiors. The results indicated that for the Japanese, work performance depended on the relatively frequent use of manuals and procedures and on relatively frequent guidance from supervisors. American and British supervisors, however, favored more contingent responses, suggesting that the preferred managerial response depends on the specific event or task they face.

Many other studies have documented cross-cultural differences in leadership and managerial style. Schmidt and Yeh (1992) found cross-national differences in leader influence strategies in Japan, Taiwan, Australia, and Great Britain. Howell, Dorfman, Hibino, Lee, and Tale (1995) found cultural differences in decision making and contingent punishment in Japan, Korea, Taiwan, Mexico, and the United States. Gerstner and Day (1994) asked students from eight different countries to rate 59 traits of a business leader; they found that the ratings correlated highly with Hofstede's indices of IN, PD, and UA.

Some studies have attempted to identify culture-specific leadership and managerial styles. Many authors, for example, have tried to describe the Japanese management style (see, for example, the review by Keys, Denton, & Miller, 1994), in hopes of adapting Japanese leadership and managerial practices to American industry. Similarly, Jou and Sung (1990) have described four managerial styles prevalent in Taiwan. No doubt much of this attention to Japan and other Asian countries was due to the widespread success of Asian companies and economies, including those of South Korea, Hong Kong, Taiwan, and mainland China. In the past five to ten years, however, the American economy and businesses appear to be doing relatively better in the world economy, while many Asian economies are struggling. These dynamic trends in the global economy are associated with an evolution in studies of managerial styles across cultures, and many authors are now questioning the long-term effectiveness of Asian managerial and leadership approaches of the past (see, for example, Keys, Denton, & Miller, 1994).

Not all cross-cultural research on this topic, however, has shown cultural differences; a substantial amount of literature documents cultural similarities in leadership behaviors as well. For example, Smith, Peterson, Misumi, and Bond (1992) examined work teams in Japan, Hong Kong, the United States, and Great Britain, and found that leaders who were rated high in behaviors related to task performance and group maintenance all achieved higher work quality. Smith (1998) also found consistent themes in a survey of managers' handling of day-to-day work events in Brazil, Mexico, Colombia, and Argentina. Many other studies (see review by Bond & Smith, 1996) show similar cross-cultural consistencies in some aspects of managerial behavior.

How are we to make sense of the literature that shows both similarities and differences across cultures in leadership and managerial behaviors? Misumi (1985) suggests that management involves general and universal functions that all effective leaders must carry out, but that the specific ways in which they are carried out may differ. Misumi contrasts functions related to task performance (P) and group maintenance (M), and suggests that both domains involve universal leadership goals that are consistent across cultures and companies. Different specific behaviors may be used to accomplish these managerial goals, however, depending on situations, companies, and cultures. This approach invites us to examine and understand human behavior on multiple levels—one level involving cross-cultural universals or similarities in functions and goals, and the other involving differences in culture- and context-specific instrumental behaviors.

Intracultural and cross-cultural research has accomplished much in the way of documenting cross-cultural consistencies and differences in leadership behaviors. Less frequent in the literature, however, are studies that examine leadership and managerial effectiveness in intercultural settings. What happens, for example, when managers from other countries and cultures—Japan, Korea, Hong Kong, France, or Germany, for example—come to the United States and are placed in a situation in which they must manage and lead American subordinates? What happens when Americans are sent to other countries? Such situations occur frequently in today's global marketplace and are often central to the effective and successful functioning of companies. Yet research has been slow to address these complex questions. One study (Thomas & Toyne, 1995) suggests that American subordinates may respond best when managers from other cultures demonstrate moderate levels of adaptation to the American culture and employee; high or low levels of adaptation have less positive effects on the subordinates. More research on this important topic is obviously necessary to capture the essence of effective intercultural management, a situation that promises to become even more important in the future.

Culture and Decision-Making Processes

Making decisions is one of the most important things a company, or any organization, does. As with many other types of behaviors, culture influences how a company makes decisions.

Many organizations in the United States use a democratic decision-making procedure. In a democratic procedure, every person involved has a say in the decision, usually by way of a vote; once votes are tallied, the decision of the majority prevails. This procedure has advantages and disadvantages. A major advantage to this procedure is that everyone has an equal say in the process. Democratic decision making is associated with an individualistic cultural viewpoint, which tends to see each person as a separate, autonomous being.

One disadvantage to this process concerns the consequences of close votes. If a proposal wins only a bare majority (51%), then a large minority (up to 49%) may be less than enthusiastic in implementing the decision. This scenario can lead, and has indeed led, to sabotage and disruption in many organizations.

The democratic process can also lead to considerable red tape and bureaucracy. Many organizations, in fact, are not so much democracies as oligarchies (Ferrante, 1992). An **oligarchy** is an organizational structure characterized by rule- or decision-making power of a few. Decisions are typically made by people "at the top," who then impose their decisions on subordinates. Sometimes the sheer size of organizations necessitates that they be oligarchies if decisions are to be made at all. If everyone were to be involved in all types of decisions, the bureaucratic process would simply be too unwieldy and time-consuming. This top-down approach to business decisions is characteristic of many American companies.

Cross-cultural research and the intercultural experiences of many business-persons reveal interesting differences in organizational decision making across cultures. One of the most studied cultures is that of Japan, because of its economic successes over the past few decades. (Similar decision-making procedures in other cultures are reviewed in Berry et al., 1992.) The Japanese process of decision making is known as the **ringi** system. In a Japanese company, there is no formal system by which every person is ensured a vote. Instead, a proposal is circulated among all people who will be affected by it, regardless of status, rank, or position. Initiatives for proposals can come from top, middle, or lower management, or from subordinates within a business section. Even before a proposal is formally circulated among all interested parties, there is often considerable discussion and debate about the proposal. All views are taken into account, so that the proposal, when written and formally circulated, addresses concerns and negative consequences raised by as many parties as possible. There is considerable consultation about the proposal on as broad a basis as possible, and consensus is achieved before the proposal is ever formally implemented. This broad-based, consensus-building procedure is called **nemawashi**. If proposals do not achieve consensus by this procedure, they do not appear formally. Proposals that have gone through this procedure and have received the blessing of all those affected are then put in the form of a formal proposal on paper. A routing of the proposal involves all section chiefs and managers before it gets to the person or persons on top, who then put their formal stamp of approval on it. Needless to say, by the time something gets to that stage, it has met with the approval of many people throughout the organization.

Like all decision-making procedures, the Japanese system has advantages and disadvantages. One of the major disadvantages is the time-consuming nature of the process. In fact, the inability of Japanese managers to make a decision on the spot in international negotiations is often a source of frustration for American negotiators, who are used to dealing with single decision makers. The Japanese negotiator, however, must contact all the people within the company affected by the impending decision prior to making that decision. An advantage of the Japanese system, however, is the speed with which decisions can be implemented. Although the Japanese typically take much more time making a decision, they can usually implement it relatively quickly. No doubt, having everyone briefed in advance about the proposal aids in speedy implementation.

Also, people in a collectivistic culture are more likely to get behind a decision that is for the good of the company, whatever their personal feelings about it.

Cross-cultural studies of organizational decision making point out other important and interesting differences between cultures. Yates, Lee, and Shinotsuka (1996), for example, found that people of East Asian cultures were more confident than Americans that their decisions were correct. To explain these findings, the authors suggest that people of East Asian cultures tend to select what may appear to be the first adequate solution to a problem that is identified, rather than considering a wide range of alternatives before deciding. Smith, Wang, and Leung (1997) obtained similar results in their study of 121 managers from mainland China, who reported strong reliance on widespread beliefs as a source of guidance when making decisions and handling various work events. Radford (Radford, Nakane, Ohta, & Mann, 1991; Radford, Mann, Ohta, & Nakane, 1993) found comparable differences between Australian and Japanese students. The Australians preferred careful, individual thought when making decisions; the Japanese preferred other strategies that involved more interpersonal dimensions. On an organizational level, Hall, Jiang, Loscocco, and Allen (1993) compared decision-making patterns in small businesses in China and the United States. They found that, in general, the Chinese organizations were more centralized than their American counterparts.

Weatherly and Beach (1998) conducted four studies that examined the relationship between organizational culture and decision making involving managers and employees from a number of commercial organizations. They found that the decisions made by an organization are generally influenced by the degree to which features of the options are compatible with features of the organization's own culture; the higher the degree of compatibility, the more likely it is that the decision will endorse that option. They also found that an organization's employees are more likely to endorse a management decision if features of the decision are compatible with features of the organizational culture. This study is important because it places organizational decision making within the larger context of organizational culture at multiple levels.

One particular problem that has plagued decision making in groups is "groupthink"—a collective pattern of thinking that hinders effective group decisions. Groupthink is generally characterized by direct pressure, self-censorship, illusions of invulnerability, unanimity, or morality, mind guarding, collective rationalization, and shared stereotypes (Janis, 1983). These types of processes may underlie social loafing and general apathy toward work and productivity. Such destructive thought patterns, however, can be transformed into constructive ones, or "teamthink" (Neck & Manz, 1994). Teamthink involves the encouragement of divergent views, open expression of concerns and ideas, awareness of limitations and threats, recognition of members' uniqueness, and discussion of collective doubts. These constructive patterns lead to more effective decision making. Such a process may be critical for many organizations in many cultures, and especially for increasingly diversified companies in the United States, because it may be one way of maintaining individuality while serving the collective common good of the organization.

In summary, cross-cultural research has contributed considerably to our knowledge of cultural similarities and differences in decision-making processes, but much more work remains to be done. Once again, the findings on decision making suggest there are both culture-specific and universal aspects to this organizational behavior. Although the particular ways in which decisions are made may vary across cultures, the underlying rationale for those decision processes—including views of decision making as extensions of the underlying organizational culture—may be similar. Future research should pursue these ideas of coexisting and complementary similarities and differences.

The areas we have covered so far, concerning how culture relates to specific work-related behaviors such as the meaning of work, motivations, leadership, and decision-making processes, are some of the more popular cross-cultural topics. In a review of industrial and organizational psychology research of the past two decades, Aycan (2000) argues that other fundamental, underresearched areas also deserve attention, such as the recruitment and selection of employees. For instance, some of the most common selection criteria in the United States are intelligence, education, and specific skills. However, in other, collectivistic cultures, these may not be the most appropriate criteria. For instance, important selection criteria in Islamic Arab countries are agreeableness and trustworthiness (Ali, 1989); in Japan, team members' approval (Huo, Von Glinow, & Lowe, 1995); and in India, belonging to the same family or homeland (Sinha, 1997). Future research on such fundamental topics are important to better understand and guide work practices in various cultural contexts.

Intercultural Issues Regarding Business and Work

As companies become increasingly dependent on other companies in other countries and cultures for business survival and success, people today are facing an ever-larger number of intercultural issues in the workplace. Add to these organizational developments the increasingly porous and flexible nature of national borders, and the result is a large number of people of different cultural backgrounds, lifestyles, values, and behaviors living and working together. These social trends and changes bring their own particular set of issues, challenges, and opportunities regarding intercultural interactions in the workplace and other work-related situations.

For multinational corporations, international business is not just international; it is intercultural. As we have seen throughout this chapter, business organizations are affected in many different ways by the cultures in which they reside. Organizational structures differ, organizational decision-making procedures differ, and people differ—in their definitions of work, work-related values, identification between self and company, and rules of interacting with other workers. Today's international business world requires that business organizations, and the people within them, gain intercultural competence as well as business competence.

In this final section of the chapter, we will discuss three broad areas in which intercultural issues have come to the fore in recent decades: international negotiation, overseas assignments, and working with an increasingly diverse workforce population.

International Negotiation

Improving communications technologies and changes in trade and tariff laws have resulted in an increasing interdependence among countries for economic and business survival. Not only multinational corporations but domestic companies too need to negotiate with companies in other countries to obtain resources, sell products, and conduct other business activities.

In the United States, Americans generally approach negotiation with a certain set of assumptions, summarized in Table 15.5 (Kimmel, 1994). In the United States, negotiation is a business, not a social activity. The objective of the negotiation is to get a job done, which usually requires a mixture of problem solving and bargaining. Communication is direct and verbal, with little deliberate or intentional use of nonverbal behaviors in the communication process.

Along with the 11 basic assumptions summarized in Table 15.5, Kimmel (1994) lists eight cultural values related to the American negotiation process:

1. *Time* is a commodity to be used efficiently to accomplish goals.
2. *Individual control.* You control your own destiny, and should do something about your life.
3. *Specialization* is desirable in work and social relationships; there is little desire for consistency or harmony.
4. *Pragmatism.* There are few absolute truths; what works is good.
5. *Democracy.* Everyone with an interest in an issue should have a say in the process.
6. *Equal opportunity.* People should have equal opportunities to develop their abilities.
7. *Independence.* Authority is resisted, and everyone has a right to privacy.
8. *Competition.* One must compete with others to get ahead; achievements are rewarded through upward mobility and income.

Negotiation processes in other cultures, however, challenge many of these traditionally American assumptions. In the arena of international negotiation, negotiators come as representatives not only of their companies but of their cultures as well. They bring all the issues of culture—customs, rituals, rules, and heritage—to the negotiating table. Factors that we are not even aware of play a role in these negotiating sessions, such as the amount of space between the people, how to greet each other, what to call each other, and what kinds of expectations we have of each other. The "diplomatic dance" that has been observed between American and Arab negotiators is but one example. People

Table 15.5 U.S. Assumptions about Negotiating

Topic	Description
Conception of the negotiation process	Negotiation is a business, not a social activity. The object is to get a job done, which usually requires a mixture of problem-solving and bargaining activities. Most negotiations are adversarial, and negotiators are trying to get as much as possible for their side. The flow of a negotiation is from prenegotiation strategy sessions to opening sessions to give-and-take (bargaining) to final compromises to signing and implementation of agreements. All parties are expected to give up some of their original demands. Success can be measured in terms of how much each party achieves its bottom-line objectives.
Type of issues	Substantive issues are more important than social and emotional issues. Differences in positions are seen as problems to be solved.
Protocol	Negotiations are scheduled occasions that require face-to-face interactions among the parties involved. Efficiency of time centering on substantive tasks is valued over ceremony and social amenities. During negotiation, standardized procedures of interaction should be followed; social interactions are informal and should occur elsewhere.
Reliance on verbal behaviors	Communication is direct and verbal. What is said is more important than how it is said, or what is not said. Communications tend to be spontaneous and reactive after presentation of initial positions.
Nature of persuasive arguments	Tactics such as bluffing are acceptable in the bargaining process. Current information and ideas are more valid than history or tradition.
Individual negotiator's latitude	The representatives who negotiate have a great deal of latitude in reaching agreements for their companies.
Bases of trust	Negotiators trust the other parties until they prove untrustworthy. Trust is judged by the behavior of others.
Risk-taking propensities	Negotiators are open to different or novel approaches to problem issues. Brainstorming is good. Avoiding uncertainty is not important in the negotiation process. Fixed ideological positions and approaches are not acceptable.
Value of time	Time is very important. Punctuality is expected. A fixed time is allotted for concluding a negotiation.
Decision-making system	Majority voting and/or authoritative decisions are the rule. Certain team members are expected to be authorized to make binding decisions.
Forms of satisfactory agreement	Oral commitments are not binding. Written contracts that are exact and impersonally worded are binding. There is the expectation of contractual finality. Lawyers and courts are the final arbitrators in any arguments after contracts have been signed.

Source: Adapted from Kimmel, 1994.

from Arab cultures tend to interact with others at a much closer distance than Americans are accustomed to. As the Arabs move closer, Americans unconsciously edge backward, whereupon the Arabs unconsciously edge forward, until they are almost chasing each other around the room.

Many studies have examined the Japanese approach to negotiation (see, for example, Allerheiligen, Graham, & Lin, 1985; Goldman, 1994; Graham, 1983, 1984, 1993; Graham & Andrews, 1987), which challenges virtually all of the American assumptions. Graham and Andrews, for example, videotaped American and Japanese participants during negotiation, then reviewed the videotapes with them to discuss negotiation processes and outcomes. One of the main concerns expressed by participants in both cultures involved language and communication processes. Indeed, even small cultural differences can have big effects on international business. In the Japanese language, for example, the word for "yes" (*hai*) is also used as a conversation regulator, signaling to others that you are listening to what they are saying (but not necessarily agreeing). American negotiators, hearing this word used as a regulator, often interpret it to mean "yes." As you can imagine, considerable conflict can and does arise when, after using this word throughout the conversation, the Japanese take a contradictory position. To the Japanese, they were merely saying "um hmm," but to the Americans, it sounded like "yes." Such misunderstandings can lead to conflict, mistrust, the breakdown of negotiations, and the loss of business and good faith relations (see Okamoto, 1993).

One interesting cultural difference between American and Japanese approaches to negotiation is in entertainment. American businesspeople are used to "sitting down at the table and hammering out a deal." Japanese businesspeople may want to have dinner, have drinks, and play golf. The Japanese are more willing to engage in these activities because they are interested in developing a relationship with their business partners as people; it also gives them a good opportunity to make judgments about the character or integrity of potential partners, which is an important aspect of their business decisions. American businesspeople are primarily concerned with "the deal" and what is right for the company's bottom line. Many American business negotiators not used to the Japanese style of negotiating become impatient with these activities, feeling as though they never get to talk business. By the same token, many Japanese negotiators, put on the spot by American negotiators, feel as though they have been thrust into a situation and forced to make a decision they cannot possibly make. Needless to say, these cultural differences in negotiation styles have led to many a breakdown in international business negotiations.

Cross-cultural research on international negotiation has spanned other countries and cultures as well, including Brazil (Allerheiligen et al., 1985; Graham, 1983, 1984), China (Allerheiligen et al., 1985), Russia (Graham, Evenko, & Rajan, 1992), Taiwan (Graham, Kim, Lin, & Robinson, 1988), Germany and Britain (Campbell, Graham, Jolibert, & Meissner, 1988), and Mexico and Canada (Adler, Schwartz, & Graham, 1987). Many of these studies, like those on the Japanese process, demonstrate how people of different cultures approach negotiation from often quite different viewpoints. For example, Tse,

Francis, and Walls (1994) examined Chinese and Canadian negotiation practices. They found that the Chinese avoided conflict more than the Canadians did, and when conflict did occur, they opted for withdrawal or consultation with superiors more than the Canadians did. Context may also play an important role in the negotiation process, as people of collectivistic cultures tend to make a larger distinction between ingroup and outgroup members than do people of individualistic cultures. Thus, negotiation processes involving collectivistic cultures may differ drastically depending on the exact nature of the relationship between the negotiators (ingroup versus outgroup) and the exact context of the negotiation (formal meeting during the day at a company versus informal meeting after work in a bar).

The available research tells us little about the degree to which negotiators adjust their cultural practices depending on whom they are negotiating with, and on what parameters such adjustment occurs. Nor has cross-cultural research done much to elucidate the ingredients of a "successful" negotiation. Furthermore, a recent review of cross-cultural studies on negotiation (Gelfand & Dyer, 2000) suggests that factors such as proximal social conditions (deadlines, negotiator relationships), the negotiators' psychological states (implicit theories and metaphors, judgment biases), and behaviors (tactics) are also important in understanding international/intercultural discussions and negotiations. Future studies are needed to examine these important issues.

Overseas Assignments

Many multinational corporations with subsidiaries and business partners in other countries are finding it increasingly necessary to send workers abroad for extended periods of time. Worker exchanges and overseas assignments are used to train employees and business units in another country in skills that are found only there. Such overseas assignments can give rise to myriad problems, not only because of all the cultural differences discussed in this chapter, but also because of limited language skills and differing expectations of the person on assignment and his or her hosts.

American companies today would not hesitate to send "the most qualified person" on assignment, either for negotiation or long-term, regardless of sex, race, or ethnicity. Many other cultures, however, are not accustomed to women in important positions in business, and may not be totally receptive to people of different perceived races or ethnicities. In many contexts, a woman would not be taken as seriously as a man, and racial/ethnic stereotypes may dominate interactions. Resulting frustrations might include not being looked at during a conversation, or having questions directed to a man when a woman is the recognized leader or expert on an assignment team.

Many of the most pressing problems for people on overseas assignments occur not at work but in other aspects of living in a foreign country. Major differences in lifestyle, customs, and behaviors often overshadow cultural differences at work. If an individual goes on overseas assignment with his or her family, there is the added problem of their adjustment to the new culture, especially if school-age children are involved. The entire spectrum of intercultural adjustment and acculturation becomes important. Even when workers do well in their work environment, they may do poorly in their home and community adjustment. And while employees may find a safe haven during the workday in a milieu with which they are somewhat familiar, their families are often left bearing the brunt of intercultural adaptation. Interested readers should recall the material presented in Chapter 10 on intercultural communication and the development of intercultural sensitivity.

On the positive side, people who go on overseas assignments have a tremendous opportunity to learn new skills and new ways of doing their work that can help them when they return. They may learn a new language and customs, broadening their perspectives. They may make new friends and business acquaintances, and this type of networking may have business as well as personal payoffs in the future. Foreign assignment is an important aspect of today's international business world that promises to play an even larger role in the global village of the future. Completing these assignments to the best of our abilities requires us to understand all the influences of culture, both in and out of the workplace. In the future, these types of skills will be even more valuable than they are today. Little systematic, formal research exists on this topic in the published literature (despite an abundance of anecdotal and case study data that are proprietary to many companies). Future research on this important topic will help in the design of intercultural adjustment programs for company employees, allowing them to be more effective in their overseas assignments.

Working with an Increasingly Diverse Workforce Population

Organizations all around the world are dealing with an increasingly diverse workforce population. For example, American companies are increasingly hosting workers from other countries. Joint ventures between American and Asian and European companies have increased over the past ten years—most visibly in automobile manufacturing, but also in computers and semiconductors, communication technology, and many other fields. One result is an influx of workers from these countries and cultures to the United States.

Many of the problems that arise when American workers go overseas also arise when foreign workers come to the United States. Often, managers from another culture come to oversee and supervise production or assembly, bringing with them all the expectations, customs, and rituals of their home country. Not surprisingly, they find that those ways of doing business do not work in the United States, because the people are different and the system is different. Similarly, many of the problems experienced by American families abroad are also experienced by the families of workers who come to the United States. To make the transition easier, many Japanese companies in the Los Angeles area have established little Japanese villages and apartments where the Japanese lifestyle and customs can be preserved. These controversial enclaves serve to maintain barriers between people, raising problems of their own.

One recent study highlights some of the problems and issues that may arise in these situations. In this study, Graham (1993) spent six months as a hidden participant observer at a Japanese automobile plant near Lafayette, Indiana (Subaru/Isuzu Automotive). During this time, the author was able to document worker resistance to Japanese management practices in the form of sabotage, protest, agitation, and confrontation. The results of this study brought into question the validity and worth of simply "transferring" the Japanese management model to the American milieu. The data also failed to support the contention that participation schemes (such as teamwork) automatically increase worker control or that decentralized authority structures increase worker autonomy.

A recent study focused on cultural differences in ways of handling disagreement. In this study (Smith, Dugan, Peterson, & Leung, 1998), managers and supervisors from a variety of organizations in 23 countries completed a questionnaire about how they handled disagreements in their work unit. The responses were aggregated for each country, and the country mean values on the questionnaire were correlated with the country's scores on Hofstede's dimensions described earlier. The results indicated that power distance (PD) significantly predicted the frequency of disagreements between work groups. In handling disagreements, people in low-PD cultures tended to rely on subordinates and coworkers. People of individualistic countries relied more on their own personal experience and training, whereas people of collectivistic cultures relied more on formal rules and procedures. Although this study involved participants in different countries, these types of psychological differences based on PD and IC may be important in understanding cultural differences within a single multicultural organization.

Despite the potential problems associated with receiving foreign workers, many of the advantages of overseas assignments also apply to receiving people from abroad. The ability to reap these benefits depends on the openness of the host organization to learn and on the goodwill and intent of the employee and the company to engage in a mutually beneficial partnership.

Even without international joint ventures and worker exchanges, many American companies are dealing with increasing diversity solely on the basis of the increasing diversity of the American population. The United States is home to people of many different races, ethnicities, and cultures. Within this "mixed salad" of cultures are generational differences, from recent immigrants to second-, third-, and multigeneration Americans of wide-ranging ethnic and cultural backgrounds. The problems that can occur when two cultures clash can be magnified many times over when people from multiple cultures are thrust together to interact toward a common goal.

Many of the issues raised in dealing with people across countries and cultures are relevant for domestic work organizations dealing with an increasingly diverse American workforce as well. People come to work with different expectations, and different expectations can lead to intercultural clashes. Cultural differences in the management of time and people, in identification with work, and in making decisions all provide areas for conflict. People in the United States come to work with differences in work-related values and the degree to which they respect or minimize power and status differences between them. People come to work with different views regarding sex differences and how to manage uncertainty.

Many successful companies have met these challenges by making explicit what kinds of communication styles, decision making, productivity, and worker behaviors are important for the success of the company. Many companies today actively train their employees in intercultural issues ranging from communication to expectations (see, for example, Goldman, 1992); the most successful of these programs undoubtedly have important positive, practical implications in many arenas of people's lives. Many companies have created temporary organizational cultures in which their employees can move and adapt without fear of losing themselves or their own personal cultures. They have designed ways not only of avoiding problems but also of handling problems effectively and constructively when they do arise. Negotiating all of these issues requires additional work and effort by companies and people alike, but organizations that can do so successfully are likely to realize long-term benefits to the bottom line.

Conclusion

The cultural differences that people bring with them to the workplace, both internationally and domestically, present us with challenges unprecedented in the modern industrialized period of history. To meet these challenges, business, government, and private organizations look to research and education about cultural diversity as it relates to work. Intercultural communication and competence training and business consulting with regard to managing diversity have become major growth industries.

Too often, the idea of managing diversity rests on the underlying assumption that diversity is an unwanted by-product of our work environment—a nuisance variable that must be dealt with in order to maximize efficiency. As we move toward a greater appreciation of cultural similarities and differences, however, we may gain a better appreciation for the different approaches to work, management, and leadership that have worked for different cultures. As we confront the challenges of diversity in the future, we need to move away from the notion of managing a nuisance variable to viewing it as a potential resource for tapping into products, services, and activities that will make companies more efficient, productive, and profitable than ever before. By tapping into diversity rather than managing it, perhaps we can increase international and intercultural cooperation not only in business but among people in general.

Glossary

Anglo-Saxon type of organization A work organization more or less opposite to the Latin type, with less centralization, more diffusion of power and decision making, and less hierarchy in the bureaucracy.

centralization The degree to which organizations concentrate their operations and decision-making capabilities in a limited number of business units or people.

complexity The degree to which organizations foster differentiation of tasks and activities within themselves.

Confucian dynamism A dimension of work-related values important to Asian companies and thought to be rooted in Confucian thought and principles.

formalization The degree to which organizations provide structure and rules for their operations.

Latin type of organization A work organization that is characterized as a classical bureaucracy, with centralized power and decision making and many hierarchical levels.

leadership The "process of influence between a leader and followers to attain group, organizational, or societal goals" (Hollander, 1985).

multinational and international corporations Work organizations that have subsidiaries, satellite offices, and work units in more than one country.

nemawashi The broad-based consensus-building procedure that occurs within the Japanese ringi system of decision making.

oligarchy An organizational structure characterized by rule- or decision-making power of a few. Decisions are typically made by people "at the top" who impose their decisions on subordinates.

organizational climate A shared perception of organizational policies, practices, and procedures, and how people feel about them.

organizational culture A dynamic system of rules involving attitudes, values, beliefs, norms, and behaviors that are shared among members of an organization.

ringi The Japanese process of decision making, which involves circulating a proposal among all people who will be affected by it, addressing concerns and negative consequences raised by as many parties as possible, consulting on as broad a basis as possible about the proposal, and achieving consensus before the proposal is ever formally implemented.

social loafing The common finding in research on group productivity in the United States that individual productivity tends to decline in larger groups.

social striving The opposite of social loafing; the finding in many cultures that working in a group enhances individual performance rather than diminishes it.

Third World type of organization A work organization characterized by greater centralization of decision making, less formalization of rules, and a more paternalistic or traditional family orientation.

InfoTrac College Edition

Use InfoTrac College Edition to search for additional readings on topics of interest to you. For more information on topics in this chapter, use the following as search terms:

culture and aggression
culture and organizational structure
culture and work values
culture and power distance
Confucian dynamism
culture and management styles

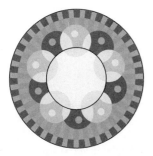

16

Conclusion

As we have seen throughout this book, the influence of culture on our lives is enormous. Culture influences the language we speak, our perceptions of the world around us, our behaviors and attitudes, the structures of our homes, our system of education, our government, and our health. Across all the topics covered in this book, culture plays a major, albeit sometimes silent and invisible, role in determining how we act and how we perceive the actions of others.

In the past, mainstream academic psychology, and many psychologists, never gave much thought to culture as a serious variable in theory and in research. Culture is to psychology what air is to us or water is to fish—all around us but invisible. We don't think about it often, but it is there, and influences everything about us. Only when we come into contact with others from different cultures, as occurs more and more often in our diverse and shrinking world, do we think twice about culture. Today, we realize that culture is a major source of psychological differences that need to be accounted for in both theoretical and empirical work.

Thus, we are in the middle of a cultural revolution of sorts in psychology, and cross-cultural studies in all aspects of psychology are much more commonplace today than ever before. When we study cultures, it is easy to get lost in the mass of "facts," especially about cultural differences. The facts derived from cross-cultural research in psychology, anthropology, and other disciplines would indeed fill the volumes of an encyclopedia on cultural differences. It would be interesting to have such an encyclopedia—a Farmer's Almanac of Culture, if you will—to help us understand the breadth and scope of culture's influence on our lives.

But even when we are surrounded by all those differences, or perhaps especially when we are surrounded by those differences, we must not forget that there are important similarities as well. The study of human behavior across cultures informs us of those similarities as well as differences. This book has sought to highlight the major similarities and differences among cultures across a broad range of psychological phenomena.

What does it all mean—to academic psychology, and to each one of us individually? Where do we go from here? In this final chapter, we would like to discuss the implications of this cultural revolution in psychology, both for mainstream academic psychology and for individuals in a diverse and interdependent world. The profound implications in both domains give rise to challenges that make this era of psychology so exciting.

Implications for Mainstream Psychology

As discussed in the introductory chapter of this book, all research is associated with certain parameters that limit the knowledge and data that are generated from that research. The research that forms the basis for much of mainstream psychology has been based largely on studies using American university students as research subjects. And many of those studies were conducted many years ago, when the American population was much more homogeneous than it is today.

For many years, there was no need to question the validity or veracity of the knowledge generated in American psychology. The knowledge gathered from those studies formed the basis of many theories and models in psychology that were indeed applicable at the time. Geographically, the United States was relatively isolated, with only Canada to the north and Mexico to the south, separated from the rest of the world by vast oceans on both east and west. With so much space and so many resources within the continental United States, Americans had little need for interdependence with others for their survival and welfare, and little interaction with different peoples. Moreover, the rest of the world tended to treat American academia as the ultimate ivory tower, glamorizing it as it does so many other American things (celebrities, sports, popular culture). American psychology, like many other academic fields, was and still is a major driving force for psychology in many other parts of the world, in terms of academic training, research, and theory.

This picture is currently changing, however. The American university student population, mirroring the population as a whole, has become increasingly diverse in race, sex, class, and lifestyle—that is, in culture. The same is true of university faculty who teach psychology. Borders between countries are becoming more porous, and instantaneous communication by phone, fax, and electronic mail enables us to interact with people in far places and disparate cultures much more easily today than ever before. With modern transportation, a few hours' plane ride can take us physically to those distant countries and cultures. Americans are also much more interdependent economically with people of other countries and cultures than ever before. Because of all these factors,

Americans are increasingly coming in contact with people of very different cultures in their everyday lives, and the American population is diversifying at a rapid pace. Finally, academic psychology has become much more prominent in other parts of the world, including Europe and Asia.

It is against this backdrop that cross-cultural psychology is such a welcome and timely addition to mainstream academic, predominantly American, psychology. As mentioned in Chapter 1, cross-cultural research actually has quite a long history in psychology, but it is only recently that it has become so important to psychology as a whole. And although research in cross-cultural psychology has produced evidence of both similarities and differences in psychological processes and behaviors, it is the cultural differences that have greater consequences for mainstream academic psychology.

Cultural differences challenge mainstream theoretical notions about the nature of people and force us to rethink our basic theories of personality, perception, cognition, emotion, development, social psychology, and other psychological processes. We are on the verge of witnessing encyclopedic-type compendia of cultural differences in almost all subfields of psychology, with ample evidence from many cultures that the truths of mainstream Americans are not necessarily applicable to the rest of the world. Many such studies and findings have been reviewed in this book.

In fact, it has become almost too easy to produce a research finding documenting a cultural difference in some aspect of psychological behavior. Indeed, the challenge facing cross-cultural psychology today and in the future is not simply to continue compiling cultural differences in various facets of psychological research. Instead, the greatest challenge of the near future is to develop theoretical models and conceptual frameworks that can explain how cultures are both similar and different, and why. The overwhelming evidence cross-cultural psychology has already gathered, and will continue to gather, brings with it an obligation to make some sense of it all.

The Challenge for Cross-Cultural Psychology

Fortunately, a small but growing number of cross-cultural psychologists have been interested in discovering how cultures come to create similarities and differences, and why. Many have turned their efforts to studying the developmental processes underlying enculturation—the process of learning the rules, values, attitudes, beliefs, behaviors, and opinions of one's first, original culture—and have made important inroads toward understanding how we acquire culture and how it influences our lives (see Chapter 5). Another important inroad involves the relationship between culture and self-concept as a mediator of psychological differences across cultures (see Chapter 11). A third avenue has been the use of meaningful dimensions of cultural variability, such as individualism–collectivism (IC), to predict and explain cultural similarities and differences.

As discussed throughout the book, many researchers have used IC to predict and explain cultural differences in a wide variety of psychological constructs (also see review by Triandis, 1995). This construct is a major plus for cross-cultural research and thinking because it allows us to go beyond nationality, race, or ethnicity in predicting and explaining differences, focusing instead on functional psychological predictions and interpretations of data. Constructs such as IC give researchers and theoreticians alike a basis on which they can understand the psychological impact of culture on both the macro-social and individual levels.

Recent advances in cross-cultural methods include the development of ways to measure IC tendencies on the individual level (reviewed in Chapter 2), and these methods have had a large and positive impact on theory building in cross-cultural psychology. Triandis (Triandis, Leung, Villareal, & Clack, 1985) refers to IC at the individual level as *idiocentrism* and *allocentrism*, and their measurement is a major plus for research. It allows researchers to ascertain empirically that their samples differ on this construct, providing an important methodological check and eliminating reliance on anecdotes, impressions, or stereotypes when interpreting findings. It also allows researchers to assess numerically the degree of within-culture variability on this important construct. Using this index, researchers can determine how much of the difference between groups is attributable to individual-level differences in IC.

Say, for example, that a researcher intends to compare two cultures and has participants complete an individual-level measurement of IC. Group differences on the dependent variable can be tested through normal procedures (for example, t-test, ANOVA, chi-square). In addition, the relationship between IC and the dependent variable can be assessed through correlational procedures. If correlations are found, their influence on the group differences obtained earlier can be tested using multiple regression or analysis of covariance (ANCOVA). The degree of contribution of IC to the group differences can be computed by comparing effect sizes of the group differences between the original and ANCOVA analyses.

In fact, this was the approach adopted in a recent study of cultural display rules of emotional expression in the United States, Japan, Russia, and South Korea (Matsumoto, Takeuchi, Andayani, Kouznetsouva, & Krupp, 1998). In that study, participants in the four countries completed an individual-based measure of IC, as well as an inventory of the rules governing their displays of seven different emotions in four separate social contexts. The analyses indicated that not only were there cross-national differences both in display rules and in IC, but that IC and display rules were correlated with each other, between and within the countries. An effect-size comparison technique was then used, based on findings from ANCOVAs testing the display rule ratings across the four countries using IC scores as covariates. These comparisons indicated that individual-level IC accounted for approximately 30% of the differences between countries in display rules.

As discussed briefly in Chapter 2, many methods of IC measurement are available to choose from, and the field is embracing these measures in cross-cultural comparisons. These developments are a major plus, as they relate culture to functional psychology, giving us a basis for understanding how and why similarities and differences occur. They allow for valuable methodological checks in our research, and for statistical assessments of the contribution of measured culture to observed differences (as in the study just described). The innovative and promising approach allows researchers to specify the exact degree of contribution of specific cultural dimensions to their variables of interest, and it allows theorists to incorporate these estimates of contribution into their models and theory building. In some cases, such as with display rules, this process may force us to consider the contribution of other factors to psychological processes.

In fact, the field has perhaps been too preoccupied with IC to the exclusion of other important dimensions. Clearly, no one dimension can capture "culture." In the study of display rules described here, for example, IC accounted for only about 30% of the variance between countries. What accounts for the other 70%? We believe that another cultural dimension, power distance (PD) or status differentiation, is just as important as IC, if not more so. Future endeavors should include developing individual-level measures of this important cultural construct and integrating it into cross-cultural research. In any case, it is this approach—specifying meaningful dimensions of cultural variability and actually measuring them—that promises to enable cross-cultural psychology to meet the challenge of developing theoretical models to explain cultural similarities and differences.

The Challenge for Mainstream Psychology

If the challenge for cross-cultural psychology is to develop theoretical models to explain cultural similarities and differences, the challenge for mainstream psychology is to integrate these cultural frameworks into mainstream academic psychology. Research on bilingualism reviewed in Chapter 10 has demonstrated that bilinguals seem to access two cultural frames of references, depending on which language they are speaking. Many of you who are bilingual may recognize this phenomenon. Although there are certainly areas of overlap and similarity, bilinguals have reported having different personalities, judging emotions differently, appraising events and the environment around them differently, and attributing the causes of events differently depending on the language used when performing these tasks. Not only do multiple cultural frameworks exist in their minds, but bilinguals have the added ability to monitor which cultural framework to adopt in each social context. Thus, they have a meta-cognitive process that allows them to engage with their "multiple personalities" in a healthy and constructive way. This ability is related to the development of intercultural sensitivity (see, for example, Bennett, 1993, reviewed in Chapter 10).

Most Americans are monolingual; most of the rest of the world is multilingual. Thus, the information obtained from research with Americans, and theories derived from Americans by Americans, may be based on a theory of mind that is not really applicable to the rest of the world. We may not stop to think about whether those theories make sense or not, because they are bounded within our own cultural framework. It is only when we look outside of ourselves that we can experience, understand, and appreciate those boundaries.

Lillard (1998) has suggested these notions in a recent review discussing ethnopsychologies. She suggests that theories of mind and folk psychologies (a set of basic beliefs about minds and behavior) are actually quite variable according to culture, although we don't often realize it. Four reasons why such folk theories differ around the world are that (1) external differences reflect internal differences in psychological meaning, (2) every culture fosters certain optional construals in their own psychologies, (3) preconditions for social cognition and attitudes vary across cultures, and (4) nuances in psychological meaning can exist despite apparent similarities. She reviewed a number of aspects of theories of mind that vary across cultures, including the structure of mind, attributional processes, and specific processes such as perception, emotion, and thought. That these various ethnopsychologies even exist suggests that mainstream American approaches to psychology do not do justice to the actual diversity of psychological processes and functions in the world.

Created largely within a monolingual, monocultural milieu, mainstream psychology has a lot of catching up to do if it is to be truly inclusive of as many people as possible in a world of diversity. The assimilation of cross-cultural findings and theories into mainstream psychology suggests a fundamental revision in ways of thinking about self and personality that have important consequences for all areas of psychology. No information or ideas that we have currently need to be thrown out; they just need to be placed within the proper context to be applicable to more people. Cross-cultural work needs to be assimilated into mainstream psychology, and mainstream psychology needs to accommodate to these ideas. The end product will be qualitatively different than the psychology to which we are currently accustomed.

What is needed is a fundamental revision in the very nature of psychology—one that incorporates culture as a normal part of its working variables, in research as well as theory. That is, we need to move from a psychology of the past to a cultural psychology of the future. In a cultural psychology, culture is not an afterthought or an exotic extension of mainstream psychology; rather, it is an integral part of mainstream psychology. And in fact, some writers have begun to take up the challenge of creating that cultural psychology (see, for example, Cole, 1996, and review by Takahashi & Hatano, 1997).

How do we take up this challenge? The fight, if you will, is not in the laboratory or the field; it is in us. The greatest challenge facing cross-cultural psychology now is to think less about producing finding after finding of cultural differences, and to think more about ways of integrating them collectively into a cohesive, comprehensive theory incorporating mainstream as well as cross-cultural psychology. This challenge applies equally to all the subfields of psychology, which are Humpty Dumpty–like splintered fragments of a larger collective. Although the need for specificity and fragmentation is understandable, so is the need for integration and synthesis. We need to look outside of psychology to help us "put the pieces back together"; otherwise, we can never envision the whole, only its parts. This integration may require us to consult with anthropology, sociology, business, medicine, and other disciplines. In developing theoretical models to integrate cultural similarities and differences, we need to go outside of psychology to know more about psychology. These almost Herculean efforts will be what is required to put Humpty Dumpty back together.

This new approach need not be forced down anyone's throat, nor need the revisions be horrendously traumatic. Little steps will turn to big steps, and big steps will be a journey. In the end, it is the walking, not the destination, that matters. Are cross-cultural psychologists up to the task? Are psychologists up to the task?

Implications for Our Everyday Lives

Finding an Intercultural Process Model to Engage with Diversity

As we learn more about both cultural similarities and differences, we need to touch base with the reasons why we study cultures in the first place. Without revisiting our motivations, the mass of facts about both similarities and differences will remain just that—a mass of facts. We need a way to take those facts and use them—to allow those facts to become means to an end, and not an end in themselves. When we revisit our motivations, we should quickly realize that the ultimate reason we study culture is to improve our lives and our relationships with others in a diverse world. This goal should be the primary reason we study culture and its influence on human behavior. If we are not able to take the information gathered so far and use it in some productive way, the great opportunity provided by this information will slip through our hands and be wasted.

Recall the two goals of psychology discussed in Chapter 1. One goal of psychology is to produce knowledge; the second is to use the knowledge that is produced to intervene in people's lives and help make them better. The knowledge that is produced in psychology is used by therapists, counselors, consultants, and teachers to intervene directly in people's lives. As our world becomes increasingly diverse in culture, heritage, and tradition, accurate information about cultural influences on psychology becomes increasingly important in our ability to deliver meaningful and effective intervention programs for the people whose lives we touch.

How can we, in our everyday lives, approach this final task? One way would be to create a Farmer's Almanac of Culture in your mind, documenting the cultural similarities and differences found in specific cultures and building your own reference book that you can retrieve at any time. This is a formidable task, as there is so much about culture to learn and so little time, energy, and storage space available. Despite the difficulties, however, this approach is not without merit, and certainly many people develop such almanacs in their minds about a small number of cultures with which they become intimately familiar. Many individuals who spend extended periods of time immersed in different cultures—through travel, business, or homestay programs—do build such an almanac, albeit unconsciously. The strength of this approach lies both in increasing our capacity to be culturally relative and in guiding our behavior in daily interactions with people from diverse backgrounds.

But none of us can create a Farmer's Almanac of Culture for all the cultures we might possibly come in contact with in our lives, and many of us do not have the opportunity to travel and immerse ourselves in other cultures to become culturally fluent in this fashion. Instead, the vast majority of us will need to rely on a process of intercultural growth that we can rely on to engage with the multitude of diversities that exist in our world today.

In fact, we discussed such a process in Chapter 10 when we described a model of intercultural sensitivity. This model depicts the various stages in which people engage with cultural differences, ranging from denial and minimization of those differences on one end to acceptance, adaptation, and integration on the other. One assumption of this model is that being more appreciative and more multicultural is preferable to being in denial or minimizing differences. Although some people may actually debate this assumption, we would argue that this assumption is valid—not only in today's diverse world, but especially in tomorrow's even more diverse world.

How do we move from one end of the spectrum in that model to the other—from denial and minimization to integration? The road from one end to the other is not an easy one, because the existence of differences makes it relatively easy for all of us to engage in denial or to minimize the importance of those differences in our lives. As we discussed in Chapter 3, our own ethnocentric and stereotypic ways of thinking, which are themselves inevitable consequences of normal, psychological functioning, make it easy for us to create negative value judgments about those differences. And it is only normal that we have at least slightly negative emotional reactions when engaging with cultural differences. These negative reactions, and the negative value judgments we are apt to make because of our ethnocentrism and stereotypic thinking, make it difficult for us to engage in healthier and more constructive methods of interacting, and keep us from truly appreciating those differences and integrating with people who exhibit those differences.

As we discussed in Chapter 10, the process of intercultural communication is complex, and conflicts based on intercultural misunderstandings are inevitable. Thus, if we are to go beyond these ethnocentric and stereotypic biases, it is extremely important to be able to control our own negative emotional reactions when engaging with intercultural differences. This point is related to the points made earlier in Chapter 3 about the role of emotion and mood in the process of person perception and stereotyping. Those who can regulate their emotional reactions will be able to engage in a more constructive intercultural process, such as the one outlined in the model of intercultural sensitivity described in Chapter 10, opening the door to more successful intercultural interactions. Those who cannot will have that door closed to them. Emotions, therefore, are central to this process, and hold the key to successful intercultural experiences.

Regulating Emotions: A Key to Personal Growth

Many of us who have experience dealing with children know that even very young children can engage in morally altruistic behaviors. They may offer their favorite blanket, toy, or food to another youngster in distress, or lend a helping hand to Mom or Dad or a sibling at play. When something happens to hurt, anger, frustrate, or upset them, however, it is a very different story. They begin to cry or throw a temper tantrum. Their thinking and worldview revert back to a more primitive way of dealing with and understanding their world. It becomes impossible for them to engage in moral or altruistic acts of kindness, because their way of thinking is locked into a more infantile mode of operation. As mentioned in Chapter 3, many psychologists refer to this process as *regression*.

Regression is not the sole domain of children and adolescents. Adults of all ages also regress at times. We all know of instances and individuals who, when hurt, upset, frustrated, or angry, cannot think straight; they rant and rave and revert back to a more primitive way of thinking, acting, and feeling. Although the outward manifestations of these processes may differ between adults and children (adults may not just pick up their toys and storm out of the room), there is considerable similarity in the underlying psychological processes.

When a negative emotion is aroused, people can easily be overcome by those feelings, which then "take over" their way of being. Even people who are usually adept at thinking critically about things, and who often act in perfectly moral and altruistic ways, may not be able to think or act in such a manner when overcome by negative emotions.

A critical moment arises in an intercultural interaction episode when negative emotions are aroused because of inevitable cultural differences. Those individuals who can somehow control or regulate those negative feelings—who can somehow put them on hold and not act directly upon them or allow them to overcome their way of thinking, acting, and feeling—will be able to engage in other processes that can help them expand their appraisal and attribution of the causes of the differences. Once emotions are held in check and not immediately acted upon, individuals can then think critically about the origins of those differences, perhaps going beyond their own cultural lenses and framework to entertain the possibility of other causes of the differences that they may not even have been aware of. If this type of critical thinking can occur, then individuals will have an active choice of accepting or rejecting alternative hypotheses concerning the causes of those differences. Hopefully, they will have the openness and flexibility to accept rival hypotheses if it turns out their initial reactions were inaccurate.

Thus, the three key ingredients of personal growth are:

1. Emotional regulation
2. Critical thinking (generation of rival hypotheses)
3. Openness/flexibility to accept rival hypotheses

For example, suppose you meet someone for the first time. You try to look directly at her and shake her hand, but she looks away from you, seemingly refusing to acknowledge your presence or shake your hand. Your immediate reaction may well be negative. At this point, it may be easy to form a negative impression about this person, based on a negative attribution about the cause of the difference in behavior from what you expected. If you are able to put that reaction on hold, however, and then to engage in critical thinking about possible causes of that behavior, you might consider a number of alternative hypotheses. Whereas direct eye contact may be a sign of respect in your culture, avoiding eye contact may be a sign of respect in her culture. Whereas shaking hands is an accepted form of greeting in your culture, such contact may be limited to intimate partners in her culture. Once you have generated these and other possible hypotheses, you will then have the choice of accepting or rejecting them. If you choose to accept an alternative cause of the unexpected behavior, hopefully you will have the openness and flexibility to change your mind regarding your initial negative reaction.

This model is inherently a growth model. By engaging in critical thinking about cultural differences and being open and flexible to new ways of thinking, you allow your ways of perceiving people to continue to grow. You continually add more and more complexity to your method of interacting with diversity. This complexity allows you to move from denial and minimization to adaptation and integration on the intercultural sensitivity model discussed earlier. This entire process is possible, however, only when you can regulate your emotions and not allow negative emotions to get the better of you.

Conversely, if our negative emotional reactions to inevitable cultural differences continue to overwhelm us and dictate how we think, feel, and act, we cannot engage in critical thinking about those differences. Rather, we regress to a previous way of thinking about those differences that is rooted in our ethnocentric and stereotypic ways of viewing the world. Instead of creating rival hypotheses that stimulate growth in our ways of thinking, we will instead only reinforce our preexisting, limited ways of thinking. Openness to new ideas and rival hypotheses is not even an option, because these new ideas don't exist. Instead, there is only a regurgitation of stereotypes and ethnocentric attitudes. This scenario is a nongrowth model.

In summary, then, the three main ingredients of personal growth in relation to cultural differences are emotion regulation, critical thinking, and openness and flexibility. Of these, emotion regulation is the key ingredient, as it is the gatekeeper of the growth process. If we cannot put our inevitable negative emotions in check, it is impossible to engage in what is clearly higher-order thinking about cultural differences.

Using Critical Thinking

Once we can deal with our emotional reactions, exactly how can we think critically about cultural differences? In this section, we present seven guidelines for this critical thinking process. These guidelines are not universal in the sense that they have been "proven" by cross-cultural research. Instead, they are our feeble attempt at taking all the information presented in this book, along with our experiences and the experiences of others interacting with people of different backgrounds, and synthesizing this information into a coherent set of guidelines that we have found useful. Others may have their own guidelines, and those may be at variance with ours. We offer these not as an end-all prescription for successful human relations, but as a platform from which to launch meaningful discussions with others about this important topic. Whether people agree or disagree with these guidelines is a question secondary to the more important issue of their contribution to our ability to talk about these emotionally charged issues.

Recognize that culture is a psychological construct. We have focused on a definition of culture as a psychological construct emphasizing the subjective (Triandis, 1972) rather than objective aspects of culture. We believe it is these subjective aspects of culture, existing in our minds as mental blueprints or programming, that are most important to understanding the contribution of culture to human behavior. Culture refers to the degree to which a group of people share attitudes, values, beliefs, and behaviors. It is communicated from one generation to the next. As such, culture is a functional entity—one we cannot see but only infer from observations of human behavior.

Culture is not race. Being born of a particular "race" does not mean that you automatically harbor the cultural values associated with that race. Culture is not nationality. Being a citizen of a country does not mean that you automatically adopt the culture associated with that country. Culture is not birthplace. Being born in a certain place does not automatically mean that you harbor the culture of your birthplace.

When we think of intercultural relations and cultural diversity, both within the United States and abroad, we mostly think of differences according to race, ethnicity, or nationality. Yet we have not used these terms and concepts in this book. This lack of focus on race, ethnicity, and nationality is a function of our view that the important aspect of people is their underlying psychological culture, not the color of their skin or the citizenship on their passport.

Some people may interpret this position as suggesting that race, nationality, and other personal characteristics are not important. That is not true. Future cross-cultural research and thinking in this area must meet the formidable challenge of integrating these concepts with psychological definitions of culture to examine their joint influence and interactive effects on human behaviors. In adopting the approach taken in this book, we hoped to highlight the important role of subjective, psychological culture in producing similarities and differences in behaviors and to bring a fresh way of thinking to old and nagging problems.

As we learn more about what culture is and is not, we need to recognize the fuzzy nature of the definition of culture, based in function rather than biology or geopolitics. By recognizing that culture is a psychological construct—our learned mental programming—we can avoid the use of race and nationality in understanding cultural differences among people. Defining culture as a meaningful psychological construct also allows us to consider the remaining guidelines.

Recognize individual differences within a culture.

Defining culture as a sociopsychological construct is not enough. With a functional definition of culture, we need to recognize individual differences within cultures. Within any culture, people differ according to how strongly they adhere to or comply with the values, standards, and mores of that culture. Some people may be true representatives of their culture; others may not be as adequately described by their culture. Yet they are all members of the culture. Even within the individualistic American culture, for example, we can find people who harbor more collectivistic cultural values. Describing all individuals within this cultural group as individualistic ignores actual cultural differences that exist among individual members.

Recognizing individual differences within cultures helps us develop flexibility in our ethnocentrism and stereotypes. One of the keys to improving intergroup and interpersonal relationships is to develop a healthy flexibility with regard to ethnocentrism and stereotypes. Recognizing individual differences in culture and how these differences are related to behaviors is one of the first steps to eliminating reliance on negative and detrimental stereotypes.

Understand our own cultural filters and ethnocentrism.

We are not always aware of our own cultural filters as we perceive, think about, and interpret events around us and the behavior of others. We are not always aware of the cultural bases of our behaviors and actions. Often, the way we see the world (worldview) is fundamentally different from the way others see the world.

One important first step in gaining an understanding of cultural influences on behavior is to recognize that we have our own perceptual filters and cultural bases for behavior. We need to stop and think about how our own cultural upbringing contributed to how we interact with the world and with others. This comparison comes to the forefront when we travel outside our culture. By clashing with the cultures of others, we are forced to think about differences in cognition and behavior. In doing so, we may come to a better understanding of our own filters and biases.

Allow for the possibility that conflicts are cultural.

One fallacy of cross-cultural study is the assumption that if you study cultures, there will be no intercultural conflicts. This is not the case. In interacting with others, conflicts and misunderstandings will undoubtedly occur. All too often, we are too quick to attribute the cause of the conflict or misunderstanding to some fault or shortcoming in the other person, or the other person's culture. And because we have a limited understanding of culture, equating it with race or nationality, we may make negative attributions about that race or nationality, when in fact the differences arose because of culture.

With a better understanding of cultural influences on behavior, we can allow for the possibility that many conflicts and misunderstandings are due to cultural differences. By doing so, we avoid personalizing the source of conflict and misunderstanding in our interactions and focus on the reasons the misunderstanding may have arisen in the first place. Of course, some conflicts do arise because of personal differences, ignorance, stupidity, or closed-mindedness. But we can consider that culture may be a contributing factor and give people the benefit of the doubt.

Recognize that cultural differences are legitimate. Simply attributing conflicts and misunderstandings to culture is not enough; we need to recognize and respect legitimate differences between our cultural upbringing and that of others. This is often a very difficult task because, within our own cultural context, we see a failure to behave in culturally appropriate ways as "bad" or "wrong." Therefore, our natural tendency is to label the same behaviors of others as "bad" or "wrong." But a person from another culture may view those same behaviors as "good" or "acceptable" or "normal." In fact, behaviors that seem bad or ignorant or stupid to us may be performed by a person of sincerity and trustworthiness. And no matter how much we want to label them as bad or ignorant or stupid, other people's cultural ways, values, and beliefs have just as much legitimacy to them as ours have to us. A step in the right direction is to respect that legitimacy and that difference and find a way to work from that level of respect.

Have tolerance, be patient, and presume good intent. How can we find ways to work things out? Once we recognize that conflicts arise because of differences in culture, and that cultural differences in others are legitimate, where do we go from there? One answer lies in examining how we traditionally deal with these conflicts.

American culture is based on preservation of an individualistic sense of self. In finding ways to maintain self-integrity, we often attribute negative characteristics to others, lashing out at them when we feel our cultural norms have been violated. This style of making attributions is related to the individualistic American culture. It is neither bad nor good; it is just the way things are.

When we are too quick to attribute negative characteristics to others, however, we deny the possibility that their intent may have been good—that it was only the behavioral manifestations of that good intent that we were at odds with. By being tolerant of transgressions and presuming good intent in intercultural interaction, we allow that possibility to exist. If we practice tolerance and presume good intent, we will be able to operate on the level of psychological culture discussed throughout this book, finding ways to explore and react to underlying intent rather than focusing solely on behaviors we find offensive.

Learn more about cultural influences on behavior. As we turn toward the future, we must continue to learn how culture influences human behavior. By recognizing the impact of culture on behavior, we face an incredible challenge and opportunity. The diverse world that faces us, both within the United States and as part of an interdependent global village, provides a rich and complex arena for human behavior. Psychology has yet to explore this arena fully. These challenges bring new opportunities and new hopes, not only for science but also for people and their lives.

As we come in contact with people of different cultures from around the world, whether through our travels or theirs, we are exposed to many different ways that culture manifests itself in behavior. As our understanding grows, we will come to appreciate even more the important role that culture plays in helping us meet the challenges of survival successfully and with integrity. Cultures will continue to change, because culture itself is not a static, fixed entity. That cultures change over time is apparent today in Europe, Russia, Asia, and indeed the United States. These changes ensure that there will never be a shortage of things to learn about cultural influences on human behavior. The important thing is that we must want to learn them.

Achieving Intercultural Success or Stagnation

So we return to the question posed earlier in this section of this chapter: How can we move from one end of the intercultural sensitivity model (denial and minimization) to the other (adaptation, acceptance, and integration)? As we have seen, the key to such movement is a personal growth process model in which our ways of thinking, person perception, and worldview are constantly being updated by the new and exciting cultural differences with which we engage in our everyday lives. The key to this process is the ability to regulate and control our emotional reactions. If we can do so, then the world's cultural diversity is an exciting research laboratory, where we can constantly test our hypotheses, explore new hypotheses, throw out theories that don't work, and create theories of the world that do. The world becomes an exciting place to be, and intercultural episodes and conflicts provide a stage for forging new relationships, new ideas, and new people—a stage for intercultural success for those individuals who can engage in the process. We call these individuals *voyagers*, because to them, life is an enjoyable journey (see Figure 16.1).

On the other hand, some people cannot control their emotional reactions. Instead of engaging in the critical thinking necessary for personal growth, they

Figure 16.1 Steps to interpersonal and intercultural success or stagnation

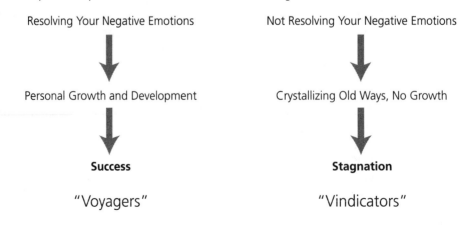

only reinforce their ethnocentric and stereotypic worldviews. Instead of expanding their knowledge and thinking patterns, they crystallize and reinforce their preexisting, limited ways of dealing with the world. Theirs is a no-growth model of stagnation, and these individuals are not engaged in a journey. Their worldviews are established solely to vindicate their preexisting ethnocentric and stereotypic ways of thinking, not to challenge those ways and grow. Therefore, we call these people *vindicators*.

The world of the voyager is neither a panacea nor utopia. These processes do not ensure that we will all live happily ever after, or that we will like and enjoy all cultural differences we come into contact with. After critically thinking about an episode or event, we may indeed come to the conclusion that someone is morally wrong, or just plain rude or selfish. Understanding differences and appreciating how they originate and their meaning to other people's lives does not mean that we have to like those differences, or accept them for our own life. What is important is not the conclusions we draw from this process, but engaging in the process itself. The distinction between voyagers and vindicators lies not in their conclusions, but in the processes they engage in to draw their conclusions.

Conclusion

In Knowing Others, We Will Come to Know Ourselves

Human behavior is too rich and complex to be "captured" by understanding the world through the eyes of a single culture. One of the major goals of this book has been to examine how culture influences our behaviors and our lives and to challenge the many truths of our cultural world. Many cross-cultural studies in the literature speak to this breadth, and to this need. We hope that this book has been like an intercultural journey for you, with travel to many other lands and cultures and meetings with many diverse peoples, and that it has helped to foster that challenge to your knowledge and worldview.

In challenging the "traditional," we cannot and should not disregard the importance of the work that produced that knowledge. But we have so much more to learn, and as time progresses, the need to learn increases. Improvements in communication bring previously distant points on the globe closer and closer together. The opening of national borders and the infusion of people from all walks of life and cultures into our workplaces and our families ensures that cross-cultural issues will remain a high priority in the years to come.

Can we keep up? Future cross-cultural research will help uncover universal and culture-specific aspects of human behavior. Scholars will increasingly have to include culture as a major determinant in theories of human behavior, and researchers will include culture as a variable in their studies. As new information is uncovered, we will undoubtedly improve our thinking about the nature of culture and cultural influences on the behavior of others. The real test of this knowledge is not in understanding the facts presented in this book, or in cognitively memorizing the intercultural process described here. It will be in our ability to control our emotional reactions at intercultural gaffes and to resolve the inevitable intercultural conflicts in our lives. In doing so, we have to know others well. In knowing others, we will come to know ourselves.

Advice for Those Breaking into This Field

In closing, we would like to offer some suggestions for people wanting to break into psychology in general, and cross-cultural psychology in particular.

Get grounded in academic psychology.   Get a solid grounding in the methods of contemporary academic psychology. Take as many classes on research methods and statistics as you can. Challenge instructors of your content courses about methods and statistics. Work in a research laboratory as an apprentice with someone who is willing to take you under his or her wing and "show you the ropes." Volunteer. Do a lot of research, make a lot of mistakes, and take time to think a lot along the way. Polish your skills at not only doing research, but learning how to think logically, rationally, and critically. Learn how to use a computer and analyze your own data. Be able to do everything in a study from start to finish, and do it well.

Get exposed to the variety of human behavior.   Get a lot of life experience. Have friends. Take time for love and relationships. Work in a clinical setting. Experience interacting with people with different psychopathologies. Experience the range of human emotions—from the ultimate joys of accomplishment to the depths of anguish and despair of loss. As a psychologist, understand people from an emotional standpoint, not only from a cognitive/research standpoint. You can't learn about the taste of strawberries by reading about it in a book; you have to experience it for yourself.

Get experience in an unfamiliar culture.   Travel, but not just as a tourist. Learn about the customs, ways, and lifestyles of different people. Learn how they think, experience emotions, and experience life. Learn another language, and get to the point where you are fluent in it. Learn to accept, appreciate, and respect cultural diversity. Become multicultural yourself. It is an entirely different plane of being.

Put it all together.   Finally, put it all together. Take your life experiences with the range of human behavior, your knowledge and appreciation of culture, and the academic skills you have learned, and integrate them into a meaningful career and life that teaches the rest of us something we don't already know. Make the world a better place. The next frontier for psychology is culture, and the next generation of psychologists armed with these skills will be those who are ready for that journey.

As you leave this book, it is our sincere hope that you leave as a voyager and not as a vindicator, and that you will use the knowledge and information you have learned not only in your academic preparation in psychology, but also in your everyday, personal lives. Good luck in that journey.

References

Abad, V., Ramos, J., & Boyce, E. (1974). A model for delivery of mental health services to Spanish-speaking minorities. *American Journal of Orthopsychiatry, 44,* 584–595.

Abebimpe, V. R. (1981). Overview: White norms and psychiatric diagnosis of black patients. *American Journal of Psychiatry, 139,* 888–891.

Abrams, D., Ando, K., & Hinkle, S. (1998). Psychological attachment to the group: Cross-cultural differences in organizational identification and subjective norms as predictors of workers' turnover intentions. *Personality and Social Psychology Bulletin, 24*(10), 1027–1039.

Abrams, K. K., Allen, L. R., & Gray, J. J. (1993). Disordered eating attitudes and behaviors, psychological adjustment, and ethnic identity: A comparison of black and white female college students. *International Journal of Eating Disorders, 14,* 49–57.

Abramson, R. P., & Pinkerton, D. S. (1995). *Sexual nature, sexual culture.* Chicago: University of Chicago Press.

Achenbach, T. M. (2001). *Child behavior checklist for ages 6 to 18.* Burlington: University of Vermont, Research Center for Children, Youth and Families.

Acioly, N. M., & Schliemann, A. D. (1986). *Intuitive mathematics and schooling in understanding a lottery game.* Paper presented at the Tenth PME Conference, London.

Adamopoulos, J. (1991). The emergence of interpersonal behavior. In S. Ting-Toomey & F. Korzenny (Eds.), *Cross-cultural interpersonal communication* (pp. 155–270). Newbury Park, CA: Sage.

Adler, N. E., Boyce, T., Chesney, M. A., Cohen, S., Folkman, S., Kahn, R. L., & Syme, S. L. (1994). Socioeconomic status and health. *American Psychologist, 49,* 15–24.

Adler, N. J., Schwartz, T., & Graham, J. L. (1987). Business negotiations in Canada (French and English speakers), Mexico and the United States. *Journal of Business Research, 15,* 411–429.

Adorno, T. W., Frenkel-Brunswick, E., Levinson, D. J., & Sanford, R. N. (1950). *The authoritarian personality.* New York: Harper & Row.

Ainsworth, M. (1967). *Infancy in Uganda: Infant care and the growth of love.* Baltimore: Johns Hopkins University Press.

Ainsworth, M. (1977). Infant development and mother-infant interaction among Ganda and American families. In P. H. Leiderman, S. R. Tulkin, & A. H. Rosenfeld (Eds.), *Culture and infancy* (pp. 119–150). New York: Academic Press.

Ajwani, J. K. (1982). A correlational study of Cattel's personality factor B. and I.Q. as measured by his culture fair test. *Indian Psychological Review, 22*(1), 9–11.

Akan, G. E., & Grilo, C. M. (1995). Sociocultural influences on eating attitudes and behaviors, body image, and psychological functioning: A comparison of African American, Asian American, and Caucasian college women. *International Journal of Eating Disorders, 18*(2), 181–187.

Akin-Ogundeji, O. (1988). An African perspective on personality: A case study of the Ibo. *Journal of Human Behavior and Learning, 5*(1), 22–26.

Alarcon, R. D. (1995). Culture and psychiatric diagnosis. *Cultural Psychiatry, 18*(3), 449–465.

Alarcon, R. D., & Leetz, K. L. (1998). Cultural intersections in the psychotherapy of borderline personality disorder. *American Journal of Psychotherapy, 52*(2), 176–190.

Albert, A. A., & Porter, J. R. (1986). Children's gender role stereotypes: A comparison of the United States and South Africa. *Journal of Cross-Cultural Psychology, 17,* 45–65.

Albright, L., Kenny, D. A., & Malloy, T. E. (1988). Consensus in personality judgments at zero acquaintance. *Journal of Personality and Social Psychology, 55,* 387–395.

Alderete, E., Vega, W. A., & Kolody, B. (2000). Lifetime prevalence of the risk factors for psychiatric disorders among Mexican migrant farmworkers in California. *American Journal of Public Health, 90*(4), 608–614.

Ali, A. J. (1989). A comparative study of managerial beliefs about work in the Arab states. *Advances in International Comparative Management, 4,* 95–112.

Al-Issa, I. (Ed.). (1995). *Handbook of culture and mental illness: An international perspective.* Madison, CT: International Universities Press.

Al-Krenawi, A., & Graham, J. R. (2000). Culturally sensitive social work: Practice with Arab clients in mental health settings. *Health & Social Work, 25,* 9–22.

Allen, L., & Santrock, J. W. (1993). *Psychology: The context of behavior.* Dubuque, IA: Brown & Benchmark.

Allen, R. F., & Dyer, F. J. (1980). A tool for tapping the organizational unconscious. *Personnel Journal,* 192–199.

Allerheiligen, R., Graham, J. L., & Lin, C. (1985, Fall). Honesty in interorganizational negotiations in the United States, Japan, Brazil, and the Republic of China. *Journal of Macromarketing,* 4–16.

Al-Mutlaq, H., & Chaleby, K. (1995). Group psychotherapy with Arab patients. *Arab Journal of Psychiatry, 6*(2), 125–136.

Al-Subaie, A., & Alhamad, A. (2000). Psychiatry in Saudi Arabia. In I. Al-Junūn (Ed.), *Mental illness in the Islamic world* (pp. 205–233). Madison, CT: International Universities Press.

Altarriba, J. (Ed). (1993). *Cognition and culture: A cross-cultural approach to cognitive psychology.* Amsterdam: North-Holland/Elsevier Science Publishers.

Altarriba, J., & Santiago-Rivera, A. L. (1994). Current perspectives on using linguistic and cultural factors in counseling the Hispanic client. *Professional Psychology: Research and Practice, 25*(4), 388–397.

Altman, I., & Taylor, D. A. (1973). *Social penetration: The development of interpersonal relationships.* New York: Holt, Rinehart & Winston.

Amelang, M., & Borkenau, P. (1982). Ueber die faktorielle Struktur und externe Validtaet einiger Fragebogen-Skalen zur Erfassung von Dimensionen der Extraversion und emotionalen Labilitaet [The factional structure and external validity of some questionnaire scales for measurement of the dimensions of extraversion and emotional lability]. *Zeitschrift fuer Differentielle und Diagnostische Psychologie, 3*(2), 119–145.

American Psychiatric Association. (1987). *Diagnostic and statistical manual of mental disorders* (3rd ed.) [DSM-III-R]. Washington, DC: Author.

American Psychiatric Association. (1994). *Diagnostic and statistical manual of mental disorders* (4th ed.) [DSM-IV]. Washington, DC: Author.

American Psychological Association. (2002). *Guidelines on multicultural education, training, research, practice and organizational change for psychologists.* Washington, DC: American Psychological Association.

Amir, Y., & Sharon, I. (1988). Are social psychological laws cross-culturally valid? *Journal of Cross-Cultural Psychology, 18*(4), 383–470.

Anderson, C. A., & Anderson, K. B. (1996). Violent crime rate studies in philosophical context: A destructive testing approach to heat and southern culture of violence effects. *Journal of Personality, 70*(4), 740–756.

Angyal, A. (1951). *Neurosis and treatment: A holistic theory.* New York: Wiley.

Anshel, M. H., Williams, L. R. T., & Hodge, K. (1997). Cross-cultural and gender differences on coping style in sport. *International Journal of Sport Psychology, 28*(2), 141–156.

APS Observer. (1997, October). *Human capital initiative: Reducing violence: A research agenda* (Report No. 5).

Argyle, M., Alkema, F., & Gilmour, K. (1978). The communication of friendly and hostile attitudes by verbal and non-verbal signals. *European Journal of Social Psychology, 1*(3), 385–402.

Argyle, M., Henderson, M., Bond, M. H., Iizuka, Y., & Contarello, A. (1986). Cross-cultural variations in relationship rules. *International Journal of Psychology, 21,* 287–315.

Argyle, M., Salter, G., Nicholson, H., Williams, M., & Burgess, P. (1970). The communication of inferior and superior attitudes by verbal and non-verbal signals. *British Journal of Sociology and Clinical Psychology, 9,* 222–231.

Armstrong, T. L., & Swartzman, L. C. (1999). Asian versus Western differences in satisfaction with Western medical care: The mediational effects of illness attributions. *Psychology and Health, 14,* 403–416.

Armstrong, T. L., & Swartzman, L. C. (2001). Cross-cultural differences in illness models and expectations. In S. S. Kazarian & D. R. Evans (Eds.), *Handbook of cultural health psychology* (pp. 63–84). San Diego: Academic Press.

Arnett, J. (2001). *Adolescence and emerging adulthood: A cultural approach.* Upper Saddle River, NJ: Prentice Hall.

Aronson, E. (2002). Building empathy, compassion and achievement in jigsaw classrooms. In J. Aronson (Ed.), *Improving academic achievement: Impact of psychological factors on education* (pp. 209–225). San Diego: Academic Press.

Asch, S. E. (1951). Effects of group pressure upon the modification and distortion of judgments. In H. Guetzkow (Ed.), *Groups, leadership and men: Research in human relations* (pp. 177–190). Pittsburgh: Carnegie Press.

Asch, S. E. (1955). Opinions and social pressures. *Scientific American, 193,* 31–35.

Asch, S. E. (1956). Studies of independence and conformity: A minority of one against a unanimous majority. *Psychological Monographs, 70*(9, Whole No. 416).

Atkeson, P. (1970). Building communication in intercultural marriage. *Psychiatry: Journal for the Study of Interpersonal Processes, 33*(3), 396–408.

Atkinson, D. R., Casa, A., & Abreu, J. (1992). Mexican American acculturation, counselor ethnicity and cultural sensitivity, and perceived counselor competence. *American Psychologist, 39,* 515–520.

Atkinson, D. R., Furlong, M. J., & Poston, W. C. (1986). Afro-American preferences for counselor characteristics. *Journal of Counseling Psychology, 33,* 326–330.

Atkinson, D. R., Maruyama, M., & Matsui, S. (1978). Effects of counselor race and counseling approach on Asian Americans' perceptions of counselor. *Journal of Counseling Psychology, 25,* 76–83.

Atkinson, D. R., Morten, G., & Sue, D. W. (1989). *Counseling American minorities* (3rd ed.). Dubuque, IA: Brown.

Atkinson, D. R., Ponce, F. Q., & Martinez, F. M. (1984). Effects of ethnic, sex, and attitude similarity on counselor credibility. *Journal of Counseling Psychology, 31*(40), 588–590.

Atkinson, J. W. (1964). *An introduction to motivation.* Princeton, NJ: Van Nostrand Reinhold.

Au, T. K. (1983). Chinese and English counterfactuals: The Sapir-Whorf hypothesis revisited. *Cognition, 15,* 155–187.

Au, T. K. (1984). Counterfactuals: In reply to Alfred Bloom. *Cognition, 17,* 289–302.

Auerbach, J. G., Yirmiya, N., & Kamel, F. N. (1996). Behavior problems in Israeli Jewish and Palestinian preschool children. *Journal of Clinical Child Psychology, 25*(4), 398–405.

Aune, K., & Aune K. (1995). Culture differences in the self-reported experience and expression of emotions in relationships. *Journal of Cross-Cultural Psychology, 27,* 67–81.

Averill, J. R. (1980). Emotion and anxiety: Sociocultural, biological, and psychological determinants. In A. O. Rorty (Ed.), *Explaining emotions* (pp. 37–72). Berkeley: University of California Press.

Aycan, Z. (2000). Cross-cultural industrial and organizational psychology: Contributions, past developments, future directions. *Journal of Cross-Cultural Psychology, 31*(1), 110–128.

Azhar, M. Z., & Varma, S. L. (1995). Religious psychotherapy in depressive disorder patients. *Psychotherapy and Psychosomatics, 53,* 165–168.

Azhar, M. Z., & Varma, S. L. (2000). Mental illness and its treatment in Malaysia. In I. Al-Junūn (Ed.), *Mental illness in the Islamic world* (pp. 163–186). Madison, CT: International Universities Press.

Azhar, M. Z., Varma, S. L., & Dharap, A. S. (1994). Religious psychotherapy in anxiety disorder patients. *Acta Psychiatry Scandinavica, 90,* 1–3.

Bachman, J. G., & O'Malley, P. M. (1984). Black-white differences in self-esteem: Are they affected by response styles? *American Journal of Sociology, 90*(3), 624–639.

Baddeley, A. D., & Hitch, G. (1974). Working memory. In G. Bower (Ed.), *Recent advances in learning and motivating* (pp. 47–89). New York: Academic Press.

Bahrick, H. P., & Hall, L. K. (1991). Lifetime maintenance of high school mathematics content. *Journal of Experimental Psychology: General, 120,* 20–33.

Bakan, D. (1966). *The duality of human existence.* Boston: Beacon Press.

Balint, M. (1959). *Thrills and regression.* London: Hogarth Press.

Bal-Tal, D., & Labin, D. (2001). The effect of a major event on stereotyping: Terrorist attacks in Israel and Israeli adolescents' perceptions of Palestinians, Jordanians and Arabs. *European Journal of Social Psychology, 31,* 265–280.

Bargh, J. (1996). Automaticity in social psychology. In E. Higgins & A. Kruglanski (Eds.), *Social psychology: Handbook of basic principles* (pp. 169–183). New York: Guilford.

Barna, L. M. (1996). Stumbling blocks in intercultural communication. In L. A. Samovar & R. E. Porter (Eds.), *Intercultural communication: A reader* (8th ed., pp. 370–379). Belmont, CA: Wadsworth.

Barnlund, D. C., & Araki, S. (1985). Intercultural encounters: The management of compliments by Japanese and Americans. *Journal of Cross-Cultural Psychology, 16*(1), 9–26.

Barnlund, D. C., & Yoshioka, M. (1990). Apologies: Japanese and American styles. *International Journal of Intercultural Relations, 14,* 193–206.

Barry, H. (1980). Description and uses of the Human Relations Area Files. In H. C. Triandis & J. W. Berry (Eds.), *Handbook of cross-cultural psychology: Vol. 2. Methodology* (pp. 445–478). Boston: Allyn & Bacon.

Barry, H., Josephson, L., Lauer, E., & Marshall, C. (1976). Agents and techniques for child training. *Ethnology, 16,* 191–230.

Bartlett, F. C. (1932). *Remembering.* Cambridge, UK: Cambridge University Press.

Basow, S. A., & Rubin, L. R. (1999). Gender influences on adolescent development. In N. G. Johnson, M. C. Roberts, & J. Worrell (Eds), *Beyond appearance: A new look at adolescent girls* (pp. 25–52). Washington, DC: American Psychological Association.

Bates, J. E., Maslin, C. A., & Frankel, K. A. (1985). Attachment security, mother-child interaction, and temperament as predictors of behavior-problem ratings at age three years. *Monographs of the Society for Research in Child Development, 50*(1–2), 167–193.

Baumrind, D. (1967). Child care practices anteceding three patterns of preschool behavior. *Genetic Psychology Monographs, 75,* 43–88.

Baumrind, D. (1971). Current patterns of parental authority. *Developmental Psychology Monograph, 4* (No. 1, Pt. 2).

Beach, L. R. (1993). Image theory: Personal and organizational decisions. In G. A. Klein & J. Orasanu (Eds.), *Decision making in action: Models and methods* (pp. 148–157). Norwood, NJ: Ablex.

Beall, A. E., & Sternberg, R. J. (1995). The social construction of love. *Journal of Social and Personal Relationships, 12,* 417–438.

Bechtold, D. W. (1988). Cluster suicide in American Indian adolescents. *American Indian and Alaska Native Mental Health Research, 1*(3), 26–35.

Beck, A. T. (1967). *Depression: Clinical, experimental and theoretical aspects.* New York: Harper and Row.

Beck, A. T. (1976). *Cognitive therapy and the emotional disorders.* New York: International Universities Press.

Beiser, M. (1985). A study of depression among traditional Africans, urban North Americans, and Southeast Asian refugees. In A. Kleinman & B. Good (Eds.), *Culture and depression: Studies in the anthropology and cross-cultural psychiatry of affect and disorder* (pp. 272–298). Berkeley: University of California Presss.

Beit-Hallahmi, B. (1972). National character and national behavior in the Middle East conflict: The case of the "Arab personality." *International Journal of Group Tensions, 2*(3), 19–28.

Bell, R. (1968). A reinterpretation of the direction of effects in studies of socialization. *Psychological Review, 75,* 81–95.

Bem, S. (1981). Gender schema theory: A cognitive account of sex-typing. *Psychological Review, 88,* 354–364.

Ben-David, A. (1996). Therapists' perceptions of multicultural assessment and therapy with immigrant families. *Journal of Family Therapy, 18,* 23–41.

Benedict, R. (1946). *The chrysanthemum and the sword.* Boston: Houghton Mifflin.

Benet-Martinez, V., & John, O. P. (1998). Los Cinco Grandes across cultures and ethnic groups: Multi trait–multi method analyses of the Big Five in Spanish and English. *Journal of Personality and Social Psychology, 75*(3), 729–750.

Benet-Martinez, V., & John, O. P. (2000). Measuring *Los Cinco Grandes* in Spain with indigenous Castilian markers. *American Behavioral Scientist, 44*(1), 141–157.

Bennett, M. J. (1993). Towards ethnorelativism: A developmental model of intercultural sensitivity. In R. Michael Paige (Ed.), *Education for the intercultural experience* (pp. 109–136). Yarmouth, ME: Intercultural Press.

Beratis, S. (1986). Suicide in southwestern Greece 1979–1984. *Acta Psychiatrica Scandinavica, 74*(5), 433–439.

Berger, C. R. (1979). Beyond initial interaction. In H. Giles & R. St. Claire (Eds.), *Language and social psychology* (pp. 122–144). Oxford, UK: Basil Blackwell.

Berger, C. R., & Calabrese, R. J. (1975). Some explorations in initial interaction and beyond: Toward a development theory of interpersonal communication. *Human Communication Research, 10,* 179–196.

Bergling, K. (1981). *Moral development: The validity of Kohlberg's Theory.* Stockholm: Almgrist & Wilsell International.

Berkman, L. F., & Syme, S. L. (1979). Social networks, host resistance, and mortality: A nine-year follow-up study of Alameda County residents. *American Journal of Epidemiology, 109,* 186–204.

Berlin, B., & Kay, P. (1969). *Basic color terms: Their universality and evolution.* Berkeley: University of California Press.

Berman, S., Ozkaragoz, T., Young, R., & Noble, E. (2002). D2 dopamine receptor gene polymorphism discriminates two kinds of novelty seeking. *Personality and Individual Differences, 33*(6), 867–882.

Bernal, G., & Scharrón-Del-Río, M. R. (2001). Are empirically supported treatments valid for ethnic minorities? Toward an alternative approach for treatment research. *Cultural Diversity and Ethnic Minority Psychology, 7,* 328–342.

Bernal, H. (1993). A model for delivering culture-relevant care in the community. *Public Health Nursing, 10*(4), 228–232.

Bernieri, F., & Gillis, J.S. (1995). The judgement of rapport: A cross-cultural comparison between Americans and Greeks. *Journal of Nonverbal Behavior, 19*(2), 115–131.

Berry, D. S., & McArthur, L. Z. (1985). Some components and consequences of a babyface. *Journal of Personality and Social Psychology, 48,* 312–323.

Berry, D. S., & McArthur, L. Z. (1986). Perceiving character in faces: The impact of age-related craniofacial changes in social perception. *Psychological Bulletin, 100,* 3–18.

Berry, J. W. (1966). Temne and Eskimo perceptual skills. *International Journal of Psychology, 1,* 207–229.

Berry, J. W. (1969). On cross-cultural comparability. *International Journal of Psychology, 4,* 119–128.

Berry, J. W. (1976). Sex differences in behavior and cultural complexity. *Indian Journal of Psychology, 51,* 89–97.

Berry, J. W. (1997). Immigration, acculturation and adaptation. *Applied Psychology: An International Review,* 46, 5–68.

Berry, J. W., & Kim, U. (1988). Acculturation and mental health. In P. Dasen, J. W. Berry, & N. Sortarious (Eds.), *Health and cross-cultural psychology: Towards applications* (pp. 207–236). Newbury Park, CA: Sage.

Berry, J. W., Kim, U., Minde, T., & Mok, D. (1987). Comparative studies of acculturation stress. *International Migration Review, 21,* 491–511.

Berry, J. W., Poortinga, Y. H., Segall, M. H., & Dasen, P. R. (1992). *Cross-cultural psychology: Research and applications.* New York: Cambridge University Press.

Berry, J. W., & Sam, D. L. (1997). Acculturation and adaptation. In J. W. Berry, M. H. Segall, & C. Kagitcibasi (Eds.), *Handbook of cross-cultural psychology: Vol 3. Social behaviour and applications* (2nd ed., pp. 291–326). Boston: Allyn & Bacon.

Berscheid, E. (1988). Some comments on love's anatomy: Or, whatever happened to old-fashioned lust? In R. J. Sternberg & M. L. Barnes (Eds.), *Anatomy of love* (pp. 359–374). New Haven, CT: Yale University Press.

Best, D., House, A., Barnard, E. A., & Spicker, S. B. (1994). Parent-child interactions in France, Germany, and Italy: The effects of gender and culture. *Journal of Cross-Cultural Psychology, 25*(2), 181–193.

Betancourt, H., & Lopez, R. S. (1993). The study of culture, ethnicity, and race in American psychology. *American Psychologist, 48*(6), 629–637.

Bickerton, D. (1981). *The roots of language.* Ann Arbor, MI: Karoma.

Biehl, M., Matsumoto, D., Ekman, P., Hearn, V., Heider, K., Kudoh, T., & Ton, V. (1997). Matsumoto and Ekman's Japanese and Caucasian facial expressions of emotion (JACFEE): Reliability data and cross-national differences. *Journal of Nonverbal Behavior, 21,* 3–21.

Biehl, M., Matsumoto, D., & Kasri, F. (in press). Culture and emotion. In U. Gielen & A. L. Comunian (Eds.), *Cross-cultural and international dimensions of psychology.* Trieste, Italy: Edizioni Lint Trieste S.r.l.

Bigler, R. S., & Liben, L. S. (1993). A cognitive-developmental approach to racial stereotyping and reconstructive memory in Euro-American children. *Child Development, 64*(5), 1507–1518.

Binion, V. J. (1990). Psychological androgyny: A black female perspective. *Sex Roles, 22,* 487–507.

Birenbaum, M., & Kraemer, R. (1995). Gender and ethnic-group differences in causal attributions for success and failure in mathematics and language examinations. *Journal of Cross-Cultural Psychology, 26*(3), 342–359.

Bissilat, J., Laya, D., Pierre, E., & Pidoux, C. (1967). La notion de lakkal dans la culture Djerma-Songhai [The concept of lakkal in Djerma-Songhai culture]. *Psychopathologie Africaine, 3,* 207–264.

Black, J. S., & Porter, L. W. (1991). Managerial behavior and job performance: A successful manager in Los Angeles may not succeed in Hong Kong. *Journal of International Business Studies, 22,* 99–113.

Blair, I. V. (2001). Implicit stereotypes and prejudice. In G. B. Moskowitz (Ed.), *Cognitive social psychology: The Princeton symposium on the legacy and future of social cognition* (pp. 359–374). Mahwah, NJ: Erlbaum.

Blau, Z. S. (1981). *Black children–white children: Competence, socialization, and social structure.* New York: Free Press.

Bletzer, K. V. (1991). Biobehavioral characteristics of a culture-bound syndrome perceived as life-threatening illness. *Qualitative Health Research, 1*(2), 200–233.

Blinco, M. A. P. (1992). A cross-cultural study of task persistence of young children in Japan and the United States. *Journal of Cross-Cultural Psychology, 21*(3), 407–415.

Block, J. (1983). Differential premises arising from differential socialization of the sexes: Some conjectures. *Child Development, 54,* 1335–1354.

Bloom, A. H. (1981). *The linguistic shaping of thought: A study in the impact of language on thinking in China and the West.* Hillsdale, NJ: Erlbaum.

Bloom, A. H. (1984). Caution—the words you use may affect what you say: A response to Au. *Cognition, 17*(3), 275–287.

Bochner, S. (1982). *Cultures in contact: Studies in cross-cultural interaction.* Oxford, UK: Pergamon.

Bochner, S. (1994). Cross-cultural differences in the self concept. *Journal of Cross-Cultural Psychology, 25,* 273–283.

Bochner, S., & Hesketh, B. (1994). Power distance, individualism/collectivism, and job-related attitudes in a culturally diverse work group. *Journal of Cross-Cultural Psychology, 25*(2), 233–257.

Bochner, S., & Osako, T. (1977). Ethnic role salience in racially homogeneous and heterogeneous societies. *Journal of Cross-Cultural Psychology, 8*(4), 477–492.

Bochner, S., & Perks, W. R. (1971). National role evocation as a function of cross-national interaction. Journal of *Cross-Cultural Psychology, 2*(2), 157–164.

Bock, P. K. (2000). Culture and personality revisited. *American Behavioral Scientist, 44*(1), 32–40.

Bodenhausen, G. V., Kramer, G. P., & Suesser, K. (1994). Happiness and stereotypic thinking in social judgment. *Journal of Personality and Social Psychology, 66*(4), 621–632.

Boehnlein, J. K., & Kinzie, J. D. (1995). Refugee trauma. *Transcultural Psychiatric Research Review, 32*(3), 223–252.

Boehnlein, J. K., Kinzie, J. D., & Leung, P. K. (1992). The natural history of medical and psychiatric disorders in an American Indian community. *Culture, Medicine & Psychiatry, 16*(4), 543–554.

Bond, M. H. (1979). Winning either way: The effect of anticipating a competitive interaction on person perception. *Personality and Social Psychology Bulletin, 5*(3), 316–319.

Bond, M. H. (1986). *The psychology of the Chinese people.* New York: Oxford University Press.

Bond, M. H. (1991). Chinese values and health: A cultural-level examination. *Psychology and Health, 5*(2), 137–152.

Bond, M. H., & Forgas, J. P. (1984). Linking person perception to behavior intention across cultures: The role of cultural collectivism. *Journal of Cross-Cultural Psychology, 15,* 337–352.

Bond, M. H., Leung, K., & Wan, K. C. (1982). The social impact of self-effacing attributions: The Chinese case. *Journal of Social Psychology, 118*(2), 157–166.

Bond, M. H., Nakazato, H., & Shiraishi, D. (1975). Universality and distinctiveness in dimensions of Japanese person perception. *Journal of Cross-Cultural Psychology, 6*(3), 346–357.

Bond, M. H., & Smith, P. B. (1996). Cross-cultural social and organizational psychology. *Annual Review of Psychology, 47,* 205–235.

Bond, M. H., & Tak-Sing, C. (1983). College students' spontaneous self concept: The effect of culture among respondents in Hong Kong, Japan, and the United States. *Journal of Cross-Cultural Psychology, 14,* 153–171.

Bond, M. H., & Tedeschi, J. T. (2001). Polishing the jade: A modest proposal for improving social psychology across cultures. In D. Matsumoto (Ed.), *Handbook of culture and psychology* (pp. 309–324). Oxford, UK: Oxford University Press.

Bond, M. H., Wan, K. C., Leong, K., & Giacalone, R. A. (1985). How are responses to verbal insult related to cultural collectivism and power distance? *Journal of Cross-Cultural Psychology, 16*(1), 111–127.

Bond, M. H., & Wang, S. (1983). China: Aggressive behavior and the problems of mainstreaming order and harmony. In A. P. Goldstein & M. H. Segall (Eds.), *Aggression in global perspective* (pp. 58–74). New York: Pergamon.

Boor, M. (1976). Relationship of internal-external control and national suicide rates. *Journal of Social Psychology, 100*(1), 143–144.

Boothby, N. (1994). Trauma and violence among refugee children. In A. Marsella, T. Bornemann, S. Ekblad, & J. Orley (Eds.), *Amidst the pain and peril: The mental health and well-being of the world's refugees* (pp. 239–259). Washington, DC: American Psychological Association.

Borkenau, P., & Ostendorf, F. (1998). The Big Five as states: How useful is the five-factor model to describe intraindividual variations over time? *Journal of Research in Personality, 32*(2), 202–221.

Born, M., Bleichrodt, N., & Van der Flier, H. (1987). Cross-cultural comparison of sex-related differences on intelligence tests: A meta-analysis. *Journal of Cross-Cultural Psychology, 18,* 283–314.

Bornstein, M. H. (1989). Cross-cultural developmental comparisons: The case of Japanese-American infant and mother activities and interactions. What we know, what we need to know, and why we need to know. *Developmental Review, 9,* 171–204.

Bornstein, M. H., Haynes, O. M., Azuma, H., et al. (1998). A cross-national study of self-evaluations and attributions in parenting: Argentina, Belgium, France, Israel, Italy, Japan and the United States. *Developmental Psychology, 34*(4), 662–676.

Bothwell, R. K., Brigham, J. C., & Malpass, R. S. (1989). Cross-racial identification. *Personality and Social Psychology Bulletin, 15*(1), 19–25.

Bouchard, T. J., Jr., & McGue, M. (1981). Familial studies of intelligence: A review. *Science, 212,* 1055–1059.

Boucher, J. D., & Brandt, M. E. (1981). Judgement of emotion: American and Malay antecedents. *Journal of Cross-Cultural Psychology, 12*(3), 272–283.

Boucher, J. D., & Carlson, G. E. (1980). Recognition of facial expression in three cultures. *Journal of Cross-Cultural Psychology, 11*(3), 263–280.

Boucher, J. D., Landis, D., & Clark, K. A. (1987). *Ethnic conflict: International perspectives*. Newbury Park, CA: Sage.

Bouhmama, D. (1984). Assessment of Kohlberg's stages of moral development in two cultures. *Journal of Moral Education, 13*, 124–132.

Bourhis, R. Y., Moise, L. C., Perreault, S., & Senecal, S. (1997). Towards an interactive acculturation model: A social psychological approach. *International Journal of Psychology, 32*, 369–386.

Bowen, M. (1966). The use of family theory in clinical practice. *Comprehensive Psychiatry, 7*, 345–374.

Bowlby, J. (1969). *Attachment and loss: Vol. 1. Attachment*. New York: Basic Books.

Bradley, G. W. (1978). Self-serving biases in the attribution process: A re-examination of the fact or fiction question. *Journal of Personality and Social Psychology, 35*, 56–71.

Brandt, M. E., & Boucher, J. D. (1985). Judgement of emotions from antecedent situations in three cultures. In I. Lagunes & Y. Poortinga (Eds.), *From a different perspective: Studies of behavior across cultures* (pp. 348–362). Lisse, Netherlands: Swets & Zeitlinger.

Brandt, M. E., & Boucher, J. D. (1986). Concepts of depression in emotion lexicons of eight cultures. *International Journal of Intercultural Relations, 10*, 321–346.

Brehm, S. S. (1985). *Intimate relationships*. New York: Random House.

Brewer, M. B., & Campbell, D. T. (1976). *Ethnocentrism and intergroup attitudes*. New York: Wiley.

Brewer, M. B., & Kramer, R. M. (1985). The psychology of intergroup attitudes and behavior. *Annual Review of Psychology, 36*, 219–243.

Brigham, J. C., & Malpass, R. S. (1985). The role of experience and contact in the recognition of faces of own and other race persons. *Journal of Social Issues, 41*(3), 139–155.

Brislin, R. (1970). Back translation for cross-cultural research. *Journal of Cross-Cultural Psychology, 1*, 185–216.

Brislin, R. (1993). *Understanding culture's influence on behavior*. Fort Worth, TX: Harcourt Brace Jovanovich.

Broman, C. L. (1996). Coping with personal problems. In H. W. Neighbors & J. S. Jackson (Eds.), *Mental health in black America* (pp. 117–129). Thousand Oaks, CA: Sage.

Brondolo, E., Rieppi, R., Kelly, K. P., & Gerin, W. (2003). Perceived racism and blood pressure: A review of the literature and conceptual and methodological critique. *Annals of Behavioral Medicine, 25*(1), 55–65.

Bronfenbrenner, U. (1979). *The ecology of human development*. Cambridge, MA: Harvard University Press.

Bronstein, P. A. (1984). Differences in mothers' and fathers' behaviors toward children: A cross-cultural comparison. *Developmental Psychology, 20*(6), 995–1003.

Bronstein, P. A., & Paludi, M. (1988). The introductory psychology course from a broader human perspective. In P. A. Bronstein & K. Quina (Eds.), *Teaching a psychology of people: Resources for gender and sociocultural awareness* (pp. 21–36). Washington, DC: American Psychological Association.

Brook, D. W., Gordon, C., & Meadow, H. (1998). Ethnicity, culture, and group psychotherapy. *Group, 22*(2), 53–80.

Broota, K. D., & Ganguli, H. C. (1975). Cultural differences in perceptual selectivity. *Journal of Social Psychology, 95*, 157–163.

Brown, R., & Lenneberg, E. (1954). A study in language and cognition. *Journal of Abnormal and Social Psychology, 49*, 454–462.

Brummett, B. H., Siegler, I. C., McQuoid, D. R., Svenson, I. K., Marchuk, D. A., & Steffens, D. C. (2003). Associations among the NEO Personality Inventory, Revised and the serotonin transporter gene-linked polymorphic region in elders: Effects of depression and gender. *Psychiatric Genetics, 13*(1), 13–18.

Bruner, J. S., Oliver, R. R., & Greenfield, P. M. (1966). *Studies in cognitive growth*. New York: Wiley.

Buck, E. B., Newton, B. J., & Muramatsu, Y. (1984). Independence and obedience in the U. S. and Japan. *International Journal of Intercultural Relations, 8*, 279–300.

Buck, R. (1984). *The communication of emotion*. New York: Guilford Press.

Bugental, D. E., Kaswan, J. W., & Love, L. R. (1970). Perception of contradictory meanings conveyed by verbal and nonverbal channels. *Journal of Personality and Social Psychology, 16*(4), 647–655.

Bui, K.-T., & Takeuchi, D.T. (1992). Ethnic minority adolescents and the use of community mental health care services. *American Journal of Community Psychology, 20*, 403–417.

Burger, J. M., & Hemans, L. T. (1988). Desire for control and the use of attribution processes. *Journal of Personality, 56*, 531–546.

Burgos, N. M., & Diaz-Perez, Y. I. (1986). An explanation of human sexuality in the Puerto Rican culture. Special issue: Human sexuality, ethnoculture, and social work. *Journal of Social Work and Human Sexuality, 4*, 135–150.

Burleson, B. R. (1997). A different voice on different cultures: Illusion and reality in the study of sex differences in personal relationships. *Personal Relationships, 4*(3), 229–241.

Burnam, A. M., Hough, R. L., Karno, M., Escobar, J. I., & Telles, C. A. (1987). Acculturation and lifetime prevalence of psychiatric disorders among Mexican Americans in Los Angeles. *Journal of Health and Social Behavior, 28*, 89–102.

Buss, D. M. (1988). The evolution of human intrasexual competition: Tactics of mate attraction. *Journal of Personality and Social Psychology, 54*, 616–628.

Buss, D. M. (1989). Sex differences in human mate preferences: Evolutionary hypotheses tested in 37 cultures. *Behavioral and Brain Sciences, 12*, 1–49.

Buss, D. M. (1994). *The evolution of desire: Strategies of human mating*. New York: Basic Books.

Butcher, J. N, Lim, J., & Nezami, E. (1998). Objective study of abnormal personality in cross-cultural settings: The Minnesota Multiphasic Personality Inventory (MMPI–2). *Journal of Cross-Cultural Psychology, 29*(1), 189–211.

Butsch, R. (1992). Class and gender in four decades of television situation comedy. *Critical Studies in Mass Communication, 9*, 387–399.

Buunk, B., & Hupka, R. B. (1987). Cross-cultural differences in the elicitation of sexual jealousy. *Journal of Sex Research, 23*(1), 12–22.

Byrne, D., & Murnen, S. K. (1988). Maintaining loving relationships. In R. J. Sternberg & M. L. Barnes (Eds.), *The psychology of love* (pp. 293–310). New Haven, CT: Yale University Press.

Callister, L., Vehvilainen-Julkunen, K., & Lauri, S. (2001). Giving birth: Perceptions of Finnish childbearing women. *American Journal of Maternal/Child Nursing, 26*(1), 28–32.

Campbell, D. T., & Levine, R. A. (1965). *Propositions about ethnocentrism from social science theories.* Unpublished monograph, Northwestern University, Evanston, Illinois.

Campbell, N. C. G., Graham, J. L., Jolibert, A., & Meissner, H. G. (1988). Marketing negotiations in France, Germany, the United Kingdom and the United States. *Journal of Marketing, 52*, 49–62.

Canino, G. J., Bird, H. R., Shrout, P. E., Rubio-Stipec, M., Bravo, M., Martinez, R., Sesman, M., & Guevara, L. M. (1987). The prevalence of specific psychiatric disorders in Puerto Rico. *Archives of General Psychiatry, 44*, 727–735.

Caprara, G. V., Barbaranelli, C. & Comrey, A. L. (1995). Factor analysis of the NEO-PI Inventory and the Comrey Personality Scales in an Italian sample. *Personality and Individual Differences, 18*(2), 193–200.

Caprara, G. V., & Perugini, M. (1994). Personality described by adjectives: The generalizability of the Big Five to the Italian lexical context. *European Journal of Personality, 8*(5), 357–369.

Carlo, G., Koller H. S., Eisenberg N., DaSilva, S. M., & Frohlich, B. C. (1996). A cross-national study on the relations among prosocial moral reasoning, gender role orientations, and prosocial behaviors. *Developmental Psychology, 32*(2), 231–240.

Carrell, L. J. (1997). Diversity in the communication curriculum: Impact on student empathy. *Communication Education, 46*(2), 234–244.

Carroll, J. B., & Casagrande, J. B. (1958). The function of language classifications in behavior. In E. E. Maccoby, T. M. Newcomb, & E. L. Hartley (Eds.), *Readings in social psychology* (pp. 18–31). New York: Holt.

Carroll, J. L., & Wolpe, P. R. (1996). *Sexuality and gender in society.* New York: HarperCollins.

Carson, R. C., Butcher, J. N., & Coleman, J. C. (1988). *Abnormal psychology and modern life* (8th ed.). Glenview, IL: Scott, Foresman.

Carter, K. A., & Dinnel, D. L. (1997). *Conceptualization of self-esteem in collectivistic and individualistic cultures.* Bellingham: Western Washington University Press.

Cashmore, J. A., & Goodnow, J. J. (1986). Influences on Australian parents' values: Ethnicity versus sociometric status. *Journal of Cross-Cultural Psychology, 17*, 441–454.

Caspi, A., Henry, B., McGee, R. O., Moffitt, T. E., & Silva, P. A. (1995). Temperamental origins of child and adolescent behavior problems: From age 3 to age 15. *Child Development, 66*, 55–68.

Caspi, A., McClay, J., Moffitt, T. E., Mill, J., Martin, J., Craig, I. W., Taylor, A., & Poulton, R. (2002). *Science, 297*, 851–854.

Cauce, A. M., Domenech-Rodírigues, M., Paradise, M., Cochran, B. N., Shea, J. M., et al. (2002). Cultural and contextual influence in mental health help seeking: A focus on ethnic minority youth. *Journal of Counseling and Clinical Psychology, 70*, 44–55.

Caudill, W. (1988). Tiny dramas: Vocal communication between mother and infant in Japanese and American families. In G. Handel (Ed.), *Childhood socialization* (pp. 49–72). New York: Aldine de Gruyter.

Caudill, W., & Frost, L. (1974). A comparison of maternal care and infant behavior in Japanese-American, American, and Japanese families. In W. P. Lebra (Ed.), *Youth, socialization, and mental health: Vol. 3. Mental health research in Asia and the Pacific* (pp. 3–15). Honolulu: University Press of Hawaii.

Caudill, W., & Weinstein, H. (1969). Maternal care and infant behavior in Japan and America. *Psychiatry: Journal for the Study of Interpersonal Processes, 32*(1), 12–43.

Cederblad, M. (1988). Behavioural disorders in children from different cultures. *Acta Psychiatrica Scandinavia Supplementum, 344*, 85–92.

Cerroni-Long, E. L. (1985). Culture as communication: Defining the parameters of analysis. *Communication and Cognition, 18*(4), 379–392.

Chambless, D. L., Sanderson, W. C., Shoham, V., Bennett-Johnson, S., Pope, K. S., Crits-Christoph, P., Baker, M., Johnson, B., Woody, S. R., Sue, S. Beutler, L., Williams, D. A., & McCurry, S. (1996). An update on empirically validated therapies. *Clinical Psychologist, 49*, 5–18.

Chan, Y. M. (2000). Self-esteem: A cross-cultural comparison of British-Chinese, White British and Hong Kong Chinese children. *Educational Psychology, 20*(1), 59–74.

Chance, S. E., Kaslow, N. J., Summerville, M. B., & Wood, K. (1998). Suicidal behavior in African American individuals: Current status and future directions. *Cultural Diversity and Mental Health, 4*, 19–37.

Chandler, T. A., & Spies, C. J. (1996). Semantic differential comparisons of attributions and dimensions among respondents from seven nations. *Psychological Reports, 79*, 747–758.

Chandra, S. (1975). Some patterns of response on the Queensland test. *Australian Psychologist, 10*(2), 185–192.

Chao, R. K. (1994). Beyond parental control and authoritarian parenting style: Understanding Chinese parenting through the cultural notion of training. *Child Development, 65*, 1111–1119.

Chao, R. K. (1996). Chinese and European American mothers' beliefs about the role of parenting in children's school success. *Journal of Cross-Cultural Psychology, 27*(4), 403–423.

Chen, G. M. (1995). Differences in self-disclosure patterns among Americans versus Chinese: A comparative study. *Journal of Cross-Cultural Psychology, 26,* 84–91.

Chen, X., Dong, Q., & Zhou, H. (1997). Authoritative and authoritarian parenting practices and social and school performances in Chinese children. *International Journal of Behavioral Development, 21*(4), 855–873.

Cheng, D., Leong, F. T. L., & Geist, R. (1993). Cultural differences in psychological distress between Asian and Caucasian American college students. *Journal of Multicultural Counseling and Development, 21,* 182–190.

Cheung, F. M., Kwong, J. Y. Y., & Zhang, J. (2003). Clinical validation of the Chinese Personality Assessment Inventory. *Psychological Assessment, 15*(1), 89–100.

Cheung, F. M., & Leung, K. (1998). Indigenous personality measures: Chinese examples. *Journal of Cross-Cultural Psychology, 29*(1), 233–248.

Cheung, F. M., Leung, K., Fan, R. M., Song, W. Z., Zhang, J. X., & Zhang, J. P. (1996). Development of the Chinese Personality Assessment Inventory. *Journal of Cross-Cultural Psychology, 27,* 181–199.

Chinese Culture Connection. (1987). Chinese values and the search for culture-free dimensions of culture. *Journal of Cross-Cultural Psychology, 18,* 143–164.

Chisholm, J. (1983). *Navajo infancy.* New York: Aldine.

Cho, M. J., Moscicki, E. K., Narrow, W. E., Rae, D. S., Locke, B. Z., & Regier, D. A. (1993). Concordance between two measures of depression in the Hispanic Health and Nutrition Examination Survey. *Social Psychiatry and Psychiatric Epidemiology, 28*(4), 156–163.

Choe, H. (1994). Korea. In K. Hurrelmann (Ed.), *International handbook of adolescence* (pp. 246–256). Westport, CT: Greenwood Press.

Choi, S.-C., Kim, U., & Choi, S.-H. (1993). Indigenous analysis of collective representations: A Korean perspective. In U. Kim & J. W. Berry (Eds.), *Indigenous psychologies: Research and experience in cultural context* (pp. 193–210). Newbury Park, CA: Sage.

Church, A. T. (2000). Culture and personality: Toward an integrated cultural trait psychology. *Journal of Personality, 68,* 651–703.

Church, A. T., & Katigbak, M. S. (1988). Imposed-etic and emic measures of intelligence as predictors of early school performance of rural Philippine children. *Journal of Cross-Cultural Psychology, 19*(2), 164–177.

Church, A. T., Katigbak, M. S., & Reyes, J. A. S. (1996). Toward a taxonomy of trait adjectives in Filipino: Comparing personality lexicons across cultures. *European Journal of Personality, 10*(1), 3–24.

Church, A. T., & Lonner, W. J. (Eds.). (1998). The cross-cultural perspective in the study of personality: Rationale and current research. *Journal of Cross-Cultural Psychology, 29*(1), 32–62.

Church, A. T., Reyes, J. A. S., Katigbak, M. S., & Grimm, S. D. (1997). Filipino personality structure and the Big Five model: A lexical approach. *Journal of Personality, 65*(3), 477–528.

Claeys, W. (1967). The factorial intelligence structure of the Congolese at the beginning of their university studies. *Psychologica Belgica, 7,* 7–15.

Clark, M. L., & Person, W. (1982). Racial stereotypes revisited. *International Journal of Intercultural Relations, 6,* 381–392.

Clymer, E. C. (1995). The psychology of deafness: Enhancing self-concept in the deaf and hearing impaired. *Family Therapy, 22*(2), 113–120.

Coates, D. L. (1999). The cultured and culturing aspects of romantic experience in adolescence. In W. Furman, B. Brown, & C. Feiring (Eds.), *The development of romantic relationships in adolescence* (pp. 330–363). New York: Cambridge University Press.

Cogan, J. C., Bhalla, S. K., Sefa-Dedeh, A., & Rothblum, E. D. (1996). A comparison study of United States and African students on perceptions of obesity and thinness. *Journal of Cross-Cultural Psychology, 27,* 98–113.

Cohen, D., Nisbett, R. E., Bowdle, B. F., & Schwartz, N. (1996). Insult, aggression, and the southern culture of honor: An "experimental ethnography." *Journal of Personality and Social Psychology, 70*(5), 945–960.

Cohen, N. (1982). Same or different? A problem of identity in cross-cultural marriages. *Journal of Family Therapy, 4*(2), 177–199.

Cole, M. (1996). *Cultural psychology: A once and future discipline.* Cambridge, MA: Harvard University Press.

Cole, M., Gay, J., Glick, J. A., & Sharp, D. W. (1971). *The cultural context of learning and thinking: An exploration in experimental anthropology.* New York: Basic Books.

Cole, M., & Scribner, S. (1974). *Culture and thought: A psychological introduction.* New York: Wiley.

Coll, C. G. (1990). Developmental outcome of minority infants: A process-oriented look into our beginnings. *Child Development, 61*(2), 270–289.

Collins, A. W., Maccoby, E. E., Steinberg, L., Hetherington, E. M., & Bornstein, M. H. (2000). Contemporary research on parenting: The case for nature and nurture. *American Psychologist, 55*(2), 218–232.

Colvin, C., Matsumoto, D., Taylor, S., & Grogan, J. (1998, August). *An organizational typology for managing change.* Paper presented at the 24th International Congress of Applied Psychology, San Francisco.

Comas-Diaz, L. (1992). The future of psychotherapy with ethnic minorities. *Psychotherapy, 29,* 88–94.

Comas-Diaz, L., & Jacobsen, F. M. (1991). Ethnocultural transference and countertransference in the therapeutic dyad. *American Journal of Orthopsychiatry, 61,* 392–402.

Compas, B., Ey, S., & Grant, K. (1993). Taxonomy, assessment, and diagnosis of depression during adolescence. *Psychological Bulletin, 114,* 323–344.

Conroy, M., Hess, D. R., Azuma, H., & Kashiwagi, K. (1980). Maternal strategies for regulating children's behavior. *Journal of Cross-Cultural Psychology, 11*(2), 153–172.

Cook, P. (1994). Chronic illness beliefs and the role of social networks among Chinese, Indian, and Anglo-Celtic Canadians. *Journal of Cross-Cultural Psychology, 25*(4), 452–465.

Cortes, D. E. (2003). Idioms of distress, acculturation and depression: The Puerto Rican experience. In K. M. Chun, P. B. Organista, & G. Marin (Eds.), *Acculturation: Advances in theory, measurement, and applied research* (pp. 207–222). Washington DC: American Psychological Association.

Costa, P. T., Jr., & McCrae, R. R. (1989). *The NEO PI/FFI manual supplement*. Odessa, FL: Psychological Assessment Resources.

Cottrell, A. B. (1990). Cross-national marriages: A review of literature. *Journal of Comparative Family Studies, 21*(2), 151–169.

Cousins, S. D. (1989). Culture and self-perception in Japan and the United States. *Journal of Personality and Social Psychology, 56,* 124–131.

Crandall, C. S., & Martinez, R. (1996). Culture, ideology, and antifat attitudes. *Personality and Social Psychology Bulletin, 22*(11), 1165–1176.

Crijnen, A. A. M., Achenbach, T. M., & Verhulst, F. C. (1999). Problems reported by parents of children in multiple cultures: The Child Behavior Checklist syndrome constructs. *American Journal of Psychiatry, 156*(4), 569–574.

Crittenden, K. S. (1991). Asian self-effacement or feminine modesty? Attributional patterns of women university students in Taiwan. *Gender and Society, 5,* 98–117.

Crittenden, P. M. (2000). A dynamic-maturational exploration of the meaning of security and adaptation. In P. M. Crittenden & A. H. Claussen (Eds.), *The organization of attachment relationships: Maturation, culture and context* (pp. 358–383). Cambridge, UK: Cambridge University Press.

Crocker, J., & Lawrence, J. S. (1999). Social stigma and self-esteem: The role of contingencies of worth. In D. A. Prentice & D. T. Miller (Eds.), *Cultural divides: Understanding and overcoming group conflict* (pp. 364–392). New York: Russell Sage Foundation.

Crook, T. H., Youngjohn, J. R., Larrabee, G. J., & Salama, M. (1992). Aging and everyday memory: A cross-cultural study. *Neuropsychology, 6*(2), 123–136.

Croteau, D., & Hoynes, W. (2000). *Media/society: Industries, images and audiences* (2nd ed.). Thousand Oaks, CA: Sage.

Csikszentmihalyi, M. (1999). Implications of a systems perspective for the study of creativity. In R. J. Sternberg (Ed.), *Handbook of creativity* (pp. 313–335). New York: Cambridge University Press.

Cunningham, M. R., Roberts, A. R., Barbee, A. P., Druen, P. B., & Wu, C. (1995). "Their ideas of beauty are, on the whole, the same as ours": Consistency and variability in the cross-cultural perception of female physical attractiveness. *Journal of Personality and Social Psychology, 68*(2), 261–279.

Dabul, A. J., Bernal, M. E., & Knight, G. P. (1995). Allocentric and idiocentric self-description and academic achievement among Mexican American and Anglo American adolescents. *Journal of Social Psychology, 135*(5), 621–630.

Daibo, I., Murasawa, H., & Chou, Y. (1994). Attractive faces and affection of beauty: A comparison in preference of feminine facial beauty in Japan and Korea. *Japanese Journal of Research on Emotions, 1*(2), 101–123.

Dalal, K. A., Sharma, R., & Bisht, S. (1983). Causal attributions of ex-criminal tribal and urban children in India. *Journal of Social Psychology, 119,* 163–171.

Damond, M. E., Breur, N. L., & Pharr, A. E. (1993). The evaluation of setting and a culturally specific HIV/AIDS curriculum: HIV/AIDS knowledge and behavior intent of African American adolescents. *Journal of Black Psychology, 19*(2), 169–189.

Darwin, C. (1859). *The origin of species.* New York: Modern Library.

Darwin, C. (1872). *The expression of emotion in man and animals.* London: John Murray.

Darwin, C. (1998). *The expression of the emotions in man and animals* (P. Ekman, Ed.) (3rd ed.). New York: Oxford University Press. (Original work published 1872)

Dasen, P. R. (1975). Concrete operational development in three cultures. *Journal of Cross-Cultural Psychology, 6,* 156–172.

Dasen, P. R. (1982). Cross-cultural aspects of Piaget's theory: The competence–performance model. In L. L. Adler (Ed.), *Cross-cultural research at issue* (pp. 163–170). New York: Academic Press.

Dasen, P. R., Dembele, B., Ettien, K., Kabran, L., Kamagate, D., Koffi, D. A., & N'Guessan, A. (1985). N'glouele, l'intelligence chez les Baoule [N'glouele: Intelligence among the Ivory Coast Baoule]. *Archives de Psychologie, 53,* 293–324.

Dasen, P. R., Lavallee, M., & Retschitzki, J. (1979). Training conservation of quantity (liquids) in West African (Baoule) children. *International Journal of Psychology, 14,* 57–68.

Dasen, P. R., Ngini, L., & Lavallee, M. (1979). Cross-cultural training studies of concrete operations. In L. Eckensberger, Y. Poortinga, & W. Lonner (Eds.), *Cross-cultural contributions to psychology* (pp. 94–104). Amsterdam: Swets & Zeitlinger.

Dasgupta, S. D. (1998). Gender roles and cultural continuity in the Asian Indian immigrant community in the U.S. *Sex Roles, 38*(11–12), 953–974.

David, K. H., & Bochner, S. (1967). Teacher ratings of I.Q. and porteus maze scores of Pitjandjara children. *Perceptual and Motor Skills, 25*(2), 639–640.

Davies, I. R. L., Sowden, P. T., Jerrett, D. T., Jerrett, T., & Corbelt, G. G. (1998). A cross-cultural study of English and Setswana speakers on a colour triads task: A test of the Sapir-Whorf hypothesis. *British Journal of Psychology, 89*(1), 1–15.

Davis, F. G. (1991). *Who is black? One nation's definition.* University Park: Pennsylvania State University Press.

Davis, S. S., & Davis, D. A. (1989). *Adolescence in a Moroccan town.* New Brunswick, NJ: Rutgers.

De, B., & Singh, R. (1972). A cross-cultural study of the Maudley Personality Inventory and the Manifest Anxiety Scale. *Behaviorometric, 2*(1), 40–44.

Deck, L. P. (1968). Buying brains by the inch. *Journal of College and University Personnel Associations, 19,* 33–37.

De-Fruyt, F., & Mervielde, I. (1998). The assessment of the Big Five in the Dutch language domain. *Psychologica Belgica, 38*(1), 1–22.

Degler, C. (1971). *Neither black nor white: Slavery and race relations in Brazil and the United States.* New York: Macmillan.

Delgado, M. (1995). Hispanic natural support systems and alcohol and other drug services: Challenges and rewards for practice. *Alcoholism Treatment Quarterly, 12,* 17–31.

del Pino Perez, A., Meizoso, M. T., & Gonzalez, R. (1999). Validity of the structured interview for the assessment of Type A behavior pattern. *European Journal of Psychological Assessment, 15*(1), 39–48.

Denham, S. A., Renwick, S. M., & Holt, R. W. (1997). Working and playing together: Prediction of preschool social-emotional competence from mother-child interaction. *Child Development, 62*(2), 242–249.

DePaulo, B. M., Rosenthal, R., Eisenstat, R. A., Rogers, P. L., & Susan, F. (1978). Decoding discrepant nonverbal cues. *Journal of Personality and Social Psychology, 36*(3), 313–323.

DePaulo, B. M., Stone, J., & Lassiter, G. D. (1985). Deceiving and detecting deceit. In B. R. Schlenker (Ed.), *The self and social life* (pp. 323–370). New York: McGraw-Hill.

De Raad, B., & Boddema-Winesemius, M. (1992). Factors in the assortment of human mates: Differential preferences in Germany and the Netherlands. *Personality and Individual Differences, 13,* 103–114.

De Raad, B., Hendriks, A. J., & Hofstee, W. K. (1992, October). Towards a refined structure of personality traits. *European Journal of Personality, 6*(4), 301–319.

De Raad, B., Perugini, M., Hrebickova, M., & Szarota, P. (1998, January). Lingua franca of personality: Taxonomies and structures based on the psycholexical approach. *Journal of Cross-Cultural Psychology, 29*(1), 212–232.

De Raad, B., Perugini, M., & Szirmak, Z. (1997). In pursuit of a cross-lingual reference structure of personality traits: Comparisons among five languages. *European Journal of Personality, 11*(3), 167–185.

de Silva, S., Stiles, D., & Gibbons, J. (1992). Girls' identity formation in the changing social structure of Sri Lanka. *Journal of Genetic Psychology, 153*(2), 211–220.

Desjarlais, R. R. (1991). Dreams, divination, and Yolmo ways of knowing. *Dreaming: Journal of the Association for the Study of Dreams, 1*(3), 211–224.

Devan, G. S. (2001). Culture and the practice of group psychotherapy in Singapore. *International Journal of Groups Psychotherapy, 51,* 571–577.

Devereux, C. E., Jr., Bronfenbrenner, U., & Suci, G. (1962). Patterns of parent behaviour in the United States of America and the Federal Republic of Germany: A cross-national comparison. *International Social Science Journal, 14,* 488–506.

Devine, P. G. (1989). Stereotypes and prejudice: Their automatic and controlled components. *Journal of Personality and Social Psychology, 56,* 5–18.

Devine, P. G., & Malpass, R. S. (1985). Orienting strategies in differential face recognition. *Personality and Social Psychology Bulletin, 11*(1), 33–40.

DeVries, M. W. (1987). Cry babies, culture, and catastrophe: Infant temperament among the Masai. In N. Scheper-Hughes (Ed.), *Child survival: Anthropological approaches to the treatment and maltreatment of children* (pp. 165–185). Boston: Reidel.

DeVries, M. W. (1989). Difficult temperament: A universal and culturally embedded concept. In W. B. Carey & S. C. McDevitt (Eds.), *Clinical and educational applications of temperament research* (pp. 81–85). Amsterdam: Swets & Zeitlinger.

DeWolff, M. S., & van IJzendoorn, M. H. (1997). Sensitivity and attachment: A meta-analysis on parental antecedents of infant attachment. *Child Development, 68,* 571–591.

Dhawan, N., Roseman, I. J., Naidu, R. K., Komilla, T., & Rettek, S. I. (1995). Self-concepts across two cultures. *Journal of Cross-Cultural Psychology, 26*(6), 606–621.

Diaz-Loving, R. (1998, January). Contributions of Mexican ethnopsychology to the resolution of the etic-emic dilemma in personality. *Journal of Cross Cultural Psychology, 29*(1), 104–118.

Diener, E., & Diener, M. (1995). Cross-cultural correlates of life satisfaction and self-esteem. *Journal of Personality and Social Psychology, 68*(4), 653–663.

Digman, J. M., & Shmelyov, A. G. (1996, August). The structure of temperament and personality in Russian children. *Journal of Personality and Social Psychology, 71*(2), 341–351.

DiMartino, C. E. (1994). Appraising social dilemmas: A cross-cultural study of Sicilians, Sicilian Americans, and Americans. *Journal of Cross-Cultural Psychology, 25*(2), 165–180.

Dinges, N. G., & Hull, P. (1992). Personality, culture, and international studies. In D. Lieberman (Ed.), *Revealing the world: An interdisciplinary reader for international studies.* Dubuque, IA: Kendall-Hunt.

Dion, K. K. (1986). Stereotyping based on physical attractiveness: Issues and conceptual perspectives. In C. P. Herman, M. P. Zanna, & E. T. Higgins (Eds.), *Ontario symposium on personality and social psychology* (Vol. 3). Hillsdale, NJ: Erlbaum.

Dion, K. K., & Dion, K. L. (1993a). Gender and ethnocultural comparisons in styles of love. *Psychology of Women Quarterly, 17,* 463–473.

Dion, K. K., & Dion, K. L. (1993b). Individualistic and collectivistic perspectives on gender and the cultural context of love and intimacy. *Journal of Social Issues, 49,* 53–69.

Doi, K. (1982). Two dimensional theory of achievement motivation. *Japanese Journal of Psychology, 52,* 344–350.

Doi, K. (1985). The relation between the two dimensions of achievement motivation and personality of male university students. *Japanese Journal of Psychology, 56,* 107–110.

Doi, T. (1973). *The anatomy of dependence.* Tokyo: Kodansha.

Domino, G. (1992). Cooperation and competition in Chinese and American children. *Journal of Cross-Cultural Psychology, 23*(4), 456–467.

Domino, G., & Lin, W. (1993). Cancer metaphors: Taiwan and the United States. *International Journal of Psychology, 28*(1), 45–56.

Dosanjh, J. S., & Ghuman, P. A. S. (1996). The cultural context of child rearing: A study of indigenous and British Punjabis. *Early Child Development and Care, 126,* 39–55.

Dosanjh, J. S., & Ghuman, P. A. S. (1997). Punjabi childrearing in Britain: Development of identity, religion and bilingualism. *Childhood, 4*(3), 285–303.

Douki, S., Moussaoui, D., & Kacha, F. (1987). *Handbook of psychiatry of expert Maghrebin.* Paris: Masson.

Draguns, J. (1997). Abnormal behavior patterns across cultures: Implications for counseling and psychotherapy. *International Journal of Intercultural Relations, 21*(2), 213–248.

Duckitt, J. (1992). Psychology and prejudice: A historical analysis and integrative framework. *American Psychologist, 47,* 1182–1194.

Duda, J. L., & Allison, M. T. (1989). The attributional theory of achievement motivation: Cross-cultural considerations. *International Journal of Intercultural Relations, 13,* 37–55.

Dunn, J. (1988). *The beginnings of social understanding.* Cambridge, MA: Harvard University Press.

Durie, M. H. (1997). Maori cultural identity and its implications for mental health services. *International Journal of Mental Health, 26*(3), 23–35.

Durrett, M. E., Otaki, M., & Richards, P. (1984). Attachment and mothers' perception of support from the father. *Journal of the International Society for the Study of Behavioral Development, 7,* 167–176.

Dyal, J. A. (1984). Cross-cultural research with the locus of control construct. In H. M. Lefcourt (Ed.), *Research with the locus of control construct* (Vol. 3, pp. 209–306). New York: Academic Press.

Eagly, A., Ashmore, R. D., Makhijani, M. G., & Longo, L. C. (1991). What is beautiful is good, but . . . : A meta-analytic review of research on the physical attractiveness stereotype. *Psychological Bulletin, 110*(1), 109–128.

Earley, P. C. (1989). Social loafing and collectivism: A comparison of the United States and the People's Republic of China. *Administrative Science Quarterly, 34,* 565–581.

Early, K. E., & Akers, R. L. (1993). "It's a White thing": An exploration of beliefs about suicide in the African American community. *Deviant Behavior, 14,* 227–296.

Eberhardt, J. L., & Randall, J. L. (1997). The essential notion of race. *Psychological Science, 8*(3), 198–203.

Ebrahimpour, M., & Johnson, J. L. (1992). Quality, vendor evaluation and organizational performance: A comparison of U.S. and Japanese firms. *Journal of Business Research, 25,* 129–142.

EchoHawk, M. (1997). Suicide: The scourge of Native American people. *Suicide and Life Threatening Behavior, 27*(1), 60–67.

Edman, J. L., & Kameoka, A. K. (1997). Cultural differences in illness schemas: An analysis of Filipino and American illness attributions. *Journal of Cross-Cultural Psychology, 28*(3), 252–265.

Edwards, P. K. (1981). Race, residence, and leisure style: Some policy implications. *Leisure Sciences, 4*(2), 95–112.

Eisenberg, D. M., Davis, R. B., Ettner, S. L., Appel, S., Wilkey, S., Van Rompay, M., & Kessler, R. C. (1998). Trends in alternative medicine use in the United States, 1990–1997: Results of a follow-up national survey. *Journal of the American Medical Association, 280,* 1569–1575.

Ekman, K. L. (1982). A comparative study of value priorities in a sample of United States Air Force personnel and their spouses. *Dissertation Abstracts International, 43*(6-B), 2037.

Ekman, P. (1972). Universal and cultural differences in facial expression of emotion. In J. R. Cole (Ed.), *Nebraska symposium on motivation, 1971* (pp. 207–283). Lincoln: University of Nebraska Press.

Ekman, P. (1973). Universal facial expressions in emotion. *Studia Psychologica, 15*(2), 140–147.

Ekman, P. (1994). Strong evidence for universals in facial expressions: A reply to Russell's mistaken critique. *Psychological Bulletin, 115,* 268–287.

Ekman, P., & Friesen, W. V. (1969). The repertoire of nonverbal behavior: Categories, origins, usage, and coding. *Semiotica, 1,* 49–98.

Ekman, P., & Friesen, W. V. (1971). Constants across cultures in the face and emotion. *Journal of Personality and Social Psychology, 17,* 124–129.

Ekman, P., & Friesen, W. V. (1986). A new pan-cultural expression of emotion. *Motivation and Emotion, 10,* 159–168.

Ekman, P., Friesen, W. V., & Ellsworth, P. (1972). *Emotion in the human face.* New York: Garland.

Ekman, P., Friesen, W., LeCompete, W. L., Ricci-Bitti, P. E., Tomita, M., Tzavaras, A., O'Sullivan, M., Diacoyanni-Tarlatzis, I., Krause, R., Pitcairn, T., Scherer, K., Chan, A., & Heider, K. (1987). Universals and cultural differences in the judgements of facial expressions of emotion. *Journal of Personality and Social Psychology, 53*(4), 712–717.

Ekman, P., & Heider, K. G. (1988). The universality of a contempt expression: A replication. *Motivation and Emotion, 12,* 17–22.

Ekman, P., Levenson, R., & Friesen, W. V. (1983). Autonomic nervous system activity distinguishes among emotions. *Science, 221,* 1208–1210.

Ekman, P., O'Sullivan, M., & Matsumoto, D. (1991a). Confusions about context in the judgment of facial expression: A reply to "Contempt and the Relativity Thesis." *Motivation and Emotion, 15,* 169–176.

Ekman, P., O'Sullivan, M., & Matsumoto, D. (1991b). Contradictions in the study of contempt: What's it all about? *Motivation and Emotions, 15,* 293–296.

Ekman, P., Sorenson, E. R., & Friesen, W. V. (1969). Pan-cultural elements in facial displays of emotion. *Science, 164,* 86–94.

Elbedour, S., Shulman, S., & Kedem, P. (1997). Adolescent intimacy. *Journal of Cross-Cultural Psychology, 28,* 5–22.

Eley, T. C. (1997). General genes: A new theme in developmental psychopathology. *Current Directions in Psychological Science, 6*(4), 90–95.

El-Islam, M. F. (1983). Cultural change and intergenerational relationships in Arabian families. *International Journal of Family Psychiatry, 4,* 321–329.

El-Islam, M. F. (1982). Arabic cultural psychiatry. *Transcultural Psychiatric Research Review, 19,* 5–24.

Elkind, D. (1978). Understanding the young adolescent. *Adolescence, 13,* 127–134.

Ellis, A. (1962). *Reason and emotion in psychotherapy.* Secaucus, NJ: Prentice-Hall.

Ellis, B., Kimmel, H., Diaz-Guerrero, R., Canas, J., & Bajo, M. (1994). Love and power in Mexico, Spain, and the United States. *Journal of Cross-Cultural Psychology, 25*(4), 525–540.

Emory, E. K., & Toomey, K. (1991). Implications for neuropsychology and temperament research. In J. H. Johnson & S. B. Johnson (Eds.), *Advances in child health psychology* (pp. 331–344). Gainsville, FL: J. Hillis Miller Health Science Center.

Enriquez, V. G. (1992). *From colonial to liberation psychology: The Philippine experience.* Manila: De La Salle University Press.

Enz, C. (1986). *Power and shared values in the corporate culture.* Ann Arbor: University of Michigan Press.

Ervin, S. M. (1964). Language and TAT content in bilinguals. *Journal of Abnormal and Social Psychology, 68,* 500–507.

Escobar, J. (1998). Immigration and mental health: Why are immigrants better off? *Archives of General Psychiatry, 55*(9), 781–782.

Espin, O. M. (1993). Feminist theory: Not for or by white women only. *Counseling Psychologist, 21,* 103–108.

Espin, O. M. (1997). *Latina realities: Essays on healing, migration, and sexuality.* Boulder, CO: Westview.

Evans, J. L., & Segall, M. H. (1969). Learning to classify by color and function: A study of concept discovery by Ganda children. *Journal of Social Psychology, 77,* 35–55.

Everett, F., Proctor, N., & Cartmell, B. (1983) Providing psychological services to American Indian children and families. *Research & Practice, 14,* 588–603.

Exline, R. V., Jones, P., & Maciorowski, K. (1977). *Race, affiliative-conflict theory and mutual visual attention during conversation.* Paper presented at the American Psychological Association meeting in San Francisco.

Eysenck, H. J. (1983). Is there a paradigm in personality research? *Journal of Research in Personality, 17*(4), 369–397.

Eysenck, S. B. G., & Abdel-Khalek, A. M. (1989). A cross cultural study of personality: Egyptian and English children. *International Journal of Psychology, 24,* 1–11.

Eysenck, S. B. G., Baban, P., Derevenco, P., & Pitariu, H. (1989). A cross cultural study of personality: Romanian and English adults. *Revue Roumaine des Science Sociales Serie de Psychologie, 33*(1), 75–80.

Eysenck, S. B. G., & Chan, J. (1982). A comparative study of personality in adults and children: Hong Kong vs. England. *Personality and Individual Differences, 3,* 153–160.

Eysenck, S. B. G., Makaremi, A., & Barrett, P. T. (1994). A cross-cultural study of personality: Iranian and English children. *Personality and Individual Differences, 16*(2), 203–210.

Fabrega, H. (1989). Language, culture, and the neurobiology of pain: A theoretical exploration. *Behavioral Neurology, 2* (4), 235–260.

Fagot, B., Leinbach, M.D. & Hagen, R. (1986). Gender labeling and adoption of sex-typed behaviors. *Developmental Psychology, 22,* 440–443.

Farver, J. M., & Howes, C. (1988). Cross-cultural differences in social interaction: A comparison of American and Indonesian children. *Journal of Cross-Cultural Psychology, 19*(2), 203–215.

Farver, J. M., Kim, Y. K., & Lee-Shin, Y. (2000). Within cultural differences: Examining individual differences in Korean American and European American preschoolers' social pretend play. *Journal of Cross-Cultural Psychology, 31*(5), 583–602.

Farver, J. M., Welles-Nystroem, B., Frosch, D. L., Wimbarti, S., & Hoppe-Graff, S. (1997). Toy stories: Aggression in children's narratives in the United States, Sweden, Germany, and Indonesia. *Journal of Cross-Cultural Psychology, 28*(4), 393–420.

Feather, N. T. (1986). Value systems across cultures: Australia and China. *International Journal of Psychology, 21,* 697–715.

Fehring, R. J., Cheever, K. H., German, K., & Philpot, C. (1998). Religiosity and sexual activity among older adolescents. *Journal of Religion and Health, 37,* 229–239.

Feingold, A. (1992). Good-looking people are not what we think. *Psychological Bulletin, 111*(2), 304–341.

Feist, J., & Brannon, L. (1988). *Health psychology: An introduction to behavior and health.* Belmont, CA: Wadsworth.

Fejes, F. (1992). "Masculinity as fact: A review of empirical mass communication research on masculinity." In S. Craig (Ed.), *Men, masculinity, and the media,* pp. 9–22. Thousand Oaks, CA: Sage.

Fernandez-Dols, J. M., & Ruiz-Belda, M. A. (1995). Are smiles a sign of happiness? Gold medal winners at the Olympic games. *Journal of Personality and Social Psychology, 69,* 1113–1110.

Fernandez-Dols, J. M., Sanchez, F. & Carrera, P. (1997). Are spontaneous expressions and emotions linked? An experimental test of coherence. *Journal of Nonverbal Behavior, 21*(3), 163–177.

Ferrante, J. (1992). *Sociology: A global perspective.* Belmont, CA: Wadsworth.

Festinger, L., Schachter, S., & Back, K. (1950). *Social pressures in informal groups: A study of human factors in housing.* New York: Harper.

Fields, J. (2001). Living arrangements of children: Fall 1996. In U.S. Bureau of the Census, *Current population reports* (pp. 70–74). Washington, DC: Government Printing Office.

Figueroa, R.A. (1980). Field dependence, ethnicity and cognitive styles. *Hispanic Journal of Behavioral Sciences, 2*(1), 35–42.

Filardo, E. K. (1996). Gender patterns in African American and White adolescents' social interactions in same-race, mixed-gender groups. *Journal of Personality and Social Psychology, 71*(1), 71–82.

Fishman, J. A. (1960). A systematization of the Whorfian hypothesis. *Behavioral Science, 5,* 323–339.

Fitzgerald, M. H., Mullavey-O'Byrne, C., & Clemson, L. (2001). Families and nursing home placements: A cross-cultural study. *Journal of Cross-Cultural Gerontology, 16*(4), 333–351.

Flanagan, O. (2000). *Dreaming souls: Sleep, dreams, and the evolution of the conscious mind.* Oxford University Press.

Fletcher, J. M., Todd, J., & Satz, P. (1975). Culture fairness of three intelligence tests and a short form procedure. *Psychological Reports, 37,* (3, Pt 2), 1255–1262.

Flores, E., Eyre, S. L., & Millstein, S. G. (1998). Sociocultural beliefs related to sex among Mexican American adolescents. *Hispanic Journal of Behavioral Sciences, 20* (1), 60–82.

Forgas, J. P. (1992). On mood and peculiar people: Affect and person typicality in impression formation. *Journal of Personality & Social Psychology, 62*(5), 863–875.

Forgas, J. P. (1994). The role of emotion in social judgments: An introductory review and an affect infusion model (AIM). *European Journal of Social Psychology, 24,* 1–24.

Forgas, J. P., & Bond, M. H. (1985). Cultural influences on the perceptions of interaction episodes. *Personality and Social Psychology Bulletin, 11*(1), 75–88.

Forgas, J. P., & Bower, H. G. (1987). Mood effects on person-perception judgments. *Journal of Personality and Social Psychology, 53*(1), 53–60.

Forgas, J. P., & Fiedler, K. (1996). Us and them: Mood effects on intergroup discrimination. *Journal of Personality and Social Psychology, 70,* 28–40.

Forgas, J. P., Furnham, A., & Frey, D. (1989). Cross-national differences in attributions of wealth and economic success. *Journal of Social Psychology, 129,* 643–657.

Forgas, J. P., & Moylan, J. S. (1991). Affective influences on stereotype judgements. *Cognition and Emotion, 5*(5/6), 379–395.

Forgas, J. P., & O'Driscoll, M. (1984). Cross-cultural and demographic differences in the perception of nations. *Journal of Cross-Cultural Psychology, 15*(2), 199–222.

Franz, C. E., & White, K. M. (1985). Individuation and attachment in personality development: Extending Erickson's theory. *Journal of Personality, 53*(2), 224–256.

Freedman, D. (1974). *Human infancy: An evolutionary perspective.* Hillsdale, NJ: Erlbaum.

Freud, S. (1961). *The interpretation of dreams.* New York: Science Editions. (Original work published 1900)

Friedman, H. S. (1978). The relative strength of verbal versus nonverbal cues. *Personality and Social Psychology Bulletin, 4*(1), 147–150.

Friedman, M., & Rosenman, R. H. (1974). *Type A behavior and your heart.* New York: Knopf.

Friesen, W. V. (1972). *Cultural differences in facial expressions in a social situation: An experimental test of the concept of display rules.* Unpublished doctoral dissertation, University of California, San Francisco.

Frome, P., & Eccles, J. (1996, March). *Gender-role identity and self-esteem.* Paper presented at the biennial meeting of the Society for Research on Adolescence, Boston.

Fuligni, A., & Stevenson, H. (1995). Time-use and mathematics achievement among American, Chinese, and Japanese high school students. *Child Development, 66,* 830–842.

Furnham, A. (1984). Value systems and anomie in three cultures. *International Journal of Psychology, 19,* 565–579.

Furnham, A., & Alibhai, N. (1983). Cross-cultural differences in the perception of female body shapes. *Psychology Medicine, 13,* 829–837.

Furnham, A., & Baguma, P. (1994). Cross-cultural differences in the evaluations of male and female body shapes. *International Journal of Eating Disorders, 15,* 81–89.

Furnham, A., Bond, M., Heaven, P., & Hilton, D. (1993). A comparison of Protestant work ethic beliefs in thirteen nations. *Journal of Social Psychology, 133*(2), 185–197.

Furnham, A., & Singh, A. (1986). Memory for information about sex differences. *Sex Roles, 15,* 479–486.

Gabrenya, W. K., Jr., Wang, Y., & Latané, B. (1985). Social loafing on an optimizing task: Cross-cultural differences among Chinese and Americans. *Journal of Cross-Cultural Psychology, 16,* 223–242.

Galambos, N., Peterson, A., Richards, M., & Gitelson, I. (1985). The Attitudes Towards Women Scale for Adolescents (AWSA): A study of reliability and validity. *Sex Roles, 5/6,* 343–356.

Galati, D., & Sciaky, R. (1995). The representation of antecedents of emotions in northern and southern Italy. *Journal of Cross-Cultural Psychology, 26*(2), 123–140.

Gallup, G. W., & Bezilla, R. (1992). *The religious life of young Americans.* Princeton, NJ: Gallup Institute.

Garcia Coll, C. T. (1990). Developmental outcomes of minority infants: A process oriented look at our beginnings. *Child Development, 61,* 270–289.

Garcia Coll., C. T., Meyer, E. C., & Brillon, L. (1995). Ethnic and minority parenting. In M. H. Bornstein & H. Marc (Eds.), *Handbook of parenting: Vol. 2. Biology and ecology of parenting* (pp. 189–209). Mahwah, NJ: Erlbaum.

Garcia Coll, C. T., Sepkoski, C., & Lester, B. M. (1981). Cultural and biomedical correlates of neonatal behavior. *Developmental Psychobiology, 14,* 147–154.

Gardner, H. (1983). *Frames of mind.* New York: Basic Books.

Garro, L. C. (1986). Language, memory, and focality: A reexamination. *American Anthropologist, 88*(1), 128–136.

Ge, X., Conger, R., Cadoret, R., Neiderhiser, J., Yates, W., Throughton, E., & Stewart, M. (1996). The developmental interface between nature and nurture: A mutual influence model of child antisocial behavior and parent behaviors. *Developmental Psychology, 32,* 574–589.

Geary, D. C. (1996). International differences in mathematical achievement: Their nature, causes, and consequences. *Current Directions in Psychological Science, 5*(5), 133–137.

Geen, R. G. (1994). Social psychological. In M. Hersen & R. T. Ammerman (Eds.), *Handbook of aggressive and destructive behavior in psychiatric patients* (pp. 51–64). New York: Plenum.

Geertz, C. (1973). *The interpretation of cultures.* New York: Basic Books.

Geertz, C. (1975). From the natives' point of view: On the nature of anthropological understanding. *American Scientist, 63,* 47–53.

Gelfand, M. J. & Dyer, N. (2000). A cultural perspective on negotiation: Progress, pitfalls, and prospects. *Applied Psychology: An International Review, 49*(1), 62–99.

Georgas, J. (1989). Changing family values in Greece: From collectivist to individualist. *Journal of Cross-Cultural Psychology, 20,* 80–91.

Georgas, J. (1991). Intrafamily acculturation of values in Greece. *Journal of Cross-Cultural Psychology, 22,* 445–457.

Gerber, E. (1975). *The cultural patterning of emotions in Samoa.* Unpublished doctoral dissertation, University of California, San Diego.

Gergen, K. J., Gulerce, A., Lock, A., & Misra, G. (1996). Psychological science in cultural context. *American Psychologist, 51*(5), 496–503.

Gerstner, C. R., & Day, D. V. (1994, Summer). Cross cultural comparison of leadership prototypes. *Leadership Quarterly, 5*(2), 121–134.

Gibbons, J., Bradford, R., & Stiles, D.A. (1989). Madrid adolescents express interest in gender roles and work possibilities. *Journal of Early Adolescence, 9*(1–2), 125–141.

Gibbons, J., Stiles, D. A., Schnellman, J. D., & Morales-Hidalgo, I. (1990). Images of work, gender, and social commitment among Guatemalan adolescents. *Journal of Early Adolescence, 10*(1), 89–103.

Gibbons, J., Stiles, D. A., & Shkodriani, G. M. (1991). Adolescents' attitudes toward family and gender roles: An international comparison. *Sex Roles, 25*(11–12), 625–643.

Gilbert, D. T., & Hixon, J. G. (1991). The trouble of thinking: Activation and application of stereotypic beliefs. *Journal of Personality and Social Psychology, 60*(4), 509–517.

Gilbert, G. M. (1951). Stereotype persistence and change among college students. *Journal of Abnormal and Social Psychology, 46,* 245–254.

Gilligan, C. (1982). *In a different voice: Psychological theory and women's development.* Cambridge, MA: Harvard University Press.

Gim, R. H., Atkinson, D. R., & Kim, S. J. (1991). Asian-American acculturation, counselor ethnicity and cultural sensitivity, and ratings of counselors. *Journal of Counseling Psychology, 38,* 57–62.

Gitter, A. G., Black, H., & Fishman, J. E. (1975). Effect of race, sex, nonverbal communication and verbal communication on perception of leadership. *Sociology and Social Research, 60*(1), 46–57.

Gladwin, H., & Gladwin, C. (1971). Estimating market conditions and profit expectations of fish sellers at Cape Coast, Ghana. In G. Dalton (Ed.), *Studies in economic anthropology* (Anthropological Studies No. 7, pp. 122–143). Washington, DC: American Anthropological Association.

Gladwin, T. (1970). *East is a big bird: Navigation and logic on Puluwat Atoll.* Cambridge, MA: Harvard University Press.

Glaser, S. R. (1983, November). *Assessing organizational culture: An interpretive approach.* Paper presented at the annual meeting of the Speech Communication Association, Washington, DC.

Gleason, H. A. (1961). *An introduction to descriptive linguistics.* New York: Holt, Rinehart & Winston.

Glover, G. (2001). Parenting in Native American families. In N. B. Webb (Ed.), *Culturally diverse parent-child and family relationships: A guide for social workers and other practitioners* (pp. 205–231). New York: Columbia University Press.

Goater, N., King, M., & Cole, E. (1999). Ethnicity and outcome of psychosis. *British Journal of Psychiatry, 175,* 34–42.

Goh, S. E., Ong, S. B., & Subramaniam, M. (1993). Eating disorders in Hong Kong. *British Journal of Psychiatry, 162,* 276–277.

Goldman, A. (1992). Intercultural training of Japanese for U.S.–Japanese interorganizational communication. *International Journal of Intercultural Relations, 16,* 195–215.

Goldman, A. (1994). The centrality of "ningensei" to Japanese negotiating and interpersonal relationships: Implications for U.S.–Japanese communication. *International Journal of Intercultural Relations, 18*(1), 29–54.

Goodnow, J. (1988). Parents' ideas, actions and feelings: Models and methods from developmental and social psychology. *Child Development, 59,* 289–320.

Goodwin, R. (1990). Sex differences among partner preferences: Are the sexes really very similar? *Sex Roles, 23,* 501–503.

Goodwin, R., & Lee, I. (1994). Taboo topics among Chinese and English friends. *Journal of Cross-Cultural Psychology, 25*(3), 325–338.

Goody, J. R. (1968). *Literacy in traditional societies.* Cambridge, UK: Cambridge University Press.

Goody, J. R. (1977). *The domestication of the savage mind.* Cambridge, UK: Cambridge University Press.

Goossens, L. (1994). Belgium. In K. Hurrelmann (Ed.), *International handbook of adolescence* (pp. 51–64). Westport, CT: Greenwood Press.

Gordon, R. A. (2001). Eating disorders East and West: A culture-bound syndrome unbound. In M. Nasser & M. A. Katzman (Eds.), *Eating disorders and cultures in transition* (pp. 1–16). New York: Brunner-Routledge.

Gorman, J. C. (1998). Parenting attitudes and practices of immigrant Chinese mothers of adolescents. *Family*

Relations: Interdisciplinary Journal of Applied Family Studies, 47(1), 73–80.

Gottfredson, L. S. (1994). The science and politics of race-norming. *American Psychologist, 49*(1), 955–963.

Graham, J. L. (1983). Brazilian, Japanese, and American Business Negotiations. *Journal of International Business Studies, 14,* 47–61.

Graham, J. L. (1984). *Smart bargaining: Doing business with the Japanese.* Cambridge, MA: Ballinger.

Graham, J. L. (1993). The Japanese negotiation style: Characteristics of a distinct approach. *Negotiation Journal, 9*(2), 123–140.

Graham, J. L., & Andrews, J. D. (1987). A holistic analysis of Japanese and American business negotiations. *Analysis of Business Negotiations, 24*(4), 63–77.

Graham, J. L., Evenko, L. I., & Rajan, M. N. (1992). A empirical comparison of Soviet and American business negotiations. *Journal of International Business Studies, 23,* 387–418.

Graham, J. L., Kim, D. K., Lin, C-Y., & Robinson, M. (1988). Buyer-seller negotiations around the Pacific rim: Differences in fundamental exchange processes. *Journal of Consumer Research, 15*(1), 48–54.

Graham, P., Rutter, M., & George, S. (1973). Temperamental characteristics as predictors of behavior disorders in children. *American Journal of Orthopsychiatry, 43*(3), 328–339.

Graham, S. (1984). Communicating sympathy and anger to black and white children: The cognitive (attributional) consequences of affective cues. *Journal of Personality and Social Psychology, 47*(1), 40–54.

Graham, S. (1992). Most of the subjects were white and middle-class: Trends in published research on African Americans in selected APA journals, 1970–1989. *American Psychologist, 47,* 629–639.

Graham, S., & Long, A. (1986). Race, class, and the attributional process. *Journal of Educational Psychology, 78,* 4–13.

Greenberg, J., Pyszczynski, T., Solomon, S., Rosenblatt, A., Veeder, M., Kirkland, S., & Lyon, D. (1990). Evidence for terror management theory: II. The effects of mortality salience on reactions to those who threaten or bolster the cultural worldview. *Journal of Personality and Social Psychology, 58,* 308–318.

Greenfield, P. M. (1997). You can't take it with you: Why ability assessments don't cross cultures. *American Psychologist, 52,* 1115–1124.

Greenfield, P. M., Reich, L. C., & Oliver, R. R. (1966). On culture and equivalence II. In J. S. Bruner, R. R. Oliver, & P. M. Greenfield (Eds.), *Studies in cognitive growth* (pp. 270–318). New York: Wiley.

Grisaru, N., Budowski, D., & Witztum, E. (1997). Possession by the "zar" among Ethiopian immigrants to Israel: Psychopathology or culture-bound syndrome? *Psychopathology, 30*(4), 223–233.

Grossmann, K., Grossmann, K. E., Spangler, S., Suess, G., & Unzner, L. (1985). Maternal sensitivity and newborn attachment orientation responses as related to quality of attachment in northern Germany. In I. Bretherton & E. Waters (Eds.), *Growing points of attachment theory. Monographs of the Society of Research in Child Development, 50* (1–2, Serial No. 209).

Grossmann, K. E., & Grossmann, K. (1990). The wider concept of attachment in cross-cultural research. *Human Development, 33*(1), 31–47.

Guarnaccia, P. J., Rivera, M., Franco, F., & Neighbors, C. (1996). The experiences of *ataques de nervios*: Towards an anthropology of emotions in Puerto Rico. *Culture, Medicine, and Psychiatry, 20,* 343–367.

Gudykunst, W. B. (1993). Toward a theory of effective interpersonal and intergroup communication: An anxiety/uncertainty management (AUM) perspective. In R. L. Wiseman, J. Koester, et al. (Eds.), *International and intercultural communication annual: Vol. 17. Intercultural communication competence* (pp. 33–71). Newbury Park, CA: Sage.

Gudykunst, W. B., Gao, G., Nishida, T., Bond, M. H., et al. (1989). A cross cultural comparison of self-monitoring. *Communication Research Reports, 6*(1), 7–12.

Gudykunst, W. B., Gao, G., Schmidt, K. L., Nishida, T., Bond, M. L., Leung, K., Wang, G., & Barraclough, R.A. (1992). The influence of individualism-collectivism, self-monitoring, and predicted-outcome value on communication in ingroup and outgroup relationships. *Journal of Cross-Cultural Psychology, 23*(2), 196–213.

Gudykunst, W. B., Matsumoto, Y., Ting-Toomey, S., Nishida, T., Kim, K., & Heyman, S. (1996). The influence of cultural individualism-collectivism, self construals, and individual values on communication styles across cultures. *Human Communication Research, 22*(4), 510–543.

Gudykunst, W. B., & Nishida, T. (1984). Individual and cultural influences on uncertainty reduction. *Communication Monographs, 51,* 23–36.

Gudykunst, W. B., & Nishida, T. (1986a). Attributional confidence in low- and high-context cultures. *Human Communication Research, 12,* 525–549.

Gudykunst, W. B., & Nishida, T. (1986b). The influence of cultural variability on perceptions of communication behavior associated with relationship terms. *Human Communication Research, 13,* 147–166.

Gudykunst, W. B., & Shapiro, R. B. (1996). Communication in everyday interpersonal and intergroup encounters. *International Journal of Intercultural Relations, 20*(1), 19–45.

Gudykunst, W. B., Sodetani, L. L., & Sonoda, K. T. (1987). Uncertainty reduction in Japanese-American/Caucasian relationships in Hawaii. *Western Journal of Speech Communication, 51,* 256–278.

Gudykunst, W. B., & Ting-Toomey, S. (1988). Culture and affective communication. [Special Issue: Communication and affect.] *American Behavioral Scientist, 31,* 384–400.

Gudykunst, W. B., Yang, S., & Nishida, T. (1987). Cultural differences in self-consciousness and self-monitoring. *Communications Research, 14*(1), 7–34.

Gudykunst, W. B., Yoon, Y., & Nishida, T. (1987). The influence of individualism-collectivism on perceptions of communication in ingroup and outgroup relationships. *Communication Monographs, 54,* 295–306.

Guilford, J. P. (1985). The structure of intellect model. In B. B. Wolman (Ed.), *Handbook of intelligence: Theories, measurements, and applications* (pp. 225–265). New York: Wiley.

Guinn, B. (1998). Acculturation and health locus of control among Mexican American adolescents. *Hispanic Journal of Behavioral Sciences, 20*(4), 492–499.

Guisinger, S., & Blatt, S. J. (1994). Individuality and relatedness: Evolution of a fundamental dialectic. *American Psychologist, 49,* 104–111.

Gumperz, J. J., & Levinson, S. C. (Eds.). (1996). *Rethinking linguistic relativity.* Cambridge, UK: Cambridge University Press.

Gurin, P. (1997). Expert report. Ann Arbor: University of Michigan. http://www.umich.edu/ ~ urel/admissions/legal/expert/gurintoc.html

Guthrie, G. M., & Bennett, A. B. (1971). Cultural differences in implicit personality theory. *International Journal of Psychology, 6*(4), 305–312.

Hadiyono, J. E. P., & Hahn, M. W. (1985). Personality differences and sex similarities in American and Indonesian college students. *Journal of Social Psychology, 125,* 703–708.

Hadley, R. F. (1997). Cognition, systematicity and nomic necessity. *Mind and Language, 12*(2), 137–153.

Haghighatgou, H., & Peterson, C. (1995). Coping and depressive symptoms among Iranian students. *Journal of Social Psychology, 135*(2), 175–180.

Hall, C. C. I., Evans, B. J., & Selice, S. (Eds.). (1989). *Black females in the United States: A bibliography from 1967 to 1987.* Washington, DC: American Psychological Association.

Hall, E. T. (1966). *The hidden dimension.* New York: Doubleday.

Hall, E. T. (1973). *The silent language.* New York: Anchor.

Hall, E. T. (1976). *Beyond culture.* New York: Anchor.

Hall, R. H., Jiang, S., Loscocco, K. A., & Allen, J. K. (1993). Ownership patterns and centralization: A China and U.S. comparison. *Sociological Forum, 8*(4), 595–608.

Hall, V. C., Howe, A., Merkel, S., & Lederman, N. (1986). Behavior, motivation, and achievement in desegregated junior high school science classes. *Journal of Educational Psychology, 78,* 108–115.

Hamid, P. N. (1994). Self-monitoring, locus of control, and social encounters of Chinese and New Zealand students. *Journal of Cross-Cultural Psychology, 25*(3), 353–368.

Hamilton, L. H., Brooks-Gunn, J., & Warren, M. P. (1985). Sociocultural influences on eating disorders in professional female ballet dancers. *International Journal of Eating Disorders, 4*(4), 465–477.

Hamilton, V. L., Blumenfeld, P. C., Akoh, H., & Miura, K. (1991). Group and gender in Japanese and American elementary classrooms. *Journal of Cross-Cultural Psychology, 22,* 317–346.

Hampel, R., & Krupp, B. (1977). The cultural and the political framework of prejudice in South Africa and Great Britain. *Journal of Social Psychology, 103,* 193–202.

Hanna, G. S., House, B., & Salisbury, L. H. (1968). WAIS performance of Alaskan Native university freshmen. *Journal of Genetic Psychology, 112*(1), 57–61.

Harkins, S. G. (1987). Social loafing and social facilitation. *Journal of Experimental Social Psychology, 23,* 1–18.

Harkins, S. G., & Petty, R. E. (1982). Effects of task difficulty and task uniqueness on social loafing. *Journal of Personality and Social Psychology, 43,* 1214–1229.

Harlow, H. F., & Harlow, M. K. (1969). Effects of various mother-infant relationships on rhesus monkey behavior. In B. M. Foss (Ed.), *Determinants of infant behavior* (Vol. 4, pp. 15–40). London: Methuen.

Harris, A. C. (1996). African Americans and Anglo American gender identities: An empirical study. *Journal of Black Psychology, 22*(2), 182–194.

Harris, M. B., & Koehler, K. M. (1992). Eating and exercise behaviors and attitudes of southwestern Anglos and Hispanics. *Psychology and Health, 7,* 165–174.

Harrison, A. O., Stewart, R. B., Myambo, K., & Teveraishe, C. (1995). Perceptions of social networks among adolescents from Zimbabwe and the United States. *Journal of Black Psychology, 21*(4), 382–407.

Harrison, A. O., Wilson, M. N., Pine, C. J., Chan, S. Q., & Buriel, R. (1990). Family ecologies of ethnic minority children. *Child Development, 61,* 347–362.

Hart, I. (1971). Scores of Irish groups on the Cattell Culture Fair Test of Intelligence and the California Psychological Inventory. *Irish Journal of Psychology, 1*(1), 30–25.

Harvey, Y. K. (1979). *Six Korean women: The socialization of shamans.* New York: West.

Haskins, R. (1989). Beyond metaphor: The efficacy of early childhood education. *American Psychologist, 44,* 274–282.

Hatfield, E. (1988). Passionate and companionate love. In R. J. Sternberg & M. L. Barnes (Eds.), *The psychology of love* (pp. 191–217). New Haven, CT: Yale University Press.

Hatfield, E., & Rapson, R. L. (1996). *Love and sex: Cross-cultural perspectives.* Boston: Allyn & Bacon.

Hatfield, E., & Sprecher, S. (1995). Men's and women's preferences in marital partners in the United States, Russia, and Japan. *Journal of Cross-Cultural Psychology, 26*(6), 728–750.

Hau, K., & Lew, W. J. (1989). Moral development of Chinese students in Hong Kong. *International Journal of Psychology, 24*(5), 561–569.

Hau, K., & Salili, F. (1991). Structure and semantic differential placement of specific causes: Academic causal attributions by Chinese students in Hong Kong. *International Journal of Psychology, 26,* 175–193.

Hays, J. R., & Smith, A. L. (1980). Comparison of WISC-R and Culture Fair Intelligence Test scores for three ethnic groups of juvenile delinquents. *Psychological Reports, 46*(3, Pt. 1), 931–934.

Healey, J. F. (1998). *Race, ethnicity, gender, and class: The sociology of group conflict and change.* Thousand Oaks, CA: Pine Forge.

Health Canada (1995). *Suicide in Canada: Update of the report of the Task Force on Suicide in Canada.* Ottawa:

Mental Health Division, Health Services Directorate, Health Programs and Services Branch.

Heaven, P. C. L., Connors, J., & Stones, C. R. (1994). Three or five personality dimensions? An analysis of natural language terms in two cultures. *Personality and Individual Differences, 17*(2), 181–189.

Heaven, P. C. L., & Rajab, D. (1983). Correlates of self-esteem among a South African minority group. *Journal of Social Psychology, 121*(2), 269–270.

Heelas, P., & Lock, A. (1981). *Indigenous psychologies: An anthropology of the self.* London: Academic Press.

Heider, E. R., & Oliver, D. (1972). The structure of the color space in naming and memory for two languages. *Cognitive Psychology, 3,* 337–354.

Heine, S. J., Lehman, D. R., Markus, H. R., & Kitayama, S. (1999). Is there a universal need for positive regard? *Psychological Review, 106,* 766–794.

Helgeson, V. S., Shaver, P., & Dyer, M. (1987). Prototypes of intimacy and distance in same-sex and opposite-sex relationships. *Journal of Social and Personal Relationships, 4,* 195–233.

Henderson, N. D. (1982). Human behavior genetics. *Annual Review of Psychology, 33,* 403–440.

Hendrick, C., & Hendrick, S. (1983). *Liking, loving, and relating.* Pacific Grove, CA: Brooks/Cole.

Henriques, G. R., Calhoun, L. G., & Cann, A. (1996). Ethnic differences in women's body satisfaction: An experimental investigation. *Journal of Social Psychology, 136,* 689–697.

Herrnstein, R. J., & Murray, C. (1994). *The bell curve: Intelligence and class structure in American life.* New York: Free Press.

Hess, J. A. (1993). Assimilating newcomers into an organization: A cultural perspective. *Journal of Applied Communication Research, 21*(2), 189–210.

Heyes, C. M. (1993). Imitation, culture and cognition. *Animal Behaviour, 46*(5), 999–1010.

Hiatt, L. R. (1978). Classification of the emotions. In L. R. Hiatt (Ed.), *Australian aboriginal concepts* (pp. 182–187). Princeton, NJ: Humanities Press.

Hiatt, R. A., Pasick, R. J., Perez Stable, E. J., McPhee, S. J., et al. (1996). Pathways to early cancer detection in the multiethnic population of the San Francisco Bay area. *Health Education Quarterly, 23,* S10–S27.

Higginbotham, H. N. (1979). Culture and mental health services. In A. J. Marsella, G. DeVos, & F. L. K. Hsu (Eds.), *Perspectives on cross-cultural psychology* (pp. 307–332). New York: Academic Press.

Higgins, L. T., Zheng, M., Liu, Y., & Sun, C. H. (2002). Attitudes to marriage and sexual behaviors: A survey of gender and culture differences in China and the United Kingdom. *Sex Roles, 46*(3–4), 75–89.

Hill, R. F., & Fortenberry, J. D. (1992). Adolescence as a culture-bound syndrome. *Social Science and Medicine, 35,* 73–80.

Hippler, A. E. (1974). The North Alaska Eskimos: A culture and personality perspective. *American Ethnologist, 1*(3), 449–469.

Hippler, A. E. (1980). Editorial. *International Association of Cross-Cultural Psychology Newsletter, 14,* 2–3.

Hirschfield, L. A. (1996). *Race in the making: Cognition, culture, and the child's construction of human kinds.* Cambridge, MA: MIT Press.

Ho, D. Y. (1998). Indigenous psychologies: Asian perspectives. *Journal of Cross Cultural Psychology, 29*(1), 88–103.

Ho, M. K. (1984). Social group work with Asian/Pacific-Americans. *Social Work with Groups, 7*(3), 49–61.

Hobson, J. A. (1999). The new neuropsychology of sleep: Implications for psychoanalysis. *Neuropsychoanalysis, 1,* 157–183.

Hoch, E. M. (1990). Experiences with psychotherapy training in India. *Psychotherapy and Psychosomatics, 53*(1–4), 14–20.

Hodgetts, R. M., Luthans, F., & Lee, S. M. (1994). New paradigm organizations: From total quality to learning to world-class. *Organizational Dynamics, 22*(3), 5–19.

Hoek, H. W., van Harten, P. N., van Hoeken, D., & Susser, E. (1998). Lack of relation between culture and anorexia nervosa: Results of an incidence study on Curacao. *New England Journal of Medicine, 338*(17), 1231–1232.

Hofstede, G. (1980). *Culture's consequences: International differences in work-related values.* Beverly Hills, CA: Sage.

Hofstede, G. (1983). Dimensions of national cultures in fifty countries and three regions. In J. B. Deregowski, S. Dziurawiec, & R. C. Annis (Eds.), *Expiscations in cross-cultural psychology* (pp. 335–355). Amsterdam: Swets & Zeitlinger.

Hofstede, G. (1984). *Culture's consequences: International differences in work-related values* (abridged ed.). Beverly Hills, CA: Sage.

Hofstede, G. (1996a). The cultural relativity of organizational practices and theories. In J. Billsberry et al. (Eds.), *The effective manager: Perspectives and illustrations* (pp. 243–262). London: Sage.

Hofstede, G. (1996b). Riding the waves of commerce: A test of Trompenaars' "model" of national culture differences. *International Journal of Intercultural Relations, 20*(2), 189–198.

Hofstede, G. (1997). *Culture and organizations.* New York: McGraw Hill.

Hofstede, G. (2001). *Culture's consequences: Comparing values, behaviors, institutions, and organizations across nations* (2nd ed.). Thousand Oaks, CA: Sage.

Hofstede, G., & Bond, M. (1988). Confucius and economic growth: New trends in culture's consequences. *Organizational Dynamics, 16*(4), 4–21.

Hofstee, W. K. B., Kiers, H. A., De Raad, B., Goldberg, L. R., et al. (1997). A comparison of Big Five structures of personality traits in Dutch, English, and German. *European Journal of Personality, 11*(1), 15–31.

Hollander, E. (1985). Leadership and power. In G. Lindzey & E. Aaronson (Eds.), *The handbook of social psychology* (3rd ed., Vol. 2, pp. 485–537). New York: Random House.

Hollon, S. D., & Beck, A. T. (1994). Cognitive and cognitive-behavioral therapies. In A. E. Bergin & S. L. Garfield

(Eds.), *Handbook of psychotherapy and behavior change* (4th ed., pp. 428–466). New York: Wiley.

Holloway, S. D., & Minami, M. (1996). Production and reproduction of culture: The dynamic role of mothers and children in early socialization. In D. W. Schwalb, B. J. Schwalb, et al. (Eds.), *Japanese childrearing: Two generations of scholarship* (pp. 164–176). New York: Guilford Press.

Holmes, L. D., Tallman, G., & Jantz, V. (1978, Fall). Samoan personality. *Journal of Psychological Anthropology, 1*(4), 453–469.

Hood, R. W., Spilka, B., Hunsberger, B., & Gorsuch, R. (1996). *The psychology of religion* (2nd ed.). New York: Guilford Press.

Hoosain, R. (1986). Language, orthography and cognitive process: Chinese perspectives for the Sapir-Whorf hypothesis. *International Journal of Behavioral Development, 9*(4), 507–525.

Hoosain, R. (1991). *Psycholinguistic implications for linguistic relativity: A case study of Chinese.* Hillsdale, NJ: Erlbaum.

Hothersall, D. (1990). *History of psychology* (2nd ed.). New York: McGraw-Hill.

Howell, J. P., Dorfman P. W., Hibino, S., Lee, J. K., & Tale, U. (1995). *Leadership in Western and Asian countries: Commonalities and differences in effective leadership processes and substitutes across cultures.* Las Cruces: New Mexico State University.

Howell, S. (1981). Rules not words. In P. Heelas & A. Lock (Eds.), *Indigenous psychologies: The anthropology of the self* (pp. 133–143). San Diego: Academic Press.

Howes, C. (1990). Can the age of entry into child care and the quality of child care predict adjustment in kindergarten? *Developmental Psychology, 26,* 292–303.

Howes, C., Whitebrook, M., & Phillips, D. (1992). Teacher characteristics and effective teaching in child care: Findings from the National Child Care Staffing Study. *Child and Youth Care Forum, 21*(6), 399–414.

Hsu, L. (1977). An examination of Cooper's test for monotonic trend. *Educational and Psychological Measurement, 37*(4), 843–845.

Hu, P., & Meng, Z. (1996). *An examination of infant-mother attachment in China.* Poster presented at the meeting of the International Society for the Study of Behavioral Development, Quebec City.

Huang, L. N., & Ying, Y. (1989). Japanese children and adolescents. In J. T. Gibbs & L. N. Huang (Eds.), *Children of color.* San Francisco: Jossey-Bass.

Hudson, W. (1960). Pictorial depth perception in subcultural groups in Africa. *Journal of Social Psychology, 52,* 183–208.

Huff, R. M. (1999). Cross-cultural concepts of health and disease. In R. M. Huff & M. V. Kline (Eds.), *Promoting health in multicultural populations: A handbook for practitioners* (pp. 23–39). Thousand Oaks, CA: Sage.

Hughes, B., & Paterson, K. (1997). The social model of disability and the disappearing body: Towards a sociology of impairment. *Disability and Society, 12*(3), 325–340.

Hui, C. H. (1984). *Individualism-collectivism: Theory, measurement, and its relation to reward allocation.* Unpublished doctoral dissertation, University of Illinois.

Hui, C. H. (1988). Measurement of individualism-collectivism. *Journal of Research in Personality, 22,* 17–36.

Hui, C. H., & Triandis, H. C. (1986). Individualism-collectivism: A study of cross-cultural researchers. *Journal of Cross-Cultural Psychology, 17,* 225–248.

Hull, P. V. (1987). *Bilingualism: Two languages, two personalities? Resources in education, educational resources clearinghouse on education.* Ann Arbor: University of Michigan Press.

Hull, P. V. (1990a). *Bilingualism: Two languages, two personalities?* Unpublished doctoral dissertation, University of California, Berkeley.

Hull, P. V. (1990b, August). *Bilingualism and language choice.* Paper presented at the Annual Convention of the American Psychological Association, Boston.

Human Synergistics. (1986). *Organizational Culture Inventory.* Isle of Man, UK: Author.

Hunt, E., & Agnoli, F. (1991). The Whorfian hypothesis: A cognitive psychology perspective. *Psychological Review, 98,* 377–389.

Huntington, R. L., Fronk, C., & Chadwick, B. A. (2001). Family roles of contemporary Palestinian women. *Journal of Comparative Family Studies, 32*(1), 1–19.

Huo, Y. P., Von Glinow, M. A., & Lowe, K. B. (1995, May). *Managing human resources across the Pacific Ocean: A tri-national comparison of staffing practices.* Second International Conference on Asia-Pacific Management, Kaosiung, Taiwan.

Husen, T. (1967). *International study of achievement in mathematics.* New York: Wiley.

Hwang, C. P., & Broberg, A. G. (1992). The historical and social context of child care in Sweden. In M. E. Lamb, K. J. Sternberg, C-P. Hwang, & A. G. Broberg (Eds). *Childcare in context: Cross-cultural perspectives* (pp. 27–53). Hillsdale, NJ: Erlbaum.

Hwu, H. G., & Compton, W. M. (1994). Comparison of major epidemiological surveys using the diagnostic interview schedule. *International Review of Psychiatry, 6,* 309–327.

Indian Health Service. (1997). *Trends in Indian health 1997.* [On-line]. http://www.ihs.gov/PublicInfo/Publications/trends97/trends

Ineichen, B. (1979). The social geography of marriage. In M. Cook & G. Wilson (Eds.), *Love and attraction* (pp. 52–62). New York: Pergamon Press.

Isaac, M., Janca, A., & Orley, J. (1996). Somatization: A culture-bound or universal syndrome? *Journal of Mental Health UK, 5*(3), 219–222.

Islam, M. R. & Jahjah, M. (2001). Predictors of young Australians' attitudes toward Aboriginals, Asians and Arabs. *Social Behavior and Personality, 29*(6), 569–579.

Itoi, R., Ohbuchi, K. I., & Fukuno, M. (1996). A cross-cultural study of preference of accounts: Relationship closeness, harm severity, and motives of account making. *Journal of Applied Social Psychology, 26*(10), 913–934.

Iwao, S., & Triandis, C. H. (1993). Validity of auto- and heterostereotypes among Japanese and American students. *Journal of Cross-Cultural Psychology, 24*(4), 428–444.

Izard, C. E. (1971). *The face of emotion*. New York: Appleton-Century-Crofts.

Izard, C. E. (1994). Innate and universal facial expressions: Evidence from developmental and cross-cultural research. *Psychological Bulletin, 115*(2), 288–299.

Izard, C. E., & Haynes, O. M. (1988). On the form and universality of the contempt expression: A challenge to Ekman and Friesen's claim of discovery. *Motivation and Emotion, 12*(1), 1–16.

Jackson, J. M., & Williams, K. D. (1985). Social loafing on difficult tasks: Working collectively can improve performance. *Journal of Personality and Social Psychology, 49,* 937–942.

Jacob, E. (1997). Context and cognition: Implications for educational innovators and anthropologists. *Anthropology and Education Quarterly, 28*(1), 3–21.

Jacobsen, L. (1996). PPR bistand til sprogskolerne—et omrade uden lovdaekning [Psychological support in language schools: An unlegislated area]. *Psykologisk—Paedagogisk Radgivning, 33*(1): 46–61.

Jaffe, Y., & Yinon, Y. (1983). Collective aggression: The group-individual paradigm in the study of collective antisocial behavior. In H. H. Blumberg, A. P. Hare, V. Kent, & M. F. Davies (Eds.), *Small groups and social interaction* (Vol. 1., pp. 267–175). Chichester, UK: Wiley.

Jahoda, G. (1984). Do we need a concept of culture? *Journal of Cross-Cultural Psychology, 15*(2), 139–151.

Jalali, B. (1982). Iranian families. In M. McGoldrick, J. Pearce, & J. Giordano (Eds.), *Ethnicity and family therapy* (pp. 288–309). New York: Guilford Press.

James, W. (1890). *The principles of psychology* (Vol. 2). New York: Holt.

Jang, K. L., McCrae, R. R., Angleitner, A., Riemann, R., & Livesley, W. J. (1998). Heritability of facet-level traits in cross-cultural twin sample: Support for a hierarchical model of personality. *Journal of Personality and Social Psychology, 74*, 1556–1565.

Janicki, M. G., & Krebs, D. L. (1998). Evolutionary approaches to culture. In C. B. Crawford & D. L. Krebs et al. (Eds.), *Handbook of evolutionary psychology: Ideas, issues and applications* (pp. 163–207). Mahwah, NJ: Erlbaum.

Janis, I. L. (1983). *Group think*. Boston: Hougton Mifflin.

Jankowiak, W. R., & Fischer, E. F. (1992*). A cross-cultural perspective on romantic love. Ethology, 32*, 149–155.

Jeanquart-Barone, S., & Sekaran, U. (1996). Institutional racism: An empirical study. *Journal of Social Psychology, 136*(4), 477–482.

Jencks, C., Smith, M., Acland, H., Bane, M. J., Cohen, D., Gintis, H., Heyns, B., & Michaelson, S. (1972). *Inequality: A reassessment of the effect of family and schooling in America*. New York: Harper & Row.

Jensen, A. R. (1968). Social class, race and genetics: Implications for education. *American Educational Research Journal, 5*(1), 1–42.

Jensen, A. R. (1969). How much can we boost IQ and scholastic achievement? *Harvard Educational Review, 39,* 1–123.

Jensen, A. R. (1971). Twin differences and race differences in I.Q.: A reply to Burgess and Jahoda. *Bulletin of the British Psychological Society, 24*(84), 195–198.

Jensen, A. R. (1973). Personality and scholastic achievement in three ethnic groups. *British Journal of Educational Psychology, 43*(20), 115–125.

Jensen, A. R. (1977). Cumulative deficit in IQ of Blacks in the rural South. *Developmental Psychology, 13*(93), 184–191.

Jensen, A. R. (1980). *Bias in mental testing*. New York: Free Press.

Jensen, A. R. (1981). *Straight talk about mental tests*. London: Methuen.

Jensen, A. R. (1983). Effects of inbreeding on mental-ability factors. *Personality and Individual Differences, 4*(1), 71–87.

Jensen, A. R. (1984). The black-white difference on the K-ABC: Implications for future tests. *Journal of Special Education, 18*(3), 377–408.

Jensen, A. R., & Johnson, F. W. (1994). Race and sex differences in head size and I. Q. *Intelligence, 18*(3), 309–333.

Jensen, A. R., & Munro, E. (1979). Reaction time, movement time, and intelligence. *Intelligence, 3*(2), 121–126.

Jensen, A. R., & Reed, T. E. (1990). Simple reaction time as a suppressor variable in the chronometric study of intelligence. *Intelligence, 14*(4), 375–388.

Jensen, A. R., & Whang, P. A. (1993). Reaction times and intelligence: A comparison of Chinese-American and Anglo-American children. *Journal of Biosocial Science, 25*(3), 397–410.

Jensen, L. A. (1997). Different worldviews, different morals: America's culture war divide. *Human Development, 40*(6), 325–344.

Jensen, S. M. (1970). A technical description of the Danish Binet test under revision. *Skolepsykologi, 7*(4), 241–248.

Jilek-Aall, L., Jilek, M., Kaaya, J., Mkombachepa, L., & Hillary, K. (1997). Psychosocial study of epilepsy in Africa. *Social Science and Medicine, 45*(5), 783–795.

Joensson, E. G., Cichon, S., Gustavsson, J. P., Greunhage, F., Forslund, K., Mattila-Evenden, M., Rylander, G., Asberg, M., Farde, L., Propping, P., & Noethen, M. (2003). Association between a promoter dopamine D-sub-2 receptor gene variant and the personality trait detachment. *Biological Psychiatry, 53*(7), 577–584.

John, O. (1989). *The BFI-54*. Unpublished test, Institute of Personality and Social Research, Department of Psychology, University of California, Berkeley.

Johnson, D. L., Johnson, C. A., & Price-Williams, D. (1967). The Draw A Man Test and Raven Progressive Matrices performance of Guatemalan boys and Latino children. *Revista Interamericana de Psicologia, 1*(2), 143–157.

Johnson, T. M. (1987). Premenstrual syndrome as a Western culture-specific disorder. *Medicine and Psychiatry, 11*(3), 337–356.

Johnston, L., Hewstone, M., Pendry, L., & Frankish, C. (1994). Cognitive models of sterotype change: IV. Motivational and cognitive influences. *European Journal of Social Psychology, 24*(2), 237–265.

Jones, E. E., & Harris, V. A. (1967). The attribution of attitudes. *Journal of Experimental Social Psychology, 3,* 1–24.

Jones, E. E., & Matsumoto, D. R. (1982). Psychotherapy with the underserved. In L. Snowden (Ed.), *Services to the underserved* (pp. 207–228). Beverly Hills, CA: Sage.

Jones, E. E., & Nisbett, R. E. (1971). The actor and the observer: Divergent perceptions of the causes of behavior. In E. E. Jones, D. E. Kanouse, H. H. Kelley, R. E. Nisbett, S. Valins, & B. Weiner (Eds.), *Attribution: Perceiving the causes of behavior* (pp. 79–94) Morristown, NJ: General Learning Press.

Joseph, R. A., Markus, H. R., & Tafarodi, R. W. (1992). Gender differences in the source of self-esteem. *Journal of Personality and Social Psychology, 63,* 1017–1028.

Joshi, S. M., & MacLean, M. (1997). Maternal expectations of child development in India, Japan, and England. *Journal of Cross-Cultural Psychology, 28*(2), 219–234.

Jou, J. Y. H., & Sung, K. (1990). Chinese value system and managerial behavior. *International Journal of Psychology, 25,* 619–627.

Juni, S. (1996). Review of the revised NEO Personality Inventory. In J. C. Conoley & J. C. Impara (Eds.), *12th mental measurements yearbook* (pp. 863–868). Lincoln: University of Nebraska Press.

Kagan, J., Snidman, N., Arcus, D., & Reznick, J. S. (1994). *Galen's prophecy: Temperament in human nature.* New York: Basic Books.

Kagitcibasi, C. (1996a). The autonomous-relational self: A new synthesis. *European Psychologist, 1,* 180–186.

Kagitcibasi, C. (1996b). *Family and human development across cultures: A view from the other side.* Mahwah, NJ: Erlbaum.

Kahneman, D., & Tversky, A. (1973). On the psychology of prediction. *Psychological Review, 80*(4), 237–251.

Kakar, S. (1978). *The inner world: A psychoanalytic study of childhood and society in India.* New Delhi: Oxford University Press.

Kamal, Z., & Lowenthal, K. M. (2002). Suicide beliefs and behavior among young Muslims and Indians in the UK. *Mental Health, Religion and Culture, 5*(2), 111–118.

Kane, C. M. (1994). Differences in the manifest dream content of Anglo-American, Mexican-American, and African-American college women. *Journal of Multicultural Counseling and Development, 22,* 203–209.

Karlins, M., Coffman, T. L., & Walters, G. (1969). On the fading of social stereotypes: Studies in three generations of college students. *Journal of Personality and Social Psychology, 13*(1), 1–16.

Karno, M., Jenkins, J. H., De la Silva, A., Sanatana, F., Telles, C., Lopez, S., & Mintz, J. (1987). Expressed emotion and schizophrenic outcome among Mexican-American families. *Journal of Nervous and Mental Disease, 175,* 145–151.

Kashima, E. S., & Kashima, Y. (1998). Culture and language: The case of cultural dimensions and personal pronoun use. *Journal of Cross-Cultural Psychology, 29,* 461–486.

Kashima, Y., Kim, U., Gelfand, M. J., Yamaguchi, S., Choi, S., & Yuki, M. (1995). Culture, gender, and self: A perspective from individualism-collectivism research. *Journal of Personality and Social Psychology, 69,* 925–937.

Kashima, Y., & Triandis, H. C. (1986). The self-serving bias in attributions as a coping strategy: A cross-cultural study. *Journal of Cross-Cultural Psychology, 17,* 83–97.

Katigbak, M. S., Church, A. T., Guanzon-Lapena, M. A., Carlota, A. J., & del Pilar, G. H. (2002). Are indigenous personality dimensions culture specific? Philippine inventories and the five-factor model. *Journal of Personality and Social Psychology, 82*(1), 89–101

Katz, D., & Braly, K. (1933). Racial stereotypes of one hundred college students. *Journal of Abnormal and Social Psychology, 28,* 280–290.

Kay, P., & Kempton, W. (1984). What is the Sapir-Whorf hypothesis? *American Anthropologist, 86,* 65–89.

Kazarian, S. S., & Persad, E. (2001). Cultural issues in suicidal behavior. In S. S. Kazarian & D. R. Evans (Eds.), *Handbook of cultural health psychology* (pp. 267–302). San Diego: Academic Press.

Keating, C. (1976). Nonverbal aspects of communication. *Topics in Culture Learning, 4,* 12–13.

Keats, D. M. (1982). Cultural bases of concepts of intelligence: A Chinese versus Australian comparison. In P. Sukontasarp, N. Yongsiri, P. Intasuwan, N. Jotiban, & C. Suvannathat (Eds.), *Proceedings of the Second Asian Workshop on Child and Adolescent Development* (pp. 67–75). Bangkok: Burapasilpa Press.

Keats, D. M., & Fang, F. X. (1987). Cultural factors in concepts of intelligence. In C. Kagitcibasi et al. (Eds.), *Growth and progress in cross-cultural psychology* (pp. 236–247). Berwyn, PA: Swets North America.

Keith, S. J., Regier, D. A., & Rae, D. S. (1991). Schizophrenic disorders. In L. N. Robins & D. A. Regier (Eds.), *Psychiatric disorders in America: The epidemiological catchment area study* (pp. 33–52). New York: Free Press.

Keitner, G. I., Fodor, J., Ryan, C. E., Miller, I. W., Epstein, N. B., & Bishop, D. S. (1991). A cross-cultural study of major depression and family functioning. *Canadian Journal of Psychiatry, 36*(4), 254–258.

Kelleher, M. J., Chambers, D., Corcoran, P., Williamson, E., & Keeley, H. S. (1998). Religious sanctions and rates of suicide worldwide. *Crisis, 19,* 78–86.

Keller, H., Chasiotis, A., & Runde, B. (1992). Intuitive parenting programs in German, American, and Greek parents of 3–month-old infants. *Journal of Cross-Cultural Psychology, 23*(4), 510–520.

Keller, M., Edelstein, W., Schmid, C., Fang, F.-X., & Fang, G. (1998). Reasoning about responsibilities and obligations in close relationships: A comparison across two cultures. *Developmental Psychology, 34*(4), 731–741.

Kelley, H. H. (1967). Attributional theory in social psychology. *Nebraska Symposium on Motivation, 15,* 192–241.

Kelley, H. H. (1973). The processes of causal attribution. *American Psychologist, 28,* 107–128.

Kelley, M., & Tseng, H. (1992). Cultural differences in child rearing: A comparison of immigrant Chinese and

Caucasian American mothers. *Journal of Cross-Cultural Psychology, 23*(4), 444–455.

Kelly, J. G. (1990). Changing contexts and the field of community psychology. *American Journal of Community Psychology, 18*(6), 769–792.

Keltikangas-Jaervinen, L., & Terav, T. (1996). Social decision-making strategies in individualist and collectivist cultures: A comparison of Finnish and Estonian adolescents. *Journal of Cross Cultural Psychology, 27*(6), 714–732.

Kemper, T. (1978). *A social interactional theory of emotions.* New York: Wiley.

Kermoian, R., & Leiderman, P. H. (1986). Infant attachment to mother and child caretakers in an East African community. *International Journal of Behavioral Development, 9*(4), 455–469.

Keys, J. B., Denton, L. T., & Miller, T. R. (1994). The Japanese management theory jungle revisited. *Journal of Management, 20*(2), 373–402.

Khaleefa, O. H., Erdos, G., & Ashria, I. H. (1996). Creativity in an indigenous Afro-Arab Islamic culture: The case of Sudan. *Journal of Creative Behavior, 30*(4), 268–282.

Kiev, A. (1972). *Transcultural psychiatry.* New York: Free Press.

Kiev, A. (1973). The psychiatric implications of interracial marriage. In I. R. Stuart & L. E. Abt (Eds.), *Interracial marriage: Expectations and realities* (pp. 162–176). New York: Grossman.

Kilmann, R. H., & Saxton, M. J. (1983). *Kilmann-Saxton culture gap survey.* Tuxedo, NY: Organizational Design Consultants.

Kim, E. Y. (1993). Career choice among second-generation Korean-Americans: Reflections of a cultural model of success. *Anthropology and Education Quarterly, 24*(3), 224–248.

Kim, M., Hunter, J. E., Ahara, A. M., Horvath, A., Bresnahan, M., & Yoon, H. (1996). Individual vs. culture-level dimensions of individualism and collectivism: Effects on preferred conversational styles. *Communication Monograph, 63,* 29–49.

Kim, U. (1992). *The parent-child relationship: The core of Korean collectivism.* Unpublished manuscript, Department of Psychology, University of Hawaii, Honolulu.

Kim, U. (2001). Culture, science, and indigenous psychologies: An integrated analysis. In D. Matsumoto (Ed.), *Handbook of culture and psychology* (pp. 51–75). Oxford, UK: Oxford University Press.

Kim, U., & Berry, J. W. (1993). Introduction. In K. Uichol & J. W. Berry (Eds.), *Indigenous psychologies: Research and experience in cultural context* (Cross-cultural research: Indigenous and methodology series, Vol. 17, pp. 1–29). Newbury Park, CA: Sage.

Kimmel, P. R. (1994). Cultural perspectives on international negotiations. *Journal of Social Issues, 50*(1), 179–196.

King, J. E., & Figueredo, A. J. (1997). The Five-Factor Model plus dominance in chimpanzee personality. *Journal of Research in Personality, 31*(2), 257–271.

Kinzie, J. D., Leung, P. K., & Bui, A. (1988). Group therapy with Southeast Asian refugees. *Community Mental Health Journal, 24*(2), 157–166.

Kinzie, J. D., Leung, P. K., Boehnlein, J., Matsunaga, D., Johnson, R., Manson, S., Shore, J. H., Heinz, J., & Williams, M. (1992). Psychiatric epidemiology of an Indian village: A 19-year replication study. *Journal of Nervous and Mental Disease, 180,* 33–39.

Kinzie, J. D., & Sack, W. (2002). The psychiatric disorders among Cambodian adolescents: The effects of severe trauma. In F. J. C. Azima & N. Grizenko (Eds.), *Immigrant and refugee children and their families: Clinical, research, and training issues* (pp. 95–112). Madison, CT: International Universities Press.

Kirmayer, L. J. (2001). Cultural variations in the clinical presentation of depression and anxiety: Implications for diagnosis and treatment. *Journal of Clinical Psychiatry, 62*(113), 22–28.

Kitayama, S., & Karasawa, M. (1997). Implicit self-esteem in Japan: Name letters and birthday numbers. *Personality and Social Psychology Bulletin, 23*(7), 736–742.

Kitayama, S., & Markus, H. R. (1991). Culture and the self: Implications for cognition, emotion, and motivation. *Psychological Review, 98,* 224–253.

Kitayama, S., & Markus, H. R. (Eds.). (1994). *Emotions and culture: Empirical studies of mutual influence.* Washington, DC: American Psychological Association.

Kitayama, S., & Markus, H. R. (1995). Culture and self: Implications for internationalizing psychology. In N. Rule & J. B. Veroff (Eds.), *The culture and psychology reader* (pp. 366–383). New York: New York University Press.

Kitayama, S., Markus, H. R., & Kurokawa, M. (2000). Culture, emotion and well-being: Good feelings in Japan and the U.S. *Cognition and Emotion, 14*(1), 93–124.

Kitayama, S., Markus, H. R., Kurokawa, M., & Negishi, K. (1993). *Social orientation of emotions: Cross-cultural evidence and implications.* Unpublished manuscript, University of Oregon.

Kitayama, S., Markus, H. R., & Matsumoto, H. (1995). Culture, self, and emotion: A cultural perspective on "self-conscious" emotions. In J. P. Tangney & K. Fisher (Eds.), *Self-conscious emotions: The psychology of shame, guilt, embarrassment, and pride* (pp. 439–464). New York: Guilford Press.

Kitayama, S., Matsumoto, H., Markus, H. R., & Norasakkunkit, V. (1997). Individual and collective processes in the construction of the self: Self-enhancement in the United States and self-criticism in Japan. *Journal of Personality and Social Psychology, 72,* 1245–1267.

Kleinman, A. (1978). Culture and depression. *Culture and Medical Psychiatry, 2,* 295–296.

Kleinman, A. (1982). Neurasthenia and depression: A study of somatization and culture in China. *Culture, Medicine and Psychiatry, 6*(2), 117–190.

Kleinman, A. (1988). *Rethinking psychiatry: From cultural category to personal experience.* New York: Free Press.

Kleinman, A. (1995). Do psychiatric disorders differ in different cultures? The methodological questions. In N. R.

Goldberger & J. B. Veroff (Eds.), *The culture and psychology* (pp. 631–651). New York: New York University Press.

Klingelhofer, E. L. (1967). Performance of Tanzanian secondary school pupils on the Raven Standard Progressive Matrices Test. *Journal of Social Psychology, 72*(2), 205–215.

Kluckholn, F., & Strodtbeck, F. (1961). *Variations in value orientations.* Evanston, IL: Row, Peterson.

Kohlberg, L. (1976). Moral stages and moralization: The cognitive-developmental approach. In J. Lickona (Ed.), *Moral development behavior: Theory, research and social issues* (pp. 31–53). New York: Holt, Rinehart & Winston.

Kohlberg, L. (1984). *The psychology of moral development: The nature and validity of moral stages* (Vol. 2). New York: Harper & Row.

Kontos, S., Howes, C., Shinn, M., & Galinksy, E. (1995). *Quality in family child care and relative care.* New York: Teachers College Press.

Kosmitzki, C. (1996). The reaffirmation of cultural identity in cross-cultural encounters. *Personality and Social Psychology Bulletin, 22,* 238–248.

Koss, J. D. (1990). Somatization and somatic complaint syndromes among Hispanics: Overview and ethnopsychological perspectives. *Transcultural Psychiatric Research Review, 27,* 5–29.

Koss-Chioino, J. D. (2000). Traditional and folk approaches among ethnic minorities. In J. F. Aponte & J. Wohl (Eds.), *Psychological intervention and cultural diversity* (2nd ed., pp. 149–166). Boston: Allyn & Bacon.

Kral, M. J. (1998). Suicide and the internalization of culture: Three questions. *Transcultural Psychiatry, 35*(2), 221–233.

Kranzler, J. H., & Jensen, A. R. (1989). Inspection time and intelligence: A meta-analysis. *Intelligence, 13*(4), 329–347.

Krappmann, L. (1996). Amicitia, drujba, shin-yu, philia, freundschaft, friendship: On the cultural diversity of a human relationship. In W. M. Bukowski, A. F. Newcomb, & W. W. Hartup (Eds.), *The company they keep: Friendship in childhood and adolescence* (pp. 19–40). Cambridge, UK: Cambridge University Press.

Krause, I. B. (1989). Sinking heart: A Punjabi communication of distress. *Social Science and Medicine, 29*(4), 563–575.

Krieger, N. (1999). Embodying inequality: A review of concepts, measures, and methods for studying health consequences of discrimination. *International Journal of Health Services, 29,* 295–352.

Kroeber, A. L., & Kluckhohn, C. (1952). *Culture: A critical review of concepts and definitions* (Vol. 47, No. 1). Cambridge, MA: Peabody Museum.

Kubany, E. S., Bauer, G. B., Pangilinan, M. E., Muraoka, M. Y., et al. (1995). Impact of labeled anger and blame in intimate relationships: Cross-cultural extensions of findings. *Journal of Cross-Cultural Psychology, 26*(1), 65–83.

Kudoh, T., & Kaji, M. (1988). *Culture and nonverbal behavior I.* Unpublished manuscript, Meisei University at Tokyo.

Kudoh, T., & Tamie, B. (1991). *Culture and nonverbal behavior II.* Unpublished manuscript, Meisei University at Tokyo.

Kuo, W. H. (1984). Prevalence of depression among Asian Americans. *Journal of Nervous and Mental Disease, 172*(8), 449–457.

Kurasaki, K. S., Sue, S., Chun, C-A., & Gee, K. (2000). Ethnic minority and intervention and treatment research. In J. E. Aponte & J. Wohl (Eds.), *Psychological intervention and cultural diversity* (2nd ed., pp. 167–182). Boston: Allyn & Bacon.

Kurman, J. (2001). Self-enhancement: Is it restricted to individualistic cultures? *Personality and Social Psychology Bulletin, 27*(12), 1705–1716.

Kush, C. J. (1996). Field-dependence, cognitive ability, and academic achievement in Anglo American and Mexican American students. *Journal of Cross-Cultural Psychology, 27*(5), 561–575.

LaFreniere, P., Masataka, N., Butovskaya, M., Chen, Q., Dessen, M. A., Atwanger, K., Schreiner, S., Montirosso, R., & Frigerio, A. (2002). Cross-cultural analysis of social competence and behavior problems in preschoolers. *Early Education and Development, 13*(2), 201–219.

LaFromboise, T. D., Trimble, J. E., & Mohatt, G. V. (1990). Counseling intervention and American Indian tradition: An integrative approach. *Counseling Psychologist, 18*(4), 159–182.

Lamb, M. E., & Sternberg, K. J. (1992). Sociocultural perspectives on nonparental child care. In M. E. Lamb, K. J. Sternberg, C-P. Hwang, & A. G. Broberg (Eds.), *Childcare in context: Cross-cultural perspectives* (pp. 1–23). Hillsdale, NJ: Erlbaum.

Lambert, E. W., Mermigis, L., & Taylor, M. D. (1986). Greek Canadians' attitudes toward own group and other Canadian ethnic groups: A test of the multiculturalism hypothesis. *Canadian Journal of Behavioral Science, 18*(1), 35–51.

Lamborn, S. D., Mounts, N. S., Steinberg, L., & Dornbusch, S. M. (1991). Patterns of competence and adjustment among adolescents from authoritarian, authoritative, indulgent, and neglectful families. *Child Development, 62,* 1049–1065.

Lammers, C. J., & Hickson, D. J. (Eds.). (1979). *Organizations alike and unlike: International and interinstitutional studies in the sociology of organizations.* London: Routledge & Kegan Paul.

Landau, M. S. (1984). The effects of spatial ability and problem presentation format on mathematical problem solving performance of middle school students. *Dissertation Abstracts International, 45*(2-A), 442–443.

Landis, D. &, O'Shea, W. (2000). Cross-cultural aspects of passionate love: An individual differences analysis. *Journal of Cross-Cultural Psychology, 31*(6), 752–777.

Lange, C. (1887). *Ueber Gemuthsbewegungen.* Leipzig: Theodor Thomas.

Langer, E. J. (1989). *Mindfulness*. Reading, MA: Addison-Wesley.

Langman, P.F. (1997). White culture, Jewish culture and the origins of psychotherapy. *Psychotherapy: Theory, Research, Practice, Training, 34*, 207–218.

Latané, B. (1981). The psychology of social impact. *American Psychologist, 36*, 343–356.

Latané, B., Williams, K., & Harkins, S. (1979). Many hands make light the work: The causes and consequences of social loafing. *Journal of Personality and Social Psychology, 37*, 322–332.

Lau, S. (1989). Sex role orientation and domains of self-esteem. *Sex Roles, 21*(5–6), 415–422.

Laurendeau-Bendavid, M. (1977). Culture, schooling, and cognitive development: A comparative study of children in French Canada and Rwanda. In P. R. Dasen (Ed.), *Piagetian psychology: Cross-cultural contributions* (pp. 123–168). New York: Gardner/Wiley.

Laurent, A. (1978). *Matrix organizations and Latin cultures.* Working Paper 78–28. Brussels: European Institute for Advanced Studies in Management.

Lazarus, R. S. (1991). *Emotion and adaptation.* New York: Oxford University Press.

Lederer, G. (1982). Trends in authoritarianism: A study of adolescents in West Germany and the United States since 1945. *Journal of Cross-Cultural Psychology, 13*(3), 299–314.

Lee, C. C., Oh, M. Y., & Mountcastle, A. R. (1992). Indigenous models of helping in nonwestern countries: Implication for multicultural counseling. *Journal of Multicultural Counseling and Development, 20*, 3–10.

Lee, F., Hallahan, M., & Herzog, T. (1996). Explaining real-life events: How culture and domain shape attributions. *Personality and Social Psychology Bulletin, 22*(7), 732–741.

Lee, H. O., & Boster, F. J. (1992). Collectivism-individualism in perceptions of speech rate: A cross-cultural comparison. *Journal of Cross-Cultural Psychology, 23*, 377–388.

Lee, S. (1995). Reconsidering the status of anorexia nervosa as a culture-bound syndrome. *Social Science and Medicine, 42*, 21–34.

Lee, S. (2001). From diversity to unity: The classification of mental disorders in 21st century China. *Cultural Psychiatry: International Perspectives, 24*(3), 421–431.

Lee, V. K., & Dengerink, H. A. (1992). Locus of control in relation to sex and nationality: A cross-cultural study. *Journal of Cross-Cultural Psychology, 23*(4), 488–497.

Lee, W. M. L., & Mixson, R. J. (1995). Asian and Caucasian client perceptions of the effectiveness of counseling. *Journal of Multicultural Counseling and Development, 23*(1), 48–56.

Lee, Y.-T., Jussin, L. J., & Mc Cauley, C. R. (Eds.). (1995). *Stereotype accuracy: Toward appreciating group differences.* Washington, DC: American Psychological Association.

Lee-Sing, C. M., Leung, Y. K., Wing, H. F., & Chiu, C. N. (1991). Acne as a risk factor for anorexia nervosa in Chinese. *Australian and New Zealand Journal of Psychiatry, 25*(1), 134–137.

Leenaars, A. A., Anawak, J., & Taparti, L. (1998). Suicide among the Canadian Inuit. In R. J. Kosky & H. S. Hadi (Eds.), *Suicide prevention: The global context* (pp. 111–120). New York: Plenum Press.

Leff, J. (1973). Culture and the differentiation of emotional states. *British Journal of Psychiatry, 123*, 299–306.

Leff, J. (1977). International variations in the diagnosis of psychiatric illness. *British Journal of Psychiatry, 131*, 329–338.

Leff, J. (1981). *Psychiatry around the globe: A transcultural view.* New York: Dekker.

Leff, J. (1986). The epidemiology of mental illness. In J. L. Cox (Ed.), *Transcultural psychiatry* (pp. 23–36). London: Croom Helm.

Leong, F. T. L., & Lau, A. S. L. (2001). Barriers to providing effective mental health services to Asian Americans. *Mental Health Services Research, 3*(4), 201–214.

Leong, F. T. L., Wagner, N. S., & Tata, S. P. (1995). Racial and ethnic variations in help-seeking attitudes. In J. G. Ponterotto & J. M. Casas (Eds.), *Handbook of multicultural counseling* (pp. 415–438). Thousand Oaks, CA: Sage.

Lerner, B. (1972). *Therapy in the ghetto: Political impotence and personal disintegration.* Baltimore: Johns Hopkins University Press.

Leung, K. (1988). Some determinants of conflict avoidance. *Journal of Cross-Cultural Psychology, 19*, 125–136.

Leung, K. (1989). Cross-cultural differences: Individual-level vs. culture-level analysis. *International Journal of Psychology, 24*, 703–719.

Leung, K. (1996). The role of beliefs in Chinese culture. In M. H. Bond (Ed.), *The handbook of Chinese psychology* (pp. 247–262). Hong Kong: Oxford University Press.

Leung, K., & Bond, H. M. (1989). On the empirical identification of dimensions for cross-cultural comparisons. *Journal of Cross-Cultural Psychology, 20*(2), 133–151.

Levin, H. M. (1996). Accelerated schools after eight years. In L. Schauble & R. Glaser (Eds.), *Innovations in learning: New environments for education* (pp. 329–352). Mahwah, NJ: Erlbaum.

Levine, J. B. (1988). Play in the context of family. *Journal of Family Psychology, 2*(2), 164–187.

Levine, J. B. (1991). The role of culture in the representation of conflict in dreams: A comparison of Bedouin, Irish, and Israeli children. *Journal of Cross-Cultural Psychology, 22*, 472–490.

Levine, R., Sato, S., Hashimoto, T., & Verma, J. (1995). Love and marriage in eleven cultures. *Journal of Cross-Cultural Psychology, 26*(5), 554–571.

LeVine, R. A. (1977). Child rearing as cultural adaptation. In P. H. Leiderman, S. R. Tulkin, & A. Rosenfeld (Eds.), *Culture and infancy* (pp. 15–27). New York: Academic Press.

LeVine, R. A. (1997). Mother-infant interaction in cross-cultural perspective. In N. L. Segal & G. Weisfeld (Eds.), *Uniting psychology and biology: Integrative perspectives on human development* (pp. 339–354). Washington, DC: American Psychological Association.

LeVine, R. A., LeVine, S. E., Dixon, S., Richman, A., Leiderman, P. H., & Keefer, C. (1996). *Child care and culture: Lessons from Africa.* Cambridge, UK: Cambridge University Press.

Levine, R. B., & Norenzayan, A. (1999). The pace of life in 31 countries. *Journal of Cross-Cultural Psychology, 30,* 178–205.

Levy, G., Lysne, M., & Underwood, L. (1995). Children's and adults' memories for self-schema consistent and inconsistent content. *Journal of Social Psychology, 135*(1), 113–115.

Levy, R. I. (1973). *Tahitians.* Chicago: University of Chicago Press.

Levy, R. I. (1983). Introduction: Self and emotion. *Ethos, 11,* 128–134.

Levy, R. I. (1984). The emotions in comparative perspective. In K. Scherer & P. Ekman (Eds.), *Approaches to emotion* (pp. 397–412). Hillsdale, NJ: Erlbaum.

Levy-Bruhl, L. (1910). *Les fonctions mentales dans les societes inferieures.* Paris: Alcan. (Trans. 1928, *How natives think.* London: Allen & Unwin.)

Levy-Bruhl, L. (1922). *Mentalite primitive.* Paris: Alcan. (Trans. 1923, *Primitive mentality.* London: Allen & Unwin.)

Levy-Bruhl, L. (1949). *Les carnets de Lucien Levy-Bruhl* [The notebooks of Lucien Levy-Bruhl]. Paris: Presses Universitaires de France.

Lewinsohn, P., Rohde, P., Seeley, J., & Fischer, S. (1993). Age-cohort changes in the lifetime occurrence of depression and other mental disorders. *Journal of Abnormal Psychology, 102,* 110–120.

Lewis, G., Croft-Jeffreys, C., & Anthony, D. (1990). Are British psychiatrists racist? *British Journal of Psychiatry, 157,* 410–415.

Lewis, M. (1989). Culture and biology: The role of temperament. In P. R. Zelazo & R. Barr (Eds.), *Challenges to developmental paradigms: Implications for theory, assessment and treatment* (pp. 203–223). Hillsdale, NJ: Erlbaum.

Lewontin, R. C. (1976). Race and intelligence. In N. J. Block & G. Dworkin (Eds.), *The IQ controversy* (pp. 78–92). New York: Pantheon.

Lewontin, R. C., Rose, S., & Kamin, L. J. (1984). *Not in our genes: Biology, ideology and human nature.* New York: Pantheon.

Liebkind, K. (1996). Acculturation and stress: Vietnamese refugees in Finland. *Journal of Cross-Cultural Psychology, 27*(2), 161–180.

Lightfoot-Klein, H. (1989). *Prisoners of ritual: An odyssey into female genital circumcision in Africa.* New York: Harrington Park Press.

Lillard, A. (1998). Ethnopsychologies: Cultural variations in theories of mind. *Psychological Bulletin, 123,* 3–32.

Lin, K., Inui, T. S., Kleiman, A. M., & Womack, W. M. (1992). Socio-cultural determinants of the help-seeking behavior of patients with mental illness. *Journal of Nervous and Mental Disease, 170,* 78–85.

Lin, P., & Schwanenflugel, P.(1995). Cultural familiarity and language factors in the structure of category knowledge. *Journal of Cross-Cultural Psychology, 26*(2), 153–168.

Lindsey, K. P., & Paul, G. L. (1989). Involuntary commitments to public mental institutions: Issues involving the overrepresentation of Blacks and assessment of relevant functioning. *Psychological Bulletin, 106*(2), 171–183.

Linton, R. (1936). *The study of man: An introduction.* New York: Appleton.

Li-Repac, D. (1980). Cultural influences on clinical perception: A comparison between Caucasian and Chinese-American therapists. *Journal of Cross-Cultural Psychology, 11,* 327–342.

Little, D. T., Oettingen, G., Stetsenko, A., & Baltes, B. P. (1995). Children's action-control beliefs about school performance: How do American children compare with German and Russian children? *Journal of Personality and Social Psychology, 69*(4), 686–700.

Liu, L. G. (1985). Reasoning counterfactually in Chinese: Are there any obstacles? *Cognition, 21*(3), 239–270.

Loewenthal, K. M. (1995). *Mental health and religion.* London: Chapman & Hall.

Loewenthal, K. M., MacLeod, A. K., & Cinnirella, M. (2002). Are women more religious than men? Gender differences in religious activity among different religious groups in the UK. *Personality and Individual Differences, 32*(1), 133–139.

Lonner, W. J., & Ibrahim, F. A. (1989). Assessment in cross-cultural counseling. In P. B. Pedersen, J. Dragus, W. Lonner, & J. E. Trimble (Eds.), *Counseling across cultures* (3rd ed., pp. 299–334). Honolulu: University of Hawaii Press.

Lopez, S. R. (1989), Patient variable biases in clinical judgment: Conceptual overview and methodological considerations. *Psychological Bulletin, 106*(2), 184–203.

Lott, D. F., & Hart, B. L. (1977, Summer). Aggressive domination of cattle by Fulani herdsmen and its relation to aggression in Fulani culture and personality. *Ethos, 5*(2), 174–186.

Love, K. G., Bishop, R. C., Heinisch, D. A., & Montei, M. S. (1994). Selection across two cultures: Adapting the selection of American assemblers to meet Japanese job performance demands. *Personnel Psychology, 47,* 837–846.

Lucy, J. A. (1992). *Language diversity and thought: A reformation of the linguistic relativity hypothesis.* Cambridge, UK: Cambridge University Press.

Lueptow, L. B., Garovich, L., & Lueptow, M. B. (1995). The persistence of gender stereotypes in the face of changing sex roles: Evidence contrary to the sociocultural model. *Ethology and Sociobiology, 16*(6), 509–530.

Luria, A. R. (1976). *Cognitive development: Its cultural and social foundations* (M. Lopes & L. Solotaroff, Trans.). Cambridge, MA: Harvard University Press. (Original work published 1974)

Luster, T., & McAdoo, H. (1996). Family and child influences on educational attainment: A secondary analysis of the High/Scope Perry Preschool data. *Developmental Psychology, 32*(1), 26–39.

Luthar, S. S., & Quinlan, D. M. (1993). Parental images in two cultures: A study of women in India and America. *Journal of Cross-Cultural Psychology, 24*(2), 186–202.

Lutz, C. (1980). *Emotion words and emotional development on Ifaluk Atoll.* Unpublished doctoral dissertation, Harvard University.

Lutz, C. (1982). The domain of emotion words in Ifaluk. *American Ethnologist, 9,* 113–128.

Lutz, C. (1983). Parental goals, ethnopsychology, and the development of emotional meaning. *Ethos, 11,* 246–262.

Lutz, C. (1988). *Unnatural emotions: Everyday sentiments on a Micronesian atoll and their challenge to Western theory.* Chicago: University of Chicago Press.

Lutz, C. (1992). Culture and consciousness: A problem in the anthropology of knowledge. In F. S. Kessel & P. M. Cole (Eds.), *Self and conciousness: Multiple perspectives* (pp. 64–87). Hillsdale, NJ: Erlbaum.

Luzzo, D. A. (1993). Ethnic differences in college students' perceptions of barriers to careers development. *Journal of Multicultural Counseling and Development, 21,* 227–236.

Lynn, R., Paspalanova, E., Stetinsky, D., & Tzenova, B. (1998). Intelligence in Bulgaria. *Psychological Reports, 82*(3, Pt. 1), 912–914.

Lyons, A., & Kashima, Y. (2001). The reproduction of culture: Communication processes tend to maintain cultural stereotypes. *Social Cognition, 19*(3), 372–394.

Ma, H. K. (1988). Objective moral judgment in Hong Kong, Mainland China and England. *Journal of Cross-Cultural Psychology, 19*(1), 78–95.

Ma, H. K. (1997). The affective and cognitive aspects of moral development: A Chinese perspective. In H. Kao & D. Sinha (Eds.), *Asian perspectives on psychology* (pp. 93–109). Thousand Oaks, CA: Sage.

Ma, K. H., & Cheung, C. (1996). A cross-cultural study of moral stage structure in Hong Kong Chinese, English, and Americans. *Journal of Cross-Cultural Psychology, 27*(6), 700–713.

Ma, S. M. (1998). *Immigrant subjectivities in Asian American and Asian Diaspora literatures.* New York: State University of New York Press.

Maccoby, E. E., & Jacklin, C. N. (1974). *The psychology of sex differences.* Stanford, CA: Stanford University Press.

Maccoby, E. E., & Martin, J. A. (1983). Socialization in the context of the family: Parent-child interaction. In E. M. Hetherington (Ed.), *Handbook of child psychology: Vol. 4. Socialization, personality, and social development* (4th ed., pp. 1–101). New York: Wiley.

MacDonald, K. (1991). A perspective on Darwinian psychology: The importance of domain-general mechanisms, plasticity, and individual differences. *Ethology and Sociobiology, 12*(6), 449–480.

MacDonald, K. (1998). Evolution, culture, and the five-factor model. *Journal of Cross-Cultural Psychology, 29*(1), 119–149.

MacLachlan, M. (1997). *Culture and health.* Chichester, UK: Wiley.

Macrae, C. N., Bodenhausen, G. V., & Milne, A. B. (1998). Saying no to unwanted thoughts: Self-focus and the regulation of mental life. *Journal of Personality and Social Psychology, 74*(3), 578–589.

Madon, S., Guyll, M., Aboufadel, K., Montiel, E., Smith, A., Palumbo, P., & Jussim, L. (2001). Ethnic and national stereotypes: The Princeton trilogy revisited and revised. *Personality and Social Psychology Bulletin, 27*(8), 996–1010.

Maehr, M., & Nicholls, J. (1980). Culture and achievement motivation: A second look. In N. Warren (Ed.), *Studies in cross-cultural psychology* (Vol. 2, pp. 221–267). London: Academic Press.

Maher, T. E., & Wong, Y. Y. (1994). The impact of cultural differences on the growing tensions between Japan and the United States. *SAM Advanced Management Journal, 59,* 40–46.

Maio, R. G., & Esses, M. V. (1998). The social consequences of affirmative action: Deleterious effects on perceptions of groups. *Personality and Social Psychology Bulletin, 24*(1), 65–74.

Major, B., Spencer, S., Schmader, T., Wolfe, C., & Crocker, J. (1998). Coping with negative stereotypes about intellectual performance: The role of psychological disengagement. *Personality and Social Psychology Bulletin, 24*(1), 34–50.

Malpass, R. S. (1993, August). *A discussion of the ICAI.* Symposium presented at the Annual Convention of the American Psychological Association, Toronto.

Malpass, R. S. (1974). Racial bias in eyewitness identification. *Personality and Social Psychology Bulletin, 1*(1), 42–44.

Malpass, R. S. (1981). Effective size and defendant bias in eyewitness identification lineups. *Law and Human Behavior, 5*(4), 299–309.

Malpass, R. S., & Kravitz, J. (1969). Recognition for faces of own and other race. *Journal of Personality and Social Psychology, 13*(4), 330–334.

Mann, L., Mitsui, H., Beswick, G., & Harmoni, R. V. (1994). A study of Japanese and Australian children's respect for others. *Journal of Cross-Cultural Psychology, 25*(1), 133–145.

Manrai, L. A., & Manrai, A. K. (1995). Effects of cultural-context, gender, and acculturation on perceptions of work versus social/leisure time usage. *Journal of Business Research, 32*(2), 115–128.

Manson, S. M., & Shore, J. H. (1981). Psychiatric epidemiological research among American Indian and Alaska Natives: Some methodological issues. *White Cloud Journal, 2,* 48–56.

Manson, S. M., Shore, J. H., & Bloom, J. D. (1985). The depressive experience in American Indian communities: A challenge for psychiatric theory and diagnosis. In A. Kleinman & B. Good (Eds.), *Culture and depression: Studies in the anthropology and cross-cultural psychiatry of affect and disorder* (pp. 331–368). Berkeley: University of California Press.

Manz, C. C. (1992). Self-leading work teams: Moving beyond self-management myths. *Human Relations, 45*(11), 1119–1140.

Maramba, G. G., & Nagayama Hall, G. C. (2002). Meta-analysis of ethnic match as a predictor of dropout, utilization, and level of functioning. *Cultural Diversity and Ethnic Minority Psychology, 8*, 290–297.

Marin, G., Gamba, R. J., & Marin, B. V. (1992). Extreme response style and acquiescence among Hispanics: The role of acculturation and education. *Journal of Cross-Cultural Psychology, 23*(4), 498–509.

Markham, R., & Wang, L. (1996). Recognition of emotion by Chinese and Australian children. *Journal of Cross-Cultural Psychology, 27*(5), 616–643.

Markoff, R. (1977). Intercultural marriage: Problem areas. In W. S. Tsent, J. F. McDermott, Jr., and T. W. Maretzk (Eds.), *Adjustment in intercultural marriage* (pp. 51–61). Honolulu: University of Hawaii Press.

Marks, D. (1997). Models of disability. *Disability and Rehabilitation: An International Multidisciplinary Journal, 19*(3), 85–91.

Markus, H. R. (1977). Self-schemata and processing information about the self. *Journal of Personality and Social Psychology, 35*, 63–78.

Markus, H. R., & Kitayama, S. (1991a). Cultural variation in self-concept. In G. R. Goethals & J. Strauss (Eds.), *Multidisciplinary perspectives on the self* (pp. 18–48). New York: Springer-Verlag.

Markus, H. R., & Kitayama, S. (1991b). Culture and the self: Implications for cognition, emotion, and motivation. *Psychological Review, 98*, 224–253.

Markus, H. R., & Kitayama, S. (1998). The cultural psychology of personality. *Journal of Cross Cultural Psychology, 29*(1), 63–87.

Markus, H. R., Mullally, P. R., & Kitayama, S. (1997). Selfways: Diversity in modes of cultural participation. In U. Neisser & D. Jopling (Eds.), *The conceptual self in context* (pp. 13–61). New York: Cambridge University Press.

Markus, H. R., & Zajonc, R. (1985). The cognitive perspective in social psychology. In G. Lindzey & E. Aaronson (Eds.), *Handbook of social psychology* (3rd ed., Vol. 1, pp. 137–230). New York: Random House.

Marmot, M. G., & Syme, S. L. (1976). Acculturation and coronary heart disease in Japanese Americans. *American Journal of Epidemiology, 104*, 225–247.

Marsella, A. J. (1979). Cross-cultural studies of mental disorders. In A. J. Marsella, G. DeVos, & F. L. K. Hsu (Eds.), *Perspectives on cross-cultural psychology* (pp. 233–262). New York: Academic Press.

Marsella, A. J. (1980). Depressive experience and disorder across cultures. In H. C. Triandis & J. Draguns (Eds.), *Handbook of cross-cultural psychology: Vol. 6. Psychopathology* (pp. 237–289). Boston: Allyn & Bacon.

Marsella, A. J., Sartorius, N., Jablensky, A., & Fenton, F. R. (1985). Cross-cultural studies of depressive disorders. In A. Kleinman & B. Good (Eds.), *Culture and depression* (pp. 299–324). Berkeley: University of California Press.

Martin, W. E., & Farris, K. K. (1994). A cultural and contextual decision path approach to career assessment with Native Americans: A psychological perspective. *Journal of Career Assessment, 2*(3), 258–275.

Marvin, R. S., VanDevender, T. L., Iwanaga, M. I., LeVine, S., & LeVine, R. A. (1977). Infant-caregiver attachment among the Hausa of Nigeria. In H. McGurk (Ed.), *Ecological factors in human development* (pp. 247–259). Amsterdam: North-Holland.

Mastor, K. A., Jin, P., & Cooper, M. (2000). Malay culture and personality: A big five perspective. *American Behavioral Scientist, 44*, 95–111.

Mathews, H. F., Lannin, D. R., & Mitchell, J. P., (1994). Coming to terms with advanced breast cancer: Black women's narratives from eastern North Carolina. *Social Science Medicine, 38*(6), 789–800.

Matsumoto, D. (1987). *Sport science approaches to training in U.S. judo.* Paper presented at the Fourth Annual National Judo Coaches Conference, United States Olympic Training Center, Colorado Springs.

Matsumoto, D. (1989). Cultural influences on the perception of emotion. *Journal of Cross-Cultural Psychology, 20*, 92–105.

Matsumoto, D. (1990). Cultural similarities and differences in display rules. *Motivation and Emotion, 14*(3), 195–214.

Matsumoto, D. (1991). Cultural influences on facial expressions of emotion. *Southern Communication Journal, 56*, 128–137.

Matsumoto, D. (1992a). American Japanese cultural differences in the recognition of universal facial expressions. *Journal of Cross-Cultural Psychology, 23*, 72–84.

Matsumoto, D. (1992b). More evidence for the universality of a contempt expression. *Motivation and Emotion, 16*(4), 363–368.

Matsumoto, D. (1993). Ethnic differences in affect intensity, emotion judgments, display rule attitudes, and self-reported emotional expression in an American sample. *Motivation and Emotion, 17*(2), 107–123.

Matsumoto, D. (1994). *Cultural influences on research methods and statistics.* Pacific Grove, CA: Brooks/Cole.

Matsumoto, D. (1996). *Culture and psychology.* Pacific Grove, CA: Brooks Cole.

Matsumoto, D. (1999). Culture and self: An empirical assessment of Markus and Kitayama's theory of independent and interdependent self-construal. *Asian Journal of Social Psychology, 2*(3), 289–310.

Matsumoto, D. (2001). Culture and emotion. In D. Matsumoto (Ed.), *The handbook of culture and psychology* (pp. 171–194). New York: Oxford University Press.

Matsumoto, D. (2002). *The new Japan: Debunking seven cultural stereotypes.* Yarmouth, ME: Intercultural Press.

Matsumoto, D., & Assar, M. (1992). The effects of language on judgments of universal facial expressions of emotion. *Journal of Nonverbal Behavior, 16*, 85–99.

Matsumoto, D., & Ekman, P. (1989). American-Japanese cultural differences in intensity ratings of facial expressions of emotion. *Motivation and Emotion, 13*, 143–157.

Matsumoto, D., & Fletcher, D. (1996). Cultural influences on disease. *Journal of Gender, Culture, and Health, 1,* 71–82.

Matsumoto, D., Grissom, R., & Dinnel, D. L. (2001). Do between-culture differences really mean that people are different? A look at some measures of cultural effect size. *Journal of Cross-Cultural Psychology, 32*(4), 478–490.

Matsumoto, D., Kasri, F., & Kooken, K. (1999). American-Japanese cultural differences in judgments of expression intensity and subjective experience. *Cognition and Emotion, 13*(2), 201–218.

Matsumoto, D., Kasri, F., Milligan, E., Singh, U., & The, J. (1997). *Lay conceptions of culture: Do students and researchers understand culture in the same way?* Unpublished paper, San Francisco State University.

Matsumoto, D., Kouznetsova, N., Ray, R., Ratzlaff, C., Biehl, M., & Raroque, J. (1999). Psychological culture, physical health, and subjective well being. *Journal of Gender, Culture, and Health, 4*(1), 1–18.

Matsumoto, D., & Kudoh, T. (1993). American-Japanese cultural differences in attributions of personality based on smiles. *Journal of Nonverbal Behavior, 17*(4), 231–243.

Matsumoto, D., Kudoh, T., Scherer, K., & Wallbott, H. (1988). Antecedents and reactions to emotions in the United States and Japan. *Journal of Cross-Cultural Psychology, 19*(3), 267–286.

Matsumoto, D., Kudoh, T., & Takeuchi, S. (1996). Changing patterns of individualism and collectivism in the United States and Japan. *Culture and Psychology, 2,* 77–107.

Matsumoto, D., Pun, K. K., Nakatani, M., Kadowaki, D., Weissman, M., McCarter, L., Fletcher, D., & Takeuchi, S. (1995). Cultural differences in attitudes, values and beliefs about osteoporosis in first and second generation Japanese-American women. *Women and Health, 23*(4), 39–56.

Matsumoto, D., Takeuchi, S., Andayani, S., Koutnetsouva, N., & Krupp, D. (1998). The contribution of individualism-collectivism to cross-national differences in display rules. *Asian Journal of Social Psychology, 1,* 147–165.

Matsumoto, D., Wallbott, H. G., & Scherer, K. R. (1987). Emotions in intercultural communication. In M. K. Asante & W. B. Gudykunst (Eds.), *Handbook of international and cultural communication.* Newbury Park, CA: Sage.

Matsumoto, D., Weissman, M., Preston, K., Brown, B., & Kupperbusch, C. (1997). Context-specific measurement of individualism–collectivism on the individual level: The IC Interpersonal Assessment Inventory (ICIAI). *Journal of Cross-Cultural Psychology, 28,* 743–767.

Matsuyama, Y., Hama, H., Kawamura, Y., & Mine, H. (1978). Analysis of emotional words. *Japanese Journal of Psychology, 49,* 229–232.

Mauro, R., Sato, K., & Tucker, J. (1992). The role of appraisal in human emotions: A cross-cultural study. *Journal of Personality and Social Psychology, 62*(2), 301–317.

May, P. A., & Dizmang, L. H. (1974). Suicide and the American Indian. *Psychiatric Annals, 4*(11), 22–28.

McCargar, D. F. (1993). Teacher and student role expectations: Cross-cultural differences and implications. *Modern Language Journal, 77*(2), 192–207.

McClelland, D. C. (1961). *The achieving society.* Princeton, NJ: Van Nostrand.

McConatha, J. T., Lightner, E., & Deaner, S. L. (1994). Culture, age, and gender as variables in the expression of emotions. *Journal of Social Behavior and Personality, 9*(3), 481–488.

McCrae, R. R. (2001). Trait psychology and culture: Exploring intercultural comparisons. *Journal of Personality, 69*(6), 819–846.

McCrae, R. R., & Costa, P. T. (1987). Validation of the Five-Factor model of personality across instruments and observers. *Journal of Personality and Social Psychology, 52*(1), 81–90.

McCrae, R. R., & Costa, P. T. (1997). Personality trait structure as a human universal. *American Psychologist, 52*(5), 509–516.

McCrae, R. R., Costa, P. T., Del-Pilar, G. H., & Rolland, J. P. (1998, January). Cross-cultural assessment of the five-factor model: The revised NEO personality inventory. *Journal of Cross Cultural Psychology, 29*(1), 171–188.

McCrae, R. R., Costa, P. T., & Yik, M. S. M. (1996). Universal aspects of Chinese personality structure. In M. H. Bond et al. (Eds.), *The handbook of Chinese psychology* (pp. 189–207). Hong Kong: Oxford University Press.

McGoldrick, M., & Preto, N. G. (1984). Ethnic intermarriage: Implications for therapy. *Family Process, 23*(3), 347–364.

McGowan, R. W., McGowan, J. S., & Omifade, A. (1997). Cultural effects: Attributions following ruminations of success and failure. *Psychological Reports, 81,* 155–159.

McGurk, H., & Jahoda, G. (1975). Pictorial depth perception by children in Scotland and Ghana. *Journal of Cross-Cultural Psychology, 6*(3), 279–296.

Mead, M. (1961). *Cooperation and competition among primitive people.* Boston: Beacon Press.

Mead, M. (1978). *Culture and commitment.* Garden City, NY: Anchor. (Original work published 1928)

Meade, R. D. (1971). Future time perspectives of college students in America and in India. *Journal of Social Psychology, 83,* 175–182.

Meglino, B. M., Ravlin, E. C., & Adkins, C. L. (1989). A work values approach to corporate culture: A field test of the value congruence process and its relationship to individual outcomes. *Journal of Applied Psychology, 74*(3), 424–432.

Mehrabi, F., Bayanzadeh, S.-A., Atef-Vahid, M.-K., Bolhari, J., Shahmohammadi, D., & Vaezi, S.-A. (2000). Mental health in Iran. In I. Al-Junūn (Ed.), *Mental illness in the Islamic world* (pp. 139–161). Madison, CT: International Universities Press.

Mehrabian, A. (1981). *Silent messages: Implication of emotions and attitudes* (2nd ed.). Belmont, CA: Wadsworth.

Mehrabian, A., & Wiener, M. (1967). Decoding of inconsistent communications. *Journal of Personality and Social Psychology, 6*(1), 109–114.

Mehryar, A. H. (1970). Authoritarianism, rigidity, and Eysenck's E and N dimensions in an authoritarian culture. *Psychological Reports, 27*(1), 326.

Meissner, C. A., & Brigham, J. C. (2001). Thirty years of investigating the own-race bias in memory for faces: A meta-analytic review. *Psychology, Public Policy, and Law, 7,* 3–35.

Merton, R. (1968). *Social theory and social structures.* New York: Free Press.

Mesquita, B., & Frijda, N. H. (1992). Cultural variations in emotions: A review. *Psychological Bulletin, 112*(2), 179–204.

Messick, D. M., & Mackie, D. M. (1989). Intergroup relations. *Annual Review of Psychology, 40,* 45–81.

Milgram, S. (1974). *Obedience to authority.* New York: Harper & Row.

Miller, J. G. (1984). Culture and the development of everyday social explanation. *Journal of Personality and Social Psychology, 46,* 961–978.

Miller, J. G. (1994). Cultural diversity in the morality of caring: Individually oriented versus duty-based interpersonal moral codes. *Cross-Cultural Research, 28,* 3–39.

Miller, J. G. (2001). Culture and moral development. In D. Matsumoto (Ed.), *The handbook of culture and psychology* (pp. 151–170). New York: Oxford University Press.

Miller, J. G., & Bersoff, D. M. (1992). Culture and moral judgment: How are conflicts between justice and interpersonal responsibilities resolved? *Journal of Personality and Social Psychology, 62,* 541–554.

Miller, K. E. (1999). Rethinking a familiar model: Psychotherapy and the mental health of refugees. *Journal of Contemporary Psychotherapy, 29,* 283–306.

Miller, K. E., Worthington, G. J., Muzurovic, J., Tipping, S., & Goldman, A. (2002). Bosnian refugees and the stressors of exile: A narrative study. *American Journal of Orthopsychiatry, 72*(3), 341–354.

Minami, M., & McCabe, A. (1995). Rice balls and bear hunts: Japanese and North American family narrative patterns. *Journal of Child Language, 22*(2), 423–445.

Mintz, J., Mintz, L., & Goldstein, M. (1987). Expressed emotion and relapse in first episodes of schizophrenia. *British Journal of Psychiatry, 151,* 314–320.

Mintz, L. B., & Kashubeck, S. (1999). Body image and disordered eating among Asian American and Caucasian college students: An examination of race and gender differences. *Psychology of Women Quarterly, 23*(4), 781–796.

Miranda, J., & Green, B. L. (1999). The need for mental health services research focusing on poor young women. *Journal of Mental Health Policy and Economics, 2,* 73–89.

Mirande, M. (1985). *The Chicano experience: An alternative perspective.* Notre Dame, IN: University of Notre Dame Press.

Miron, M. (1975). A study of cross-cultural factorial structure of intelligence. *Psychologia: An International Journal of Psychology in the Orient, 18*(2), 92–94.

Misumi, J. (1985). *The behavioral science of leadership: An interdisciplinary Japanese research program.* Ann Arbor: University of Michigan Press.

Miura, I. T., Okamoto, Y., Kim, C. C., Steere, M., et al. (1993). First graders' cognitive representation of number and understanding of place value. Cross-national comparisons: France, Japan, Korea, Sweden, and the United States. *Journal of Educational Psychology, 85*(1), 24–30.

Miyake, K. (1993). Temperament, mother-infant interaction, and early emotional development. *Japanese Journal of Research on Emotions, 1*(1), 48–55.

Miyake, K., Chen, S., & Campos, J. J. (1985). Infant temperament, mother's mode of interaction, and attachment in Japan: An interim report. In I. Bretherton & E. Waters (Eds.), *Growing points of attachment theory. Monographs of the Society of Research in Child Development, 50*(1–2, Serial No. 209).

Moghaddam, F. M., Ditto, B., & Taylor, D. M. (1990). Attitudes and attributions related to psychological symptomatology in Indian immigrant women. *Journal of Cross-Cultural Psychology, 21,* 335–350.

Moghaddam, F. M., Taylor, D. M., Lambert, E. W., & Schmidt, E. A. (1995). Attributions and discrimination: A study of attributions to the self, the group, and external factors among whites, blacks, and Cubans in Miami. *Journal of Cross-Cultural Psychology, 26*(2), 209–220.

Monteith, M., Sherman, J. & Devine, P. (1998). Suppression as a stereotype control strategy. *Personality and Social Psychology Review, 1,* 63–82.

Moore, J. T. (1988, March). *Pride against prejudice: The biography of Larry Doby.* New York: Greenwood Press.

Morelli, G. A., Oppenheim, D., Rogoff, B., & Goldsmith, D. (1992). Cultural variations in infant sleeping arrangements: Questions of independence. *Developmental Psychology, 28,* 604–613.

Morgan, L. H. (1877). *Ancient society: Or, researches in the line of human progress from savagery through barbarism to civilization.* Chicago: C. H. Kerr.

Morinaga, Y., Frieze, I. H., & Ferligoj, A. (1993). Career plans and gender-role attitude of college students in the United States, Japan, and Slovenia. *Sex Roles, 29*(5–6), 317–334.

Morinis, A. (1985). The ritual experience: Pain and the transformation of consciousness in ordeals of initiation. *Ethos, 13*(2), 150–174.

Morris, M. H., Avila, R. A., & Allen, J. (1993). Individualism and the modern corporation: Implications for innovation and entrepreneurship. *Journal of Management, 19*(3), 595–612.

Morris, M. W., & Peng, K. (1994). Culture and cause: American and Chinese attributions for social and physical events. *Journal of Personality and Social Psychology, 67*(6), 949–971.

Muela, S. H., Ribera, J. M., & Tanner, M. (1998). Fake malaria and hidden parasites: The ambiguity of malaria. *Anthropology and Medicine, 5*(1), 43–61.

Mukai, T., & McCloskey, L. (1996). Eating attitudes among Japanese and American elementary schoolgirls. *Journal of Cross-Cultural Psychology, 27*(4), 424–435.

Mulatu, M. S., & Berry, J. W. (2001). Health care practice in a multicultural context: Western and non-Western assumptions. In S. S. Kazarian & D. R. Evans (Eds.), *Handbook of cultural health psychology* (pp. 45–61). San Diego: Academic Press.

Mulder, M. (1976). Reduction of power differences in practice: The power distance reduction theory and its applications. In G. Hofstede & M. S. Kassem (Eds.), *European contributions to organization theory* (pp. 79–94). Assen, Netherlands: Van Gorcum.

Mulder, M. (1977). *The daily power game.* Leyden, Netherlands: Martinus.

Mule, P., & Barthel, D. (1992). The return to the veil: Individual autonomy and social esteem. *Sociological Forum, 7*(2), 323–333.

Munro, D. (1979). Locus-of-control attribution: Factors among Blacks and Whites in Africa. *Journal of Cross-Cultural Psychology, 10*(2), 157–172.

Munroe, R. H., Shimmin, H. S., & Munroe, R. L. (1984). Gender understanding and sex role preference in four cultures. *Developmental Psychology, 20*(4), 673–682.

Murase, T. (1986). Naikan therapy. In T. S. Lebra & W. P. Lebra (Eds.), *Japanese culture and behavior* (pp. 388–398). Honolulu: University of Hawaii Press.

Murdock, G. P., Ford, C. S., & Hudson, A. E. (1971). *Outline of cultural materials* (4th ed.). New Haven, CT: Human Relations Area Files.

Muret-Wagstaff, S., & Moore, S. G. (1989). The Hmong in America: Infant behavior and rearing practices. In J. K. Nugent, B. M. Lester, & T. B. Brazelton (Eds.), *The cultural context of infancy: Vol. 1. Biology, culture and infant development* (pp. 319–339). Norwood, NJ: Ablex.

Murphy, H. B. M. (1982). Culture and schizophrenia. In I. Al-Issa (Ed.), *Culture and psychopathology* (pp. 221–249). Baltimore: University Park Press.

Murphy, J. M. (1976). Psychiatric labeling in cross-cultural perspective. *Science, 191,* 1019–1028.

Murstein, B., Merighi, J., & Vyse, S. (1991). Love styles in the United States and France: A cross-cultural comparison. *Journal of Social and Clinical Psychology, 10*(1), 37–46.

Myers, D. (1987). *Social psychology* (2nd ed.). New York: McGraw-Hill.

Myers, F. R. (1979). Emotions and the self: A theory of personhood and political order among Pintupi aborigines. *Ethos, 7,* 343–370.

Myers, J. K., Weissman, M. M., Tischler, G. L., Holzer, C. E., Leaf, P. J., Orvaschel, H., Anthony, J. C., Boyd, J. H., Burke, J. D., Kramer, M., & Stolzman, R. (1984). Six month prevalence of psychiatric disorders in three communities: 1980 to 1982. *Archives of General Psychiatry, 41,* 959–967.

Narayanan, L., Menon, S., & Levine, E. L. (1995). Personality structure: A culture-specific examination of the five-factor model. *Journal of Personality Assessment, 64*(1), 51–62.

Narayanan, S., & Ganesan, V. (1978). The concept of self among the Irulas of Palamalai. *Journal of Psychological Researches, 22*(2), 127–134.

Nayak, S., Shiflett, S., Eshun, S., & Levine, F. (2000). Culture and gender effects in pain beliefs and the prediction of

pain tolerance. *Cross-Cultural Research: The Journal of Comparative Social Science, 34*(2), 135–151.

Neck, C. P., & Manz, C. C. (1994). From groupthink to teamthink: Toward the creation of constructive thought patterns in self-managing work teams. *Human Relations, 47*(8), 929–951.

Nelson, S. H., McCoy, G. F., Stetter, M., & Vanderwagen, W. C. (1992). An overview of mental health services for American Indians and Alaska Natives in the 1990s. *Hospital and Community Psychiatry, 43,* 257–261.

Nemoto, T., Wong, F. Y., Ching, A., Chng, C. L., Bouey, P., Henrickson, M., & Smeber, R. E. (1998). HIV seroprevalence, risk behaviors, and cognitive factors among Asian and Pacific Islander American men who have sex with men: A summary and critique of empirical studies and methodological issues. *AIDS Education and Prevention, 10*(3), 31–47.

Nenty, H. J. (1986). Cross-culture bias analysis of Cattell Culture-Fair Intelligence Test. *Perspectives in Psychological Researches, 9*(1), 1–16.

Nenty, H. J., & Dinero, T. E. (1981). A cross-cultural analysis of the fairness of the Cattell Culture Fair Intelligence Test using the Rasch model. *Applied Psychological Measurement, 5*(3), 355–368.

Newton, N., & Newton, M. (1972). Childbirth in cross-cultural perspectives. In J. G. Howells (Ed.), *Modern perspectives in psycho-obstetrics* (pp. 76–94). New York: Brunner/Mazel.

Ng, H. S., Cooper, M., & Chandler, P. (1998). The Eysenckian personality structure: A "Giant Three" or "Big Five" model in Hong Kong? *Personality and Individual Differences, 25*(6), 1111–1131.

Ng, W. G., & Lindsay, R. L. (1994). Cross-race facial recognition: Failure of the contact hypothesis. *Journal of Cross-Cultural Psychology, 25*(2), 217–232.

Nguyen, H. H., Messe, L. & Stollack, G. (1999). Toward a more complex understanding of acculturation and adjustment: Cultural involvements and psychosocial functioning in Vietnamese youth. *Journal of Cross-Cultural Psychology, 30*(1), 5–31.

Nichols, R. K., & McAndrew, T. F. (1984). Stereotyping and autostereotyping in Spanish, Malaysian, and American college students. *Journal of Social Psychology, 124,* 179–189.

Niedenthal, P., & Beike, D. (1997). Interrelated and isolated self-concepts. *Personality and Social Psychology Review, 1*(2), 106–128.

Noel, D. L. (1968). A theory of the origin of ethnic stratification. *Social Problems, 16*(2), 157–172.

Nomura, N., & Barnlund, D. (1983). Patterns of interpersonal criticism in Japan and United States. *International Journal of Intercultural Relations, 7*(1), 1–18.

Nurmi, J., Liiceanu, A., & Liberska, H. (1999). Future-oriented interests. In F. D. Alsaker, & A. Flammer (Eds.), *The adolescent experience: European and American adolescents in the 1990s* (pp. 85–98). Mahwah, NJ: Erlbaum.

Nurmi, J., Poole, E. M., & Seginer, R. (1995). Tracks and transitions: A comparison of adolescent future-oriented goals, explorations, and commitments in Australia, Israel, and Finland. *International Journal of Psychology, 30*(3), 355–375.

Nyborg, H., Eysenck, S. B. G., & Kroll, N. (1982). Cross-cultural comparison of personality in Danish and English children. *Scandinavian Journal of Psychology, 23,* 291–297.

Nydell, M. K. (1998). *Understanding Arabs: A guide for Westerners.* Yarmouth, ME: Intercultural Press.

Oakes, P. J., Haslam, S. A., & Turner, J. C. (1994). *Stereotyping and social reality.* Oxford, UK: Basil Blackwell.

Oesterheld, J. R. (1997). Acceptability of the Conners Parent Rating Scale and Child Behavior Checklist to Dakotan/Lakotan parents. *Journal of the American Academy of Child and Adolescent Psychiatry, 36*(1), 55–64.

Oettingen, G. (1997). Culture and future thought. *Culture and Psychology, 3*(3), 353–381.

Ogbu, J. U. (1981). Origins of human competence: A cultural-ecological perspective. *Child Development, 52,* 413–429.

Okamoto, K. (1993). *Nihonjin no YES wa Naze No Ka? [Why is a Japanese yes a no?].* Tokyo: PHP Research Laboratory.

Okechuku, C. (1994). The relationship of six managerial characteristics to the assessment of managerial effectiveness in Canada, Hong Kong and People's Republic of China. *Journal of Occupational and Organizational Psychology, 67*(1), 79–86.

Okonkwo, R. (1997). Moral development and culture in Kohlberg's theory: A Nigerian (Igbo) evidence. *IFT Psychologia: An International Journal, 5*(2), 117–128.

Olah, A. (1995). Coping strategies among adolescents: A cross-cultural study. *Journal of Adolescence, 18,* 491–512.

Omi, M., & Winant, H. (1994). *Racial formation in the United States: From the 1960s to the 1990s* (2nd ed.). New York: Routledge.

Opler, M. K., & Singer, J. L. (1959). Ethnic differences in behavior and psychopathology. *International Journal of Social Psychiatry, 2,* 11–23.

Oquendo, M. A. (1996a). Psychiatric evaluation and psychotherapy in the patient's second language. *Psychiatric Services, 47*(6), 614–618.

Oquendo, M. A. (1996b). Psychiatric evaluation in a second language: Commentary reply. *Psychiatric Services, 47*(9), 1002.

O'Reilly, C. A. (1989). Corporations, culture, and commitment: Motivation and social control in organizations. *California Management Review, 31,* 9–25.

O'Reilly, C. A., Chatman, J. A., & Caldwell, D. (1988). *People, jobs, and organizational culture.* Working paper, University of California at Berkeley, School of Business Administration.

O'Reilly, C. A., Chatman, J., & Caldwell, D. F. (1991). People and organizational culture: A profile-comparison approach to assessing person-organization fit. *Academy of Management Journal, 34,* 487–516.

Organista, P. B., Organista, K. C., & Kurasaki, K. (2003). The relationship between acculturation and ethnic minority health. In K. M. Chun & P. B. Organista (Eds.), *Accul-turation: Advances in theory, measurement, and applied research* (pp. 139–161). Washington, DC: American Psychological Association.

Orlinsky, D. E., Grawe, K., & Parks, B. K. (1994). Process and outcome in psychotherapy: Noch einmal. In A. E. Bergin & S. L. Garfield, (Eds), *Handbook of psychotherapy and behavior change* (4th ed., pp. 270–376). New York: Wiley.

Orpen, C. (1971a). Prejudice and adjustment to cultural norms among English-speaking South Africans. *Journal of Psychology, 77,* 217–218.

Orpen, C. (1971b). The effect of cultural factors on the relationship between prejudice and personality. *Journal of Psychology, 78,* 73–79.

Orr, E., & Ben-Eliahu, E. (1993). Gender differences in idiosyncratic sex-typed self-images and self-esteem. *Sex Roles, 29*(3–4), 271–296.

Oster, H., & Ekman, P. (1979). Facial expressions of emotion. *Annual Reviews of Psychology, 30,* 527–554.

Osterman, K., Bjorkquist, K., & Lagerspetz, K. (1994). Peer and self-estimated aggression and victimization in 8 year old children from five ethnic groups. *Aggressive Behavior, 20,* 411–428.

Osterweil, Z., & Nagano-Nakamura, K. (1992). Maternal views on aggression: Japan and Israel. *Aggressive Behavior, 18,* 263–270.

O'Toole, A. J., Deffenbacher, K. A., Valentin, D., & Abdi, H. (1994). Structural aspects of face recognition and the other-race effect. *Memory and Cognition, 22*(2), 208–224.

O'Toole, A. J., Peterson, J., & Deffenbacher, K. A. (1996). An "other-race effect" for categorizing faces by sex. *Perception, 25*(6), 669–676.

Oyserman, D. (1993). The lens of personhood: Viewing the self and others in a multicultural society. *Journal of Personality and Social Psychology, 65*(5), 993–1009.

Oyserman, D., Coon, H. M., & Kemmelmeier, M. (2002). Rethinking individualism and collectivism: Evaluation of theoretical and assumptions and meta-analyses. *Psychological Bulletin, 128,* 3–72.

Oyserman, D., Gant, L., & Ager, J. (1995). A socially contextualized model of African American identity: Possible selves and school persistence. *Journal of Personality and Psychology, 69*(6), 1216–1232.

Padilla, A. M., Wagatsuma, Y., & Lindholm, K. J. (1985). Acculturation and personality as predictors of stress in Japanese and Japanese Americans. *Journal of Social Psychology, 125,* 295–305.

Paguio, L. P., Robinson, B. E., Skeen, P., & Deal, J. E. (1987). Relationship between fathers' and mothers' socialization practices and children's locus of control in Brazil, the Philippines, and the United States. *Journal of Genetic Psychology, 148*(3), 202–313.

Palmer, S. (1971). Characteristics of suicide in 54 non-literate societies. *Life Threatening Behavior, 1*(3), 178–183.

Pang, O. V. (1991). The relationship of test anxiety and math achievement to parental values in Asian American and European American middle school students. *Journal of Research and Development in Education, 24*(4), 1–10.

Paniagua, F. A. (1998). *Assessing and treating culturally diverse clients: A practical guide.* Newbury Park, CA: Sage.

Paniagua, F. A. (2000). Culture-bound syndromes, cultural variations and psychopathology. In I. Cuellar & F. A. Paniagua (Eds.), *Handbook of multicultural mental health: Assessment and treatment of diverse populations* (pp. 139–169). San Diego: Academic Press.

Papousek, H., & Papousek, M. (1997). Preverbal communication in humans and the genesis of culture. In U. C. Segerstrale & P. M. Molnar (Eds.), *Nonverbal communication: Where nature meets culture* (pp. 87–107). Hillsdale, NJ: Erlbaum.

Papps, F., Walker, M., Trimboli, A., & Trimboli, C. (1995). Parental discipline in Anglo, Greek, Lebanese, and Vietnamese cultures. *Journal of Cross-Cultural Psychology, 26*(1), 49–64.

Pargament, K. I., & Maton, K. I. (2000). Religion in American life. In J. Rappaport & E. Seidman (Eds.), *Handbook of community psychology* (pp. 495–522). New York: Kluwer Academic/Plenum.

Parkin, M. (1974). Suicide and culture in Fairbanks: A comparison of three cultural groups in a small city of interior Alaska. *Psychiatry: Journal for the Study of Interpersonal Processes, 37*(1), 60–67.

Parsonson, K. (1987). Intermarriages: Effects on the ethnic identity of the offspring. *Journal of Cross-Cultural Psychology, 18*(3), 363–371.

Pascual, L., Haynes, O. M., Galperin, Z. C., & Bornstein, H. M. (1995). Psychosocial determinants of whether and how much new mothers work: A study in the United States and Argentina. *Journal of Cross-Cultural Psychology, 26*(3), 314–330.

Patel, P. G. (1996). Linguistic and cognitive aspects of the orality-literacy complex in ancient India. *Language and Communication, 16*(4), 315–329.

Patterson, M. L. (1995). Invited article: A parallel process model of nonverbal communication. *Journal of Nonverbal Behavior, 19*(1), 3–29.

Patzer, G. L. (1985). *The physical attractiveness phenomena.* New York: Plenum Press.

Paunonen, S. V., & Ashton, M. C. (1998). The structured assessment of personality across cultures. *Journal of Cross-Cultural Psychology, 29*(1), 150–170.

Paunonen, S. V., Jackson, D. N., Trzebinski, J., & Forsterling, F. (1992). Personality structure across cultures: A multimethod evaluation. *Journal of Personality and Social Psychology, 62*(3), 447–456.

Pelto, P. J. (1968, April). The differences between "tight" and "loose" societies. *Trans-action,* pp. 37–40.

Pelto, P. J., & Pelto, G. H. (1975). Intra-cultural diversity: Some theoretical issues. *American Ethnologist, 2,* 1–18.

Peng, K., Nisbett, R. E., & Wong, Y. C. (1997). Validity problems comparing values across cultures and possible solutions. *Psychological Methods, 2*(4), 329–344.

Pennebaker, J. W., Rime, B., & Blankenship, V. E. (1996). Stereotypes of emotional expressiveness of northerners and southerners: A cross-cultural test of Montesquieu's hypothesis. *Journal of Personality and Social Psychology, 70*(2), 372–380.

Pe-Pua, R. (1989). Pagtatanong-Tanong: A cross-cultural research method. *International Journal of Intercultural Relations, 13,* 147–163.

Pervin, L. (Ed.). (1989). *Goal concepts in personality and social psychology.* Hillsdale, NJ: Erlbaum.

Peterson, M. (1997). Work, corporate culture, and stress: Implications for worksite health promotion. *American Journal of Health Behavior, 21*(4), 243–252.

Peterson, M. F., & Smith, P. B. (1997). Does national culture or ambient temperature explain cross-national differences in role stress? No sweat! *Academy of Management Journal, 40*(4), 930–946.

Petrie, K., Dibble, C., Long-Taylor, M., & Ruthe, G. (1986). A New Zealand information subtest for the WAIS-R. *New Zealand Journal of Psychology, 15*(1), 23–26.

Pfeiffer, K. T. (1994). Alaskan native suicide. *Dissertation Abstracts International Section A: Humanities and Social Sciences, 54*(8-A), 3214.

Pfeiffer, W. M. (1982). Culture-bound syndromes. In I. Al-Issa (Ed.), *Culture and psychopathology* (pp. 201–218). Baltimore: University Park Press.

Phalet, K., & Claeys, W. (1993). A comparative study of Turkish and Belgian youth. *Journal of Cross-Cultural Psychology, 24,* 319–343.

Phillips, D. A., Voran, M., Kisker, E., Howes, C., & Whitebrook, M. (1994). Child care for children in poverty: Opportunity or inequity? *Child Development, 65*(2), 472–492.

Phinney, J. S. (1996). When we talk about American ethnic groups, what do we mean? *American Psychologist, 51*(9), 918–927.

Phinney, J. S., & Chavira, V. (1992). Ethnic identity and self-esteem: An exploratory longitudinal study. *Journal of Adolescence, 15,* 271–281.

Phinney, J. S., Horenczyk, G., & Liebkind, K. (2001). Ethnic identity, immigration and well-being: An interactional perspective. *Journal of Social Issues, 57*(3), 493–510.

Phinney, J. S., & Rosenthal, D. (1992). Ethnic identity in adolescence: Process, context, and outcome. In G. Adams, T. Gulotta, & R. Montemayor (Eds.), *Identity formation during adolescence* (pp. 145–172). Newbury Park, CA: Sage.

Piaget, J. (1952). *The origins of intelligence in children.* New York: International Universities Press.

Piaget, J. (1954). *Construction of reality in the child.* New York: Basic Books.

Piedmont, R. L., & Leach, M. M. (2002). Cross-cultural generalizability of the spiritual transcendence scale in India. *American Behavioral Scientist, 45,* 1888–1901.

Piers, G., & Singer, M. B. (1971). *Shame and guilt: A psychoanalytic and a cultural study.* New York: Norton.

Pike, K. L. (1954). *Language in relation to a unified theory of the structure of human behavior, Pt. 1* (Preliminary ed.). Glendale, CA: Summer Institute of Linguistics.

Piker, S. (1998). Contributions of psychological anthropology. *Journal of Cross-Cultural Psychology, 29*(1), 9–31.

Pines, A. M. (2001). The role of gender and culture in romantic attraction. *European Psychologist, 6*(2), 96–102.

Pinker, S. (1995). *The language instinct: How the mind creates language*. New York: HarperCollins.

Pittam, J., Gallois, C., Iwawaki, S., & Kroonenberg, P. (1995). Australian and Japanese concepts of expressive behavior. *Journal of Cross-Cultural Psychology, 26*(5), 451–473.

Plaks, J. E., Stroessner, S. J., Dweck, C. S., & Sherman, J. W. (2001). Person theories and attention allocation: Preferences for stereotypic versus counterstereotypic information. *Journal of Personality and Social Psychology, 80*(6), 876–893.

Plomin, R. (1990). *Nature and nurture: An introduction to human behavioral genetics*. Pacific Grove, CA: Brooks/Cole.

Pollack, R. H., & Silvar, S. D. (1967). Magnitude of the Mueller-Lyer illusion in children as a function of the pigmentation of the fundus oculi. *Psychonomic Science, 8,* 83–84.

Ponce, F. Q., & Atkinson, D. R. (1989). Mexican-American acculturation, counselor ethnicity, counseling style, and perceived counselor credibility. *Journal of Counseling Psychology, 36,* 203–208.

Ponchillia, S. V. (1993). The effect of cultural beliefs on the treatment of native people with diabetes and visual impairment. *Journal of Visual Impairment and Blindness, 87*(9), 333–335.

Ponterotto, J. G., Alexander, C. M., & Hinkston, J. A. (1988). Afro-American preferences for counselor characteristics: A replication and extension. *Journal of Counseling Psychology, 35*(2), 175–182.

Pontius, A. A. (1997). Lack of sex differences among east Ecuadorian school children on geometric figure rotation and face drawings. *Perceptual and Motor Skills, 85*(1), 72–74.

Poole, G., & Ting, K. (1995). Cultural differences between Euro-Canadian and Indo-Canadian maternity patients. *Journal of Social Psychology, 135*(5), 631–644.

Poortinga, H. Y. (1989). Equivalence of cross-cultural data: An overview of basic issues. *International Journal of Psychology, 24,* 737–756.

Poortinga, H. Y. (1990). *Presidential address IACCP: Towards a conceptualization of culture for psychology*. Unpublished paper, Tilburg University, The Netherlands.

Poortinga, Y. H., Van de Vijver, F. J. R., Joe, R. C., & van de Koppel, J. M. H. (1987). Peeling the onion called culture: A synopsis. In C. Kagitcibasi et al. (Eds.), *Growth and progress in cross-cultural psychology* (pp. 22–34). Berwyn, PA: Swets North America.

Porter, J. R., & Washington, R. E. (1993). Minority identity and self-esteem. *Annual Review of Sociology, 19,* 139–161.

Porter, R. Y. (2000). Understanding and treating ethnic minority youth. In J. E. Aponte & J. Wohl (Eds.), *Psychological intervention and cultural diversity* (2nd ed., pp. 167–182). Boston: Allyn & Bacon.

Posada, G., Gao, Y., Wu, F., Posado, R., Tascon, M., Schoelmerich, A., Sagi, A., Kondo-Ikemura, K., Haaland, W., & Synnevaag, B. (1995). The secure-base phenomenon across cultures: Children's behavior, mothers' preferences and experts' concepts. In E. Waters, B. E. Vaughn, G. Posada, & K. Kondo-Ikemura (Eds.), *Caregiving, cultural, and cognitive perspectives on secure-base behavior and working models: New growing points of attachment theory and research. Monographs of the Society for Research on Child Development, 60*(2–3, Serial No. 244), 27–48.

Prasadaro, P. S. D. V., & Matam, S. P. (2001). Clinical psychology in India. *Journal of Clinical Psychology in Medical Settings, 8*(1), 31–38.

Pratt, G. (1993). Should I take this job? The organizational culture dimension to career decisions. *Educational Psychology in Practice, 8*(4), 222–224.

Price-Williams, D., & Ramirez, M., III (1977). Divergent thinking, cultural differences, and bilingualism. *Journal of Social Psychology, 103,* 3–11.

Priest, R. (1991). Racism and prejudice as negative impacts on African American clients in therapy. *Journal of Counseling and Development, 70,* 213–215.

Primm, A. B., Lima, B. R., & Rowe, C. L. (1996). Cultural and ethnic sensitivity. In W. R. Breakey (Ed.), *Integrated mental health services: Modern community psychiatry* (pp. 146–159). New York: Oxford University Press.

Prince, R. (1980). Variations in psychotherapeutic procedures. In H. C. Triandis & J. Draguns (Eds.), *Handbook of cross-cultural psychology: Vol. 6. Psychopathology* (pp. 291–349). Boston: Allyn & Bacon.

Prince, V. (1985). Sex, gender, and semantics. *Journal of Sex Research, 21,* 92–96.

Pugh, J. F. (1991). The semantics of pain in Indian culture and medicine. *Culture, Medicine and Psychiatry, 15*(1), 19–43.

Puloka, M. H. (1997). A commonsense perspective on the Tongan folk healing. *International Journal of Mental Health, 26*(3), 69–93.

Punamaeki, R. L., & Joustie, M. (1998). The role of culture, violence, and personal factors affecting dream content. *Journal of Cross-Cultural Psychology, 29*(2), 320–342.

Punetha, D., Giles, H., & Young, L. (1987). Ethnicity and immigrant values: Religion and language choice. *Journal of Language and Social Psychology, 6,* 229–241.

Quah, S., & Bishop, G. D. (1996). Seeking help for illness: The roles of cultural orientation and illness cognition. *Journal of Health Psychology, 1,* 209–222.

Rabbie, J. M., & Horwitz, M. (1982). Conflicts and aggression among individuals and groups. In H. Hirsch, H. Brandstatter, & H. Kelley (Eds.), *Proceedings of the XXII International Congress of Psychology, Leipzig, DDR: No. 8. Social Psychology*. Amersterdam: Noord-Holland.

Rack, P. (1982). *Race, culture and mental disorder*. London: Tavistock.

Radford, M. H. B. (1989). *Culture, depression, and decision-making behavior: A study with Japanese and Australian clinical and non-clinical populations*. Unpublished doctoral dissertation, Flinters University of South Australia.

Radford, M. H. B., Mann, L., Ohta, Y., & Nakane, Y. (1993). Differences between Australian and Japanese students in decisional self-esteem, decisional stress, and coping styles. *Journal of Cross-Cultural Psychology, 24*(3), 284–297.

Radford, M. H. B., Nakane, Y., Ohta, Y., & Mann, L. (1991). Differences between Australian and Japanese students in reported use of decision processes. *International Journal of Psychology, 26*(1), 35–52.

Ramirez, J. M. (1993). Acceptability of aggression in four Spanish regions and a comparison with other European countries. *Aggressive Behavior, 19*(3), 185–197.

Ramirez, J. M., Lagerspetz, K. M. J., Fraczek, A., Fujihara, T., Theron, W. H., Musazadeh, Z., & Andreu, J. M. (2001). Moral approval of aggressive acts by urban students. In J. M. Ramirez & D. S. Richardson (Eds.), *Cross-cultural approaches to aggression and reconciliation* (pp. 61–71). Huntington, NY: Nova Science Publishers.

Rao, V., & Rao, V. (1985). Sex-role attitudes across two cultures: United States and India. *Sex Roles, 13*(11–12), 607–624.

Rattan, M. S., & MacArthur, R. S. (1968). Longitudinal prediction of school achievement for Metis and Eskimo pupils. *Alberta Journal of Educational Research, 14*(1), 37–41.

Reece, D. (1996). Covering and communication: The symbolism of dress among Muslim women. *Howard Journal of Communications, 7*(1), 35–52.

Reed, T. E., & Jensen, A. R. (1992). Conduction velocity in a brain nerve pathway of normal adults correlates with intelligence levels. *Intelligence, 16*(3–4), 259–272.

Reed, T. E., & Jensen, A. R. (1993). A somatosensory latency between the thalamus and cortex also correlates with level of intelligence. *Intelligence, 17*(4), 443–450.

Regier, D. A., Farmer, M. E., Rae, D. S., Myers, J. K., Kramer, M., Robins, L. N., George, L. K., Karno, M., & Locke, B. Z. (1993a). One-month prevalence of mental disorders in the United States and sociodemographic characteristics: The Epidemiologic Catchment Area study. *Acta Psychiatrica Scandinavica, 88*, 35–47.

Regier, D. A., Narrow, W. E., Rae, D. S., Manderscheid, R. W., Locke, B. Z., & Goodwin, F. K. (1993b). The de facto US mental and addictive disorders service system: Epidemiologic Catchment Area prospective 1-year prevalence rates of disorders and services. *Archives of General Psychiatry, 50*, 85–94.

Reichers, A. E., & Schneider, B. (1990). Climate and culture: An evolution of constructs. In B. Schneider (Ed.), *Organizational climate and culture* (pp. 5–39). San Francisco: Jossey-Bass.

Reid, P. T., & Trotter, K. H. (1993). Children's self-presentations with infants: Gender and ethnic comparisons. *Sex Roles, 29*(3–4), 1993.

Remland, M. S., Jones, T. S., & Brinkman, H. (1995). Interpersonal distance, body orientation, and touch: Effects of culture, gender, and age. *Journal of Social Psychology, 135*(3), 281–297.

Repetti, R. L., Taylor, S. E., & Seeman, T. E. (2002). Risky families: Family social environments and the mental and physical health of offspring. *Psychological Bulletin, 128*(2), 330–366.

Resnik, H. L., & Dizmang, L. H. (1971). Observations on suicidal behavior among American Indians. *American Journal of Psychiatry, 127*(7), 882–887.

Reynolds, D. K. (1980). *The quiet therapies.* Honolulu: University of Hawaii Press.

Rhi, B.-Y. (2000). Culture, spirituality, and mental health. *Cultural Psychiatry: International Perspectives, 24*(3), 569–579.

Richardson, D. S., & Huguet, P. (2001). Beliefs about and experience with aggression in the United States and France. In J. M. Ramirez & D. S. Richardson (Eds), *Cross-cultural approaches to aggression and reconciliation* (pp. 73–85). Huntington, NY: Nova Science Publishers.

Riemann, R., Angleitner, A., & Strelau, J. (1997). Genetic and environmental influences on personality: A study of twins reared together using the self- and peer-report NEO-FFI scales. *Journal of Personality, 65*(3), 449–475.

Riesman, P. (1977). *Freedom in Fulani social life: An introspective ethnography* (M. Fuller, Trans.). Chicago: University of Chicago Press. (Original work published 1974)

Rivers, W. H. R. (1905). Observations on the senses of the Todas. *British Journal of Psychology, 1*, 321–396.

Robbins, M. C., DeWalt, B. R., & Pelto, P. J. (1972). Climate and behavior: A biocultural study. *Journal of Cross-Cultural Psychology, 3*(4), 331–344.

Robbins, S. R. (1987). *Organization theory: Structure, design and applications.* Englewood Cliffs, NJ: Prentice-Hall.

Robertson, A., & Cochrane, R. (1976). Attempted suicide and cultural change: An empirical investigation. *Human Relations, 29*(9), 863–883.

Robins, L. N., Helzer, J. E., Weissman, M. M., Ovraschel, H., Gruenberg, E., Burke, J. D., & Reiger, D. (1984). Lifetime prevalence of specific psychiatric disorders in three sites. *Archives of General Psychiatry, 41*, 949–958.

Robins, L. N., & Regier, D. A. (1991). *Psychiatric disorders in America: The Epidemiologic Catchment Area study.* New York: Free Press.

Rodenhauser, P. (1994). Cultural barriers to mental health care delivery in Alaska. *Journal of Mental Health Administration, 21*, 60–70.

Roemer, M. I. (1991). *National health systems of the world.* New York: Oxford University Press.

Rogers, C. R. (1942). *Counseling and psychotherapy.* Boston: Houghton Mifflin.

Rogler, L. H., Malgady, R. G., & Rodriguez, O. (1989). *Hispanics and mental health: A framework for research.* Malabar, FL: Krieger.

Rohner, R. P. (1984). Toward a conception of culture for cross-cultural psychology. *Journal of Cross-Cultural Psychology, 15*, 111–138.

Rohner, R. P., & Pettengill, S. M. (1985). Perceived parental acceptance-rejection and parental control among Korean adolescents. *Child Development, 56*, 524–528.

Rolland, J. S. (1993). Mastering family challenges in serious illness and disability. In F. Walsh et al. (Eds.), *Normal family processes* (2nd ed., pp. 444–473). New York: Guilford Press.

Romano, J. L. (1988). Stress management counseling: From crisis to intervention. *Counseling Psychology Quarterly, 1*(2–3), 211–219.

Romero, G. J., & Garza, R. T. (1986). Attributes for the occupational success/failure of ethnic minority and nonminority women. *Sex Roles, 14,* 445–452.

Rosch, E. (1973). On the internal structure of perceptual categories. In T. E. Moore (Ed.), *Cognitive development and the acquisition of language* (pp. 111–144). San Diego: Academic Press.

Rosch, E. (1978). Principles of categorization. In E. Rosch & B. B. Lloyd (Eds.), *Cognition and categorization* (pp. 28–48). Hillsdale, NJ: Erlbaum.

Rose, M. H. (1995). Apprehending deaf culture. *Journal of Applied Communication Research, 23*(2), 156–162.

Roseman, I. J., Dhawan, N., Rettek, S. I., Nadidu, R. K., & Thapa, K. (1995). Cultural differences and cross-cultural similarities in appraisals and emotional responses. *Journal of Cross-Cultural Psychology, 26,* 23–48.

Rosenberg, E. L., & Ekman, P. (1994). Coherence between expressive and experiential systems in emotion. *Cognition and Emotion, 8*(3), 201–229.

Rosenthal, M.K. (1992). Nonparental child care in Israel: A cultural and historical perspective. In M. E. Lamb, K. J. Sternberg, C-P. Hwang, & A. G. Broberg (Eds.), *Childcare in context: Cross-cultural perspectives* (pp. 305–330). Hillsdale, NJ: Erlbaum.

Rosmus, C., Halifax, N. S., Johnston, C., Chan-Yip, A., & Yang, F. (2000). Pain response in Chinese and non-Chinese Canadian infants: Is there a difference? *Social Science and Medicine, 51*(2), 175–184.

Ross, B. M., & Millson, C. (1970). Repeated memory of oral prose in Ghana and New York. *International Journal of Psychology, 5,* 173–181.

Ross, J., & Ferris, K. R. (1981). Interpersonal attraction and organizational outcome: A field experiment. *Administrative Science Quarterly, 26,* 617–632.

Ross, L. (1977). The intuitive psychologist and his shortcomings: Distortions in the attribution process. In L. Berkowitz (Ed.), *Advances in experimental social psychology* (Vol. 10, pp. 174–221). New York: Academic Press.

Rosselló, J., & Bernal, G. (1999). The efficacy of cognitive-behavioral and interpersonal treatments for depression in Puerto Rican adolescents. *Journal of Consulting and Clinical Psychology, 67,* 734–745.

Rossiter, J. C. (1994). The effect of a culture-specific education program to promote breastfeeding among Vietnamese women in Sydney. *International Journal of Nursing Studies, 31*(4), 369–379.

Rotheram-Borus, M. J., & Petrie, K. J. (1996). Patterns of social expectations among Maori and European children in New Zealand. *Journal of Cross-Cultural Psychology, 27*(5), 576–597.

Rotter, J. B. (1954). *Social learning and clinical psychology.* Englewood Cliffs, NJ: Prentice-Hall.

Rotter, J. B. (1966). Generalized expectancies for internal versus external control of reinforcement. *Psychological Monographs, 80* (Whole No. 609).

Rousseau, B. M. (1990). Normative beliefs in fund-raising organizations: Linking culture to organizational performance and individual responses. *Group and Organization Studies, 15*(4), 448–460.

Rubin, G. (1995). Maitrise des emotions, emprise et analite [Emotion control, mastery, and anality]. *Revue-Francaise-de-Psychoanalyse, 59*(3), 803–809.

Russell, G. L., Fujino, D. C., Sue, S., Cheung, M., & Snowden, L. R. (1996). The effects of the therapist-client ethnic match in the assessment of mental health functioning. *Journal of Cross-Cultural Psychology, 27*(5), 598–615.

Russell, J. A. (1991). Culture and the categorization of emotions. *Psychological Bulletin, 110,* 426–450.

Russell, J. A. (1994a). Is there universal recognition of emotion from facial expression? A review of the cross-cultural studies. *Psychological Bulletin, 115*(1), 102–141.

Russell, J. A. (1994b). Afterword. In J. Russell, J. Fernandez-Dols, A. Manstead, & J. Wellenkamp (Eds.), *Everyday conceptions of emotion* (pp. 571–574). Dordrecht, Netherlands: Kluwer Academic Publishers.

Russell, J. A. (1995). Facial expressions of emotion: What lies beyond minimal universality? *Psychological Bulletin, 118*(3), 379–391.

Russell, J. A. (1997). Reading emotions from and into faces: Resurrecting a dimensional-contextual perspective. In J. A. Russell, J. M. Fernandez-Dols, et al. (Eds.), *The psychology of facial expression: Studies in emotion and social interaction* (2nd series, pp. 295–320). New York: Cambridge University Press.

Sachdev, P. S. (1990). Whakama: Culturally determined behavior in the New Zealand Maori. *Psychological Medicine, 20*(2), 433–444.

Sackett, P. R., & Wilk, S. L. (1994). Within-group norming and other forms of score adjustment in preemployment testing. *American Psychologist, 49*(11), 929–954.

Saco-Pollit, C. (1989). Ecocultural context and developmental risk: Birth in the high altitudes (Peru). In J. K. Nugent, B. M. Lester, & T. B. Brazelton (Eds.), *The cultural context of infancy: Vol. 1. Biology, culture and infant development* (pp. 3–25). Norwood, NJ: Ablex.

Sagi, A., Lamb, M. E., Lewkowicz, K. S., Shoham, R., Dvir, R., & Estes, D. (1985). Security of infant-mother, -father, and metapelet attachments among kibbutz reared Israeli children. In I. Bretherton & E. Waters (Eds.), *Growing point in attachment theory. Monographs of the Society for Research in Child Development, 50*(1–2, Serial No. 209).

Sagi, A., van IJzendoorn, M. H., Aviezer, O., Donnell, F., & Mayseless, O. (1994). Sleeping out of home in a kibbutz communal arrangement: It makes a difference for infant-mother attachment. *Child Development, 65,* 992–1004.

Sagi, A., van IJzendoorn, M. H., Scharf, M., Joels, T., Koren-Karie, N., Mayseless, O., & Aviezer, O. (1997). Ecological constraints for intergenerational transmission of attachment. *International Journal of Behavioral Development, 20,* 287–299.

Sakamoto, Y., & Miura, T. (1976, March). An attempt to understand Japanese personality from a family psychiatry point of view. *Australian and New Zealand Journal of Psychiatry, 10*(1-A), 115–117.

Salovey, P., & Birnbaum, D. (1989). Influence of mood on health related cognitions. *Journal of Personality and Social Psychology, 57,* 539–551.

Sam, D. L. (1994). The psychological adjustment of young immigrants in Norway. *Scandinavian Journal of Psychology, 35,* 240–253.

Sampson, E. E. (1988). The debate on individualism: Indigenous psychologies and their role in personal and societal functioning. *American Psychologist, 43,* 15–22.

Sanchez, A. R., & Atkinson, D. R. (1983). Mexican-American cultural commitment, preference for counselor ethnicity, and willingness to use counseling. *Journal of Counseling Psychology, 30*(2), 215–220.

Santa, J. L., & Baker, L. (1975). Linguistic influences on visual memory. *Memory and Cognition, 3*(4), 445–450.

Santiago-Rivera, A. L., & Azara, L. (1995). Developing a culturally sensitive treatment modality for bilingual Spanish-speaking clients: Incorporating language and culture in counseling. *Journal of Counseling and Development, 74*(1), 12–17.

Saraswathi, T. (1999). Adult-child continuity in India: Is adolescence a myth or an emerging reality? In T. Saraswathi (Ed.), *Culture, socialization, and human development: Theory, research, and applications in India* (pp. 213–232). Thousand Oaks, CA: Sage.

Sargent, C. (1984). Between death and shame: Dimensions of pain in Bariba culture. *Social Science and Medicine, 19*(12), 1299–1304.

Sashkin, M., & Fulmer, R. (1985, August). *Measuring organizational excellence culture with a validated questionnaire.* Paper presented at the meeting of the Academy of Management, San Diego.

Sato, T. (1998). Agency and communion: The relationship between therapy and culture. *Cultural Diversity and Mental Health, 4,* 278–290.

Satoh, K. (1996). Expression in the Japanese kindergarten curriculum. *Early Child Development and Care, 123,* 193–202.

Saudino, K. J. (1997). Moving beyond the heritability question: New directions in behavioral genetic studies of personality. *Current Directions in Psychological Science, 6*(4), 86–90.

Scarr, S. (1993). Biological and cultural diversity: The legacy of Darwin for development. *Child Development, 64,* 1333–1353.

Scarr, S., & McCartney, K. (1983). How people make their own environments: A theory of genotype environment effects. *Child Development, 54,* 424–435.

Scarr, S., & Weinberg, R.A. (1976). I.Q. test performance of black children adopted by white families. *American Psychologist, 31,* 726–739.

Schaller, M., Conway, L. G., & Tanchuk, T. L. (2002). Selective pressures on the once and future contents of ethnic stereotypes: Effects of the communicability of traits. *Journal of Personality and Social Psychology, 82*(6), 861–877.

Schein, E. H. (1985). *Organizational culture and leadership: A dynamic view.* San Francisco: Jossey-Bass.

Scherer, K. R. (1997a). Profiles of emotion-antecedent appraisal: Testing theoretical predictions across cultures. *Cognition and Emotion, 11*(2), 113–150.

Scherer, K. R. (1997b). The role of culture in emotion-antecedent appraisal. *Journal of Personality and Social Psychology, 73*(4), 902–922.

Scherer, K. R., Matsumoto, D., Wallbott, H., & Kudoh, T. (1988). Emotional experience in cultural context: A comparison between Europe, Japan, and the USA. In K. Scherer (Ed.), *Facets of emotion: Recent research* (pp. 5–30). Hillsdale, NJ: Erlbaum.

Scherer, K. R., Summerfield, A., & Wallbott, H. (1983). Cross-national research on antecedents and components of emotion: A progress report. *Social Science Information, 22,* 355–385.

Scherer, K. R., & Wallbott, H. G. (1994). Evidence for universality and cultural variation of differential emotion response patterning. *Journal of Personality and Social Psychology, 66*(2), 310–328.

Scherer, K. R., Wallbott, H. G., & Summerfield, A. B. (Eds.). (1986). *Experiencing emotion: A cross-cultural study.* Cambridge, UK: Cambridge University Press.

Schimmack, U. (1996). Cultural influences on the recognition of emotion by facial expressions. *Journal of Cross-Cultural Psychology, 27,* 37–50.

Schmidt, S. M., & Yeh, R. (1992). The structure of leader influence: A cross-national comparison. *Journal of Cross-Cultural Psychology, 23*(2), 251–264.

Schmit, M. J., Ryan, A. M., Stierwalt, S. L., & Powell, A. B. (1995). Frame-of-reference effects on personality scale scores and criterion-related validity. *Journal of Applied Psychology, 80*(5), 607–620.

Schwartz, N., Strack, F., Kommer, D., & Wagner, D. (1987). Soccer, rooms, and the quality of life: Mood effects on judgments of satisfaction with life in general and with specific domains. *European Journal of Social Psychology, 17*(1), 69–79.

Schwartz, S. (1990). Individualism-collectivism: Critique and proposed refinements. *Journal of Cross-Cultural Psychology, 21,* 139–157.

Schwartz, S. H. (1978). Temporal instability as a moderator of the attitude behavior relationship. *Journal of Personality and Social Psychology, 36*(7), 715–724.

Schwartz, S. H. (1994). Are there universal aspects in the structure and contents of human values? *Journal of Social Issues, 50*(4), 19–45.

Schwartz, S. H., & Bilsky, W. (1987). Toward a universal psychological structure of human values. *Journal of Personality and Social Psychology, 53,* 550–562.

Scribner, S. (1974). Developmental aspects of categorized recall in a West African society. *Cognitive Psychology, 6*(4), 475–494.

Scribner, S. (1979). Modes of thinking and ways of speaking: Culture and logic reconsidered. In I. O. Freedle (Ed.),

New directions in discourse processing (pp. 223–243). Norwood, NJ: Ablex.

Seelye, H. N., & Brewer, B. M. (1970). Ethnocentrism and acculturation of North Americans in Guatemala. *Journal of Social Psychology, 80,* 147–155.

Segall, M. H. (1979). *Cross-cultural psychology: Human behavior in global perspective.* Pacific Grove, CA: Brooks/Cole.

Segall, M. H. (1984). More than we need to know about culture, but are afraid to ask. *Journal of Cross Cultural Psychology, 15*(2), 153–162.

Segall, M. H., Campbell, D. T., & Hersokovits, J. (1963). Cultural differences in the perception of geometric illusions. *Science, 193,* 769–771.

Segall, M. H., Campbell, D. T., & Hersokovits, J. (1966). *The influence of culture on visual perception.* Indianapolis: Bobbs-Merrill.

Segall, M. H., Dasen, P. R., Berry, J. W., & Poortinga, Y. H. (1990). *Human behavior in global perspective: An introduction to cross-cultural psychology.* New York: Pergamon Press.

Seiffge-Krenke, I., & Shulman, S. (1990). Coping style in adolescence: A cross-cultural study. *Journal of Cross-Cultural Psychology, 21*(3), 351–377.

Shahim, S. (1992). Correlations for Wechsler Intelligence Scale for Children–Revised and the Weschler Preschool and Primary Scale of Intelligence for Iranian children. *Psychological Reports, 70,* 27–30.

Shakin, M., Shakin, D., & Sternglanz, S. H. (1985). Infant clothing: Sex labeling for strangers. *Sex Roles, Vol. 12*(9–10), 955–964.

Shand, N., & Kosawa, Y. (1985). Culture transmission: Caudill's model and alternative hypotheses. *American Anthropologist, 87*(4), 862–871.

Shane, S., Venkataraman, S., & MacMillan, I. (1995). Cultural differences in innovation championing strategies. *Journal of Management, 21*(5), 931–952.

Shapiro, P. N., & Penrod, S. (1986). Meta-analysis of facial identification studies. *Psychological Bulletin, 100*(2), 139–156.

Shayer, M., Demetriou, A., & Perez, M. (1988). The structure and scaling of concrete operational thought: Three studies in four countries and only one story. *Genetic Psychology Monographs, 114,* 307–376.

Shea, J. D. (1985). Studies of cognitive development in Papua New Guinea. *International Journal of Psychology, 20,* 33–61.

Shepperd, J., & Wright, R. (1989). Individual contributions to a collective effort: An incentive analysis. *Personality and Social Psychology Bulletin, 15,* 141–149.

Sherif, M., & Sherif, C. W. (1953). *Groups in harmony and tension.* New York: Harper & Row.

Shiang, J. (1998). Does culture make a difference? Racial/ethnic patterns of completed suicide in San Francisco, CA, 1987–1996 and clinical applications. *Suicide and Life Threatening Behavior, 28,* 338–354.

Shikanai, K. (1978). Effects of self-esteem on attribution of success and failure. *Japanese Journal of Experimental Social Psychology, 18*(1), 35–46.

Shirakashi, S. (1985). Social loafing of Japanese students. *Hiroshima Forum for Psychology, 10,* 35–40.

Shore, B. (1991). Twice born, once conceived: Meaning construction and cultural cognition. *American Anthropologist, 93*(1), 9–27.

Shweder, R. A. (1979a). Rethinking culture and personality theory: I. A critical examination of two classical postulates. *Ethos, 7*(3), 255–278.

Shweder, R. A. (1979b). Rethinking culture and personality theory: II. A critical examination of two more classical postulates. *Ethos, 7*(4), 279–311.

Shweder, R. A. (1980). Rethinking culture and personality theory: III. From genesis and typology to hermeneutics and dynamics. *Ethos, 8*(1), 60–94.

Shweder, R. A. (1991). *Thinking through cultures: Expeditions in cultural psychology.* Cambridge, MA: Harvard University Press.

Shweder, R. A. (1994). Liberalism as destiny. In B. Puka et al. (Eds.), *Moral development: A compendium: Vol. 4. The great justice debate: Kohlberg criticism* (pp. 71–74). New York: Garland.

Shweder, R. A. (2000). The psychology of practice and the practice of the three psychologies. *Asian Journal of Social Psychology, 3*(3), 207–222.

Shweder, R. A., & Bourne, E. J. (1984). Does the concept of the person vary cross-culturally? In R. A. Shweder & R. A. LeVine (Eds.), *Culture theory: Essays on mind, self, and emotion* (pp. 158–199). Cambridge, UK: Cambridge University Press.

Shweder, R. A., Mahapatra, M., & Miller, J. G. (1987). Culture and moral development. In J. Kagan & S. Lamb (Eds.), *The emergence of morality in young children* (pp. 1–83). Chicago: University of Chicago Press.

Signorella, M. L., & Liben, L. S. (1984). Recall and reconstruction of gender-related pictures: Effects of attitude, task difficulty, and age. *Child Development, 55*(2), 393–405.

Simmons, C. H., vom Kolke, A., & Shimizu, H. (1986). Attitudes toward romantic love among American, German and Japanese students. *Journal of Social Psychology, 126,* 327–336.

Simonton, D. K. (1996). Presidents' wives and First Ladies: On achieving eminence within a traditional gender role. *Sex Roles 35,* (5–6), 309–336.

Singelis, T. M. (1994). The measurement of independent and interdependent self-construals. *Personality and Social Psychology Bulletin, 20* (5), 580–591.

Singelis, T. M. (2000). Some thoughts on the future of cross-cultural social psychology. *Journal of Cross-Cultural Psychology, 31*(1), 76–91.

Singelis, T. M., & Sharkey, W. (1995). Culture, self-construal, and embarrassability. *Journal of Cross-Cultural Psychology, 26*(6), 622–644.

Singelis, T. M., Triandis, C. H., Bhawuk, S. D., & Gelfand, M. J. (1995). Horizontal and vertical dimensions of individualism and collectivism: A theoretical and measurement refinement. *Cross-Cultural Research, 29*(3), 241–275.

Sinha, D. (1993). Indigenization of psychology in India and its relevance. In U. Kim & J. W. Berry (Eds.), *Indigenous psychologies: Research and experience in cultural context* (pp. 30–43). Newbury Park, CA: Sage.

Sinha, J. B. P. (1979). The authoritative leadership: A style of effective management. *Indian Journal of Industrial Relations, 2*(3), 381–389.

Sinha, J. B. P. (1997). A cultural perspective on organizational behavior in India. In P. C. Earley & M. Erez (Eds.), *New perspectives on international industrial/organizational psychology*. San Francisco: New Lexington Press.

Slavin, M. O., and Kriegman, D. (1992). *The adaptive design of the human psyche: Psychoanalysis, evolutionary biology, and the therapeutic process.* New York: The Guilford Press.

Slee, R., & Cook, S. (1994). Creating cultures of disability to control young people in Australian schools. *Urban Review, 26,* 15–23.

Smith, J. R., Griffith, E. J., Griffith, K. H., & Steger, J. M. (1980). When is a stereotype a stereotype? *Psychological Reports, 46,* 643–651.

Smith, P. B. (1998, October). *Leadership in high power distance cultures: An event management perspective.* Paper presented at the Third Latin-American Reunion of Cross-Cultural Psychology, Toluca, Mexico.

Smith, P. B., & Bond, M. H. (1999). *Social psychology: Across cultures* (2nd ed.) Boston: Allyn & Bacon.

Smith, P. B., Dugan, S., Peterson, M. F., & Leung, K. (1998). Individualism–collectivism and the handling of disagreement: A 23-country study. *International Journal of Intercultural Relations, 22*(3), 351–367.

Smith, P. B., Dugan, S., & Trompenaars, F. (1996). National culture and the values of organizational employees. *Journal of Cross-Cultural Psychology, 27*(2), 231–264.

Smith, P. B., Dugan, S., & Trompenaars, F. (1997). Locus of control and affectivity by gender and occupational status: A 14-nation study. *Sex Roles, 36*(1–2), 51–77.

Smith, P. B., Peterson, M. F., & Misumi, J. (1994). Event management and work team effectiveness in Japan, Britain and USA. *Journal of Occupational and Organizational Psychology, 67,* 33–43.

Smith, P. B., Peterson, M., Misumi, J., & Bond, M. (1992). A cross-cultural test of the Japanese PM leadership theory. *Applied Psychology: An International Review, 41,* 5–19.

Smith, P. B., Peterson, M. F., & Schwartz, S. H. (2002). Cultural values, sources of guidance, and their relevance to managerial behavior. *Journal of Cross-Cultural Psychology, 33*(2), 188–208.

Smith, P. B., Wang, Z. M., & Leung, K. (1997). Leadership, decision-making, and cultural context: Event management within Chinese joint ventures. *Leadership Quarterly, 8*(4), 413–431.

Snarey, J. R. (1985). Cross-cultural universality of social development: A critical review of Kohlbergian research. *Psychological Bulletin, 97,* 202–232.

Sniderman, M. P., Northrup, A. D., Fletcher, F. J., Russell, H. P., & Tetlock, E. P. (1993). Psychological and cultural foundations of prejudice: The case of anti-Semitism in Quebec. *Canadian Review of Sociology and Anthropology, 30*(2), 242–270.

Snowden L. R. (2001). Barriers to effective mental health services for African Americans. *Mental Health Services Research, 3,* 181–187.

Snyder, C. R. (1974). Acceptance of personality interpretations as a function of assessment procedures. *Journal of Consulting and Clinical Psychology, 42*(1), 150.

Snyder, C. R., & Higgins, R. L. (1988). Excuses: Their effective role in the negotiation of reality. *Psychological Bulletin, 104,* 23–35.

Snyder, M. (1974). Self-monitoring of expressive behavior. *Journal of Personality and Social Psychology, 30*(4), 526–537.

Sodowsky, G. R., & Carey, J. C. (1987). Asian immigrants in America: Factors related to adjustment. *Journal of Multicultural Counseling and Development, 15,* 129–141.

Solis-Camara, P., & Fox, R. A. (1995). Parenting among mothers with young children in Mexico and the United States. *Journal of Social Psychology, 135*(5), 591–599.

Song, M. J., & Ginsburg, H. P. (1987). The development of informal and formal mathematical thinking in Korean and U.S. children. *Child Development, 58,* 1286–1296.

Soudijn, K. A., Hutschemaekers, G. J. M., & Van de Vijver, F. J. R. (1990). Culture conceptualizations. In F. J. R. Van de Vijver and G. J. M. Hutschemaekers (Eds.), *The investigation of culture: Current issues in cultural psychology* (pp. 19–39). Tilburg, Netherlands: Tilburg University Press.

Sow, I. (1977). *Psychiatrie dynamique africaine.* Paris: Payot.

Sow, I. (1978). *Les structures anthropologiques de la folie en Afrique noire.* Paris: Payot.

Sowell, T. (1983). *The economics and politics of race.* New York: Quill.

Spadone, R. A. (1992). Internal-external control and temporal orientation among Southeast Asians and White Americans. *American Journal of Occupational Therapy, 46*(8), 713–718.

Spearman, C. E. (1927). *The abilities of man.* New York: Macmillan.

Spencer, H. (1876). *Principles of sociology.* New York: Appleton.

Sponsel, L. E. (1998). Yanomami: An arena of conflict and aggression in the Amazon. *Aggressive Behavior, 24*(2), 97–122.

Sprecher, S., & Chandak, R. (1992). Attitudes about arranged marriage and dating among men and women from India. *Journal of Sex Research, 32,* 3–15.

Srull, T. K. (1983). Organizational and retrieval processes in person memory: An examination of processing objectives, presentation format, and the possible role of self-generated retrieval cues. *Journal of Personality and Social Psychology, 44,* 1157–1170.

Steele, C. (1998). How stereotypes shape intellectual identity and performance. *American Psychologist, 52*(6), 613–629.

Steele, C., & Aronson, J. (1995). Stereotype threat and the intellectual test performance of African Americans.

Journal of Personality and Social Psychology, 69, 797–811.

Steele, S. (1990). *The content of our character: A new vision of race in America.* New York: HarperCollins.

Steinberg, L., Lamborn, S. D., Darling, N., Mounts, N. S., & Dornbusch, S. M. (1994). Over-time changes in adjustment and competence in adolescents from authoritative, authoritarian, indulgent, and neglectful families. *Child Development, 65,* 754–770.

Steinberg, L., Lamborn, S., Dornbusch, S., & Darling, N. (1992). Impact of parenting practices on adolescent achievement: Authoritative parenting, school involvement, and encouragement to succeed. *Child Development, 63,* 1266–1281.

Steinberg, L., Mounts, N., Lamborn, S., & Dornbusch, S. (1991). Authoritative parenting and adolescent adjustment across various ecological niches. *Journal of Research on Adolescence, 1,* 19–36.

Steinberg, S. (1989). *The ethnic myth: Race, ethnicity, and class in America.* Boston: Beacon Press.

Stephan, W. G., Stephan, C. W., & de Vargas, M. (1996). Emotional expression in Costa Rica and the United States. *Journal of Cross-Cultural Psychology, 27*(2), 147–160.

Steptoe, A., Sutcliffe, I., Allen, B., & Coombes, C. (1991). Satisfaction with communication, medical knowledge, and coping styles in patients with metastatic cancer. *Social Science and Medicine, 32*(6), 627–632.

Steptoe, A., & Wardle, J. (Eds.). (1994). *Psychosocial processes and health: A reader.* Cambridge, UK: Cambridge University Press.

Sternberg, R. J. (1986). *Intelligence applied: Understanding and increasing your intellectual skills.* New York: Harcourt Brace Jovanovich.

Sternberg, R. J. (1988). Triangulating love. In R. J. Sternberg & M. L. Barnes (Eds.), *The psychology of love* (pp. 119–138). New Haven, CT: Yale University Press.

Sternberg, R. J., & Lubart, T. I. (1995). *Defying the crowd: Cultivating creativity in a culture of conformity.* New York: Free Press.

Sternberg, R. J., & Lubart, T. I. (1999). The concept of creativity: Prospects and paradigms. In R. J. Sternberg (Ed.), *Handbook of creativity* (pp. 3–15). New York: Cambridge University Press.

Stevenson, H. W., et al. (1985). Cognitive performance and academic achievement of Japanese, Chinese, and American children. *Child Development, 56*(3), 718–734.

Stevenson, H. W., Chen, C., & Lee, S. (1993). Mathematics achievement of Chinese, Japanese, and American children: Ten years later. *Science, 259,* 53–58.

Stevenson, H. W., Lee, S., & Stigler, S. Y. (1986). *Beliefs and achievements: A study in Japan, Taiwan, and the United States.* Unpublished manuscript.

Stevenson, H. W., Stigler, J. W., Lee., S., Lucker, G. W., Kitamura, S., & Hsu, C.-C. (1985). Cognitive performance and academic achievement of Japanese, Chinese, and American children. *Child Development, 56*(3), 718–734.

Stewart, A. J., & Malley, J. E. (1987). Role combination in women: Mitigating agency and communion. In F. J. Crosby et al. (Eds.), *Spouse, parent, worker: On gender and multiple roles* (pp. 44–62). New Haven, CT: Yale University Press.

Stewart, S. M., Bond, M. H., Zaman, R. M., McBride-Chang, C., Rao, N., Ho, L. M., & Fielding, R. (1999). Functional parenting in Pakistan. *International Journal of Behavioral Development, 23*(3), 747–770.

Stewart, V. (1973). Tests of the "carpentered world" hypothesis by race and environment in American and Zambia. *International Journal of Psychology, 8,* 83–94.

Stiff, J. B., Hale, J. L., Garlick, R., & Rogan, R. G. (1990). Effects of cue incongruence and social normative influences on individual judgements of honesty and deceit. *Southern Communication Journal, 55,* 206–229.

Stigler, J. W., & Baranes, R. (1988). Culture and mathematics learning. In E. Rothkopf (Ed.), *Review of research in education* (Vol. 15, pp. 253–306). Washington, DC: American Educational Research Association.

Stigler, J. W., Lee, S., & Stevenson, H. W. (1986). Digit memory in Chinese and English: Evidence for a temporally limited store. *Cognition, 23,* 1–20.

Stigler, J. W., & Perry, M. (1988). Mathematics learning in Japanese, Chinese, and American classrooms. *New Directions for Child Development, 41,* 27–58.

Stiles, D. A., Gibbons, J. L., & Schnellman, J. (1990). The smiling sunbather and the chivalrous football player: Young adolescents' images of the ideal women and men. *Journal of Early Adolescence, 7,* 411–427.

Stipek, D. J., & Gralinski, J. H. (1991). Gender differences in children's achievement-related beliefs and emotional responses to success and failure in mathematics. *Journal of Educational Psychology, 83*(3), 361–371.

Stone, L. (1990). *Road to divorce: England 1530–1987.* New York: Oxford University Press.

Strathman, A., Gleicher, F., Boninger, D., & Edwards, C. (1994). The consideration of future consequences: Weighing immediate and distant outcomes of behavior. *Journal of Personality and Social Psychology, 66,* 742–752.

Streltzer, J. (1997). Pain. In W. Tseng & J. Streltzer (Eds.), *Culture and psychopathology: A guide to clinical assessment* (pp. 87–100). New York: Brunner/Mazel.

Strodtbeck, F. L. (1964). Considerations of meta-method in cross-cultural studies. *American Anthropologist, 66*(3), 223–229.

Stropes-Roe, M., & Cochrane, R. (1990). The child-rearing values of Asian and British parents and young people: An inter-ethnic and inter-generational comparison in the evolution of Kohn's 13 qualities. *British Journal of Social Psychology, 29,* 149–160.

Stryker, S. (1986). Identity theory: Developments and extensions. In K. Tardley & T. Honess (Eds.), *Self and identity* (pp. 89–107). New York: Wiley.

Su, L., Yang, Z., Wan, G., Luo, X., & Li, X. (1999). The Child Behavior Checklist used in Chinese children aged 6–11. *Chinese Journal of Clinical Psychology, 7*(2), 70–73.

Suchman, R. G. (1966). Cultural differences in children's color and form perception. *Journal of Social Psychology, 70,* 3–10.

Sue, D. (1998). The interplay of sociocultural factors in the psychological development of Asians in America. In D. R. Atkinson & G. Morten (Eds.), *Counseling American minorities* (5th ed., pp. 205–213). New York: McGraw-Hill.

Sue, D., Sue, D. W., & Sue, S. (1990). *Understanding abnormal behavior* (3rd ed.). Boston: Houghton Mifflin.

Sue, D. W. (1994). Asian-American mental health and help-seeking behavior: Comment on Solberg et al. (1994), Tata and Leong (1994), and Lin (1994). *Journal of Counseling Psychology, 41,* 292–295.

Sue, D. W., & Ivey, A. E., & Pedersen, P. B. (1996). A theory of multicultural counseling and therapy. Pacific Grove, CA: Brooks/Cole.

Sue, D. W., & Sue, D. (1999). *Counseling the culturally different: Theory and practice* (3rd ed.). New York: Wiley.

Sue, S. (1977). Community mental health services to minority groups: Some optimism, some pessimism. *American Psychologist, 32,* 616–624.

Sue, S. (1991, August). *Ethnicity and mental health: Research and policy issues.* Invited address presented at the annual meeting of the American Psychological Association, San Francisco.

Sue, S. (1998). In search of cultural competence in psychotherapy and counseling. *American Psychologist, 53,* 440–448.

Sue, S., Akutsu, P. D., & Higashi, C. (1985). Training issues in conducting therapy with ethnic-minority-group clients. In P. Pedersen (Ed.), *Handbook of cross-cultural counseling and therapy.* New York: Greenwood Press.

Sue, S., Fujino, D. C., Hu, L. T., Takeuchi, D. T., & Zane, N. W. S. (1991). Community mental health services for ethnic minority groups: A test of the cultural responsiveness hypothesis. *Journal of Counseling Psychology, 59,* 533–540.

Sue, S., & Morishima, J. K. (1982). *The mental health of Asian Americans.* San Francisco: Jossey-Bass.

Sue, S., & Zane, N. (1987). The role of culture and cultural techniques in psychotherapy: A reformation. *American Psychologist, 42,* 37–45.

Sue, S., Zane, N., & Young, K. (1994). Research on psychotherapy with culturally diverse populations. In A. E. Bergin & S. L. Garfield (Eds.), *Handbook of psychotherapy and behavior change* (4th ed., pp. 428–466). New York: Wiley.

Suggs, D. N., & Miracle, A. W. (Eds.). (1993). *Culture and human sexuality: A reader.* Pacific Grove: Brooks/Cole.

Suhail, K., & Nisa, Z. (2002). Prevalence of eating disorders in Pakistan: Relationship with depression and body shape. *Eating and Weight Disorders, 7*(2), 131–138.

Sun, L., & Stewart, S. (2000). Psychological adjustment to cancer in a collective culture. *International Journal of Psychology, 35*(5), 177–185.

Suomi, S. J. (2000). A biobehavioral perspective on developmental psychopathology: Excessive aggression and sero-tonergic dysfunction in monkeys. In A. J. Sameroff, M. Lewis, & S. Miller (Eds), *Handbook of developmental psychopathology* (2nd ed., (pp. 237–256). New York: Plenum.

Super, C. M., & Harkness, S. (1986). The developmental niche: A conceptualization at the interface of child and culture. *International Journal of Behavioral Development, 9,* 545–569.

Super, C. M., & Harkness, S. (1994). The developmental niche. In W. Lonner & R. Malpass (Eds.), *Psychology and culture* (pp. 95–99). Boston: Allyn & Bacon.

Sussman, L. K., Robins, L. N., & Earls, F. (1987). Treatment-seeking for depression by black and white Americans. *Social Science and Medicine, 24,* 187–196.

Swartz, L. (1985). Anorexia nervosa as a culture-bound syndrome. *Social Science and Medicine, 20,* 725–730.

Szapocznik, J., Scopetta, M. A., & Tillman, W. (1979). What changes, what stays the same and what affects acculturative change? In J. Szapocznik & M. C. Herrera (Eds.), *Cuban Americans: Acculturation, adjustment and the family* (pp. 12–21). Miami: Universal.

Tafarodi, R. W., & Swann, W. B., Jr. (1996). Individualism-collectivism and global self-esteem: Evidence for a cultural trade-off. *Journal of Cross-Cultural Psychology, 27*(6), 651–672.

Tajfel, H. (1982). Social psychology of intergroup relations. *Annual Review of Psychology, 33,* 1–39.

Tajfel, H., & Turner, J. C. (1986). The social identity theory of intergroup behavior. In S. Worchel & W. G. Austin (Eds.), *Psychology of intergroup relationships* (pp. 7 –24). Chicago: Nelson-Hall.

Takahashi, K. (1990). *Affective relationships and their life-long development* (Vol. 10). Hillsdale, NJ: Erlbaum.

Takahashi, K., & Hatano, G. (1997). A landmark toward the construction of cultural psychology. *Human Development, 40,* 355–359.

Takahashi, K., & Majima, N. (1994). Transition from home to college dormitory: The role of preestablished affective relationships in adjustment to a new life. *Journal of Research on Adolescence, 4*(3), 367–384.

Takahashi, Y. (1997). Culture and suicide: From a Japanese psychiatrist's perspective. *Suicide and Life Threatening Behavior, 27*(1), 137–145.

Takaki, R. (1998). *Strangers from a different shore: A history of Asian Americans* (rev. ed.). Boston: Back Bay Books.

Takano, Y. (1989). Methodological problems in cross-cultural stidies of linguist relativity. *Cognition, 31,* 141–162.

Takano, Y., & Noda, A. (1993). A temporary decline of thinking ability during foreign language processing. *Journal of Cross-Cultural Psychology, 24*(4), 445–462.

Takano, Y., & Noda, A. (1995). Interlanguage dissimilarity enhances the decline of thinking ability during foreign language processing. *Language Learning, 45*(40), 657–681.

Takano, Y., & Osaka, E. (1997). "Japanese collectivism" and "American individualism": Reexamining the dominant view. *Japanese Journal of Psychology, 68*(4), 312–327.

Takeuchi, D. T., Bui, K.-V. T., & Kim, L. (1993). The referral of minority adolescents to community health centers. *Journal of Health and Social Behavior, 34*(2), 153–164.

Takeuchi, D. T., Higginbotham, N., Marsella, A., Gomes, K., Kwan, L., Ostrowski, B., et al. (1987). Native Hawaiian mental health. In A. B. Robillard & A. J. Marsella (Eds.), *Contemporary issues in mental health research in the Pacific Islands* (pp. 149–176). Honolulu: University of Hawaii Press.

Takeuchi, D. T., Sue, S., & Yeh, M. (1995). Return rates and outcomes from ethnicity-specific mental health programs in Los Angeles. *American Journal of Public Health, 85,* 638–643.

Takeuchi, D. T., & Uehara, E. S. (1996). Ethnic minority mental health services: Current research and future conceptual directions. In B. L. Levin & J. Petrila (Eds.), *Mental health services: A public health perspective* (pp. 63–80). New York: Oxford University Press.

Talamantes, M. A., Lawler, W. R., & Espino, V. (1995). Hispanic American elders: Caregiving norms surrounding dying and the use of hospice services. *Hospice Journal, 10*(2), 35–49.

Tanaka-Matsumi, J. (2001). Abnormal psychology and culture. In D. Matsumoto (Ed.), *The handbook of culture and psychology* (pp. 265–286). New York: Oxford University Press.

Tanaka-Matsumi, J., & Draguns, J. G. (1997). Culture and psychopathology. In J. W. Berry, M. H. Segall, & C. Kagitcibasi (Eds.), *Handbook of cross-cultural psychology: Vol. 3. Social behavior and applications* (2nd ed., pp. 449–491). Boston: Allyn & Bacon.

Tata, S. P., & Leong, F. T. (1994). Individualism-collectivism, social-network orientation, and acculturation as predictors of attitudes toward seeking professional psychological help among Chinese Americans. *Journal of Counseling Psychology, 41,* 280–287.

Taylor, C. R., & Stern, B. B. (1997). Asian-Americans: Television advertising and the "model minority" stereotype. *Journal of Advertising, 26*(2), 47–61.

Taylor, J. (1992). *Paved with good intentions: The failure of race relations in contemporary America.* New York: Carroll & Graf.

Tedlock, B. (1987). Zuni and Quiche dream sharing and interpreting. *Dreaming: Anthropological and psychological interpretations* (pp. 105–131). Cambridge, UK: Cambridge University Press.

Tedlock, B. (1992). The role of dreams and visionary narratives in Mayan cultural survival. *Ethos, 20*(4), 453–476.

ter Bogt, T. F., Meeus, W. H., Raaijmakers, Q. A., & Vollebergh, W. A. M. (2001). Youth centrism and the formation of political orientations in adolescence and young adulthood. *Journal of Cross-Cultural Psychology, 32*(2), 229–240.

Terav, T., & Keltikangas, J. L. (1998). Social decision-making strategies among Finnish and Estonian adolescents. *Journal of Social Psychology, 138*(3), 381–391.

Terrell, M. D. (1992, August). *Stress, coping, ethnic identity and college adjustment.* Paper presented at the annual meeting of the American Psychological Association, Washington, DC.

Tharp, R. G. (1991). Cultural diversity and treatment of children. *Journal of Consulting and Clinical Psychology, 5*(3), 381–392.

Thomas, A., & Chess, S. (1977). *Temperament and development.* New York: Brunner/Mazel.

Thomas, A., & Sillen, S. (1972). *Racism and psychiatry.* New York: Brunner/Mazel.

Thomas, D. C., & Toyne, B. (1995). Subordinates' responses to cultural adaptation by Japanese expatriate managers. *Journal of Business Research, 32,* 1–10.

Thompson, N., Stradling, S., Murphy, M., & O'Neill, P. (1996). Stress and organizational culture. *British Journal of Social Work, 26*(5), 647–665.

Thornton, B. (1984). Defensive attribution of responsibility: Evidence for an arousal-based motivational bias. *Journal of Personality and Social Psychology, 46,* 721–734.

Thurstone, L. L. (1938). *Primary mental abilities.* Chicago: University of Chicago Press.

Ting-Toomey, S. (1991). Intimacy expressions in three cultures: France, Japan, and the United States. *International Journal of Intercultural Relations, 15,* 29–46.

Ting-Toomey, S. (1996). Managing intercultural conflicts effectively. In L. A. Samovar & R. E. Porter (Eds.), *Intercultural communication: A reader* (8th ed., pp. 392–404). Belmont, CA: Wadsworth.

Tobin, J. J., & Friedman, J. (1983). Spirits, shamans, and nightmare death: Survivor stress in a Hmong refugee. *American Journal of Orthopsychiatry, 53,* 434–448.

Tolman, A., & Reedy, R. (1998). Implementation of a culture-specific intervention for a Native American community. *Journal of Clinical Psychology in Medical Settings, 5*(3), 381–392.

Tolson, T. F., & Wilson, M. N. (1990). The impact of two- and three-generational Black family structure on perceived family climate. *Child Development, 61*(2), 416–428.

Tom, D., & Cooper, H. (1986). The effect of student background on teacher performance attributions: Evidence for counterdefensive patterns and low expectancy cycles. *Basic and Applied Social Psychology, 7,* 53–62.

Tomada, G., & Schneider, B. H. (1997). Relational agression, gender, and peer acceptance: Invariance across culture, stability over time, and concordance among informants. *Developmental Psychology, 33*(4), 601–609.

Tomasello, M. (1993). On the interpersonal origins of self-concept. In U. Neisser et al. (Eds.), *The perceived self: Ecological and interpersonal sources of self-knowledge. Emory symposia in cognition, 5* (pp. 174–184). New York: Cambridge University Press.

Tomkins, S. S. (1962). *Affect, imagery, and consciousness: Vol. 1. The positive affects.* New York: Springer.

Tomkins, S. S. (1963). *Affect, imagery, and consciousness: Vol. 2. The negative affects.* New York: Springer.

Torrey, E. F. (1972). *The mind game: Witchdoctors and psychiatrists.* New York: Emerson Hall.

Trankina, F. J. (1983). Clinical issues and techniques in working with Hispanic children and their families. In

G. J. Powell (Ed.), *The psychological development of minority group children* (pp. 307–329). New York: Brunner/Mazel.

Triandis, H. C. (1972). *The analysis of subjective culture.* New York: Wiley.

Triandis, H. C. (1989). The self and social behavior in differing cultural contexts. *Psychological Review, 96,* 506–520.

Triandis, H. C. (1994). *Culture and social behavior.* New York: McGraw-Hill.

Triandis, H. C. (Series Ed.). (1995). *New directions in social psychology: Individualism and collectivism.* Boulder: Westview Press.

Triandis, H. C. (1996). The psychologist measurement of cultural syndromes. *American Psychologist, 51*(4), 407–415.

Triandis, H. C. (1998). Vertical and horizontal individualism and collectivism: Theory and research implications for international comparative management. In J. L. C. Cheng & R. B. Peterson (Eds.), *Advances in international comparative management* (Vol. 12, pp. 7–35). Stamford, CT: JAI Press.

Triandis, H. C., Bontempo, R., Betancourt, H., Bond, M., Leung, K., Brenes, A., Georgas, J., Hui, C. H., Marin, G., Setiadi, B., Sinha, J. B., Verma, J., Spangenberg, J., Touzard, H., & de Montonollin, G. (1986). The measurement aspects of individualism and collectivism across cultures. *Australian Journal of Psychology, 38,* 257–267.

Triandis, H. C., Bontempo, R., Villareal, M. J., Asai, M., & Lucca, N. (1988). Individualism and collectivism: Cross-cultural perspectives on self-ingroup relationships. *Journal of Personality and Social Psychology, 4,* 323–338.

Triandis, H. C., & Lambert, W. W. (1958). A restatement and test of Schlosberg's theory of emotion with two kinds of subjects from Greece. *Journal of Abnormal and Social Psychology, 56,* 321–328.

Triandis, H. C., Leung, K., Villareal, M., & Clack, F. (1985). Allocentric versus idiocentric tendencies: Convergent and discriminate validation. *Journal of Research in Personality, 19,* 395–415.

Triandis, H., Marin, G., Lisansky, J., & Betancourt, H. (1984). Simpatia as a cultural script of Hispanics. *Journal of Personality and Social Psychology, 47,* 1363–1375.

Triandis, H. C., McCusker, C., & Hui, C. H. (1990). Multimethod probes of individualism and collectivism. *Journal of Personality and Social Psychology, 59,* 1006–1020.

Tribe, R., & De Silva, P. (1999). Psychological intervention with displaced widows in Sri Lanka. *International Review of Psychiatry, 11,* 184–190.

Trickett, E. J. (1996). A future for community psychology: the contexts of diversity and the diversity of contexts. *American Journal of Community Psychology, 24,* 209–234.

Trommsdorff, G., & Iwawaki, S. (1989). Students' perceptions of socialization and gender role in Japan and Germany. *International Journal of Behavioral Development, 12*(4), 485–493.

Trompenaars, F. (1993). *Riding the waves of culture.* London: Brealey.

Tronick, E. Z. (1989). Emotions and emotional communication in infants. *American Psychologist, 44*(2), 112–119.

Tronick, E. Z., Morelli, G. A., & Ivey, P. K. (1992). The Efe forager infant and toddlers pattern of social relationships: Multiple and simultaneous. *Developmental Psychology, 28,* 568–577.

True, M. M. (1994). *Mother-infant attachment and communication among the Dogon of Mali.* Unpublished doctoral dissertation, University of California at Berkeley.

Trull, T. J., & Geary, D. C. (1997). Comparison of the Big-Five factor structure across samples of Chinese and American adults. *Journal of Personality Assessment, 69*(2), 324–341.

Tse, D. K., Francis, J., & Walls, J. (1994). Cultural differences in conducting intra- and inter-cultural negotiations: A Sino-Canadian comparison. *Journal of International Business Studies, 25*(3), 537.

Tseng, W. (1977). Family diagnosis and classification. *Annual Progress in Child Psychiatry and Child Development,* 434–454.

Tseng, W., & McDermott, J. F. (1981). *Culture, mind and therapy: An introduction to cultural psychiatry.* New York: Brunner/Mazel.

Tullett, A. D. (1997). Cognitive style: Not culture's consequence. *European Psychologist, 2* (3), 258–267.

Tulviste, P. (1978). On the origins of the theoretic syllogistic reasoning in culture and in the child. *Acta et commentationes Universitatis Tortuensis, 4,* 3–22.

Turner, V. (1993). Body, brain, and culture. *Brain, culture, and the human spirit: Essays from an emergent evolutionary perspective* (pp. 77–108). Lanham, MD: University Press of America.

Tuss, P., Zimmer, J., & Ho, H. (1995) Causal attributions of underachieving fourth-grade students in China, Japan, and the United States. *Journal of Cross-Cultural Psychology, 26*(4), 408–425.

Tversky, A., & Kahneman, D. (1981). The framing of decisions and the psychology of choice. *Science, 211,* 453–458.

Tylor, E. B. (1865). *Researches into the early history of mankind and development of civilization.* London: John Murray.

Uba, L. (1994). *Asian Americans: Personality patterns, identity, and mental health.* New York: Guilford Press.

Uehara, E. S., Takeuchi, D. T., & Smukler, M. (1994). Effects of combining disparate groups in the analysis of ethnic differences: Variations among Asian American mental health service consumers in level of community functioning. *American Journal of Community Psychology, 22*(1), 83–99.

U.S. Census Bureau. (2002). *Current population reports: Poverty in the United States: 2001.* Washington, DC: Government Printing Office.

U.S. Committee for Refugees (2000). *World refugee survey.* http://www.refugees.org/news/press_releases/2000/061300a.htm

U.S. Department of Health and Human Services (1999). *Mental Health: A Report of the Surgeon General—Executive Summary.* Rockville, MD: U.S. Department of

Health and Human Services, Substance Abuse and Mental Health Services Administration, Center for Mental Health Services, National Institutes of Health, National Institute of Mental Health.

Uziel-Miller, N. D., Lyons, J. S., Kissiel, C., & Love, S. (1998). Treatment needs and initial outcomes of a residential recovery program for African American women and their children. *American Journal on Addictions, 7,* 43–50.

Valadez, J. R. (1998). Applying to college: Race, class, gender differences. *Professional School Counseling, 1*(5), 14–20.

Van den Berghe, P. L. (1981). *The ethnic phenomenon.* New York: Elsevier.

Van de Vijver, F. J. R., & Leung, K. (1997a). Methods and data analysis of comparative research. In J. W. Berry, Y. H. Poortinga, & J. Pandey (Eds.), *Handbook of cross-cultural psychology* (2nd ed., Vol. 1, pp. 257–300). Boston: Allyn & Bacon.

Van de Vijver, F. J. R., & Leung, K. (1997b). *Methods and data analysis for cross-cultural research.* Newbury Park, CA: Sage.

van IJzendoorn, M. H. (1996). "Attachment patterns and their outcomes": Commentary. *Human Development, 39*(4), 224–231.

van IJzendoorn, M. H., & Sagi, A. (1999). Cross-cultural patterns of attachment: Universal and contextual dimensions. In J. Cassidy & P. R. Shaver (Eds.), *Handbook of attachment: Theory, research, and clinical applications* (pp. 713–734). New York: Guilford Press.

van Ommeren, M., Sharma, B., Sharma, G. K., Komproe, K., Cardena, E., & de Jong, J. T. V. N. (2002). The relationship between somatic and PTSD symptoms among Bhutanese refugee torture survivors: Examination of comorbidity with anxiety and depression. *Journal of Traumatic Stress, 15*(5), 415–421.

Vasquez, M. J. T., & de las Fuentes, C. (1999). American-born Asian, African, Latina, and American Indian adolescent girls: Challenges and strengths. In N. G. Johnson, M. C. Roberts, & J. Worrell (Eds.), *Beyond appearance: A new look at adolescent girls* (pp. 151–173). Washington, DC: American Psychological Association.

Vaughn, B. E., Lefever, G. B., Seifer, R., & Barglow, P. (1989). Attachment behavior, attachment security, and temperament during infancy. *Child Development, 60*(3), 728–737.

Vega, W. A., Koloy, B., Aguilar-Gaxiola, S., Alderete, E., Catalano, R., & Caraveo-Anduaga, J. (1998). Lifetime prevalence of DSM-III-R psychiatric disorders among urban and rural Mexican Americans in California. *Archives of General Psychiatry, 55,* 771–778.

Verkuyten, M., & Hagendoorn, L. (1998). Prejudice and self-categorization: The variable role of authoritarianism and in-group stereotypes. *Personality and Social Psychology Bulletin, 24*(1), 99–110.

Vinacke, W. E. (1949). The judgment of facial expressions by three national-racial groups in Hawaii: I. Caucasian faces. *Journal of Personality, 17,* 407–429.

Vinacke, W. E., & Fong, R. W. (1955). The judgment of facial expressions by three national-racial groups in Hawaii: II. Oriental faces. *Journal of Social Psychology, 41,* 184–195.

Von Raffler–Engel, W. (1981). Developmental kinesics: How children acquire communicative and non-communicative nonverbal behavior. *Infant Mental Health Journal, 2*(2), 84–94.

Vontress, C. E. (1991). Traditional healing in Africa: Implications for cross-cultural counseling. *Counseling and Development, 70,* 242–249.

Vornberg, A. J., & Grant, T. R. (1976). Adolescent cultural acquaintance experiences and ethnic group attitudes. *Adolescence, 6*(44), 601–608.

Vrij, A., & Winkel, F. W. (1994). Perceptual distortions in cross-cultural interrogations: The impact of skin color, accent, speech style, and spoken fluency on impression formation. *Journal of Cross-Cultural Psychology, 25*(2), 284–295.

Wagner, D. A. (1977). Ontogeny of the Ponzo illusion: Effects of age, schooling and environment. *International Journal of Psychology, 12,* 161–176.

Wagner, D. A. (1980). Culture and memory development. In H. Triandis & A. Heron (Eds.), *Handbook of cross-cultural psychology: Vol. 4. Developmental psychology* (pp. 187–232). Boston: Allyn & Bacon.

Wagner, J. A., III. (1995). Studies of individualism-collectivism: Effects on cooperation in groups. *Academy of Management Journal, 38*(1), 152–172.

Wainryb, C., & Turiel, E. (1994). Dominance, subordination, and concepts of personal entitlements in cultural contexts. *Child Development, 65*(6), 1701–1722.

Walker, C. E. (1977). Continuing professional developmental: The future for clinical psychology. *Clinical Psychologist, 30*(2), 6–7, 22.

Walker, L. J. (1984). Sex differences in the development of moral reasoning: A critical review. *Child Development, 57,* 522–526.

Walker, L. J. (1991). Sex differences in moral reasoning. In W. Kurtines & J. L. Gewirtz (Eds.), *Handbook of moral behavior and development: Research* (pp. 333–364). Hillsdale, NJ: Erlbaum.

Walkey, H. F., & Chung, C. R. (1996). An examination of stereotypes of Chinese and Europeans held by some New Zealand secondary school pupils. *Journal of Cross-Cultural Psychology, 27*(3), 283–292.

Wallace, J. M., & Williams, D. R. (1997). Religion and adolescent health-compromising behavior. In J. Schulenberg, J. L. Maggs, & K. Hurrelmann (Eds.), *Health risks and developmental transitions during adolescence* (pp. 444–468). New York: Cambridge University Press.

Wallbott, H., & Scherer, K. (1986). How universal and specific is emotional experience? Evidence from 27 countries on five continents. *Social Science Information, 25,* 763–795.

Wallbott, H., & Scherer, K. (1988). Emotion and economic development: Data and speculations concerning the relationship between emotional experience and socioeconomic factors. *European Journal of Social Psychology, 18,* 267–273.

Wallbott, H., & Scherer, K. (1995). Cultural determinants in experiencing shame and guilt. In J. Tangney & K. Fischer (Eds.), *Self-conscious emotions.* New York: Guilford Press.

Walsh Escarce, M. E. (1989). A cross-cultural study of Nepalese neonatal behavior. In J. K. Nugent, B. M. Lester, & T. B. Brazelton (Eds.), *The cultural context of infancy: Vol. 1. Biology, culture and infant development* (pp. 65–86). Norwood, NJ: Ablex.

Walters, T. K. (1994). Acculturative stress, social support, and trauma in a community sample of Cambodian refugees. *Dissertation Abstracts International: Section B: The Sciences and Engineering, 54*(8-B), 4374.

Wang, A. V. (1994). Passionate love and social anxiety of American and Italian students. *Psychology: A Journal of Human Behavior, 31*, 9–11.

Wassenaar, D. R., Van der Veen, M., & Pillay, A. L. (1998). Women in cultural transition: Suicidal behavior in South African Indian women. *Suicide and Life Threatening Behavior, 28*, 82–93.

Watkins, D., Akande, A., Cheng, C., & Regmi, M. (1996). Cultural and gender differences in the self-esteem of college students: A four-country comparison. *Social Behavior and Personality, 24*(4), 321–328.

Watkins, D., & Cheung, S. (1995). Culture, gender, and response bias: An analysis of responses to the Self-Description Questionnaire. *Journal of Cross-Cultural Psychology, 26*(5), 490–504.

Watkins, D., & Regmi, M. (1996). Within-culture and gender differences in self-concept: An investigation with rural and urban Nepalese school children. *Journal of Cross-Cultural Psychology, 27*(6), 692–699.

Watson, D. (1982). The actor and the observer: How are their perceptions of causality divergent? *Psychological Bulletin, 92*, 682–700.

Watson-Gegeo, K. A. (1992). Thick explanation in the ethnographic study of child socialization: A longitudinal study of the problem of schooling for Kwara'ae (Solomon Islands) children. In W. A. Corsaro & P. Miller (Eds.), *New directions for child development: Interpretive approaches to children's socialization* (pp. 51–66). San Francisco: Jossey-Bass.

Weatherly, K. A., & Beach, L. R. (1998). Organizational culture and decision making. In L. R. Beach et al. (Eds.), *Image theory: Theoretical and empirical foundations* (pp. 211–225). Mahwah, NJ: Erlbaum.

Weber, E. U., & Hsee, C. H (2000). Culture and individual judgment and decision making. *Applied Psychology: An International Review, 49*(1), 32–61.

Weber, G. G. (1997). Cross-cultural menopause: A study in contrasts. In D. E. Stewart (Ed.), *A clinician's guide to menopause: Clinical practice* (pp. 45–62). Washington, DC: Health Press International.

Weiner, B. (1974). *Achievement motivation and attribution theory.* Morristown, NJ: General Learning Press.

Weiner, B., Frieze, I., Kukla, A., Reed, L., Rest, S., & Rosenbaum, R. M. (1987). Perceiving the causes of success and failure. In E. E. Jones, D. E. Kanouse, H. H. Kelley, R. E. Nesbett, S. Valins, & B. Weiner (Eds.), *Perceiving the causes of behavior* (pp. 95–120). Morristown, NJ: General Learning Press.

Weisner, T. S., & Gallimore, R. (1977). My brother's keeper: Child and sibling caretaking. *Current Anthropology, 18*(2), 169–190.

Weiss, S. C. (1980). Porteus Maze performances on non-literate and literate Campas from Eastern Peru. *Journal of Social Psychology, 112*(2), 303–304.

Weisz, J. R., Sigman, M., Weiss, B., & Mosk, J. (1993). Parent reports of behavioral and emotional problems among children in Kenya, Thailand, and the United States. *Child Development, 64*, 98–109.

Weisz, J. R., Suwanlert, S., Chaiyasit, W., Weiss, B., Walter, B. R., & Anderson, W. W. (1988). Thai and American perspectives on over- and under-controlled child behavior problems: Exploring the threshold model among parents, teachers and psychologists. *Journal of Consulting and Clinical Psychology, 56*(4), 601–609.

Weldon, E., & Gargano, G. M. (1988). Cognitive loafing: The effects of accountability and shared responsibility on cognitive effort. *Personality and Social Psychology Bulletin, 14*, 159–171.

Wessells, M. & Monteiro, C. (2001). Psychosocial interventions and post-war reconstruction in Angola: Interweaving Western and traditional approaches. In D. J. Christie, V. Richards (Eds), *Peace, conflict, and violence: Peace psychology for the 21st century*, (pp. 262–275). Upper Saddle River, NJ, US: Prentice Hall.

Westaby, J. D. (1995). Presence of others and task performance in Japan and the United States: A laboratory investigation. *International Journal of Psychology, 30*(4), 451–460.

Wheeler, L., & Kim, Y. (1997). What is beautiful is culturally good: The physical attractiveness stereotype has different content in collectivistic cultures. *Personality and Social Psychology Bulletin, 23*(8), 795–800.

Wheeler, L., Reis, H. T., & Bond, M. H. (1989). Collectivism and individualism in everyday social life: The middle kingdom and the melting pot. *Journal of Personality and Social Psychology, 57*(1), 79–86.

White, G. M. (1980). Conceptual universals in interpersonal language. *American Anthropologist, 88*, 759–781.

Wierzbicka, A. (1986). Human emotions: Universal or culture-specific? *American Anthropologist, 88*, 584–594.

Wierzbicka, A. (1994). Semantic universals and primitive thought: The question of the psychic unity of humankind. *Journal of Linguistic Anthropology, 4*(1), 23.

Williams, J. E., & Best, D. L. (1982). *Measuring sex stereotypes: A thirty-nation study.* Beverly Hills, CA: Sage.

Williams, J. E., & Best, D. L. (1990). *Measuring sex stereotypes: A multination study.* Beverly Hills, CA: Sage.

Williams, J. E., & Best, D. L. (1994). Cross-cultural views of women and men. In W. Lonner & R. Malpass (Eds.), *Psychology and culture.* Boston: Allyn & Bacon.

Williams, J. E., Satterwhite, R. C., & Best, D. L. (1999). Pancultural gender stereotypes revisited: The five factor model. *Sex Roles, 40*(7–8), 513–525.

Williams, L., Anshel, M., & Quek, J. (1997). Cognitive style in adolescent competitive athletes as a function of culture and gender. *Journal of Sport Behavior, 20*(2), 232–245.

Willman, E., Feldt, K., & Amelang, M. (1997). Prototypical behavior patterns of social intelligence: An intercultural comparison between Chinese and German subjects. *International Journal of Psychology, 32*(5), 329–346.

Wilson, M. N., Kohn, L. P., & Lee, T. S. (2000). Cultural relativistic approach toward ethnic minorities in family therapy. In J. E. Aponte & J. Wohl (Eds.), *Psychological intervention and cultural diversity* (2nd ed., pp. 167–182). Boston: Allyn & Bacon.

Wing, D. M., Crow, S. S., & Thompson, T. (1995). An ethnonursing study of Muscogee (Creek) Indians and effective health care practices for treating alcohol abuse. *Family and Community Health, 18*(2), 52–64.

Winton, W. M. (1986). The role of facial response in self-reports of emotion: A critique of Laird. *Journal of Personality and Social Psychology, 50*, 808–812.

Wittmer, J. (1971). Old order Amish and non-Amish youth: A personality comparison utilizing the 16 PF. *Personality, 2*(4), 305–313.

Wlodarek, J. (1994). Poland. In K. Hurrelmann (Ed.), *International handbook of adolescence* (pp. 309–321). Westport, CT: Greenwood Press.

Wober, M. (1974). Toward an understanding of the Kiganda concept of intelligence. In J. W. Berry & P. R. Dasen (Eds.), *Culture and cognition* (pp. 261–280). London: Methuen.

Wohl, J. (1989). Integration of cultural awareness into psychotherapy. *American Journal of Psychotherapy, 43*, 343–355.

Wolf, R. M. (1965). The measurement of environments. In C. W. Harris (Ed.), *Proceedings of the 1964 Invited Conference on Testing Problems*. Princeton, NJ: Educational Testing Service.

Wolff, B. B., & Langley, S. (1968). Cultural factors and the response to pain: A review. *American Anthropologist, 70*(3), 494–501.

Wolpoff, M., & Caspari, R. (1997). *Race and human evolution: A fatal attraction*. New York: Simon & Schuster.

Wong, P. T. P., Derlaga, V. J., & Colson, W. (1988). The effects of race on expectancies and performance and attributions. *Canadian Journal of Behavioral Science, 20*, 29–39.

Wood, P. B., & Chesser, M. (1994). Black stereotyping in a university population. *Sociological Focus, 27*(1), 17–34.

Wood, P. C., Hillman, S. B., & Sawilowsky, S. S. (1995). Comparison of self-esteem scores: American and Indian adolescents. *Psychological Reports, 76*(2), 367–370.

World Health Organization (1948). *Constitution of the World Health Organization*. Geneva: Author.

World Health Organization. (1973). *Report of the International Pilot Study of Schizophrenia* (Vol. 1). Geneva: Author.

World Health Organization. (1979). *Schizophrenia: An international follow-up study*. New York: Wiley.

World Health Organization. (1981). *Current state of diagnosis and classification in the mental health field*. Geneva: Author.

World Health Organization. (1983). *Depressive disorders in different cultures: Report of the WHO collaborative study of standardized assessment of depressive disorders*. Geneva: Author.

World Health Organization. (1991). *World health statistics quarterly*. Geneva: Author.

Wright, D. B., Boyd, C. E., & Tredoux, C. G. (2001). A field study of own-race bias in South Africa and England. *Psychology, Public Policy, and Law, 7*(1), 119–133.

Wylie, R. C. (1979). *The self concept: Vol. 2. Theory and research on selected topics*. Lincoln: University of Nebraska Press.

Wynn, K. (1992). Addition and subtraction in human infants. *Nature, 358*, 749–750.

Yamaguchi, S. (1994). Collectivism among the Japanese: A perspective from the self. In U. Kim & H. Triandis (Eds.), *Individualism and collectivism: Theory, method, and applications* (pp. 175–188). Thousand Oaks, CA: Sage.

Yamaguchi, S., Kuhlman, D. M., & Sugimori, S. (1995). Personality correlates of allocentric tendencies in individualist and collectivist cultures. *Journal of Cross-Cultural Psychology, 26*(6), 658–672.

Yamaguchi, S., Okamoto, K., & Oka, T. (1985). Effects of coactor's presence: Social loafing and social facilitation. *Japanese Psychological Research, 27*, 215–222.

Yamamoto, J., & Kubota, M. (1983). The Japanese-American family. In G. J. Powell (Ed.), *The psychological development of minority group children* (pp. 307–329). New York: Brunner/Mazel.

Yamamoto, K., Soliman, A., Parsons, J., & Davies, O. L. (1987). Voices in unison: Stressful events in the lives of children in six countries. *Child Psychology and Psychiatry, 28*(6), 855–864.

Yamashita, I., & Koyama, T. (1994). Neurotic spectrum disorders in Japan. In J. E. Mezzich, Y. Honda, & M. O. Kastrup (Eds.), *Psychiatric diagnosis: A world perspective* (pp. 96–101). New York: Springer-Verlag.

Yamauchi, H., & Li, Y. (1995). Comparative study of aggressive motives of Japanese and Chinese college students. *Psychologia: An International Journal of Psychology in the Orient, 38*(4), 209–219.

Yan, W., & Gaier, L. E. (1994). Causal attributions for college success and failure: An Asian-American comparison. *Journal of Cross-Cultural Psychology, 25*, 146–158.

Yanchi, L. (1988). *The essential book of traditional Chinese medicine: Vol 1. Theory*. New York: Columbia University Press.

Yang, K. S. (1982). Causal attributions of academic success and failure and their affective consequences. *Chinese Journal of Psychology* [Taiwan], *24*, 65–83. (The abstract only is in English.)

Yao, L. E. (1985). A comparison of family characteristics of Asian American and Anglo American high achievers. *International Journal of Comparative Sociology, 26*(3–4), 198–206.

Yap, P. M. (1974). *Comparative psychiatry: A theoretical framework.* Toronto: University of Toronto Press.

Yates, J. F., Lee, J.-W., & Shinotsuka, H. (1996). Beliefs about overconfidence, including its cross-national variation. *Organizational Behavior and Human Decision Processes, 65*(2), 138–147.

Yee, H. A., Fairchild, H. H., Weizmann, F., & Wyatt, E. G. (1993). Addressing psychology's problems with race. *American Psychologist, 48*(11), 1132–1140.

Yeh, M., Takeuchi, D. T., & Sue, S. (1994). Asian-American children treated in the mental health system: A comparison of parallel and mainstream outpatient service centers. *Journal of Clinical Child Psychology, 23*(1), 5–12.

Yi, J.-S. & Park, S. (2003). Cross-cultural differences in decision-making styles: A study of college students in five countries. *Social Behavior & Personality, 31*(1), 35–48.

Ying, Y-W., Akutsu, P. D., Zhang, X., & Huang, L. N. (1997). Psychological dysfunction in Southeast Asian refugees as mediated by sense of coherence. *American Journal of Community Psychology, 25*(6), 839–859.

Ying, Y-W., & Hu, L.-T. (1994). Public outpatient mental health services: Use and outcome among Asian Americans. *American Journal of Orthopsychiatry, 64*(3), 448–455.

Young, D. M. (1997). Depression. In W.-S. Tseng & J. Streltzer (Eds.), *Culture and psychopathology: A guide to clinical assessment* (pp. 28–45). New York: Brunner/Mazel.

Youniss, J., & Smollar, J. (1989). Adolescents' interpersonal relationships in social context. In T. J. Berndt & G. W. Ladd (Eds.), *Peer relationships in child development* (pp. 300–316). New York: Wiley.

Yrizarry, N., Matsumoto, D., & Wilson-Cohn, C. (1998). American-Japanese differences in multiscalar intensity ratings of universal facial expressions of emotion. *Motivation and Emotion, 22*(4), 315–327.

Yu, E. S. H. (1974). Achievement motive, familism, and hsiao: A replication of McClellend-Winterbottom stud-ies. *Dissertation Abstracts International, 35,* 593A (University Microfilms No. 74–14, 942).

Zaccaro, S. J. (1984). The role of task attractiveness. *Personality and Social Psychology Bulletin, 10,* 99–106.

Zahn-Waxler, C., Friedman, J. R., Cole, M. P., Mizuta, I., & Hiruma, N. (1996). Japanese and United States preschool children's responses to conflict and distress. *Child Development, 67,* 2462–2477.

Zane, N., Hatanaka, H., & Park, S. (1994). Ethnic-specific mental health services: Evaluation of the parallel approach for Asian-American clients. *Journal of Community Psychology, 22*(2), 68–81.

Zane, N., Hatanaka, H., Park, S., & Akutsu, P. (1994). Ethnic-specific mental health services: Evaluation of the parallel approach for Asian-American clients. *Journal of Community Psychology, 22*(2), 68–81.

Zhang, M., Yan, H., & Phillips, M. R. (1994). Community-based psychiatric rehabilitation in Shanghai: Facilities, services, outcome, and culture-specific characteristics. *British Journal of Psychiatry, 165*(24), 70–79.

Zhang, Y., Young, D., & Lee, S. (2002). Chinese Taoist cognitive psychotherapy in the treatment of generalized anxiety disorder in contemporary China. *Transcultural Psychiatry, 39*(1), 115–129.

Zimbardo, P. G., & Boyd, J. N. (1999). Putting time in perspective: A valid, reliable individual-differences metric. *Journal of Personality and Social Psychology, 77*(6), 1271–1288.

Zuckerman, M. (1990). Some dubious premises in research and theory on racial differences: Scientific, social, and ethical issues. *American Psychologist, 45*(12), 1297–1303.

Zukow-Goldring, P. (1995). *Sibling interaction across cultures.* New York: Springer-Verlag.

Zuniga, M. E. (1997). Counseling Mexican American seniors: An overview. *Journal of Multicultural Counseling and Development, 25,* 142–155.

Name Index

Abad, V., 374
Abdel-Khalek, A. M., 326
Abebimpe, V. R., 344
Abrams, D., 447, 450
Abrams, K. K., 212
Abramson, R. P., 20
Abreu, J., 375
Achenbach, T. M., 355
Acioly, N. M., 148
Adamopoulos, J., 397
Adkins, C. L., 447
Adler, N. E., 205
Adler, N. J., 462
Adorno, T. W., 84
Ager, J., 318
Ainsworth, M. D., 162
Ajwani, J. K., 126
Akan, G. E., 212
Akande, A., 193, 413
Akers, R. L., 215
Akin-Ogundeji, O., 334
Akoh, H., 50
Akutsu, P. D., 359, 370, 376
Alarcon, R. D., 353, 367
Albert, A. A., 186
Albright, L., 393
Alderete, E., 359, 360
Alexander, C. M., 375
Alhamad, A., 349
Ali, A. J., 459
Alibhai, N., 204
Al-Issa, I., 351
Alkema, F., 281
Al-Krenawi, A., 371, 372, 373, 374
Allen, B., 205
Allen, J. K., 449, 458
Allen, L. R., 195, 196, 212
Allen, R. F., 445
Allerheiligen, R., 462
Allison, M. T., 415
Al-Mutlaq, H., 378
Al-Subaie, A., 349
Altarriba, J., 114, 383
Altman, I., 397
Al-Zharany, S., 414
Amelang, M., 126, 329
Amir, Y., 24, 425
Anawak, J., 214
Andayani, S., 233, 472
Anderson, C. A., 417
Anderson, K. B., 417
Ando, K., 447
Andrews, J. D., 462

Angleitner, A., 329
Angyal, A., 316
Anshel, M. H., 193
Anthony, D., 358
Araki, S., 266
Arcus, D., 158
Argyle, M., 281, 422
Armstrong, T. L., 218, 222
Arnett, J., 152, 402
Aronson, E., 89
Aronson, J., 122
Asai, M., 31
Asch, S. E., 421
Ashmore, R. D., 392
Ashria, I. H., 112
Ashton, M. C., 333
Assar, M., 276
Atkeson, P., 403
Atkinson, D. R., 374, 375, 376
Atkinson, J. W., 307, 308
Au, T. K., 271
Auerbach, J. G., 355
Aune, K., 233
Averill, J. R., 258
Avila, R. A., 449
Aycan, Z., 459
Azara, L., 382
Azhar, M. Z., 378
Azuma, H., 138

Baban, P., 326
Bachman, J. G., 42
Back, K., 396
Baddeley, A. D., 76
Baguma, P., 204
Bahrick, H. P., 76
Bajo, M., 399
Bakan, D., 316
Baker, L., 270
Balint, M., 316
Bal-Tal, D., 79
Baltes, B. P., 150
Baranes, R., 145, 146, 148, 265
Barbaranelli, C., 330
Barbee, A. P., 394
Bargh, J., 79
Barglow, P., 166
Barna, L. M., 292, 293
Barnard, E. A., 139
Barnlund, D. C., 266
Barrett, P. T., 326
Barry, H., 7, 192

Barthel, D., 188
Bartlett, F. C., 106
Basow, S. A., 196
Bates, J. E., 166
Baumrind, D., 136
Beach, L. R., 446, 458
Beall, A. E., 400
Bechtold, D. W., 214
Beck, A. T., 366
Beike, D., 317
Beiser, M., 355
Beit-Hallahmi, B., 334
Bem, S., 193
Ben-David, A., 382
Benedict, R., 321, 422
Ben-Eliahu, E., 196
Benet-Martinez, V., 329, 333
Bennett, A. B., 329
Bennett, M. J., 473
Beratis, S., 214
Berger, C. R., 290
Bergling, K., 175
Berkman, L. F., 206
Berlin, B., 270, 271
Berman, S., 328
Bernal, G., 368, 369
Bernal, H., 155
Bernal, M. E., 314
Bernieri, F., 396
Berry, D. S., 393
Berry, J. W., 6, 7, 10, 21, 22, 183, 189, 190, 191, 192, 194, 201, 203, 317, 333, 334, 345, 360, 432, 449, 457
Berscheid, E., 397
Bersoff, D. M., 174, 175
Best, D. L., 72, 139, 183, 184, 185, 187
Beswick, G., 424
Betancourt, H., 17, 334
Bezilla, R., 152
Bhawuk, S. D., 52
Biehl, M., 234, 237, 238, 239
Bigler, R. S., 107
Bilsky, W., 53
Binion, V. J., 182
Birenbaum, M., 150
Birnbaum, D., 75
Bishop, G. D., 218
Bishop, R. C., 448
Bisht, S., 176
Bissilat, J., 127

Bjorkquist, K., 418
Black, H., 281
Black, J. S., 454
Blair, I. V., 79
Blankenship, V. E., 233
Blatt, S. J., 317
Blau, Z. S., 122
Bleichrodt, N., 190
Bletzer, K. V., 114
Blinco, M. A. P., 176
Block, J., 191
Bloom, A. H., 270, 271
Bloom, J. D., 346, 355
Blumenfeld, P. C., 50
Bochner, S., 65, 67, 90, 126, 305, 447
Boddema-Winesemius, M., 400
Bodenhausen, G. V., 75, 79
Boehnlein, J. K., 360, 361
Bond, M. H., 59, 160, 209, 210, 304, 308, 316, 326, 329, 387, 391, 395, 408, 410, 417, 422, 423, 443, 445, 455
Boninger, D., 117
Bontempo, R., 31
Boor, M., 214
Boothby, N., 381
Borkenau, P., 329, 331
Born, M., 190
Bornstein, M. H., 141, 153, 154, 415
Boster, F. J., 50
Bothwell, R. K., 108, 395
Bouchard, T. J., Jr., 121
Boucher, J. D., 65, 236, 247, 248, 255
Bouhmama, D., 175
Bourhis, R. Y., 360
Bourne, E. J., 288, 304, 306
Bowdle, B. F., 418
Bowen, M., 316
Bower, H. G., 75
Bowlby, J., 162, 316
Boyce, E., 374
Boyd, C. E., 108
Boyd, J. N., 117
Bradford, R., 187
Bradley, G. W., 308, 406
Braly, K., 70, 71
Brandt, M. E., 247, 248, 255

Brannon, L., 203, 206, 208
Brazelton, T. B., 159
Brehm, S. S., 397
Breuer, N. L., 222
Brewer, B. M., 67
Brewer, M. B., 50, 172, 386
Brigham, J. C., 108, 395
Brillon, L., 152
Brinkman, H., 193
Brislin, R., 40, 65, 78, 182, 191
Broberg, A. G., 145
Broman, C. L., 371
Brondolo, E., 206
Bronfenbrenner, U., 135, 139
Bronstein, P. A., 139, 174
Brook, D. W., 381
Brooks-Gunn, J., 212
Broota, K. D., 103
Brown, B., 52, 53
Brummett, B. H., 329
Bruner, J. S., 105
Buck, E. B., 422
Buck, R., 74
Budowski, D., 349
Bugental, D. E., 281
Bui, A., 369, 370
Bui, K.-T., 372
Burger, J. M., 74
Burgess, P., 281
Burgos, N. M., 422
Buriel, R., 134
Burleson, B. R., 193
Burnam, A. M., 360
Buss, D. M., 396, 399
Butcher, J. N., 343, 357
Butsch, R., 78
Buunk, B., 248
Byrne, D., 397

Calabrese, R. J., 290
Caldwell, D. F., 431, 446
Calhoun, L. G., 205
Callister, L., 118
Campbell, D. T., 67, 98, 172
Campbell, N. C. G., 462
Campos, J. J., 164
Canas, J., 399
Canino, G. J., 359
Cann, A., 205
Capara, G. V., 330
Carey, J. C., 360
Carlo, G., 176
Carlota, A. J., 330
Carlson, G. E., 236
Carroll, J. B., 269
Carroll, J. L., 396
Carson, R. C., 343, 348, 349, 352, 355
Carter, K. A., 314, 315
Cartmell, B., 373
Casa, A., 375
Casagrande, J. B., 269
Cashmore, J. A., 422

Caspari, R., 16
Caspi, A., 95, 160
Cauce, A. M., 377
Caudill, W., 153, 158
Cederblad, M., 141
Chadwick, B. A., 188
Chaleby, K., 378
Chambers, D., 215
Chambliss, D. L., 369
Chan, J., 326, 328
Chan, S. Q., 134
Chan, Y. M., 324
Chance, S. E., 215
Chandak, R., 402
Chandler, P., 330
Chandler, T. A., 415
Chandra, S., 126
Chan-Yip, A., 117
Chao, R. K., 137, 149
Chasiotis, A., 140
Chatman, J. A., 431, 446
Chavira, V., 155
Cheever, K. H., 152
Chen, C., 146
Chen, G. M., 266
Chen, S., 164
Chen, X., 137
Cheng, C., 193
Cheng, D., 347, 371
Chess, S., 158
Chesser, M., 70
Cheung, C., 174
Cheung, F. M., 334, 357
Cheung, M., 376
Cheung, S., 193
Chisholm, J., 158
Chiu, C. N., 349
Cho, M. J., 359
Choe, H., 152
Choi, S.-C., 334
Choi, S.-H., 334
Chou, Y., 393
Chun, C.-A., 369
Chung, C. R., 69, 70
Church, A. T., 126, 321, 322, 327, 330, 334, 335
Cicero, 119
Cinnirella, M., 193
Clack, F., 50, 472
Claeys, W., 126, 308
Clark, K. A., 65
Clark, M. L., 70
Clemson, L., 112
Clymer, E. C., 19
Coates, D. L., 176
Cochrane, R., 214, 422
Coffman, T. L., 70
Cogan, J. C., 212
Cohen, D., 418
Cohen, N., 403
Cole, E., 358
Cole, J., 232
Cole, M., 106, 109, 474
Cole, M. P., 95, 176

Coleman, J. C., 343
Coll, C. G., 136
Collins, A. W., 154
Colson, W., 409, 410
Colvin, C., 431
Comas-Diaz, L., 196, 375, 376
Compas, B., 345
Compton, W. M., 346
Comrey, A. L., 330
Connors, J., 330
Conroy, M., 138
Contarello, A., 422
Conway, L. G., 78
Cook, P., 217
Cook, S., 19
Coombes, C., 205
Coon, H. M., 50, 315
Cooper, H., 410
Cooper, M., 330
Corbelt, G. G., 272
Corcoran, P., 215
Cortes, D. E., 361
Costa, P. T., 329, 330, 331, 337
Cottrell, A. B., 402
Cousins, S. D., 305
Crandall, C. S., 212, 213
Crijnen, A. A. M., 355
Crittenden, K. S., 406, 408
Crittenden, P. M., 163, 164
Crocker, J., 90, 325
Croft-Jeffreys, C., 358
Crook, T. H., 107
Croteau, D., 78
Crow, S. S., 221
Csikszentmihaly, M., 113
Cunningham, M. R., 394

Dabul, A. J., 314
Daibo, I., 393
Dalal, K. A., 176
Damond, M. E., 222
Darling, N., 137
Darwin, C., 171, 226, 227
Dasen, P. R., 6, 22, 127, 169, 192
Dasgupta, S. D., 193
DaSilva, S. M., 176
David, K. H., 126
Davies, I. R. L., 272
Davies, O. L., 345
Davis, D. A., 144
Davis, F. G., 17
Davis, S. S., 144
Day, D. V., 455
De, B., 327
Deal, J. E., 323
Deaner, S. L., 233
Deck, L. P., 392
De Fruyt, F., 329
Degler, C., 17
De las Fuentes, C., 196
Delgado, M., 222
Del Pilar, G. H., 329, 330

Del Pino Perez, A., 207
Demetriou, A., 169
Dengerink, H. A., 323
Denham, S. A., 136
Denton, L. T., 455
DePaulo, B. M., 281, 393
De Raad, B., 329, 335, 400
Derevenco, P., 326
Derlaga, V. J., 409, 410
De Silva, P., 381
De Silva, S., 187, 188
Desjarlais, R. R., 115
Devan, G. S., 378
De Vargas, M., 231
Devereux, C. E., Jr., 138, 139
Devine, P. G., 79, 80, 108
DeVries, M. W., 160
DeWalt, B. R., 417
DeWolff, M. S., 163
Dharap, A. S., 378
Dhawan, N., 251, 305
Diaz-Guerrero, R., 399
Diaz-Loving, R., 322
Diaz-Perez, Y. I., 422
Dibble, C., 126
Diener, E., 324
Diener, M., 324
Digman, J. M., 330
DiMartino, C. E., 176
Dinero, T. E., 126
Dinges, N. G., 275
Dinnel, D. L., 43, 314, 315
Dion, K. K., 392, 398, 402
Dion, K. L., 398, 402
Ditto, B., 411, 414
Dizmang, L. H., 214
Doi, K., 308, 422
Doi, T., 311, 317, 334
Domino, G., 217, 423
Dong, Q., 137
Dorfman, P. W., 455
Dornbusch, S. M., 137
Dosanjh, J. S., 152
Douki, S., 353
Draguns, J., 340, 347, 351, 354
Druen, P. B., 394
Duckitt, J., 83
Duda, J. L., 415
Dugan, S., 324, 328, 444, 465
Dunn, J., 141
Durie, M. H., 379
Durrett, M. E., 164
Dweck, C. S., 73
Dyal, J. A., 323
Dyer, F. J., 445
Dyer, M., 397
Dyer, N., 463

Eagly, A., 392
Earley, P. C., 451
Earls, F., 372
Early, K. E., 215

Eberhardt, J. L., 17
Ebrahimpour, M., 452
Eccles, J., 196
EchoHawk, M., 214
Edelstein, W., 174
Edman, J. L., 217, 413
Edwards, C., 117
Edwards, P. K., 175
Eisenberg, D. M., 203
Eisenberg, N., 176
Eisenstat, R. A., 281
Ekman, P., 44, 105, 211, 227, 228, 230, 231, 232, 236, 237, 238, 239, 240
Elbedour, S., 399
Eley, T. C., 329
El-Islam, M. F., 347, 422
Elkind, D., 152
Elliot, J., 83
Ellis, A., 366
Ellis, B., 399
Ellsworth, P., 227
Emory, E. K., 161
Enriquez, V. G., 335
Enz, C., 445
Erdos, G., 112
Ervin, S. M., 274
Escobar, J., 360
Eshun, S., 118
Espin, O. M., 196, 197
Espino, V., 222
Esses, M. V., 82
Evans, B. J., 195
Evans, J. L., 105
Evenko, L. I., 462
Everett, F., 373
Ey, S., 345
Eyre, S. L., 112
Eysenck, S. B. G., 326, 328, 329

Fabrega, H., 118
Fagot, B., 193
Fairchild, H. H., 16
Fang, F. X., 126, 174
Fang, G., 174
Farris, K. K., 112
Farver, J. M., 176, 419
Feather, N. T., 327
Fehring, R. J., 152
Feingold, A., 392
Feist, J., 203, 206, 208
Fejes, F., 186
Feldt, K., 126
Fenton, F. R., 345
Ferligoj, A., 192
Fernandez-Dols, J. M., 237
Ferrante, J., 457
Ferris, K. R., 392
Festinger, L., 396
Fiedler, K., 75
Fields, J., 142
Figueredo, A. J., 331
Figueroa, R. A., 327

Filardo, E. K., 424
Fischer, E. F., 402
Fischer, S., 345
Fishman, J. E., 272, 281
Fitzgerald, M. H., 112
Flanagan, O., 116
Fletcher, D., 31, 208, 209, 210
Fletcher, F. J., 68
Fletcher, J. M., 126
Flores, E., 112
Fong, R. W., 227
Ford, C. S., 7
Forgas, J. P., 70, 72, 75, 76, 289, 387, 395, 411, 412
Forsterling, F., 330, 412
Fortenberry, J. D., 350
Francis, J., 463
Franco, F., 349
Frankel, K. A., 166
Frankish, C., 77
Franz, C. E., 317
Freedman, D., 158
Freud, S., 115, 316, 366
Frey, D., 411, 412
Friedman, H. S., 281
Friedman, J., 377
Friedman, J. R., 95, 176
Friedman, M., 207
Friesen, W. V., 211, 227, 228, 230, 231, 236, 240
Frieze, I. H., 192
Frijda, N. H., 249
Frohlich, B. C., 176
Frome, P., 196
Fronk, C., 188
Frosch, D. L., 419
Frost, L., 153
Fujino, D. C., 369, 376
Fukuno, M., 193
Fuligni, A., 143
Fulmer, R., 446
Furlong, M. J., 376
Furnham, A., 186, 204, 398, 411, 412, 413, 445

Gabrenya, W. K., Jr., 451
Gaier, L. E., 150, 408
Galambos, N., 188
Galati, D., 248
Galinsky, E., 144
Gallimore, R., 166
Gallois, C., 233
Gallup, G. W., 152
Galperin, Z. C., 141
Gamba, R. J., 42
Ganesan, V., 334
Ganguli, H. C., 103
Gant, L., 318
Gao, G., 326
Garcia Coll, C. T., 143, 152, 159

Gardner, H., 127
Gargano, G. M., 452
Garlick, R., 281
Garovich, L., 195
Garro, L. C., 270
Garza, R. T., 411, 412
Gay, J., 106
Ge, X., 154
Geary, D. C., 146, 147, 329
Gee, K., 369
Geen, R. G., 417
Geertz, C., 10, 300
Gelfand, M. J., 52, 463
Georgas, J., 50
George, S., 160
Gerber, E., 255, 257
Gergen, K. J., 3, 24
Gerin, W., 206
German, K., 152
Gerstner, C. R., 455
Ghuman, P. A. S., 152
Giacalone, R. A., 417
Gibbons, J., 187, 188
Gilbert, D. T., 79
Gilbert, G. M., 70
Giles, H., 422
Gilligan, C., 173, 175, 304
Gillis, J. S., 396
Gilmour, K., 281
Gim, R. H., 376
Ginsburg, H. P., 146
Gitelson, I., 188
Gitter, A. G., 281
Gladwin, C., 148
Gladwin, H., 148
Gladwin, T., 148
Glaser, S. R., 446
Gleason, H. A., 270
Gleicher, F., 117
Glick, J. A., 106
Glover, G., 197
Goater, N., 358
Goldberg, L. R., 329
Goldman, A., 361, 462, 466
Goldsmith, D., 139
Goldstein, M., 344
Gonzalez, R., 207
Goodnow, J. J., 136, 422
Goodwin, R., 390, 400
Goody, J. R., 171
Goossens, L., 152
Gordon, C., 381
Gordon, R. A., 349
Gorman, J. C., 137
Gorsuch, R., 152
Gottfredson, L. S., 129
Graham, J. L., 462, 465
Graham, J. R., 371, 372, 373, 374
Graham, P., 160
Graham, S., 407, 410

Gralinkski, J. H., 74
Grant, K., 345
Grant, T. R., 90
Grawe, K., 370
Gray, J. J., 212
Green, B. L., 362
Greenberg, J., 75
Greenfield, P. M., 38, 105, 123
Griffith, E. J., 70
Griffith, K. H., 70
Grilo, C. M., 212
Grimm, S. D., 334
Grisaru, N., 349
Grissom, R., 43
Grogan, J., 431
Grossmann, K. E., 164
Guanzon-Lapena, M. A., 330
Guarnaccia, P. J., 349
Gudykunst, W. B., 50, 266, 267, 290, 294, 326
Guilford, J. P., 119
Guinn, B., 218
Guisinger, S., 317
Gulerce, A., 3
Gumperz, J. J., 272
Gurin, P., 82
Guthrie, G. M., 329

Hadiyono, J. E. P., 422
Hadley, R. F., 272
Hagen, R., 193
Hagendoorn, L., 84
Haghighatgou, H., 345
Hahn, M. W., 422
Hale, J. L., 281
Halifax, N. S., 117
Hall, C. C. I., 195
Hall, E. T., 48, 116, 336, 424
Hall, G. C., 375
Hall, L. K., 76
Hall, R. H., 458
Hall, V. C., 407, 410
Hallahan, M., 411, 413
Hama, H., 255
Hamid, P. N., 323, 328
Hamilton, L. H., 212
Hamilton, V. L., 50
Hampel, R., 84
Hanna, G. S., 126
Harkins, S., 451, 452
Harkness, S., 155
Harlow, H. F., 161
Harlow, M. K., 161
Harmoni, R. V., 424
Harris, A. C., 192, 196, 418
Harris, M. B., 212
Harris, V. A., 306
Harrison, A. O., 134, 388
Hart, B. L., 334
Hart, I., 126
Harvey, Y. K., 348

Hashimoto, T., 401
Haskins, R., 145
Haslam, S. A., 79
Hatanaka, H., 370
Hatano, G., 474
Hatfield, E., 397, 399, 402
Hau, K., 174, 406, 407
Haynes, O. M., 140, 236
Hays, J. R., 126
Healey, J. F., 63, 81, 83, 84
Heaven, P. C. L., 330, 334, 445
Heelas, P., 317
Hegel, G. W. F., 171
Heider, E. R., 271
Heider, K. G., 236
Heine, S. J., 324
Heinisch, D. A., 448
Helgeson, V. S., 397
Hemans, L. T., 74
Henderson, M., 422
Henderson, N. D., 121
Hendrick, C., 397
Hendrick, S., 397
Hendriks, A. J., 329
Henriques, G. R., 205
Henry, B., 160
Herrnstein, R. J., 124, 125
Hersokovits, J., 98
Herzog, T., 411, 413
Hesketh, B., 447
Hess, D. R., 138
Hess, J. A., 448
Hetherington, E. M., 154
Hewstone, M., 77
Heyes, C. M., 155
Hiatt, L. R., 256
Hiatt, R. A., 222
Hibino, S., 455
Hickson, D. J., 433
Higashi, C., 376
Higginbotham, H. N., 355, 375, 376
Higgins, L. T., 193
Higgins, R. L., 74
Hill, R. F., 350
Hillary, K., 218
Hillman, S. B., 324
Hilton, D., 445
Hinkle, S., 447
Hinkston, J. A., 375
Hippler, A. E., 171, 334
Hippocrates, 204
Hirschfield, L. A., 17, 20
Hiruma, N., 95, 176
Hitch, G., 76
Hixon, J. G., 79
Ho, D. Y., 321
Ho, H., 150
Ho, M. K., 403
Hobson, J. A., 115, 116
Hoch, E. M., 379
Hodge, K., 193
Hodgetts, R. M., 452

Hoek, H. W., 349
Hofstede, G., 13, 31, 48, 49, 51, 185, 188, 208, 239, 266, 315, 389, 417, 433, 434, 435, 436, 439, 440, 441, 442, 443, 444, 445
Hofstee, W. K., 329
Hollander, E., 453
Hollon, S. D., 366
Holloway, S. D., 153
Holmes, L. D., 334
Holt, R. W., 136
Hood, R. W., 152
Hoosain, R., 270
Hoppe-Graff, S., 419
Horenczyk, G., 155
Horowitz, M., 418
Hothersall, D., 366
Hough, R. L., 360
House, A., 139
House, B., 126
Howe, A., 410
Howell, J. P., 455
Howell, S., 257
Howes, C., 144, 145, 176
Hoynes, W., 78
Hrebickova, M., 335
Hsee, C. H., 112
Hsu, L., 403
Hu, L. T., 369, 370
Hu, P., 163
Huang, L. N., 196, 359
Hudson, A. E., 7
Hudson, W., 102, 103
Huff, R. M., 203
Hughes, B., 19
Huguet, P., 418
Hui, C. H., 49, 51, 53
Hull, P., 275, 276
Hunsberger, B., 152
Hunt, M., 409
Huntington, R. L., 188
Huo, Y. P., 459
Hupka, R. B., 248
Husen, T., 146
Hutschemaekers, G. J. M., 10
Hwang, C. P., 145
Hwu, H. G., 346

Ibrahim, F. A., 355
Iizuka, Y., 422
Ineichen, B., 396
Inui, T. S., 374
Isaac, M., 347
Islam, M. R., 74
Itoi, R., 193
Ivey, A. E., 369
Ivey, P. K., 165
Iwanaga, M. I., 162
Iwao, S., 69
Iwawaki, S., 186, 233
Izard, C., 227, 236, 239

Jablensky, A., 345
Jacklin, C. N., 190
Jackson, D. N., 330
Jackson, J. M., 452
Jacob, E., 114
Jacobsen, F. M., 375, 376
Jacobsen, L., 155
Jaffe, Y., 418
Jahjah, M., 74
Jahoda, G., 10, 103
Jalali, B., 373
Janca, A., 347
Jang, K. L., 329
Janicki, M. G., 94
Janis, I. L., 458
Jankowiak, W. R., 402
Jantz, V., 334
Jeanquart-Barone, S., 85
Jencks, C., 121
Jensen, A. R., 120, 121, 122
Jensen, L. A., 175
Jerrett, D. T., 272
Jerrett, T., 272
Jiang, S., 458
Jilek, M., 217
Jilek-Aall, L., 217
Jin, P., 330
Joe, R. C., 30
Joensson, E. G., 329
John, O. P., 329, 333
Johnson, C. A., 126
Johnson, D. L., 126
Johnson, F. W., 122
Johnson, J. L., 452
Johnson, T. M., 350
Johnston, C., 117
Johnston, L., 77
Jolibert, A., 462
Jones, E. E., 306, 369, 405
Jones, T. S., 193
Joseph, R. A., 304, 309
Josephson, L., 192
Joshi, S. M., 139
Jou, J. Y. H., 455
Joustie, M., 115, 193
Juni, S., 329
Jussin, L. J., 69

Kaaya, J., 217
Kacha, F., 353
Kagan, J., 158
Kagitcibasi, C., 134, 136, 317
Kahneman, D., 111
Kaji, M., 281
Kakar, S., 136
Kamal, Z., 153
Kamel, F. N., 355
Kameoka, A. K., 217, 413
Kamin, L. J., 16
Kane, C. M., 115
Kaplowitz, S., 414
Karasawa, M., 310, 325
Karlins, M., 70

Karno, M., 344, 360
Kashima, E. S., 266
Kashima, Y., 77, 266, 315, 409, 410
Kashiwagi, K., 138
Kashubeck, S., 325
Kaslow, N. J., 215
Kasri, F., 44, 234, 237
Kaswan, J. W., 281
Katigbak, M. S., 126, 330, 334
Katz, D., 70, 71
Kawamura, Y., 255
Kay, P., 269, 270, 271
Kazarian, S. S., 214, 215
Keating, C., 284
Keats, D. M., 126
Kedem, P., 399
Keeley, H. S., 215
Keith, S. J., 343
Keitner, G. I., 345
Kelleher, M. J., 215
Keller, H., 140
Keller, M., 174, 175
Kelley, H. H., 405
Kelley, M., 138, 140
Kelly, J. G., 380
Kelly, K. P., 206
Keltikangas, J. L., 417
Keltikangas-Jaervinen, L., 112
Kemmelmeier, M., 50, 315
Kemper, T., 258
Kempton, W., 269
Kenny, D. A., 393
Kermoian, R., 165
Keys, J. B., 455
Khaleefa, O. H., 112
Kiers, H. A., 329
Kiev, A., 350, 402, 403
Kilmann, R. H., 445
Kim, C. C., 147
Kim, D. K., 462
Kim, E. Y., 448
Kim, L., 372
Kim, M., 267
Kim, S. J., 376
Kim, U., 138, 317, 322, 334, 360
Kim, Y. K., 176, 393
Kimmel, H., 399
Kimmel, P. R., 460, 461
King, J. E., 331
King, M., 358
King, M. L., 87
Kinzie, J. D., 359, 360, 361, 369
Kirmayer, L. J., 347
Kisker, E., 145
Kissiel, C., 222
Kitayama, S., 48, 245, 246, 301, 302, 303, 309, 310, 312, 313, 316, 322, 324, 325

Kleinman, A. M., 312, 342, 343, 344, 346, 347, 350, 354, 374
Klingelhofer, E. L., 126
Kluckhohn, C., 6, 9, 10, 46, 48, 389
Knight, G. P., 314
Koehler, K. M., 212
Kohlberg, L., 173
Kohn, L. P., 373
Koller, H. S., 176
Kolody, B., 359
Komilla, T., 305
Kommer, D., 75
Kontos, S., 144
Kooken, K., 44, 237
Kosawa, Y., 153
Kosmitzki, C., 318, 319
Koss, J. D., 347
Koss-Chioino, J. D., 371
Koutnetsouva, N., 233, 472
Koyama, T., 347
Kraemer, K., 150
Kral, M. J., 214
Kramer, G. P., 75
Kramer, R. M., 50, 386
Kranzler, J. H., 121
Krappmann, L., 144
Krause, I. B., 349
Kravitz, J., 108
Krebs, D. L., 94
Krieger, N., 206
Kriegman, D., 317
Kroeber, A. L., 6, 9, 10, 46
Kroll, N., 326
Kroonenberg, P., 233
Krupp, B., 84
Krupp, D., 233, 472
Kubany, E. S., 400, 401
Kubota, M., 142
Kudoh, T., 240, 241, 252, 281, 315, 394
Kuhlman, D. M., 326
Kuo, W. H., 359
Kupperbusch, C., 52, 53
Kurasaki, K. S., 359, 369, 377
Kurman, J., 310
Kurokawa, M., 312, 313
Kush, C. J., 149
Kwong, J. Y. Y., 357

Labarre, W., 321
Labin, D., 79
LaFreniere, P., 176
LaFromboise, T. D., 374
Lagerspetz, K., 418
Lamb, M. E., 144, 145
Lambert, E. W., 68, 90
Lambert, W. W., 227
Lamborn, S. D., 137
Lammers, C. J., 433
Landau, M. S., 417
Landis, D., 65, 398
Langley, S., 117

Langman, P. F., 367
Lannin, D. R., 217
Larrabee, G. J., 107
Lassiter, G. D., 393
Latané, B., 451
Lau, A. S. L., 370
Lau, S., 196
Lauer, E., 192
Laurendeau-Bendavid, M., 170
Laurent, A., 438
Lauri, S., 118
Lavallee, M., 169
Lawler, W. R., 222
Lawrence, J. S., 325
Laya, D., 127
Lazarus, R. S., 73
Leach, M. M., 327
Lederer, G., 327
Lederman, N., 410
Lee, C. C., 379
Lee, F., 411, 413
Lee, H. O., 50
Lee, I., 390
Lee, J. K., 455
Lee, J.-W., 458
Lee, S., 146, 147, 319, 341, 347, 349, 350, 378
Lee, S. M., 452
Lee, T. S., 373
Lee, V. K., 323
Lee, W. M. L., 372
Lee, Y.-T., 69
Leenaars, A. A., 214
Lee-Shin, Y., 176
Lee-Sing, C. M., 349
Leetz, K. L., 367
Lefever, G. B., 166
Leff, J., 256, 343, 344, 346, 354, 355
Lehman, D. R., 324
Leiderman, P. H., 165
Leinbach, M. D., 193
Leong, F. T. L., 347, 370, 371, 377
Leong, K., 417
Lerner, B., 369
Lester, B. M., 159
Leung, K., 31, 50, 59, 324, 334, 408, 410, 458, 465, 472
Leung, P. K., 360, 369
Leung, Y. K., 349
Levenson, R., 211
Levin, H. M., 108
Levine, E. L., 334
Levine, F., 118
Levine, J. B., 115, 116
Levine, R., 401
Levine, R. A., 67, 135, 141, 162
Levine, R. B., 214
Levine, S., 162
Levinson, S. C., 272
Levy, G., 108

Levy, R. I., 248, 255, 257, 258
Levy-Bruhl, L., 171
Lew, W. J., 174
Lewinsohn, P., 345
Lewis, G., 358
Lewis, M., 160
Lewontin, R. C., 16, 121
Li, X., 355
Liben, L. S., 76, 107
Liberska, H., 176
Liebkind, K., 155, 361
Lightfoot-Klein, H., 179
Lightner, E., 233
Liiceanu, A., 176
Lillard, A., 474
Lim, J., 357
Lima, B. R., 372
Lin, C., 462
Lin, K., 374
Lin, P., 270
Lin, W., 217
Lindholm, K. J., 360
Lindsay, R. L., 395
Lindsey, K. P., 358
Linton, R., 9
Li-Repac, D., 356
Lisansky, J., 334
Little, D. T., 150
Liu, L. G., 271
Liu, Y., 193
Livesley, W. J., 329
Lock, A., 3, 317
Loewenthal, K. M., 193, 342
Long, A., 407, 410
Longo, L. C., 392
Lonner, W. J., 184, 321, 327, 355
Lopez, R. S., 17
Lopez, S. R., 356
Loscocco, K. A., 458
Lott, D. F., 334
Love, K. G., 448
Love, L. R., 281
Love, S., 222
Lowe, K. B., 459
Lowenthal, K. M., 153
Lubart, T. I., 112, 113
Lucca, N., 31
Lucy, J. A., 270, 272
Lueptow, L. B., 195
Lueptow, M. B., 195
Luo, X., 355
Luria, A. R., 110, 171
Luster, T., 137
Luthans, F., 452
Lutz, C., 114, 255, 256, 257, 311
Luzzo, D. A., 448
Lynn, R., 125
Lyons, A., 77
Lyons, J. S., 222
Lysne, M., 108

Ma, K. H., 174, 175
MacArthur, R. S., 126
Maccoby, E. E., 136, 154, 190
MacDonald, K., 321, 330
Mackie, D. M., 50, 386
MacLachlan, M., 204
MacLean, M., 139
MacLeod, A. K., 193
MacMillan, I., 113
Macrae, C. N., 79
Madon, S., 70
Maehr, M., 307
Mahapatra, M., 174
Maio, R. G., 82
Majima, N., 176
Major, B., 90
Makaremi, A., 326
Makhijani, M. G., 392
Malgady, R. G., 357
Malloy, T. E., 393
Malpass, R. S., 7, 108, 184, 395
Mann, L., 325, 424, 458
Manrai, A. K., 116
Manrai, L. A., 116
Manson, S. M., 346, 355
Manz, C. C., 452, 458
Maramba, G. G., 375
Marin, B. V., 42
Marin, G., 42, 334
Markham, R., 236
Markoff, R., 403
Marks, D., 19
Markus, H. R., 48, 245, 246, 300, 301, 302, 303, 304, 309, 310, 312, 313, 316, 322, 324, 393
Marmot, M. G., 207
Marsella, A. J., 339, 342, 345, 346, 350, 354, 355
Marshall, C., 192
Martin, J. A., 136
Martin, W. E., 112
Martinez, F. M., 375
Martinez, R., 212, 213
Marvin, R. S., 162
Maslin, C. A., 166
Mastor, K. A., 330
Matam, S. P., 378
Mathews, H. F., 217
Maton, K. I., 152
Matsumoto, D., 12, 31, 42, 43, 44, 48, 50, 52, 53, 54, 59, 208, 209, 210, 211, 216, 229, 233, 234, 235, 236, 237, 238, 239, 240, 241, 249, 252, 276, 281, 310, 315, 316, 319, 324, 328, 394, 431, 472
Matsuyama, Y., 255

Mauro, R., 243, 251, 253
May, P. A., 214
McAdoo, H., 137
McAndrew, T. F., 69, 70
McArthur, L. Z., 393
McCabe, A., 266
McCargar, D. F., 151
McCartney, K., 95
McCauley, C. R., 69
McClelland, D. C., 307
McCloskey, L., 213
McClure, J., 409
McConatha, J. T., 233
McCoy, G. F., 359
McCrae, R. R., 329, 330,
    331, 332, 337
McCusker, C., 51
McDermott, J. F., 201, 375,
    376, 380
McGee, R. O., 160
McGoldrick, M., 403
McGowan, J. S., 413
McGowan, R. W., 413
McGue, M., 121
McGurk, H., 103
Mead, M., 48, 143, 230,
    321, 389
Meade, R. D., 117
Meadow, H., 381
Meeus, W. H., 176
Meglino, B. M., 447
Mehrabi, F., 346
Mehrabian, A., 280, 281
Mehryar, A. H., 327
Meissner, C. A., 108
Meissner, H. G., 462
Meizoso, M. T., 207
Meng, Z., 163
Menon, S., 334
Merighi, J., 398
Merkel, S., 410
Mermigis, L., 68
Merton, R., 81
Mervielde, I., 329
Mesquita, B., 249
Messe, L., 360
Messick, D. M., 50, 386
Meyer, E. C., 152
Milgram, S., 421, 423
Miller, J. G., 174, 175, 288,
    306
Miller, K. E., 361, 380
Miller, T. R., 455
Millson, C., 106
Millstein, S. G., 112
Milne, A. B., 79
Minami, M., 153, 266
Minde, T., 360
Mine, H., 255
Mintz, J., 344
Mintz, L. B., 325, 344
Miracle, A. W., 20
Miranda, J., 362
Mirande, M., 83
Miron, M., 126

Misra, G., 3
Misumi, J., 455
Mitchell, J. P., 217
Mitsui, H., 424
Miura, I. T., 147
Miura, K., 50
Miura, T., 334
Mixson, R. J., 372
Miyake, K., 164, 165
Mizokawa, D. T., 408
Mizuta, I., 95, 176
Mkombachepa, L., 218
Moffitt, T. E., 160
Moghaddam, M. F., 90, 411,
    414
Mohatt, G. V., 374
Moise, L. C., 360
Mok, D., 360
Montei, M. S., 448
Moore, J. T., 83
Moore, S. G., 159
Morales-Hidalgo, I., 187
Morelli, G. A., 139, 165
Morgan, L. H., 171
Morinaga, Y., 192
Morinis, A., 114
Morishima, J. K., 344
Morris, M. H., 449
Morris, M. W., 411, 414
Morten, G., 374
Mosk, J., 355
Mountcastle, A. R., 379
Mounts, N. S., 137
Moussaoui, D., 353
Moylan, J. S., 75
Muela, S. H., 218
Mukai, T., 213
Mulatu, M. S., 203
Mulder, M., 48
Mule, P., 188
Mullally, P. R., 309
Mullavey-O'Byrne, C., 112
Munro, D., 323, 328
Munro, E., 121
Munroe, R. H., 186
Munroe, R. L., 186
Muramatsu, Y., 422
Murasawa, H., 393
Murase, T., 379
Murdock, G. P., 7
Muret-Wagstaff, S., 159
Murnen, S. K., 397
Murphy, H. B. M., 344
Murphy, J. M., 342
Murphy, M., 446
Murray, C., 124, 125
Murstein, B., 398
Muzurovic, J., 361
Myambo, K., 388
Myers, D., 309
Myers, F. R., 257
Myers, J. K., 345

Nadidu, R. K., 251
Nagano-Nakamura, K., 419

Naidu, R. K., 305
Nakane, Y., 325, 458
Nakazato, H., 329
Narayanan, L., 334
Narayanan, S., 334
Nayak, S., 118
Neck, C. P., 452, 458
Negishi, K., 312, 313
Neighbors, C., 349
Nelson, S. H., 359
Nemoto, T., 222
Nenty, H. J., 124, 126
Newton, B. J., 422
Newton, M., 118
Newton, N., 118
Nezami, E., 357
Ng, D., 409
Ng, H. S., 330
Ng, W. G., 395
Ngini, L., 169
Nguyen, H. H., 360
Nicholls, J., 307
Nichols, R. K., 69, 70
Nicholson, H., 281
Niedenthal, P., 317
Nisa, Z., 213
Nisbett, R. E., 39, 405, 418
Nishida, T., 266, 290, 326
Noble, E., 329
Noda, A., 276, 277
Noel, D. L., 63
Norasakkunkit, V., 324
Norenzayan, A., 214
Northrup, A. D., 68
Nurmi, J., 176
Nyborg, H., 326
Nydell, M. K., 142

Oakes, P. J., 79
O'Driscoll, M., 70, 72
Oesterheld, J. R., 355
Oettingen, G., 114, 150
Ogbu, J. U., 134
Oh, M. Y., 379
Ohbuchi, K. I., 193
Ohta, Y., 325, 458
Oka, T., 451
Okamoto, K., 451, 462
Okamoto, Y., 147
Okechuku, C., 454
Okonkwo, R., 152
Olah, A., 176
Oliver, D., 271
Oliver, R. R., 105
O'Malley, P. M., 42
Omifade, A., 413
O'Neill, P., 446
Ong, S. B., 349
Opler, M. K., 344
Oppenheim, D., 139
Oquendo, M. A., 356
O'Reilly, C. A., 431, 446
Organista, K. C., 359
Organista, P. B., 359
Orley, J., 347

Orlinsky, D. E., 370
Orpen, C., 84
Orr, E., 196
Osaka, E., 315
Osako, T., 67
O'Shea, W., 398
Ostendorf, F., 331
Oster, H., 105
Osterman, K., 418
Osterweil, Z., 419
O'Sullivan, M., 236
Otaki, M., 164
Oyserman, D., 50, 315, 318
Ozkaragoz, T., 328

Padilla, A. M., 360
Paguio, L. P., 323
Palmer, S., 214
Paludi, M., 174
Pang, O. V., 150
Paniagua, F. A., 340, 344,
    351, 353, 371
Papousek, H., 94
Papousek, M., 94
Papps, F., 140
Pargament, K. I., 152
Park, S., 370
Parkin, M., 214
Parks, B. K., 370
Parsons, J., 345
Parsonson, K., 403
Pascual, L., 140
Paspalanova, E., 125
Patel, P. G., 107
Paterson, K., 19
Patterson, M. L., 286
Patzer, G. L., 392, 393, 396
Paul, G. L., 358
Paunonen, S. V., 330, 333
Pedersen, P. B., 369
Pelto, G. H., 10
Pelto, P. J., 9, 10, 11, 48, 417
Pendry, L., 77
Peng, K., 39, 411, 414
Pennebaker, J. W., 233
Penrod, S., 395
Pe-Pua, R., 5
Perez, M., 169
Perks, W. R., 90
Perreault, S., 360
Perry, M., 150
Persad, E., 214, 215
Person, W., 70
Perugini, M., 329, 330, 335
Peterson, A., 188
Peterson, C., 345
Peterson, M. F., 446, 455,
    465
Petrie, K. J., 126, 176
Pettengill, S. M., 138
Petty, R. E., 452
Pfeiffer, W. M., 350, 351
Phalet, K., 308
Pharr, A. E., 222
Phillips, D. A., 144, 145

Phillips, M. R., 379
Philpot, C., 152
Phinney, J. S., 17, 18, 155
Piaget, J., 119, 167
Pidoux, C., 127
Piedmont, R. L., 327
Pierre, E., 127
Pike, K. L., 21
Piker, S., 321
Pillay, A. L., 193
Pine, C. J., 134
Pines, A. M., 400
Pinker, S., 272
Pinkerton, D. S., 20
Pitariu, H., 326
Pittam, J., 233
Plaks, J. E., 73
Plomin, R., 121
Pollack, R. H., 101, 102
Ponce, F. Q., 374, 375
Ponchillia, S. V., 221
Ponterotto, J. G., 375
Pontius, A. A., 190
Poole, E. M., 176
Poole, G., 217
Poortinga, Y. H., 6, 11, 12,
    22, 30, 38, 39, 40, 44,
    45, 192
Porter, J. R., 186, 325
Porter, L. W., 454
Porter, R. Y., 374
Posada, G., 164
Poston, W. C., 376
Powell, A. B., 337
Prasadaro, P. S. D. V., 378
Pratt, G., 448
Preston, K., 52, 53
Preto, N. G., 403
Price-Williams, D., 126, 277
Priest, R., 372
Primm, A. B., 372
Prince, R., 379
Prince, V., 181
Proctor, N., 373
Pugh, J. F., 117
Puloka, M. H., 349
Punamaeki, R. L., 115, 193
Punetha, D., 422

Quah, S., 218
Quek, J., 193

Raaiijmakers, Q. A., 176
Rabbie, J. M., 418
Rack, P., 372
Radford, M. H. B., 325, 347,
    458
Rae, D. S., 343
Rajab, D., 334
Rajan, M. N., 462
Ramirez, J. M., 419, 420
Ramirez, M., III, 277
Ramos, J., 374
Randall, L. J., 17
Rao, V., 186

Rapson, R. L., 402
Rattan, M. S., 126
Ravlin, E. C., 447
Reece, D., 192
Reed, T. E., 121, 122
Reedy, R., 371, 379
Regier, D. A., 343, 358, 359,
    362
Regmi, M., 193, 314
Reich, L. C., 105
Reichers, A. E., 432
Reid, P. T., 192
Reis, H. T., 391
Remland, M. S., 193
Renwick, S. M., 136
Repetti, R. L., 95
Resnick, H. L., 214
Retschitzki, J., 169
Rettek, S. I., 251, 305
Reyes, J. A. S., 334
Reynolds, D. K., 379
Reznick, J. S., 158
Rhi, B.-Y., 342
Ribera, J. M., 218
Richards, M., 188
Richards, P., 164
Richardson, D. S., 418
Riemann, R., 329
Rieppi, R., 206
Riesman, P., 257
Rime, B., 233
Rivera, M., 349
Rivers, W. H. R., 100
Robbins, L. N., 345, 359, 372
Robinson, B. E., 323
Robinson, M., 462
Rodenhauser, P., 379
Rodriguez, O., 357
Roemer, M. I., 220
Rogan, R. G., 281
Rogers, C., 366
Rogers, P. L., 281
Rogler, L. H., 357
Rogoff, B., 139
Rohde, P., 345
Rohner, R. P., 10, 138
Rolland, J. P., 329
Rolland, J. S., 329
Romano, J. L., 403
Romero, G. J., 411, 412
Rosch, E., 104, 271
Rose, M. H., 19
Rose, S., 16
Roseman, I. J., 251, 253,
    305
Rosenberg, E. L., 237
Rosenman, R. H., 207
Rosenthal, D., 155
Rosenthal, M. K., 144
Rosenthal, R., 281
Rosmus, C., 117

Ross, B. M., 106
Ross, J., 392
Ross, L., 287, 306
Rosselló, J., 369
Rossiter, J. C., 222
Rothblum, E. D., 212
Rotherram-Borus, M. J., 176
Rotter, J. B., 323
Rousseau, B. M., 445
Rowe, C. L., 372
Rubin, G., 107
Rubin, L. R., 196
Runde, B., 140
Russell, G. L., 376
Russell, H. P., 68
Russell, J. A., 226, 236, 237,
    238, 255, 256, 257,
    311
Ruthe, G., 126
Rutter, M., 160
Ryan, A. M., 337
Ryckman, D. B., 408

Sachdev, P. S., 349
Sack, W., 361
Sackett, P. R., 129
Saco-Pollit, C., 159
Sagi, A., 162, 163, 164, 166
Sakamoto, Y., 334
Salama, M., 107
Salili, F., 406, 407, 409
Salisbury, L. H., 126
Salovey, P., 75
Salter, G., 281
Sam, D. L., 360
Sampson, E. E., 317
Sanchez, A. R., 375
Santa, J. L., 270
Santiago-Rivera, A. L., 382
Santrock, J. W., 195, 196
Sapir, E., 269, 321
Saraswathi, T., 402
Sargent, C., 118
Sartorius, N., 345
Sashkin, M., 446
Sato, K., 243, 251
Sato, S., 401
Sato, T., 379
Satoh, K., 113
Satterwhite, R. C., 185
Satz, P., 126
Saudino, K. J., 329
Sawilowsky, S. S., 324
Saxton, M. J., 445
Scarr, S., 95, 123, 154
Schachter, S., 396
Schaller, M., 78
Scharrón-Del-Rio, M. R.,
    368
Schein, E. H., 432
Scherer, K. R., 13, 50, 236,
    241, 242, 243, 244,
    245, 251, 252, 253
Schimmack, U., 239
Schliemann, A. D., 148

Schmader, T., 90
Schmid, C., 174
Schmidt, E. A., 90
Schmidt, S. M., 455
Schmit, M. J., 337
Schneider, B., 432
Schneider, B. H., 419
Schnellman, J. D., 187
Schuster, B., 412
Schwanenflugel, P., 270
Schwartz, N., 75, 418
Schwartz, S. H., 10, 53, 185,
    455
Schwartz, T., 462
Sciaky, R., 248
Scopetta, M. A., 360
Scribner, S., 106, 107, 110
Seeley, J., 345
Seelye, H. N., 67
Seeman, T. E., 95
Sefa-Dedeh, A., 212
Segall, M. H., 6, 22, 31, 97,
    98, 101, 105, 192
Seginer, R., 176
Seifer, R., 166
Seiffge-Krenke, I., 176
Sekaran, U., 85
Selice, S., 195
Senecal, S., 360
Sepkoski, C., 159
Shahim, S., 125
Shand, N., 153
Shane, S., 113
Shapiro, P. N., 395
Shapiro, R. B., 290
Sharkey, W., 314
Sharma, R., 176
Sharon, I., 24, 425
Sharp, D. W., 106
Shaver, P., 397
Shayer, M., 169
Shea, J. D., 170
Shepperd, J., 452
Sherif, C. W., 75
Sherif, M., 75
Sherman, J. W., 73
Shiang, J., 215
Shiflett, S., 118
Shikanai, K., 310
Shimizu, H., 398
Shimmin, H. S., 186
Shinn, M., 144
Shinotsuka, H., 458
Shiraishi, D., 329
Shirakashi, S., 451
Shkodriani, G. M., 188
Shmelyov, A. G., 330
Shore, B., 155
Shore, J. H., 346, 355
Shulman, S., 176, 399
Shweder, R. A., 174, 245,
    288, 304, 306, 322
Sigman, M., 355
Signorella, M. L., 76
Sillen, S., 344

Silva, P. A., 160
Silvar, S. D., 101, 102
Simmons, C. H., 398
Simonton, D. K., 113
Singelis, T. M., 52, 314, 315, 317
Singer, J. L., 344
Singh, R., 327
Singh, U., 186
Sinha, J. B. P., 334, 453, 459
Skeen, P., 323
Slavin, M. O., 317
Slee, R., 19
Smith, A. L., 126
Smith, J. R., 70
Smith, P. B., 324, 328, 422, 423, 444, 446, 455, 458, 465
Smollar, J., 144
Smukler, M., 359
Snarey, J. R., 174, 175
Sniderman, M. P., 68
Snidman, N., 158
Snowden, L. R., 371, 376
Snyder, C. R., 74, 326
Sodetani, L. L., 290
Sodowsky, G. R., 360
Soliman, A., 345
Song, M. J., 146
Sonoda, K. T., 290
Sorenson, E. R., 228, 236
Soudijn, K. A., 10
Sow, I., 334
Sowden, P. T., 272
Sowell, T., 87
Spadone, R. A., 323
Spangler, S., 164
Spearman, C. E., 119
Spencer, H., 171
Spencer, S., 90
Spicker, S. B., 139
Spies, C. J., 415
Spilka, B., 152
Sponsel, L. E., 192, 417
Sprecher, S., 399, 402
Srull, T. K., 75
Steele, C., 122
Steele, S., 87
Steere, M., 147
Steger, J. M., 70
Steinberg, L., 137, 154
Steinberg, S., 87
Stephan, C. W., 231
Stephan, W. G., 231
Steptoe, A., 205
Stern, B. B., 78
Sternberg, K. J., 144, 145
Sternberg, R. J., 112, 113, 128, 397, 400
Stetinsky, D., 125
Stetsenko, A., 150
Stetter, M., 359
Stevenson, H. W., 143, 146, 147
Stewart, A. J., 317

Stewart, J. E., 317
Stewart, R. B., 388
Stewart, S. M., 137, 218
Stewart, V., 102
Stierwalt, S. L., 337
Stiff, J. B., 281
Stigler, J. W., 145, 146, 147, 148, 150, 265
Stigler, S. Y., 146
Stiles, D. A., 187, 188
Stipek, D. J., 74
Stollack, G., 360
Stone, J., 393
Stone, L., 402
Stones, C. R., 330
Strack, F., 75
Stradling, S., 446
Strathman, A., 117
Strelau, J., 329
Streltzer, J., 117
Strodtbeck, F. L., 31, 48, 389
Stroessner, S. J., 73
Stropes-Roe, M., 422
Stryker, S., 300
Su, L., 355
Subramaniam, M., 349
Suchman, R. G., 105
Suci, G., 139
Sue, D., 196, 345, 367, 377, 378, 379
Sue, D. W., 345, 367, 369, 371, 374, 377, 378, 379
Sue, S., 344, 345, 369, 370, 374, 375, 376
Suess, G., 164
Suesser, K., 75
Suggs, D. N., 20
Sugimori, S., 326
Suhail, K., 213
Summerfield, A., 241, 242
Summerville, M. B., 215
Sun, C. H., 193
Sun, L., 218
Sung, K., 455
Suomi, S. J., 95
Super, C. M., 155
Susan, F., 281
Susser, E., 349
Sussman, L. K., 372
Sutcliffe, I., 205
Swann, W. B., Jr., 325, 328
Swartz, L., 349
Swartzman, L. C., 218, 222
Syme, S. L., 206, 207
Szapocznik, J., 360
Szarota, P., 335
Szirmak, Z., 329

Tafarodi, R. W., 304, 325, 328
Tajfel, H., 50, 74, 386
Takahashi, K., 163, 165, 176, 474
Takahashi, Y., 215
Takaki, R., 319

Takano, Y., 271, 276, 277, 315
Takeuchi, D. T., 214, 359, 369, 370, 372
Takeuchi, S., 233, 315, 472
Tak-Sing, C., 304
Talamantes, M. A., 221
Tale, U., 455
Tallman, G., 334
Tamie, B., 281
Tanaka-Matsumi, J., 351, 354, 360
Tanchuk, T. L., 78
Tanner, M., 218
Taparti, L., 214
Tata, S. P., 371, 377
Taylor, C. R., 78
Taylor, D. A., 397
Taylor, D. M., 90, 411, 414
Taylor, J., 87
Taylor, M. D., 68
Taylor, S., 431
Taylor, S. E., 95
Tedeschi, J. T., 316
Tedlock, B., 114, 115
Telles, C. A., 360
Terav, T., 112, 417
Terrell, M. D., 201
Tetlock, E. P., 68
Teveraishe, C., 388
Thapa, K., 251
Tharp, R. G., 381
Thomas, A., 158, 344
Thomas, D. C., 456
Thompson, N., 446
Thompson, T., 221
Thornton, B., 406
Thurstone, L. L., 119
Tillman, W., 360
Ting, K., 217
Ting-Toomey, S., 50, 293, 294, 295, 397
Tipping, S., 361
Tobin, J. J., 377
Todd, J., 126
Tolman, A., 371, 379
Tolson, T. F., 142
Tom, D., 410
Tomada, G., 419
Tomasello, M., 154
Tomkins, S. S., 74, 227
Toomey, K., 161
Torrey, E. F., 380
Toyne, B., 456
Trankina, F. J., 142
Tredoux, C. G., 108
Triandis, H. C., 10, 11, 31, 46, 48, 49, 50, 51, 52, 53, 69, 207, 208, 210, 227, 305, 315, 334, 388, 389, 390, 391, 409, 410, 441, 471, 472, 479
Tribe, R., 381

Trickett, E. J., 380
Trimble, J. E., 374
Trimboli, A., 140
Trimboli, C., 140
Trommsdorff, G., 186
Trompenaars, F., 324, 328, 444, 445
Tronick, E. Z., 154, 165
Trotter, K. H., 192
True, M. M., 162
Trull, T. J., 329
Trzebinski, J., 330
Tse, D. K., 462
Tseng, H., 138, 140
Tseng, W., 201, 375, 376, 380, 404
Tucker, J., 243, 251
Tullett, A. D., 114
Tulviste, P., 110
Turiel, E., 193
Turner, J. C., 74, 79
Turner, V., 94
Tuss, P., 150
Tversky, A., 111
Tylor, E. B., 9, 171
Tzenova, B., 125

Uba, L., 359, 372
Uehara, E. S., 359
Underwood, L., 108
Unzner, L., 164
Uziel-Miller, N. D., 222

Valadez, J. R., 112
Van de Koppel, J. M. H., 30
Van den Berghe, P. L., 83
Van der Flier, H., 190
Van der Veen, M., 193
Vanderwagen, W. C., 359
VanDevender, T. L., 162
Van de Vijver, F. J. R., 10, 30, 59
Van Harten, P. N., 349
Van Hoeken, D., 349
Van IJzendoorn, M. H., 162, 163, 164, 165, 166
Van Ommeren, M., 361
Varma, S. L., 378
Vasquez, M. J. T., 196
Vaughn, B. E., 166
Vega, W. A., 359, 360
Vehvilainen-Julkunen, K., 118
Venkataraman, S., 113
Verhulst, F. C., 355
Verkuyten, M., 84
Verma, J., 401
Villareal, M. J., 31, 50, 472
Vinacke, W. E., 227
Vollebergh, W. A. M., 176
Vom Kolke, A., 398
Von Glinow, M. A., 459
Von Raffler, W., 285
Vontress, C. E., 334
Voran, M., 145

Vornberg, A. J., 90
Vrij, A., 67
Vyse, S., 398

Wagatsuma, Y., 360
Wagner, D., 75
Wagner, D. A., 101, 106
Wagner, J. A., III, 452
Wagner, N. S., 371
Wainryb, C., 193
Walker, C. E., 281
Walker, L. J., 173
Walker, M., 140
Walkey, H. F., 69, 70, 409
Wallace, J. M., 152
Wallbott, H. B., 13, 50, 236, 241, 242, 243, 244, 245, 252
Walls, J., 463
Walsh Escarce, M. E., 159
Walters, G., 70
Walters, T. K., 112
Wan, G., 355
Wan, K. C., 408, 410, 417
Wang, A. V., 374, 398
Wang, L., 236
Wang, S., 160
Wang, Y., 451
Wang, Z. M., 458
Wardle, J., 205
Warren, M. P., 212
Washington, R. E., 325
Wassenaar, D. R., 192
Watkins, D., 193, 314
Watson, D., 405
Watson-Gegeo, K. A., 141
Weatherly, K. A., 458
Weber, E. U., 112

Weber, G. G., 95
Weinberg, R. A., 123
Weiner, B., 405, 412
Weinstein, H., 153
Weisner, T. S., 166
Weiss, B., 355
Weiss, S. C., 126
Weissman, M., 52, 53, 54, 315, 319
Weisz, J. R., 355
Weizmann, F., 16
Weldon, E., 452
Welles-Nystroem, B., 419
Westaby, J. D., 452
Whang, P. A., 121
Wheeler, L., 391, 393
White, K. M., 317
Whitebrook, M., 144, 145
Whorf, B. L., 269
Wiener, M., 281
Wierzbicka, A., 245, 312
Wilk, S. L., 129
Williams, D. R., 152
Williams, J. E., 72, 183, 184, 185, 187
Williams, K. D., 451, 452
Williams, L. R. T., 193
Williams, M., 281
Williamson, E., 215
Willman, E., 126
Wilson, M. N., 134, 142, 373
Wilson-Cohn, C., 238
Wimbarti, S., 419
Wing, D. M., 221
Wing, H. F., 349
Winkel, F. W., 67
Winton, W. M., 237

Wittgenstein, L., 38
Wittmer, J., 327
Witztum, E., 349
Wlodarek, J., 152
Wober, M., 127
Wohl, J., 367, 382
Wolf, R. M., 122
Wolfe, C., 90
Wolff, B. B., 117
Wolpe, P. R., 396
Wolpoff, M., 16
Womack, W. M., 374
Wong, P. T. P., 409, 410
Wong, Y. C., 39
Wood, K., 215
Wood, P. B., 70
Wood, P. C., 324
Worthington, G. J., 361
Wright, D. B., 108
Wright, R., 452
Wu, C., 394
Wyatt, E. G., 16
Wylie, R. C., 309
Wynn, K., 272

Yamaguchi, S., 315, 326, 419, 451
Yamamoto, J., 142
Yamamoto, K., 345
Yamashita, I., 347
Yan, H., 379
Yan, W., 150, 408
Yanchi, L., 203
Yang, F., 117
Yang, S., 326
Yang, Z., 355
Yao, L. E., 149
Yap, P. M., 350

Yates, J. F., 458
Yee, H. A., 16
Yeh, M., 370
Yeh, R., 455
Yik, M. S. M., 329
Ying, Y., 196
Ying, Y.-W., 359, 370
Yinon, Y., 418
Yirmiya, N., 355
Yoon, Y., 266
Yoshioka, M., 266
Young, D., 378
Young, D. M., 346
Young, K., 369
Young, L., 422
Young, R., 328
Youngjohn, J. R., 107
Youniss, J., 144
Yrizarry, N., 238
Yu, E. S. H., 308

Zaccaro, S. J., 452
Zahn-Waxler, C., 95, 176, 419
Zajonc, R., 393
Zane, N., 369, 370, 374, 375, 376
Zhang, J., 357
Zhang, M., 379
Zhang, X., 359
Zhang, Y., 378
Zheng, M., 193
Zhou, H., 137
Zimbardo, P. G., 117
Zimmer, J., 150
Zuckerman, M., 16, 17, 34
Zukow-Goldring, P., 141
Zuniga, M. E., 377

Subject Index

Abnormal behavior, 339–363
  assessment of, 352–357
  cross-cultural studies on, 342–351
  culture-bound syndromes and, 348–351
  defining, 340–342
  indigenous healing systems and, 355, 378–380
  treatment of, 365–383
  See also Psychological disorders
Aborigines, Australian, 98
Academic achievement, 145–151
  attributions about, 406–410
  biological factors and, 146–147
  cross-national differences in, 145–147
  language differences and, 147
  parental/familial values and, 148–149
  school systems and, 147–148
  student appraisals and, 149–150
  teaching styles and, 150–151
  See also Education
Academic psychology, 484
Accommodation, 168, 177
Acculturation, 138, 156
Achievement motivation, 307–308, 337
Active genotype-environment interactions, 96, 131
Adjective Check List (ACL), 183–184, 185
Affirmative action policies, 81–82
Affluence, 13
African Americans
  extended families of, 142
  gender differences among, 195–196
  intelligence tests and, 120, 122–123, 124–125

mental health services and, 369–370, 371, 372, 375
psychological disorders among, 358
African cultures
  attachment studies in, 165
  concept of intelligence in, 126–127
  indigenous personality model for, 333–334
  pain perception in, 118
  personality construct of, 333–334
  problem-solving process and, 109–110
  social support in, 388
  visual perception and, 102–103
Aggression, 417, 426
  cross-cultural studies on, 417–420
  gender differences and, 191–192
Agreeableness, 329
Alcoholism, 221
Allocentrism, 52, 326–327, 472
Alternating way, 404
Amae, 311, 334
Ambivalent attachment, 163, 177
American Indian Depression Schedule (AIDS), 355
American Psychiatric Association (APA), 352
American Psychological Association (APA), 369
Amok, 348, 350
Analysis of covariance (ANCOVA), 472
Analysis of variance (ANOVA), 42
Androgyny, 196, 198
Anger, 229, 242–243, 250, 252
  expressed in intimate relationships, 400–401
  physical experience of, 242–243

Anglo-Saxon type of organization, 433, 467
Animals, 331–332
Animism, 167–168, 177
Anorexia nervosa, 212, 349
Anthropological medicine, 94–95
Anti-Semitism, 68
Anxiety, 211, 293
Applied psychologists, 3
Appraisal, 73, 91
  of emotions, 250–253
Arab Americans
  extended families of, 142
  mental health services and, 371, 372, 373
Arranged marriages, 402
Asch studies, 421, 423
Asian Americans
  cardiovascular disease among, 207
  cultural reaffirmation effect in, 319
  gender role differences among, 196
  health-related attitudes among, 216–217, 218
  mental health services and, 369–370, 371, 372, 374, 375
  parenting behaviors of, 138
  psychological disorders among, 358–359
  self-construals of, 314
  student attitudes among, 149–150
Asian cultures
  achievement motivation in, 307–308
  attractiveness studies in, 393–394
  Confucian dynamism in, 443
  decision-making processes in, 457–458
  health-related attitudes in, 216–217, 218
  individualism-collectivism studies of, 50
  parenting styles in, 137, 138
  psychotherapy and, 368

self-construals in, 303, 314
Assimilation, 168, 177
Ataque de nervios, 349
Attachment, 161–166, 177
  Bowlby's theory of, 162
  child development and, 165–166
  cross-cultural studies on, 162–166
  secure ideal of, 163–166
  styles of, 162, 163
Attitudes, 11
Attractiveness
  cross-cultural studies on, 393–395
  personality judgments based on, 392–393
  See also Interpersonal attraction
Attributions, 74, 91, 404–417, 426
  academic achievement and, 406–410
  cross-cultural studies on, 406–417
  defensive, 406
  defined, 404
  emotions and, 239–240, 252–253
  stereotypes and, 74, 77
  traditional American patterns of, 405–406
Australian Aborigines, 98
Authoritarian parents, 136, 156
Authoritarian personality, 84
Authoritative parents, 136, 137, 156
Autostereotypes, 69, 91
Avanga, 349
Avoidant attachment, 163, 177

Back translation, 40, 59
Banding process, 129
Bantu people, 102–103
Behavior
  abnormal, 339–363
  aggressive, 417–420
  biological bases of, 93–97
  cultural influences on, 481–482

eating and dieting, 212–213
nonverbal, 280–282
social, 385–427
suicidal, 213–215
Beliefs, 11
Bell Curve, The (Herrnstein and Murray), 124–125
Bem Sex Role Inventory, 196
Bias, 33
confirmation, 111
researcher, 44–45
self-serving, 308, 406
Bilingualism, 273–278
intercultural sensitivity and, 473
psychological differences and, 274–277
Sapir-Whorf hypothesis and, 273–274
United States and, 277–278
Biological factors
behavior influenced by, 93–97
IQ scores and, 120–122, 147
math achievement and, 146–147
personality and, 328–329
See also Genetics
Biomedical model, 202, 224
Blind spot, 97, 131
Blue-Eyed/Brown-Eyed exercise, 83–84
Body conceptions, 204–205
Bulimia, 212
Businesses. *See* Organizations

California Psychological Inventory (CPI), 275–276
Capitulation, 403
Cardiovascular disease, 207–208
Career advice, 484–485
Carpentered world theory, 100, 131
Categorization, 73, 91, 131
cultural influences on, 104–106
emotions and, 256
stereotypes and, 73–74, 105
Cattell Culture Fair Intelligence Test, 123, 124
Causal interpretations, 43–44
Centralization, 432, 467
Centration, 167, 177

Channels, 283, 297
Child Behavior Checklist (CBCL), 355
Child development
attachment and, 165–166
day care and, 145
See also Developmental processes
Child rearing, 135–143
cross-cultural studies on, 138–140
economic factors in, 140–141
extended families and, 142–143
intercultural marriages and, 403
styles of, 136–138
See also Parenting
Children
assessing behavior problems in, 355
temperament of, 157–161
China
achievement motivation in, 307–308
concept of health in, 202–203
concept of intelligence in, 126
diagnosis of mental disorders in, 346–347
language of, 270
parenting styles in, 137
personality construct of, 334
teaching styles in, 150–151
See also Asian cultures
Chinese Classification of Mental Disorders (CCMD), 346, 353
Chinese Culture Connection, 443
Chinese Personality Assessment Inventory (CPAI), 334, 357
Chi-square, 42
Civil Rights Act (1991), 129
Classification process. *See* Categorization
Classism, 81
Climate, 13
Clinical psychologists, 381–382
Cocktail party phenomenon, 73
Coexistence, 404
Cofigurative cultures, 143, 156
Cognition, 104–114, 131
categorization and, 104–106

creativity and, 112–113
decision making and, 111–112
face recognition and, 107–108
gender and, 190–191
language and, 268–273
memory and, 106–107
problem solving and, 109–111
Cognitive-behavioral therapy, 366–367
Cognitive development, 167–172, 177
cross-cultural studies on, 168–170
great divide theories of, 171–172
Piaget's stage theory of, 167–171
Cognitive schemas, 393, 426
Cognitive template, 306, 337
Cognitive therapy, 366–367
Collaborative learning, 155
Collectivistic cultures, 48
concept of face in, 294
conformity and, 423
cooperation and, 424
creativity and, 113
emotions and, 234, 239, 245
empirical studies on, 50–51
health issues related to, 207–208, 210
ingroup/outgroup relationships and, 388–390, 391
meaning of work in, 450
methods for measuring, 51–54
psychotherapy and, 368
self-construals in, 303, 315–316
self-esteem in, 325
theoretical studies on, 49–50
work-related values and, 437
See also Individualistic cultures
Colors
categorization of, 104–105
language and, 270–271
Communication, 261–262, 278–296
barriers to, 292–293
channels of, 283
components of, 278–283
concepts for improving, 293–295

cultural influences on, 283–288
emotional regulation and, 295–296
encoding and decoding of, 282
intercultural, 289–292
intracultural, 288–289
messages conveyed through, 283
nonverbal behaviors in, 279, 280–282
signals used in, 283
styles of, 266
topics and contexts of, 266–267
verbal behaviors in, 279, 280–282
See also Language; Nonverbal behaviors
Communication technology, 13
Community psychology, 380–381
Companionate love, 397, 426
Complexity, 432, 467
Compliance, 420, 426
cross-cultural studies on, 421–423
domestic research on, 421
Componential intelligence, 128
Comprehensive health systems, 221
Compromise, 403–404
Computers, 13
Concept, defined, 73, 91
See also Self-concept
Concept formation, 73
cultural diversity and, 104–106
stereotypes and, 73–74
Concrete operations stage, 168
Confirmation bias, 111
Conflict
intercultural, 290–292, 403–404, 480–481
intimate relationships and, 400–401, 402–404
Conformity, 420, 426
cross-cultural studies on, 421–423
domestic research on, 421
gender differences and, 191
Confucian dynamism, 443, 467
Conscientiousness, 329, 330

Consciousness, 114–118
  dreams and, 115–116
  pain perception and,
    117–118
  time orientation and,
    116–117
Consensus, 405, 426
Conservation, 167, 177
Consistency, 405, 426
Construals of self. *See* Self-
    construals
Consummate love, 397, 426
Contact hypothesis, 395
Contempt, 229, 236–237,
    250
Context, 336–337
Context constructionistic
    way, 404
Contextual intelligence, 128
Contextualization, 48
Context variables, 31
Conventional morality, 173,
    177
Cooperation, 420, 423–424,
    426
Coping, 73, 211
Corporations. *See*
    Organizations
Correlational interpreta-
    tions, 43–44
Counting systems, 147,
    264–265
Creative adjustment, 404
Creativity
  cultural influences on,
    112–113
  intelligence and, 127
Critical thinking
  guidelines for, 478–482
  intercultural communica-
    tion and, 296
  personal growth and,
    477–478
Cross-cultural approach, 4,
    27
Cross-cultural communica-
    tion. *See* Intercultural
    communication
Cross-cultural comparison
    studies, 30, 32, 59
Cross-cultural psychology
  career advice related to,
    484–485
  contemporary challenges
    for, 471–473
  contributions of, 22–25
Cross-cultural research, 3–
    5, 27
  contemporary challenges
    for, 471–473
  cultural response sets
    and, 41–42
  data analysis issues in,
    41–43

definitions of culture
    and, 34–35
effect size analysis and,
    42–43
equivalence issues in,
    32–33
guidelines for evaluating,
    54–58
importance of under-
    standing, 29–30
individualism-
    collectivism and,
    471–473
interpretation issues in,
    43–45
language/translation
    issues in, 40–41
limitations of, 26
meaning of variables in,
    38–40
measuring culture in,
    46–54
methodological issues in,
    34–41
noncultural demograph-
    ics and, 36–38
nonequivalent data in,
    45
operationalization of
    variables in, 38–40
psychology and, 3–5, 23–
    25
researcher bias in, 44–45
sampling adequacy in,
    35–36
setting and procedure in,
    41
theoretical issues in,
    33–34
types of, 30–32
Cross-cultural studies
  on abnormal behavior,
    342–351
  on aggression, 417–420
  on attachment, 162–166
  on attractiveness, 393–
    395
  on attributions, 406–417
  on conformity and
    compliance, 421–423
  on cooperation, 423–424
  on decision making,
    111–112
  on dreams, 115–116
  on emotions, 231–235,
    236–250, 251–253,
    255–258
  on gender, 182–193
  on health, 208–211
  on ingroup/outgroup re-
    lationships, 390–391
  on intelligence, 119–126
  on interpersonal
    attraction, 397–401

on language, 266–267,
    269–272, 274–277
on leadership and
    management, 454–
    456
on math achievement,
    145–147
on moral reasoning, 174–
    176
on negotiation processes,
    462–463
on optical illusions, 100–
    103
on organizational
    culture, 443–449
on parenting styles, 138–
    140
on personality, 322–329,
    332–333, 357
on person perception,
    393–396
on Piaget's stage theory,
    168–170
on problem solving, 109–
    111
on suicidal behavior,
    214–215
on temperament, 158–
    161
on time orientation, 116–
    117
of work-related values,
    433–441, 442
Cross-cultural validation
    studies, 31, 59
Cultural cognition, 155
Cultural context, 336–337
Cultural display rules, 118,
    230–235, 260
  cross-cultural studies on,
    231–235
Cultural diversity
  abnormal behavior and,
    339–363
  aggressive behavior and,
    417–420
  attachment and, 161–166
  attributional styles and,
    406–417
  biological characteristics
    and, 94–97
  categorization and, 104–
    106
  challenges of, 1–2
  child-rearing practices
    and, 135–143
  clinical training and,
    381–382
  cognitive development
    and, 168–170
  creativity and, 112–113
  decision making and,
    111–112
  dreams and, 115–116

emotions and, 238–241,
    243–247, 248–249,
    252–253, 255–258
face recognition and,
    107–108
gender and, 182–193
health and, 201–224
ingroup/outgroup
    relationships and,
    387–391
intelligence and, 119–129
language and, 263–268
leadership/management
    styles and, 453–454
legitimacy of, 481
mainstream psychology
    and, 470–471
memory and, 106–107
moral reasoning and,
    174–176
pain perception and,
    117–118
perception and, 97–104
problem solving and,
    109–111
psychotherapy and, 368–
    369
suicidal behavior and,
    213–215
temperament and, 157–
    161
time orientation/
    perspective and, 116–
    117
visual perception and,
    98–104
work-related values and,
    433–441, 442
See also Cross-cultural
    studies
Cultural effect size
    statistics, 43
Cultural factors, 12–13
  health and, 205–216
  math achievement and,
    147–151
  prejudice and, 84
Cultural filters, 480
Cultural identity, 318
Culturally competent
    services, 374–376
Cultural psychology, 322,
    335, 474
Cultural reaffirmation
    effect, 318–319
Cultural relativism, 340, 362
Cultural response sets, 41–
    42, 59
Cultural trait psychology,
    322
Culture, 10–12, 27
  abstract nature of, 7–8
  aspects of life touched
    by, 7

attributions and, 404–417

behavior influenced by, 21–22

bilingualism and, 273–278

biological factors and, 93–97

cognition and, 104–114

common usages of word, 6–7

consciousness and, 114–118

cyclical and dynamic nature of, 8–9

definitions of, 9–12, 34–35

developmental processes and, 157–178

disability and, 19

education and, 145–151

emotion and, 225–260

enculturation process and, 133–156

ethnicity and, 17–18

factors influencing, 12–13

gender and, 19, 179–199

health and, 201–224

importance of defining, 5–6

individual differences and, 13–14, 480

individualism-collectivism dimension of, 48–54

intelligence and, 119–129

language and, 263–278

measuring in research, 46–54

nationality and, 18

objective elements of, 46

organizations and, 429–467

perception and, 97–104

personality and, 14–15, 320–335

popular culture vs., 15

as psychological construct, 479

psychotherapy and, 365–368

race and, 16–17, 34–35, 479

religion and, 152–153

self-concept and, 300–320

sexual orientation and, 20

social behavior and, 385–427

subjective elements of, 46–48

Culture, Medicine and Psychiatry (journal), 353–354

Culture-affiliation hypothesis, 275, 297

Culture-bound syndromes, 348–351, 362

Culture-bound theories, 33–34

Culture-free intelligence tests, 123, 124

Culture-specific principles, 4, 27
    pancultural principles vs., 20–21

Cycle of reciprocity, 8, 9

Data
    analyzing, 41–43
    evaluating, 57
    nonequivalent, 45

Data analysis, 41–43
    cultural response sets and, 41–42
    effect size analysis and, 42–43
    evaluation process and, 57

Day care, 144–145
    child development and, 145
    variations in, 144–145

Decentering, 40, 59

Decision making
    cultural influences on, 111–112
    organizational, 456–459

Decoding process, 282, 297
    cultural influences on, 286–288
    rules related to, 239, 260, 286–287
    See also Encoding process

Decoding rules, 239, 260, 286–287

Defensive attributions, 406, 426

Democratic decision-making process, 456–457

Demographics, noncultural, 36–38

Depression, 211, 345–347, 355

Depth perception, 103

Descriptive definitions of culture, 6

Developmental niche, 155

Developmental processes, 157–178
    attachment and, 161–166
    cognitive development and, 167–172
    cross-cultural research on, 176

moral reasoning and, 172–176
    temperament and, 157–161

Diagnostic and Statistical Manual of Mental Disorders (DSM-IV), 352–353

Diagnostic Interview Schedule (DIS), 355

Difficult temperament, 158, 160, 178

Dimensions of culture, 46–48

Disability, culture of, 19

Discrimination, 80–81, 91
    institutional, 81–83
    prejudice and, 81
    reducing, 88–89

Disease
    attitudes and beliefs related to, 216–218
    body conceptions and, 204–205
    cross-cultural studies on, 208–211
    cultural differences in defining, 202–203
    culturally sensitive treatment approaches for, 221–223
    health care systems for, 220–221
    individualism and, 207–208
    psychosocial determinants of, 205–206
    social isolation and, 206–207
    See also Health

Disgust, 229, 243, 250, 252

Display rules. *See* Cultural display rules

Distinctiveness, 405, 426

Domains of culture, 46–47

Downsizing, 453

Dreams, 115–116

Drug abuse, 222

Dynamic nature of culture, 10

Easy temperament, 158, 178

Eating disorders, 211–213

Ecological-level studies, 31, 59

Economic factors
    child-rearing practices and, 140–141
    emotions and, 245
    health and, 205–206, 209
    See also Socioeconomic status

Education
    categorization and, 105

cognitive development and, 170–171
    enculturation and, 145–151
    math achievement and, 145–147
    memory and, 106–107
    parental/familial values and, 148–149
    school systems and, 147–148
    student attitudes and, 149–150
    teaching styles and, 150–151
    See also Academic achievement

Effect size analysis, 42–43

Egocentrism, 167, 178

Emics, 20–21, 27, 348

Emotion antecedents, 247–250, 260
    cultural differences in, 248–249
    cultural similarities in, 247–248
    latent vs. manifest content and, 249–250

Emotion appraisal, 250–253, 260
    cultural differences in, 252–253
    cultural similarities in, 250–252

Emotions, 225–260
    American view of, 254–255
    antecedents of, 247–250
    appraisal of, 250–253
    categorization of, 256
    concept and definition of, 255–256
    controlling or regulating, 89, 295–296, 477–478
    cross-cultural studies on, 231–235, 236–250, 251–253, 255–258
    cultural construction of, 245–247
    cultural display rules and, 230–235
    decoding rules and, 287
    experience of, 241–247
    expressed, 344
    facial expressions of, 226–230
    functionalist approach to, 245
    importance of, 225–226
    indigenous, 311–312
    intensity of, 237, 239–240
    language of, 256, 257
    latent content of, 249–250

Emotions *(continued)*
location of, 257
meaning of, 257–258
perception of, 236–241
recognition of, 236, 237–239
self-concept and, 310–312
stereotypes and, 74–75, 233
subjective experience of, 237
universality of, 226–230, 236, 241–243
Empirically supported treatments (EST), 368
Encoding process, 282, 297
cultural influences on, 283–286
rules related to, 284–286
See also Decoding process
Enculturation, 133–156
child rearing and, 135–143
day care and, 144–145
definition of, 134, 156
education and, 145–151
ethnocentrism as consequence of, 63–65
extended families and, 142–143
friendships and, 144
parents and, 135–143
peer groups and, 143–144
religion and, 152–153
siblings and, 141
socialization and, 133–135
temperament and, 159–160
English language, 263–265
Ensembled individualism, 317
Entrepreneurial health systems, 220–221
Environment
culture influenced by, 13
genetic interactions with, 95–96
IQ scores and, 121, 122–123
Equivalence, 32–33, 59
definitions of variables and, 38–40
language/translation issues and, 40–41
noncultural demographics and, 36–38
research setting/procedures and, 41
Ethnic identity, 155
Ethnicity
culture and, 17–18
gender differences and, 195–197

intelligence tests and, 120–126
stereotypes based on, 71
See also Race
Ethnic minorities
intelligence tests and, 120
mental health services and, 368–377
psychological disorders among, 358–362
Ethnocentrism, 62–68, 91
cognitive development and, 172
decoding rules and, 286
definitions of, 62–63
enculturation and, 63–65
flexible vs. inflexible, 66
monolingualism and, 277–278
psychological factors contributing to, 67–68
recognizing in oneself, 65–67, 85–86, 480
stereotypes and, 77–78
Ethnographies, 32, 59–60, 255
Ethnopsychologies, 474
Etics, 20–21, 27, 348
European Americans
eating disorders among, 212, 213
individualism-collectivism studies of, 51
mental health services and, 369–370
parenting behaviors of, 138–139
self-construals of, 314
student attitudes among, 149–150
Evocative genotype-environment interactions, 96, 131
Exosystem, 135
Experiential intelligence, 128
Expressed emotion, 344
Expression of Emotion in Man and Animals, The (Darwin), 227
Extended families, 142–143
External locus of control, 323
Extroversion, 329
Eyewitness testimony, 108
Eysenck Personality Questionnaire (EPQ), 325–326

Face, concept of, 294–295
Face recognition
cultural influences on, 107–108

person perception and, 395
Facial expressions
categorization of, 104
cross-cultural studies on, 231–235
cultural display rules and, 230–235
illustrated, 229
intensity of, 237, 239–240
recognition of, 236, 237–239
universality of, 226–230, 236, 241–243
See also Nonverbal behaviors
Fago, 311
False uniqueness effect, 309, 337
Families
child-rearing practices in, 135–143
educational influence of, 148–149
extended, 142–143
Fear, 229, 250, 252
Feelings. *See* Emotions
Filial piety, 308, 337
Five Factor Model (FFM) of personality, 185, 329–332
Flexible ethnocentrism, 66, 91
Folk psychologies, 474
Foreign language effect, 276–277, 297–298
Foreign language processing difficulties, 276, 298
Formalization, 432, 467
Formal operations stage, 168
Friendships, 144
Front-horizontal foreshortening theory, 100, 131
Functionalist approach to emotion, 245
Fundamental attribution error, 287, 306, 337, 405–406, 426

g (general intelligence) factor, 119
Gender, 19, 179–199
cross-cultural studies on, 182–193
cultural influences on, 193–195
definitions related to, 181–182
ethnicity and, 195–197
mainstream psychology and, 180–181
mate selection and, 399–400

parenting behaviors and, 139
psychological differences and, 189–193
self-concept and, 187–188
work-related values and, 188–189
Gender identity, 182, 198
Gender role ideology, 187–188, 198
Gender roles, 19, 182, 197, 198
cross-cultural studies on, 187–188
ethnicity and, 196–197
ideologies associated with, 187–188
Gender stereotypes, 182, 198
on aggressiveness, 191–192
on conformity and obedience, 191
cross-cultural research on, 183–187
General Collectivism Index (GCI), 51
General intelligence (*g*) factor, 119
Generalizations, 78–79, 87–88
Generation gap, 8
Generations
cultural rules communicated through, 12
stereotypes perpetuated through, 78
Genetic definitions of culture, 6
Genetics
environment interactions with, 95–96
IQ scores and, 120–122
personality and, 328–329
See also Biological factors
Gestures, 284, 298
Global village, 430
Goodness of fit, 158, 160, 178
Grammar, 262
Grandparents, 142–143
Great divide theories, 171, 178
Greek culture, 50
Gross domestic product (GDP), 209
Group psychotherapy, 378
Groups, 11
Groupthink, 458
Guilt, 243, 250, 252

Happiness, 229, 249, 250, 252, 312–313
Hardiness, 203, 224

Health, 201–224
  attitudes and beliefs
    related to, 216–218
  body conceptions and,
    204–205
  cross-cultural studies on,
    208–211
  cultural discrepancies
    and, 211
  culturally sensitive
    treatment approaches
    and, 221–223
  definitions and views of,
    202–203
  eating disorders and,
    211–213
  economic factors and,
    205–206, 209
  health care delivery
    systems and, 220–221
  model of cultural influ-
    ences on, 219–220
  psychosocial determi-
    nants of, 205–206
  social isolation and, 206–
    207
  See also Mental health
Health care delivery
  systems, 220–221
Health psychology, 205
Heart disease, 207–208
Heterostereotypes, 69, 91
High-context cultures, 116,
  336
Historical definitions of
  culture, 6
Horizontal individualism/
  collectivism, 52
Horizontal-vertical illusion,
  98, 99, 100–101
Hospice services, 222
Hypotheses, 56

Identity
  cultural, 318
  ethnic, 155
  gender, 182
  sexual, 182
Idiocentrism, 52, 472
Illness. See Disease
Imitation, 154
Immigrants
  cultural reaffirmation
    effect and, 318–319
  intelligence testing of,
    120
  psychological disorders
    among, 360–361
INDCOL scale, 51
Independent construal of
  self, 302, 303, 337
India
  time orientation in, 117
  visual perception in,
    100–101, 103

Indigenous emotions, 311–
  312, 337
Indigenous healing systems,
  355, 362, 378–380,
  383
  abnormal behavior and,
    355, 378–380
  mental health services
    and, 376–377
Indigenous personalities,
  321–322, 333–335,
  337
Individualism
  culture and, 13–14, 480
  emotions and, 254–255
  health issues related to,
    207–208, 209, 210
Individualism-collectivism
  (IC), 48–54
  conformity and, 423
  cooperation and, 424
  cross-cultural psychology
    and, 471–473
  emotions and, 234, 239,
    244–245
  empirical work on, 50–
    51
  health issues related to,
    207–208, 209, 210
  ingroup/outgroup
    relationships and,
    388–390, 391
  leadership/management
    styles and, 454
  measurement of, 51–54
  self-construals and, 315–
    316
  self-esteem and, 325
  theoretical work on, 49–
    50
  work-related values and,
    437, 439, 440, 447
Individualism-Collectivism
  Interpersonal
  Assessment Inventory
  (ICIAI), 53–54
Individualistic cultures, 48
  conformity and, 423
  cooperation and, 424
  creativity and, 113
  emotions and, 234, 239,
    245
  empirical studies on, 50–
    51
  health issues related to,
    207–208, 209, 210
  ingroup/outgroup
    relationships and,
    388–390, 391
  meaning of work in, 450
  methods for measuring,
    51–54
  self-construals in, 302,
    315–316
  self-esteem in, 325

theoretical studies on,
  49–50
work-related values and,
  437, 439
See also Collectivistic
  cultures
Infatuation, 397, 426
Inflexible ethnocentrism,
  66, 91
InfoTrac College Edition,
  27
Ingroup relationships, 385–
  392, 426
  cross-cultural studies on,
    390–391
  cultural differences in,
    387–391
  definition of, 386
  emotional expression
    and, 234–235
  individualism-
    collectivism and, 388–
    390, 391
  structure and format of,
    387–388
  See also Outgroup
    relationships
Institutional discrimina-
  tion, 81–83, 85, 91
Instructional learning, 154–
  155
Intelligence, 119–129
  cross-cultural research
    on, 119–126
  cultural differences in
    concept of, 126–127
  recent developments in
    theories about, 127–
    128
  traditional definitions of,
    119
  types of, 127–128
  See also IQ
Intelligence tests, 119–126
  biological factors and,
    120–122
  environmental factors
    and, 121, 122–123
  ethnic minorities and,
    120
  selection issues and,
    128–129
Intercultural communica-
  tion, 289–292
  barriers to, 292–293
  competence in, 294
  conflict and, 290–292
  emotional regulation
    and, 295–296
  improvement of, 293–
    295
  micromomentary
    analysis of, 291
  uncertainty and, 289–
    290

Intercultural marriages,
  401–404
Intercultural sensitivity,
  473, 476
Intercultural success,
  482–483
Interdependent construal of
  self, 302–304, 337
Intergroup attitudes
  ethnocentrism and,
    62–68
  psychological factors
    contributing to, 67–68
Internal locus of control,
  323
International Association
  for the Evaluation of
  Education Achieve-
  ment (IEA), 146
International Association of
  Cross-Cultural
  Psychology, 22
International Classification
  of Diseases, Tenth
  Edition (ICD-10), 353
International negotiations,
  460–463
International organizations,
  430
International Pilot Study of
  Schizophrenia (IPSS),
  343–344
Interorganizational-level
  culture, 431–432
Interpersonal attraction,
  396–404, 426
  cross-cultural studies on,
    397–401
  domestic research on,
    396–397
  intercultural marriages
    and, 401–404
  intimate relationships
    and, 396–397
  See also Attractiveness
Interpersonal space, 285
Interpretation, 43–45
  cause-effect vs.
    correlational, 43–44
  dealing with non-
    equivalent data, 45
  evaluation process and,
    57–58
  researcher bias and,
    44–45
  stereotypes based on,
    86–87
Interrelated self-concept,
  317
Intimate relationships
  cross-cultural studies on,
    397–401
  intercultural marriages
    and, 401–404
  interpersonal attraction
    and, 396–397

Intracultural communication, 288–289
Intraorganizational-level culture, 431
Introspection, 257, 260
IQ (intelligence quotient), 120–125
   biological factors and, 120–122
   environmental factors and, 121, 122–123
   math achievement and, 147
   selection issues and, 128–129
   See also Intelligence
Irreversibility, 167, 178
Isolated self-concept, 317

Japan
   achievement motivation in, 308
   attachment studies in, 165–166
   cultural display rules in, 231
   decision-making process in, 457
   emotion appraisal in, 252
   health-related attitudes in, 216–217
   indigenous emotions of, 311
   individualism-collectivism studies in, 50
   language of, 263–265
   negotiation processes in, 462
   nonverbal behaviors in, 285
   parenting behaviors in, 138
   personality construct of, 334
   suicide in, 213–214
   teaching styles in, 50, 150–151
   See also Asian cultures
Jigsaw classroom, 89
Journal of Cross-Cultural Psychology, 22
Joy, 242, 243

Kinship sentiments, 83
Knowledge factors, 294
Kohlberg's theory of morality, 173
Koro, 350

Labeling of emotions, 256
Language, 261–278
   bilingualism and, 273–278

cognition and, 268–273
cross-cultural studies on, 266–267, 269–272, 274–277
emotions and, 256, 257
ethnocentrism and, 277–278
intercultural communication and, 292
lexicons of, 262, 263–265
math achievement and, 147
mental health services and, 372–373
pragmatics of, 262, 265–267
psychological testing and, 356
Sapir-Whorf hypothesis and, 268–273
structure of, 262–263
translation issues and, 40–41
See also Communication; Verbal behaviors
Latah, 350
Latent content, 249–250
Latino Americans
   gender role differences among, 196–197
   mental health services and, 369–370, 371, 374, 375
   psychological disorders among, 359
   self-construals of, 314
Latin type of organization, 433, 467
Leadership, 453–456
   cross-cultural studies on, 454–456
   cultural differences in, 453–454
   definition of, 453, 467
Learning
   memory and, 106–107
   teaching styles and, 150–151
   See also Education
Lexicons, 262, 263–265
   counting systems, 264–265
   self/other referents, 263–264, 265
Linguistic relativity, 268–273
   challenges to, 270–272
   research supporting, 269–270
   See also Sapir-Whorf hypothesis
Locus of control, 323–324, 337

Logical thinking, 110–111
Love
   cross-cultural studies on, 397–401
   intercultural marriages and, 401–404
   types of, 397
Low-context cultures, 116, 336

Machismo, 196, 198
Macrosystem, 135
Management, 453–456
   cross-cultural studies on, 454–456
   cultural differences in, 453–454
Manifest content, 249–250
Marriage
   arranged, 402
   intercultural, 401–404
   mate selection and, 399–400
   See also Intimate relationships
Masculinity (MA), 48
   health issues related to, 208–209
   work-related values and, 189, 439, 441, 442
Matching hypothesis, 397, 426
Mate selection, 399–400
Math achievement, 145–151
   biological factors and, 146–147
   cross-national differences in, 145–147
   social/cultural factors influencing, 147–151
   See also Academic achievement
Media stereotypes, 78
Medical delivery systems, 220–221
Medical model, 380
Memory
   culture and, 106–107
   stereotypes and, 76
   types of, 75–76
Mental health, 339–363
   assessment of, 352–357
   culture-bound syndromes and, 348–351
   defining abnormality and, 340–342
   ethnic minorities and, 358–360
   indigenous healing systems and, 355, 378–380
   migrants and, 360–361
   refugees and, 361

suicidal behavior and, 213–215
treatment methods and, 365–383
See also Psychological disorders
Mental health services, 368–377
   barriers to seeking treatment by, 371–372
   community-based approach to, 380–381
   cross-cultural studies on, 368–369
   culturally competent treatment and, 374–376
   ethnic differences in response to, 369–371
   indigenous healing practices and, 376–377
   language difficulties and, 372–373
   treatment issues and, 372–374
Mental processes. See Cognition
Mesosystem, 135
Messages, 283
Meta-analysis, 422
Methodology (research), 34–41
   definitions of culture and, 34–35
   evaluation process and, 56–57
   language/translation issues and, 40–41
   meaning of variables and, 38–40
   noncultural demographics and, 36–38
   operationalization of variables and, 38–40
   research setting/procedures and, 41
   sampling adequacy and, 35–36
Mexican Americans
   gender role differences among, 196–197
   psychological disorders among, 359
   self-construals of, 314
Microsystem, 135
Migrants
   psychological disorders among, 360–361
   See also Immigrants
Milgram studies, 421, 423
Mindfulness, 293–294
Minnesota Multiphasic Personality Inventory (MMPI), 357

Minority group-affiliation hypothesis, 275
Mixing way, 404
Monolingualism, 273, 277–278
Moral reasoning, 172–176
cross-cultural studies on, 174–176
Kohlberg's theory of morality, 173
Morita therapy, 379
Morphemes, 263
Mortality
social isolation and, 206–207
socioeconomic status and, 206
Motivation
achievement, 307–308
employee productivity and, 451–453
hierarchical model of, 330, 331
visual perception and, 103
Motivational factors, 294
Mueller-Lyer illusion, 98, 99, 100–102
Multicultural identities, 318–319
Multinational and international corporations, 430, 467
See also Organizations

Naikan therapy, 379
National health systems, 220–221
Nationality
culture and, 18
stereotypes based on, 71
Native Americans
concept of health among, 203
gender role differences among, 197
language studies among, 269–270
mental health services and, 369–370, 371, 372, 374
psychological disorders among, 359–360
Negotiation processes, 460–463
American assumptions about, 460, 461
cross-cultural studies on, 462–463
Nemawashi procedure, 457, 467
NEO Five Factor Inventory, 337

Neonatal Behavior Assessment Scale (NBAS), 159
Neurocultural theory of emotional expression, 232
Neuroticism, 329, 330
New Guineans, 100–101, 228
Noncultural demographics, 36–38
Nonequivalent data, 45
Nonhuman primates, 331–332
Nonverbal behaviors, 280–282
cultural influences on, 283–288
definition of, 280
facial expressions and, 226–230
intercultural communication and, 292–293
types of, 280
See also Communication; Facial expressions
Normative definitions of culture, 6
Norms, 11
North American Free Trade Agreement (NAFTA), 430

Obedience, 420, 426
culture and, 423
domestic research on, 421
gender differences and, 191
Obesity, 211–213
Objective elements of culture, 46
Oligarchy, 457, 467
On the Origin of Species (Darwin), 226–227
Openness, 329
Operationalization, 38, 60
Optical illusions, 98–101, 131
Oral traditions, 106, 107
Organizational climate, 432, 467
Organizational culture, 430–432
contemporary research on, 441, 443–449
cross-cultural studies on, 443–449
definition of, 431, 467
measurement of, 445–446
practical implications of, 446–449

Organizations, 429–467
climate in, 432
culture in, 430–432, 441, 443–449
decision-making processes in, 456–459
institutional discrimination and, 81–83
intercultural issues for, 459–466
leadership and management styles in, 453–456
meaning of work in, 450
motivation and productivity in, 451–453
multinational and international, 430
national character of, 433
negotiation processes in, 460–463
overseas assignments within, 463–464
structure of, 432–433
workforce diversity in, 464
work-related values in, 433–441, 442
Osteoporosis, 216–217
Outgroup relationships, 385–392, 426
cross-cultural studies on, 390–391
cultural differences in, 387–391
definition of, 386
emotional expression and, 234–235
individualism-collectivism and, 388–390
structure and format of, 387–388
See also Ingroup relationships
Overpathologizing, 356, 362
Overseas assignments, 463–464

Pain perception, 117–118
Pancultural principles, 20–21
Parenting, 135–143
cross-cultural studies on, 138–140
economic factors in, 140–141
educational success and, 148–149
goals and beliefs about, 135–136

intercultural marriages and, 403
styles of, 136–138
See also Child rearing
Passionate love, 397, 398, 426
Passive genotype-environment interactions, 95–96, 131
Pathogens, 202, 224
Peer groups, 143–144
Perception, 97–104, 131
cultural influences on, 98–104
emotional, 236–241
experience and, 97–98
gender differences and, 190–191
optical illusions and, 98–101
pain, 117–118
self-, 304–305
stereotypes based on, 86–87
See also Person perception
Permissive parents, 136, 137, 156
Personality, 320–335
authoritarian, 84
bilingualism and, 275
cross-cultural studies on, 322–329, 357
culture and, 14–15, 321–322
definitions of, 320–321, 337
Five Factor Model of, 329–332
genetics and, 328–329
indigenous conceptions of, 321–322, 333–335
locus of control and, 323–324
measurement of, 325–326, 332–333
prejudice and, 84
psychopathology and, 357
self-esteem and, 324–325
Personality tests, 332–333, 357
Person perception, 392–404, 426
attractiveness and, 392, 393–395
cross-cultural studies on, 393–396
definition of, 392
domestic research on, 392–393
language and, 276
physical appearance and, 392–393

Phonemes, 262
Phonology, 262
Physical attractiveness. *See* Attractiveness
Physiological symptoms emotional experience and, 242–243, 244
somatization and, 347
Piaget's stage theory, 167–171
cross-cultural studies on, 168–170
developmental stages in, 167–168
Ponzo illusion, 98, 99, 101
Popular culture, 15
Population density, 13
Postconventional morality, 173, 178
Postfigurative cultures, 143, 156
Posttraumatic stress disorder (PTSD), 361
Power distance (PD), 48
creativity and, 113
health issues related to, 208–209, 210
work-related values and, 434–435, 436, 447, 465
Pragmatics, 262, 265–267
Preconceptions, 293
See also Stereotypes
Preconventional morality, 173, 178
Prefigurative cultures, 143, 156
Prejudice, 80, 91
components of, 80
discrimination and, 81
factors contributing to, 83–85
methods for reducing, 86–88
origins of, 83–85
Preoperational stage, 167–168
Present State Examination (PSE), 354
Primacy effect, 106
Problem-solving process, 109–111, 131
Productivity, 451–453
Pronouns, 266
Psychoanalysis, 367
Psychological anthropology, 321
Psychological definitions of culture, 6
Psychological disorders, 339–363
assessment of, 352–357
cross-cultural research on, 342–351

culture-bound syndromes and, 348–351
defining abnormality and, 340–342
depression, 345–347
diagnosis of, 352–354
ethnic minorities and, 358–360
indigenous healing systems and, 355
measurement tools for, 354–356, 357
mental health services and, 368–377
migrants and, 360–361
psychotherapy and, 365–368, 378
refugees and, 361
schizophrenia, 343–345
somatization, 347
treatment of, 365–383
Psychological factors
bilingualism and, 274–277
biology and, 93–95
ethnocentrism and, 67–68
gender and, 189–193
health and, 205–206
stereotypes and, 72–77
Psychologists, 2–3
clinical training of, 381–382
community-oriented, 380–381
emotions as viewed by, 254
Psychology
career advice related to, 484–485
clinical training in, 381–382
contemporary challenges for, 473–475
cross-cultural research and, 3–5
cultural revolution in, 23–24, 469–475
gender differences and, 180–181
intelligence defined in, 119
two goals of, 2–3, 475
Psychopathology, 357
See also Psychological disorders
Psychotherapy, 365–368
community-based, 380–381
contemporary, 366–367
cultural limitations of, 367–368
diverse cultures and, 368–369

global practice of, 378
indigenous healing practices and, 376–377, 378–380
traditional, 366
See also Mental health services

Qigong-induced mental disorder, 350

Race
culture and, 16–17, 34–35, 479
intelligence tests and, 120–126
stereotypes based on, 71
visual perception and, 102
See also Ethnicity
Racism, 81, 85
Recency effect, 106
Reciprocity cycle, 8, 9
Reciprocity hypothesis, 397, 426
Refugees, 361
Regression, 295, 477
Regulators, 285, 298
Relationships
ingroup vs. outgroup, 385–392
intimate, 396–404
Reliability, 38, 60
Religion
cross-cultural research and, 37
enculturation and, 152–153
psychotherapy and, 378
suicide and, 215
Research. *See* Cross-cultural research
Researcher bias, 44–45
Research psychologists, 3
Retinal pigmentation, 101–102
Rightsizing, 453
Ringi system, 457, 467
Rochester Interaction Record (RIR), 391
Rokeach Value Survey, 398, 422
Romantic love, 397, 398, 426
Running amok, 348

Sadness, 229, 242, 243, 250, 252
Sample, 35, 60
Sampling, 35–36, 60
Sapir-Whorf hypothesis, 118, 268–273
analysis of, 272–273
bilingualism and, 273–274

challenges to, 270–272
explanation of, 268–269
research supporting, 269–270
Schedule for Affective Disorders and Schizophrenia (SADS), 355
Schizophrenia, 343–345, 354
Scholastic achievement. *See* Academic achievement
School systems, 147–148
See also Education
Secure attachment, 163–165, 178
Selection issues, 128
Selective attention, 72–73, 91
Self-concept, 300–320, 337
achievement motivation and, 307–308
cultural influences on, 300–302
dualities of self and, 316–318
emotions and, 310–312
evaluation of research on, 313–316
gender differences in, 187–188
happiness and, 312–313
independent vs. interdependent, 302–304
indigenous emotions and, 311–312
multicultural identities and, 318–319
self-enhancement and, 308–310
self-perception and, 304–305
social explanation and, 306–307
Self-construals
evaluation of research on, 313–316
independent vs. interdependent, 302–304
Self-contained individualism, 317
Self-enhancement, 308–310, 338, 416
Self-esteem
personality and, 324–325
self-enhancement and, 308–310
Self-monitoring, 326
Self/other referents, 263–264, 265
Self-perception, 304–305

Self-serving bias, 308, 338, 406, 426
Self-worth, 324
Semantic memory, 76, 91
Semantics, 262
Sensorimotor stage, 167
Serial position effect, 106, 131
Sex, 19, 181, 197, 198–199
  See also Gender
Sexism, 81
Sex roles, 19, 181–182, 197, 199
  See also Gender roles
Sexual identity, 182, 199
Sexual orientation, 20
Shame, 243, 244–245, 250, 252
Siblings, 141
Signals, 283
Similarity hypothesis, 397, 427
Sinbyong, 348
"Sinking heart" condition, 349
Skill factors, 294
Slow-to-warm-up temperament, 158, 178
Smiling faces, 240–241
Social behavior, 385–427
  aggression and, 417–420
  attributions and, 404–417
  compliance and, 420, 421–423
  conformity and, 420, 421–423
  cooperation and, 420, 423–424
  ingroup/outgroup relationships and, 385–392
  interpersonal attraction and, 396–404
  obedience and, 420, 421, 423
  person perception and, 392–404
Social class
  health and, 205–206
  IQ scores and, 122, 125
  See also Economic factors
Social cognition, 287–288
Social explanation, 306–307
Social factors
  health and, 205–206
  math achievement and, 147–151
  prejudice and, 83–84
Social identity theory, 74
Social integration, 209–210
Social isolation, 206–207
Socialist health systems, 221

Socialization, 133–156
  child rearing and, 135–143
  day care and, 144–145
  definition of, 134, 156
  education and, 145–151
  enculturation and, 133–135
  ethnocentrism as consequence of, 63–65
  extended families and, 142–143
  friendships and, 144
  peer groups and, 143–144
  religion and, 152–153
  siblings and, 141
  temperament and, 159–160
Socialization agents, 135, 156
Social loafing, 451–453, 467
Socially disengaged emotions, 310, 338
Socially engaged emotions, 311, 338
Social schemas, 393, 427
Social striving, 451–453, 467
Socioeconomic status (SES), 37
  emotions and, 245
  health and, 205–206
  intelligence tests and, 125
  mental illness and, 358, 362
  See also Economic factors
Somatization, 347, 362
Sorting tasks, 105
South Africans, 84
Spatial abilities, 190
Stagnation, intercultural, 482–483
Status differentiation (SD), 48
Stereotypes, 69–79, 91
  appraisal and, 73
  attribution and, 74
  categorization and, 73–74, 105
  concept formation and, 73–74
  content of, 70–72
  decoding process and, 287
  definition of, 69
  development of, 72–77
  emotions and, 74–75, 233
  ethnocentrism and, 77–78
  examining limitations in, 86–88
  gender, 182

intercultural communication and, 293
  memory and, 75–76, 107
  recognizing, 85–86
  reinforcement of, 77
  selective attention and, 72–73
  types of, 69–70
Stereotype threat, 122, 131
Stoicism, 118
Strange Situation measure, 163
Stress, 293
Structural definitions of culture, 6
Student attitudes, 149–150
Subjective elements of culture, 46–48
Subjective experience of emotion, 237, 260
Substance abuse, 222
Substantive processing, 76
Suicidal behavior, 213–215
Surprise, 229, 250
Survival, ensuring, 11
Susto, 350, 351, 375
Syllogisms, 110
Symbolizing three dimensions in two theory, 101, 131
Syntax, 262
System of rules, 10–11

Tasks, sorting, 105
Teaching styles, 150–151
Teamthink, 458
Technology
  culture influenced by, 13
  global village and, 430
Teenage parents, 142–143
Temperament, 157–161, 166, 178
  cross-cultural studies on, 158–161
  enculturation and, 159–160
  traditional knowledge about, 158
Temporary culture, 449
Thematic Apperception Test (TAT), 102, 274–275
Theories
  culture-bound, 33–34
  evaluating, 56
Therapy. *See* Psychotherapy
Third World type of organization, 433, 467
Thought processes. *See* Cognition
Tightness, 48
Time orientation/ perspective, 116–117
Tolerance, 481

Translation issues, 40–41, 256
Twin studies, 121
Type A personality, 205, 207

Uncertainty avoidance (UA), 48
  creativity and, 113
  health issues related to, 208–209
  work-related values and, 435, 437, 438–439
Uncertainty reduction, 294
Underpathologizing, 356, 362
Uninvolved parents, 136, 137, 156
United States
  attribution patterns in, 405–406
  concept of intelligence in, 127
  conformity, compliance, obedience studies in, 421
  cross-cultural research in, 5, 26
  eating disorders in, 212, 213
  emotions as viewed in, 254–255
  ethnicity and gender in, 195–197
  ethnocentrism in, 277–278
  false uniqueness effect in, 309
  health-related attitudes in, 216–217
  individualism-collectivism studies in, 50
  interpersonal attraction studies in, 396–397
  mental health services in, 368–377
  negotiation processes in, 460, 461
  parenting behaviors in, 138–139
  person perception studies in, 392–393
  psychotherapy with diverse cultures in, 368–369
  self-construals in, 302, 314
  social support in, 388
  teaching styles in, 50, 150–151
  time orientation in, 117
  treatment of abnormal behavior in, 368–377

Universality studies, 227, 260
Unpackaging studies, 30–31, 60

Validity, 38, 60
Value judgments, 44, 60
   decoding rules and, 287
   researcher bias and, 44–45
Values, 11
   parental/familial, 148–149
   work-related, 188–189, 433–441
Variables
   conceptual definitions of, 38–40
   context, 31
   operationalization of, 38–40

Verbal behaviors
   communication process and, 279, 280–282
   cultural influences on, 283–288
   See also Communication; Language
Vertical individualism/collectivism, 52
Vindicators, 482, 483
Visual perception
   cultural influences on, 98–104
   See also Perception
Voyagers, 482

WAIS test, 38
Welfare-oriented health systems, 221
Whakama, 349

Within-group norming, 129
Witiko, 349
Word problems, 110
Work
   cultural meaning of, 450
   diversity of workforce at, 464–466
   intercultural issues related to, 459–466
   motivation and productivity at, 451–453
   organizational culture and, 430–432, 441, 443–449
   overseas assignments for, 463–464
   values related to, 433–441
   See also Organizations

Work-related values, 433–441
   gender and, 188–189
   individualism-collectivism and, 437, 439, 440
   masculinity and, 189, 439, 441, 442
   power distance and, 434–435, 436
   uncertainty avoidance and, 435, 437, 438–439
World Health Organization (WHO), 202, 343–345
World Health Statistics Quarterly, 208

Zar, 349

TO THE OWNER OF THIS BOOK

We hope that you found *Culture and Psychology,* Third Edition, useful. So that this book can be improved in a future edition, would you take the time to complete this sheet and return it? Thank you.

School and address: _____

Department: _____

Instructor's name: _____

1. What I like most about this book is: _____

   _____

   _____

2. What I like least about this book is: _____

   _____

   _____

3. My general reaction to this book is: _____

   _____

   _____

4. The name of the course in which I used this book is: _____

   _____

5. Were all of the chapters of the book assigned for you to read? _____

   _____

   If not, which ones weren't? _____

   _____

6. In the space below, or on a separate sheet of paper, please write specific suggestions for improving this book and anything else you'd care to share about your experiences in using the book.

   _____

   _____

   _____

   _____

OPTIONAL:

Your name: _____ Date: _____

May we quote you, either in promotion for *Culture and Psychology,* Third Edition, or in future publishing ventures?

       Yes: _____   No: _____

       Sincerely yours,

       David Matsumoto
       Linda Juang

- - - - - FOLD HERE -

- - - - - FOLD HERE -